Retailing Principles

FAIRCHILD BOOKS

Retailing Principles
Global, Multichannel, and Managerial Viewpoints

Second Edition

Lynda Rose Poloian
Southern New Hampshire University

Fairchild Books | New York

Fairchild Books
An imprint of Bloomsbury Publishing Inc

175 Fifth Avenue
New York
NY 10010
USA

50 Bedford Square
London
WC1B 3DP
UK

www.fairchildbooks.com

First published 2003

© Bloomsbury Publishing Inc, 2013

Library of Congress Cataloging-in-Publication Data
Poloian, Lynda Rose
Retailing Principles:
Global, Multichannel, and Managerial Viewpoints/ Poloian, Lynda Rose p.cm
2012937631

ISBN: 978-1-56367-742-7

Typeset by Precision Graphics
Cover Design: Sarah Silberg
Cover Art Credit: © jjaakk/iStockphoto
Printed and bound in Canada

For Eleanor G. May and my loyal office assistants, Gabrielle and Muffin

Contents

Extended Table of Contents

Preface

Retailing Principles: Global, Multichannel, and Managerial Viewpoints was known as *Retailing Principles: A Global Outlook* and *Retailing: New Perspectives* in previous editions. The title changes confirm the reality that retailing is an industry in which change is inevitable, and that participants either embrace it or suffer the consequences. Since the last edition was published, the global economy has faced extraordinary turmoil, and it remains in a state of flux. Retailers, suppliers, and customers—including our students—participate in a complex marketplace where retail transactions take place through multiple selling channels and innovation and speed fuel a societal sense of urgency. New technologies, analytical tools, cross-channel tactics, pricing strategies, and product style trends cause retailers here and abroad to react. When retailers are propelled into action, profoundly insightful leadership is needed. These factors justify the title adjustments. Expanded coverage reflects retail's technology-driven, multidimensional momentum and the acknowledgment that global connectivity is here to stay. Many students will live, study, and build careers in the international marketplace.

This book is written for students in colleges and universities, online or in class, who are taking their first course in retailing. Some possess a rudimentary knowledge of marketing; others have worked part-time in retailing and are ready to enhance their knowledge of business practices. Several already have "taken ownership" of a career in retailing and want to experience the academic and experiential facets of their degrees. Other users include students in marketing, business management, international business, fashion merchandising, and vocational programs. With the addition of managerial-oriented material in two new chapters, the book is appropriate for master's programs—especially those directed to students with nonbusiness undergraduate degrees. The text delivers solid information in a straightforward manner and is an equally useful reference for training directors and managers of retail organizations.

Organization and Scope

Current and forecasted information, comprehensive coverage of retail issues, exposure to strategic planning, operational nuance, and management practices are presented in a pragmatic way.

Unit One, *The State of the Industry* covers the past and present status of the retail industry, and stresses the importance placed on the customer. Chapter 1, "Roots and Rudiments," lays the groundwork by explaining basic facts, terminology, retail's place in the supply chain, retail ownership, and retail history. Chapter 2, "The Retail Environment: Dynamics of Change," considers events in the economic, political, legal, social, and competitive realms that affect retail planning. Chapter 3, "Strategic Planning: Adapting to Change," leads off by enumerating the steps of the strategic planning process followed by a survey of ten critical areas of change affecting retailers and customers this decade. Several retail companies that are adapting to change are introduced here; other examples are woven in throughout the text. Chapter 4, "Customer Behavior," is new to this unit and reminds us that retailing is and always will be a people business. Basic theories of consumer behavior and the changing roles and status of today's globally oriented and technologically savvy customers are covered.

Unit Two, *Retail Structures and Multichannel Strategies,* examines strategies used by retailers as they compete through omnichannel methods. Chapters are devoted to retail stores, direct marketing and selling, electronic retailing, and international retailing. Chapter 5, "Brick-and-Mortar Retailing," identifies and describes retailers that operate from traditional stores. Chapter 6, "Direct Marketing and Selling," explores catalogue selling, telemarketing, direct mail tactics, and several nonstore retail formats. Chapter 7, "Electronic Retailing," contains useful information about online and other digital media that are evolving at breathtaking speed. Coverage of retail involvement with social networking, mobile retailing, and Web analytics is new to this edition. Chapter 8, "Global

Retailing," looks at reasons for global expansion, qualities of successful global retailers, and how international initiatives merge with multichannel practices.

Unit Three, *Store Location and Planning,* comprises three chapters that deal with the physical structures in which retailing transpires and how they are made amenable to customers. Chapter 9, "Site Selection," discusses the importance of selecting an appropriate store location—whether it's a city center or freestanding store, a London high street or a Moroccan souk. Advanced geo-spatial research methods and a discussion of emerging retail sites round out the subject matter. Chapter 10, "Shopping Centers and Malls," is devoted entirely to venues ranging from strip malls to megamalls. Roles played by mall developers and managers are included. In Chapter 11, "Store Design and Visual Merchandising," topics including store image, atmosphere, traffic flow, design principles, and displays are made clear. Sections on safety and security—including organized retail crime—complete the chapter.

Unit Four, *Retail Management,* begins with Chapter 12, "Principles of Management," which explains theories, organizational leadership skills, and contemporary practices of management. Chapter 13, "Human Resource Management," specializes in activities essential to recruiting, hiring, training, motivating, and assessing retail management and staff. Chapter 14, "Financial Analysis and Management," merges the fundamentals of financial planning at a retail level with accounting and fiscal control practices. Chapter 15, "Merchandising Management," addresses dollar and unit planning and the role retail buyers play in the process. Product sourcing and private label programs also are explained.

Unit Five, *Marketing the Merchandise,* applies marketing concepts—product, pricing, distribution, and promotion—to retailing. Contemporary pricing strategies and tactics are covered in Chapter 16, "Pricing for Profit." In Chapter 17, "Planning Retail Promotion," essential aspects of advertising, sales promotion, and personal selling culminate in a discussion of customer service. Chapter 18, "Monitoring the Supply Chain," examines logistics, physical distribution, and inventory control practices, including the ways in which technology helps create operational efficiencies. The Appendix, "Retail Career Directions," presents career-planning strategies and suggests avenues for career search, including several online resources.

Highlights of This Edition

Retailing Principles: Global, Multichannel, and Managerial Viewpoints takes a more integrated approach than did its predecessors in describing the fundamental principles upon which successful retail companies operate. This manifests in several ways:

1. Two new chapters introduce students to general management practices—knowledge expected of all who pursue a retail degree.
   - "Principles of Management," Chapter 12, familiarizes students with theories and practices of management as they have evolved over time. Examining the qualities that make an effective manager should lead to introspection for prospective retail executives.
   - "Financial Analysis and Management," Chapter 14, describes the responsibilities of a chief financial officer (CFO) as well as the basics of financial planning. Using retail examples, students review income and balance statements, cash flow, and other tools that support a strong company.
   - These topics are intended not to substitute for a course in these disciplines, but rather to increase awareness of the knowledge and skills needed to run a profitable company.
2. Global retail profiles at the end of each unit were chosen to reflect unit themes, ignite interest, encourage critical thinking, and explore topics through independent research.
3. Enhanced coverage of the retail environment includes the events that brought about the global recession and strategies used by retailers to cope with the ensuing consequences. Examples are given of economic decisions that have changed the face of retailing and the purchasing habits of customers.
4. Direct marketing and selling are treated as important choices in the omnichannel approach to retailing practices globally.
5. Ethical issues are woven into text material in several pertinent areas, including the sections on consumerism in Chapter 4 and global sourcing in Chapters 15 and 18.

6. Technology as a stimulus for change underlies the development of every chapter. The rapid growth of m-commerce is covered in Chapter 7, "Electronic Retailing," as well as the use of social networking sites as a retail advertising option.

7. For the first time, *Retailing Principles: Global, Multichannel, and Managerial Viewpoints* appears in full, totally engaging color!

Pedagogical Features

Throughout this text, every attempt has been made not only to include international references, profiles, and examples but also to encourage students to think less ethnocentrically. Readers may not be familiar with all of the retailers mentioned in the book. However, introducing these and other companies that may be new to us presents a fine opportunity to do extra research. Several international examples are used in contexts where knowledge of a specific retailer is not as important as the concept being discussed.

Four of the end-of-unit Global Retail Profiles examine retail companies that operate internationally or globally. The fifth is a study of retailing in China, chosen because of that country's importance to global commerce and because China, despite its rapid evolution into an economic powerhouse, remains less well understood by many Westerners than other emerging countries. Profiles are followed by study questions to encourage thoughtful analysis of the material. Sources used to compile the profiles include professional study tours, interviews, and personal discussions with retail executives, as well as my own international teaching and business experiences.

Pedagogical features carried over from previous editions, but updated and improved for this book, include From the Field vignettes in each chapter. They bring a strong dose of reality to the reader in brief bursts of information. Relevant industry incidents and perspectives from leading trade and consumer publications link to concepts presented in the chapter. Two From the Field pieces in Chapter 17 were specially chosen to focus on small businesses.

All of the Did You Know? (DYK) and Cyberscoop (CYB) boxes are fresh in this edition. DYKs spotlight retail trivia that illuminate a point or example, break up the tedium of reading, and foster interest in retailing. CYBs are used in much the same way and encourage students to work online. As this text went to press, all Web sites mentioned in the CYBs were accessible. Because of constant upgrading, redesigning, and natural attrition, some may not be available as you read this. The author and publisher regret any inconvenience this may cause students and instructors.

Other special learning features include concise learning objectives at the beginning of each chapter and a summary at the end of each chapter, followed by a list of key terms and a selection of questions for review and discussion. Throughout the text, key terms are set in bold type at their first occurrence, where they are defined. Eighty percent of the text material and 95 percent of the more than 200 photographs, figures, and tables are new to this edition. Many of the photos throughout the text are from my personal collection and present a unique perspective. An Instructor's Guide featuring course outlines, suggestions for projects and activities, and a test bank is available for use in conjunction with the text. A PowerPoint presentation provides chapter highlights and includes some illustrations not found in the text.

What is retailing? Where has it come from? Where is it going? Who are the players? How do they operate? These are just some of the questions that students should ask in a course on the principles of retailing. I hope they'll be answered by the end of your term and that the text was beneficial—both to instructors as you prepared for class, and to your students who participated in it.

Acknowledgments

Without a doubt this has been the longest revision this author has ever undertaken. No, I do not mean that the book holds an ungodly thousand pages, but rather it has been a one-year project that took five, with time off in the middle to write another book. I know it was worth it but it would not have been were it not for the family of executives, editors, advisors, and specialists that brought our book to fruition.

At Bloomsbury (a.k.a. Fairchild Books), the cumulative experience of my team members cannot help but make this text our best one ever. They have given freely of their talents, time, and encouragement. I heartily thank the following individuals: Olga Kontzias, executive editor, for her consistently fair and professional treatment over the many years of our association and Sylvia Weber, development editor, who has taught me more about managing people (nag, nag, nag), projects, and life than I ever expected. My off-premises development editor, Donna Frassetto and I belong to a mutual admiration society despite the fact that we have never met in person. Having worked with her on two books, I've come to appreciate her fastidious editing and her gracious coaching. Donna strives for 100 percent perfect, but don't tell Sylvia! Art editor Sarah Silberg and photo editor Avital Aronowitz are the power behind the creative rendering of this work. I honor their skills and am grateful for their patience. Avital contributed several of her own photos—such a professional touch. Copyeditor Lauren Wool's keen eye caught even the smallest of errors. Jessica Katz, the production editor, skillfully oversaw the metamorphosis of the manuscript into a bound book. Joseph Hancock, retailing professor at Drexel University, joined the team in the last inning. When work was piling up and deadlines were looming, we needed an extra retail eye and he was there—complete with A&F photo.

Numerous colleagues, trade associations, retailers, researchers, and talented friends supported my efforts to complete this book. Thanks go to present and past members of the Southern New Hampshire University community. Graduate Sara Bilodeau Misuraca served as my research assistant on the previous edition and went on to a management position in retailing that she has written about in the Appendix. Colleagues from other universities have also helped fine-tune the manuscript. Tony Hernandez of Ryerson University in Toronto made significant contributions to Chapter 9, "Site Selection." Eleanor May, Professor Emerita of the University of Virginia's Darden School of Business, read and thoughtfully commented not only on her wheel of retailing section, but on Chapter 1 in its entirety.

Many retailers and trade organizations have provided material for this edition. At Global Retail Symposiums, held annually at the Terry Lundgren Center for Retailing at the University of Arizona, I met and learned from many global retailers. Through study tours sponsored by the American Collegiate Retailing Association I became privy to retail information not accessible in other ways. The resources of the National Retail Federation, Retail Industry Leaders Association, Direct Marketing Educational Foundation, Direct Selling Association, and International Council of Shopping Centers also have been of great value during the preparation of this text. Equally useful have been the reports, white papers, and articles from online publications *McKinsey Quarterly, Internet Retailer,* and *Multichannel Merchant,* as well as business and research firms Adobe, Aberdeen Group, Kantar Retail, A.T. Kearney, SRI, and ESRI. The use of current research ensured that the book is timely, accurate, insightful, and a good read at that.

Special thanks are offered to the following colleagues and friends:

- Andy Correa, owner of A.G.A. Correa & Son in Edgecomb, Maine, and preeminent provider of customer service, for exemplifying the small business perspective in Chapter 17. From the Field 17.2 describes his retail venture.
- Craig and Char Curry. To Craig, for not only lending me his MBA library, but also sharing his inimitable managerial anecdotes and wine. To Char, for ongoing creative inspiration and her special French grocery photograph.

- Kevin Green, vice president of strategy at Digital Influence Group for sharing first-hand experience in managing his social media staff.
- Nancy Kyle, president of the New Hampshire Retail Merchants Association, long-time supporter of academic retail projects, and guru of organized retail crime (ORC).
- Evelyn and Gerry Letendre, for their generosity and support in providing the means to stage the Bahama photo shoot. Without you and *Diamond Days* this could never have happened.
- Fred, manager of Ritz Photo for his extemporaneous and valuable tutorial on photo editing.
- Gordon Lothrop, for his authentic photos of a Moroccan souk and his worldly perspective gained from years of travel.
- Joan Olson, owner of Olson Jewelers, for sharing her direct-mail advertisement and taking care of her yoga-mate.
- Nancy and Mark Rines, owners of City Music stores in Massachusetts, lent their decades of retail experience. Nancy worked with me on several occasions to ensure the perspective of the entrepreneur was accurately reflected in Chapter 17's focus on small business. Look for her insights in From the Field 17.1. To you, Nancy, namaste.
- Lorelei and Kees Van Ingen, for their international hospitality and our many discussions about retailing in the Netherlands.

This edition is more balanced and better directed to the needs of students because of the diversity of comments made by the reviewers. I would particularly like to thank those whose detailed comments contributed greatly to the validity of this text. The reviewers selected by the publisher include Joseph Hancock, Drexel University; Julie Hengle, The Art Institute of Ohio-Cincinnati; Vanessa Jackson, University of Kentucky; Pandora Neiland, IADT Seattle; Rogene Nelsen, Fontbonne University; and Helen Smith, The Art Institute of Phoenix.

And finally my gratitude goes to The Wolf, The Kids, The Katts, Katryn and The Yogis, and Karen my Reiki teacher, who unfailingly bring me fresh insights, courage, light, peace, and love.

Lynda Rose Poloian
May 2012

Unit One

The State of the Industry

Without knowing where the retailing industry came from, how can we appreciate what it is today or contemplate how it will mold the future? That question spurs our exploration of the topics in this unit. Chapter 1 describes the underpinning of marketing theory and practice, immerses us in the language of retailing, and examines various rationales for how the industry works, as preparation for a glimpse into its history and present status.

Retailing affects and is transformed by changes in customers and the economy—just a few of the topics related in Chapter 2. Monitoring the retail environment is a constant and occasionally overwhelming task because it is always in a state of flux. Awareness of social, demographic, and legal shifts, as well as global trends, helps retailers initialize the strategic planning process, the subject of Chapter 3.

Thorough analysis of past practices and present business climate brings clarity that helps retailers construct a foundation from which to set goals and objectives for their companies. Planning and implementing successful tactics fuels and sustains retail growth and profitability. The single most important aspect of retailing remains understanding and satisfying the often unpredictable customer, as discussed in Chapter 4. This was true when ancient trade routes were established, and it remains so amid the continually evolving online delivery systems in use today.

Chapter 1

Roots and Rudiments

Learning Objectives

After completing this chapter you should be able to:

- Define basic retailing and marketing terms.
- Identify retail marketing channels and members of the supply chain.
- List the major retail sectors and functional areas.
- Delineate basic types of retail stores and services.
- Apply popular theories to the evolution of retail businesses.
- Categorize retailers by type of ownership.
- Describe how history has shaped contemporary retail organizations.

a

b

Figure 1.1
It's only fitting to begin our retail study with Walmart, the largest retailer in the world. In keeping with its proactive environmental stance, many stores feature skylights and photovoltaic solar panels that generate passive and electrically generated power, respectively (a). The interiors of Walmart's superstores boast full-service pharmacies and aisles packed with over-the-counter remedies (b).

Retailing is all around us. It is as old as ancient trade routes and outdoor markets and as new as mobile commerce. It includes elegant Tiffany and eclectic garage sales. Retailing is small-town and big-city, local and regional, national, international, global, and electronic. It is the most important link in the journey from producer to consumer, since much of a country's wealth—its gross domestic product—is accrued through some form of retailing.

The **gross domestic product (GDP)** is the total value of all goods and services produced by a country during a specific time period. It is expressed in units of currency. This should not be confused with the GDP growth rate, which is an indicator of economic health and is expressed as a percentage increase or decrease in GDP from the previous measurement cycle. To clarify the distinction, consider that China's estimated GDP growth rate for 2011 was an enviable 9.2 percent, whereas its total estimated GDP for 2011 was $11.29 trillion. In contrast, GDP growth in the United States during 2011 was an anemic 1.5 percent. However, the U.S. GDP of $15.04 trillion in 2011, reflecting the larger value of goods and services in the U.S.[1] (Adding an additional wrinkle to this picture is the fact that consumer spending currently accounts for about 70 percent of the U.S. GDP, a variable that has had important consequences during economic fluctuations.[2])

Retailers search for excellence in every phase of their operations, and challenges involving the economy, communications, technology, distribution, and competition abound. Above all, retailing is a people business. Skills in dealing with people at all levels are among the most valued in the industry. Success depends on understanding customers' needs, motivations, and lifestyles no matter what retailing venue is employed. Automobile salespeople who do not understand why one person wants a customized black Cadillac Escalade SUV while another prefers a blue Toyota Prius cannot succeed at their jobs.

Retail employees need excellent written and oral communication skills. A misunderstood e-mail or contentious sales presentation might diminish goodwill or incur financial loss. A loyal customer who is verbally assaulted when making a return can easily find another retailer with which to do business. Web sites with confusing language do not hold the shopper's interest. Retailers that prosper in a highly competitive, technological world are those that nurture effective communication.

High-performing retailers demand state-of-the-art business intelligence systems as well as the expertise to use technological tools to full capacity. **Business intelligence (BI)** is information gathered from a variety of internal and external sources to help businesses make sound decisions. Computer programs that simply supply information on sales, inventory, and commission earnings are no longer enough. Retailers must efficiently monitor all facets of business and gather and use information that helps them serve customers more efficiently and effectively while earning a profit.

The historical context of modern retailing practices is highlighted in the final section of this chapter, and throughout the text in examples. Understanding the origins of the industry helps us gain both a deeper appreciation for the state of the industry today and a broader perspective on the ever-evolving retail experience.

Definitions and Dynamics

Every discipline and industry has its own terminology, and retailing is no exception. Because retailing is such an important part of business, falling within the broader scope of marketing, the language of retailing reflects an integration of marketing terms. The first part of this chapter serves as a review of marketing terminology and concepts for those who have taken a basic marketing course, and as an introduction to key principles for those who have not. Following this marketing orientation, segments focusing on retail sectors, business functions, and scope; the many types of stores and retail service businesses; and the educational benefits of retailing round out the first section.

Retailing in a Marketing Context

Marketing is at the heart of every business function. **Marketing** is a process that uses product, price, promotion, and distribution to address customer needs effectively and turn a profit. **Marketing mix** is the unique blend of product, price, promotion, and distribution techniques that are used to reach and satisfy a target market. A **target market** is a group of people with similar characteristics and needs who are likely to purchase. Marketers emphasize that people are crucial to the success of all marketing initiatives.

The process of tracing the existence of a product in the marketplace, by examining the stages through which it passes and the time it spends in each stage, is called the **product life cycle**. The cycle consists of four stages: introduction, growth, maturity, and decline. Knowing which stage a product occupies helps retailers determine the appropriate steps to ensure a long life in the marketplace.

Formats including stores, catalogues, and online retailers also experience a life cycle, and the speed with which retail concepts enter and exit the cycle grows shorter with each decade. As an example, consider the movie rental business. Video rental stores made their debut in the 1980s and were strong for about 20 years. However, the online company Netflix dramatically changed the way people rented movies, taking the market away from retailers that operated rental services. The cycle continues to evolve, with viewers now streaming movies directly from the Internet to their home entertainment systems. Criticized for not having new releases available in a timely manner, Netflix arranged exclusive licensing arrangements with several film distributors, effectively preempting cable channels from having first dibs on films from major studios.[3] Today, Netflix accounts for 29.7 percent of all prime-time network download traffic, making the company the largest source of online video.[4] Life is short for many formats as new technologies emerge, customer purchasing habits change, and competition intensifies.

Without knowledge of marketing channels, it is difficult to understand the role played by retailing in the distribution process. A **marketing channel** is the route taken by a product as it travels from producer to final consumer. Marketing channels can be direct or indirect and are also called channels of distribution. Various participants involved in the channel include manufacturers, wholesalers, and retailers. Retailers are the last link in the process that delivers goods to customers. A look at contemporary channels provides further clarification. **Business-to-consumer (B2C)** describes the retail channel through which retail stores, catalogs, or online retailers sell goods to final consumers. Typical retail marketing channels are discussed in the next section. **Business-to-business (B2B)** describes an industrial or commercial channel such as one through which an apparel manufacturer sells to a wholesaler, distributor, or retail company.

All of the businesses involved throughout the marketing channel comprise the **supply chain**. Specific members of the supply chain that provide goods and services to the retailer are called **vendors**. Apparel manufacturers and service providers such as advertising agencies are considered vendors. The term *resource* is used interchangeably with vendor. Though differentiating the members of the supply chain can be confusing, all work together to try to ensure customer satisfaction. Success stems from selecting the appropriate channel that will fulfill customers' needs most efficiently and effectively. Understanding the concept of economic utility is fundamental to this task.

Economic Utility

There would be little satisfaction for customers if manufacturers created new items but did not consider customers' wants and needs. This is the core of marketing and it stresses that consumer satisfaction should be the basis for all retail planning. **Economic utility** further explains this concept, and is defined as the ability of a product to satisfy consumers' needs and wants. The four basic economic utilities referenced by economists are time, place, form, and possession. In an industrial world, where most people can no longer be self-sufficient, the key to success is having the right goods in the right place at the right time. If a marketing system works well, it provides for the four basic utilities, which are explained in a retailing context as follows:

- Time utility occurs when retailers have merchandise that customers want exactly when they want it.
- Place utility occurs when retailers locate their stores—or Web sites—in a way that offers easy access to their customers.
- Form utility refers to the power of retailers to create a satisfying merchandise assortment within their stores or places of business.
- Possession utility occurs when merchandise is sold to the customer.

Build-A-Bear is a specialty retailer that is unusually successful at providing all four types of economic utility. The growing 400-unit chain usually locates its stores in high-traffic, family-oriented shopping centers (place). Build-A-Bear opened its first airport store at Florida's Orlando International Airport in 2011, expanding on the benefits of place utility.[5] The opportunity to design, stuff, dress, and name a personalized bear with readily available materials provides a unique and entertaining experience (time and form). Companies like Build-A-Bear and Disney appeal to shoppers of all ages. As illustrated in Figure 1.2, possession utility is evident as this experiential retailer delights its customer.

Retailing Defined

When marketing is conducted at the level of the final consumer, it is considered retailing. **Retailing** is the selling of goods or services directly to the customer for personal, nonbusiness use. This definition implies that retail transactions involve individual units or small quantities of merchandise or limited use of a service. Retailers are businesses or individuals who by definition sell more than 50 percent of their goods or services to final consumers. Efficient distribution is one of the most critical competitive elements for retailers. Fine-tuning relationships with vendors, managing inventory, streamlining transportation modes, refining technology, and fulfilling customer expectations are all ways to help retailers become successful.

Figure 1.2
Disney parks and stores combine the best of all retail worlds. A satisfied customer expresses the joy of ownership as he emerges from a Disney store in Disneyland.

Similar to the marketing mix, the retail mix specifically pertains to store, service, and nonstore settings like catalogs and online stores. **Retail mix** describes the various activities in which retailers are engaged as they attempt to satisfy customers. Location selection, facilities planning, merchandising, pricing, promoting, distributing goods, and human resource management are important aspects of the retail mix. Applications of the retail mix are cited throughout this text.

You'll want to become familiar with common merchandising terms since these terms appear frequently in observations and reports about retailers. One way that retailers differentiate themselves is through merchandise assortment. A **merchandise assortment** consists of all the goods in a store, defined in terms of breadth and depth of stock. **Breadth of stock** refers to the number of different product lines carried in a store. **Depth of stock** measures the number of similar styles or models in each product line. Merchandise assortments are often described as "narrow and deep" or "broad and shallow." A **product line** is a group of closely related items produced by a manufacturer. For example, Juicy Couture jeans and Apple iPhones are each product lines. To expand this example, a **merchandise classification** is a group of related goods in a store, such as all brands of jeans and types of smartphones carried by a retailer. The term *category* is also used to define closely related items, especially in large retail establishments such as supermarkets. Merchandise assortment varies by type of retailer, merchandising policies of the company, and consumer demand.

Definitions help us organize the parlance of a discipline, but they do not necessarily make a topic come alive. The many dimensions of retailing will become clearer, the industry more vibrant, and the message more personal as chapters unfold.

Retailing's Place in the Marketing Channel

Just where does retailing belong in the vast marketing channel that brings New Zealand kiwi fruit to Harrod's food hall in London and hand-painted silk scarves from Malaysia to fashion retailers in Colombia? Are retailers always involved as goods move from manufacturer to user? There is no single answer to these questions because the distinction between retailers and wholesalers—and others in the supply chain—has blurred in recent years.

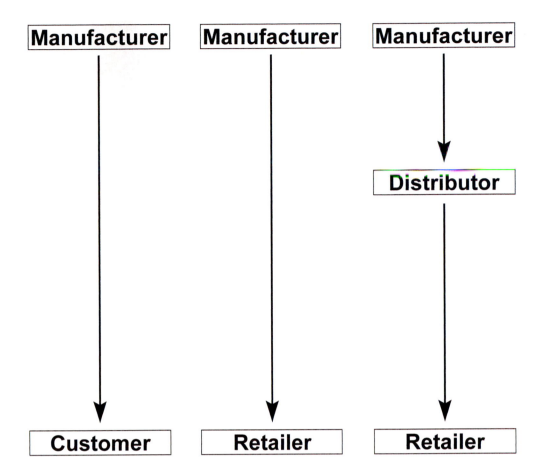

Figure 1.3
Common Retail
Marketing Channels

A firm does not have to be a retailer by definition in order to engage in retailing. Even though the largest percentage of consumer goods is marketed through the retail sector, many other firms throughout the channel engage in the functions traditionally performed by retailers. Warehouse clubs such as Costco or Sam's Club are examples of firms that sell to more than one member of the supply chain. **Warehouse clubs** are large-format, bare-bones retail stores that sell a broad assortment of merchandise to small businesses as well as to families and individuals. In other words, they sell through both B2C and B2B channels. Direct, indirect, and multiple channels may be used to reach the customer. Figure 1.3 illustrates typical retail marketing channels.

Manufacturer to Consumer

Manufacturers play a number of retail roles—supplier, partner, inventory control specialist, shipping agent, and promotion consultant, to name a few. The more functions they undertake, the more control they can exert over the channel and ultimately the more profits they can generate. Manufacturer to customer is the shortest, most direct channel. No intermediaries such as wholesalers are used. Some nonstore retailers that reach customers through catalogues or online also belong to this category. **Nonstore retailers** are those that sell through means other than traditional storefronts. Included in this channel are diverse types of retailers such as the following:

- *Direct sellers*. Retailers that sell to customers one-on-one are included in this category. As examples, Mary Kay Cosmetics sells through party plans and Cutco Cutlery via in-home consultations.
- *Direct marketers*. Retailers that manufacture some or all of their own products—and reach many of their customers through catalogues, direct-mail pieces, telemarketing, or online venues—are included in this category. Omaha Steaks is an example and has now opened brick-and-mortar stores, which it advertises in newspaper inserts.

- *Factory outlet stores.* Stores that are owned by the manufacturer belong to this group. Factory outlets are company-owned stores that sell manufacturers' overruns, seconds, irregulars, and sample products. Examples include Hanes, Calvin Klein, and Mikasa.
- *Artisans.* Individuals that design and produce goods and sell to customers operate through direct channels. Independent furniture and pottery makers as well as fine artists who sell their own works belong in this category. Artisans make and sell their wares in specialized indoor and outdoor markets, as shown in Figure 1.4.
- *Couture fashion designers.* Company figureheads who create one-of-a-kind garments at extremely high prices and deal directly with a limited number of high-income customers use this channel. Karl Lagerfeld and Christian Lacroix are examples.

The marketing strategies of manufacturers that sell directly to consumers are highly customer-oriented, because they are not selling to middlemen. In some situations the name brand or reputation is extremely important. In other instances, such as shoes sold in factory outlets, the emphasis is on price, and brand is of less importance.

Manufacturer to Retailer to Consumer

An indirect route, but one in which the retailer is the only middleman, is the one from manufacturer directly to retailer, and then to customer. Retailers are a very important link in the distribution chain because most goods are marketed through some type of retail outlet. Industry-dominant retailers, such as Walmart, generally buy directly from producers because of the vast quantities of goods they purchase. In this instance, Walmart is considered a channel captain because of the power it has to influence the flow of goods within its marketing channel. To appreciate the size and scope of Walmart stores, see the cost-saving, environmentally friendly roof and the wide aisle that leads to the in-store pharmacy in Figure 1.1.

This channel is also selected for fads and fashion items that have a relatively short life. Retailers that sell metallic silver nail polish or artfully designed snowboards for their respective strong seasons probably bought directly from the makers of these products.

Manufacturer to Wholesaler to Retailer to Consumer

The longest channel travels from manufacturer to wholesaler to retailer before it reaches the consumer. When retailers began taking over the distribution functions formerly performed by wholesalers in the mid-20th century, most wholesalers lost their dominant position in the channel. However, even now certain circumstances call for the use of a longer channel. In home electronics, many wholesale transactions go through a manufacturer's representative. A **manufacturer's representative** (often referred to as a "rep") is an independent businessperson who works in a specific territory selling related but noncompeting products to more than one account.

Some wholesale firms also sell directly to consumers in small quantities. A typical example is a fashion wholesaler that occasionally opens its doors to the public and sells merchandise at or slightly above wholesale prices through what are popularly called "sample sales." New wholesale and retail tactics—particularly those that involve the Internet—are changing the definition of retailing. Some companies successfully leverage manufacturing, wholesaling, and retailing functions concurrently, as you will see next.

Vertical Integration

To gain control, manufacturers are becoming retailers and retailers are becoming manufacturers while continuing their dominance in both marketplaces. This practice is called **vertical integration** and occurs when two or more supply chain members are owned by the same company. Several examples illustrate this competitive tactic.

- Verizon, one of the largest telephone and wireless communications providers in the United States, opened retail stores and kiosks to sell cellular phones and accessories.
- Fifth & Pacific Companies (formerly Liz Claiborne) and Nine West are manufacturers that have added retailing to their business portfolios through development of new concepts or through purchase of existing retailers. Both companies sell at wholesale to other retailers and operate retail stores under their own brand or other names. In addition, Fifth & Pacific manufactures a Liz Claiborne line of women's apparel exclusively for JCPenney that now owns the fashion brand.
- Sherwin-Williams produces the paints it sells to contractors as well as homeowners through its chain of 3,300 retail stores. It also sells to retailers such as Walmart and home improvement chains.[6]
- Under Armour, the high-performing athletic apparel and footwear manufacturer, sells to retail chains such as Foot Locker and Finish Line.[7] The company reaches additional customers online and through its growing retail store network.
- Dell Computers is vertically integrated and sells directly to customers, controlling all supply chain functions itself.

Conversely, the industry is ripe with retailers that have become manufacturers. The Gap and Limited Brands are two of many retail companies that use vertical integration as a cost-saving measure.

To expand on this concept companies turn to e-commerce. Consumer product manufacturers such as Procter & Gamble use their Web sites to educate consumers, offer coupons, and sell merchandise. They also sell wholesale to retail outlets. Brand building and customer convenience are the primary objectives of manufacturing companies that maximize online contact with the retailers they supply as well as their ultimate consumers. From the Field 1.1 presents a view of P & G's virtual world.

Multichannel Retailing

Trading through more than one selling channel has become paramount to retailers whose goals are to provide customer convenience, compete effectively, grow, and achieve profitability. The practice of trading using two or more methods of distribution concurrently is known as **multichannel retailing**. Stores, catalogues, and Web sites are the most frequently used points of contact. The inception of e-commerce was a precipitating factor in the upsurge of interest in this approach. The use of the term "omnichannel" retailing is becoming increasingly prevalent as the multichannel

//////////////////////////////////

Cyberscoop

Ralph Lauren Corp. is a vertically integrated company that represents almost every aspect of the marketing channel. Its products are sold from manufacturer to consumer, manufacturer to retailer to consumer, and through multiple channels. Can you identify Ralph Lauren's numerous divisions and the various channels that are used to sell his company's products? To start your research, visit www.ralphlauren.com and examine the company's history and practices.

concept evolves to a more inclusive and universal business model. **Omnichannel retailing** is the optimal practice of aligning merchandising, logistics, technologies, and all other functions fully in order to serve customers consistently well across all selling options. Avon, Next (an apparel retailer based in the United Kingdom), Coldwater Creek, REI, Cabela's, and Yves Rocher each sell in stores, through catalogues, and online, and are prime examples of multichannel practitioners. Catalogue covers for Yves Rocher, a producer and retailer of skin care, makeup, and fragrance lines, are illustrated in Figure 1.5. More on this integrative viewpoint appears in Unit Two, Retail Structures and Multichannel Strategies. Several ways of classifying retailers follow.

Cyberscoop

Many statistics on the size, scope, and classifications of retailing are available from the United States government. Visit www. census.gov and click on "Business" then "Data by Sector" and then "Retail Trade." Browse through these industry categories to see just how large retailing is in the United States.

Retail Sectors

This textbook concentrates primarily on firms that are classified as retailers, rather than on manufacturers or wholesalers with retail operations. The phrase "classified as," in this context, is not a reference to "merchandise classifications" described earlier. Some former manufacturers and wholesalers are now considered retailers; once a company begins to realize more than 50 percent of its sales at retail, it changes its channel position from manufacturing or wholesaling to retailing.

According to the National Retail Federation, each type of retailer falls into one of the following eleven sectors, based on merchandise carried or type of store:

1. Discount stores.
2. Department stores.
3. Clothing and accessories stores.
4. Jewelry stores.
5. Sporting goods, book, hobby, and music stores.
6. Electronics and appliance stores.
7. Furniture and home furnishings stores.
8. Warehouse clubs and superstores.
9. Building equipment and supplies stores.
10. Food and beverage stores.
11. Health and personal care stores.[8]

Each is vitally important to the economy as a whole. Various types of retail stores are discussed in Chapter 5; direct marketing, direct selling, and electronic retailing are covered in Chapters 6 and 7.

Retail Business Functions

The six universal functions of all retail businesses are merchandising, operations, promotion, finance, human resource management, and information technology.

- *Merchandising* includes all sourcing, buying, and—in some smaller stores—selling activities. **Sourcing** is the identification and utilization of resources for the manufacture of goods. Developing the product, planning the assortment, purchasing, educating sales staff, and making the product available for sale are a few of the responsibilities in this sector and are discussed in Chapter 15, Merchandising Management.
- *Operations* involves all aspects of managing the physical plant. Operations staff oversee maintenance, scheduling, customer services, shipping and receiving, warehousing, inventory control, and store security. Facilities development is part of operations, but in most large companies, separate real estate divisions handle this aspect of business. Several of these areas are discussed in Chapter 12, Principles of Management, and related material is infused throughout the text. In many chains, selling is an aspect of operations. This topic is covered in Chapter 17, Planning Retail Promotion.
- *Promotion* includes advertising, visual merchandising, public relations, personal selling, and sales promotion events. Visual merchandising is explored in Chapter 11, Store Design and Visual Merchandising; other related topics are found in Chapter 17, Planning Retail Promotion.
- *Finance* involves controlling the company's assets and includes accounting, record-keeping, forecasting, budgeting, taxation, and deriving capital. Chapter 14, Financial Analysis and Management, takes a look at these and other aspects of finance.
- *Human resource management* involves the recruiting, hiring, training, and assessment of personnel. The administration of benefits, liaising with unions, and general employee welfare are included. Chapter 13 covers the important human factor in retailing.
- *Information technology* crosses all functional areas and is of particular importance in planning, control, management, merchandising, and customer service. Internet-based communications, tools, and online store technology platforms are another part of this area.

Functional areas do not exist in isolation. Without frequent communication and collaboration between areas, no retail operation can work efficiently no matter how strong each part may be individually. The six functional areas are illustrated in Figure 1.6.

Scope of Retailing

Think for a moment about what you're wearing on your feet today. Where did you purchase your shoes? Maybe at a specialty store like Footlocker? **Specialty stores** are retail outlets that present large selections of highly focused limited lines of merchandise in small or large facilities. If you wanted to pick up some running gear, a fishing pole, and a sports watch in addition to your shoes,

Figure 1.5
Multichannel beauty products retailer Yves Rocher uses stores, its Web site, and catalogues to reach customers. Headquartered in France, the company operates in more than 80 countries and grows many of the botanicals used in its product lines.

Figure 1.6
Major Functional Areas
in Retailing

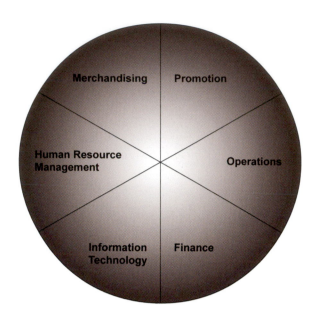

you might have shopped at a category killer, like Sports Authority. **Category killers** are specialty superstores that focus on limited merchandise classifications and great breadth and depth of assortments. If you are brand- and value-conscious, maybe a Target superstore was your destination. **Superstores** are huge retail stores, usually over 150,000 square feet, typically combining general merchandise and food under one roof. Whether you are on a tight budget this semester or not, you might have visited Dollar General, a discounter. **Discounters** are retailers that buy and sell at low prices and depend on high volume and low overhead to be profitable. With little time to shop, you might have ordered your new outdoor boots through a catalogue like L.L.Bean. If you're into something very hip, the Zappo's Web site might have been your choice.

Continuing with this mental exercise, let's assume you have decided to shop at Nordstrom, a department store known for its shoe department. **Department stores** are retail companies that occupy large facilities and carry broad assortments of goods organized by use, function, and brand. By design, stores are designated full-line or limited-line. **Full-line department stores** carry both soft goods like apparel, accessories, and shoes and hard goods like home electronics and furniture. **Limited-line department stores** focus on a few closely related categories of merchandise. Nordstrom is an upmarket limited-line department store, since it features apparel and services such as bistros and coffee bars for fashion-conscious customers.

Thanks to the efforts of store planners and visual merchandisers, you are enticed to enter the store. The objective is to catch your attention: "Look here, touch me, walk this way!" If you thought you were making a relatively simple purchase, guess again. You may have been interested in athletic shoes, but as soon as you eyed the hot new dress-shoe styles you totally forgot your quest for utilitarian footwear. Your next decision involves the type of shoe you want from among myriad brands, styles, colors, and price points, all further complicating the situation. Will it be the Jimmy Choo or Christian Louboutin designer styles? Now consider why you chose Nordstrom. Was the store convenient to home, work, or school? Were you at the shopping center anyway and just happened to see the store sign? Maybe a friend told you about a great sale the store was having. Possibly the newest Jimmy Choo styles weren't carried at another store you visited. Why did you decide to buy footwear in the first place? Do you have a special event coming up, or were you bored with your existing shoe wardrobe?

These questions and others underscore the fact that for most products and services, the choice of retail outlets is vast, and the customer's decision is often based on a complex network of factors. If you are looking for a broad selection of styles, you will probably go to a specialty store or a department store like Nordstrom that has a vast assortment of high-style shoes. If you need to be educated on the suitability of styles for various social functions, you may choose a store where salespeople have the expertise to assist you. If you do not own a car but can get to a nearby mall by public transportation, then location and accessibility may determine your choice of retailer. Personal finances may override all other factors involving your purchase decision; you may choose not to buy at all, postpone your purchase, or decide to shop at a secondhand consignment shop.

Take this scenario further and you will probably come up with dozens of places where you have shopped or could shop for shoes. This exercise demonstrates the omnipresence of retailing, the importance of accessibility, and the many other factors that affect purchasing decisions. When you apply any of these incidents or questions to your own shopping behavior, then you are beginning to *think retailing*.

Service Retailing

Although many service retailers operate from storefronts, many do not. Some retail services involve physical products, but many are intangible. They are all important to the retail landscape. For this reason, service retailers are included in this introduction.

Classification of Services

Service retailers are categorized in several ways. **Pure service retailers** conduct business transactions not involving merchandise. If retail services entail merchandise, they are considered owned or rented services. Services can be businesses in their own right or exist as marketing strategies for other retail businesses. Some retail services are also customer services, because they enhance the purchase of tangible products in classic stores. These include gift-wrapping, credit services, and options to order online and pick up at a nearby store, for example, and are discussed in more detail in Chapter 17. Several examples illustrate the distinctions between the various types of service retailers.

Pure Services   Banking institutions, hotels and restaurants, skin care spas, and pet care agencies are pure services. Many also have added retail product lines to their venues and most are chains. The retail challenges for service businesses differ from those experienced in conventional store retailing, as shown by the following example.

Coin-operated laundries are concentrating more on the customer as they join the ranks of national chains. Consider the case of SpinCycle, based in Scottsdale, Arizona, which wanted to expand nationally. Running a retail service business is somewhat different from conventional retailing. For example, laundromats usually operate with cash-based, coin-operated systems. This works well when operations are small and localized, but management must be prepared to compensate for the personal touch that is lost when companies move out of mom-and-pop status. They also must plan for better security. SpinCycle did this by providing on-site customer service managers and by making the store environment an appealing one. Television sets were added along with better lighting and ambiance. Wash-and-fold services allow customers to drop off and pick up their laundry at their convenience. Earlier this decade, SpinCycle grew its business by acquiring former mom-and-pop operations, announcing plans to open approximately 150 stores per year.[9] The company grew to a chain of 172 stores in 16 states. Los Angeles company PWS acquired SpinCycle in 2003 and continues to expand its presence.[10] PWS owns 3,000 coin-operated laundry chains in the United States.[11]

Service companies must provide excellent customer service. When service businesses expand or are acquired by larger firms, the challenge to provide consistently satisfactory service increases.

Owned-Goods Services   Services such as appliance, watch, or car repair are in this category. These are services that are performed on products previously purchased. Changing customer attitudes have inspired improvements in some retail service industries. For example, auto body repair shops—and those that provide quick oil changes or are muffler specialists—are upgrading their images and forming chains. For many people, customer service at auto repair shops is sporadic at best and nonexistent at worst. Forward-thinking companies are training employees in customer-service skills, providing clean and attractive waiting areas, offering refreshments, and helping customers with insurance claims.

Rented-Goods Services   When people need party tents, cars for vacations in Europe, or floor-sanding machines, they usually rent them rather than outlay a substantial amount of money to buy them. Sales of rented goods correlate positively to periods of economic growth. The stronger the economy, the more likely it is that a BMW Z4 instead of a Ford Taurus will be rented for a California vacation. Retailers who provide rental merchandise have to be concerned with equipment mainte-nance, timely delivery, and the training of courteous customer service representatives.

Service Marketing Initiatives
Many retailers add services when they explore ways to serve their customers better and find competitive advantages. Category killers Home Depot and Lowe's offer installation services for time-strapped homeowners, as well as in-store and Web-based training for do-it-yourselfers. Most building-supply retailers advertise their services through store signage, flyers, and their Web sites. For some consumers, picking out tile for a bathroom floor is a pleasure but the thought of self-installation is daunting. Seeing a sign immediately adjacent to a travertine marble display offering help at a reasonable price could turn the shopping expedition into a sale of both the product and the service. Building-supply retailers realize that cannibalization could be a problem, since many independent contractors offering installation services are wholesale customers to the retailer, but might choose to purchase their supplies elsewhere if DIY chains enter the service sector extensive-ly. **Cannibalization** is the loss of sales from one retail sector to another caused by the introduction of competing products or services.

Many service businesses do not operate out of stores, but even if they did, customers might not have the time to visit them to arrange for services. Indeed, most still operate by phone to coordinate services. But retail services are continuing to develop, expand, form national and inter-national chains, and engage customers online. Time-conscious consumers are often willing to pay for the opportunity to free up time for themselves. Customers also are demanding more services from all retailers. Rising standards of living in many parts of the world, along with the growth of the Internet, means more opportunities for service businesses and more satisfaction for customers.

Educational Dimension
You probably are well aware of the transactional aspects of retailing, but you may never have thought of your local retail store as a school. If not, make it a point to observe young children rid-ing in supermarket baskets, their inquisitive eyes darting from shelf to shelf or glued to a plasma screen brandishing a special of the week at the checkout. In doing so, you will quickly recognize the educational dimension of retailing. Through such questions as "What is that?" and "Can I eat this?" children learn. Product knowledge is often followed by a lesson in simple economics. "No, it's too much money" may be said in reference to brightly colored, novel-shaped, but more expen-sive cereals. A retail store is often the place where a child learns social patterns—that is, behaviors that are appropriate to a specific time and place, but that also change over time. As examples, a 10-year-old accompanying his mother to the supermarket in 1960 soon learned that she was the decision-maker when it involved selecting groceries and fresh vegetables. In 1980, a five-year-old may have watched her father make the selections, reflecting an increase in single-parent or at-home-father families. In 1990, it may have been a teenage son or daughter who shopped for the whole family and made independent product choices because both parents worked full-time. For families today, whoever arrives home first may bear the responsibility of calling on the cell phone or logging on to the Web to order groceries or prepared foods for delivery.

We are all introduced to new products or new uses for existing ones through point-of-purchase displays in stores. **Point-of-purchase (POP)** displays are fixtures or special racks and printed materi-als positioned close to customer interface areas in a store. POP displays communicate to a shopper that an old brand of frozen pizza has been improved or a new Stephenie Meyer vampire novel has been released. New products or hot items are often located on end-caps in self-service stores. **End-caps** are display areas located at the ends of shopping-aisle shelving. They are often used in superstores, discount, and warehouse-type stores, as illustrated in Figure 1.7. In-store displays help us obtain valuable product information.

Figure 1.7
Fast-selling soda is restocked frequently on this end-cap at Target.

Electronic media provide other forms of retail education. If we are looking for a new notebook computer, we can read product reviews and blogs to learn about other shoppers' experiences, or we can easily access comparison-shopping Web sites to make a more informed decision. Banner, display, and pop-up ads have become the POP vehicle for online stores.

By watching programmed 30-minute commercials we may know more about exercise equipment than any previous generation, but the equipment still might hold laundry rather than be used to keep us fit once purchased. Some aspects of consumer behavior may not change despite the temptations of technology.

Basic economics, psychology, and sociology are added to the list of lessons learned in almost all retail stores. Education is an inherent part of retailing, and it is not only for the very young.

Retail Evolution

Constant motion and change are other characteristics of retailing that are explained by various theories, all whose very names evoke action: wheel of retailing, retail dissemination, accordion theory, and geographic movement. Each explanation of retail presence and evolution considers the competitive nature of retailing and the ways retailers relentlessly confront change in the marketplace.

Wheel of Retailing

The **wheel of retailing theory** describes a cyclical pattern of retail evolution consisting of three phases: entry, trading up, and vulnerability. According to this theory, retailers usually enter the marketplace as low-price, low-margin, and low-service operators, and mature over time into more elaborate and higher-cost establishments. As they do so, they become increasingly vulnerable to new, lower-priced, lower-margin, lower-service competitors that in turn may go through the same process.[12] The wheel of retailing has similarities to marketing's product life cycle in that products, services, and even retail stores go through stages of the cycle over varying lengths of time. Along the way, many forces, including consumer shifts and competition, affect the pace. The wheel of

Figure 1.8
Wheel of Retailing

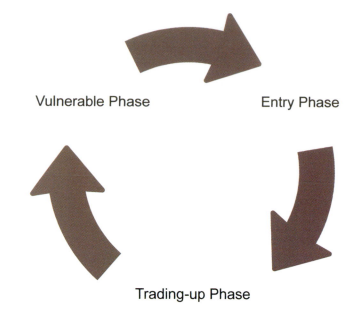

retailing theory describes the dynamic nature of the retailing industry and is graphed in Figure 1.8. The constant motion and competition indicative of the three phases of the wheel are explored below using the example of electronics retailer Circuit City.

Phase One: Entry

Circuit City began in 1949 as Wards Company, the first television retailer in Richmond, Virginia (not to be confused with Montgomery Ward, the department store chain and catalogue retailer, later known as Wards). After several years and various incarnations, the name Circuit City was selected in 1984.[13] These stores were successful in part because they were readily accessible, had plentiful parking, were modern and well-lighted, had knowledgeable staff, and carried a broader assortment of home electronics and computers than existing electronics retailers. Its image of technological savvy and competitive pricing helped Circuit City move the entire home electronics industry up from its humble beginnings.

Phase Two: Trading Up

Through internal growth and several advantageous regional acquisitions, Circuit City became the first home electronics retailer to attain a national presence. Seeing an opportunity to diversify its interests, Circuit City tested in 1994 what the company called a "revolutionary automotive retailing concept." Its CarMax Auto Superstore featured only premium used cars, but two years later the company experimented with selling new cars at select locations.[14] By 2002, Circuit City had spun off the seventy-one–store division into an independent, separately traded company. CarMax sold only automobiles that were less than six years old with not more than 60,000 miles on the gauge.[15] By this time, a new competitor, Best Buy, had begun to wield more power and Circuit City was looking for ways to refocus on its core business.

Strong consumer acceptance compelled other retailers to compete for a share of Circuit City's lucrative business. Mass merchandisers like Target and Walmart were able to surpass Circuit City through astute pricing and aggressive promotion. **Mass merchandisers** are large-format chain stores with broad geographic coverage that carry large assortments of general merchandise and food. Large discount stores with broad distribution networks are considered mass merchandisers. Volume buying, competitive pricing, aggressive expansion, effective merchandise controls, and forward-thinking management are among their tools of competition.

Circuit City stores were made more appealing to customers as décor, merchandise, and customer services were improved. At one time, the company was a multibillion-dollar operation with 721 retail stores in the United States, 770 in Canada operating as The Source by Circuit City, as well as an active online presence and Firedog, its product installation and computer-service business.[16]

Phase Three: Vulnerability

Most retailers discover that rapid expansion, intense price competition, constantly eroding market share, a waning economy, and decreasing sales are difficult to counter individually. When all factors converge concurrently, as they did for Circuit City, we see the wheel of retailing in action. Eventually the electronics pioneer became vulnerable to the strengths and strategies of the new breed of home electronics category killers—especially Best Buy.

The downturn in the global economy further strained the company, which had already been weakened by the intense competition it had endured before the economic recession. Circuit City filed for Chapter 11 bankruptcy protection in late 2008. To defend against bankruptcy, the company announced the closure of 21 percent of its existing stores and the layoff of 6,800 employees.[17] Several outside companies considered acquiring the company, including an international firm. In early 2009, however, with no buyer on the horizon, Circuit City closed its remaining 567 U.S. stores and dismissed 34,000 employees.[18] Soon after, the company sold its Canadian stores to Bell Canada Enterprises.[19]

On a brighter note, the company Systemax bought www.circuitcity.com at auction in 2009 and continues to operate the business exclusively online.[20] The Web-based store, which uses the familiar logo, has expanded its merchandise mix and upgraded customer service.[21] This silver lining does not, of course, assuage the loss experienced by tens of thousands of employees whose jobs were eliminated in the earlier bankruptcy filing and store closures.

Competitive Nature of the Wheel

In some instances, the development of entirely new types of retail institutions has kept the wheel turning. By the 1970s, department stores had become complacent, top-heavy with excess management, and vulnerable to competition. Enterprising retailers responded to the demand voiced by growing numbers of customers for easy access, ample parking, and more aggressive pricing. Market share of department stores eroded as discount stores like Kmart made advances. Smaller off-price specialty discount retailers that focused on apparel found a niche in the 1980s. **Off-price retailers** are specialty discount stores that sell branded products at 20 to 60 percent less than traditional specialty or department stores. Off-price apparel stores like T.J. Maxx applied innovative buying practices and offered discount pricing on popular apparel labels.

This sequence of events illustrates the ever-intensifying competitive pressure that makes the wheel turn, thus hastening retail formats through the cycle faster than ever before. Feel the motion of the wheel as you observe current changes in retailing.

Apparent Immunity to the Wheel

The longevity of some retail institutions cannot be explained by the wheel of retailing. These institutions have withstood the test of time and seem immune to competition. The vending machine industry, specialty food stores, and catalogues are examples. As retailing professor emerita Eleanor May has noted, "specialty catalogs are showing some maturity problems and electronic retailing some immaturity problems."[22] Will online retailing become archaic, displaced by newer retail formats? Or will it achieve its place in a truly integrative retail world? Either eventuality will create further activity on the wheel.

The wheel theory is one explanation of the dynamic nature of retailing. In the next section, other possible determinants of change are considered.

Retail Dissemination

How do retail stores and other formats spread throughout the marketplace? How do new concepts enter the retail arena? Why do retailers decide to spin off part of their business so that they can compete more effectively? These are valid questions as we explore several viewpoints regarding retail dissemination.

Originally used to describe how fashion trends disseminate across consumer markets, so-called "trickle" theories also explain retail movement. Dissemination can occur in three ways: trickle down, trickle up, and trickle across. These theories acknowledge the importance of trend innovation and acceptance as well as economic impact.

Trickle Down

Some retailers initially target high-income markets. They eventually face competition from merchants who copy their strategies to appeal to lower-income groups. To generate more sales, these upmarket retailers trade down to appeal to a lower-income market, even though this new market was not originally their chosen segment. Apparel line Vera for Vera Wang at Kohl's and the variety of well-priced designer options in Target's "Go International" offerings are indicative of trickle down in action. In addition to the company's higher-priced merchandise lines, Ralph Lauren has partnered with JCPenney, producing goods under its American Living label at prices more customers can afford. The opening of mid-market stores by high-end retailers illustrates another aspect of trickle down. Saks, Inc. operates tony Saks Fifth Avenue but also Saks Off 5th, its off-price division.

Trickle Up

The trickle-up process occurs when a trend that begins in or appeals to a lower economic group is identified by customers and retailers and filters up to a higher economic strata—or perhaps taste level—of society. This could be a plausible explanation for the tactics of highly focused businesses. Retailers that take ordinary products, such as coffee and candy, and elevate them to elite experiences illustrate the trickle-up process. Gourmet coffee retailer Starbucks and chocolatier Godiva have both accomplished this. Denim jeans, once the wardrobe staple of farmers and other laborers, have risen to designer fashion status, commanding higher prices than when they were considered utilitarian apparel.

Trickle Across

Jeans are virtually a commodity in mass markets and are a theme of specialty stores at all price levels. Acknowledgment of these trends possibly dilutes the credibility of the trickle-down theory to explain their dissemination; an alternative case can be made that denim's widespread popularity is representative of a trickle-across model.

The trickle-across process occurs when trends are observed across many economic and taste levels at about the same time and speed. In this circumstance, products at varying price and quality levels are available from many types of retailers at approximately the same time. Try to find an Internet-capable cell phone today—whether in a specialty or discount store; in a catalogue, on a Web site, or on a home shopping channel; in San Diego, Santiago, or Singapore—and you probably can.

Retail stores that provide a broad range of merchandise to an equally diverse customer base need to identify trends and interpret them expediently for their markets. Because many retailers carry nearly the same merchandise, knowledge of the trickle-across process is essential.

Accordion Theory

In addition to the trickle perspectives, the **accordion theory** explains the way retail organizations expand and contract in response to changes in the market. When retail organizations grow and retrench in rhythm with changes in the economy (mimicking the in-and-out motion of the musical instrument) this is an example of the accordion theory. During periods of economic decline—like the one that began in 2007—many retailers consolidate their resources, close stores, curb expansion plans, and terminate employees. When the economy is booming, a greater expansiveness of retail growth strategies is evident. Companies seek new locations, grow their Web businesses, and hire new executives and staff. These tactics appear to be cyclical and follow the ebb and flow of available capital and sales.

Geographic Movement

Another indication of the dynamic nature of retailing is geographic movement. Mobility of families caused by employment relocation, growth of industrial parks, and changes to urban and suburban locations always heralds changes in retail growth and development.

Often, retailers follow consumers in order to meet their needs. At other times, gentrification of residential and shopping areas has precipitated change. Occasionally, development in emerging geographic locations occurs in response to entertainment or sporting event trends. Several examples illustrate these points.

Usually new industrial developments first draw major employers, then housing, people, transportation systems, and, of course, retailing. However, planned communities also play a part in geographic movement, creating a customer base by their very existence. For example, the Easton Town Center in Columbus, Ohio, was one of the first lifestyle centers in the United States. A **lifestyle center** is a planned area designed to encompass retail, entertainment, and living in an expansive, themed, outdoor setting. Originally intended to service suburban families in the area, the Easton Town Center includes apartments and condominiums, trendy retailers like Restoration Hardware and Pottery Barn, restaurants like Cheesecake Factory, and entertainment venues, as well as peripheral development. A joint venture between Steiner & Associates and Limited Brands, the 1.7 million-square-foot mixed-use project boasts 170 retailers and several additions that have been made to the nostalgic, downtown-like center since its opening in 1999.[23]

A major movement by retailers into new urban areas in New York City's Harlem shows what happens when old economic structures begin to erode, making way for the redevelopment of areas previously considered undesirable by retailers. Figure 1.9 illustrates Swedish apparel retailer H&M, one of the major tenants on a main shopping street in Harlem. Read more about H&M in the Global Retail Profile following Unit IV.

Equally impressive is the extensive development by global apparel retailers. H&M, as well as Spain's Mango bring high fashion at moderate prices to broad geographic markets. Read about the international expansion plans of these companies in From the Field 1.2.

Bank branches in supermarkets and health clinics in drugstores not only indicate changes in retail banking and medical services but show how innovative service providers meet the immediate needs of customers by overcoming the limits of geography. Equally impressive are airport-based massage services and electronic kiosks that vend numerous electronic gadgets. Consumer demand and innovative retailing work together to change location stereotypes.

Figure 1.9
Stroll along a major street in Harlem and find popular retailers like Staples, Marshall's, and H&M that are committed to revitalization projects in New York. Nearby is none other than Starbucks, dispelling the myth that the area was not ripe for expansion.

Types of Retail Ownership

Retailers are also categorized by the way in which the company is owned. Major forms of retail store ownership include independent retailers, corporate chains, franchise operations, leased departments, government-owned stores, and consumer cooperatives. Several nontraditional forms of ownership add to the variety.

Independent Retailers

Single stores, multiunit operations, and service businesses owned by an individual, a partnership, a small group, or a family are called **independent retailers**. Retail stores owned by only one person are also called sole proprietorships. Independent retail stores can be incorporated under a variety of legal arrangements. About 80 percent of individual stores in the United States are independently owned, forming the largest ownership group in the United States. Although they account for only a small portion of total retail revenue, they are important to the economy because they provide jobs for many and hold potential for growth. According to U.S. Census figures, there are more than 27.2 million small businesses in the United States, the majority of which operate without employees.[24] Sole-proprietor operations and single-unit boutiques fall into this category. There are untold millions of small retailers worldwide and some may embody the next hot retail concept.

Complicating the definition, many large regional or national retailers are also considered independents. Using a census of business approach, when the majority of the company stock rests with a few key individuals or within a family, the company is defined as independent. Nordstrom, in Seattle, Washington, and L.L. Bean in Freeport, Maine, are retailers that fit this definition. Size may not have a bearing on independent ownership status, but gender might. According to the National Women's Business Council, there are 7.8 million women-owned businesses in the United States, comprising 34.4 percent of all retail businesses.[25]

Corporate Chains

In any regional shopping center, 80 to 95 percent of the stores usually belong to large corporate chains. A group of stores with identical or similar formats under central ownership is classified as a **corporate chain**. Normally, executive functions, including merchandise buying, emanate from central headquarters. In this text, a corporate chain is considered any chain of more than 25 units of which a person, family, or partnership is the majority shareholder. Three types of corporate chains are unified, segmented, and holding company formats. Many of the examples presented on the next pages are indicative of the largest corporate chains in the world, which control many hundred to several thousand stores in their respective chains.

Unified Format

JCPenney, Macy's, and Kohl's are examples of retailers that own and operate all or the majority of their stores under the name of the parent company. The broad scope of unified format companies assures that each name has high customer recognition. Unified companies have central headquarters—JCPenney in Plano, Texas, Macy's in New York City, and Kohl's in Menomonee, Wisconsin—where most strategic decisions are made. There are always exceptions. JCPenney operates all of its department stores under its name but spun off its furniture and decorative home products business and opened its Home Store division. Macy's changed the names of several of its existing holdings and acquisitions to Macy's in the mid-2000s, but still runs Bloomingdale's as a separate division. Macy's operated regional headquarters in Cincinnati, Miami, San Francisco, and Atlanta until 2009, when it created one centralized headquarters for buying, merchandise planning, stores organization, and marketing in New York City. Other functions including human resources and property development remain in Cincinnati.[26] Operating more efficiently during the economic downturn and achieving its goal of total company consolidation were the main reasons behind this move.

Segmented Format

Many corporate chains have grown by purchasing other chains or establishing their own. The stores may not all adopt the name of the parent company, and some have rich histories of name and strategy changes. The Gap acquired Banana Republic but developed several other chains, such as GapKids, that closely resembled the parent company's namesake. Other holdings, such as Old Navy, were developed by the company to stand on their own merits. As the economy soured in 2008, Gap announced that it would bring Gap Kids, BabyGap, GapMaternity, and GapBody stores back into its flagship brand stores.[27]

Holding Company Format

Huge conglomerates called **retail holding companies** are composed of many individual companies doing business under a variety of names. Retailing may or may not be the primary focus of a holding company. Many multinational holding companies are extremely large and powerful and do business across many related and unrelated product categories. **Multinational companies** conduct manufacturing, service, or retail businesses—or a mix of all three—in their home countries, as well as many other countries. As examples, the French company Louis Vuitton Moet Hennessy (LVMH) owns several couture fashion houses—including Fendi, Marc Jacobs, Céline, Donna Karan, and its signature Louis Vuitton leather-goods company—through its Louis Vuitton division. The company also owns Sephora fragrance and cosmetics stores, Thomas Pink shirtmakers, the DFS chain of duty-free shops, and jeweler Bulgari. Through its Moet Hennessy division, it owns major wine and spirits companies. All divisions operate or distribute internationally.

In several instances, companies that began as manufacturers have evolved into holding companies, shifting emphasis from one part of the marketing channel to another. Many apparel manufacturers, including Jones Apparel Group and Calvin Klein, run factory outlets or other specialty store divisions and have acquired or developed retail stores.

As retail emphasis shifts, so do corporate names. Dayton Hudson Company, which represented a consolidation of the Dayton Company and J. L. Hudson, changed its name to Target in 2000 to better reflect the contributions of its discount store division to corporate profits. At one time Target also owned Marshall Field's, the Chicago-based department store, which was sold to Macy's. The retail logo, illustrated in Figure 1.10, was retired when Macy's absorbed the famous brand.

The purchase of Kmart by Sears in 2004 came as a surprise to many observers of the retail scene, since nonretailer Edward Lampert, a real estate baron and investor, engineered the transaction. Lampert's company became a majority shareholder in Kmart when the company was in financial difficulty and its stock prices were low.

Figure 1.10
Marshall Field's, a popular department store in the Midwest for more than a century, is now part of retail history. The name on this Minneapolis store was changed to Macy's when the Field's chain was acquired by that company.

Sears was ripe for investment when Lampert bought the troubled retailer and took control of the entire company. Conscious of the power and high recognition of the Sears brand, he renamed the new parent company Sears Holdings.

Along with its global holdings, Royal Ahold, the Dutch retailer, owns several U.S. supermarket chains including Stop & Shop and Giant. Using sovereign wealth funds, the company Istithmar, based in the United Arab Emirates, bought apparel retailer Barneys New York. Investment capital emanating from governments is called **sovereign wealth funds**. The chief investor in Talbot's, the specialty clothing chain for professional women, is Aeon Group of Japan. These examples illustrate the complexities of holding company structure, the presence of strong multinational involvement, and the trend toward consolidation in the retail industry.

Franchise Operations

Franchising is one means by which retailers expand, assuming less risk than those companies that open businesses independently. **Franchising** is a contractual arrangement by which individuals or companies agree to own and operate a business in accordance with the brand standards of the host company.

Individuals or companies that purchase franchises are called *franchisees*. Host companies that sell franchise rights are called *franchisors*. Franchisors usually offer time-tested formats, strong brand recognition, management training, business plans, and many corporate support services. Accounting, hiring, training, site selection, advertising, and marketing assistance are available, as well as legal rights to use the brand name. However, purchasers of franchises need adequate capital and managerial experience to run a successful operation.

According to the International Franchise Association (IFA), there are more than 3,000 franchise companies in the United States. Revenues exceed 11 percent of the private-sector economic output.[28] Usually, for a flat fee and an ongoing percentage of sales paid by the franchisee, the host company will provide a methodically planned retail store or service that is completely ready to begin operation. Such an outlet is called a **turnkey operation**. Franchise fees can run from a low of $10,000 for a lesser-known name to $30,000 or more for a Dunkin' Donuts, to several hundred thousand dollars for a McDonald's.

One of the first franchises was sold in 1863, when the Singer Sewing Machine Company offered small stores the right to use its trade name and buy products from Singer. Times have changed. Many products and services—from hair salons to car washes, bagel shops to childcare centers—are franchised. Workout franchises such as Jazzercise and Gold's Gym are also popular. Fast-food franchises are making inroads in unconventional locations. Subway, Taco Bell, and Domino's Pizza have all established franchise agreements with high schools and universities. Quiznos sandwich shops recruit store managers on college campuses and encourage students to help with grand openings.

Franchising is an effective way to enter the global market. Collective Brands, owner of the Payless ShoeSource chain, has opened stores with various franchise partners in several Middle Eastern countries, including Saudi Arabia, as well as in Guam, Saipan, Canada, the Caribbean, and South and Central America.[29] The company expected to open 15 franchised stores in Indonesia in 2011.[30] Via franchise agreements, Gap moved into Mexico, Cyprus, Israel, Jordan, and Romania in 2009 as the company celebrated its 40th anniversary. In 2010 it opened other franchised stores in Australia, Bulgaria, and Thailand, followed in 2011 by a unit in Kazakhstan. Gap expects its franchise store numbers to grow from 200 to 400 by 2015.[31]

Franchises large and small are also making inroads online. Instant Imprints, a San Diego–based screen printing, sign, and advertising specialties franchise, offers prospective franchisees the option of setting up shop through iStores, an online service, or through conventional stores. Also an international retailer, Instant Imprints operates about 100 stores in three countries.[32]

Leased Departments

A unique form of ownership that is rarely apparent to customers, leased departments add to the products and services in most major department stores and an increasing number of discount and specialty stores. **Leased departments** are merchandise or service specialty areas that are owned and operated by companies other than the host store. Leased departments are often chains themselves. Some examples of departments that frequently are leased include jewelry, shoes, gift-wrapping, florist, beauty or eye-care shops, and restaurants. Meldisco, a division of Footstar, is an example of a leased shoe department chain. The company operates more than 2,000 licensed footwear departments, including those in some Rite Aid stores,[33] and it serviced all Kmart stores until the company took its shoe operation back in-house in 2009.[34] Retailers welcome the diversity that leased departments bring to their merchandise mix, particularly in areas that are difficult to stock, manage, or service.

Most customers do not realize that the leased department is not the store's own, which is the intent. For example, sushi bars and fishmonger departments are often a separate operation in grocery markets. The jewelry departments in Macy's are leased but appear as an integral part of the store. Problems could surface if leased departments did not meld or if managerial inconsistencies were apparent. Leased departments usually pay a per-square-foot fee and a percentage of sales to the host store. They are similar to concessions but differ in intent. **Concessions** are independently owned and operated departments that cross many product and service lines and are less dependent on special levels of management expertise than leased departments.

In some countries an entire retail store, or floor, may be composed of concessions or leased departments. Founded in 1902, Nordiska Kompaniet (NK) operates two major department stores in Sweden that have 100 leased departments. Some of the popular global brands carried are Hermes accessories, Mulberry apparel, and Orrefors crystal.[35] In the early 1990s, NK converted from a traditional department store format because of increased competition and operating costs, and declining profits. NK had a well-established name and high traffic in its stores. When the transition was made, many buyers and department managers became entrepreneurs, taking ownership in the departments where they were once employed. Many merchandise areas in Japanese department stores are also set up as concessions.

Government-Owned Stores

Though individual examples are few, government-owned stores are a significant contributor to the retail economy. **Government-owned stores** are those that are owned and operated by local, state, or federal governments. Examples cover a broad spectrum of store types and locales. Military families shop at base exchanges or post exchanges, government-owned facilities where food and general merchandise are purchased at lower prices than at comparable civilian stores. The U.S. Army Air Force Exchange (AAFES)—now called simply "The Exchange"—is ranked number 113 in *Stores* magazine's listing of the "Top 250 Global Retailers" and recorded sales of $8.2 billion in fiscal 2010 that ended in January 2011.[36] The retail operations of the Navy Exchange Service Command (NEXCOM) are highlighted in From the Field 1.3.

As other examples, in some states, including New Hampshire, liquor stores are state owned and all proceeds on wines and spirits go into the state coffers. In Singapore, some general merchandise and food stores are government-owned. Until 2002 when China opened its markets to global trade, all retail firms had the Chinese government as a retail partner.

Consumer Cooperatives

Although not a widespread phenomenon in the United States, consumer cooperatives are an important form of retail ownership in Europe and Scandinavia. **Consumer cooperatives** are stores in which customers own a stake, receive lower prices on merchandise, and may participate in profit sharing. Cooperatives are run similarly to credit unions in the United States. Through a board of directors, members of a credit union approve management to operate banking transactions. For a modest membership fee, consumers join and are then able to use financial services, receive preferred rates on personal loans, and vote for credit union directors. Operating along similar principles, consumer cooperatives usually sell general merchandise and food.

Lower prices, profit sharing, and ready access are the motivations for belonging to a cooperative. Migros in Switzerland is an example of a consumer cooperative with a large membership and a strongly expressed social consciousness. Approximately 2 million out of 7.2 million Swiss are member/owners of Migros. It is the largest retailer in Switzerland and, regardless of the economy, gives back 1 percent of its annual sales to cultural activities, many involving education.[37]

From the Field 1.3   Competing in a Sea of Change

Despite the sinking economy, the Navy Exchange Service Command (NEXCOM) is sailing in relatively calm waters these days, with $2.6 billion in revenue posted for 2011.*

Established in 1946, NEXCOM operates more than 100 NEX complexes, including almost 300 retail locations and approximately 170 stores based on Navy ships. Additionally, NEXCOM has more than 1,200 service operations, including gas stations, food outlets, barbershops and salons, and laundry/dry cleaners.+ With stores in Europe, Asia, Africa, Cuba, the Middle East, and the Pacific Rim, few retailers can compare to NEXCOM's global presence.

What differentiates NEXCOM from mainstream retailing is primarily its military core, witnessed most profoundly through its philosophy, mission, and financial management. The NEXCOM mission is to serve enlisted soldiers and their families by providing quality-of-life enhancements via retail outlets and services. Making products and opportunities available to military personnel takes precedence over making profits. However, NEX is profitable: 70 percent of store profits are set aside for the Navy's Morale, Welfare and Recreation (MWR) budget, and 30 percent are invested back into store operations to fund new growth, remodels, or improvements.

A true multichannel player, NEXCOM sells Navy uniforms at brick-and-mortar stores as well as through direct-to-consumer channels, including catalogs, the online store (www.mynavyexchange.com) and the Uniform Support Center (USC).

Stores range in size from 70,000 square feet to the 144,000-square-foot flagship in Pearl Harbor, Hawaii. Inventory flows to NEX stores from three domestic and six international distribution centers. NEXCOM is ac-tively engaged in conserving natural resources in its stores, gas stations, and vending machines.

On the merchandising side, NEXCOM strives to offer the best prices on the largest assortment possible—everything from Coach handbags to household cleaners. Surveys conducted by NEXCOM indicate shoppers save an average of 20 percent on products, not including sales tax.

In an interview, Rear Admiral Robert J. Bianchi commented on some of NEXCOM's unique challenges. One is the inability to advertise merchandise and prices using traditional media. NEX can only advertise to its authorized patrons, thus restricting media channels to direct mail, military-associated publications, Web sites, and military TV outlets. Another is following its consumers as they travel the world while on duty. Bianchi believes that by expanding brand presence on the Internet, NEXCOM will be in a better position to serve its customers.

The rear admiral also believes that NEXCOM is no less affected by economic trends than the rest of the retail industry. Understanding competition plays an important part in how NEXCOM plans pricing, promotional scheduling, store design, location, and merchandise mix strategies.

Adapted and condensed from Connie Robbins Gentry, "Competing in a Sea of Change," *Chain Store Age*, October 2008: 23–30.
Sources for updates:
* "Resale Snapshot–December 2011," *Exchange and Commissary News*, March 2012. www.ebmpubs.com/ECN_pdfs/ecn0312_ResaleSnapshot.pdf.
+"Handbook for Military Life: Pay and Benefits," *Military Times*, http://militarytimes.com/projects/benefits-handbook/pay-benefits/other-benefits.

Membership in a cooperative should not be confused with membership in a warehouse club. Members of warehouse clubs do not own shares or participate in profit sharing, although both warehouse club and cooperative members enjoy the benefit of low pricing and other services.

Nontraditional Owners

The quest for increased sales, profits, and growth has drawn nontraditional owners into retailing. Nonprofit organizations such as churches, hospitals, art galleries, and museums are prime examples. One of the most interesting is the Metropolitan Museum of Art Store, which operates shops in New York City as well as satellite stores in many other cities. The company is a multichannel retailer, offering a wealth of products—most inspired by the artwork and exhibits found in the museum's collections—through its stores, catalogues, and Web site. This nontraditional retail owner is illustrated in Figure 1.11.

Other examples illustrate profit-oriented firms from other industries that have become retail owners. The presence of an NBC Television Network store in New York City, as well as online, shows us that even media giants are exploring new methods of brand building and revenue generation. At the NBC Experience Store in Rockefeller Center, customers can browse interactive displays and purchase items inspired by their favorite shows.

Health and fitness centers, yoga studios, and dance studios are examples of service retailers that have added merchandise to their businesses. The large numbers of members that these businesses draw make it feasible to provide exercise-related merchandise on the premises. My favorite editor takes her dogs to a veterinary hospital chain that includes an array of pet foods and products, including Dyson vacuum cleaners—used for removing those ever-present dog hairs from rugs and furniture. She was astonished to see the vacuum in this setting, but its presence suggests that all businesses need new revenue drivers. Business revenues grow because of retail expansion. Nontraditional ownership is expected to increase as more businesses explore the benefits of retail ownership.

Retailing History

No attempt is made to present a comprehensive chronology of retailing in this chapter; instead, an anecdotal approach brings the history of retailing to life. This section emphasizes retailing in the United States, but the establishment of major institutions was similar in many industrialized societies, and several international examples are included.

The Marketplace

Visit an outdoor market to experience the essence of retail trade. Markets are as old as time and indeed predate recorded history. Anthropologists have written about the migratory patterns of peoples based on the types of pottery remnants found near trade routes. Six thousand years ago in Mesopotamia, pottery designs varied from village to village, showing us that tastes and preferences were as important to consumers then as they are now.

To trade profitably, surplus stock is necessary. This is the basis for the exchange process, which is fundamental to all marketing. As nations evolved from agrarian to industrial economies and food consumption was no longer tied to the cycles of nature, there was less need for traditional marketplaces. However, many exist today despite the availability of more modern retail facilities. For example, the Grand Bazaar in Istanbul and some of the souks in Morocco and the Middle East are centuries old and still in use. By studying present-day outdoor markets in the developing countries of Africa or Asia, one can get an idea as to what earlier trade arenas looked like. Everything from fresh fish to peanut butter is available, but customers may have to bring their own containers. Even chicken—dressed or still alive—makes its way to the dinner table from the outdoor market.

In the United States and other developed countries, the open marketplace may have waned in popularity, but the fascination with it persists. Many frequent flea markets or swap meets; others prefer to buy their produce at farm stands or collaboratives. Farmers' markets are staging a comeback in small towns and major U.S. cities, from Portland, Oregon, to Portland, Maine. In London, England, markets have never waned in popularity, but they have become highly specialized. On weekends, Petticoat Lane is the place to go for apparel and general household goods, but if antique lithograph prints are sought, the Brick Mill Lane market is a better choice. It is said in partial jest that you can find your grandmother's lost silverware for sale in stalls on Portobello Road. The marketplace has played an important part in retailing through the centuries, around the world.

Pre–Industrial Revolution

Retail formats of a more formal type evolved in the 17th and 18th centuries, although they were not as sophisticated as they would become later. Trading posts, seaports, roving peddlers, and general stores paved the way for contemporary retail stores and nonstore operations.

Trading Posts

The first North American retailers were probably Native Americans. They sold to the early settlers skins of animals they had trapped and killed. Although settlers were mostly self-sufficient, the ability to buy fur skins gave them more time for other chores and to look for other material goods. Trading posts in the United States and Canada evolved as central places where fur trappers bartered for products imported from Europe. They were located along navigable waterways or at intersections of trails, areas that were also natural locations for villages.

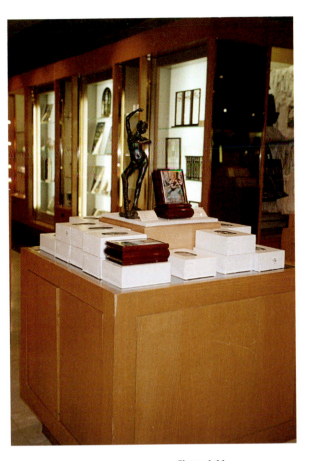

Figure 1.11
Many products at the Metropolitan Museum of Art stores are inspired by artifacts from the museum's collections. The success of this concept illustrates the growing importance of retail revenue on previously not-for-profit organizations.

When settlers arrived, the trappers who had preceded them served customers in what could be called—with a stretch of the imagination—retail stores.

One Canadian retailer traces its roots to the Hudson's Bay Company (HBC), which was established in 1670, trading "knives, kettles, beads, needles, and blankets" in exchange for furs. The six original HBC department stores opened in 1912.[38] Adding a contemporary twist, HBC was acquired by the U.S. company NRCD Equity Partners in 2008. NRCD also owns the U.S. retailer Lord & Taylor, an upmarket department store, along with several Canadian store chains.[39] Hudson's Bay Company is considered North America's oldest retail brand and is now simply called The Bay—or, in French, La Baie. The company expected to go public in early 2013.[40]

Port City Retail Centers

The shipping industry practiced global trade long before it was a popular concept. Ports from London to New York, Cartegena in Colombia to Cádiz in Spain, were important centers of trade where markets served the growing population. Some merchants imported finished furniture, cloth, and clothing from Europe, or spices and silks from Asia. Carpenters made and sold products for the home, and tailors offered custom-made garments to the wealthy.

Early apparel shops in coastal cities were called "slop shops." The term was not derogatory but referred to the ready-made apparel (called "slops") worn by merchant sailors.

Yankee Peddlers

Called Yankee peddlers because their original homes were in New England, these early retailers purchased a variety of goods from importers, auctioneers, and at fairs. They traveled the countryside, first with packs on their backs and later with horses and wagons, selling everything from needles and pins to groceries, housewares, patent medicines, and magic elixirs—usually derived from a strong alcohol base—to their country customers. As the settlers moved inland, so did the Yankee peddler. Success depended on his strength, the size of his wagon, his ability to traverse terrible terrain, the demand for his products, and the ability of customers to pay.

The appearance of the traveling merchant was a highlight in settlers' lives. He brought not only needed goods but also news of events in the cities. Certainly not exclusive to the United States, itinerant merchants have long played an important role in the dissemination of products and information in villages remote from bustling cities.

Life was hard on the road, and eventually peddlers settled down, often joining forces with settlers who ran local trading posts. At other times peddlers opened their own small stores in growing communities.

General Stores

The birth of the general store was the most important retail event of the latter part of the 18th century. The Brick Store in Bath, New Hampshire, opened in 1790 and is considered the oldest general store still in operation in the United States.[41] General stores served not only as emporia for supplies but also as centers for community gatherings, providing a rare chance to socialize with neighbors who often lived miles away. Shopkeepers carried groceries, dry goods, medicines, and other household goods. They also traded for or bought products produced in the geographic areas where they were located. Their assortments came from trips to wholesale centers, wholesale merchants, and local farms or producers.

The following excerpt from a book on general stores in Downeast Maine encapsulates the essence of the general store:

> The old yellow general store—which had meant so much to me—its front windows adorned with Tetley Tea signs and local notices, had been the community information center, the neighborhood gathering place. Certainly the store's demise left a void, but more importantly it had served as a nucleus, or core, to which all of the town's appendages—its widely scattered population—adhered. Put another way: The village store, like a good school system, or perhaps a strong local government, acted like a centripetal force that helped to fuse the townspeople's whims and differences into a community.[42]

Shopkeepers did not operate on a one-price policy. Instead, they bargained with their customers for the optimum price. They also started the first charge account systems, often giving credit to farmers for as long as a year. Payment was made when the crops came in, fish were sold, or the sheep were shorn.

The Industrial Revolution

When economies were dominated by agriculture, the general store was able to address the few needs that were not met by farmers themselves. As countries became industrialized, people were more likely to work away from their homes. The growth of the textile industry in the United States contributed significantly to this shift, and also to the production of fabric that eventually would fuel the ready-to-wear market. Amoskeag Manufacturing Company in Manchester, New Hampshire, was once the largest textile mill in the world. Two of its biggest accounts were Marshall Field & Company and the JCPenney Company, which purchased great quantities of fabric for their stores.[43]

Growing affluence increased demand for a broader assortment of goods in all categories. Families now purchased goods in stores, rather than relying on home production. As life in industrialized cities changed, so did the nature of retail stores. Two important retail concepts flourished: specialty shops and department stores.

Predominance of Specialty Stores

Single-line stores such as shoe and millinery (hat) shops developed at this time. Home production could not keep up with demand so factories that specialized in popular merchandise lines were established in cities in Europe and the United States. Early specialty stores were small shops owned independently in much the same manner as many of today's boutiques. They were clustered together in easily accessible city locations, usually central business districts. The downtowns attracted residents from every part of town, and public transportation facilitated trips to larger retail venues.

Industrialization helped create urban areas that became retail hubs in the developing world. Although the shopping center movement would not officially begin for a few decades, Providence, Rhode Island, boasts the oldest indoor shopping center in the United States. The three-story Greek Revival-style building opened in 1828.[44]

Birth of Department Stores

The first true department stores in the United States, including Chicago's Marshall Field & Company, Philadelphia's Wanamaker's, and New York's R. H. Macy, opened during the 1850s. This began the golden age of department stores, when retailers mastered what we now call the "wow factor."

London's Harrods, considered the largest department store in the world, was founded by Charles Henry Harrod in 1849.[45] Trade had been conducted since the early 1600s on its Brompton Road site. Through gradual acquisition of the space surrounding the original modest grocery shop, Harrods now encompasses an entire city block.

Surviving various fires, several owners, and other challenges, the company was held by Mohamed Al Fayed from 1985 to 2010, when it was sold to the Qatari royal family for £1.5 billion (about $2.2 billion).[46] Harrods' motto tells us that the store carries "everything, for everybody, everywhere." This sentiment captures concisely the extensive merchandise assortment that in the 1930s included one of the first TV models and yachts made to order. Harrods' customers could choose from funeral services, and in later years, banking and real estate.[47]

Another early retailer was James Cash Penney, who began his career in Kemmerer, Wyoming, a mining and sheep ranching town. His first venture, a butcher shop, was not profitable because Penney extended too much credit to his customers. His second attempt at retailing in 1902 was a general merchandise store called The Golden Rule. It was successful—due not only to his customer service orientation but also to the fact that prior experience had taught him to operate on a cash-only basis. He provided a large assortment of quality goods in one location and stayed open long hours. Penney kept his doors open until the last sheep rancher or miner was off the streets of Kemmerer. Penney's first year's sales were $28,898, not a small sum at that time in a town with a

Cyberscoop

If you're interested in vintage catalogues, you'll enjoy this Web site, which features a variety of oldies but goodies including those from Sears and JCPenney. Go to www.wishbookweb.com for a bit of research and a touch of nostalgia.

population of 1,000.[48] The company eventually grew to 1,102 department stores in the United States and Puerto Rico. In 2011, JCPenney recorded $17.3 billion in sales.[49]

Department stores have withstood many ups and downs in the last 150 years. Their popularity, which peaked in the 1960s, began to diminish due to high operational costs, competition, redundant merchandise, and changes in customer lifestyles.

The 20th Century

Chain stores were a product of the late 19th and early 20th centuries. Some of the early ventures, such as Walgreen's drugstores, are still with us today. Founded in 1901, the stores featured soda fountains, a requisite of drugstores until the 1960s.[50] The top-volume drugstore chain today, Walgreen Company recorded sales of $72.2 billion in fiscal year 2011.[51] As of August 2011, the company had 8,210 stores in operation.[52]

General merchandise chains and variety stores also formed in this era and included companies like S. S. Kresge (which opened Kmart in 1962), Montgomery Ward, and Sears. The latter created one of the earliest catalogues, directed to a rural population that could not get to markets as easily as their city counterparts.

In the United States, grocery chains were also a product of the late 19th century, although they did not match the size and scope of today's supermarkets. **Supermarkets** are self-service food and grocery stores of under 100,000 square feet that may carry some nonfood items but do not have extensive specialty departments. As early as 1880, the Great Atlantic and Pacific Tea Company, better known as A&P, had 95 stores

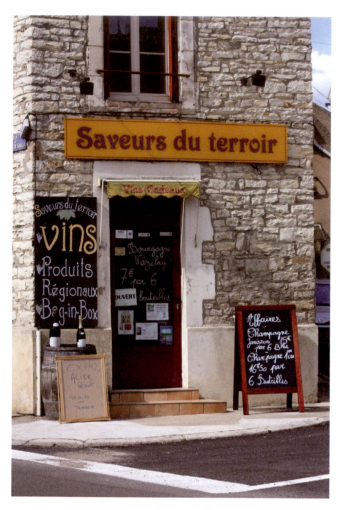

Figure 1.12
Neighborhood grocery stores were staples of the retail community in the United States early 20th century, and still are important to shoppers in smaller towns and many other countries. This corner store in the French countryside offers various necessities, fresh foods, and of course local wine to customers and tourists. (Courtesy of Charlene Curry)

that stretched from Boston to Milwaukee. Single-unit mom-and-pop grocery stores served neighborhoods and predominated in this era. In many parts of the world, the small grocery is still an important part of the retail community, as seen in Figure 1.12. Larger units did not evolve until the 1930s. Stores were located on the periphery of cities and towns where parking was more plentiful, rents were less expensive, and more square footage was available. The invention of the automobile allowed growing ranks of mobile consumers to shop less frequently but purchase more products on their shopping junkets. Better refrigeration and more attention to product development and packaging also aided the growth of the supermarket.

After the turn of the 20th century, chain stores were plentiful in the United States. By 1914 there were over 20,000 individual stores belonging to retail chains. A&P then had 800 stores, the United Cigar Stores Company had 900, and Woolworth's had 774.[53] Growth is usually negatively affected by economic downturns and war; indeed, the Great Depression in the United States was prefaced by the stock market crash of 1929. Despite this, major chains continued to dominate the retail landscape. At its peak in the 1930s, A&P had 16,000 stores—more than top retailer Walmart does today.[54]

Rationing of consumer products such as sugar, coffee, and textile fabric during World War II (1939–1945) subsequently slowed retail expansion. It was not until after the war that retailers were again able to move forward.

Post–World War II Retail Growth

The second and largest spurt in retail growth took place in the late 1940s and early 1950s. With the war finally over, enlisted men and women from the United States and Canada returned home to growing economies and fresh products on the shelves. Retailers were eager and willing to help in both instances. Those in Europe and Asia were in the process of rebuilding their countries, including their commercial districts, which were often in ruins due to devastating bombings.

During this period in the United States, suburban living peaked in popularity. People poured out of cities to nearby areas where the trappings of expanding middle-class prosperity—new ranch houses, station wagons, and backyard barbecue equipment—were rapidly becoming a way of life. Real-estate developers and highway systems linked city jobs to suburban living.

Instead of refurbishing their old downtown stores, department store owners followed the newly moneyed populace to their burgeoning suburban communities. This was, in retrospect, another example of the wheel of retailing in action, as department stores adapted to change in order to maintain growth and withstand competition.

Between 1950 and 1970, suburban shopping centers became community landmarks. The Southdale Center opened in Minnesota in 1956 and is considered the first fully enclosed, climate-controlled, regional shopping center in the country. Almost no suburb was without a center, and one-stop shopping became the norm. Department stores were often shopping center anchors but served an expanding middle-class market. Working class families had almost as much money to spend as their white-collar neighbors, but believed that department stores portrayed a high-price image. Discount stores evolved to better meet the needs of shoppers who were more dollar- than status-conscious.

Approaching the Millennium

While the suburbs flourished, urban blight also prevailed. Years of suburban growth in the 1950s and 1960s left many central city districts looking neglected. The shopping center movement shifted retail power to the suburbs, while urban areas planned for renewal. The latter decades of the 20th century witnessed the birth of advanced technologies that would forever change business practices.

Demise of Downtowns

Urban department stores suffered most, and the 1980s and 1990s saw the demise of many significant downtown retailers. To compete, some adopted store-within-a-store concepts to break up their cavernous spaces and bring more intimate shopping experiences to customers. Industry consolidation closed many department stores' doors. Shopping center development in suburban areas posed other challenges, as department stores had to contend with increased competition from specialty stores and discounters. To this day, some department stores have survived in part by practicing promotional pricing techniques much like their discount store counterparts.

Urban Renewal and Redevelopment

Beginning in the 1970s and continuing to this day, urban renewal became a national goal. With funding from both government and private sources, some city centers once again began to look clean, fresh, and exciting. Middle-class and upper-class suburbanites slowly began to move back to the city. By the early 1980s, cities from coast to coast were once again places where people lived, shopped, and worked. Smaller cities also benefited from the surge in revitalization efforts. Some have re-created their historic pasts through architectural restoration and development of new buildings that play on historical themes. San Diego's gaslight district is a downtown area that embraces turn-of-the-20th-century attributes in a welcoming urban setting. Nearby is the Horton Center, San Diego's downtown shopping mall.

Contrasting Sentiments Toward Redevelopment

Western Europe has traditionally maintained a different perspective on redevelopment. The past is revered, and it is customary to rebuild centuries-old establishments. Historical preservation laws ensure that old buildings in England are not torn down but instead are restored. This has not always been the attitude in the United States, but fortunately, as times change, so does public sentiment regarding the role preservation plays in retail progress.

Advances in Technological Infrastructure

The last three decades of the 20th century witnessed the establishment of new management tools that went beyond existing technologies, becoming the precursors to modern systems. Electronic data interchange systems became the industry standard, replacing earlier approaches for managing supply and sales data. **Electronic data interchange (EDI)** is a computer-guided communication network between retailer, manufacturer, and other supply chain members. Today, Internet-based wireless tools are surpassing EDI as technologies continue to develop. Industry consolidation and the advent of many new specialty formats, including online stores, marked retailing in the 1990s.

The 21st Century and Beyond

Retailing unquestionably has become more complex since the latter half of the 20th century, when growth seemed limitless, world economies were fairly stable, and competitive battles revolved around the question of who could get to the next hot spot first. The first decade of the new millennium saw two boom-to-bust business cycles: greater emphasis on energy conservation, the green movement, and the consequences of dwindling natural resources, as well as major conflicts and socially defining movements. The impact on retailing in all its multichannel forms has been great. Major changes in ownership, including the demise of sometimes century-old retail companies, became commonplace. Approximately 3,800 to 4,300 stores announced closings in 2009 and this trend continued in 2010.[55] Despite these challenges, double-digit annual growth of online stores continued, with periodic glimmers of improvement in markets worldwide. Volatility characterizes markets as retailers grapple with declining sales, consumer wariness, and pressure from shareholders to perform. Such turbulence is indicative of change and may herald the promise of retail innovation in the future.

Retailing in this century demands as much science as art if the goals of customer satisfaction, productivity, growth, and profit are to be met. The importance of retailing to national and global economies is emphasized throughout this text. One in five Americans works in retailing and there are 1.6 million retail establishments in the United States.[56]

The rules, players, loci of exchange, methods, and customers are all changing. In the future, challenges will be met differently. Lessons from history are valuable as retailers make informed decisions faster than their competition. Welcome to the world of retailing.

Summary

Retailing exists everywhere people gather, and the industry changes constantly to meet the needs of customers. Product knowledge that we possess is largely due to the marketing efforts of retailers and our own efforts to educate ourselves in the retail arena.

Retailing is presented throughout this book in a marketing context. In order to be classified as a retailer, a company must sell more than 50 percent of its goods or services directly to individual consumers. Many manufacturers and wholesalers also engage in retailing. A major direction in the 21st century is multichannel retailing, in which retailers draw upon several sales channels concurrently to reach their customers. Omnichannel retailing represents the evolution of multichannel retailing.

The six functional areas of retailing are merchandising, operations, promotion, finance, human resources, and information technology. Each must work in synergy with the others to assure smooth operations.

The cyclical pattern of retail evolution, according to the wheel of retailing theory, consists of three stages: entry, trading up, and vulnerability. The wheel theory is not the only one that explains the element of change in retailing. Trickle-up, trickle-down, and trickle-across processes and the accordion theory also are offered as explanations. Geographic movement and mobility of customers are precursors of change, as retailers follow customers, or customers follow retailers, to new locations.

Retailers are categorized by type of ownership. Independent owners include small businesses as well as larger chains. Corporate chains dominate shopping centers and are the revenue drivers in retailing. Franchises enable retail owners to work with an established brand, thus diminishing risk. Other ownership options include leased departments, government-owned stores, and consumer cooperatives. Nontraditional retail owners include museums, media companies, hotels, and service businesses.

History permeates many discussions in this introductory chapter. Retailers learn from past trends and challenges, and find solutions that allow them to adapt to change.

Key Terms

Accordion theory
Breadth of stock
Business intelligence (BI)
Business-to-business (B2B)
Business-to-consumer (B2C)
Cannibalization
Category killers
Concessions
Consumer cooperatives
Corporate chain
Department stores
Depth of stock
Discounters
Economic utility
Electronic data interchange (EDI)
End-caps
Franchising
Full-line department stores
Government-owned stores
Gross domestic product (GDP)
Independent retailers
Leased departments
Lifestyle center
Limited-line department stores
Manufacturer's representative
Marketing
Marketing channel
Marketing mix

Mass merchandisers
Merchandise assortment
Merchandise classification
Multichannel retailing
Multinational companies
Nonstore retailers
Off-price retailers
Omnichannel retailing
Point-of-purchase (POP)
Product life cycle
Product line
Pure service retailers
Retail holding companies
Retailing
Retail mix
Sourcing
Sovereign wealth funds
Specialty stores
Supermarkets
Superstores
Supply chain
Target market
Turnkey operation
Vendors
Vertical integration
Warehouse clubs
Wheel of retailing theory

Questions for Discussion

1. Does a company need to be a retailer by definition in order to engage in retailing? Give examples from the text and your own experience of nontraditional retailers that sell to ultimate consumers. How does retailing affect you?

2. Describe the areas of responsibility that fall under each of the six functional areas in retail organizations.

3. How do retailers select marketing channels? Give examples of typical channels used by retailers of fashion apparel and home electronics.

4. Explain the concept of multichannel retailing. Why has this become a strategic imperative for retail companies? How does this differ from vertical integration?

5. The scope of retailing is vast; different types of stores and nonstore methods to reach the customer are constantly evolving. What are the essential differences between specialty stores and category killers? What types of retailers satisfy your needs best? Why?

6. What are the challenges faced by service retailers and how do these differ from the challenges faced by retail companies that are product-centered?

7. How does the wheel of retailing theory explain the evolution of retail companies? What other dynamics help explain the spread of retailing?

8. Several ownership options are available to retailers. What are the advantages of each?

9. It is said that history often repeats itself. How do retailers benefit from having knowledge of retail history? Over time, what types of events diminish opportunities for retail expansion?

Endnotes

1. GDP figures for United States and China. *CIA World Factbook*, accessed June 2, 2011, CHINA: https://www .cia.gov/library/publications/the-world-factbook/geos/ch.html, THE UNITED STATES: https://www.cia.gov/ library/publications/the-world-factbook/geos/us.html, U.S. Department of Commerce, Bureau of Economic

Analysis. "GDP Growth Slows in the First Quarter." May 26, 2011, http://www.bea.gov/newsreleases/national/gdp/2011/pdf/gdp1q11_2nd_fax.pdf .

2. Lucia Mulikani. "Retail Sales Slow, Still Point to Growth Pickup." Reuters. February 15, 2011. www.reuters.com/assets/print?aid-USTRE70ROSG20110215.

3. Sara Yin. "Netflix Inks Content Deal for 2011." *PC Magazine*. December 1, 2010. www.pcmag.com/print_article2/0,1217,a=257589,00.asp.

4. Matthew Lasar. "Netflix Now 'The King' of North American Internet Traffic." May 11, 2011. http://arstechnica.com/tech-policy/news/2011/05/netflix-now-owns-30-percent-of-north-american-fixed-internet-traffic.ars.

5. Business Wire. "Build-A-Bear Workshop to Open First Store at Airport." April 27, 2011. http://www.businesswire.com/news/home/20110427006425/en/Build-A-Bear-Workshop-Open-Store-Airport.

6. Ralph E. Winter. "For Sherwin-Williams, a Rosy Outlook in Recession." *Wall Street Journal*. December 24, 2008, B7.

7. Jean E. Palmieri. "Under Armour Boosts Apparel Offering to Back Footwear." *Women's Wear Daily*. December 11, 2008, 20.

8. National Retail Federation. "2008 Holiday Survival Kit (derived from U.S. Department of Commerce data)," 7. www.nrf.com/modules.php?name=Documents&op=viewlive&sp_id=1931&ei=2LLaT_unOPCo0AHK4YDiCg&usg=AFQjCNHquDc95l4Xhey4bxc1BA1D8iTH_g.

9. www.spin-cycle.com/corporate/news/journaltwo (accessed September 1999)

10. *Phoenix Business Journal*. "Spin-Cycle Laundromat Chain Sold to L.A. Firm." August 8, 2003. www.bizjournals.com/phoenix/stories/2003/08/04/daily56.html.

11. "PWS About Us & Services," PWS, accessed November 26, 2008, www.pwslaundry.com/p-223-about-us-html.

12. Malcome P. McNair, "Significant Trends and Developments in the Postwar Period," in *Competitive Distribution in a Free, HighLevel Economy and Its Implications for the University*, ed. A.B. Smith. (Pittsburg: University of Pittsburg Press, 1958) 1–25.

13. http://investor.circuitcity.com/history.cfm (accessed November 26, 2008)

14. Circuit City. *Annual Report* 1996: 7.

15. *Boston Globe*. "CarMax Stock Gains as Used-Vehicle Sales Rise." September 21, 2006, D6.

16. http://investor.circuitcity.com/history.cfm (accessed November 26, 2008)

17. Miguel Bustillo. "Circuit City Braces for Dismal Holiday." *Wall Street Journal*. November 4, 2008, B3.

18. Miguel Bustillo. "Retailer Circuit City to Liquidate." *Wall Street Journal*. January 17-18, 2009, B1.

19. Miguel Bustillo. "Circuit City to Sell Canadian Stores." *Wall Street Journal*. March 3, 2009, B5.

20. Internet Retailer. "CircuitCity.com is Alive and Well, Systemax Tells Stock Analysts." August 13, 2009, www.internetretailer.com/2009/08/13/circuitcity-com-is-alive-and-well-systemax-tells-stock-analysts.

21. "About Us," Circuit City, accessed June 7, 2011, www.circuitcity.com/sectors/aboutus/index.asp.

22. Eleanor May. Interview. Rindge, New Hampshire. October 2009.

23. http://www.eastontowncenter.com (accessed January 16, 2013)

24. "Frequently Asked Questions," U.S. Small Business Administration, accessed January 12, 2009, web.sba.gov/faqs/faqindex.cfm?areaID=24.

25. National Women's Business Council. "Women Business Owners and their Enterprises." *Fast Facts*. March 2011. www.nwbc.gov. (Data source: *U.S. Census' 2007 Survey of Business Owners*.)

26. David Moin. "Four Go Down to One: Macy's Cuts Divisions and 7, 000 Employees," *Women's Wear Daily*, February 3, 2009, 1, 8.

27. Jeanine Poggi. "Gap to Bring Subbrands Into Full-line Stores," *Women's Wear Daily*. June 11, 2008, 2.

28. Julie Bennett. "A Year of Growth, New Rules, and Experimentation," *Wall Street Journal*. November 6, 2008, D7.

29. Collective Brands, Inc. "Payless ShoeSource," accessed June 8, 2011, www.collectivebrands.com/business-units/payless.

30. Anthony Deautsch and Jonathan Birchall, "Collective Brands Targets Indonesia," *Financial Times*, December 12, 2010, http://www.ft.com/cms/s/0/dd5a287e-060c-11e0-976b-00144feabdc0.html#axzz1xpfzjI4c.

31. Gap, Inc. "Gap Inc's Global Runway," April, 4, 2011. www.gapinc.com/content/gapinc/html/media/pressrelease/2011/med_pr_Design_Leadership_Change_Brand.html.

32. Jan Norman, "Businesses Use Web Without Abandoning Physical Presence," *The Orange County Register*, September 2, 2008, accessed September 3, 2008, www.newsobserver.com/1595/v-print/story/1203214.html.

33. "Welcome," Footstar, accessed December 4, 2008, www.footstar.com/meldisco.html.

34. Sandra Guy. "Kmart Fashions a Shoe-in." *Chicago Sun-Times*, February 19, 2009, www.suntimes.com/business/1439358,CST-FIN-kmart19.article.

35. www.nk.se/templates/html.aspx?id=7904 (accessed December 4, 2008)

36. Deloitte. "Global Powers of Retailing 2012." Top 250 Global Retailers 2010. ©2012 Deloitte Global Services Limited, www.deloitte.com.

37. Robert Brooks. "Migros 'Culture Percent' Celebrates 50 Years." May 25, 2007, accessed January 12, 2009, www.swissinfo.ch/eng/front/Migros.

38. "Our History," Hudson Bay Company, accessed November 27, 2008, www2.hbc.com/hbc/history/default .asp.

39. David Moin. "NRDC Heading North: Buys Hudson's Bay Co., Sees L & T in Canada." *Women's Wear Daily*. July 17, 2008, 1, 14.

40. Kevin Woodward, "Hudson's Bay Projects 70% E-commerce Growth as it Prepares to Go Public," October 19, 2012, www.internetretailer.com/2012/10/19/hudsons_bay_projects_70_e-commerce_growth_it_prepares_go.

41. Marty Basch, "Cold Enough? Tired? Come and Sit by the Fire." *Boston Sunday Globe*. January 27, 2008, M9–M10.

42. Allan Lockyer, *Clamdiggers and Downeast Country Stores: Eastern Maine's Vanishing Culture* (Orono, Maine: Northern Lights, 1993), 96.

43. Tamara Hareven and Randolph Langenbach, *Amoskeag: Life and Work in an American Factory City* (New York: Pantheon Books, 1978), 335.

44. Tim Lehnert. "Providence's Place in Mall History." *Boston Sunday Globe*. July 15, 2007, M12.

45. "The History of Harrods." www.harrods.com/content/misc/boutiques/best-of-British/history-of-harrods. Harrods. (accessed August 1, 2012)

46. Ruth Sunderland, "Harrod's Sold for £1.5 bn as Mohamed Al Fayed Retires," *Guardian*. May 8, 2010, 1, http://www.guardian.co.uk/business/2010/may/08/harrods-sold-mohamed-al-fayed.

47. Ibid.

48. *The Illustrated JCPenney*, ed. Robert Pasch and Cynthia McGrath. JCPenney. Plano, Texas. Undated.

49. JCPenney 2012 Proxy Statement (Form 10-K) Item 6. Selected Financial Data "Five-Year Financial Summary." http://media.corporate-ir-net/media_files/IROL/70/70528/reports/JCP_2011I10K/HTML

50. www.walgreens.com/history7.jsp (accessed November 27, 2008)

51. Walgreens Annual Report 2011. "Financial Highlights." 1.news.walgreens.com/images/20007/WALGREENS_ 2011_AR.pdf

52. Ibid. "Company Highlights." 1.

53. Michael Moynihan, "Big Box Panic," *Reason*, January 2008, 4. http://reason.com/news/printer/123497 .html.

54. Ibid: 5.

55. Elaine Misonzhnik, "Store Closings Likely to Peak in First Half of 2010," *Retail Traffic*, October 13, 2009, www.retailtrafficmag.com/retailing/trends/store-closings/index.html.

56. Kathy Grannis, National Retail Federation. "Financial Crisis Freezes Consumer Spending in October, According to NRF." November 14, 2008, accessed November 27, 2008, www.nrf.com/modules.php? name=News&op=viewlive&sp_id=601.

Chapter 2

The Retail Environment: Dynamics of Change

Learning Objectives

After completing this chapter you should be able to:

- Identify how changes in the economy affect retailers and consumers.
- Examine how retailers react to and influence legal and political actions.
- Describe several ways demographic changes influence retailing.
- Survey the status of the green movement and how it influences retailers and consumers.
- Describe how social change, ethical issues, and unpredictable events affect retail decision making.
- Explain how advances in technology precipitate change.
- Explore the nature and influence of competition in retailing.

  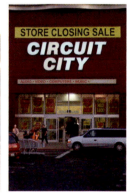

Figure 2.1
Well-known retailers were adversely affected by the economic downturn in 2008, an uncontrollable aspect of the retail environment. Many—including Circuit City, Mervyns, Sharper Image, shown here as well as Goody's Family Clothing, Steve and Barry's, and Linens 'n Things—closed their doors.

Retailers must be trend-watchers in every sense of the word. Changes in economics, demographics, political movements, legislation, society, environmental consciousness, technology, and competition all affect business. Individuals do not have control over these components of the retail environment, nor do retail companies to any great extent. Using the world as a laboratory to help predict customer behavior—and ultimately to develop effective retail strategies—is essential. However, this task is not an easy or exact science. It is important to adopt a geocentric rather than ethnocentric view when analyzing the retail environment, since all nations and economies are dependent on one another. A **geocentric** perspective is one that views the world as a whole—the locus for ideas and decision making. An **ethnocentric** perspective views individual cultures or countries in a narrow focus and perpetuates the viewpoint of one's own culture or country. Retailers run their businesses effectively today and plan for the future by acknowledging uncontrollable forces and dealing with them in ethical ways.

This chapter tracks changes in several areas of the retail environment. Many statistics on the U.S. market are included, and where appropriate, several international examples are used. The material validates the premise that the same environmental factors affect business decisions around the world.

During the first decade of the new millennium, volatility in financial markets affected business performance, raised concerns for retailers and consumers alike, and permeated discussions worldwide. For this reason, the chapter begins with the economy and its role in shaping change.

Retailing and the Economy

Feel the pulse of the economy and you will feel the pulse of retailing. Inflation, recession, war, peace, and prosperity are all reflected at the point of sale. Retail sales and strategies change in response to events such as bank closings, tax increases or reductions, stock market volatility, and credit and currency crises. Displacements in major industries and openings of new businesses also affect retail planning. **Displacement** is the reduction of a workforce involving the dismissal or layoff of employees.

How do executives of department stores cope during a recession? What happens to local bookstores when wholesale prices increase or when direct competition from large chains, Amazon.com, or e-books encroaches on sales? Can the costly service orientation of specialty stores allow them to survive the onslaught of off-price fashion merchants? When sales decline during a holiday selling period and jewelry stores are anticipating 30 percent of their annual sales during the month of November and December, what happens when sales goals are not met? These are the kinds of questions that retailers routinely ask. Although specific problems vary from year to year, the need to work within an ever-changing economy remains constant. Retailers must be attuned to current global, national, regional, and local economic conditions if they expect to create and sustain profitable operations.

The economy is the first component blamed when retail sales are down. Retail analysts recognize that this is both a truth and an oversimplification, since the mechanics of the economy are complex. The causes and effects of inflation, deflation, recession, and depression are critical for retailers and consumers to understand. Monitoring key economic trends such as consumer confidence, new home construction, buying power, consumer price index, gross domestic product output, availability of credit, and other indicators is equally imperative. Fluctuation in interest and currency exchange rates echoes other changes in the economy. We begin by explaining several economic activities.

Interest Rates

Carefully monitored in the United States by the Federal Reserve and globally by the International Monetary Fund, interest rates affect retail sales and development, as well as consumer credit. Fluctuations in the prime rate affect many aspects of the business sector. The **prime rate** is the interest rate charged to commercial lending institutions by the Federal Reserve Bank. By late 2012, the prime rate was 3.25 percent, the same as in early 2009. The prime had been as high as 6.0 in 2008.[1]

Changes in mortgage lending rates and credit card interest rates greatly affect consumers. If it is difficult to qualify for mortgage loans due to uncertainty in the economy, then prospective homeowners will defer buying new homes. Credit card interest rates vary depending on the credit worthiness and payment history of the cardholder and the credit card company's affiliations with commercial partners such as airlines or retailers. Rates are also affected by the condition of the economy and consumer behavior.

Fluctuating Economic Conditions

Economic conditions like inflation, deflation, and periods of recession or depression—as well as currency market fluctuations—are watched carefully because they affect retail and wholesale prices and customer purchasing power. By examining each factor in turn, we can better understand how they interrelate.

Inflation

Inflation is an abnormal increase in the volume of money and credit in a country, resulting in substantial and continuing increases in price levels. The rate of inflation changes with time and is affected by other factors, including rapid expansion of the economy. In the United States, inflation was considered very high in the early 1980s, when it was close to 5 percent. In 2002, it hovered at approximately 2.5 percent. In 2011, the global inflation rate for consumer prices was 2 percent in advanced economies and 7 percent in emerging countries. The International Monetary Fund (IMF) estimated that inflation would drop to 1.5 percent in advanced countries and below 5 percent in emerging and developing countries in 2012. High prices of fuel, food, and raw materials used in manufacturing precipitated the rise in inflation in this era.[2]

To appreciate the progression of price increases over time, consider the following historical example. In 1949, a pound of hamburger cost approximately 59 cents. This price is documented on the vintage grocery receipt illustrated in Figure 2.2. In 1980, the same amount of meat cost about $1.69. In 2002, the average rate per pound was $2.99 and by 2009 the price was approximately $3.99.

Inflation affects the importation of goods and consumer spending. Without imports coming into a country from foreign markets, there is no incentive for domestic firms to moderate prices. If there are no imports, prices are set at what the market will bear, which is generally higher than in a competitive marketplace. Retail profit declines because the basic costs of doing business increase, along with vendors' prices. To cover their costs, retailers increase prices and customers pay more for some products, perhaps more than they are intrinsically worth. Because many retailers depend on imports as a large percentage of their inventories, the rate of inflation is considered during the merchandise planning process.

The **consumer price index (CPI)** is an economic indicator that measures changes in the cost of living due to inflation. The U.S. Bureau of Labor Statistics defines the CPI as "a measure of the average change over time in the prices paid by urban customers for a market basket of consumer goods and services."[3] The figure is released monthly by the U.S. government and is based on price fluctuations of a group of retail products—including food and beverages, apparel, medical care needs, and recreation equipment and services—that are purchased by actual families and individuals.

The index is calculated using a historic three-year period as a baseline, which is equal to 100. Increases or reductions in the CPI for the current time period are calculated using percentage points. For example, a CPI of 110 equates to a 10 percent increase in prices; a CPI of 90 indicates a 10 percent decrease in prices.[4] Consumer prices in the United States had increased 2.1 percent in the 12 months ending in September 2012; the CPI was 231.317.[5]

When the index increases, people are able to purchase less for their money since retail prices have gone up. The worry of most people is that wages will not keep up with increases in prices. This is why many workers receive cost-of-living increases annually when their salaries are reviewed. Inflation causes wholesale prices to increase as well. Retailers must pass along price increases to their customers or expect lower profits.

Customers often change their buying patterns during periods of inflation. People eat at Taco Bell more often than at Red Lobster, and shop at discounters more frequently than department stores. Coupon use becomes a way of life. As the cost of living increases, so does the sale of **generic goods**—products that do not bear brand names of manufacturers or retailers and are cheaper than comparable branded goods. Most generic products feature simple packaging with nondescript labels.

Deflation

Deflation is a reduction in the amount of money available in a country, creating a decline in prices and wages. In a period of deflation, economic growth slows, unemployment rates rise, and manufacturing activity decreases. Compounding the problem, wholesale and retail prices move downward during deflation, in response to contraction within the economy. Deflation is the opposite of inflation. In October 2008, women's apparel prices fell 2.5 percent, the biggest decline on record for that month of the year.[6]

Some observers viewed the deflation that accompanied the 2008 economic slump as a positive influence on the U.S. economy. Wages had not kept pace with the rate of inflation since 2003, causing workers to rely more heavily on credit cards to cover the cost of essential items. Declines in retail prices thus offered a possibility that the buying power of the average citizen might improve, at least for a limited period.

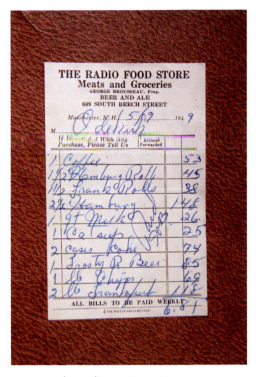

Figure 2.2
This vintage grocery sales slip helps demonstrate inflation over time. Hamburger meat cost about 59 cents per pound in 1949. What is its price today?

Recession

A **recession** is a period during which there is less money in the economy than there was previously. In periods of recession, retailers generate low or no business growth, and business closures increase. This hurts retailers, because sales may be down while the basic costs of doing business (such as wages, energy, and credit) remain at prerecession levels. In the manufacturing sector, recession is anticipated when wholesale orders for products slow appreciably.

Many countries, including Japan, the United States, Germany, and the United Kingdom, coped with recession in the 1990s. The United States experienced two recessions during the first decade of the 21st century. The first, caused by major problems in the technology sector (the dot-com crash), began in 2000. This situation was made worse by the terrorist attacks of September 11, 2001, and ensuing turmoil in financial markets.

The multifaceted financial crisis that began in late 2007 stemmed from poorly regulated subprime mortgage lending and the subsequent selling of mortgage debt to investors. Although the deep disruption in financial markets, sluggish retail environment, and growing consumer unease were evident to many, this major economic downturn was not officially named a recession by the U.S. government until December 2008.[7] Not limited to a specific sector, as in the earlier burst of the technology bubble, this latest recession was broader and deeper, causing repercussions worldwide.

Precipitating Factors We would be remiss if we did not look more closely at the conditions that precipitated the recent downturn and its impact on all members of the supply chain. Between late 2007 and late 2008, many adverse reactions occurred almost simultaneously:

- Stock markets crumbled, imperiling retirement and other investment savings of many individuals.
- Oil prices spiked to record levels and then fell within a few months; this translated to anxiety at the gas pumps for all Americans.
- Venerable financial institutions failed, including small banks and huge investment banking firms. Individuals worried about protecting assets; retailers were concerned about credit lines and sources of capital.
- Consumer confidence sank to its lowest level in 32 years.[8]
- The unemployment rate had risen to 10.2 percent by October 2009, nearly double the average rate recorded in the years leading up to the recession.[9]
- Congress passed several corporate bailout programs and the U.S. government purchased entire mortgage lending associations, thus becoming a partner in other businesses.
- Consumer stimulus packages were passed but took a back seat to the resolution of major failures in the automotive, banking, and insurance industries.

Retail and Consumer Response Reactions from retailers and customers are grim during a recession, as commerce is stultified and families retrench in fear of lost jobs, savings, or comfortable retirements. Beginning in 2008, consumers' instincts to reallocate disposable income and not spend discretionary income greatly paralyzed the efforts of retailers to remain solvent. **Disposable income** is the amount of money remaining after taxes for major household expenditures such as sustenance foodstuffs, basic clothing, and shelter. **Discretionary income** is the amount of money that remains for nonessential purchases after life-sustaining items have been purchased.

Several tendencies are evident in human behaviors and retail responses during a recession:

- Consumers generally spend less on goods and services during a recession than in prosperous times. People might purchase less expensive grocery items to feed their families or use coupons extensively when shopping. Extras or luxury goods may not be purchased at all.
- People expect bigger markdowns on merchandise during periods of recession. The behavior of shoppers during the major "black Friday" kickoff of the holiday season illustrates this point. Many retailers stage special limited time promotions while opening their stores at 4:00 or 5:00 a.m. to customers. The deepest discounts, which cause some customers to start lining up the night before, are curtailed by noon or 1:00 p.m. Customer demand peaks during the promotional sweep and then declines during the remainder of the day.

- Customers find a less extensive selection of products in stores. Retailers carry leaner inventories during these times. The objective is to stock the best-selling items in quantity and underrepresent speculative or risky merchandise.
- Human resources are affected negatively. To cut payroll costs, retailers displace staff, hire fewer part-time or seasonal workers, and expect more hours from salaried employees. For example, one Macy's store hired approximately 45 seasonal workers during the 2008–2009 holiday period, compared with 120 the previous year.
- Over-staffing affects profits. If retailers attempt to keep employees working while sales are declining, eventually this will affect profitability. During a recession, retailers need to maintain a delicate balance between continuing employment for talented and loyal workers and keeping operational costs down.
- Retailers offer fewer services. Reducing nonessential services for customers may also be part of general retrenchment during a recession.

Impact of Recession   During major recessions, many retailers succumb to economic pressures and are forced to close their operations. Some file for bankruptcy protection. **Bankruptcy protection** is a legal filing that gives an ailing company time to restructure debt, secure new financing, or reorganize while remaining in business. Let's review some of the retail reverberations from the period between 2007 and 2010:

- Several companies filed for bankruptcy protection and eventually closed their retail doors, including Linens 'n Things, Circuit City, Sharper Image, Mervyn's, Steve and Barry's, and Boscov's. Three of these retailers are illustrated in Figure 2.1. General Growth Properties (GGP)—one of the largest shopping center developers and management companies—filed for bankruptcy protection in April 2009 as it sought to find ways to postpone debt payments. By January 2010, it had restructured loans and secured a significant development opportunity in Columbia, Maryland.[10] In late 2010, the company emerged from bankruptcy and began concentrating on paring down its 169 malls, with the intent to use revenue from the sales to further pay down its debts.[11] By September 2012 GGP had sold approximately 3.9 million square feet of gross leasable area and was well on its way to reducing its debts.[12]
- Shoppers turned to consignment stores, pawnshops, deep discounters, and warehouse clubs. Discount specialty retailers like Dress Barn and Fashion Bug attracted budget-conscious women looking for value.
- Retailers closed or tried to sell poor-performing divisions. Home Depot announced that it would close Expo, its upscale home improvement and decorating chain; Talbot's sold its J. Jill women's casual apparel chain.
- Most retailers recorded double-digit sales drops over the prior year and took major strides to improve margins and draw customers. Price cuts were taken extensively. DSW shoe stores increased the discount on designer footwear to 75 percent before the 2008–2009 holiday selling period. The typical discount had been 50 percent the previous year.[13]
- Some specialty boutiques downscaled their luxury lines; others went out of business. Luxury retailers that had been previously less affected by the recession also recorded poor sales.

Although few retailers thrive during a recession, some are better equipped to meet the needs of limited budgets, dwindling savings, and underemployment. Walmart, McDonald's, and Family Dollar Stores were among the few retailers to experience sales growth during the recession.[14] Another discounter, Dollar General, continued on its growth trajectory during the height of the recession by adding 4,000 jobs in 2009 and expanding its operations to 8,800 stores.[15] Dollar General opened 625 new stores and launched its e-commerce site in 2011.[16] The company reported $14.81 billion in sales for fiscal 2011.[17] Though not totally immune to the downturn, discounters and quick-serve restaurants fared better than most retailers.

Craft retailer Michaels operates over 1,000 stores and found that sales on craft supplies increased in the last two months of 2008 as more customers turned to making holiday gifts and decorations.[18] More information on refining strategic direction in times of economic downturn appears in Chapter 3.

Did You Know?
When gas prices spiked to $4.00 per gallon in May 2011, some small service businesses added fuel surcharges to compensate for the rising costs of doing business. One piano tuner, whose business involved driving 150 miles per day, added eight percent to his fee. It covered costs but didn't add to profits. Think about auto parts and appliance delivery trucks, home health workers, and grocery delivery services as you consider how price increases affect retail services.
Source: Kris Maher, "Gas Prices Drive a Shift," *Wall Street Journal*, June 18–19, 2011, A3.

Monitoring Economic Indicators

Retailers track many economic indicators in addition to the CPI mentioned earlier. Other indexes, which also relate to the rate of inflation and are of particular note to retailers, are import and export prices and the international consumer price indexes. In addition, buying power, gross domestic product (GDP), consumer confidence levels, and unemployment trends are regularly watched. Two examples illustrate the use and importance of economic indicators.

The amount of money a family has available for purchases after taxes is called **buying power**. Also called purchasing power, this measure indicates ability and inclination to spend at retail. Walmart looked for buying power equivalent to $18,000 or more per household when the company surveyed potential locations for new stores in Asia.[19] This figure would be substantially higher in the United States and other developed markets.

Retail companies monitor GDP—a key economic indicator, introduced in Chapter 1—especially when considering expansion. In the United States, consumer spending accounts for 70 percent of the GDP; a downturn in the economy thereby has a strong impact on retail sales when people refrain from spending.[20] Early in 2010, the International Monetary Fund (IMF) predicted that as the recession lessened, global growth would reach 3.9 percent by the end of the year. The U.S. economy was projected to grow 2.7 percent in 2010 and then contract slightly to 2.4 percent in 2011. In contrast, the European economy was projected to grow more slowly: Germany at 1.5 percent and Britain at 1.3 percent in 2010, with 1.9 and 2.7 percent increases, respectively, in 2011.[21] Retailers have learned through experience, however, that such projections often fail to anticipate the vagaries in world events that contribute to economic gains and losses.

Consumer confidence is an index used to assess customers' sentiments toward making retail transactions. It serves as a vote of confidence in the economy when enough momentum is maintained for customers to feel secure and willing to spend their money. The consumer confidence index has been based on a 100-point scale since 1985.[22] At the start of the current recession, the index dropped from 61.4 in September to 38 in October 2008, its lowest point since the United States began using the index.[23] The downward trajectory represented a growing discontent among shoppers and paralysis at the cash registers. By January 2010, the index stood at 55.9, a moderate improvement, but by May 2011 it had climbed only to 60.8, significantly lower than had been predicted.[24] In June 2012 it stood at 62.0.

Currency Exchange Fluctuations

The worth of many world currencies is linked to the U.S. dollar because historically, the dollar has been considered less volatile than other currencies. This is due to the size of the U.S. economy, stability of its currency, and solid performance of its stock and financial markets over time. When a currency becomes hardly worth the paper it is printed on, devaluation has occurred. **Devaluation** is a reduction in the international exchange value of a currency. This condition happens for many reasons, including bank failures, stock market crashes, unrestricted foreign investments, poor financial management, and panic.

In the past several years the dollar has declined and rebounded against two major benchmark currencies: the euro and the pound sterling. When the euro was introduced in 2002, the objective was to keep its value equal with that of the dollar. Since that time, the euro has outpaced the dollar, at one point reaching a high of $1.34 against it. The British pound was worth over $2.00 in the same period. As the 2008 recession deepened and foreign markets were affected, exchange rates became more volatile. By mid-2012, the pound was worth approximately $1.54 and the euro $1.22,[25] although financial concerns in the eurozone threatened to undermine some of the latter's advances.

When the Canadian dollar gained strength against the U.S. dollar in 2008, many Canadian shoppers flocked to the United States to take advantage of the exchange rate. Conversely, when certain U.S. prescription drug prices and medical services were cheaper in Canada than they were in the United States, Americans routinely filled their orders by **outshopping**, the practice of purchasing goods from retailers that are located outside of a customer's usual shopping territory.

Another classic example of the effects of devaluation is the 1997 Asian currency crisis. It affected not only several Pacific Rim countries but also the nations with which they did business.

Examining the factors that converged to create this financial crisis teaches an important lesson in global economics.

The problem began in Thailand and ballooned throughout the Pacific Rim. Most severely affected were Thailand and Indonesia, with the economies of Malaysia, the Philippines, Hong Kong, Korea, and Japan also implicated. Poor bank management was one reason for the Thai economy's problems. The country's banks had borrowed money at lower interest rates abroad than were available domestically and, with little hesitation, were granting loans to businesses. Transactions were often in dollars, not baht, the local currency. When loan repayment time came and the local currency had lost strength, companies had to provide more baht to pay their debts. Many could not and defaulted on their loans. The baht declined further against the dollar despite efforts to strengthen the currency. Panic spread as international agencies were called upon to help the situation.

Other reasons precipitating declines in currency values include:

- Increased interest rates.
- Excessive bad debts.
- Trade imbalances.
- Bank failures.
- Stock market declines.
- Countries that default on loans.

Crises of the magnitude expressed in the previous examples affect retailing. When consumer buying power is diminished, retail revenue declines. It is important to recognize that although the 1997 crisis began in Asia, and the 2007 recession began in the United States, economic reverberations were felt around the world. Japan reported in late 2008 that it was in recession for the first time since 2001. GDP had declined for the entire year prior to the announcement.[26] The earthquake and tsunami in early 2011 put more pressure on Japan's economy and the stability of its currency. The United Kingdom, Mexico, Australia, and much of Europe indicated similar downturns early in 2009. When currency values fluctuate, so do shopping habits. Political events also bring about changes that affect planning and operations of all businesses.

Political, Trade, and Legal Influences

Expecting that new leadership will influence economic and social policies in the United States, many companies take a wait-and-see attitude during a presidential election year. The emergence of new world powers and trade alliances between nations calls for new legal parameters. Leadership changes in remote parts of the world also may affect global trade.

Changes in political regimes, trade alliances, and global trade organizations all herald change in the retail environment. A look at the ways political change affects retailing illustrates this point.

Political Leadership Change

The election of Barack Obama as President of the United States in 2008—and the ensuing shift from Republican to Democratic leadership—brought both hope and uncertainty to the U.S. business community. Regardless of political party preferences, citizens hoped that the stimulus package passed by Congress in the early days of the administration would help change the economic climate for the better. Retailers were concerned that Obama's pro-union stance would pressure large retailers to revisit their own position on union membership for their employees and recruitment efforts in stores. Corporations wondered whether new taxes would make turning profits more difficult or whether new directives regarding health care coverage would adversely affect their employee benefit programs.

On a lighter note, a new first lady can also influence retailing, especially in the fashion sector. Michelle Obama, with her zest for strong color, contemporary silhouettes, and sleeveless dresses, had an immediate and marked influence on designers, manufacturers, retailers, and consumers. Her impact on fashion is documented in Figure 2.3.

Other first ladies have also made their mark on the fashions of their time. In a study dubbed "The Politics of Style," respondents were asked to rate former first ladies and wives of U.S. presidential

Figure 2.3
Political change precipitates fashion change; throughout her tenure as First Lady, Michelle Obama influenced apparel, accessories, shoes, jewelry, hairstyles, and more.

candidates by their level of stylishness. Using criteria that included overall awareness, appeal, and influence, top-ranking Jacqueline Kennedy was considered stylish by 48 percent of those surveyed.[27]

Political motivations frequently are the basis for establishing trade alliances between countries, a topic we'll look at next.

Trade Alliances

Many alliances exist throughout the world. NAFTA, CAFTA-DR, EU, and WTO are more than just an alphabet soup of letters. These acronyms represent several important agreements that have been negotiated in recent years.

North American Free Trade Agreement (NAFTA)

The **North American Free Trade Agreement (NAFTA)** is an alliance that promotes trade among the United States, Canada, and Mexico. Delicate maneuverings and years of talks between the participating governments preceded NAFTA, which went into effect in 1993. Essentials of the agreement included:

- Elimination of tariffs on most products crossing the borders of the three countries. A **tariff** is a duty or tax imposed by a government on an import.
- Elimination of quota requirements on most apparel made from yarn and fabric from any of the three countries. A **quota** is a limitation imposed on the quantities of a product imported from other countries.
- Elimination of duties on yarn made in Mexico used in items involved in 807 programs. Taking their name from an item number in the U.S. Tariff Schedules, **807 programs** are Caribbean initiative programs offering low taxation on goods, among other incentives, to encourage manufacturing in selected countries.

NAFTA provides several advantages to retailers in member countries. In Mexico, retailers can purchase more U.S. goods for their stores because of relaxed import regulations. Mexicans had long practiced cross-border shopping, but with more imports from the United States available, this is no longer necessary. However, this practice continues to be the norm—particularly in border towns like Juarez, Mexico, and El Paso, Texas; or Nogales, Mexico, and Nogales, Arizona. Merchandise deliveries to Mexico were quicker, and delays at the border minimized, until the threat of terrorism tightened border security after 9/11.

Since the inception of the agreement, trade between the United States and Mexico has more than doubled, but not all observers view NAFTA in a positive light. Detractors say that the mechanisms for intercountry trade were in place long before NAFTA was implemented. Some analysts believe the impact on all parties has been minimal and that the number of jobs gained or lost has been equalized. In U.S. communities where firms closed factories to move their manufacturing facilities to Mexico, residents and politicians do not regard NAFTA as having a neutral effect; rather, they believe the loss of jobs has been excessive and damaging to local economies. In a study done prior to the presidential primary elections in 2008, those interviewed had different disapproval ratings depending on whether they lived in a Mexican border state or in the American heartland. Fifty-nine percent of respondents in Ohio disapproved of NAFTA while only 40 percent of survey participants in Texas shared a negative view of the trade alliance.[28]

Despite strong sentiments for or against NAFTA, one constant remains: the economies of the United States and Mexico are inexorably linked. Because more than 80 percent of Mexican exports enter the U.S. market, Mexico is vulnerable to the effects of recession in the United States.[29]

Dominican Republic–Central America–United States Free Trade Agreement (CAFTA-DR)

Considered an extension to NAFTA, the **Dominican Republic–Central America–United States Free Trade Agreement (CAFTA-DR)** signed by then-President George W. Bush, went into effect in 2006. In addition to the Dominican Republic and the United States, four Central American countries are included in the agreement: Costa Rica, El Salvador, Guatemala, and Honduras. Like NAFTA, its intent is to eliminate or reduce tariffs on products being traded among participants.[30]

European Union (EU)

The 27 countries that comprise the **European Union (EU)** form not only a trade alliance but also a trading bloc. A **trading bloc** is a major geographic trading area that tends to have close political, cultural, or economic ties. In the case of the EU, the buying power of almost 500 million people is a consumer force of significance. Only 16 member nations use the euro, the EU's common currency. The euro celebrated its tenth birthday on January 1, 2009.[31]

Online shopping is an important revenue driver for the EU, generating $112 billion in 2010. EU officials estimate that Internet sales could grow to $184.6 by 2015. In 2010, 275 million Europeans used the Internet to shop, with 303 million expected by 2015.[32] Some customers have voiced concerns about language difficulties, tax issues, and payment problems, which serve as deterrents to cross-border shopping. Growth of this magnitude has motivated the EU to solidify consumer rights throughout the member nations.

Standardization of trade policies, pricing, tax structures, and services has been a challenge for members since the EU's inception in 1992. Through its various committees, the EU handles disputes within its jurisdiction. Recently, the EU has been shaken by financial instability of some member nations, which has spread an atmosphere of uncertainty throughout the eurozone. More about international trade emanating from and within the eurozone is presented in Chapter 8.

World Trade Organization (WTO)

The **World Trade Organization (WTO)** is an international governing body made up of representatives from over 150 countries that grants preferred trading partner status, regulates trade, and settles disputes among members. Once approved by the WTO, a country that engages in trade freely with another country is considered a **preferred trading partner (PTP)**.

Whether China would be granted preferred trading partner status by the WTO was hotly debated at the start of the new millennium. The situation became political when financial and ethical issues converged, since China is the largest source of imported apparel and textile products for the United States.[33] Many government and industry leaders in the United States and other sympathetic countries objected to sweatshop and other human-rights violations that have occurred in China.

Yet most wholesalers and retailers recognized that purchasing goods made in China provides substantial cost savings for their companies and consumers. There were many sides to this preferred trading partner issue, but China was granted full status in the WTO late in 2001.

Another aspect of political intervention focuses on the initiatives of manufacturers and retailers to support domestic manufacturing programs. **Protectionism** is a government policy that protects domestic manufacturers by placing restrictions on foreign producers of the same goods. Lobbyists work to influence legislators at the state and national levels on issues ranging from protectionism to government financial support. Protectionist policies may decline as retailers and manufacturers become more committed to international partnerships and as the global economy regains strength.

Whether customers truly care about purchasing only products made in their home countries is yet to be determined. Despite patriotic feelings, most consumers realize that the best prices and values are to be had on goods produced in countries with low labor rates. The events of 9/11 evoked new expressions of dedication to the United States and its products by many citizens and businesses, but strong sentiments have diminished as the years passed—or have they? Many American apparel manufacturers and citizens were irate that U.S. Olympic team members would be wearing outfits that were made in China for the opening ceremonies of the Summer Olympics in London in 2012.

The opposite sentiment was apparent in the waning days of 2008 when the top three U.S. automobile manufacturers were pleading for governmental funding in the wake of the deep recession. Their requests precipitated a round of antiprotectionist reactions from some U.S. consumers disappointed with the performance of U.S. cars compared to imports and disenchanted with the lack of initiative taken by auto companies to produce fuel-efficient green vehicles. These consumers voiced their intent not to buy American cars or support legislation until the auto industry's practices changed. As these examples show, strong sentiments are apparent both for and against protectionism.

Certain mechanisms are used to curtail the movement of goods and selection of trading partners. A **trade embargo** is a restriction set by a government on the importation of goods. Many trade embargoes are politically motivated. For example, the United States does not trade with Cuba because of that country's communist government. Ironically, although Cuba's political ideology is in direct opposition to the capitalistic way of doing business in the United States, the U.S. dollar is unofficially but widely exchanged for goods and services in Cuba.

These are only some of the many ways political issues and alliances influence trade. Globalization has created sources of power that fall outside political and governmental interests. Huge companies that operate on many continents wield great influence. Many U.S. retailers and manufacturers doing business in foreign countries and, conversely, foreign companies doing business in the United States fall into this category. Consumer and human-rights activists, industry trade associations, and retailers themselves have influenced current laws affecting retailers.

Retailing and the Law

When retailers make decisions, they pay close attention to local, state, federal, and, increasingly, international laws. Manufacturing, wholesaling, importing or exporting, hiring help, advertising practices, and credit and lending policies are regulated by government agencies. Consumers are becoming more knowledgeable about laws that are applicable to retailers and are quick to identify their rights. The penalties for violations of laws are pecuniarily harmful to retailers, and infractions can also affect store image. Fortunately for both parties, most retailers recognize that doing business legally and ethically is best. The legal power of the individual can be viewed in historical and contemporary ways through the consumerism movement.

Consumerism

Consumer advocacy can be traced to medieval England, when an edict required certain products to be imprinted with an identification hallmark (an early trademark) so that producers would bear the responsibility for defects. **Consumerism** is a social movement advocating fair interaction between people and merchants. After World War II, the movement became a significant force in the United States. Consumers were no longer as willing to accept a retailing attitude of **caveat emptor**, which, translated from Latin, means "let the buyer beware." The expression applies to all merchandise sold, with or without a warranty or return option. As consumer-rights legislators worked to gain support, politicians who would hold manufacturers and retailers accountable for faulty merchandise won votes. The 1960s and 1970s saw many changes as consumerism took on new meaning for industry, and customer satisfaction became a central focus for retailers—a perspective expressed in what is known as the marketing concept.

Impact on Retailing   Evidence of the impact of the consumer movement is seen in the use of informative labels, advertising that warns people of potential health hazards, and increased product quality safety standards. Privacy, especially as it affects Internet commerce, is of growing importance. Many laws directly regulate retailing operations and functions. How credit is given, customers are billed, Internet-purchased goods are taxed, and sales are run are all of concern.

Product safety standards originated from the consumerism movement. The recall of millions of dollars' worth of toys containing lead paint and tainted food products, as well as questions about the safety of other products—including children's jewelry and construction sheetrock that were manufactured in China—have received close scrutiny in recent years.

Global Ethical Orientation   American consumerism has shifted from a self-centered orientation to a more global one. Customers are no longer only interested in fair practices regarding their rights as consumers. They are also concerned that workers around the world be treated ethically.

Sweatshop and fair-wage issues permeated the discussions of ethical issues in the 1990s and continue to this day. Several companies have been cited for underpaying factory workers, illegally withholding wages, physically abusing workers, employing children, and running unsafe operations. The following examples illustrate this point, occasionally with an ironic subtext:

- In 1998, a group of demonstrators representing the Campaign for Labor Rights protested Nike's alleged involvement in human-rights violations abroad. Busloads of primarily young people converged on a sidewalk in the Georgetown section of Washington, D.C., to hand out literature and drum up media and consumer support. When questioned, several of the protesters mentioned that they had no particular interest in Nike or the cause but just wanted something to do on a Saturday.
- American Apparel is known for operating a "sweatshop-free" company; apparently it has not handled illegitimate workers in its factories with the same good intentions. In 2009, the U.S. Immigration and Customs Enforcement Agency determined that about one-third of American Apparel's 5,600 workers in its Los Angeles factories had improper documentation or problems with their I-9 identity documents. Situations like this highlight a greater issue. American manufacturers are encouraged to produce their goods in the United States, but American workers often will not work for lower wages or under the same conditions that illegal immigrants will tolerate. Consumers want low prices on the apparel they buy, but don't usually get them if the goods are produced in the United States.[34]
- In 2011, the Swiss parliament enacted new legislation that fixes prices on books sold through brick-and-mortar and online stores. Publishers and importers are now required to set firm-and-final prices on books. The act, designed to reduce unfair competition between booksellers, does provide some leeway by allowing retailers to offer discounts of up to 5 percent as a general discount and in special cases such as bulk or library sales.[35]
- Late in 2009, several U.S. retailers were asked to cease and desist from using forced child labor in Uzbekistan's cotton industry. According to the International Labor Rights Forum, L.L. Bean, J. Crew, Abercrombie & Fitch, and Gymboree were accused of dealing with cotton suppliers that utilized child labor to produce raw materials for garment manufacture. Both L.L. Bean and J. Crew responded within 24 hours to the accusations, and contacted their suppliers to bar the use of cotton made by forced child labor.[36] One year later, Abercrombie & Fitch and Gymboree still had not commented publicly about their alleged involvement in the Uzbek cotton child-labor issue.[37]

Did You Know?
Fewer toxic toys and textiles are finding their way to European retail shelves thanks to a partnership between Chinese and EU officials. The number of unsafe products withdrawn from shelves or recalled from consumers in 2010 increased 13 percent to 2,244 products against the previous year. Imports from China accounted for 58 percent of products removed, a slight decrease from earlier figures.
Source: EUbusiness Ltd., "Toxic Toys and Textiles on the Decrease in EU Stores," May 2011, www.eubusiness.com/news-eu/china-consumer.9xa.

Dilemmas such as these are addressed by retail and apparel industry groups, governments, and concerned individuals worldwide. In response to the Uzbekistan report, the American Apparel and Footwear Association (AAFA) joined forces with other trade groups to write letters to Washington government officials and the Dubai Cotton Exchange, encouraging them to work with the Uzbek government to eliminate the use of forced child labor in Uzbekistan.[38]

Ethical individuals oppose grievous working conditions in any country, but it is also important to acknowledge that cultural norms, local standards of living, and work ethic may differ in other parts of the world. For example, in some Southeast Asian countries, semiskilled workers are paid the U.S. equivalent of 50 cents an hour for their work; however, a good breakfast costs only 40 cents. Companies in these countries may provide transportation, medical care, and other amenities for their employees, as well as working conditions that are comfortable, although perhaps not ideal by U.S. standards. One must be careful not to judge too quickly and to have all the facts before taking sides in protest against such situations. However, when conditions are proven deleterious to health, unsafe or inhumane, then every legal and ethical avenue should be used to instigate change, improve the working environment, and prosecute those responsible.

Bribery is another issue that straddles legal and ethical lines. A **bribe** is a payment made to an individual, a company, or a government in order to secure special business privileges. These might include contracts, favorable pricing, legal oversights, or any number of other incentives. Attitudes toward giving and receiving bribes differ radically by country. Bribes are expected in some countries and rarely used in others. They are illegal in some places and overlooked in others though laws prohibiting them may exist. The cultural values, choice of trading partners, presence of laws, degree of punishment, size of bribes, and ethical orientations of participants are only some of the factors that affect the decision to pay or receive bribes.

Counterfeiting is another ethical infraction that occurs globally. **Counterfeiting** is the intentional falsification of an established brand, design, or symbol for the purpose of illicit financial gain. The practice is increasing across all merchandise categories, and it is becoming more difficult to intercept suspicious shipments, as discussed in From the Field 2.1.

Laws Affecting the Retail Trade

In every business situation, the law imposes limits beyond which retailers cannot venture. Retailers often complain that there are too many legal constraints in business. However, consumerism is strong and people want protection from unfair and unscrupulous practices.

The National Retail Federation (NRF) monitors legislation at the local, state, and federal levels that affects retailers and lobbies in Washington on behalf of its members. The objectives of the trade association are to keep Congress informed of the impact laws have on retailing and to be aware of retailers' positions on key issues. Legislative issues influenced by the NRF and its affiliate state merchant associations represent a broad spectrum of interests, including consumer safety, pricing regulation, economic stimulus initiatives, taxes, bankruptcy reform, health insurance, and trade stimulus initiatives. The NRF and its affiliated state associations employ lobbyists to ensure that the retail position is heard in Congress and in state legislatures.

A chronology of federal laws that are important to the retail industry in the United States appears in Table 2.1. The need to assimilate vast amounts of legal information intensifies as retailers expand globally. Examples of important local, federal, and international laws affecting retail trade follow.

Antitrust Laws   Several laws enacted in the United States regulate mergers and restrain trade activity; these include the Sherman, Clayton, and Antimerger Acts. Called antitrust laws, they are administered by the Federal Trade Commission (FTC). Occasionally, the FTC invokes antitrust laws in order to prevent monopolies from forming. The case involving Whole Foods Market and its purchase of Wild Oats Market in 2007 illustrates the intent of antitrust laws, if not always the outcome. The FTC contended that the merger resulted in unfair competition in natural and organic food markets and sought to reverse the acquisition. Whole Foods believed that the merger strengthened the company and benefited consumers. In early 2009, the FTC opened the issue for discussion with Whole Foods and temporarily placed a moratorium on the antitrust suit.[39] Shortly thereafter,

From the Field 2.1   Los Angeles and Long Beach Ports Are on the Front Lines of a Crackdown on Counterfeit Goods

The massive Long Beach warehouse is as well stocked as any big-box discount store, filled with brand-new electronics, designer jeans, famous-label handbags, and toys. In addition there are cartons and cartons of cigarettes, seemingly enough to supply a small kingdom. There are no shoppers, however. All of the goods in this 500,000 square foot warehouse—mostly counterfeits, along with banned items such as elephant ivory and drug paraphernalia—were seized by federal agents.

Smuggling is on the rise—with seizures by U.S. Customs and Border Protection up 35 percent in fiscal year 2010 from 2009—and the ports of Los Angeles and Long Beach are the front line. The twin ports account for about 40 percent of all seizures by U.S. CBP, which reflects their status as the nation's busiest port complex. They're also the main cargo gateway from Asia, whose workshops are as good at making knockoffs as they are at making the real thing. Customs officials acknowledge that they are struggling to intercept the vast quantities of illegal goods that make their way into the ports each day.

Thanks to technological advances such as sophisticated 3D printers, counterfeiting iPhones, PlayStation game consoles, and other goods has never been easier. Selling them has gotten easier too, as the advent of online markets such as Craigslist and eBay has allowed smugglers to bypass borders and sell directly to consumers.

Apprehending contraband shipments, meanwhile, has never been harder. About 50,000 cargo containers a day, laden with $1 billion in goods, move through the local ports' 13,300 acres of channels, wharves, and terminals. Each 40-foot container is large enough to carry about 12,300 shoe boxes, 20,000 toy dolls, or 6,600 dresses on hangers.

Smugglers have also gotten wiser, mixing in their wares with legitimate shipments to make detection more difficult. "We're not seeing containers that are just filled with contraband like we used to. We're seizing smaller amounts, but we're finding it more often," said Todd Hoffman, the Customs and Border Protection director at the ports of Los Angeles and Long Beach.

For instance, CBP officials seized 22,000 cartons of counterfeit Marlboro Light 100s and Marlboro Gold cigarettes, worth $1.1 million, which were found alongside legitimate cargo in a container with a shipping invoice that read "hang tags and hang plugs." Authorities also have found knockoffs of True Religion and other designer jeans that had distinctively stitched pockets concealed by innocuous denim patches, and cases in which cheap replicas covered counterfeit handbags by Kate Spade and Louis Vuitton, according to a customs officer.

Investigators raided several discount stores in downtown Los Angeles, where they snared more than $10 million worth of bogus iPods and other counterfeit and stolen merchandise. The fakes arrived through the harbor as parts meant to be reassembled and labeled before being sold, said Ron Boyd, chief of the Los Angeles Port Police's 200-member force.

To intercept illegal goods, customs officials rely on both electronic scans of containers as well as physical inspections. At the L.A. and Long Beach ports, all containers are screened with mobile scanners or pass-through machines resembling giant metal detectors, which test for radiation that might indicate the presence of explosives—or, after the radiation leaks caused by the earthquake and tsunami, problematic cargo from Japan. Several factors contribute to the decision to open a container for inspection, including the country from which the cargo originates, shipping manifests that arouse suspicions, and whether the importer has certified its foreign suppliers through a federal program, as Target Corp. has done.

Nearly all counterfeit and contraband items are destroyed by outside contractors under federal government supervision. There are some exceptions. If brand-owning businesses give permission, seized items can be donated to help the needy in other countries. For example, a seized shipment of several thousand pencils with fake National Football League team logos were sent to classrooms in Africa through World Vision Africa. "There could be a classroom full of Dallas Cowboy fans there soon," quipped Jaime Ruiz, spokesman for the CBP in Southern California, "although they might not realize it."

Adapted and condensed from Ronald D. White, *Los Angeles Times*, April 8, 2011.

Whole Foods Market settled the dispute with the FTC—agreeing to sell 31 stores in 12 states and give up its rights to the Wild Oats brand—but the merger remains in effect.[40]

In other applications of the laws, category killers have pressured manufacturers to stop providing their products to discount stores. Citing unfair use of size and power, the FTC found the category killers guilty of manipulating the supply chain in order to control competition and increase prices. The public's right to competitive prices and choice sometimes must be upheld legally.

International Laws   Laws enacted in the United States are not the only ones that affect retailers. Regulations proposed by the European Union have had an effect on direct marketers, including those retailers doing catalogue and online business in Europe: the European Commission's Directive on Data Privacy went into effect in late 1998, and enforcement began in early 2002. Attitudes regarding the use of customer data vary greatly by country. The United States has had less restrictive attitudes toward the collection and sharing of data than its European counterparts.[41]

Consumer Product Safety Laws   The Consumer Product Safety Improvement Act (CPSIA) was passed in 2008 after an onslaught of cases involving hazardous materials found in children's products. The bill was drafted after many children were harmed by toys, cribs, pacifiers, and

Table 2.1   Selected U.S. Legislation Important to the Retail Industry

Date	Act	Description
1890	Sherman Act	Prohibited monopoly or conspiracy in restraint of trade.
1914	Clayton Act	Made specific acts in restraint of trade unlawful.
1914	Federal Trade Commission Act	Established the enforcing agency for governing unfair methods of competition.
1931	Resale Price Act	Agreement legalized resale price maintenance between manufacturers and retailers.
1935	Unfair Practices Acts	Prohibited sales below cost.
1936	Robinson-Patman Act	Prohibited unlawful price discrimination.
1938	Wheeler-Lea Act	Expanded the FTC's responsibility to include unfair or deceptive acts or practices and gave it the power to take action whenever it is in the public interest, even when there is no proof of competitive injury.
1938	Fair Labor Standards Act	Established minimum wages.
1939	Wool Products Labeling Act	Required that products containing wool carry labels showing the fiber content.
1950	Antimerger Act	Regulated mergers that might substantially lessen competition.
1951	Fur Products Labeling Act	Required that all fur products carry labels correctly describing the fur composition.
1953	Flammable Fabrics Acts	Prohibited the manufacture or sale of fabrics or apparel that were dangerously flammable.
1960	Hazardous Substances Labeling Act	Required proper labeling on packages of hazardous household products.
1960	Textile Fiber Identification Act	Required fiber content identification on all apparel.
1963	Equal Pay Act	Required compliance with regulations on child labor and employee health and safety.
1964	Civil Rights Act, Title VII	Required equal pay for similar work, regardless of sex, race, color, religion, or national origin.
1966	Fair Packaging and Labeling Act	Permitted the voluntary adoption of industry-accepted uniform packaging standards and required clearer labeling of consumer goods.
1966	Child Protection Act of 1966	Amended the Hazardous Substances Labeling Act (1960) to ban all hazardous substances and prohibit sales of potentially harmful toys and other articles to children.
1967	Flammable Fabrics Act	Amended the 1953 act and expanded textile legislation to include the Department of Commerce Flammability Standards for additional products.
1968	Consumer Credit Protection Act (Truth in Lending)	Required full disclosure of the terms and rates charged for loans and credit.
1968	Age Discrimination in Employment Act	Prevented discrimination against employing anyone on basis of age; extended retirement age to 70.
1970	Poison Prevention Packaging Act	Provided standards for child-resistant packaging of hazardous substances.
1971	Care Labeling Act	Stated that all apparel selling for over $3 carry labels with washing or dry-cleaning instructions.

Table 2.1 *continued.*

Date	Act	Description
1972	Consumer Products Safety Act	Established the Consumer Product Safety Commission and empowered it to set safety standards for a broad range of consumer products.
1974	Equal Credit Opportunity Act	Ensured that the various financial institutions and other firms engaged in the extension of credit make credit available without discrimination on the basis of sex or marital status.
1975	Magnuson-Moss Act	Established disclosure requirements and minimum federal standards for written warranties.
1975	Consumer Goods Price Act	Outlawed legalized resale price-setting.
1977	Foreign Corrupt Practices Act	Prohibited U.S. companies from making payments (bribes) to high-ranking foreign government officials.
1984	Toy Safety Act	Granted power to the government to recall dangerous toys from the market.
1986	Tax Reform Act	Eliminated deductions for sales tax and for interest payments on revolving or installment credit.
1989	Omnibus Trade Bill	Included the switch to a harmonized system of tariff codes, a reduction of licensing requirements for exports to U.S. allies, and a strengthening of U.S. import restrictions.
1992	Americans with Disabilities Act (ADA)	Required that employers make provisions for disabled people in the workplace.
1996	Family and Medical Leave Act (FMLA)	Granted workers 12 weeks of unpaid leave to address personal or family health needs.
2001	Patriot Act	Placed limitations on cash transactions to help stop the flow of money to terrorist groups.
2002	Terrorism Risk Insurance Act	Provided federal aid to help insurers handle terrorism-related claims.
2002	Sarbanes-Oxley Act	Required all publicly traded companies to diligently document all safeguards against internal financial malfeasance.
2004	CAN-Spam Act	Clarified actions of companies that contact customers by e-mail.
2006	Fair and Accurate Credit Transaction Act (FACTA)	Required businesses to shorten credit card account numbers on their transaction receipts to protect customers against fraud.
2008	Consumer Product Safety Improvement Act	Regulated hazardous substances used in manufacturing and mandated testing of children's products; updated in 2009.
2010	Organized Retail Theft Investigation and Prosecution Act	Passed by the House of Representatives; budget crisis prevented it being heard in the Senate.
2010	Wall Street Reform and Consumer Protection Act	Directed at financial reform; included provision for preventing employers from taking adverse action against whistleblowers.
2010	Patient Protection and Affordable Care Act	Had several implications for small and large businesses that provide health care benefits.
2011	Consumer Product Safety Improvement Act Reform Bill	Extension of the earlier Consumer Product Safety Improvement Act

jewelry containing lead or other toxic substances. Many of the products under scrutiny were those that had been painted with lead paint. Hundreds of thousands of products were recalled in the process.

Although earnest in intent and necessary in order to protect children, many retailers argued that legislation overshot its mark. The act mandated that retailers were responsible for testing products for the presence of toxic substances. Retailers' reactions were strong since they felt that the cost of testing would be high and would affect financial stability in already difficult times. Small retailers were especially vulnerable to the additional costs of doing business and the extra workforce and facilities required to do the testing. Since some toxic products were already on shelves and others were in transit from manufacturers before the recalls were made public, retailers were responsible for removing products from their stores. Goods could not be shipped back to manufacturers, so losses were high for many firms.

The act was amended in 2009 when the Consumer Product Safety commission ruled that retailers would not be liable for certain categories of merchandise including:

- Items containing lead that are inaccessible to children.
- Products made of natural materials, such as cotton.
- Electronic items that cannot be manufactured without lead.[42]

A reform bill of the CPSIA that further defined circumstances under which toxic items would be removed from commerce, along with the ways in which safer substances could be used during manufacturing to protect children was signed into law by President Obama in 2011.[43]

Government and retailers work together to implement laws that protect customers and users of products, but that are also fair to retailers that act conscionably.

Laws Regulating Price Setting   In 2007, the U.S. Supreme Court voted against Section 1 of the Sherman Act, an anti-trust provision banning minimum pricing agreements set by manufacturers. The case involved Kay's Kloset, a Texas boutique no longer in business, and a manufacturer of leather products that insisted on setting minimum prices on its goods that were sold in the store. The boutique owner filed suit in federal court against the manufacturer, stating that in order to ensure the flow of goods, the retailer should be able to mark down and sell merchandise at any price it wished. Kay's won a close to $4 billion judgement that was later upheld by the Fifth Circuit Court of Appeals. However, the Supreme Court ruled in favor of the manufacturer by replacing the provision of the older Sherman Act with "the rule of reason." This ruling contended that the retailer's practice of undercutting prices was anticompetitive.[44] This decision enraged retailers that believed only they should make pricing decisions for their businesses. Reacting to the imposed pricing guidelines, consumer groups and retailers—including eBay—lobbied to have the federal ruling overturned.[45]

In a decision that proponents believe will help lower prices for consumers, the House Judiciary Committee voted in early 2010 to adopt legislation that would reinstate a ban on retail price-fixing deals by manufacturers. The move particularly helps small and middle-sized retailers because it gives them more competitive clout to reduce prices and compete with larger retailers.[46]

Although the design and intent of the supply chain is to facilitate distribution of goods to retailers and consumers, occasionally legal intervention is necessary to ensure a balance of power.

Laws Regulating Sales Tax   A variety of legal decisions regarding sales taxes are made at state and local levels. For example, in 2007 the mayor of New York City spearheaded a proposal to eliminate the 4 percent city tax on apparel. Although the state of New York continued to collect its own 4 percent tax, city retailers applauded this move as a means of stemming the loss of sales to neighboring New Jersey.

Five states currently do not have sales tax: Alaska, Delaware, Oregon, New Hampshire, and Montana.[47] New Hampshire has its own tax issue, however. Bordering state Massachusetts requested that New Hampshire take responsibility for collecting the 5 percent sales tax it feels it is due from Massachusetts consumers who shop across the border in New Hampshire stores. Retailers in New Hampshire and consumers in Massachusetts objected to the ramifications of the proposed taxation. Opponents believed that collecting Massachusetts taxes would increase costs for customers and businesses. Consumers felt they should be free to purchase goods wherever they please.[48] Subsequently, the Massachusetts Supreme Court ruled that the state has no right to collect sales taxes from New Hampshire retailers.[49]

Taxation of goods sold on the Internet has also come under close scrutiny. Online retailers initially seemed immune to sales-tax collection. But as Web-based sales expanded, states intervened to mandate sales tax collection on retail transactions. In the Web's brief history, courts have ruled that a state must collect taxes only from retailers that have a physical presence in that state. In 2009, the Hawaii legislature initiated a bill that would require online retailers to collect the same 4 percent tax paid by brick-and-mortar store shoppers. Proponents felt that encouraging a harmonized tax base would level the competitive playing field for all retailers and generate income for the state.[50]

Adamantly against taxation of online purchases, Amazon.com severed affiliate relationships in Connecticut and Arkansas since those states were on the cusp of enacting laws that would require Amazon to collect sales tax from customers via their affiliates. However, times change and Amazon now supports the Congressional Streamlined Sales Tax initiative, which proposes to standardize states' sales tax laws.[51] Formerly, Amazon collected taxes only from customers in states where the company had a physical presence. The company has been receptive to initiatives that will expand its tax collection policies more fully.

Aspects of the legal environment challenge retailers at every turn. Changes in the characteristics of a market also indicate new opportunities for retailers or the need to modify tactics.

Demographic Changes

As business leaders study the changing retail landscape, they always turn to demographics. **Demographics** are statistics on human populations, including age, gender, ethnic origin, education, income, occupation, type of housing, and other descriptors. Some types of demographic information help retailers interpret changes in the number of consumers, while others help categorize potential target markets by age, gender, or ethnicity. When demographic information is combined with other statistics, ability and willingness to purchase can be determined. Retailers may gain insight regarding taste preferences by understanding generational differences.

Population Trends

Population numbers, growth, density, and migration patterns are all statistics retailers utilize when seeking out new markets, whether they be in Chicago or China. Large retail companies generally look at areas with high population growth when planning new stores because they depend on present numbers and future growth to sustain business. However, size alone may not indicate a viable market. Growth rates and population density may be more important measures. **Population density** specifies the number of people per square mile or kilometer in a specific geographic area. Population density may indicate great opportunity for retailers if the area under scrutiny is understored. For example, Hong Kong has one of the world's most dense populations, with 6,726 people per square kilometer. To compare, Canada has 3.71 and the United States has about 33.86 people per square kilometer.[52] In this case, Hong Kong is a small geographic area and the United States a large one, but both markets are relatively saturated. Canada has a large geographic area but the majority of its population is concentrated close to the U.S. border. **Level of saturation** describes the degree to which retailers that trade in a common geographic area are able to maintain a fair share of business. Understanding the comparative worth of this kind of information is important.

Factors such as birth and death dynamics, population shifts, immigration figures, health standards, and marriage and divorce rates also help retailers understand a population. Other significant statistics include the number of households in the retailer's market, the composition of those households, and the number of dual-career households.

Migration within the United States slowed during the recent recession, making analysis of population shifts less predictable. Some state populations remained unchanged; others experienced

Did You Know?
Does anybody reading this live in Plato, Missouri? If so, you live in the population center of the United States! The mean center of the population "is determined by imagining a flat, weightless and rigid map of the United States that would balance perfectly if all 308,745,538 residents counted in the 2010 Census were of identical weight." Source: Newsroom: 2010 Census, "Plato, Mo. Celebrates Recognition as the 2010 Census U.S. Center of Population," May 9, 2011, www.census. gov/newsroom/releases/ archives/2010_census/cb11-cn135.html

declines. A few highlights from the 2010 U.S. Census indicate the major surges in growth between 2000 and 2010:

- The South and West accounted for 84.4 percent of total population growth. Nevada reported a 35.1 percent growth rate, the highest in the area, and Las Vegas—one of the fastest growing cities in the country—grew 41.8 percent.
- Florida, long a haven for retirees, experienced a decline in the number of people moving to the state during the recession, reversing a long-term trend. However, the fastest growing metro area in the country was Palm Coast, Florida, at 92 percent. The Cape Coral area also grew significantly.
- Other locations showing high growth were Raleigh, North Carolina; Provo, Utah; and Austin, Texas.
- Locations experiencing the biggest population losses were New Orleans, Louisiana; Youngstown, Ohio; Detroit, Michigan; Cleveland, Ohio; and Pittsburg, Pennsylvania. New Orleans' 11.3 percent loss was attributed to the effects of Hurricane Katrina in 2005.
- New York, Los Angeles, and Chicago remain the largest cities in the United States—a distinction they have shared for the past decade—although Chicago did document a decline in population.[53]

International immigration was 10 percent lower between 2007 and 2008 than it was in the previous seven years.[54] Many people who had emigrated from Mexico—as well as Central and South America—began returning to their countries of origin. This was due to job losses in the United States, housing issues, and the crackdown on employment of illegal immigrants. Despite this trend, 23.7 percent of all immigrants entering the United States in 2010 were from Mexico.[55]

Approximately 3 percent of global citizens live and work outside their home countries for a year or more. Many leave their developing countries for more advanced ones because greater earning power allows them to funnel a portion to relatives back home. In 2010, their remittances were about $325 billion.[56] The flow of immigrants reflects a complex and compelling story as people around the world adjust to changes in their economies and their personal livelihoods.

Age Mix

To understand the significance of shifts in the age of the U.S. population, we need to look at them in relation to the baby boomers. The 76 million people born between 1946 and 1964 are considered **baby boomers**. Because of the size of this group and members' buying power, they have dominated consumer-behavior discussions for the past three decades, and will continue to do so.

Children of early baby boomers, usually those born between 1965 and 1977, are identified as **generation X**. This time span was a period of slow population growth called the "baby-bust years." With members now in their thirties and early forties, this group is also known as the Sesame Street generation, having been the first generation to grow up with ever-present media influences.

Those born between 1978 and 1992, who include contemporary young adults, teens, and older school-age children, are members of **generation Y**. They will influence retail sales for decades to come. The youngest generation Y members are also called millennials, since they are the first generation to come of age in the 2000s. They are media-savvy and confident online. What does generation Y mean to retailers? More clothes, electronic games and gadgets, computers, and educational necessities. Stores like Forever 21, Arden B., Wet Seal, Delia's, and Abercrombie & Fitch target young-adult customers.

Girls between late childhood and teenage years fall into the category called **'tweens.** Justice, Aeropostale, and other like-minded retailers speak their language. Through money earned at part-time jobs or given as allowances, 'tweens have spending power and they are using it. Retailers that know how to talk and market to young consumers thrive. Although the downturn in the economy put a damper on the shopping enthusiasm of the oldest 'tweens, there have been relatively fewer cutbacks in part-time staff in many businesses that employ young workers. The youngest 'tweens usually earn money as babysitters or through informal neighborhood house and garden jobs, and have generally escaped the fallout from the recession except in areas where families were hard-hit by home foreclosures and job losses.

The oldest of the baby boomers turned 65 in 2011. The youngest of the group will be 50 in 2014—almost senior citizens! They will defy whatever previous generations thought old age meant. Walk through any department store and you will see mature shoppers buying golf, ski, or yoga clothes. They'll buy vitamins and herbal supplements, and use Botox for cosmetic purposes. The term *elderly* hardly applies to this burgeoning group, who are active, vigorous, and full of unique wants and needs.

Groups of senior citizens in the United States are growing. Between 2000 and 2025, the number of people 75 to 84 years old will increase by one-third; the number of individuals 85 and older will almost double. Defying the myth that older people are not active online, one study showed that 48 percent of people over 66 shop online at least quarterly.[57] That percentage continues to grow, as does the presence of seniors on Facebook. Although most older adults continue to rely on e-mail as their preferred form of electronic communication, texting is on the increase.

Retailers that study all aspects of the age mix are better able to provide appropriate and desired merchandise and services. Many use generational and specific age ranges for the purpose of market segmentation. **Market segmentation** is the process of breaking down a large population into smaller, accessible groups that share similar characteristics, lifestyles, or needs.

Ethnic Diversity

Retailers also look at changes in the ethnic composition of markets. Ethnic markets are viable segments, and some retailers seek to satisfy the specific needs of these groups. In the United States, important ethnic markets include African-American, Asian, and Hispanic consumers. Conversely, as ethnic minorities become more mainstreamed, some differences in product selectivity dissipate.

According to the Census Bureau, half of the U.S. population will be non-Caucasian by 2042. Immigration and lower birthrates in the Caucasian population are contributing to this trend. In many areas of the country, diversity is becoming more apparent: changes in populations' ethnic composition have been particularly noticeable in Denver, Las Vegas, Orlando, and Los Angeles.[58]

The buying power of ethnic groups lends credence to their importance to retailers. By 2012, the buying power of African Americans is expected to reach $1.1 trillion. African-American households earning annual incomes of $75,000 or more are designated as "affluent." This group represents 17 percent of the total African-American market and accounts for 45 percent of its buying power.[59] According to the 2010 census, African Americans make up 12.6 percent of the U.S. population.[60]

The buying power of U.S. Hispanics was $870 billion in 2008.[61] Those of Hispanic or Latino origin accounted for 16.3 percent of the U.S. population in 2010. The percentage increases annually and is attributed to births more than immigration. The Hispanic population controls more disposable income than other minority groups, according to researchers at the University of Georgia's Selig Center. By 2012, the amount of disposable income among this group is expected to reach $1.3 trillion.[62]

Home Depot is proactive in reaching the Hispanic market. Most of its stores signs are bilingual, and the company has created Spanish television commercials, direct-mail pieces, and e-mail campaigns. In late 2008, it launched a fully transactional Spanish-language site. Research showed that Hispanic customers were more comfortable using Spanish and that they were more likely to comparison-shop online than non-Hispanic customers before making a purchase.[63] However, four months later, the company closed the site—a surprise to many who followed the company's development in Hispanic markets—citing insufficient sales and ineffective site visits as the primary reasons for the closure. The company said that 50 percent of the visitors to the Web site were from other countries.[64] This finding seemed discordant with the company's intentions to bring a Spanish-language site to its American customers. Home Depot runs independent Web sites to support its stores in Canada and Mexico. The home-improvement retailer learned through further research that its Spanish-speaking customers liked to shop in the stores, but preferred to speak with sales associates in Spanish. As a result, Home Depot is adding more bilingual employees to its sales team.[65]

Asian-American households have always been important to retailers because they tend to have higher household incomes, savings rates, and often more education than their non–Asian-American counterparts. Asian-American families that emigrated from South Asia have average annual household incomes of $90,000. They tend to purchase high-end electronics and dine out frequently.[66]

Individuals of Asian ethnicity made up about 5 percent of the U.S. population in 2010. Between 2000 and 2010, the Asian segment grew 43 percent, making it the fastest growing racial group in the United States.[67]

Ethnic products have appeal in the marketplace. For example, ethnic restaurants are widely accepted. Chinese and Italian restaurants have been part of most communities in the United States for a century or more. Japanese, Thai, and Mexican restaurants gained popularity in the 1980s. The 1990s brought an upsurge in popularity of lesser-known Asian cuisines, including Vietnamese and Malaysian. A rebirth of interest in Greek, Polish, Russian, and other foods is also apparent and will provide new opportunities for forward-thinking retailers in this century.

Ethnic marketing is evident in supermarkets that allocate considerable square footage to products that appeal to specific groups residing in the neighborhood, as well as to the general populace who appreciate global cuisine.

Gender Issues

Differences in product preferences and shopping habits between men and women have always been observed. They serve as legitimate bases for segmentation. Other gender variables including outreach to gay markets address new opportunities for retailers.

Women in the Workforce

The number of women in the workforce has increased over the past few decades, generating greater need for one-stop shopping, fast food, time-saving devices, clothing for work, and childcare services. The availability of childcare for working parents is an important issue, and many have problems finding appropriate care. Some retailers have addressed this issue and offer partial reimbursement for day-care expenses; others set up day-care consortiums with other businesses in their area.

Gay and Lesbian Influence

Members of the extended gay community have become much more a part of the mainstream marketplace than they were in past decades. The acronym LGBT designates the lesbian, gay, bisexual, and transgender community. Several trends indicate opportunities for outreach to this community by retailers:

- The LGBT community is composed of people who are affluent and well educated.
- Population centers are in urban areas like New York, San Francisco, and Miami.
- Members of the LGBT community find affinity with brands and retailers that support them.[68]

Occupational and Educational Outlook

Recession has a huge impact on the job outlook for college graduates. Retail layoffs, business closings, downscaling, and declining sales affect retailers' recruitment and hiring plans. However, as the economy rebounds, the retail sector is expected to generate new jobs.

Goal attainment continues to rise across all educational levels in the United States. High school graduates; individuals possessing some college education but no degree; and associate, bachelor, postgraduate, and professional degree holders have shown significant growth in recent decades, according to U.S. Census reports. This trend is expected to escalate, influenced by the economic climate. Thus, students looking ahead to the prospects of entering a restrained job market may decide to earn a higher-level degree if finances permit, in hopes of improving their chances of landing a good first job.

Having a college degree affects future income and expenditure habits. College-educated individuals in well-paying positions have more discretionary income to spend on retail products.

Income Dynamics

In the United States, family income varies by ethnic group, by gender, and from state to state. Real median household income was $49,445 in 2010.[69] The breakdown of median household income across ethnic and racial groups is detailed in Table 2.2.

Table 2.2 Median Family Income by Race/Ethnicity, 2010

Ethnicity	Median Family Income
White	$51,846
Black	$32,068
Hispanic origin	$37,759
Asian	$64,000
Native Americans and Alaska Natives	$54,620

Source: U.S. Census Bureau. Newsroom. "Income, Poverty, and Health Insurance Coverage in the United States: 2010." Summary of Key Findings. September 13, 2011. Table: "Real Median Household Income for 2010." http://www.census.gov/newsroom/releases/archives/income_wealth/cb11-157.html

Economists speculate that in periods of economic boom, the disparity between the rich and the poor decreases, but in actuality this is not true. Personal and household income varies widely, depending on which part of the world is being studied. The Boston Consulting Group determined that households throughout the world with incomes of over $1 million increased 14 percent in 2006. That year, the United States had the most millionaire households, 4.6 million, but Switzerland and the Middle East had a higher concentration of millionaires despite smaller populations.[70] When BCG replicated the study in 2008, the picture had changed radically, but not surprisingly. Due to the global downturn, the number of millionaires worldwide had dropped 17.8 percent. Europe and North America were the most negatively affected. Asset managers do not expect wealth to reach prerecession levels until at least 2013.[71]

Gender discrepancies in earnings exist. Figure 2.4 illustrates the ratio of female-to-male earnings over time. In 2009, the median income per capita in the United States was $27,041.[72] According to the Bureau of Labor Statistics, full-time female workers earned 77 percent of what male workers earned. But there was some good news for women: "women don't gain as much in a boom, but don't lose as much in a recession," researchers reported.[73] Anecdotal evidence supported this view, suggesting that women were able to navigate the recession more successfully, in part because higher-paid men were more likely to lose jobs when employers cut their workforce.

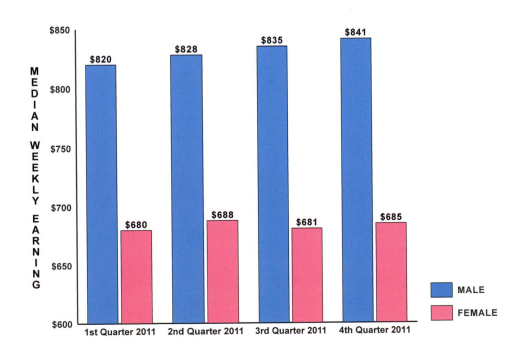

Figure 2.4
Male-to-Female Earnings Ratio
(U.S. Census Bureau)

Customers' decisions to buy or not to buy affect a retailer's survival. These decisions also reflect changes in customers' disposable and discretionary incomes. Retailers are interested in discretionary income because its availability facilitates the purchase of luxury and impulse goods. Environmental factors, including recession, also contribute significantly to the decrease in available discretionary income.

Earlier in this chapter, we looked at factors that contribute to a recession. Several other circumstances contributed to the rising standard of living in the late 20th to early 21st century:

- Increased numbers of dual-income families.
- Higher level of sophistication among the educated.
- Higher paying jobs in technological fields.
- Increased wealth due to stock market growth.

Reflecting on these radically different circumstances should alert readers to cyclical patterns that occur in the economy and their influence on lifestyles. Exclusive shops in such communities as Beverly Hills, California; Scottsdale, Arizona; and Palm Beach, Florida respond to the needs of wealthy people who share one or more of these attributes. Similar shopping streets that target high-income customers exist in major cities around the world. Avenue des Champs-Élysées in Paris and Causeway Bay in Hong Kong are examples. When the effects of a severe economic downturn reach this upper tier of society, even upscale shopping venues are vulnerable, as illustrated in Figure 2.5.

At the other extreme are retailers who perceive opportunities among middle- and lower-income families. Some have responded with deep discount stores and used-goods shops.

Income data alone do not identify potential customers. They do not indicate buying power or whether an individual has interest in purchasing from a retailer. Equally important are customers' values and attitudes. The relationship between income and social class is discussed in Chapter 4.

Societal Changes

Changes in lifestyle are molded by the behavior, attitudes, and values of society; economic wherewithal; and a host of other factors. These are the guideposts that retailers follow in order to meet the needs and preferences of their clientele. Several changes in the social fiber are affecting retailers and customers in the United States.

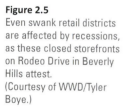

Figure 2.5
Even swank retail districts are affected by recessions, as these closed storefronts on Rodeo Drive in Beverly Hills attest.
(Courtesy of WWD/Tyler Boye.)

Green Awareness

The impact of the environmental movement in the United States has waxed and waned over the past 50 years but continues to increase this decade. Concern for the environment also varies by country, with wealthier countries generally devoting more attention to environmental issues than developing nations. Retailers show concern for ecosystems and demonstrate their responsibility to the green movement in many ways:

- *Eco-friendly products.* Many retailers stock recyclable and biodegradable products. Some retail chains were founded on the premise of providing only goods that are environmentally safe and that are tested without cruelty to animals. The Body Shop created an entire image and social responsibility platform around environmental issues. Its positions against product testing on animals and for rainforest preservation have received much publicity worldwide.
- *Ecopsychology.* The inclination to live a more basic existence manifests in several ways. Choosing to purchase clothing made from natural fabrics may be closely related to environmental consciousness as well as a more earth-oriented approach to life. Some psychologists call this mindset "ecopsychology" and consider it part of our need to bond with the universe and identify our roots. For many, it involves a return to organic fruits and vegetables, herbal medicines, and marketplace shopping.
- *Waste and conservation issues.* Hazardous waste disposal issues have been addressed by legislatures. Retailers are concerned when the products they sell come under scrutiny. Some of these products include automobile tires and batteries, oil, appliances, and electronics. Retailers take a proactive approach to the education of customers by providing brochures and signs outlining proper disposal procedures. Some retailers take on the task of safe disposal themselves—for an additional fee.
- *Earth-friendly construction.* Retailers practice energy conservation through improvements in building; lighting; and heating, ventilation, and air-conditioning (HVAC) systems. Customers are not always aware that efficiencies in these areas are part of retailers' commitment to the environment. LEED, an acronym for Leadership in Energy and Environmental Design, is a program that sets environmental standards for builders. LEED certification is a standard aspired to by builders of all types, including those that construct retail stores and shopping centers.

The green movement is changing the merchandise sourcing and building initiatives of retailers. Perpetuated by an increased awareness of global warming, the need for sustainability, and reduced wastefulness, customers have sought new products and services and retailers have responded. Examples of how green values influence strategic planning appear in Chapter 3.

Time Deprivation

Most people, regardless of vocation, complain of having minimal free time. As careers have come to consume more of a person's day, productivity has become paramount. Multitasking individuals have altered the meaning of busy, and smartphones for some have come to seem like a new body part. Whether it is because time is short or because electronic devices are now an integral part of our social fiber, a profusion of retail products and services is demanded by time-starved families. In demand are after-school programs for children; pet resorts, day care, walkers, and sitters; and grocery and meal-delivery services. Time-management and stress-reduction seminars are no longer directed only to busy executives. Hectic lives are as common in other countries as they are in the United States.

Economic Uncertainty

Many people choose to adopt a more value-conscious way of shopping, even if they can afford more. The downward spiral of the economy in 2008–2009, and its lingering legacy of uncertainty into 2011, encouraged this tendency. By 2012 the United States had seen some positive changes in the housing market and manufacturing sectors that normally signal increases in household spending. However the instability of many EU economies is believed to effect trade worldwide for at least two years. Consumers want products that offer more inherent quality for the prices they are willing to pay. Some shop in new, less pricey venues, while others have relaxed their standards toward dressing for work or other activities. Expect this trend to continue.

//////////////////////////////////
Cyberscoop
If you haven't visited www.groupon.com, do so now. It's free and easy to register, and you're able to see what bargains are available in your specified geographic area. Once you complete your profile, Groupon selects offers that parallel your stated interests and emails you when hot prospects appear. How do you think this service competes with paper coupons?

Dollar-Stretching Tactics

Most value-conscious consumers employ one or more of the following dollar-stretching tactics:

- With coupons in hand, customers belonging to all socioeconomic groups peruse supermarket shelves. Many won't buy a product unless they have a coupon for it, or can purchase it at a discounted price. Interest in the Web site Groupon.com peaked in recent years among consumers eager to share in the savings on products, services, and entertainment in their immediate trading areas.
- Retailers that consistently offer well-made products at fair prices attract value-conscious customers.
- Children's used-clothing shops, once-worn designer apparel boutiques, and previously owned furniture stores are shopped at more frequently.
- Flea markets, yard sales, and auctions also fuel a thrifty philosophy.

Whatever stigma may have formerly been associated with purchasing other people's cast-offs has been dissipated, as shoppers discover their dollars go further on good-quality used clothing and furniture than on new products. The slowdown experienced during the 2008–2009 holiday period—and the meager improvement in the 2009–2010 and 2010–2011 seasons—caused some analysts to speculate on the long-term effects on retailing of consumer reticence to spend, ongoing mistrust of financial markets, and the apparent formation of new values.

Wardrobe and Attitude Adjustments

If sales are up or down in men's and women's career wear, the economy probably influences the decline, but so do professional-dress trends in the workplace. The casual Friday trend of the late 1990s reflected the loosening of the strict dress codes that had been popular in decades past. The underlying premise—that people and their worth to a company would be defined less in terms of physical appearance and more in terms of competencies—was perceived as positive change. New status looks emerged as casual clothing was selected for the workplace. Gap polo shirts and J. Crew chinos became suitable work wear in many corporate offices. In some industries, even T-shirts and jeans are viewed as acceptable options.

A resurgence of interest in dressing more traditionally in suits, rather than more casual separates, occurred at about the same time as the economic downturn and the events of 9/11. The resurgence of conservative dress reflected patriotic sentiment, the need to cope with a troubled economy, and perhaps a desire to maintain dignity in the face of chaos. By 2009, recession-strapped workers were making do with their wardrobes and purchasing new items only if they were truly needed or the garments were marked down to a significantly lower price. Some adjusted their brand preferences by forgoing a designer suit for a less-expensive label. A similar trend toward simpler, more conservative investment dressing in somber colors was evident in some fashion markets.

Today, dressing down has become an accepted option for most social and personal occasions. Observe this the next time you attend a wedding or dine in a fine restaurant. More relaxed attitudes toward speech and e-mail behavior—including acceptance of the lower-case pronoun "i" and extensive abbreviations when texting—exemplify a more casual viewpoint toward communication, too.

Changing Aspirations

In 1998, data from a study indicated five ways that the American character was expected to change in the 21st century. People were expected to:

1. Be more tolerant of alternative lifestyles and cultures.
2. Be more focused on international issues.
3. Place more importance on marriage and children.
4. Place more emphasis on giving back to the community.
5. Be more religious.[74]

Pollsters Yankelovich, Skelly, and White were evidently on target; many of their findings are recognized attributes in today's society. All of these perspectives address ways that individuals look beyond their immediate needs to focus on the needs of others. People worldwide consistently put aside their own problems and economic uncertainty to give freely their time, possessions, and money to aid survivors of earthquakes, tropical storms, and floods. Fortunately for all, altruistic causes have gained momentum in families, across nations, and around the world.

Retail companies participate in their communities and the society as a whole in socially responsible ways. Many sponsor fundraisers for charity, form philanthropic partnerships, and contribute to those in need through cause marketing programs. **Cause marketing** is the practice of staging promotions that benefit charitable organizations or communities, and also build positive public relations for the sponsoring retailer. More companies are becoming involved in positive social change. From breast cancer, heart disease, and autism research to animal-welfare charities, important causes are gaining momentum. Macy's supports the "Go Red" program that fights heart disease. Toys "R" Us and Babies "R" Us encourage donations for the nonprofit organization Autism Speaks. Customers can donate to the cause in stores or online. Safeway, the California-based supermarket chain, has undertaken a major initiative to purchase meat only from companies that engage in humane treatment of the animals it brings to market. It also has doubled the number of eggs it sells from chickens raised free-range rather than in cramped cages.[75] Such programs might not have developed if retailers had not been open to cause marketing and paid heed to the changing attitudes of their customers.

Competition is one aspect of the retail environment that cannot be changed. Retailers cope with encroaching competition in many ways.

Retail Competition

Department stores compete with other department stores, but also with specialty stores, off-price discount stores, catalogues, and online retailers. Every retailer is eager to increase sales; none hesitates to invade another's domain. Competition may be horizontal or vertical. **Horizontal competition** involves retailer against retailer. **Vertical competition** involves a retailer against a wholesaler or manufacturer that also engages in retailing. Vertical competition has become more intense since the advent of online shopping. Competition also comes from outside the industry, as people decide whether to spend their annual bonuses on improving their family rooms or on a much-needed vacation—that is, at least in good times. Retail competition occurs domestically and internationally.

Retailers use many different approaches to find competitive advantages. Some combat the competition head on, while others find niches or identify unmet needs in the marketplace. Internally, retailers may use merchandising and store-location techniques. Externally, growth strategies may be the objective.

Internal Techniques

Selling the brand, offering unique or unexpected merchandise, providing incomparable service, or trading in an unusual way helps retailers stand out from the crowd. Several examples illustrate these techniques:

- *Private label merchandise.* Building a brand that competes on the basis of its intrinsic worth and a strong retail name is a valuable competitive advantage. **Private label merchandise** is the term given to goods that are manufactured to a retailer's specifications and bear the retailer's name or other brand names created by the retailer. Whether merchandise bears the company name or is part of a brand policy that uses several different in-house labels, the approach is cost-effective when implemented well.
- *Scrambled merchandising.* Carrying products unrelated to a store's traditional or expected merchandise mix is called **scrambled merchandising**. This type of merchandising occurs when, for example, a supermarket adds a rack of grooming products to its regular stock of meat, produce, and groceries, or a drugstore adds apparel and gifts to its expected health and beauty aids. These retailers are practicing scrambled merchandising to gain or maintain

/////////////////////////////////
Cyberscoop
Attention golfers: Since 1999, CVS Caremark and its many vendor sponsors have hosted the CVS Caremark Charity Classic golf tournament featuring world-class golfers. The event, held in Rhode Island, has raised over $14 million for 500 local and national charities. Go to www.cvs caremarkcharityclassic .com to learn more about the charities and the ways customers obtain tickets to help the cause.

Figure 2.6
Shoppers may not expect to find fresh flowers at Sam's Club but are delighted when they do; this is scrambled merchandising in action.

a competitive edge and to increase sales. Another example of scrambled merchandising is illustrated in Figure 2.6.

- *Product differentiation.* Retailers add name brands, limited merchandise lines, or new departments in order to differentiate their operations. As examples, Kmart for several years sold moderately priced sheets and draperies designed by Martha Stewart in its stores. At the same time, Macy's carried a more upscale line of Martha Stewart kitchen utensils and home furnishings. Hair salons depart from their traditional service focus by adding nail boutiques, holistic beauty product boutiques, jewelry, and apparel in order to gain a competitive advantage.

- *Location strategies.* Seeking a competitive advantage by locating where throngs of people gather in a historic landmark gives some retailers an opportunity to stand out in a crowd. Pop-up stores and other temporary locations are new ways that retailers can test-market their wares before committing to a permanent location. A **pop-up store** is a retail operation at a temporary location that is used to test the market or fulfill a time-sensitive need in the marketplace. Sears Canada exemplified this approach when it opened four pop-up stores on university campuses in Ontario; the temporary retail spaces brimmed with dorm bedding, décor, and apparel for the back-to-school season.[76]

External Techniques

Outside of the store, retailers practice aggressive—sometimes predatory—tactics by purchasing competing firms or staging market-share battles.

- *Buy the competition.* Retailers may attempt to control competition by purchasing rival firms, believing that if they own their competition, profits can be funneled into one corporate pocket. Many turn their attention to offshore markets that are economically, demographically, and psychographically ready to receive foreign retailers. More on ownership tactics appears in Chapter 3.

- *Grow market share.* Seeking dominance by gaining market share at the expense of fellow retailers is a strategy used by some retailers. **Market share** is the proportion of industry-wide product sales earned by one company. This competitive approach is a chief tool used by retailers during a recession.

Competitive battles will escalate in this century and will exist as long as free enterprise exists. As the world becomes smaller and communication improves, competition will come from distant shores and from within our own countries. Retailers that recognize the need for constant environmental monitoring, the development of coping strategies, and the scientific study of competition will succeed. They must have high ethical standards and deal with unexpected events.

Unpredictable Events

In addition to demographic and social changes, environmental concerns, and knowledge of competition, unexpected events affect customers and retailers. From riots to raging storms, accidents to earthquakes, disease to terrorism, all are uncontrollable aspects of the world in which we live, work, and trade.

Acts of Nature

Natural disasters influence retailing in positive and negative ways. In 2005, Hurricane Katrina brought out the best and the worst in people living both in and away from the affected areas. Families and businesses in and around New Orleans suffered in both the short and long term, as the city was ravaged by storm, flooding, and subsequent looting. By necessity, retailers were some of the first responders as they coped with damaged facilities and merchandise, and devised ways to help their employees get through the first critical days and weeks while also donating to the community.

Walmart, which employed about 15,000 associates in several stores in the hurricane-affected area, reported major damage. However, the retailer offered three days' pay, a $1,000 grant, and jobs in other Walmart stores for employees affected by Katrina. Dress Barn sent $3 million in apparel for distribution to needy families and also set up a gift-matching program for individuals who wanted to contribute financially to the recovery effort.[77]

As hurricane damage was assessed, 13 malls in Louisiana and one in Mississippi were forced to close, including the sprawling Riverwalk Marketplace located on the Mississippi River in New Orleans. Billions of dollars in real estate and merchandise was lost, and the physical and emotional toll on employees and customers was high. Other shopping centers remained open to provide shelter for displaced families.[78]

In the aftermath, most businesses displayed ethical behavior and resisted the temptation to price gouge. **Price gouging** is taking advantage of consumers by marking up prices on retail products to an unreasonably high level. One year later, recovery efforts were under way in New Orleans and other affected cities, although it was estimated that one-third of jobs in the area had been lost.[79]

Deaths of Celebrities

Public displays of concern over the death of international celebrities can paralyze some retailers and provoke extraordinary sales for others. The untimely death of Britain's Princess Diana in 1997 generated an outpouring of sympathy as people the world over dealt with feelings of shock and grief. One year later, sales of commemorative merchandise were still strong. "Princess" Beanie Babies were known to sell for $300 or more in the United States—if they could be found at all. Elton John's remake of "Candle in the Wind" became one of the top-selling CDs of all time. Interest in Diana has resurfaced periodically, most recently in 2007—the tenth anniversary of her death—and 2011, upon the marriage of her son, Prince William, to Kate Middleton.

Acts of War and Terrorism

The prolonged military engagements of the past decade have greatly affected individual and collective sentiment, in ways that have influenced sales and promotional activities.

Perhaps the most profoundly unsettling event of many U.S. generations was the 9/11 terrorist attacks in the United States. The events that occurred on that day—and in successive months and years in the United States and other countries—continue to affect our lives and business practices. Shortly after, patriotic feelings encouraged retailers to display the American flag in support of troops in retail stores, catalogues, and on Web sites. From the Field 2.2 highlights the impact of 9/11 then and now.

Retailers cannot predict events such as those chronicled here. However, adversity prepares companies and individuals to find and deliver the resources, talent, and teamwork to rebuild stores and spirit. The final environmental factor acknowledged in this chapter is technology.

Impact of Technology

All elements of the retail environment described so far are of considerable importance to retailers, but no other aspect is having such a profound effect as is technology. It has given retailers the means for instant sales and inventory updates, accurate and speedy credit and check approvals, video conferencing and training capabilities, online purchasing, and countless other tools to help retailers make better decisions and operate more efficiently. Technology has also changed the way customers shop. While some shopkeepers might still misinterpret the behavior of customers who patently comparison-shop on their iPhones while examining a stunning product, what was once atypical behavior is now expected and accepted. Not only has technological advancement made online re-

Did You Know?
Royalty and celebrity often combine to influence fashion direction and retail sales. Minutes after England's Prince William married Kate Middleton, the U.S. retailer David's Bridal was poised to launch look-alike wedding gowns. Inspired by her diamond drops, QVC commissioned Kenneth Jay Lane to design earrings to be sold for less than $50.
Source: Anne D'Innocenzio, "Copy-Kates: Firms rush to produce cheaper versions of the royal gown," *The Star*, April 30, 2011, www.thestar.com/printarticle/983532.

From the Field 2.2   The Impact of Terrorism on Retailing

As with all mind-boggling and devastating events, we remember where we were, what we were doing, and whom we first called when we learned about the World Trade Center, Pentagon, and Pennsylvania tragedies on September 11, 2001. Contemplating how the events affected lives and our nation was paramount in our minds. To consider otherwise would have been disrespectful to those lost, as well as their families.

Yet acts of terrorism and war also affect the economy in general, and retail business specifically. On September 13, 2001, consumer confidence levels reached their lowest point in eight years. The country experienced a $100 billion dollar economic jolt, and that figure did not include property or human life losses.[i] Several premises set the tone for deeper understanding of the effects of the terrorist attacks:

- There would be short-term and long-term economic impacts on retail businesses.
- The areas closest to the terrorist incidents would be more deeply affected than those that were farther away.
- There would be both negative and positive effects on retail sales.
- The events would change business practices and consumer behavior domestically and globally.

Airline, hotel, and tourism-related businesses were some of the first hurt. With airline fleets grounded almost immediately after the attacks, ticket sales stagnated. Restaurant sales plummeted as families stayed home out of fear and out of concern as they monitored newscasts. While networks and cable channels broadcasted 24-hour news, advertising revenues declined by $700 million during the first week after September 11.[ii]

An estimated 114,700 workers were laid off between September 15 and December 29, 2001 as a direct or indirect result of 9/11.[iii] Despite the efforts of multiple service agencies, many people from New York City and its environs were still without jobs six months later. Retail workers in lower Manhattan and food service workers in airports near and far suddenly joined the ranks of the unemployed.

A 75-store shopping mall that included Victoria's Secret, J. Crew, Coach, and Sephora stores, located beneath the World Trade Center, ceased to exist. The mall had generated average revenue of $900 per square foot, making it one of the most productive shopping centers in the country at that time.[iv]

The direct marketing sector was paralyzed as postal deliveries were curtailed. The Direct Marketing Association reported that catalogue retailers suffered declines of 50 percent or more immediately after the attacks. The need for increased security, insurance, transportation safeguards, and new privacy measures would further compromise the ability of direct marketing firms to fulfill orders.[v]

Reactions to the attacks shed light on the impact of the events. Positive and negative responses are highlighted in several examples culled from news media reports:

- Cell phone sales at Radio Shack were up 20 percent, Walmart reported record sales of American flags and emergency supplies, and sales of sympathy cards at American Greetings increased immediately following the crisis.[vi]

- Sales at Macy's and Bloomingdale's in New York City fell 40 percent two weeks after the attacks.[vii]
- The use of e-mail and online shopping increased dramatically.

The global outpouring of sympathy was evidenced by unbridled generosity and the desire to display a strong pro-American statement. Citizens were encouraged to buy in order to build the economy and send a message to terrorist organizations that their agenda had not succeeded.

Merchandising opportunities abounded for manufacturers and designers to produce patriotically themed products. Emblematic gowns, shoes, sweaters, T-shirts, pajamas, jewelry, and even diapers quickly found their way into the marketplace. Many companies donated all or part of their proceeds from the sale of goods to appropriate charities.

Seven months after the attacks, most of the physical evidence had been removed from the actual sites. Mental and spiritual healing would take much longer.

More than a decade later, rebuilding of the retail infrastructure at Ground Zero has been slower than anticipated, but progress is being made. Early in 2008, the Port Authority of New York and New Jersey, along with the Australian company Westfield Group, announced plans to develop 500,000 square feet of retail space spread over several sites surrounding the Trade Center footprint. Groundbreaking for the memorial on the original site took place in 2006.

However, the dismal state of the economy, construction delays, bickering between government agencies and insurers, and problems leasing space have compromised completion of the development. This brief update shows the status of the four main World Trade Center buildings:

- One WTC—55% leased since 2011; expect completion of building in 2014.
- Two WTC—Development put on hold.
- Three WTC—Development halted at eight stories since no tenants available—needs 400,000 sq. feet leased to continue.
- Four WTC—51% leased, mostly by government agencies; due for completion in 2013.

Should Three WTC not lease property, there is speculation that the eight completed floors could become rental space.

It is distressing that a tragedy of this magnitude should serve as an explicit example of the uncontrollable environment in which business is done. Efforts to respect the sacredness of the Trade Center site while carefully planning for the future deserve the support of all.

Endnotes

[i] Jon E. Hilsenrath, "Terror's Toll on the Economy," *Wall Street Journal*, October 9, 2001, B1.
[ii] Ibid.
[iii] Carlos Tejada, "Terror Effects," *Wall Street Journal*, February 19, 2002.
[iv] "Ground Zero Planners Urge Profusion of Shops," *Wall Street Journal*, June 29, 2005, B1, B4.
[v] Michael A. Turner, "DMA Perspective: Economic Impact of the Attack on America on US Direct Marketing." *The DMA Interactive*, accessed September 18, 2001, www.thedma.org/library/whitepapers/attackonamerica.shtml.
[vi] Hilsenrath, B1.
[vii] Hilsenrath, B4.
[viii] Elliot Brown. "New Hitch in Ground Zero Plans: No Takers." *Wall Street Journal*. July 25, 2012. C1.

tailing and other home-based electronic shopping methods possible, it has also mandated new ways for retailers to interact and engage with their customers. E-retailing is the focus of Chapter 7.

Elements of the retail environment do not operate in isolation. Retailers must be sociologists, economists, demographers, ecologists, and perhaps philosophers if they are to understand and benefit from the changes in the retail environment.

Summary

Complex variables guide retailing policy. Economic factors, political events, trade alliances, legal actions, changing demographics, societal values, competition, unpredictable events, and technology all affect retailing. Collectively, these elements make up the retail environment, which is constantly changing.

Inflation, deflation, recession, and other economic dynamics influence retail planning. Changes in political leadership, formation of trade alliances, and passage of laws influence retailing around the world.

Retailers follow demographic changes in household composition, age mix, population size, ethnic groups, and family income statistics. Information on gender issues, as well as occupational and educational trends, is also useful. Retailers reflect the behaviors, values, and attitudes of their target markets. As examples, sales of ethnic products grow because of changes in a population's composition and people's changing values. Online retailing evolves because the technology is available and some individuals prefer to shop from home or work.

Some influences on changing societal values are (1) green awareness, (2) time deprivation, (3) economic uncertainty, and (4) changing aspirations.

Competition for consumers' dollars has never been greater, or come from so many directions. Internal techniques designed to beat the competition include merchandising and store-planning techniques. External techniques include purchasing competing stores or increasing market-share growth.

Unpredictable events such as natural disasters, death of celebrities, and acts of war and terrorism also affect retail sales. In the 21st century the most important element in the retail environment is technology. Ethical concerns and choices influence retailers worldwide.

Key Terms

807 programs
Baby boomers
Bankruptcy protection
Bribe
Buying power
Cause marketing
Caveat emptor
Consumer confidence
Consumerism
Consumer Price Index (CPI)
Counterfeiting
Deflation
Demographics
Devaluation
Discretionary income
Displacement
Disposable income
Dominican Republic–Central American–United
  States Free Trade Agreement (CAFTA–DR)
Ethnocentric
European Union (EU)
Generation X
Generation Y
Generic goods

Geocentric
Horizontal competition
Inflation
Level of saturation
Market segmentation
Market share
North American Free Trade Agreement (NAFTA)
Outshopping
Population density
Pop-up store
Preferred trading partner (PTP)
Price gouging
Prime rate
Private label merchandise
Protectionism
Quota
Recession
Scrambled merchandising
Tariff
Trade embargo
Trading bloc
'Tweens
Vertical competition
World Trade Organization (WTO)

Questions for Discussion

1. How does a recession affect retailers and customers? How has the recent one affected you?
2. What impact does political change have on retailing?
3. What types of legislation are of concern to retailers this decade?
4. How do demographics and changes in social values affect retailing? Discuss several examples.
5. Are luxury-goods retailers more interested in disposable or discretionary income? Why?
6. How are retailers and consumers responding to the green movement?
7. What are several ways retailers differentiate their stores from the competition? Give examples of internal and external competitive tactics.
8. How do unpredictable events challenge retailers and provide new directions for retailers?

Endnotes

1. "Bonds, Rates & Yields," *Wall Street Journal*, June 9, 2011, C4. and "Borrowing Benchmarks," *Wall Street Journal*, February 25, 2009, C12.

2. International Monetary Fund, "Tensions From the Two-Speed Recovery, Unemployment, Commodities and Capital Flows." *World Economic Outlook April 2011*, http://elibrary.imf.org/view.imf081/11381-9781616350 598/11381-97816165098/chol.xml

3. U.S. Bureau of Labor Statistics, Consumer Price Index for April 2011, Table A. "Percent Changes in CPI for Urban Consumers (CPI-U)= US City-Average," http://data.bls.gov/cpi/cpid1104.pdf

4. Ibid, 4.

5. *Wall Street Journal.* "Borrowing Benchmarks" *Inflation.* U.S. Consumer Price Index. November 15, 2012. C5.

6. Liza Casabona. "Down, Down, Down: Deflation Fears Climb as Apparel Prices Slide," *Women's Wear Daily*, November 20, 2008, 1, 10.

7. Jon Hilsenrath and Sudeep Reddy, "Fed Signals More Action as Slump Drags On," *Wall Street Journal*, December 2, 2008, A1.

8. Alexandra Steigrad. "Consumer Confidence Sinks to Record Low," *Women's Wear Daily*, December 31, 2008, 2.

9. Sudeep Reddy, "Fed Forecasts a Much Deeper Downturn," *Wall Street Journal*, February 19, 2009, A2.

10. *Retailer Daily.* "GGP Obtains 'Historic' Development Opportunity-Update," February 4, 2010, 1–2, www.retailerdaily.com/entry/13206/ggp-files-for-chapter-11-blames-broken-credit-markets.html

11. A.D. Pruitt and Kris Hudson, "Hey, Malls Here! Get Your Used Malls Here!" *Wall Street Journal*, April 20, 2011, C8.

12. "General Growth Properties Reports Third Quarter Results," Chicago, Illinois. October 31, 2012. Acquisitions and Dispositions. www.ggp.com/Content/Corporate/docs/PressReleasePDF/Earnings%20Release%20 FINAL.pdf.

13. Jennifer Saranow and Christopher Lawton, "The Bright Side: Deep Discounts From Retailers," *Wall Street Journal*, November 13, 2008, D1, D2.

14. Rob Curran and Kejal Vyas, "Wal-Mart, McDonald's Lone Dow '08 Gainers," *Wall Street Journal*, January 2, 2009, C6.

15. Associated Press, "Discount Retailer to add More Jobs and Stores," *Wall Street Journal*, February 5, 2010, B3.

16. Annual Report 2011: Opening New Doors. "About Dollar General." p. 2. http://files.shareholder.com/downloads/DOLLAR/2006161069xox557676/Obde3b65-7dic-4abb-8904-bacf416c5b38/Dollar_General= 2001_AR_N_P5.pdf

17. "Fast Facts." http://newscenter.dollargeneral.com/company+facts. ©2011 Dollar General Corp.

18. Claire Cain Miller, "For Craft Sales, the Recession Is a Help," *New York Times*, December 23, 2008, www.nytimes.com/2008/12/23/business/23craft.html

19. Bob L. Martin, "Global Retailing: a Revolution in the Making," Presentation. Global Retail Symposium, Lundgren Center for Retailing, University of Arizona, Tucson, March 1996.

20. Ellen Simon, "A Consumer Spending Q & A: Why it Matters," *Boston Sunday Globe*, November 3, 2008, G5.

21. Bob Davis, "IMF Sees 3.9 Percent Global Growth," *Wall Street Journal*, January 27, 2010, A9. (Source: International Monetary Fund.)

22. Conference Board, "The Conference Board Consumer Confidence Index Increases Moderately," January 26, 2010, www.conference-board.org/economics/consumerConfidence.cfm.

23. Chantal Todé, "Low Confidence is An All-time Record," *DM News*, November 3, 2008, 4.

24. Conference Board Consumer Research Center, "Consumer Confidence Takes a Dive," May 31, 2011, http://dshort.com/articles/Conference-Board-Confidence-Index.html. (Source: Conference Board Consumer Research Center.)

25. "Market Data." *Wall Street Journal*, Currencies and Commodities. July 13, 2012. C5.

26. Hiroko Tabuchi, "Japan Enters Recession as Firms Cut Spending," *Wall Street Journal*, November 17, 2008, A9.

27. The WWD List, "The Politics of Style," *Women's Wear Daily*, September 11, 2008, 20. (Source: E-Poll Market Research.)

28. Amy Chozick and Nick Timiraos, "NAFTA Bashing Ends at Texas Line," *Wall Street Journal*, March 3, 2008, A13.

29. David Luhnow, "U.S. Stymies Mexico's Growth for 2009," *Wall Street Journal*, January 9, 2009, A5.

30. Kristi Ellis, "Bush Signs CAFTA Pact," *Women's Wear Daily*, August 3, 2005, 2.

31. *Wall Street Journal*. "On Euro's 10th Birthday, No Music," December 16, 2008, C1, C2.

32. "E-retail Sales in Europe 2009–2015," *Internet Retailer*, accessed March 6, 2011, www.internetretailer.com/trends/sales. (Source: Forrester Research, February 2011.)

33. Kristi Ellis, "Apparel Imports Rise in February," *Women's Wear Daily*. April 13, 2011, 6.

34. Sarah Gilbert, "American Apparel: The Downside to Sweatshop-Free Labor," *Daily Finance*, July 1, 2009, www.dailyfinance.com/story/company-news/american-apparel-the-downside-to-sweatshop-free-labor.html.

35. Silvio Venturi and Pascal G. Favre, "New Legislation Introduced to Allow Publishers to Fix Book Prices," International Law Office (ILO), May 5, 2011, www.internationallawoffice.com/newsletters/detail.aspx?g=7205fe89-d33c-4373-9d

36. International Labor Rights Forum, "2010 Sweatshop Hall of Shame," http://laborrightsblog.typePad.com/international-labor-rights/2010/01/index.html.

37. Tim Newman, "Big Campaign Victories and More Work Ahead!" International Labor Rights Forum, January 11, 2010, http://laborrightsblog.typepad.com/international_labor_right/2010/01/big-campaign-victories-and-more-work-ahead.html.

38. Nate Herman, "AAFA Urges U.S. Government to Work to Resolve Uzbek Cotton Issue," July 21, 2009, www.apparelandfootwear.org/LegislativeTradeNews/details.asp.

39. "Whole Foods Action Halted," *Wall Street Journal*, January 30, 2009, B2.

40. Timothy W. Martin, "Whole Foods to Sell 31 Stores in FTC Deal," *Wall Street Journal*, March 7-8, 2009, B5.

41. Tony Seideman, "Threat of Sanctions Heats Up Debate Over European Privacy Rules," *Stores*, June 2001, 92.

42. Consumer Product Safety Commission, "CPSC Grants One Year Stay of Testing and Certification Requirements for Certain Products," Release #09-115, January 30, 2009.

43. GovTrack. Congress Bills H.R. 2715. "H.R. 2715: To provide the Consumer Product Safety Commission with greater discretion in enforcing the consumer product safety laws, and for other purposes." Bill Overview. 112th Congress 2001–2012. http://www.govtrack.us/congress/bills/112/hr2715

44. Robert Wilonsky. "The Curious Price-Fixing Case of Kay's Kloset Makes a Return to the Supreme Court." November 16, 2010. 1 http://blogs.dallasobserver.com/unfairpark/2010/11/the_curious_antitrust_case_of.php?print=true

45. Liza Casabona. "Retailers Lobby Over Minimum Pricing," *Women's Wear Daily,* December 5, 2008, 2.

46. Judith Burns, "Update: U.S. House Panel Approves Ban on Retail Price-Fixing Deals," *Dow Jones Newswires*, January 13, 2010. www.foxbusiness.com/story/markets/industries/retail/updates.html

47. Rosemary Feitelberg and Sharon Edelson, "Bloomberg Seeks to Eliminate NYC Apparel Tax," *Women's Wear Daily*, January 18, 2007, 3.

48. Jenn Abelson, "State Chases Sales Tax in N.H.," *Boston Globe*, February 3, 2009, 1.

49. Retail Merchants Association of New Hampshire. "MA Supreme Court Rules in Favor of Town Fair Tire," August 25, 2009.

50. Mark Niesse, Associated Press, "Hawaii Proposes to Collect Sales Taxes on Internet Sales," *Boston Globe*, March 2, 2009.

51. Sam Gustin, "Amazon to Connecticut, Arkansas: 'Drop Dead' Over Sales Tax," *Wired*, June 13, 2011, www.wired.com/epicenter/2011/06/amazon-conn-ark.

52. "Population Density 2011," CIA World Factbook 2011, www.photius.com/rankings/geography/population_density_person_per_sq_kn_2011.0.htm.

53. U.S. Census Bureau Newsroom. "U.S. Census Bureau Releases Data on Population Distribution and Change in the U.S. Based on Analysis of 2010 Census Results," March 24, 2011, www.census.gov/newsroom/releases/archives/2010_census/cb11-cn124.html.

54. Conor Dougherty, "Recession Slows Migration in U.S," *Wall Street Journal*, December 23, 2008, A4.

55. Abhijit Naik, "US Immigration Facts," March 7, 2011, http://www.buzzle.com/articles/immigration-statistics-in-the-united-states.html. (Source: US Immigration Facts and Statistics: 2011 Edition.)

56. Phillip Martin, "PBR Discuss Online: Remittances, and the Recession's Effects on International Migration," May, 26, 2011. Population Reference Bureau (transcript), 1, www.prb.org/Articles/2011/remittances-recession-migration.aspx.

57. "Total U.S.Online Shoppers by Age," *Internet Retailer*, www.internetretailer.com/trends/consumers. (Source: Forrester Research, Inc. 2010.)

58. Conor Dougherty, "Whites to Lose Majority Status in U.S. by 2042," *Wall Street Journal*, August 14, 2008, A3.

59. Baar, Aaron, "Affluent African-Americans Buoy Community Buying Power," Media Post Publications, February 13, 2008, http:/ publications.mediapost.com/index.cfm. (Source: Robert Brown. et al. "The African-American Market in the U.S.," Paper Packaged Facts, 2008.)

60. U.S. Census Bureau Newsroom, "2011 Census Shows America's Diversity," March 24, 2011, www.census.gov/newsroom/releases/archives/2010_census/cb11-cn125.html.

61. Lauren Bell, "Power Market: U.S. Hispanics by the Numbers," *DM News*, July 28, 2008, 5. (Source: Hispantelligence)

62. Conor Dougherty and Miriam Jordan, "Surge in U.S. Hispanic Population Driven by Births, Not Immigration," *Wall Street Journal*, May 1, 2008, A3.

63. Chantal Todé, "New Site Furthers Home Depot's Hispanic Strategy," *DM News*, November 24, 2008, 6.

64. Ann Zimmerman, "Home Depot Spanish Site is Shuttered," *Wall Street Journal*, May 2, 2009, http://online.wsj.com/article/SB124122625291179435.html.

65. Ibid.

66. Heanine Poggi, "Retail Has Room to Grow in Ethnic Markets," *Women's Wear Daily*, June 11, 2007, 21.

67. U.S. Census Bureau Newsroom. "Income, Poverty and Health Insurance Coverage in the United States: 2010." Summary of Key Findings. Table: "Real Median Household Income for 2010." September 13, 2011. http://www.census.gov/newsroom/releases/archives/income_wealth/cb11_157.html

68. Dianna Dilworth, "The Gay-Friendly Factor," *DM News*, December 8, 2008, 18.

69. U.S. Census Bureau. "Income, Poverty and Health Insurance Coverage in the United States: 2010." Summary of Key Findings. Table: "Real Median Household Income for 2010." September 13, 2011. http://www.census.gov/newsroom/releases/archives/income_wealth/c11-157.html.

70. Robert Frank, "Wealth Gap Widens Globally," *Wall Street Journal*, October 6–7, 2007, B4.

71. Joe Rauch, "World Wealth Down 11 Percent, Fewer Millionaires," *Reuters*, www.reuters.com/article/idUSTRE59E13320090915. (Source: Boston Consulting Group, 2009.)

72. U.S. Census Bureau, "People QuickFacts: Per Capita Money Income in Past 12 Months (2009 dollars) 2005–2009," http://quickfacts.census.gov/qfd/states/ooooo.html.

73. David Leonard, "Wage Gap Between Men and Women Shrinks," *Wall Street Journal*, February 17, 2003, 3.

74. "The American Character," *Wall Street Journal,* March 5, 1998, A14.

75. Lauren Etter, "Safeway Embraces Animal Welfare," *Wall Street Journal*, February 12, 2008, B9.

76. Sears Canada Inc., "Sears Opens Four Pop-Up University Stores," September 3, 2008, http://biz.yahoo.com/cnw/080903/sears_pop_up_stores.html.

77. "Retailers, Landlords Tally Storm Losses While Rallying to Help Victims," *SCT Xtra*, September 12, 2005, 1.

78. "Katrina Shuts 14 Malls Indefinitely, but Others Serve as Relief Centers," *SCT Xtra*. September 19, 2005, 1.

79. Sharon Donovan, "One Year After Katrina New Orleans Retailers Try to Adapt, Preserve," *Women's Wear Daily*, August 29, 2006, 1, 12.

Chapter 3

Strategic Planning: Adapting to Change

Learning Objectives

After completing this chapter you should be able to:

- Delineate the important components of strategic planning.
- Identify critical aspects of change and determine how they affect strategy development.
- Examine ownership change as a strategic initiative.

a

b

Figure 3.1
Bold signage in Target stores informs customers of monetary incentives when they participate in the retailer's credit card program (a). The Target dog is the ultimate brand symbol (b).

The basic principles of retailing do not change as rapidly as the methods used to reach customers and engage them in the exchange process: goods and services for money. Change is apparent in all of our lives, and the retail sphere is not exempt. If anyone had told us ten years ago that My Virtual Model technology would enable us to key in our body type, facial structure, hair style, and hair color to ensure better-fitting, more suitable apparel when shopping online, we would have laughed. Although we have been using our cell phones forever, we still marvel at the technology that enables us to access the Internet via our phones, download a few apps, and order a pizza directly from Pizza Hut's Facebook page—if you're a member.

Many of us wish we lived in homes where rooms vacuum themselves; Roomba, a personal robot developed by I Robot, makes this service possible.[1] Phones can be programmed to translate speech in real-time into foreign languages. Using GPS technology when we travel abroad allows us to navigate with ease in unfamiliar places. Talking and interactive window displays once seemed beyond our comprehension, yet are now in use. Retailers can store their volumes of data in the cloud and harness the power of the Internet to learn more about their customers than ever before. Many believe that we live in an electronic era that is as important to the future direction of the world as the industrial revolution was 150 years ago.

Increasingly, successful retailers are those that carefully monitor the environment for changes like these and that operate in a multichannel world. Global expansion is another initiative that increases visibility for many retailers. Ownership changes cause some time-tested retailers to disappear and others to become stronger. Because of the relevance of these topics, all appear again as either a whole chapter, major sections of chapters, or continuing themes throughout this text.

Did You Know?
Amazon purchased a warehouse in Dublin, Ireland in 2011 to retrofit for a state-of-the-art cloud computing data center. Tesco, the top-ranked supermarket company in the United Kingdom and previous owner, had used the facility for storage—such a small retail world. (Source: Kantar Retail IQ, "Amazon Buys Dublin Site for Cloud Data Center." February 10, 2011, www.kantarretailiq .com/ContentIndex/News DisplayLW.aspx?id324592.)

All situations occurring in the retail environment are worthy of consideration when planning retail strategies. Retail objectives are reached with less risk if thoughtful plans are put forth. Let's begin with an overview of strategic planning.

Retail Strategy Development

Planning has become a science, practiced by proactive organizations. Advance planning requires collecting information that may be crucial to decision making. Past history, present status, and future direction of a company are considered.

The Strategic Planning Process

Strategic planning is the process of gathering and analyzing information from a variety of internal and external sources for the purpose of reducing risk before special business plans are executed. The strategic planning process necessitates the assessment of strengths and weaknesses, which change over time. Maintaining a delicate balance between success and failure while the retail environment is constantly changing is not easy. Strategic planning involves five fundamental steps:

1. Performing a **situation analysis** to determine the strengths and weaknesses of a company, specific business plan, or proposed product.
2. Identifying a **differential advantage**, which involves pinpointing the unique characteristics of a business or product that may give it a superior position in the marketplace.
3. Developing a **mission statement**, usually a brief paragraph that concisely describes a business and its reason for existence.
4. Preparing company goals and objectives. **Goals** are statements that indicate general company aims or end results. **Objectives** are specific goal-directed initiatives stated by a company.
5. Planning detailed strategies. **Strategies** are action plans that are implemented by a company to reach common goals and objectives.

Details about these five steps follow, along with examples of the ways retailers are using strategic planning to develop their businesses.

Step One: Performing a Situation Analysis

Assessing the strengths and weaknesses of a retail company is the starting point for strategic planning. Completing a situation analysis involves surveying the environment in which the retail organization operates and identifying the opportunities and threats the company faces. This is often accomplished by the use of SWOT analysis. **SWOT analysis** lists a company's strengths, weaknesses, opportunities, and threats (SWOT) and is used to determine future direction.

For example, when warehouse Costco decided to sell herbal supplements, such as ginseng and St. John's wort, it viewed its past success selling traditional vitamins as a strength. The company added herbal supplements to its shelves adjacent to other health and beauty aids. Employees' lack of knowledge about herbal remedies was a potential weakness. Although the trend toward using alternative medicines was perceived as an opportunity, the presence of General Nutrition Center (a strong vitamin and herbal supplement retailer) in its trading area posed a possible threat.

Retailers find ways to develop strengths by focusing on established channels of distribution, thereby shortening the learning curve when they launch similar products. In the previous example, if Costco employees lacked product knowledge, they could be offered the chance to attend herbal medicine seminars or vendor-training sessions. The threat of being in a location where an established retailer of herbal medicines is already trading would not require changes to Costco's plans. However, the retailer could choose to provide higher-quality products, competitive pricing, or a combination of these incentives.

Step Two: Identifying a Differential Advantage

The strategic planning process cannot proceed without articulating a differential advantage, which is closely related to positioning. **Positioning** is the perception a customer has of a company or product in relation to others. Retailers work hard to instill a positive perception in the minds of

Did You Know?

Simon Property Group made history and discovered a differential advantage when its Florida Mall in Orlando became the first retail property to offer free self-service electric-vehicle chargers as a customer service. Eventually Simon intends to add a modest fee for the opportunity to drive in, plug in, and charge up your electric vehicle while you shop at the mall. (Source: Carisa Chappell, "Simon Unveils Electric Charging Stations," April 7, 2011, www.reit.com/Articles/Electric-Vehicle-Charging-Stations-Debut-at-Simon-Mall.aspx.)

Figure 3.2
With its "Always Low Prices" theme, Walmart is appropriately positioned in the marketplace.

customers. As examples, Neiman Marcus is positioned as a company with a high level of fashion sophistication. Walmart is known for its everyday low-pricing policies, as illustrated in Figure 3.2. Special qualities like these constitute differential advantages when they distinguish a seller or product as better than the competition. Customers with a clear image can easily identify the intentions of each retailer.

Step Three: Developing a Mission Statement

Building a mission statement involves succinctly focusing on a retailer's core business, its reason for existence, and its differential advantage. What business are we in? What customers do we want to serve? What image do we want to portray? Retailers should ask all these questions as they prepare to draft mission statements.

Limited Brands owns several companies, including Victoria's Secret, Bath & Body Works, and other specialty stores. The company addresses several attributes in its short and succinct mission statement: "Limited Brands is committed to building a family of the world's best fashion brands offering captivating customer experiences that drive long-term loyalty and deliver sustained growth for our shareholders."[2]

Whether simple or detailed, the mission statement is a foundation for goals and objectives. Many companies also prepare a **vision statement,** which is a detailed and forward-thinking descriptive piece. The company's intentions for a five-year period, its ethical platform, and how it expects to treat its customers and employees are examples of topics included in a vision statement.

Step Four: Preparing Company Goals and Objectives

Company goals are general, and stated with a clear focus. They may take several directions. An established discount store may be most concerned with achieving a high sales volume. A new specialty retailer selling only electronic equipment for home media rooms may be more interested in establishing itself as an expert in installation.

Objectives are specific and should be written so that end results are easy to measure. An example involving inventory shrinkage illustrates the difference between general and more specific objective writing. **Shrinkage** is the reduction in the value of stock due to employee theft, shoplifting, and human error. A retail company might state this objective: "To decrease shrinkage by 2 percent next year." This is a measurable objective, but too broad. It would be better to state it this way: "To reduce inventory shrinkage by 1 percent in the next fiscal year by implementing a new video surveillance technology." Tying the objective to a concrete plan of action is more meaningful and easier to measure. Once objectives have been carefully constructed, the next step is to devise strategies that bring the objectives to fruition.

Step Five: Planning Detailed Strategies

Developing strategies involves seeing the big picture. Retailers may make decisions involving location, channels of distribution, management, operations, human resources, pricing policies, product and service offerings, store image, and promotional efforts. These examples illustrate controllable elements that are analyzed as retailers acknowledge present status and plot future direction. Retailers have little or no control over competition, government laws, customers, or technology; equally uncontrollable are economic, political, social, and environmental conditions. These aspects were presented in Chapter 2 and are vital to the strategic planning process.

Every retailer, regardless of size, develops its own plan for satisfying its customers and earning a profit. Several strategies used by Marks & Spencer to adapt to the challenging retail environment during the first two years of the recession are highlighted in From the Field 3.1. Ranked #55 in the *2010 Top 250 Global Retailers* listing, M&S generated sales of $15.2 billion through its operations in 41 countries.[3] M&S expects to complete its UK growth plan so that by 2015, 95% of the population will be within a 30-minute drive of a M&S store. In the multichannel sector, it intends to grow online wine, flower and Food-to-Order sales and to further develop its international presence.[4] The British department store and food retailer considers financial as well as human resource tactics in the planning process.

When the steps in the planning process are followed, a company acknowledges its strengths and weaknesses and surveys the opportunities and threats that will guide the company's course of action. Developing strategies is not the end of the planning process, but rather the beginning of a period in which initiatives are executed. Plans are never finite and are reevaluated as internal and external factors change. Planning, therefore, is an ongoing process.

Critical Aspects of Change and Retail Solutions

Determining how current and anticipated trends will challenge business in coming months and years is a continuing activity for retailers. The following discourse presents deeper insight into the dynamics of planning strategically.

Challenging Economic Periods

The U.S. economy was in recession—as was much of the world—when this text was written. Retailers experienced declining sales, curtailed expansion plans, reluctantly dismissed employees, replaced company leaders, reduced operational costs, and reassessed their strategic plans. Downturns in the economy often herald company closures but also bring unprecedented waves of innovation. From a SWOT analysis perspective, one would view a recession as a threat, but also as an opportunity to find creative ways to reach customers and reclaim sales. Many retailers respond aggressively to sales slumps by devising survival tactics. Others are not as fortunate. Several examples of strategic initiatives illustrate these points.

Taking Aggressive Markdowns

Movado Watch Group, makers and retailers of fine watches, was one of many retailers that reduced prices substantially to maintain sales volume early in the recent recession. During the week following Christmas in 2008, Movado offered savings of up to 70 percent off the manufacturer's suggested retail prices, a strategy that was successful in bringing customers into stores. **Manufacturer's suggested retail prices (MSRPs)** are prices determined by manufacturers as suitable for the market and at a level that allows a profitable retail return. In Movado's case, sales volume quotas were met company-wide and by individual stores. The tactic of driving sales volume by sacrificing gross margin was viewed as a strategic move for the company. **Gross margin** is the difference

From the Field 3.1   M&S Chief Upbeat Despite Layoffs, Poor Sales

Despite sagging sales, planned store closures, and layoffs, Stuart Rose, chairman of Marks & Spencer, is optimistic about the future. The head of Britain's largest clothing retailer indicated during a conference call that it was time for M&S to tighten its operations, and that there is a light at the end of the recessionary tunnel. "We think it's going to be tough going forward, and we need to keep our business lean and mean," he said. "We think we've taken robust action to take the business through a difficult year." Rose added that cost control was the new M&S byword.

M&S also confirmed 1,230 job cuts, both from store floors and the London headquarters. M&S employs a total of 75,000 people and the 450 layoffs at the head office represent about 15 percent of the workforce there. Most of the job losses will come from 27 planned store closures.

"We are aware that the proposed changes set out will be difficult for those members of staff impacted. But, given that we expect challenging economic conditions to continue for at least the next 12 months, we believe we are taking the right action to maintain the strength of our business," Rose said.

During the conference call, Rose could not conceal his optimism, even in the face of the downbeat news. There was even a hint of Franklin D. Roosevelt in his speech. "I believe that, for the rest of the year, a combination of falling prices and interest rates [will put] more cash into people's pockets," Rose said. "The biggest single word that needs to be addressed is confidence. The government has got to keep sending the message out that it will get better."

Adapted and condensed from Samantha Conti, *Women's Wear Daily*, January 8, 2009, 16.

---

between net sales and the cost of merchandise sold, expressed as a percentage. Movado reduced inventory levels to make way for new merchandise by hastening the flow of goods.

Curtailing Expansion Plans

Hoping to protect assets during the economic downturn, many retailers put their expansion plans on hold.[5] Cosmetic retailer Ulta and Walgreens drugstores were among those that cancelled new store openings in 2009.

With 467 stores currently operating in the United States and 100 more planned by the end of fiscal 2012, Ulta, illustrated in Figure 3.3, is a fast-growing cosmetics chain.[6] At the height of the recession, however, the company scaled back its real-estate strategies in order to concentrate on the

Figure 3.3
Ulta, the Chicago-based cosmetics chain, features both salons and beauty products in its more than 200 stores.

internal elements of its operation, over which the company had more control. The strategy paid off. For the 12-month period that ended April 30, 2011, Ulta earned $1.52 billion in revenue and demonstrated a 5.31 percent profit margin, along with a rising stock price.[7] Apparently the company's show of perspicacity at the right time helped it grow as the economy improved.

Walgreens, a well-established retailer, downgraded its store growth projection for 2010 to 4–4.5 percent. That year, the company opened 388 stores, about two-thirds the number of units it opened in 2009.[8] Its sales for the fiscal year that ended August 31, 2010 were $67.4 billion—a 6.4 percent increase. Nonetheless, the company's decision illustrates that longevity in the marketplace does not exempt a company from implementing retrenchment strategies when times are tough. Although its sales increased, the company held by its decision to slow new store development.

Modifying Pricing Models

To counter the downward trend in luxury goods and to expand their markets during challenging periods, some retailers develop lines of merchandise that can be sold at lower prices. Designer Michael Kors offers customers shoes at $150, $295, and $595 in the company's signature boutiques.[9] This practice, called **price lining,** involves setting distinguishable prices, which are determined by company policy, often as part of a good-better-best approach. Although Coach refused to cut prices on its designer handbags during the recession, to avoid eroding its image as a luxury brand, it offered less expensive styles for the 2008–2009 holiday selling period. Sales were down over the previous year, but the declines were not as steep as those of other luxury retailers.

Liquidating the Company

Several retailers, already experiencing difficulty during the early stages of the recession, decided to close their doors as the economic downturn escalated. They included electronics retailer Circuit City, regional electronic chain Tweeter, mid-market department store Mervyns, regional apparel chain Goody's Family Clothing, West Coast–based department store Gottshalks, specialty store Sharper Image, and home-goods chain Linens 'n Things. Liquidation is a strategy of last resort, although some consider it a natural response to an overstored marketplace and hard times. **Liquidation** is the process of selling off all inventory in preparation for closing down a company or one of its divisions or assets.

Making Human Resource Cutbacks

Retailers around the globe react similarly to economic downturns. In 2009, British manufacturer and retailer Burberry, long a high performer in the luxury apparel and accessories market, announced a layoff of 540 people, comprising approximately 9 percent of its employees. It also closed two factories in the United Kingdom in response to the ailing economy and currency devaluation of the British pound.[10] Despite human resource cutbacks, Burberry continued to expand its presence in Asia, opening 50 franchised stores in China, and improved online marketing and sales.[11] Building momentum, for its fiscal year ending in March 2012 the company earned $1.1 billion in revenue and plans to open about 15 stores in emerging markets and those with high tourism. New stores will be 12 to 14 percent larger than existing units.[12]

Although unsettling, layoffs are one of the ways retailers adapt to economic change. Large retailers are not exempt from the use of this strategy. Starbucks, once expected to operate 40,000 cafes worldwide, was severely affected by the failing economy in 2008–2009. The company closed hundreds of stores, both in the United States and internationally, and laid off thousands of employees.[13] Then, in early 2010, Starbucks surprised customers and investors when it introduced its instant coffee, Via. The move increased sales by 4.1 percent, putting the recession-stressed retailer back in the competitive coffee game.[14] Over the past five years, even Walmart—the top retailer in the world and among the most profitable—announced that it would dismiss 700–800 people from its Bentonville, Arkansas, headquarters as part of a belt-tightening measure.[15]

Developing Budget-Conscious Formats

Openings of cheap-chic apparel stores and adoption of low-price designer fashions by discount and mid-market specialty retailers resonate well with customers who need or want to cut back on their apparel expenditures. Renewed interest in second-hand and consignment shops, and the growth of vintage apparel shops, are other strategic moves propelled to significance by eroding credit markets and consumer confidence. For example, Target is renowned for bringing value-driven private label merchandise and cutting-edge international designer fashions to its customers at affordable prices. Giving new dimension to the second-hand clothing concept, Rescue, located on upscale Newbury Street in Boston, is a buy-sell-trade boutique. The shop carries only current fashion and favors designers like Gucci, Dior Homme, Proenza Schouler, and U.K. brand Topshop/Topman.[16] These trends not only illustrate options for budget-minded customers; they show a shift in emphasis for customers who are not strapped for cash but chose to renounce materialism.

Size, degree of market affinity, position on the pricing spectrum, and degree of promotional drive are critical variables in retailing success but none of these characteristics alone grants retailers immunity from the volatile global economy. Adaptability, willingness to put previous plans on hold, and ability to foster innovation are valuable traits for retailers during tough times.

Technological Advances

We live in a time when technology reinvents itself as frequently as we change our clothes. This revolution continues to leave its stamp on retailing. Technology now makes it possible to distribute goods through marketing channels faster and more efficiently than ever before. It also helps customers shop in more convenient and well-informed ways and have fun through electronic marketing. Through technology, retailers assess customer needs more effectively. Embracing change in this sector is mandatory for companies planning for growth while engaging their customers. Advances in several technology-driven areas suggest strategic directions for retailers.

Fantasy Becomes Reality

Interactive dressing-room mirrors linked to the Internet (illustrated in Figure 3.4), vapor curtain projection devices in stores, personal sound studios (where you can record your voice and save it to an MP3 player as you produce your Grammy-caliber song), interactive displays and billboards, and electronic kiosks represent only a few of the emerging technologies that are changing the way we perceive merchandise and conduct our shopping experiences.

Although few of us have experienced all of these advanced customer services, the technologies are available and many are designed to reach us both in our homes and on the run. This fact alone is enough to jog our minds into a new way of thinking about how we will live, work, and shop in the future.

a

b

Figure 3.4
Technology takes dressing rooms to new dimensions with Icon Nicholson's interactive versions. Using a touch screen, customers can change the color of an item they are trying on or select an entire new item (a). Web-enabled shoppers can solicit comments from friends at home or those shopping elsewhere (b).

Internet Development

No other facet of retail development has changed as rapidly or presented as many new opportunities and formats to the customer as online selling. From avatars to Zappos.com, customers are intrigued with what the Web has to offer—and it's not only fresh access to merchandise. The power of search engines has exposed us to new information—not always accurate, but lots of it—and merchandise from around the world. Lives are changed by online services, from dating to downloads, as well as communication-enhancing e-mail and tweets. Facebook, Twitter, and YouTube are constant companions, and each delivers retail information in its respective ways. To be sure you're not without the latest 3D action video game, you can shop at GameStop's storefront without ever leaving Facebook. Blogs, customer reviews, and the option to order online and pick up in store expand the scope of retailing. As customers change their buying habits, retailers respond with strategies that reach customers where and when they are receptive—or logged on.

The Cashless Society

Companies that produce products for an anticipated cashless society are important to consumers and the retail industry. **Electronic cash cards (e-cash)** load and hold cash values in any currency via an ATM, computer, or cell phone. Instead of carrying cash for buying lunch or admission to a movie or for gaining access to your apartment complex, use your card. Presently well beyond the realm of simple debit cards, smart technology was the basis for prepaid phone cards and store loyalty cards that emerged in the late 20th century, when about 80 percent of all retail transactions were still done in cash. By the early 2000s, the United States was fast becoming a cashless society. The adoption rate of cash cards varies by country and by the types of consumers that are comfortable using this technology. Many people are concerned about invasion of privacy when electronic transactions are tracked and personal information is revealed. More on this topic follows in the section on safety and privacy. Although electronic banking may never totally replace credit card options and paper money, paperless and cashless transactions are increasing in importance.

Information Technology (IT)

Retailers review past performance, analyze alternatives, plan inventories, and facilitate collaboration with vendors using IT. **Information technology (IT)** encompasses computer-based decision support systems that are used to make business operations more efficient. Other applications include human resources scheduling, predictive modeling, store location and design planning, logistics management, security, and customer relationship management programs. **Customer relationship management (CRM)** involves gathering and using database information to reach customers more effectively, identify their needs more specifically, and focus promotional and selling initiatives more precisely. Retailers have long been aware that 80 percent of their sales come from 20 percent of their customers. Tapping into information stored in databases can help stores tailor offers to core shoppers and also to those they elevate to select-client status. The best data-gathering systems go beyond basic demographic information. Information about special life events, personal favorites, and significant dates are equally important to collect at the point of impulse. **Point of impulse (POI)** is a version of point of sale (POS) that more accurately reflects customer behavior information as well as sales data that is captured electronically when it occurs.

Quick response technology represents another way retailers are making their operations more efficient. **Quick response (QR)** is the umbrella term for integrated supply chain distribution systems that allow rapid replenishment of merchandise. In some instances, QR systems have shortened product concept-to-delivery times from months to weeks. Integrated with online systems, they enable retailers and vendors to communicate crucial information faster and more accurately. Wireless Internet access systems enhance IT capabilities, and using this technology effectively is another way to gain a competitive advantage. Read more about these customer-directed uses in Chapter 7, Electronic Retailing.

Multichannel Retailing

Electronic retailing has grown rapidly since the mid-1990s and continues to shape our shopping behavior. Included in this sector are online stores, television home shopping channels, and mobile

//////////////////////////////////

Cyberscoop

One of the reasons *Fast Company* named Starbucks 7th in its "10 Most Innovative Companies" survey is because Starbucks listens to its customers. After soliciting input from customers, 98,000 ideas were submitted and 100 suggestions—including donating unsold pastries to charity and giving name badges to baristas—were adopted. Go to MyStarbucksIdea.com and Starbucks.com to see what's happening in the customer relationship management sector (Source: "The 10 Most Innovative Companies in Retail," *Fast Company*, March 15, 2011, www.fastcompany.com/1738961/the-10-most-innovative-companies-in-retail.)

commerce. Electronic retailing is only one aspect of a greater strategic direction: multichannel retailing. Also involved are direct selling companies like Tupperware and Mary Kay Cosmetics. **Direct selling** is the practice of selling to consumers through one-on-one situations or parties usually held in homes or workplaces. In contrast, direct marketing offers reach us by catalogues, direct mail pieces, telephone, or online. The Direct Marketing Association offers a detailed definition of the many facets of direct marketing on its Web site, stating: **Direct marketing** is "an integrative process of addressable communication that uses one or more advertising media to effect, at any location, a measurable sale, lead, retail purchase, or charitable donation, with this activity analyzed on a database for the development of ongoing mutually beneficial relationships between marketers and customer, prospects, or donors."[17] Because of the significant impact of electronic retailing, direct marketing, and direct selling on multichannel retailing, these topics are covered fully in Unit Two. Here are three examples to pique your interest:

1. *Online shopping.* Everyone in your classroom probably has a Facebook page, uses the Internet to do research, and shops online. Have you ordered a pair of jeans online from Levi's finished precisely to your length requirement? Did Forever 21 e-mail you to let you know they were having a sale? Do any of your friends still read books in hard- or softcover formats, or do they use an e-reader?

   Despite the dismal holiday season in 2008–2009, Amazon.com thrived and actually ran out of its Kindle electronic book readers because demand was so great. By the 2009–2010 holiday season, Amazon was in the throes of price wars with publishers and other companies, including Apple and Sony, which had launched their own electronic book readers. The 2010–2011 holiday period saw Amazon fielding pressure from Apple's iPad and Barnes & Noble's Nook; however, it remained the market leader in the e-book category. Currently the world's top Web-only retailer, Amazon's sales were estimated at $48.1 billion for 2012.[18] The newest retail entrant in the e-book category is Toronto's Kobo, Inc. The company began shipping its touch-screen reader in mid-2011 and followed other market leaders by removing the "buy" links from their Apple apps shortly thereafter. This tactic made it more difficult for some customers to access digital books on their Apple apparatus, but illustrates the competitiveness between companies.[19] Apparel, computers, books, and music sell well on the Web, but the potential for uderrepresented products and services is presently vast.

2. *Direct-access shopping.* A host of other electronic innovations are changing the way products are presented to the public. Prolific product placement is apparent in films and on TV. Soon, viewers who see a hot outfit worn by a favorite *American Idol* participant may be able to immediately call up product information on the Internet via TV remote access, touch screen, or cell phone, and place their orders. If we can vote for our favorite vocalist in real time, should we not be able to order merchandise simultaneously?

3. *Mobile commerce.* Text a request for a free burger coupon and access your cell phone's built-in GPS to get the exact directions to the new boutique you've been dying to check out—such options are second nature for today's younger shoppers and are rapidly spreading to less digitally attuned markets. If you have a newer iPhone, use the touch screen and don't bother texting. If you're having trouble using your phone when it's cold, grab a pair of gloves with metal-fabric fingertips that make your mobile ordering easier—even when it's 10 degrees below zero. And of course, there are apps galore.

   Integrated technologies form the underpinnings of cross-channel communication and make international operations more efficient. Many multichannel retailers are also international retailers.

Global Retail Expansion

Global retailing is one of the major platforms from which this text is written. The more we understand the dynamics of the global economy, the more we realize how interdependent we are with other countries.

Global expansion is not a new concept, but it is a major growth vehicle for many retailers. McDonald's, for one, has operated units all over the globe for several decades. In fact, the company's international stores often fare better than those in the United States, particularly during difficult economic periods in its domestic markets. Approximately half of the company's 31,000 locations are in international markets. This strategy spreads the financial risk for companies like McDonald's.[20]

Many retail analysts believe that, along with multichannel retailing, we will see a proliferation of global retailers in the 21st century. Most retailers address the possibility of globalization as they prepare their strategic plans. The top 20 global retailers are listed in Table 3.1.

Reasons for Global Expansion

Several factors influence global expansion. The following list refers primarily to **mature retail companies**, which are large, well-developed retailers that have the financial resources and managerial expertise to consider global expansion. There is some evidence that smaller companies are also expanding internationally, particularly those that sell online. Several conditions that precipitate international expansion lend insight into the strategic process:

- *Overstored home markets*. When expansion is complete in retailers' existing markets or there is a limited geographic area for further growth, many retailers look beyond their home borders. In some retail locations, sales growth is imperiled when competition is too intense, giving retailers just cause for global expansion. When too many retailers in the same retail trading area are competing for the same customers the resulting condition is called **overstored**.

Table 3.1 Top 20 Global Retailers 2010

Rank	Company	Country of Origin	Fiscal 2009 Group Revenue* (in US$ millions)	Primary Formats
1	Walmart Stores, Inc.	U.S.	408,214	Hypermarket/supercenter/warehouse club
2	Carrefour S.A.	France	121,861	Hypermarket/supercenter/superstore
3	Metro AG	Germany	91,389	Cash & carry/warehouse club
4	Tesco plc	U.K.	90,435	Hypermarket/supercenter/superstore
5	Schwarz Untermehmens Treuhand KG	Germany	77,221	Discount store
6	The Kroger Co.	U.S.	76,733	Supermarket
7	Costco Wholesale Corp.	U.S.	71,422	Cash and carry/warehouse club
8	Aldi Einkauf GmbH & Co. HG	Germany	67,709	Discount store
9	The Home Depot, Inc.	U.S.	66,176	Home improvement
10	Target Corp.	U.S.	65,357	Discount department store
11	Walgreen Co.	U.S.	63,335	Drugstore/pharmacy
12	Rewe-Zentral AG	Germany	71,001	Supermarket/superstore
13	CVS Caremark Corp.	U.S.	98,729	Drugstore/pharmacy
14	Edeka Zentrale AG & Co. KG	Germany	58,658	Supermarket
15	Groupe Auchan	France	55,326	Hypermarket/supercenter/superstore
16	Seven & i Holdings Co., Ltd.	Japan	54,741	Convenience
17	Best Buy Co.	U.S.	49,694	Electronics specialty
18	Aeon Co., Ltd.	Japan	54,133	Hypermarket/supercenter/superstore
19	Lowe's Companies, Inc.	U.S.	47,220	Home improvement
20	Woolworths Ltd.	Australia	45,604	Supermarket

Source: Excerpted and condensed from "Global Powers of Retailing 2012." Top "250 Global Retailers, 2010" in Deloitte Touche Tohmatsu Limited, January 2012, p. G11 www.deloitte.com/consumerbusiness

*May include sales from nonretail operations.

From the Field 3.2   Growing Pains: Rampant Development in India Has Produced a Mixed Bag of Shopping Centers.

Nghrija Chakraborty swears by such brands as Levi's and Puma, and is an all-around shopping enthusiast. But the New Delhi resident works up little enthusiasm over many of India's new malls. "A decade back, my opportunities as a shopper were much limited," said the 26-year-old, who works for the offshore offices of a Texas law firm. "Today there are these huge shopping malls at every tenth step that you take."

Chakraborty's disposable income has risen alongside the surging retail options and a roaring Indian economy. But none of this sends her on any sprees at these new shopping centers. She continues to frequent the city's flea markets while only sometimes buying at the malls. She says her expectations have risen with the increasing shopping options; malls that offer unattractive stores and that are poorly maintained simply do not get her money.

Meet a quintessential Indian shopper. Chakraborty is brand-conscious and has the money to flirt with choices, but is still an enigma for retailers trying to catch a piece of the Indian retail dream. India's retail market will approach $450 billion by 2015, according to a McKinsey & Co. study. That year, some 300 million shoppers will be patronizing organized retail, a number equivalent to the U.S. population today.

In recent years, foreign retailers and developers have flocked to the country to cash in on this potential, triggering skyrocketing rents. "Its one of the last frontiers for the shopping center industry, said retail consultant Ian Thomas, who heads Vancouver, British Columbia–based Thomas Consultants. His firm is working with Indian real estate goliath Indiabulls Group on a 15-city mall rollout program over the next five to seven years. "The country has an incredible market size, an emerging middle class, which is astronomical in numbers."

Yet for some the going had not been easy. Build-A-Bear Workshop abandoned India after failing to make a dent. Straps, an Indian chain that sold Wonderbra lingerie, closed its doors. "Foreign players entering India today face stifling regulations, a clouded political atmosphere, soaring real estate costs, and fiercely competitive domestic retailer groups," said an A.T. Kearney annual report that lists the most-attractive emerging market retail destinations. In 2008, Vietnam ended India's three year reign as the top destination, the report says.

India is essentially where China was a decade ago. The country's retail landscape is filled with mom-and-pop stores that appear along busy shopping hubs. These traditional stores are entrenched in the Indian psyche, and compete with the newer formats by pocketing rupees from shoppers like Chakraborty. Part of their survival story is related to India's socialist economy and government regulations. Single-brand stores such as Gap, Louis Vuitton, and Nike got a head start against Walmart and others needing to find a local partner.

Still, restrictions on foreign retailers have not dampened the enthusiasm of India's real-estate developers, which have been constructing shopping centers at a feverish pace for the past eight years. Chakraborty says that the first few centers that sprung up had very few brand names and poor accessibility for the handicapped. In the past three years or so, developers have brought in experienced partners, architects, and consultants from overseas as they work to improve shopping destinations.

The next two or three years will witness a sea change in the industry, says Phil McArthur, Ivanhoe Cambridge's senior vice president for India. "Hypermarkets from Europe and Asia will open [and] specialty malls will emerge in the lifestyle categories, he said. "India will become one of the most important countries in the world."

Adapted and condensed from Madhusmita Bora, *Shopping Centers Today*, December 2008, 145–148.

- *Competitive changes*. In strong economies, stiff competition may propel retailers to enter less robust economic areas when they see growth potential. When economies are weak in their home countries, some retailers enter foreign countries seeking fresh sources of revenue while spreading financial risk. This has been true for some U.S. retailers that saw sales and profits draining from their domestic business during the recession. With less inviting expansion possibilities at home, many retailers are looking to expand abroad, particularly in Asian and South American countries that have been developing rapidly. According to *Stores* magazine, "The most likely candidates for global expansion are specialty retailers rather than food, mass merchandise, or department store retailers. U.S.-based specialty retailers are well developed, often clearly differentiated, well executed, have substantial financial resources, and are facing saturation and slow growth at home."[21]

- *Attractive new markets*. Developing countries present opportunities for established retailers to find multitudes of similarly minded international consumers. Countries moving out of emerging nation status by becoming fully industrialized economies are considered **developing countries**. Usually developing countries are in transition from an agricultural economy to a more diversified and robust one. Countries on the rise include Brazil, Russia, India, and China. These countries grouped together are usually called **BRIC** in news coverage. Jim O'Neil, chairman of Goldman Sachs Asset Management, sees South Africa as the fifth BRIC country. He believes Mexico, South Korea, Turkey, and Indonesia should be added to the original BRIC countries and be called "growth markets," and that Poland, Saudi Arabia, Iran, and Argentina should be considered emerging markets.[22] From the Field 3.2 describes some of the strategic challenges for new shopping centers in India.

- *Demanding investors*. Pressure from company shareholders for sustained high growth sometimes compels retailers to seek expansion opportunities abroad. This circumstance occasionally prompts the acquisition of retail companies in other countries.
- *Customer sophistication*. Because of worldwide media efforts, increased travel, and better education, many people have developed global brand awareness as well as **import snobbery**—the tendency to believe that better, more desirable products come from other countries. The broad reach of the Internet through social networking sites has also contributed to this phenomenon. Retailers of all sizes are increasingly developing online stores that are accessible from anywhere in the world. Internet users numbered over 2 billion worldwide in 2011—45 percent of whom are from the Asia-Pacific region.[23] This trend illustrates the strong potential for future retail development in this geographic area and also explains why retailers include online stores in their strategic plans.

Other Contributing Factors

Trade agreements and a general lessening of bureaucracy in many parts of the world are making global expansion easier. The size and scope of mature global players have made expansion not only possible, but also much easier than it was even two decades ago. Tremendous capabilities in technology, distribution, and product sourcing have expedited global moves by Walmart and Carrefour, the French hypermarket company. Walmart is profiled at the end of Unit One and Carrefour at the end of Unit Three. Extended coverage of global retailing is presented in Chapter 8.

Supply Chain Dynamics

Retail companies use vertical integration and depend less on middlemen, thereby shortening their marketing channels and making them more efficient. The specialty divisions of The Limited and Gap are not simply retail chains. They are aware that control of the manufacturing process creates higher profits.

Discounters such as Walmart have effectively shortened their supply chains through extensive private label manufacturing programs, strict vendor selection criteria, and the elimination of most wholesalers. These are some of the strategic directions taken by Walmart that have brought the company to the stellar position it now holds. The company generates more than three times the revenue of its nearest competitor, Carrefour.

Supply-chain members are increasingly dependent on one another as they bring goods to the marketplace. In difficult economic times, declining retail sales pressure suppliers to find new sources of revenue or face closure.

Customer-Centric Perspective

People are now able to shop where and when they please. While visiting the museums that make up the Smithsonian Institution in Washington, D.C., they might stop into one of its many gift shops. If waiting for a flight at an airport, they can check out The Body Shop or pick up a bistro bag lunch before boarding. Instead of calling a toll-free number on their cell phones, catalogue shoppers directly access online retailers using the Web. Some college students gather in dorm rooms for Party Lite candle parties and consider a weekend visit to a flea market a good time. Our needs to socialize and examine products before we purchase them are hard habits to break. Considering human nature, we might not want to change them anyway. Aware of constant and multiple changes in consumer habits and preferences, retailers make plans with customers in mind.

A distinct shift has occurred. Reaching a greater numbers of customers may not be as important as serving existing customers better. Cultivating more customers is necessary, but not at the expense of alienating a loyal clientele. Today's retailers are embracing customer-centrism in a variety of ways.

Experiential Retailing

Experiential retailing dominates the retail culture, as customers demand more than the expected exchange of products for currency. **Experiential retailing** encompasses all contemporary methods

Figure 3.5
Experiential retailing is evident at the Forum Shops in Las Vegas, where customers are captivated by the special effects, a plethora of shops, and access to the casino.

used to engage customers at emotional, sensory, and participatory levels as they shop. Entertainment may take grand or modest forms, but novelty and excitement are important to shoppers worldwide. The hand-painted sky ceiling at the Forum in Las Vegas, illustrated in Figure 3.5, is so realistic that visitors forget they are in a building. The lighting system is programmed to portray dawn to dusk every hour. This is no chance occurrence: once hooked on the imagery, most customers remain in the facility to experience the entire light cycle, shopping as they stroll in the mall. It is the experience that counts, not only the utilitarian aspects of need fulfillment.

Frequent Shopper Incentives

Inspired by airline frequent-flyer programs, retailers of all kinds use frequent-shopper programs, incentives, and exclusive services. Increased technological capabilities are crucial to the execution of newer customer services, including those offered online. Several examples underscore the variety of incentives available to encourage customers to shop more:

- Neiman Marcus's Inner Circle program offers incentive points for dollars spent in its stores. Awards ranging from designer chocolates to European vacations are enticing. Customers must spend thousands of dollars in a calendar year in order to be eligible for more valuable gifts.
- Barnes & Noble encourages heavy readers to enroll in its frequent-shopper program, where for a $25 annual fee members can receive greater discounts on their store and online purchases than nonmembers.
- The restaurant chain T.G.I.Friday's has a punch card geared to the lunch crowd: after five punches, the next lunch is free.
- Based on the amount of their annual expenditures, customers at Macy's qualify for different "star" levels of in-store credit cards. Graduation to a higher level promises greater savings on future purchases, advance knowledge of special sales and events, and free gift-wrapping, for example.

Customers are at the center of effective customer service programs, but retailers also anticipate increased market share, sales, and profitability as a result of these programs. Target directs its customer-incentive message graphically, as illustrated in Figure 3.1.

Personal Shoppers

Personal shopping programs are another way retailers nurture relationships with customers. Formerly the domain of stores like Saks Fifth Avenue, Neiman Marcus, and upscale specialty boutiques, more intimate involvement with customers also benefits mid-market department stores and home improvement centers. Personal shoppers help preselect apparel for customers on tight schedules and those who value highly customized service. Home Depot has in-store interior decorators available to help customers design new rooms or decorate their offices.

Customer-Friendly Environment

On the selling floor, easy access to merchandise, appropriate fixtures, and supportive electronic kiosks are other ways customer service is delivered. Locating goods on the selling floor where they better match customers' shopping patterns is another useful tactic. **Cross-merchandising** is the practice of allocating the same merchandise to two or more areas of the store instead of one. For example, Bloomingdale's features Godiva candy displays in several areas of the store. The retailer might position individual bars and small-boxed candies along with cashmere sweaters, making the suggested multiple purchase seem almost irresistible.

Electronic kiosks enhance and extend the customer experience. Customers can access more extensive merchandise assortments than they can in a store by tapping into online resources via in-store kiosks. Ordering unconventional sizes of apparel or shoes, arranging for home delivery of large or heavy items, or planning for store pickup at a convenient time are services sought by many customers who prefer the expedience of online communications. Other customers prefer self-initiated options rather than seeking out the help of a sales associate. These are all examples of the changing relationship between retailers and customers.

Emphasis on Branding

The importance of branding in retailing accentuates all strategic initiatives. **Branding** is the process of developing, building, and maintaining a name in the marketplace. High recognition and demand for a product or store by consumers are goals of companies that use branding as a strategy. Branding is directed to customers in several ways:

- Emphasis is placed on nationally or globally recognized labels.
- National or global brands are featured along with private-label brands.
- When the brand is the store itself, emphasis is usually placed on private-label merchandise.

National and global brands are those that use manufacturers' labels, such as Speedo, Seiko, Timberland, or UGG. Some private-label store brands are so well established and distributed that they become national or global brands; examples include Gap, Burberry, and JCPenney's Arizona brand. Because of globalization, multichannel retailing, and better distribution, the distinction between brand types or origins may be less important to customers.

The store as brand was one of the key concepts to emerge in the 1990s and will continue in the 21st century. The significance of this shift from product to store is profound. The building of a retail brand takes time, effort, investment, and consumer acceptance; it is fundamental to the success of most retailers today.

The Store as Brand

Companies as diverse as Gap, Zara, H&M, Tesco, and Costco speak clearly and loudly wherever their logos appear. Each company is an international retailer and has a strong online presence. Although Gap, Zara, and H&M specialize in apparel, Tesco in food and general merchandise, and Costco in broad assortments of hard and soft goods in a warehouse setting, all share high brand recognition. Hershey's branding strategy culminated in its New York City store, located just off Times Square. The company exemplifies manufacturers that have moved into retailing. (The brand is so widely known, we don't even have to mention that it is a candy company!) Several other techniques attest to the power of branding.

//////////////////////////////////
Cyberscoop
Gap expanded its online business to Austria, Estonia, Finland, Luxembourg, Malta, Portugal, Slovakia, and Slovenia in 2011. Customers can gather their purchases at both Gap and Banana Republic sites in one shopping cart, pay in pounds sterling, and expect delivery in 2–3 days. The non–multilingual need not worry—www.gap.eu and www.bananarepublic.eu operate in English. Visit these sites to see how Gap's branding appeals to you.
(Source: Kantar Retail IQ, "Gap Expands E-Commerce in eight European Countries," February 10, 2011, www.kantarretailiq .com/ContentIndex/News DisplayLW.aspx?id=324585)

Table 3.2   Top 10 Global Apparel Brands by Brand Value

Ranking	Brand	Country of Origin	Brand Value (in US$ millions)
1	Nike	United States	13,917
2	H&M	Sweden	13,006
3	Zara (Inditex)	Spain	10,335
4	Ralph Lauren	United States	3,378
5	Esprit	Germany	3,375
6	Adidas	Germany	3,088
7	Uniqlo	Japan	2,916
8	Next	United Kingdom	2,567
9	Hugo Boss	Germany	2,445
10	MetersBonwe	China	1,446

Excerpted from "BrandZ Top 100 2011: Sectors/Commentary." Source: Millward Brown Optimor; includes data from BrandZ, Kantar Worldpanel, and Bloomberg.

Building Brand Equity

It is not only name recognition that makes a brand. Reputation, the relationship between quality and price, consistency of product workmanship, and strong customer service also contribute to customers' perceptions of the brand. Retailers capitalize on their brand equity by opening new chains. For example, the mall retailer Hot Topic launched a spin-off chain, Torrid, that sells similar edgy items for fashionable plus-sized young women. Customer perspectives of Hot Topic carried over to the new format. **Brand equity** is the level of consumer recognition a brand, label, or store has in the marketplace.

Many companies manufacturer the products they sell and most have built their brands through their own retail store chains. The top 10 fashion apparel companies, listed by brand value, appear in Table 3.2.

Co-Branding

When two separate retailers (brands) join forces for the purpose of reaching customers more effectively and increasing sales for both parties, this partnership is called **co-branding**. Co-branding strategies are used to create new partnerships that are stronger than the individual companies. Three examples stress this point:

- *External partnerships.* Fast-food operators Wendy's and Kentucky Fried Chicken (KFC) are not owned by the same parent company but share a sign and quarters in Taipei, Taiwan, where space is expensive and at a premium.
- *Internal partnerships.* Co-branding is also done internally when two brands from the same company share retail space. KFC and Taco Bell restaurants share freestanding facilities in many of the markets they serve.
- *Noncompeting partnerships.* Starbucks cafes and Barnes & Noble superstores are not competitors, but their branding partnership may keep customers in the stores longer, buying more books. The arrangement also addresses psychological needs. For some, a stop at Barnes & Noble that includes a sip of cappuccino is a pleasant respite from an otherwise harried existence. Starbucks' presence suggests a subtle, but perhaps important reason why customers make repeat visits to this bookseller.

Resurgence of Entrepreneurship

Revitalization of the entrepreneurial spirit is expected to continue as more individuals choose to strike out on their own as retailers. For some, the opportunity has come because of downsizing at the corporate level or a forced layoff due to a tepid economy. For others, it is fulfillment of a life-long dream to own and operate a business and control one's own destiny. Despite the long hours, stress, and financial uncertainty this entails, many are drawn to small-business ownership. Sole proprietors are particularly drawn to specialty store retailing, often in smaller shopping centers, peripheral downtown locations, and resort sites, where rents are sometimes more affordable. Sole proprietors attract shoppers looking for unusual merchandise and personal service.

Innovation in retailing often comes from the small-business sector and historically has been responsible for job growth. However, the mechanisms for growth must be in place and the climate for business ripe before retailers set up shop. Entrepreneurship statistics showed that the top five countries demonstrating the greatest ease in doing business in 2011 were Singapore, Hong Kong, New Zealand, the United Kingdom, and the United States. Several criteria were selected to define "ease in doing business"; the three most frequently cited were facilitation in starting a business, paying taxes, and trading across borders. Kazakhstan ranked first on the list of most improved countries. Included in the top ten countries were three African nations—Rwanda, Cape Verde, and Zambia; Peru, Vietnam, and Hungary brought further geographic diversity to the ranking.[24]

The growth of small business in the United States has slowed since 2008 due to the financial downturn, fluctuations in retail trade, and changing shopping habits of consumers. Many owners have sold their businesses, often at prices much lower than they anticipated. The median asking price for a firm that was eventually sold was $195,000 in 2010 and $175,000 in 2011. The median sale price was $155,000 in 2010 and $150,000 in 2011.[25] Despite these sobering findings, many entrepreneurs maintain a positive outlook.

The Internet has become an entrepreneurial stronghold. There, almost anyone with something to sell can set up a Web page. For some, the opportunity to work from home is the principal reason for taking this route. Others relish the excitement of being on the cusp of retail change.

Concern for Safety and Privacy

The events of 9/11 changed the way we view the world and our place in it. More than a decade later, the threat of terrorist attacks continues to shape our behavior in airports and our attitudes toward personal safety and privacy. People who travel have learned to pack lightly, bring unwrapped holiday gifts with them, or postpone their purchases until they reach their destinations. Retailing was not exempt from a reassessment of its practices, including customer contact methods, movement of goods, and security of shopping centers. In a greater sense, consumer sentiment also lagged and some people began to focus less on materialistic pleasures and more on the quality of our sometimes short, fragile lives.

Increased concerns for privacy parallel those of personal safety. We are more cautious about using our credit card numbers online. Many of us object when unsolicited telephone calls disturb us on our landlines or cell phones. We are more likely to accept offers from retailers if we have had positive experiences with them in the past and have established a trusting business relationship.

Retail crime is another deterrent to smooth retail transactions. The problem affects both retailers and consumers since in-store crimes potentially erode store image and the safety of shoppers. **Organized retail crime (ORC)** involves groups of people in multiple locations and jurisdictions that commit planned crimes against retailers. Shrinkage is a growing problem that resulted in retail losses due to crime or waste of $119 billion worldwide in 2011. Total losses in the United States were $41.7 billion in 2011. Employee theft accounts for 35 percent; shoplifting and organized retail crime combined account for 43.2 percent of the global total.[26]

The threat of terrorist attacks worldwide, concerns regarding individual privacy, and ORC against retailers affect the safety and security of individuals. In response, policies to enhance well-being are being enacted by businesses, governments, and other organizations. These initiatives change the way we think, act, and do business.

The Green Movement

The environment is a focal point for strategic planning for all retailers that have committed to protect the earth and acknowledge the growing environmental awareness of their customers. People articulate their needs for green products and many seek out companies that engage in ecologically sound retail practices. Building energy-efficient structures from which to trade, minimizing their carbon footprints, and developing planet-friendly products while turning a profit are goals of many retailers. **Carbon footprint** is the amount of carbon dioxide and other toxic emissions given off by manufacturing processes, utilities, households, and transportation. For example, manufacturing a Patagonia jacket creates a 66-pound carbon footprint; producing a Toyota Prius creates a 97,000-pound footprint.[27]

Environmentalism has surged and ebbed in popularity in the past several decades, but today the green movement is gaining momentum through the support of retailers, consumers, politicians, and government agencies, as well as those who are directly involved in the manufacture and distribution of sustainable building materials and products. From the consumer's perspective, there are several levels of green—from evergreen to never green. Several examples highlight changes in retail and customer perspectives.

Focusing on Natural Products

Many people concerned with wellness choose to purchase organic or naturally derived products, ranging from foods (human and pet) to personal care, household, and cleaning products. Whole Foods Market operates stores in North America and the United Kingdom. Concerned with energy efficiency, the company uses solar panels in some of its stores to supplement electric power.[28] One study of the green preferences of generation Y found that Whole Foods Market was ranked first in terms of eco-friendly brands. Whole Foods Market maintains a list of 80 ingredients—including artificial colors and flavors, and bleached flour—that it bans from products on its shelves. Not immune to economic downturns, the company changed tactics when it began to emphasize price and value without ignoring its natural-foods emphasis.

Foods are not the only products sought after in the quest for natural. Many people are avoiding unnecessary chemicals in any form. Fine bath soaps that use wholesome, organic ingredients mixed with fresh scents of sage, sandalwood, honey, and lemon have made their mark not only on health-conscious individuals but mainstream markets.

Fashioning Recyclables

Companies and individuals are finding ways to not only use the unusable, but also create attractive, saleable green products. Throwaway juice pouches and cookie packages may not sound like materials used to create fashion, but innovative green manufacturers are rising to the occasion. Terra-Cycle, a company better known as a maker of fertilizer and soy-based fireplace logs, recycles food wrapper castaways into quirky—and attractive—backpacks, umbrellas, totes, and other containers. Prices are reasonable and meet the criteria of many environmentally responsible consumers.[29]

Partnering for a Sustainable Future

Green strategies do not occur in a vacuum. Many initiatives require supply chain partnerships. Marks & Spencer, mentioned earlier in this chapter, relied on its 75,000 employees around the world to embrace the company's five-year ecological plan put forth in 2007. That document stated the company's position and intentions on topics that included climate change, waste, carbon neutrality, sustainability, and ethical and health issues. The company partnered with 2,000 vendors and suppliers to develop sound merchandise-sourcing practices and included customers and employees in its many green initiatives. M&S called this confluence of input and energy its "Virtuous Circle."[30]

Customer Attitudes toward Green Products

Some retailers have been successful in selling at similar prices both organic products and merchandise made from less environmentally conscious materials.

From the Field 3.3   Retail Key to Green Movement

In his keynote address to a rapt gathering at the International Council of Shopping Centers' (ICSC) inaugural RetailGreen conference in 2008, futurist and energy expert David Houle laid out his vision of an energy-independent shopping center. "Green is now mainstream—there's no way to avoid it," he said. "We are seeing major changes in thinking all over the world."

Houle said renewable energy "is the greatest wealth-creation opportunity in history." Citing a series of TV energy ads by T. Boone Pickens, Houle said that annual global investment in alternative energy has risen from $10 billion in 1995 to $70 billion in 2006, and was expected to reach $100 billion in 2008. ([Update: according to Bloomberg New Energy Finance, global investment was $186.5 billion in 2009 and $243 billion in 2010. Apparently the recession did not hamper steady growth in this sector.*]

In retail, "green" is not only becoming essential for lower operating costs, it serves to motivate shoppers. "It ties in with branding," Houle said. For example, Prius owners consistently said they bought the car to make personal statements; "the same will go for [environmentally conscientious] shopping centers," he said. Based on environmental initiatives that save Walmart more than 20 percent on energy costs, shopping centers and other retailers "can almost blindly get to 20 percent savings" using existing technology, according to Houle.

Doing some industry crystal-ball gazing, Houle predicted that energy prices will push the development of shopping centers into the middle of self-sustaining residential communities, instead of to the periphery. "It's already happening. People are driving golf carts to go shopping." Newer centers will feature more service businesses so people will only have to drive occasionally, he said. At some point, center parking spaces may be topped with solar panels such as those at Google's corporate headquarters.

Shopping centers should be able to fully power themselves some day with solar power or wind turbines that, thanks to breakthroughs in energy-storage technology, can retain energy for future use instead of sending their excess to power grids, he said. At some point, center parking spaces equipped with electric-car chargers could provide a value-added option. Houle predicted that by 2050, 40 percent of the world's energy will come from renewable sources.

Adapted, and title shortened, from SCT Newswire Home, International Council of Shopping Centers, September 16, 2008, www.icsc.org/srch/apps/newsdsp.php?storyid=2450&region=main.
*Renewable Energy World, "2010 Clean Energy Investment Hits a New Record," January 11, 2011, www.renewableenergyworld.com/rea/news/print/article/2011/01/2010-clean-energy-investment-hits-a-new-record. Source: Bloomberg New Energy Finance (BNEE), London.

C&A is a value-driven department store chain in Europe. The head of sourcing for C&A stated that customers are concerned about the environment but they do not want to pay more for goods.[31] Many customers worldwide share this sentiment.

Shopping-center developers see environmental consciousness as a motivator for customers who seek green shopping experiences. More architects are specifying sustainable design and buildings customers will embrace. Speaking at an International Council of Shopping Centers (ICSC) conference in 2008, energy expert David Houle forecasted completely energy-independent shopping centers, cost savings for retailers, and environmental thinking as a motivator for customers of the future. Despite the economic slowdown and a number of construction projects that have been canceled or delayed, the initiative to build green remains a priority with mall developers. Read more about the future of green shopping centers in From the Field 3.3.

Continued Industry Consolidation

Establishing dominance, gaining market share, increasing geographic coverage, and benefiting from economies of scale in purchasing and distribution are major objectives for retailers. **Economies of scale** are savings or efficiencies achieved by producing or purchasing large quantities of goods or sharing services. To achieve these objectives, some retailers consolidate their businesses with their competitors. **Consolidation** is the act of combining two or more companies for the purpose of achieving greater dominance in the marketplace. Consolidation is occurring in banking, health care, insurance, telecommunications, manufacturing, and other industries, including retailing. The trend will continue as companies seek ownership and reorganization changes that enable better financial performance. With consolidation there will be fewer major companies, but those that exist will be larger, more efficient, and able to contend effectively with economic pressures.

Critical aspects of change influence the decisions made by retailers. Some aspects are precipitated by consumers and invite adaptation by savvy retailers. Other changes are externally instigated and perhaps present greater challenges to retailers and customers alike. The future belongs to retailers that present a strong identity; place customers in the center of the planning vortex; sharpen their marketing efforts; remain attuned to safety, privacy, and green issues; and expand in global and multichannel ways. As fresh ways of thinking and survival skills are embraced, proactive retailers will consider some of the following tactics:

- Reduce their store numbers or sizes.
- Expand their formats or reallocate space.
- Contract or expand workforces as conditions dictate.
- Focus more on profit than on sales volume generation.
- Target customers more succinctly and take more risks.
- Adopt enlightened attitudes toward developing management talent.
- Integrate technology to the fullest.

The impact of change on store retailers is highlighted in Chapter 5, along with subsequent adaptive strategies.

Mergers, acquisitions, divestiture, bankruptcy, and diversification are strategies related to ownership and performance. These tactics are widely used, and are more prevalent in times of economic downturn. Few large retailers are left untouched by ownership change at some point in their histories. Forms of ownership were introduced in Chapter 1. The many facets of ownership change are presented next.

Ownership Changes as Strategic Initiatives

Although deep recessions increase frenetic merger and acquisition activity and make retailers more vulnerable to takeovers and bankruptcy, the core reasons for implementing ownership change remain consistent. All retailers must eventually cope with a maturing industry, overstored retail markets, increased competition, and changing public sentiments. Some fear the possibility of bankruptcy proceedings; others simply seek survival by forging new partnerships or ownership structures. The mechanics of ownership are complex as retailers evaluate strategic options.

Mergers, Acquisitions, and Divestiture

Mergers, acquisitions, and divestitures of companies are popular growth and competition strategies used by retailers. **Mergers** involve the pooling of resources by two or more companies in order to become one. **Acquisition** describes the buying of one company by another in either a friendly or hostile manner. This practice is also called a buyout or a takeover. Hostile takeovers receive more public attention than innocuous mergers. An ownership change that occurs when one company purchases large quantities of outstanding stock in another company, thereby giving controlling interest to the acquiring company, is called a **hostile takeover**. Some retailers use divestiture to refocus their operations and remain solvent in the face of increased competition. **Divestiture** is the selling of one business to another company.

Although mergers, acquisitions, and divestitures have been an established practice for decades, a new wave of aggressive activity began in the mid-1980s. The beginning of the 21st century saw a similar acceleration of ownership change, heightened by economic recession. Changes in ownership affect retailers and customers in many ways. Precipitating factors, advantages and disadvantages of mergers and acquisitions, and uses of divestiture follow.

Causes and Effects of Mergers and Acquisitions

Many newly formed retail entities are successful; others are not. A look at the causes and effects of mergers and acquisitions will help clarify these business practices. Mergers and acquisitions are initiated for several reasons:

- Companies are less expensive to purchase during stock market declines, periods of currency fluctuations, or political unrest.
- Retailers with available capital in stable and thriving economies desire new investments that will generate returns.
- Mature retail companies may need to acquire other companies in order to grow their businesses and remain competitive.
- Companies may decide to diversify their retail formats by acquiring companies outside of their core concept.

Advantages of Mergers and Acquisitions

Mergers and acquisitions benefit retailers in many ways:

- Mergers bring an opportunity to capitalize on the strengths of both companies.
- The increased base of retail knowledge created when two companies join forces may make the organization more competitive.
- Economies of scale may be realized in many functional and managerial areas.
- Companies may significantly increase market share.
- Prime retail locations may be gained.
- The company's retail position may be strengthened in the marketplace.
- Partnership conflicts may be eliminated.
- The business can expand for long-range investment potential.

Disadvantages of Mergers and Acquisitions

There are several negative effects of mergers and acquisitions:

- Long-standing customers may be reticent to shop at what they perceive as a new store.
- Changes of ownership causing changes in policies and procedures may be unsettling to employees.
- Long-standing retail chains may lose their identity in the proceedings. History was made when Federated Department Stores decided to fold many of its regional chains into its nationally recognized Macy's division.
- When mergers abound, human resource cutbacks are inevitable.
- Takeover activity may bring in nonretailers as retail partners.

Dynamics of Divestiture

When retailers make the decision to sell off existing companies or divisions, several factors are considered. Divestiture is used to:

- Enable companies to sell off unrelated businesses and concentrate on their core concepts.
- Help retailers raise capital in times of economic distress.
- Preclude possible bankruptcy proceedings or facilitate the reorganization process.

Acquisition and Divestiture Parameters

Retailers attempting to acquire other companies do so with care. They must be able to negotiate well and not pay too much for a company. Attention must be paid to locations, leasing arrangements, financial details, and competition. The process of preparing in-depth evaluations before a merger or acquisition can occur is called **due diligence**.

Sound and sensible business decisions are the best reasons for undertaking mergers or acquisitions. However, some merger participants have been accused of greed and ego gratification—perhaps the most negative attributes of a capitalist economy. No socially responsible business organization should condone selling assets to cover excessive debt, causing the loss of thousands of jobs in the process.

Leveraged buyouts, bankruptcy, and other aspects of ownership or company dissolution force changes in strategic direction for many retail companies. Commonly, retail suitors that are not directly involved in the retailing industry become owners, as discussed in the next section.

Rise of Private Equity Ownership

A major trend in the past decade was the emergence of nonretail companies as retail partners. Real-estate investment companies like Vornado Realty Trust, and private equity firms such as Bain Capital Partners, Texas Pacific Group, and Apollo Management became active participants in retail ownership. For example Vornado was the key investor in Toys "R" Us when it was sold in 2005. Bain Capital Partners owns several retail properties, including Burlington Coat Factory, Guitar Center, and one-third of Home Depot's wholesale supply business. Apollo Management owns Claire's Stores, General Nutrition Centers, Zales jewelers, and Rent-a-Center. The company owned Linens 'n Things when the home goods retailer filed for bankruptcy protection in 2008.

Did You Know?
Just when you think a company is secure in its ownership, the game changes. The investment community expected Toys "R" Us to go public in 2012, as the company had filed forms for an initial public offering (IPO) in 2010. The decision to delay was attributed to the uncertainty of the stock market and internal company conditions.
(Source: Dhanya Skariachan and Clare Baldwin, "RPT-IPO VIEW—Toys R Us IPO Slow Going; Now Seen in 2012," *Reuters*, July 10, 2011, www .reuters.com/assets/print?aid= UKNIE76902K20110710)

At the start of the 21st century, investment partners opened doors for retailers that needed infusions of cash to continue to grow their businesses. Such partners became less of an advantage later in the decade as many countries grappled with recession and investment capital became scarce or nonexistent.

Leveraged Buyouts

The most complicated and controversial acquisitions or hostile takeovers are called **leveraged buyouts.** These are purchases in which the acquiring company borrows large sums of money, using the yet-to-be-owned assets or debt as collateral, in order to finance the deal. A classic case involved Canadian real-estate developer Robert Campeau. It started with his acquisition of Allied Stores in 1986 and continued until his final disposition in 1990 as head of a multibillion-dollar empire. His actions affected many retail institutions and individuals, and reverberations continued into the 1990s. This saga involved Campeau, Allied, Federated, Macy's, and scores of other companies, and was considered one of the most embroiled ownership transitions in retail history.

Bankruptcy Proceedings

Bankruptcy proceedings are not new, but escalate during periods of economic slowdown. **Bankruptcy** is a legal declaration to inform the public of the financial insolvency of a company. Filing for **Chapter 11** bankruptcy protection allows a company to enter a grace period in which it attempts to reorganize its financial affairs. After filing, companies have 120 days to prepare a plan for reorganization and may wait up to 180 days after the receipt of the plan to obtain acceptance from the court. Extensions of up to 18 months may be granted upon just cause.[32] Many retailers believe that a fair assessment of retail performance and turnaround efforts is dependent on experiencing a full year's sales cycle. In contrast, **Chapter 7** of the federal bankruptcy code indicates that a company is unable to sustain its business, and seeks to file bankruptcy in order to liquidate stock and close its doors.

Indications of a retailer's impending failure may include changes in a store's regular ordering, irregular or slow payments to vendors, sparse inventories, and employee layoffs. These conditions may be apparent whether the retailer is a huge corporation or a single store. Both divestiture and bankruptcy protection practices became strategic devices wielded by some companies that attempt to sustain sinking businesses.

Developing entirely new formats is another way retailers remain competitive and expand their holdings. All strategies are important to retailers that are in the mature phase of their existence.

Impact of Ownership Change

The bubbling brew of merger, acquisition, and divestiture activity and related issues has not cooled in the second decade of the new millennium. New patterns have emerged as retailers vie for position in the industry. Three examples illustrating trends in ownership changes are reviewed here. The acquisition activities of Proffitt's and Ralph Lauren Polo and the diversification and subsequent divestiture of Limited Brands show many dimensions of strategic planning involving ownership.

Proffitt's Purchase of Saks Fifth Avenue

When Proffitt's purchased Saks Fifth Avenue (SFA) for $2.14 billion in 1998, some viewed this as the action of an upstart. Proffitt's, however, had been preparing for the acquisition for some time. The Birmingham, Alabama retailer had previously purchased several strong regional department stores, including McRae's in 1994; Parks-Belk in 1995; and Parisian, Younkers, and Herberger's in 1996. It also merged with Chicago retailer Carson Pirie Scott in 1997. All became part of the Saks Department Store Group (SDSG) when RBM Venture Company, headed by R. Brad Martin, completed a merger between Proffitt's and Saks Holdings, Inc., owner of Saks Fifth Avenue. Investcorp, a Bahrain company, had operated Saks Fifth Avenue since 1990. Before that, the company was owned by B.A.T. Industries in the United Kingdom.

The SFA acquisition propelled Proffitt's—intent on becoming a national powerhouse—toward its goal of attracting a more upscale market. Because of the high recognition and regard for the Saks brand, Proffitt's officially changed its name to Saks, Inc. in 1998.[33] By 2004, the company operated approximately 390 stores in the United States and one in Saudi Arabia. At that point, changing market conditions and stagnant performance led the company to begin divesting its mid-market department store businesses.[34]

In 2008, looking to divest divisions not related to its core Saks business, the company dissolved Club Libby Lu, an experiential retail chain with a preteen customer base. Steve Sadove, chairman and CEO of Saks, Inc., gave the following rationale for the closure: "...it was a better strategic fit with our department store business...now we can focus 100 percent of our time and resources on executing the strategies of our core Saks Fifth Avenue business."[35] Other sources cited poor performance and eroding retail markets due to the recession.

As sales declined among top luxury retailers, the company faced possible acquisition by other retailers. In this situation, some retailers invoke a poison pill to protect their namesake assets and shareholders, and avoid a takeover. A **poison pill** is a tactic that allows other shareholders to purchase stock at a reduced price, thus thwarting a takeover by a major shareholder. Although Saks did not implement this option, it is often exercised when an unfriendly takeover is imminent.

As this book went to press, the company operated 45 SFA stores in the United States and two SFA stores in Mexico City. In addition it has licensed stores in Saudi Arabia, Dubai (United Arab Emirates), and Bahrain. One of the Saks stores in the Middle East is illustrated in Figure 3.6. A store is planned for San Juan, Puerto Rico and is slated to open in 2014.[36] This evolutionary tale illustrates the intricacies of acquisition strategy and the complexities of ownership from both a historical and contemporary viewpoint.

Ralph Lauren Polo's Acquisition of Club Monaco

Ralph Lauren Polo made an unprecedented move when it acquired the Canadian specialty retailer Club Monaco in 1999. Club Monaco carries understated, contemporary merchandise that is stylish, yet ageless, for women, men, and the home. Its growth potential was optimal, and Ralph Lauren Polo felt an affinity for the retailer since both cater to customers with refined taste levels. Buoyed by the infusion of capital, Club Monaco now operates 120 stores worldwide.[37] The company had earlier expanded to Hong Kong, Korea, and Dubai and, through a strategic partnership with Browns Shop 24 in London, had opened an in-store shop there in early 2011.[38]

Figure 3.6
Saks Fifth Avenue extends its luxury brand in the Middle East through strategic partnerships. Saks' two-level store at the Bur Juman Centre in Dubai, United Arab Emirates is the largest in the mall.

Limited Brands' Diversification, Divestiture, and Acquisition

The practice of acquiring or developing companies or stores that are not directly related to a firm's core business is called **diversification**. Some department store groups have added specialty store chains; mass merchandisers followed suit, adding stores and retail services. Specialty store chains have built their businesses selling apparel, later acquiring accessory, lingerie, bath-product shops, sporting-goods chains, and catalogues. Diversification strategy works best when the economy is strong and competition is low. The example of Limited Brands illustrates these points.

When it formed its Intimate Brands division in the mid-1990s, The Limited created an environment where Victoria's Secret, Bath & Body Works, C.O. Bigelow, White Barn Candle, and Henri Bendel could flourish. The Limited sold its Brylane catalogue businesses to French company Redoute to concentrate on its store business, and earlier had spun off Abercrombie & Fitch, which remains a separate entity. In 2002, however, The Limited bought back its outstanding stock in Intimate Brands and changed its corporate name to Limited Brands. Later in the decade, the Victoria's Secret brand Pink was launched (eventually becoming a group of stand-alone stores), Express, Limited Stores, and C.O. Bigelow were divested, and the Canadian lingerie chain, La Senza, was acquired.[39]

Continuing the saga, as of 2012, Limited Brands operated 2,902 stores in the United States and Canada as well as international franchised stores and online. Victoria's Secret store and online sales combined account for almost 60 percent of Limited Brands $10.36 billion revenue.[40]

Diversification and divestiture remain tools that retailers use to gain or reacquire a competitive edge. Timing, company goals, and conditions in the retail environment dictate which technique should be used. As these examples have shown, acquisitions, bankruptcies, and ownership conflicts are propelled by a variety of factors. One fact remains constant: the face of retailing will change. Stores that survive challenges may become larger, more powerful, and more profitable operations; conversely, they may become smaller, more highly focused, and likewise profitable firms. These dynamics are expected to continue to influence retail strategy in the 21st century, bringing more surprises for retailers and customers alike.

Summary

Today's merchants plan ahead for their businesses to grow. Strategic planning involves five key steps: (1) performing a situation analysis, (2) identifying a differential advantage, (3) developing a mission statement, (4) formulating goals and objectives, and (5) planning strategies that can be executed. To achieve customer satisfaction and earn a profit, retailers everywhere must acknowledge this vital process, implement plans, and monitor results on a continuous basis.

Change is occurring in several critical areas. The economy affects retail decision-making worldwide. Currently, retailers are grappling with diminishing resources and an inability to secure credit or capital investments, while attempting to remain solvent and continue to satisfy their customers.

Advances in technology offer more choices of where to shop—including online—but also change the means by which retailers more efficiently manage their businesses. Retailers use information technology to gain a competitive edge.

Multichannel retailing is the strategy of choice for most retailers. Direct marketing and direct selling are no longer viewed as alternatives to classic retail stores, but rather an integral part of overall retail strategy. The sophisticated databases of direct marketers allow them to reach customers more effectively, and often over the Internet.

Global expansion by mature retail companies happens for several reasons: saturated home markets, increased competition, availability of new markets, demands of investors, and increased customer sophistication.

Customers fulfill more than basic shopping needs in the retail marketplace. Experiential retailing is a new approach taken by retailers that provide exceptional opportunities to fully engage customers in the shopping experience while building loyalty. Retailers of all types and sizes will continue to seek closer relationships with their customers through a variety of programs. Shorter supply chains help retailers cut the costs of doing business throughout the industry.

Branding is an important concept for retailers in the 21st century. Whether developing private-label brands or featuring national and global brands, retailers set goals to serve customers well and operate profitably. Many retailers position their stores as brands and build brand equity by expanding existing brands or acquiring others.

Terrorism and crime leave indelible marks on our way of life and the way we do business throughout the world. Consumers' increased need for privacy and personal security have created new challenges and perhaps new opportunities for retailers.

The green movement is challenging retailers not only to develop environmentally friendly products, but also to construct energy-efficient stores, utilize sustainable materials, and help spread the green message as they develop products.

Ownership change prevails as mergers, acquisitions, divestitures, bankruptcies, and diversification are used as strategic tools. As this trend unfolds, fewer moderate and large-sized companies exist, but those that do are more powerful. The reasons for mergers and acquisitions are essentially economic ones. Retailers must sell nonperforming units and purchase those that will give them a competitive advantage. In saturated markets, these strategies help retailers continue to grow their businesses; during severe economic downturns, ownership change may be the only course of action that can ensure the continuity of a company or its brands.

The impact of proactive strategic planning on retail performance should not be underestimated. Risk reduction, sustained growth, and profitability are at stake. Flexibility and the ability to adapt to change are essential ingredients in the planning process.

Key Terms

Acquisition (See also *hostile takeover*.)
Bankruptcy (See also *Chapter 11*.)
Branding
Brand equity
BRIC
Carbon footprint
Chapter 7
Chapter 11
Co-branding
Consolidation
Cross-merchandising
Customer relationship management (CRM)
Developing countries
Differential advantage
Direct marketing
Direct selling
Diversification
Divestiture
Due diligence
Economies of scale
Electronic cash (e-cash) cards
Experiential retailing
Goals
Gross margin

Hostile takeover
Import snobbery
Information technology (IT)
Leveraged buyouts
Liquidation
Manufacturer's suggested retail prices (MSRPs)
Mature retail companies
Merger
Mission statement
Objectives
Organized retail crime (ORC)
Overstored
Point of impulse (POI)
Poison pill
Positioning
Price lining
Quick response (QR)
Shrinkage
Situation analysis
Strategic planning
Strategies
SWOT analysis
Vision statement

Questions for Review and Discussion

1. Why is strategic planning important to retailers? Discuss the kinds of information that may surface while conducting a situation analysis.
2. What is the purpose of a mission statement? How does it differ from a vision statement? Go online and find mission or vision statements for your favorite retailer.
3. Discuss three impact areas that are expected to affect strategic thinking and planning this decade. How will these changes affect customers and retailers?
4. Why is multichannel retailing an important strategic direction?

5. Why is the concept of retail branding an important one? Explain several ways in which branding strategies are implemented.

6. Why has extensive merger, acquisition, and divestiture activity in retailing occurred in recent years? What are the effects of these strategies on retailers and consumers?

7. Is bankruptcy used as a strategic tool or as a last resort? Justify your position.

8. How have changes in ownership status affected Saks, Inc., Club Monaco, and Limited Brands?

Endnotes

1. "New Roomba's Pricey, But Cleans Better," *Boston Globe*, November 24, 2008, D6.

2. "About Us," Limited Brands, accessed July 23, 2011, www.limitedbrands.com/our_company/about_us/default.aspx.

3. Deloitte. *Global Powers of Retailing 2012* "Top 250 Global Retailers 2010." January 2012. www.deloitte.com/consumerbusiness

4. "About Us." "Our Plan." 2010–2015. p. 1–2. Marks & Spencer. http://corporate.marksandspencer.com/aboutus/our_plan

5. Molly Prior, "Retailers Put the Brakes on New Store Openings for 2009," *Women's Wear Daily*, January 9, 2009, 8.

6. "Ulta Beauty Announces First Quarter 2012 Results." News Release. June 5, 2012. Ulta. http://ir.ulta.com/phoenix.zhtml?c=213869&p=irol_newsArticle_pf&id=1702772

7. "Ulta Salon, Cosmetics & Fragrance, Inc. Profile and Key Statistics," Yahoo! Finance, accessed June 27, 2011, http://finance.yahoo.com/q/pr?s=ULTA+Profile and http://finance.yahoo.com/q/ks?s-ULTA+Key+Statistics.

8. "Order Online, Pick Up In Store Convenience Comes to Walgreens Stores Throughout Chicagoland with Rollout of New Web Pickup Service," Walgreens, June 27, 2011, http://walgreens2009.tekgroupweb.com/article_print.cfm?article_id5441.

9. Teri Agins, "A Glimpse of the Future of Luxury," *Wall Street Journal*, January 29, 2009, D8.

10. Cecilie Rohwedder, "Burberry Cuts Jobs Amid Luxury Slump," *Wall Street Journal*, January 21, 2009, B2.

11. Michael Haddon, "Burberry Sales Helped By Expansion in China," *Wall Street Journal*, April 20, 2011, B7.

12. "Preliminary Results for the Year Ended 31 March 2012," p 1, 14. May 23, 2012 Burbury Group, plc, www.burberryplc.com

13. Janet Adamy, "At Starbucks, A Tall Order For New Cuts, Store Closures," *Wall Street Journal*, January 29, 2009, B1.

14. Julie Jargon, "Starbucks Growth Revives, Perked by Via," *Wall Street Journal*, January 21, 2010, B7.

15. Miguel Bustillo, "Wal-Mart Figures Time Is Ripe for Chicago Push," *Wall Street Journal*, February 11, 2009, B1.

16. "How It Works," Rescue Buy Sell Trade, accessed July 20, 2011, www.rescuebuyselltrade.com/how-it-works.html.

17. "What is Direct Marketing?" Direct Marketing Association, accessed January 25, 2009, www.the-dma.org/aboutdma/whatisthedma.shtml.

18. Greg Bensinger. "Competing with Amazon on Amazon." *Wall Street Journal*, June 27, 2012. B1.

19. Jeffrey A Tractenberg, "Booksellers Alter App Sales," *Wall Street Journal*, July 26, 2011, B6.

20. Janet Adamy, "McDonald's to Expand, Posting Strong Results," *Wall Street Journal*, January 27, 2009, B1, B5.

21. "Top Retail Trends 2010: Globalization of U.S. Retailers Accelerates," *Stores*, January 2010, 2, www.stores.org/Current_Issue/2010/01/Top%20Retail%20Trends%202010.asp.

22. "BRIC Nations No Longer Emerging Markets" *Economic Times*. April 13, 2011, http://articles.economictimes.indiatimes.com/2011-04-13/news/29413703_1_bric-members-bric-nations-bric-countries.

23. "Internet Users in the World, Distribution by World Regions—2011," Internet World Stats, March 31, 2011,www.internetworldstats.com/stats.htm.

24. "Executive Summary: Table 1.2 Rankings on the Ease of Doing Business." IFC and the World Bank, November 4, 2010, 4–5. http://web.worldbank.org. (Source: Doing Business database.)

25. Sarah Needleman, "Sales of Small Firms Are Up," *Wall Street Journal*, July 14, 2011, B8.

26. *Global Retail Theft Barometer 2011*, (Nottingham, U.K.: Centre for Retail Research, 2011), www.retailresearch.org/grtb,globaltrends.php.

27. Jeffrey Ball, "Six Products, Six Carbon Footprints," *Wall Street Journal*, October 6, 2008, R1, R3.

28. "Green Giants, The Top Eco-Friendly Brands Favored by Gen Y," *Women's Wear Daily*, August 21, 2008, 16. (Source: Outlaw Consulting, San Francisco.)

29. Arden Dale, "Green Products Gain From New Price Equation," *Wall Street Journal*, June 24, 2008, B7.

30. M. V. Greene, "The 'Virtuous Circle:' Marks & Spencer Involves Partners in its Eco Plan," *Stores*, accessed January 8, 2009, www.stores.org/Current_issue/2008/12/GreenSidebar6.asp.

31. Ellen Groves, "Moving Forward," *Women's Wear Daily*, October 28, 2009, 6.

32. "How Chapter 11 Works," United States Courts, accessed July 21, 2011, www.uscourts.gov/FederalCourts/Bankruptcy/BankruptcyBasics/Ch.11.aspx.

33. "Saks Incorporated History" (excerpts from company brochure), Saks Incorporated, May, 2000, 1–6.

34. The Associated Press, "Saks to Close 11 Stores in Seven States," October 1, 2004, www.msnbc.msn.com/id/6152586.

35. Saks Incorporated, "Saks Incorporated to Discontinue Club Libby Lu Operations," accessed November 6, 2008, http:// phx.corporate-ir.net/phoenix.zhtml?c=110111&p=irol-newsArticle_print&ID=12223.

36. Walter Leob. "Saks Fifth Avenue—CEO Upbeat Reflects Exciting Merchandise in Stores." Forbes. June 26, 2012. http://www.forbes.com/sites/walterleob/2012/06/26/saks-fifth-avenue-ceo-upbeat-reflects-exciting-merchandise-in-stores/

37. "Summary," Club Monaco Corporation, accessed July 25, 2011, www.clubmonaco.com.

38. Lauren Milligan, "Join the Club," *Vogue*, February 11, 2011, www.vogue.co.uk/news/2011/02/11/club-monaco-launches-in-britain-at-browns.

39. Limited Brands, "Limited Brands Reports May 2011 Sales," June 2, 2011, www.prnewswire.com/news-releases/limited-brands-reports-may-2011-sales-123011213.html.

40. Retail Sails. "Profile—Limited Brands, Inc." p 1–2. June 30, 2012 http://retailsails.com/monthly-sales-summary/ltd/.

Chapter 4

Customer Behavior

Learning Objectives

After completing this chapter you should be able to:

- Discuss how individual and group variables shape retail shopping behavior.
- Relate how demographics and psychographics influence customer behavior.
- Describe current societal factors that have changed customer behavior.
- Identify the steps customers go through in making decisions about purchases.
- Relate the three types of decision-making time frames to the four classifications of goods and services.

Figure 4.1
Customers come in all shapes and sizes, as do retailers. The trick is to match them up in such a way that mutual needs are satisfied and met.

Although many of us have become used to thinking of retail shoppers as consumers, a key presenter at a National Retail Federation conference held in the early 2000s, suggested referring to them as customers, not consumers. Elliot Ettenberg, then chairman and chief executive office (CEO) of Bozell Retail Worldwide—and presently CEO of Ettenberg & Company Ltd., a Quebec-based strategic think-tank, cited the root definitions of these terms.[1] *Consumer* implies a user, or someone who acquires, but *customer* means a person to be dealt with. If retailers are to successfully meet the needs of contemporary customers, this mind shift is necessary, he believes. This text acknowledges the nuance as an important paradigm shift and puts an emphasis on the latter term.

Understanding customer behavior is a precursor to retailing excellence, yet customers today have less predictable purchasing habits than ever before. It is more difficult to understand their motivations, priorities, and lifestyles. Some observers argue that human decision making can never be exactly predicted. As Michael Goldberg, associate professor of economics at the University of

New Hampshire, put it, "How and when individuals revise their ways of thinking about the past and future cannot be programmed into a computer."[2]

In a customer behavior context, **lifestyles** describe the way people live, work, play, and spend their money. In the 21st century, society is more enlightened, media influence has intensified, and online stores have added a new dimension to the shopping experience. Great value is placed on instant and constant communication, ethnicity as well as diversity, rapidly expanding technologies, and the opportunity to shop in multichannel and global environments—even while dealing with global economic problems.

Retailers serve people from varied backgrounds. We don't necessarily want to look, think, eat, or dress alike—although cultural, peer, and family pressure certainly has an impact on product selection. Customer behavior involves a complex assortment of individual and group influences, which are presented in this chapter from several vantage points.

Individual and Group Influences on Customer Behavior

The fields of psychology and sociology provide insight into the complexities of human behavior. Within these disciplines is a wealth of information for retailers. Many sources of influence impinge on the decisions that individuals make.

Individual Influences

Every purchase is based on individual needs or wants. Classic psychological theories attempt to categorize and explain human complexities. They involve need determination, physiological and psychological bases of behavior, and personality.

Biogenic and Psychogenic Needs

Human needs are divided into two broad categories: biogenic and psychogenic. **Biogenic needs** are physiological needs for food, warmth, shelter, and sex. **Psychogenic needs** stem from the socialization process and involve intangibles such as status, acquisition, or love. Both types affect behavior.

Three psychogenic needs, originally defined by James Baylor, provide more insight regarding human behavior:

1. *Affectional*—The need to love and be loved; to form relationships.
2. *Ego-bolstering*—The need to build ourselves up in our own minds or in the eyes of others; to develop self-esteem or desire status.
3. *Ego-defensive*—The need to protect ourselves, our families, and our fragile egos.[3]

Psychogenic needs are often the basis for advertising campaigns. Cologne, liquor, and cosmetic ads frequently play on affectional needs; insurance, personal, and health care products on ego-defensive needs; designer clothing and high-performance automobiles on ego-bolstering needs. Perhaps the Prada bags in Figure 4.2 will give your ego a boost?

Maslow's Hierarchy of Needs

From the annals of human psychology, Dr. Abraham Maslow's **hierarchy of needs** states that people seek to satisfy needs in an ascending order of importance: biogenic, social, and psychogenic. The hierarchy is illustrated in Figure 4.3. Although not intended to predict shopping behavior, Maslow's theory helps retailers understand the buying motivations of customers. The theory provides a valuable frame of reference as shown in the following contexts.

In the early years of retailing, trading posts sold basic goods such as fur skins for bodily warmth and axes to cut down trees for shelter and heat. Satisfying fundamental human needs was most important to customers of this era.

Affluent individuals of the 1980s chose their Porsche automobiles and Rolex watches to fulfill the higher-level ego needs for self-esteem. Parents lavished possessions on their children in what some psychologists and sociologists claim was one of the greatest attempts in history to buy love, substituting a new bike or action figure for an evening of shared activities. Today, customers may be somewhat less ostentatious, but many have discretionary incomes that equal or surpass those in the 1980s and 1990s. Their self-esteem may emanate from more intrinsic than extrinsic sources.

Figure 4.2
Designer handbags by
Prada address a woman's
ego-bolstering psychogenic
needs and perhaps her
quest for status.

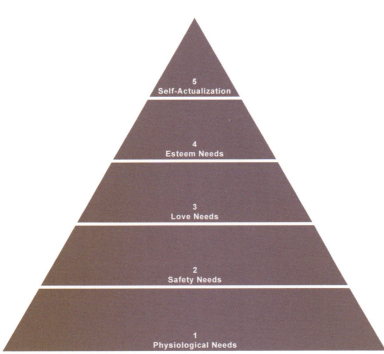

Figure 4.3
Maslow's Hierarchy of
Needs
Source: Abraham H.
Maslow, "A Theory of
Human Motivations,"
Psychological Review 50
(1943): 370–396.

Those who achieve self-actualization care little for status merchandise as a means of achieving self-fulfillment. **Self-actualization** is the desired result when a person becomes all that he or she is capable of being. At this level, people feel secure and do not have the need to state their accomplishments through possessions. This group is the most difficult of all for retailers to serve. The search for self-actualization is reflected in the proliferation of products that encourage introspection, spirituality, and expansion of self and soul. Most people never reach a truly self-actualized state.

The image of what individuals hope to become is closely allied with aspirational wants. **Aspirational wants** are those that relate to products and services that people perceive will help them achieve higher status in life.

Maslow's theory is useful for determining market segments and positioning products, but is not the only basis for retail strategy development. People have diverse backgrounds and complex psychological needs. How do we explain why some people buy the most expensive computer equipment, yet drive used compact cars? What about those who live in lavishly furnished homes but seldom eat out in fine restaurants? It is necessary to probe the depths of the human psyche further before the nuances and changes in contemporary behavior are considered.

Personality Types

Because shopping is a form of self-expression, understanding personality types is helpful to retailers. People with certain types of personalities respond to retail sales situations in particular ways. Although such responses are complex, some general themes can be noted. Extroverts, who outwardly express their ideas, are talkative and enjoy social contact and attention. Because of this they often enter into lengthy discussions during sales presentations. As long as the sale is open they have the attention of the salesperson. Introverts are more emotionally contained and less loquacious. They respond negatively to high-pressure tactics because they do not enjoy directed personal attention. Training sales associates to use selling techniques that consider different personality types can have a bearing on customer retention.

Those of us born in the northeastern United States have always been chided about being unwelcoming to outsiders, thrifty to a fault, resourceful, and introspective. Evidently, there is some truth in these stereotypes. Researchers who explore regional differences in personality traits have developed profiles that certainly put a new spin on understanding customer behavior. Looking at characteristics such as neuroticism, openness, agreeableness, conscientiousness, and extroversion, researchers were able to superimpose personality traits over data involving crime rates, health, and economic development to see if there were correlations. They found that, for example, Minnesotans ranked high in agreeableness and extroversion, and ranked lower in crime. People in the Northeast were considered more neurotic and less open, but not as conscientious as they might think they are.[4]

So what does this mean for retailers? Personality differences that influence shopping behavior, customer taste preferences, and willingness to spend may be more quantifiable than expected. The more information retailers can gather about potential customers living near planned or existing store locations, the better their chances of success will be.

Group Influences

Our attitudes are also shaped by our interactions with others. Friends and family, peers, and professional associates affect our behavior—some to a greater degree than others.

Reference Groups

An individual's self-image is developed from both external and internal influences. Reference groups guide the decision-making process. **Reference groups** are social or professional associations with which a person identifies and to which he or she looks when forming opinions. Fraternities and sororities, business affiliations, country clubs, and church memberships are examples of formal reference groups. Roommates, classmates, and even spectators at a soccer game can be informal reference groups. The following examples show how reference groups influence individual purchases. Sara, following the custom of other young, environmentally concerned managers in her firm, chose a Honda Insight LX Hybrid as her first car. Jay, after hearing his fraternity brothers rave about the latest release from Pittsburgh rapper Mac Miller, downloaded it to his iPhone. Society sets certain norms of behavior to which its members are pressured to conform. Very little is bought at retail that does not reflect social influences.

The Family

Family members exert more influence on buying behavior than any other group within a given culture or socioeconomic class. As family structure changes, so do retail strategies. Often it is difficult to determine who makes purchasing decisions. Children are sophisticated, possess media savvy, and often sway household purchasing decisions. Frequently, teens in the family are the experts when selecting and setting up items such as the wall-mounted LCD TV.

Studying individual and group differences helps retailers understand the diverse needs of their customers. Many other factors influence customer behavior.

Factors Affecting Shopping Behavior

People make purchasing decisions on the basis of who they are, who they want to be, where and how they live, and how much they earn. Age, gender, social class, and family makeup influence shopping behaviors. Special activities in which individuals choose to participate, unique combinations of interests they hold, and opinions they voice on innumerable topics also affect their behavior. Demographic and psychographic factors often intertwine and present new avenues of customer understanding for retailers. Classification of people on the basis of their lifestyles, activities, interests, and opinions is called **psychographics**.

Demographic Factors

Introduced in Chapter 2, the following demographic trends contribute to the shaping of customer demand:

- Population growth and distribution.
- Family and household composition.
- Labor force participation rates.
- Educational attainment levels.
- Household income distribution.
- Age groups.
- Ethnic diversity.

This section presents enhanced coverage of select demographic factors in relation to shopping behavior. Demographic data also are routinely used by retailers as the basis for market segmentation.

Age Influences on Shopping Behavior

Age is a powerful determinant of customer behavior. It affects individual interests, tastes, purchasing ability, and choice of shopping venues. Population distribution among different age groups is used to indicate where opportunities exist for new retail institutions. Growing interest in the youth market and in senior citizens provides untapped opportunities for retailers.

Children and 'Tweens   Through allowances and gifts, children have money to spend, and they often make purchases with little parental consultation. They have considerable clout in the marketplace. Children aged 6–12 frequently purchase products such as fashion apparel, lip gloss, and video games. Their habits are more like those of teenagers who grew up in decades past than of younger children, and for that reason they are often referred to as 'tweens. Reflecting this change, sales of classic products like Barbie dolls have declined somewhat. However, the brand is still highly sought by youngsters globally. A life-size Barbie house located inside select Toys "R" Us stores is designed to capture the attention of younger shoppers. It carries not only dolls, but also Barbie apparel for girls, and is illustrated in Figure 4.4.

The Internet has changed children's allocation of free time greatly. According to a multifaceted report released by the Joan Ganz Cooney Center and Sesame Workshop, 23 percent of children under the age of five use the Internet. Of that group, 82 percent of children use it at least weekly. Many three-year-olds watch videos online. A Nielsen study used in the report found that 36 percent of children between the ages of eight and ten use the Internet and television simultaneously, consuming 5–8 hours daily depending on how often they use media concurrently.[5]

Figure 4.4
For more than 50 years, Barbie has remained a popular brand for young girls, as evidenced by Barbie's presence online and in stores like Toys "R" Us.

The significance of this information is profound when we consider the amount of exposure young children have to educational content and marketing messages in the old and new media. Are they becoming more educated, more intelligent young consumers, or are they limiting play and exploration of the outside world in their young lives?

Global toy sales were expected to reach $84.1 billion in 2011, only 1 percent higher than the previous year's figure. One in every 11 children aged 3–6 in the United Kingdom received a "toy" tablet for Christmas in 2011. Pre-school electronic learning increased 43 percent last year.[6] The youngest generation of tablet users will surely influence future sales.

Brick-and-mortar retailers address the needs of children and their parents by providing child-oriented shopping environments that include experiential play areas, computer interaction, child care, and rest facilities.

Young Adults   The influence of generation Y—which includes the cohort known as millennials—on technology and its related must-have products is already legendary. This group, ranging in age from 19 to 34 years in 2011, comprises about 30 percent of the adult population.[7] They shop most intensely online, send or receive scores of text messages each day, and spend more time online than watching TV.

A survey that looked at the life choices of young adults and their relative importance found that 27 percent of individuals aged 23–28 were more concerned with paying off all their debts than purchasing a new car. In the career-or-family track, 73 percent were more interested in building their careers compared with 27 percent who were desirous of having children.[8] Provided with more insight, retailers can adjust their channels of distribution, merchandise mixes, advertising, and price levels to meet the needs of their young adult customers.

Sterling Silver Seniors   Americans aged 65–84 are the fastest growing segment within the mature market.[9] A viable but not always visible market to retailers, senior citizens today have the means to shop, if not always the incentive.

The oldest baby boomers turned 65 in 2011. This group is expected to spend about $50 billion on consumer goods by the end of this decade. Along with the expenditures will come some special needs for those dealing with the health issues and other aspects of aging. Walgreen's, Rite Aid, and Family Dollar are making senior-friendly changes in their stores. In preparation for this, the companies' executives participated in training exercises intended to put them in the shoes of older folks. One activity required a vice president to wear glasses that blurred his vision, put un-popped popcorn in his shoes, and bind his thumbs to his palms to simulate some of the challenges older people face. The program, put on by Kimberly-Clark Corp., alerted participants to the comfort levels seniors require, changes in the products they'll need, and where and how they will shop. Changes in store layouts, lighting, parking accommodations, and even the colors used in store decor are being evaluated and made more amenable to older eyes and bodies.[10]

Gender Differences and Influences

Men and women have different shopping habits. We realize this every time we see female shoppers at the mall with fathers, husbands, sons, or male friends. Having said that, more men than ever before are shopping for themselves, as well as for spouses, girlfriends, children, or other family members. A study showed that one in two men bought clothing for themselves, and the same number purchased apparel for their wives or significant others. Nine out of ten men shopped for apparel for their children.[11] Would it surprise you to learn that men shop at Cabela's for outdoor camouflage gear for their children? Men are the primary target market for Cabela's, but merchandise is directed toward the entire family, as illustrated in Figure 4.5.

Women tend to spend more time shopping, and they spend more time shopping online than they do in stores—with two notable exceptions. Teenage girls and young women aged 13 to 24 spend more time in stores than any other age category, and women 56 to 70 shop online for a greater period of time than any other female age group. These findings are from a study by Cotton Incorporated that included 5,000 individuals from ten countries (Brazil, China, Colombia, Germany, India, Italy, Japan, Thailand, United Kingdom, and United States).[12] We can conclude that the shift from time spent in stores to time spent online is a global trend.

Figure 4.5
Camouflage for the entire family is available at Cabela's. Do you think Dad is doing the shopping in the Scarborough, Maine store? Maybe.

In another study, Microsoft, Mindshare, and Ogilvy & Mather coined the term "digital divas" to describe the 16 percent of the 6,000 U.S. women surveyed who were the most engaged in on-line shopping and related activities. Although these results were reported in 2008, we expect the percentage to grow, particularly as the major woes of the recession dissipate and designer apparel Web sites like Ruelala and Glitz flourish. The behavioral profile of the "digital divas" appears in Table 4.1.

As women increasingly pursue advancement in their careers—earning tremendous financial clout in the process—the days of shopping as a principal leisure pursuit are waning. Time is of the essence for most women and their families. They seek convenience, fewer hassles, quality mer-chandise, and good value, and their desires are reflected at the point-of-sale regardless of where, when, and with whom they shop.

Table 4.1   Profile of "Digital Divas"*

Percentage	Characteristics
92%	Pass along information about deals of finds to others
76%	Want to be part of a special or select panel
58%	Would chuck a TV if they had to get rid of one digital device (only 11 percent would ditch their laptops)
51%	Are moms
22%	Shop at least once a day

*171: average number of contacts in their e-mail or mobile lists.

Source: Jack Neff, Mindshare/Ogilvy & Mather, "Wired Women an Untapped Goldmine for Package Goods," *Advertising Age*, November 3, 2008, http://adage.com/print?article_id=132150.

Social Class Segments

Based on the assumption that like-minded individuals tend to have similar habits, needs, and wants, social class theorists segment people into groups according to demographic data such as income, occupation, and level of education. Social-class designators such as lower-upper, upper-middle, and lower-middle provide a framework but do not accurately or adequately predict all customer behavior. An overview of social class–related characteristics appears in Table 4.2.

Informed retailers study the similarities of each group before designing a retail mix. They also watch opinion leaders for clues to their behavior. **Opinion leaders** are trendsetters whose opinions are respected within a group. By acknowledging similar shopping tastes and habits, retailers have a better chance of attracting more customers and increasing market share.

For example, members of the lower-middle class tend to be blue-collar workers who live in apartments or small homes in older neighborhoods. Spending money on children's needs, family vacations, movies, and sporting events is typical of their social class. In contrast, upper-middle class individuals are more likely to hold middle-management positions and live in larger, suburban houses. Their probable activities involve spending money on dining out, attending concerts, and escaping for the weekend.

Table 4.2   U.S. Social Class Structure and Expected Retail Purchasing Behavior

Social Class	Approximate Percentage of Population	Membership & Occupation	Purchasing Values	Behavior
Upper-upper class	1%	"Old money;" socially prominent aristocrats, professionals, and financiers.	Live well; value philanthropy and civic involvement.	Services; "old money" not as ostentatious as "nouveau riche."
Lower-upper class	1%	"Nouveau riche," high-tech entrepreneurs and other business owners. Professionals in high-level executive positions, as well as celebrities and professional athletes.	Strive for financial success; environmentally concerned; may engage in volunteer or philanthropic causes.	Travel extensively; purchase multiple cars, yachts, and homes. Shop frequently and buy fine jewelry and designer apparel.
Upper-middle class	19%	College-educated; upwardly mobile, managerial and professional occupations.	Home ownership; child-oriented; living the good life.	Home goods; branded apparel; electronic games and devices of all types.
Middle class	31%	Lower-level management and supervisory positions; small business owners, teachers, healthcare workers.	Desire respectability, neat homes; want college education for children.	Less expensive clothes, may have more money in savings than upper-middle-class families; buy electronic goods, do-it-yourself products.
Working class	30%	Blue-collar trade and technical workers; some are high-hourly-wage workers.	Try to enjoy life, stay afloat.	Big cars or trucks; major entertainment includes watching sports, reality TV.
Lower class	17%	Low-skilled workers; live just above poverty level. Long-term unemployed may live below poverty level. Welfare recipients.	Try to stay afloat; some are fatalistic and apathetic.	Necessities only, low disposable income.

Sources: Adapted from R. P. Coleman, "The Continuing Significance of Social Class Marketing," *Journal of Consumer Research* 267 (1983) and William Thompson and Joseph Hickey, *Society in Focus* (Boston: Allyn & Bacon, 2005).

Household Composition

The trend toward marriage at a later age, as well as more single and divorced people; multiparent, gay, and lesbian families; and sequential marriages in the United States have created changes in household composition and family lifestyles. These changes also have an impact on buying behavior.

Women wield significant economic power and earn $12 trillion globally in salaries and wages annually. In the United States, 30 percent of working women earn all or almost all of their family's income.[13] Dual-income households have more discretionary dollars to spend for goods but less time available to shop for them. Retailers that provide quality timesaving products and services to these customers will meet with success.

By examining the ways families evolve over time, retailers become better attuned to the needs of their customers. The family life cycle theory helps explain changes in the family constellation. As an example, the purchasing behavior of unmarried singles is radically different from that of single parents, although both are technically single. Both may be apartment-dwellers, but unmarried singles tend to spend money on car payments, electronic goods, clothes, and sporting equipment. Singles with children focus on children's clothing, toys, and medical and dental expenses. In most cases they spend less on entertainment and social pursuits. Family life cycle, which uses demographic information to help retailers understand more about their customers, is detailed in Table 4.3.

Lifestyle Psychographics

We humans are a complex species displaying many crossover tendencies in our behaviors. The person who skips lunch in order to take a yoga class can be the same person who eats at a gourmet French restaurant that evening. It is impossible to pigeonhole such an individual. Segmentation methods that consider the specific activities and interests in which people are involved and the opinions they hold bring more understanding to these manifold issues. Among the more well-known psychographic segmentation tools are SRI's VALS framework and the lifestyle trend reports developed by Faith Popcorn's BrainReserve.

VALS Segments

Research firm SRI International, now owned and operated by Strategic Business Insights (SBI), has developed descriptive categories to help businesses better understand their customers. The Menlo Park, California, company has identified eight VALS segments, derived from people's responses to the VALS questionnaire. Originally VALS was an acronym for Values and LifeStyles but now questionnaires survey individual's psychological traits, levels of motivation, and resources key demographics. SRI kept the VALS brand because of its high recognition.[14] Motivation is drawn from three primary areas: ideals, achievement, or self-expression. Resources go well beyond financial and also include education, attitudes toward leadership, health status, and a wealth of personality traits, for example. The VALS segments are described briefly here and illustrated in Figure 4.6.

1. *Innovators*—Possess the most resources; are open to new ideas and products.
2. *Thinkers*—Not interested in status; purchase goods for purposes of convenience and at moderate cost.
3. *Achievers*—Drawn to top-quality merchandise; read business and self-improvement publications.
4. *Experiencers*—Are fashion-conscious; tend to be impulse buyers.
5. *Believers*—Behave ethnocentrically; are resistant to change; buy lower-cost products.
6. *Strivers*—Concerned with personal image; use credit extensively for designer goods that they probably cannot afford.
7. *Makers*—Purchase value-oriented, basic merchandise; not interested in luxury goods.
8. *Survivors*—Use coupons and follow sales; read tabloids and believe advertising.[15]

Looking at smaller psychographic segments rather than at mass markets is one way to avoid the tendency to overgeneralize that accompanies most theories of social class and family life cycles. Many users of psychographic tools believe they are more important than demographics for understanding customer behavior. SBI believes that psychographic and demographic information

Table 4.3 Family Life Cycle Categories and Retail Implications

Status	Characteristics	Implications for Retailers
Young and Single	Never married, independent, frequently in early stages of career; moderate discretionary income.	Never marrieds living alone buy new cars, furniture, small appliances geared toward a first apartment, and career clothing; entertainment and electronic goods figure prominently.
Single, Living at Home	Never married or divorced, living in home of parents; high to low discretionary income, respectively.	Never marrieds living with parents may enjoy ample discretionary income; they may purchase better cars, computers, vacations, and clothes than those in the "Young and Single" category.
Single Heads of Households	Divorced or never married single people, often low discretionary income.	Divorced singles may regress financially after a divorce. A Bloomingdale's shopper may turn to Family Dollar for personal and household needs. Homeowners may become apartment-dwellers. The outlook for never-married heads of household may be more bleak due to child support or alimony payments; reduced standards of living.
Newly Married	Independent, present- and future-oriented; good discretionary income; usually dual incomes.	Setting up a new household is a priority; new furniture, appliances, and floor coverings are important. Many couples save for or purchase starter homes. Other couples postpone or choose not to have children, thus making them prime targets for luxury goods and travel.
Not Married but Cohabiting	May be less future-oriented than the newly married; usually dual incomes.	Maintaining sense-of-self in the relationship may be more important than making joint purchases for the home. Clothing and entertainment expenditures are significant.
Homosexual Partners	May function as traditional married or cohabiting partners; may have children in the household.	Homosexual partners tend to behave as other families and are in various social classes; more likely to live in urban areas but dispersion to smaller cities is occuring.
Full Nest I (one or two incomes)	Present- and future-oriented, youngest child under 6 years old; moderate discretionary income.	Child- and family-oriented, these couples spend a good portion of their income for toys, education, family travel, and household necessities.
Full Nest II (two incomes usual)	Present- and future-oriented, youngest child over 6 years old; somewhat more discretionary income than those in "Full Nest I" category.	Needs of growing children still dominate with clothing and electronic goods gradually replacing the emphasis on toys. Saving for college expenses may become paramount at this point.
Full Nest III (two incomes usual)	Future-oriented, may have some thoughts of retirement, may have youngest child living at home but most children are independent.	New furniture is often purchased, and decorating services are utilized, after most children have left the nest. Emphasis on travel as a couple with more dinners out. Couples married for the second or third time may see increased durable and nondurable goods as well as educational expenditures in all "Full Nest" categories.
Empty Nest I (two incomes)	No children at home, may have thoughts of retirement; good dual income.	Often affluent, people in this category may tend to travel, join golf clubs, indulge their grandchildren, and purchase future retirement homes. Situation may change if parental care becomes part of their responsibility in this and other categories.
Empty Nest II	Likely to be retired, though many may still be in the workforce full- or part-time, present-oriented; income fixed to ample.	Health care products may become more important. More affluent empty nesters may spend their money on travel, lesiure activities, and meals eaten out. Other less affluent retirees may be more restricted to purchase of basic necessities.
Sole Survivor I (spouse deceased)	Actively employed, present-oriented, more likely to be female than male; good income.	The employed sole survivor may experience a reflowering of ambition and expenditure patterns. Clothing, vacations, and leisure pursuits become joyful priorities.
Sole Survivor II (spouse deceased)	Retired, present-oriented, some may experience a sense of futility; others retain vitality; income poor to adequate to ample.	Some retired sole survivors tend to rely on long-time shopping habits rather than seek change. Others remain involved in activities for a longer time than past generations. Health care products and medicines may dominate spending. Many eventually reside in retirement homes, assisted living facilities, nursing homes, or with adult children, indicating distinct shifts of consumer behavior patterns.

Sources: Cushman & Wakefield and Hanley & Baker.

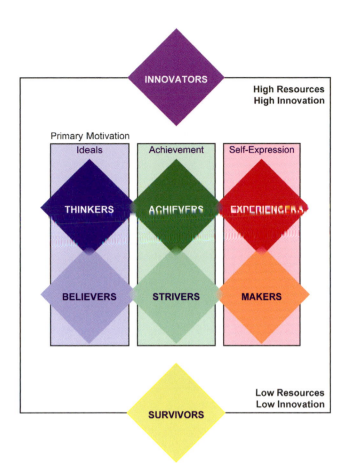

Figure 4.6
VALs Segments
Source: Strategic Business
Insights (SBI), www.
strategicbusinessinsights.
com/VALS.

that correlates significantly with consumer products, activities, and needs provides the best basis for analysis. In addition to determining VALS types, the company delves much deeper into customer behavior research.[16]

Faith Popcorn's Trend Reports

Faith Popcorn, founder of a trend-reporting and marketing-research firm called BrainReserve, monitors social and lifestyle trends to predict customer behavior. Information is compiled in part by 10,000 individuals worldwide whom Popcorn considers "visionaries," due to their expertise in many aspects of society, education, business, economics, and pop culture.

Psychographic trends such as those interpreted by BrainReserve are always in a state of flux. Astute observers of customer behavior use their knowledge to help businesses identify target markets and tailor merchandise to customers. BrainReserve has clients all over the planet that represent major consumer sectors, including retailing. McDonald's, Target, Avon, KFC, and Radio Shack are among the company's clients. In a special 2011 report, Popcorn highlighted the shift to "end-of gender," or EN-GEN. Her premise is that men and women in the near future will be treated less as specific genders and collectively more like humans. Her six points are presented in Table 4.4.

Societal Factors

Different, and sometimes conflicting, ideologies in world cultures gain acceptance, experience rejection, or undergo adaptation over time. Religious movements grow or wane in influence, and attitudes toward affluence and frugality shift. Meanwhile, customers' unprecedented need for speed of service continues to accelerate. These shifts affect the ways retailers address their customers, as many of the following situations illustrate.

Religious Influences

Personal beliefs vary, and individuals have different perspectives on this sensitive aspect of society and culture. From a retailing perspective, however, it is evident that religious movements and beliefs influence retail sales. For example, as the number of Muslims in the United States grows, so

Cyberscoop
Faith Popcorn's
BrainReserve tracks social
and cultural trends. To
see what's new and how
it may ultimately affect
customer behavior, go to
www.faithpopcorn.com
and explore her site. Which
trends best describe your
lifestyle?

Table 4.4 Faith Popcorn's 2011 Report—The Year of EN-GEN: The EN-GEN (End of Gender) Revolution Begins

Trend	Commentary	Examples
1. The Merger of Artistry and Technology	Remember when products for women were pink and products for guys grunted with a macho, four-wheel-drive aesthetic?	The new norm is Apple—simple, elegant EN-GEN design that pays attention to every single detail.
2. Beyond the Bento Box	Traditionally, men and women have kept the genders as separate as the way food is served in a walled-off bento box. But in the EN-GEN world, men and women will be liberated to experiment with interests and ideas normally associated with the opposite sex.	In Japan—where many trends originate—men are starting to arrange flowers, a classically female activity, to reduce stress. We'll be seeing women finally entering the male worlds of math and engineering in big numbers, and men taking on more caregiver roles.
3. Electric Shock	The electric vehicle is an EN-GEN car because it combines the more female values of environmentalism and concern for the world with male love of technology and innovation.	Sales of electric autos and hybrids will surprise even the most optimistic forecasters.
4. Recession Lift	The liberating forces of EN-GEN, combined with the brutal economy that makes it difficult for older men to compete, will come together.	The need to be competitive in the job market will trigger a boom in male plastic surgery.
5. Veganomics	As EN-GEN creates more sensitivity to the sources of our food and the consumer products we buy, expect a dramatic growth in vegan values—and not just in food.	Vegan-friendly retailing, including fashion and home furnishings, will emerge. MooShoes, a store in New York City, is selling cruelty-free, animal-friendly vegan shoes and accessories. Sudu, a store with a similar product range, is opening in Boston.
6. Robot Frenzy	Robots are the ultimate genderless technology.	Expect robotic breakthroughs in medicine, manufacturing, prosthetic devices, the military, and more.

Source: www.faithpopcorn.com.

do sales of Islamic halal products. To be considered halal, meat must come from animals that have been blessed before being slaughtered by hand. Non-Muslim customers who develop a taste for halal foods perpetuate the trend in much the same way those who enjoy ethnic Jewish foods have helped move kosher products into the mainstream. New retail markets develop as a result.

Bob Stein, vice president of list management for direct marketing company Trinity Direct, learned that Catholic customers are very similar to mainstream customers with a few notable differences: "They like to shop by mail, read magazines and books, donate to their favorite charities and are very responsive to a variety of direct mail offers." He adds that "they are generally an older audience, 65 or more..."[17] Stein noticed that practicing Catholics behaved differently than those who are not as involved in their faith, suggesting that marketers need to use care when addressing direct-mail offers to markets that encompass divergent views and behaviors.

An incident in France brought the world's attention to the wearing of *burqas,* which are traditional Islamic women's garments that cover the body completely from head to toe. Female Muslim students were prohibited from wearing headscarves in 2004, because the French government does not allow religious symbols to be worn in schools. A resolution regarding a partial ban on burqas being worn in public places, such as schools and hospitals, was passed by Parliament. When the law was implemented in 2011, it made France the first country in Europe to ban full-face veils.[18]

Attitudes toward Affluence and Frugality

The pressure of providing a living for one's family usually supersedes worry about whether the next pair of jeans purchased will be Lucky or Juicy Couture. Yet much in the lives of customers revolves around the accumulation of wealth and the preoccupation with how to spend it. Saving money,

Figure 4.7
What kind of shopper
frequents L.L. Bean?
Traditional outdoor types,
serious mountain climbers,
or those who place their
trust in the company's
Bean boots? Probably all
three. This larger-than-life
depiction of the famous
boot is located outside the
Freeport, Maine flagship
store.
(Kees Van Ingen)

reducing consumption, and being happily frugal seem discordant with the media depiction of affluent contemporary life in industrialized societies. Yet most families were rudely awakened in late 2008 as the effects of recession began to be felt by rich and poor alike.

In a want-driven society, it is important to understand different lifestyles, because mass marketing techniques do not work as they did when most customers shared the same basic needs. Different segments interpret the "good life" in different ways. For example, outdoor enthusiasts on a limited budget who see themselves as weekend adventurers may shop for clothes and equipment at their local Walmart. Those that seek functional, timeless merchandise turn to L.L. Bean. A classic—although oversized—Bean boot is illustrated in Figure 4.7. Although they may pay a bit more, customers who take an earth-friendly stance may shop Patagonia's Web site, and die-hard hunting and fishing enthusiasts will shop at Cabela's or Bass Pro Shops and pay top dollar for the quality they seek. Affluence—or the lack of it—affects lifestyle choices and purchasing decisions. When belt-tightening occurs, formerly upmarket shoppers may revert to shopping for outdoor gear in Walmart rather than miss out completely on the opportunity to hike up Mount Monadnock.

In less profound economic downturns, the luxury markets have been relatively immune to the pressures to perform experienced by mid-market retailers. However, during the recession that began in late 2007, even luxury retailers felt the pinch of sluggish sales, fewer customers, and the shift of even well-off families to discount shopping. This lengthy economic downturn affected the luxury market in several ways:

- In one study, high-income customers admitted they had shopped at Target, Costco, Macy's, Nordstrom, and Walmart.[19] Whatever concerns about trading-down they had felt in robust economic times apparently had diminished.
- In the early stages of the recession, the American Affluence Research Center asked affluent women what brand of cocktail dress they preferred. They indicated private labels from Nordstrom and Bloomingdale's, although they had preferred designers Prada and Vera Wang prior to the downturn.[20]
- Some very wealthy people who still are cash-strong have shown empathy for those who have lost jobs, homes, and savings by curtailing big-ticket purchases of their own on moral and ethical grounds. Perhaps this indicates a subtle revolt against conspicuous consumption.[21]

Did You Know?
In mid-2011, a Nielsen's
Quarterly Global Online
Consumer Confidence
Survey indicated that 58
percent of global online
consumers said their
economies were still in
recession, and more than
half of those polled believed
this would continue through
mid-2012. Spare cash was
a problem worldwide: 31
percent of U.S. shoppers,
25 percent of shoppers in
the Middle East and Africa,
and 22 percent of shoppers
in Europe said they had no
money for discretionary
spending—not a pretty
picture.
(Source: "More Consumers
Worldwide Slip Back to
Recessionary Sentiment Levels
in Q2," *Nielsen Wire*, July 17,
2011, http://blog.nielsen
.com/nielsenwire/consumer/
more-consumers-worldwide-
slip-back-to-recessionary-
sentiment-levels-in-q2.)

- As the wealthy see their investment portfolios grow, they tend to indulge their taste for luxury goods; as portfolios plummet, high-income earners also curtail their expenditures, as seen by the performance of several upmarket retailers. After huge dips in the stock market in August 2011, stock shares fell 16–18 percent for Saks, Nordstrom, Tiffany, and Coach. Luxury shoppers represent approximately half of all income earned in the United States and comprise 48 percent of expenditures. Therefore, this small but powerful group significantly affects the well-being of the retailers they patronize.[22]

Many retail analysts contend that the recent changes in customer behavior transcend socio-economic position. Today's customers are looking for value, using discounts and coupons, reducing expenditures, postponing big-ticket purchases, and trading down whenever possible. For some, this cautious, thrifty approach to shopping has become so inculcated into their way of life that they may not resume heavier spending once the economy rebounds.

Perception of Time

Many people in the United States live life on fast-forward. This approach carries over into shopping behaviors. U.S. customers expect huge assortments, value for their money, and above all, instant gratification. The perception of time as a fleeting and precious commodity varies somewhat in other countries. Differences in this and other customer buying habits are charted in Table 4.5.

Although most customers value timesaving services, the importance placed on decorous behavior while waiting also varies by culture. Customer queues are a well-established aspect of British life. A **queue** is a British term for a line of people. Proper behavior is expected when lining up at bus stops, ticket, service, or checkout counters. Though lines may move slowly, obvious impatience is frowned upon. Customers who fail to stay on queue or who attempt to merge or cut into an established line risk the wrath of proper Brits.

The simple activity of getting through a checkout line quickly is a priority of most time-starved customers. Toe-tapping, finger-drumming, mouse-clicking, and multi-tasking characterize people in a hurry. Retailers respond to the need for speed in various ways. The policy of opening additional registers when more than three people are in line is practiced by some, while others offer self-checkout lanes. Retailers are also developing systems for upgraded product identification tags and radio frequency identification (RFID) scanning while items are still in the shopping cart.

Stereotyping rarely works, which is why customer research is growing in importance. Psychographic profiles may vary by country, but all provide insight on customer behavior. Lifestyle changes provide new opportunities for retailers in areas they may not have considered a decade ago.

Global Influence of American Pop Culture

Whether it's music, fashion, cell phones, or films, people around the world have different perceptions of what's hot and what's not in the United States. Americans hear a lot about changing sentiments regarding the political crosscurrents in our society and how we are viewed in other parts of

Table 4.5 Differences in Consumer Buying Habits in the United States and Emerging Markets

Consumer Behavior	United States	Asia	Latin America
Consumers enjoy shopping experience	Not as much	Yes	Yes
Shopping is more of a social occurrence	Not as much	Yes	Yes
Family is involved in shopping experience	Less	More	More
Mobility factor	More	Less	Less
Time constraint factor	More	Less	Less

the world. Global perceptions extend to our brands, products, entertainment, art, music, and the way we live—all parts of pop culture. Brands like Coca-Cola and retailers like Gap have become so well known globally that they are considered icons. Although many Chinese express an aversion to U.S. entertainment, young people in China favor American music. Similarly, while some people in India say they don't like U.S. entertainment, Bollywood's film industry, based in Mumbai, has for years mimicked Hollywood and even recently become a major investor in major U.S. film studios.

Understanding Ethnic Markets

As the size and composition of ethnic groups change, so do the needs of customers. Ethnic markets present opportunities for retailers that celebrate diversity. Those that segment their markets based on the special needs of ethnic groups are better able to serve those customers. Hispanic, Asian, African-American, and Native American groups are important ethnic markets in the United States, and buying power is growing across all of these groups.

Hispanics

Although the term *Hispanic* is used to describe a variety of Spanish-speaking peoples, care should be taken not to lump customer habits and lifestyles together. Latinos on the West Coast differ from Latinos on the East Coast, and Hispanics from Mexico differ from their counterparts from Cuba, for example. Hispanic lifestyles are unique in several ways. As a whole, Hispanic families tend to value family relationships and camaraderie within their extended families more than other ethnic groups in the United States, or the population as a whole. Dressing for church and Sunday dinner is a custom still respected by most Hispanic families, whereas it seems to be the exception to the rule in most mainstream American communities. Spanish is the first language for many Hispanics living in the United States.

The following example illustrates how some Hispanic people have adopted mainstream American values. In 1987, Tianguis was the first of nine supermarkets in California developed by the Vons Companies to service the strong Hispanic population in the greater Los Angeles area. Tianguis featured an in-house tortilleria, bilingual advertising and signage, and enough ethnic delicacies to tempt Latino as well as other palates. By 1995, the company recognized that its customers wanted value and cost savings as much as they wanted ethnic products. Tianguis became Expo, with a format more like that of a warehouse club. The change in customer sentiment was attributed to a mainstreaming of taste among Hispanic customers. Concerns about pricing also paralleled those of non-Hispanic customers. In 2007 the company was sold; the new owners subsequently restored the Latino orientation—illustrating how some retail endeavors eventually come full circle.

Florida State University researcher Felipe Korzenny believes that much of the Hispanic market is misunderstood and that Hispanics in the United States have developed new bonds with people from Latin America due to their mutual history—400 years of domination by Spain. "The less acculturated are more responsive to advertising than the more acculturated," says Korzenny, who is director of the Center for Hispanic Marketing Communication. "The more acculturated Hispanics are, [the more] they become a little bit more cynical and less attentive to advertising."[23]

Asians and African Americans

Asian-American household incomes are higher than those of other ethnic groups in the United States, including white Americans, and their buying power is significant. Gender differences surface when Asian customers are studied in Pacific Rim countries. One survey, conducted by Asia Market Intelligence, examined the grocery shopping habits of men in twelve Asian markets. Results showed that 31 percent of the decision-makers across all markets were male, compared with 10 percent in the West. The findings were attributed to the role Asian men play in the shopping experience. More men grocery shop with their families, and they make more spontaneous decisions about what goes into the shopping cart.[24]

Cultural values remain strong as Asian families emigrate to other countries, and many maintain their shopping habits long after they assimilate to another culture. Since most supermarket advertisements in the United States target female shoppers, replication of these study results in U.S. markets might suggest the need for more promotions directed toward men in areas heavily populated by Asian-Americans.

Did You Know?
Hispanic buying power exceeded $1 trillion in 2010 and is expected to reach $1.5 trillion by 2015. This represents approximately 25 percent of total annual retail sales in the United States. Hispanic shoppers account for one in six Americans.
(Source: Convenience Store News. "Hispanic Shoppers Bring Increased Buying Power as Numbers Rise," *Convenience Store News*, www.csnews.com/print-topstory-hispanic_shoppers_bring_increased_buying_power_as-numbers-rise. [Statistical sources: 2010 U.S Census Report and Publisher Packaged Facts, *Latino Shoppers: Demographic Patterns and Spending Trends Among Hispanic Americans*, 8th Edition.])

Figure 4.8
African-American women owners of retail businesses are a visible presence in their communities. Here the manager of The Brownstone hosts a group of students in Harlem.

Another study looked at the online shopping behavior of individuals in Taiwan. Results showed that male shoppers spent NT$7,000 (about US$2,100) per year compared with NT$4,000 (about US$1,200) spent by women. Favorite products also differed. Men preferred purchasing computers and consumer electronics online, while women favored cosmetics and beauty products.[25]

Different shopping behaviors are also observed in African-American markets. A research study done by a University of Tennessee scholar found that black female catalogue shoppers valued certain service attributes, products, and pricing techniques more than white women. As examples, the African-American women surveyed spent an average of 5 percent more than white women at shopping malls but expressed increased dissatisfaction with customer service in stores. As a result, many turned to catalogue shopping. African-American women purchased certain items—such as hats, dolls, and toys—more often than white women. African-American women were also more price-sensitive and spent less per year than white consumers. This may reflect the fact that fewer catalogues are directed to African Americans, and their names appear less frequently on company mailing lists. Two catalogues that target black customers are *Essence By Mail* and *J.C. Penney Fashion Influences*.[26] Results of this study indicate that the African-American market is underserved, and that it offers great potential for retailers that make the effort to understand their customers.

African Americans increasingly are opening businesses and becoming involved in the communities they serve. An example is Paulette Gay, humanitarian, merchant, and owner of the Scarf Lady Boutique in New York City's Harlem for more than 15 years. She was well known for donating scarves to cancer patients in her New York neighborhood who had lost their hair due to chemotherapy. She taught the patients how to wear them and was an inspiration to many of her customers. Ms. Gay passed away in December 2010—a victim of cancer.[27] Another Harlem retail venue is located in a historic townhouse that has been re-configured to house several boutiques and designers as featured in Figure 4.8.

Ethnic diversity within neighborhoods provides merchandising opportunities for retailers. Supermarkets routinely customize their assortments of food to suit various ethnic groups, and the food aisles in most supermarkets are packed with items that appeal not only to a single ethnicity, but to those of many others. Cultural differences in customer buying habits are apparent in large and small communities around the world. The need to discern differences in attitudes and shopping behaviors is important to retailers.

Customer Behavior Variables

Knowledge of patterns of expenditures, frequency and intensity of shopping expeditions, and different shopping situations adds to retailers' knowledge of their clientele.

Family Expenditures

People shop for certain products and services more intensely at different stages of their lives. They shop differently because of income, regardless of age or circumstance. **Engel's Laws of Family Expenditures,** a theory developed by 19th-century German statistician Ernst Engel, offers one view of how people spend their incomes on goods and services. Engel observed that:

1. As a family's income *increases,* the percentage of that income spent on food *decreases.*
2. As a family's income *increases,* the percentage of that income spent on clothing remains *roughly constant.*
3. As a family's income *increases,* the percentage of that income spent on housing and household operations remains *roughly constant.* One exception to this rule is a decrease in the proportion spent on utility payments.
4. As a family's income *increases,* the percentage of that income spent on all other goods *increases.*

In all scenarios notice that it is the *percentage* of income that is being compared—not the amount. As family income increases, the actual money spent for all goods increases. During a recession, when family income may decrease, the percentage spent on food may not change but the actual cash expenditures will. When income decreases, the percentage of money spent on clothing usually declines rather than remaining constant, as it does when income increases. During the recession that began in 2007, many individuals dropped their landline telephones in favor of lower-cost cell-phone plans. Some reduced the cost of heating oil by switching to wood or wood-pellet stoves. Interpretation of Engel's Laws keeps pace with changing economic times.

Classification of Goods and Services

Although Engel's Laws provide an understanding of the ebbs and flows of family finances, they do not indicate where, when, or in exactly what way they affect purchases. To help answer these questions, goods and services can be broken down into four categories: shopping goods, specialty goods, convenience goods, and impulse goods.

Shopping Goods

High-priced merchandise, which is usually purchased after the buyer compares the offerings of more than one retailer, falls into the category of **shopping goods**. Important major personal and household purchases comprise this category. The decision to buy is premeditated, and most items under consideration are big ticket. **Big ticket** refers to merchandise that is expensive such as cars or furniture. People usually comparison shop, seek out product information, and consult knowledgeable friends and relatives before making final decisions on these items. Purchasing furniture, a cruise, or a diamond is a shopping experience.

Specialty Goods

Buying specialty goods is referred to as destination shopping. Products bearing name brands or with special features that buyers will go out of their way to purchase are called **specialty goods**. Customers are less likely to settle for substitutes should the specific item they seek be unavailable. Possession of the merchandise desired is often more important than price. Insisting that you absolutely must have a pair of Puff Daddy's Sean John shoes or need to drive an hour for a loaf of Swedish rye bread are examples of specialty shopping. Brand and retailer preferences are strong when specialty shopping.

Convenience Goods

Low-cost items that are purchased with minimal effort or time are called **convenience goods**. Products are purchased by habit with little preplanning. Picking up bread, soda, and the latest edition of *In Style* at 7-Eleven on the way home from work, or frequenting the nearest dry cleaner are examples that fit this category.

Impulse Goods

Items that are purchased on the spur of the moment are called **impulse goods**. Purchasing a single rose at a supermarket checkout or that cool-looking graphic tee from the latest Miley Cyrus and Max Azria line in Walmart are examples. Virtually no forethought goes into an impulse purchase, but impulse does not necessarily mean low ticket. Because of the availability of credit and our hedonic needs, expensive goods also fit this category. **Hedonic needs** are emotionally based and concerned with serving the ego. Whether our budget advises it or not, purchasing clothing or even an automobile on a whim is not unheard of, nor is taking off to a distant city for the weekend. Impulse purchases are a retailer's best friend. In-store visual merchandising encourages this kind of ego gratification.

As these examples show, certain retailers regard income and life-cycle factors less and base their segmentation strategies on shopping situations and behavioral aspects of customers.

Rate of Adoption

Not all customers plan to purchase items in the same stage of the product life cycle, introduced in Chapter 1. To be the first in their social group to have an iPad tablet was important to some individuals. Others did not care if the trend ever reached their doorstep. They remained impervious to peer pressure and retail sales promotion techniques.

Adopter categories separate customers into five major types: innovators, early adopters, early majority, late majority, and laggards. Most people fit into the two majority categories. Figure 4.10 illustrates when in the product life cycle each type of customer would be most likely to make a purchase. As examples, shoppers identified as early adopters would have been the first to adopt shirtwaist-inspired designer dresses for the 2011 fall season. Laggards have probably not yet purchased a pair of skinny jeans or an Aéropostale shirt.

A special group of early adopters are dubbed "technologically advanced families" (TAFs) by one research firm. TAFs are likely to purchase newly released items such as the latest Kindle Fire or new Kobe e-reader. These customers recognize that they pay more at retail for cutting-edge products, but high prices do not deter them. They want to experience the fun and timesaving advantages of such purchases more than they want to practice deferred gratification. When prices go down, later in the product life cycle, the majority of shoppers will purchase these items. Their need for up-to-the-moment technology is not as great. According to the researchers, TAFs comprise 16.2 percent of U.S. households. They are younger and well-educated, and have high household incomes and more children than average families in the United States.[28]

Shopping Frequency

Today's customers are shopping more frequently and visiting more retail stores. During the recession, more people from all over the income spectrum shopped discount stores.

These findings have far-reaching implications. Customers have changed. They do not want to pay top dollar for household consumable products and basic apparel. Many have turned away from department stores in favor of discount stores. This tendency has helped fuel the closure of some weaker regional department store chains in the United States, and the mergers and acquisitions of others. The increase in the number of stores visited may indicate an increased competitive environment and the tendency of more customers to comparison shop.

Henkel Consumer Goods looked into the behavioral aspects of supermarket shoppers and discovered three segments that, because they were described in terms of shopping styles rather than demographics, they more accurately predicted customer behavior. Read about the Shoptimizers, Mainstreeters, and Carefrees in From the Field 4.1.

Figure 4.9
Adoption categories and their relationship to the product life cycle
Source: Adapted from Everett M. Rogers, *Diffusion of Innovations,* 3rd ed. (New York: The Free Press, 1995).

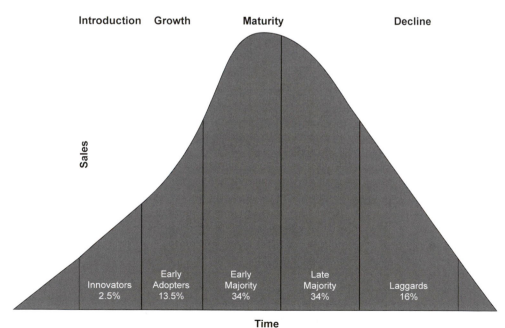

A wealth of knowledge about customer habits is available to retailers. Most large organizations employ outside market research agencies to feel the pulse of their customers. Smaller stores conduct more informal research, but are no less sensitive to the changing natures of their customers.

The Purchase Decision-Making Process

By studying the decision-making process customers go through when choosing whether or what to buy, retailers can develop strategies that lead to sales and diminish buyer's remorse. People go through the process at different speeds and may skip some steps, depending on the price or importance of the product. Different decision-making circumstances also affect the process.

Steps in the Decision-Making Process

Six steps in the decision-making process usually lead customers to purchase goods or services in the absence of any constraints, such as overpricing or poor quality.

1. *Stimulus.* The decision to buy is not unprovoked. A signal can come in a number of different ways, either from the external environment or from within. As examples, an online advertisement or e-mail notice from Amazon.com or Barnes & Noble might alert readers to a new paperback. The whiff of coffee emanating from Starbucks could very well trigger the purchase of a pound of Colombian coffee beans. A casual stop at Best Buy's Web site may act as a reminder of the entertainment unit you need for your dorm room.
2. *Problem awareness.* An unfulfilled need or want demands resolution. Your ancient Toyota finally died and you must invest in a new vehicle. This is an example of an obvious problem requiring action.
3. *Information search.* At this point, customers seek facts and figures to expedite the decision-making process. Collecting brochures, talking to opinion leaders, seeking out advertising materials, or going online to comparison shop is initiated during this stage. If you are looking for software to create your own music, you might first shop computer stores in your area to compare prices. Then you will likely go online to gather product information. You will probably talk to knowledgeable friends and fellow musicians before moving to the next stage of the decision-making process.
4. *Evaluation of alternatives.* Studying the information collected and ranking choices accordingly comprise the next phase of the process. Cost of product, ease of shopping, speed of delivery, service policies, and reputation of the company and their brands are some of the factors that may influence your decision.
5. *Purchase.* The decision is made. The scale has been tipped in favor of one particular good or service and the transaction is completed. Will that be cash, check, credit, or debit—or are you using a gift card? How about Pay-Pal?
6. *Postpurchase behavior.* The shopping experience should be satisfying. Retailers reinforce this in many ways. If the product proved inadequate, the first shopping experience will probably be the last.

More detail and nuances exist in these steps, depending on the price and complexity of the purchase. Time frames are also important in the decision-making process.

Decision-Making Time Frames

Basically, customers engage in three types of purchase decisions: (1) extended, (2) limited, and (3) routine. All three consider the degree of involvement experienced by customers and the time frame in which the steps leading up to the transaction occur.

Extended Decision Making

When a customer goes through all six steps in the process, extended decision making occurs. Usually a major purchase is involved, such as a college education or an automobile. Because of the expense and risk, a lot of information is needed to properly evaluate the alternatives. Buying a home is a complex decision and involves the extended decision-making process. About 50 percent of people do research before purchasing, and the more costly the item, the greater the likelihood this research is done. One study showed that 64 percent of individuals considering a consumer electronics purchase did research, but only 31 percent of people planning health and beauty aid purchases investigated the marketplace.[29] Figure 4.10 compares consumers' purchasing plans for a six-month period, contrasting expectations outlined in February of 2010 with those in January and February of 2011. Notice that the items listed are big ticket, requiring individuals to take more time considering the purchase.

Limited Decision Making

The main difference between the limited decision-making process and the extended process is the amount of time spent on each of the six steps. For example, if you were satisfied with your last two

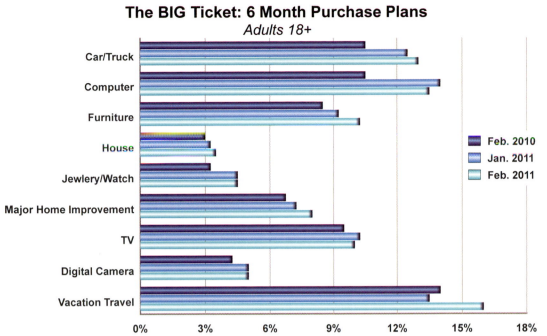

The BIG Ticket: 6 Month Purchase Plans
Adults 18+

Categories (top to bottom): Car/Truck, Computer, Furniture, House, Jewlery/Watch, Major Home Improvement, TV, Digital Camera, Vacation Travel

Legend:
- Feb. 2010
- Jan. 2011
- Feb. 2011

X-axis: 0% 3% 6% 9% 12% 15% 18%

Figure 4.10
The BIG Ticket: 6-Month Purchase Plans of Adults 18 Years of Age and Older (Source: http://.big consumerblog.worldpress.com/category/consumer-behavior-trends)

Chevy trucks and the service you received, you likely will go to the same dealer when you are in the market for a new truck. Your previous experience shortens the process of limited decision making.

Routine Decision Making

When customers buy products or services on a regular basis, routine decision making occurs. Going through the steps requires less conscious effort and customers may not shop extensively to check available alternatives. Brand recognition and shopping ease are important when making a routine purchase. Routine decision making is also affected by type of product. People do not put much effort into shopping for low-ticket items such as a loaf of bread. However, if an individual is brand-conscious, Pepperidge Farm may be the only package that is seen as the customer races through a convenience store.

Shopping Classification Relationships

The shopping category into which a product or service falls influences a customer's decision-making process. Convenience goods are generally purchased routinely, but shopping goods require extended decision making. Specialty goods are often purchased with limited decision making, but the extended process is used when the product or service is expensive or is bought for the first time. Impulse goods are purchased so spontaneously that it appears the decision-making process is almost nonexistent. It does occur, but responses to stimuli may be deep in the subconscious. Color, odors, and textures may conjure up past experiences and urge us to buy. Even hunger may affect shopping habits, something to which any famished college student—who has gorged on a huge bag of chips while waiting at a checkout counter—can attest.

Decision-making time frames are directly related to personal selling tactics, visual merchandising techniques, branding strategies, and price.

Postpurchase Implications

After parting with significant amounts of cash, many customers experience anxiety and need positive reinforcement from friends, family, and retailers. They want to feel confident that their purchase decision was a sound one.

Anxiety that occurs when people have mixed feelings or beliefs is called **cognitive dissonance.** First postulated by Leon Festinger in the late 1950s, cognitive dissonance is a concept that evolved from the field of psychology, not from the realm of marketing research. However, the concept has relevance for retailing. Postpurchase dissonance is reduced when retailers support the purchase decision. A follow-up telephone call or e-mail supporting the customer's decision, a handwritten thank-you note, or a small gift strengthens the bond with the customer and encourages repeat business. Liberal return policies and postpurchase service options also strengthen the sale. Customers want to be assured that they have made the right decision and have patronized the right retailer.

To borrow loosely from the Latin poet Virgil: a customer is a fickle and changeable thing. Customers are an unpredictable lot, but retailers must accurately interpret customer demand if they expect to sell.

Summary

Group and individual influences converge as customers attempt to satisfy their shopping needs and retailers try to anticipate them. Demographic, psychological, and social influences affect human behavior in the marketplace. Needs and wants change with age, income, education, and membership in ethnic, business, or professional groups.

Many influences affect customer behavior including age of shopper, gender differences, social class membership, and household composition

Because the market changes constantly, retailers must cultivate customer intelligence in many ways. The VALS framework from SRI and Faith Popcorn's BrainReserve trends offer contemporary views of customers' psychological traits and lifestyles, respectively. Retailing and marketing companies worldwide use these psychographic tools.

Religious beliefs, attitudes toward affluence and frugality, time constraints and pressures, pop culture, and membership in ethnic groups also affect customer behavior. As family income increases or decreases, the percentages of income spent on most discretionary products and services will vary.

Items classified as convenience goods are purchased routinely. Anything classified as specialty or shopping goods requires a more lengthy decision-making process. Impulse purchases are made at the spur of the moment and may involve low- or high-priced items.

Certain types of shoppers tend to purchase goods and services in particular stages of the product life cycle. For example, innovators were the first to purchase Amazon's Kindle e-reader when it was released in the introductory stage of the product life cycle. The customer decision-making process traces the six steps by which people recognize a stimulus, become cognizant of a need, conduct a search, become informed, evaluate alternatives, make a purchase, and receive postpurchase reinforcement.

The three types of purchasing decisions are extended, limited, and routine. Each considers the degree of involvement and time invested by customers. Retailers use a number of techniques to reduce cognitive dissonance, that is, postpurchase anxiety or buyer's remorse.

Key Terms

Aspirational wants	Lifestyle
Big ticket items	Opinion leaders
Biogenic needs	Psychogenic needs
Cognitive dissonance	Psychographics
Convenience goods	Queue
Engel's Laws of Family Expenditures	Reference groups
Hedonic needs	Self-actualization
Hierarchy of needs	Shopping goods
Impulse goods	Specialty goods

Questions for Discussion

1. What are three psychogenic needs? Locate several retail advertisements that acknowledge these needs, for in-class discussion.
2. What are reference groups? Give an example of how one of your reference groups has influenced a purchase you made.
3. Choose two demographic trends to which you can relate. How do retailers use demographic information to reach customers? Name some specific retailers that fulfill your needs and wants.
4. How is social class theory used to help retailers identify target markets? In what ways does it fail to provide adequate customer information?
5. How is family life cycle information useful to retailers? Where do you presently fit in the cycle? Is your shopping behavior similar to the examples presented in Table 4.3?
6. Which of Faith Popcorn's trends evokes your lifestyle, values, or anticipated direction? Explain how your choice relates to your shopping behavior.
7. How do religious beliefs and movements affect retailers and customers? Is this an important aspect of your culture or lifestyle? If so, how does religion affect your shopping behavior?
8. Is there a high degree of ethnic diversity in the city or town where you live, or in one you have visited? How do retailers in that area answer the needs of ethnic groups?
9. Define and differentiate among the following:
   a. Convenience goods
   b. Shopping goods
   c. Specialty goods
   d. Impulse goods
10. What are the six steps in the customer decision-making process? Using a product that you have purchased recently, trace your behavior through the six steps.
11. Have you ever experienced cognitive dissonance? How did you feel? What can retailers do to counter the negative effects of cognitive dissonance?

Endnotes

1. Elliot Ettenberg Biography. Eagles Talent Speakers Bureau ©2012 http://www.eaglestalent.com/Elliot-Ettenberg.
2. Crystal Ward Kent, "Inquiring Minds, Highlights From UNH Research," *University of New Hampshire Magazine*, Winter 2008, 12. (Source: *Imperfect Knowledge* by Michael Goldberg and Roman Frydman.)
3. James Baylor, "Motivation, Cognition, Learning: Basic Factors on Consumer Behavior," *Journal of Marketing*, January 1958.
4. Stephanie Simon, "The United States of Mind, Researchers Identify Regional Personality Traits Across America," *Wall Street Journal*, September 23, 2008, A26. (Source: *Perspectives on Psychological Science*.)
5. A.L. Gutnick, M. Robb, I. Takeuchi, and J. Kotler, *Always Connected: The New Digital Media Habits of Young Children*, (New York: The Joan Ganz Cooney Center at Sesame Workshop, 2011), 16–18.
6. NPD Group, "The European Toy Market in 2011." November, 2011. Source: NPD EPOS Retail Tracking. 5, 8. www.npd.com
7. Jack Loechner, "Generational Disparities in Internet Use," *MediaPost*, January 7, 2011, www.mediapost.com/publications/article/142164.
8. "Relative Importance of Life Choices Among Young Adults," *DMNews*, April 6, 2009, 7. (Source: Lieberman Research Worldwide on Behalf of Charles Schwab, January 2009.)
9. Melissa Campanelli, "U.S. Buyer is Changing: DMCNY," *DMNews*, May 14, 2007, 2.
10. Ellen Byron, "Seeing Store Shelves Through Senior Eyes," *Wall Street Journal*, September 14, 2009, B1, B2.
11. Cotton Incorporated, Lifestyle Monitor, "The Alpha Shopper, Men Demonstrate an Increased Confidence in Apparel Shopping," *Women's Wear Daily*, April 10, 2008, 2.
12. Cotton Incorporated. Lifestyle Monitor, "Bucking the Downward Trend: E-Savvy Sites Vital to Healthy Business," *Women's Wear Daily*, October 2, 2008, 2. (Source: Cotton Incorporated, Cotton Council International, and Synovate, 2008.)

13. Valerie Seckler, "Women Amass Clout—and Expectations," *Women's Wear Daily*, September 2, 2009, 10. (Source: "Women Want More," by Michael Silverstein and Kate Sayre, Harper Business.)

14. VALS FAQ. "What does VALS stand for?" www.stratigicbusinessinsights.com/vals/help.shtml.

15. "The VALS Segments," SRI Consulting Business Intelligence, www.sricbi.com/VALS/types.html.

16. Ibid. "VALS Fact Sheet."

17. "Lifestyle Segments Offer Prime Targets," *DMNews*, July 14, 2008, 21.

18. "Factbox: Policy on Muslim Scarves and Veils in Europe," *Reuters*, April 13, 2011, www.canada.com/story_print.html?id-4595216&sponsor=hp-storytoolbox.

19. "The WWD List, Spending Habits," *Women's Wear Daily*, March 19, 2009, 16. (Source: Unity Marketing; survey respondents were people with $250,000 annual incomes or more.)

20. Valerie Seckler, " Affluent Signal Less Lush Life Ahead," *Women's Wear Daily*, April 1, 2009, 10.

21. Sean Gregory, "How Today's Consumers Shop Differently," *Time*, February 22, 2009, 2, www.time.com/time/printout/0,8816,1881098.00.html.

22. Ellen Byron and Karen Talley, "Luxury Sales at Risk," *Wall Street Journal*. August 10, 2011, B1.

23. "Looking at Hispanic Behavior Online," *EMarketer*, June 26, 2009, www.emarketer.com/Articles/Print.aspx?1007150.

24. Louise Lee, "Men in Asia Grocery Shop, Survey Finds," *Wall Street Journal*, February 19, 1999, B5A.

25. Roger Chou, "Taiwan Online Shopping Market Estimated at NT$311 Billion," *Taiwan News*, July 15, 2009, www.etaiwannews.com/etn/print.php.

26. Allison Young, "Clothing and Catalog Usage Variables and African American Attitudes Towards Afrocentric Apparel Catalogs," American Collegiate Retailing Association Spring Conference, Toronto, Canada, May 2000.

27. Harlem World Magazine. "Home Going Service for Paulette 'Scarf Lady' Gay" January 21, 2011. http://harlemworldmag.com/2011/01/21/home-going-service-for-paulette-scarf-lady-gay/

28. Cristina Lourosa, "Understanding the User," *Wall Street Journal*, June 15, 1998, R18. (Source: Yankee Group, Boston.)

29. AMP Agency, "Inside the Buy: AMP Agency's 2011 AMPlified Research Study, 3, www.ampagency.com/wp-content/uploads/pdfs/InsideTheBuy.pdf.

Unit One: Global Retail Profile
Walmart, United States

Walmart's inviting electronics department is designed to compete with category killers like Best Buy. For many reasons, including an efficient distribution system, a proactive global strategy, and a competitive pricing model, Walmart is the number one retailer in the world.

Prologue

Selected weekends at Walmart's headquarters in Bentonville, Arkansas, a mixed group of more than a thousand executives, employees, suppliers, employment candidates, and invited guests gather for the famous Saturday morning meeting. Before being seated in the auditorium our group of guest educators was asked to report at 7:00 a.m. to clear security and to prepare for a 3-hour meeting. Headquarters is a humble but efficient building, site of the intense planning and negotiating taking place in the largest corporation in the world. A series of Waltonisms—brief quotations that convey the essence of the founder and the current corporate culture—festoon the vast auditorium. Here are a few samples:

- "Never get so set in your ways that you can't change."
- "Listen to your associates; they're our best idea generators."
- "Teach it. Preach it. Prove it."

The gathering was a combination pep rally and revival meeting with hoopla, humor, and heavy hitting of the numbers that spell profits and progress for the company. H. Lee Scott, chief executive officer (CEO) at the time, welcomed everyone, and asked one of his team to give the Walmart cheer. It was delivered with passion and centered on the slogan "It's about the customer, always." Scott called upon key executives to report on the status of international sales, domestic business, human resources, sustainability initiatives, and trends. Here is a smattering of what we heard and saw as a giant map of the world displayed on stage came to life:

- "Walmex net profit up 27 percent."
- "Sixty-two million dozen eggs were sold during the pre-Easter 4-day sales period."
- "Sam's in Shenzhen will be the best in the world."

Scott introduced several guests in the audience and when he came to our group, ventured over to where we were sitting, chatted with us informally, and, over the next 15 minutes asked if we had any questions for him. We were in the presence of one of the most charismatic leaders in the business world, and we, too, were impressed. The meeting adjourned after the Walmart Choir sang an uplifting selection as well as the Walmart song.[1] It seems only fitting that the highest revenue earning retailer and largest private employer in the world is the subject of the first company profile.

Background and Distinguishing Characteristics

Walmart, which operates over 10,000 stores in 27 countries, had sales of over $443 billion in the fiscal year ending January 31, 2012.[2] In its home market and abroad, the company is aggressive and innovative, always looking for the next competitive advantage. It never rests on past triumphs and faces change with alacrity. Walmart's strengths in operations, merchandising, distribution, and information technology are legendary. Identifying how this industry leader began trading, and the principles upon which it operates should help you understand the impact of its current global position.

Founded in 1962 in Rogers, Arkansas, by flamboyant Sam Walton, the discounter advanced rapidly despite the fact that its full presence in the United States was not realized until it expanded coast-to-coast in the 1990s. Key reasons for Walmart's lofty position and some of its distinguishing characteristics are listed here:

- Merchandise is sourced domestically and internationally very efficiently and at lowest possible cost.
- Relationships with vendors large and small are important and tightly controlled.
- State-of-the-art distribution systems designed to handle logistics, communications, and information technology are impressive.
- It pioneered the practice of bringing service with a smile to discounting.
- Worldwide employment now tops 2.2 million associates.
- All levels of the organization are involved in decision making.
- Location strategy has been nonconformist compared with that of other retailers.
- Environmental issues, social responsibility, and concern for customers are high priorities.

The last point has generated considerable publicity. In 2005 Walmart opened experimental stores that illustrate its commitment to using sustainable resources in the construction and maintenance of its stores and warehouses. A prototype superstore in Rogers, Arkansas, installed photovoltaic panels on the roof to generate solar power and also added many skylights so that during daylight hours, natural sunlight could illuminate the store interior. Saving energy, conserving natural resources, and reducing waste and pollution are foremost environmental objectives.

Walmart announced in 2012 that it reuses more than 80 percent of the waste produced in stores and other company buildings in the United States. That figure is up from 64 percent in 2007.[3]

On a customer-centric note, Walmart welcomes tourists arriving at its stores in their RVs and encourages them to spend a night in the parking lot. In some locations Walmart greeters have knocked on doors to let travelers know that the store is open and coffee is brewing. In others, welcoming notes are placed under windshield wipers.[4] These traveling customers who come from every corner of North America are sometimes called "boondockers"—in a friendly way, of course.

Walmart was long an advocate of the large-frog-small-pond theory in terms of its location strategy. Stores were located in Familyville, USA—smaller cities and towns located on the fringes of metropolitan areas. The company saturated each regional market before moving into a new territory so as not to tax its delivery and stock replenishment systems. But as times changed so have selling formats, expansion plans, and strategic direction.

Store Formats and Sales

Walmart operates several store formats in the United States. As of January 31, 2012 these units included:

- 3,029 supercenters
- 629 discount stores
- 611 Sam's Clubs
- 196 Neighborhood Markets, including Amigo and Supermercado
- 14 small formats, including Walmart Express, Super Ahorros, and one Walmart on Campus[5] (University of Arkansas)

Walmart operates online stores in the United States, United Kingdom, Canada, Brazil, and Japan. The International division has over 1,000 more stores than Walmart U.S.A. and accounts for 29 percent of total company sales.[6]

Evolution of Strategies

Departing from its original location strategies, the company gradually opened stores in highly populated urban areas. Walmart opened its first inner-city store on the outskirts of Los Angeles in 1998, followed by a store in the middle of that city in 2001. The latter is located in a three-story building that previously housed a Macy's department store.[7] A first store for New York City has long been in the planning stages. Once Walmart achieved its goal of dominating rural markets, it looked to alternative sites for continued growth.

Walmart test-marketed smaller supermarkets in Bentonville in 1998. Neighborhood Markets are less than half the size of customary 100,000-square-foot supermarkets; feature drugstores, seasonal merchandise, food, and groceries; and carry approximately 20,000 different items compared to 100,000 items in a supercenter. Store designs are more personalized to the locales in which they operate.[8] More convenience for the customer was the principal reason for introducing the format, and saturation of the market was another. Finding a niche between convenience stores and its own superstores was the company's objective.

Walmart's early online selling efforts were considered lackluster by many industry experts. Customers have experienced several reincarnations since the company launched its Web site in 2000. The original goals of the Web site were to communicate product information, expand customer relationships, and heighten awareness of Walmart. Since then the company has revamped its Web site several times, changing its presentation of merchandise radically with each revamp. As the company improves its Web presence, it is counting on online success in both its international and U.S. markets.

Today the Web site serves as a selling companion to the company's stores, with merchandise and services equally important in both formats. Walmart is the sixth largest online retailer, with estimated sales of $4.9 billion in 2011.[9] The company is confident that sales will grow as more customers worldwide are introduced to the everyday-low-pricing and shopping convenience offered online, and predicts its e-commerce sales in China will reach $300 billion by 2016.[10]

Walmart received kudos for its mobile commerce initiatives and was ranked fourth in *Internet Retailer's* "2012 Mobile Commerce Top 300 Guide." Sales that year were close to $128 million, a 178 percent increase over the previous year.[11]

In 2011 Walmart launched its "Pick Up Today" program, which encourages customers to order online from among 40,000 different products and pick up their items—excluding food—at their closest Walmart store in about 4 hours.[12] Perhaps they'll remain in the store and shop for awhile, too.

International Operations

Saturation of the U.S. market coupled with increased competition stateside are two reasons for Walmart's aggressive international expansion. Available capital and forward-thinking company executives solidified the company's global thrust. As of early 2012, Walmart owned 5,651 stores internationally. Some of the countries in Walmart's portfolio and their store count in order of most to least follow:

- Mexico—2,088
- United Kingdom—541
- Central America—622
- Brazil—512
- Japan—419
- China—370
- Africa—347
- Canada—333
- Chile—316
- India—15[13]

In the course of its expansion, Walmart has had to respond to many operational challenges and adapt to differences in customer behavior in several countries. The following examples illustrate the challenges faced by the company as it entered new markets:

- **Mexico**—Walmart first became an international retailer when it opened a discount store in Mexico City in 1991. A decade later, Sam's Club began a joint venture with Cifra SA, a supermarket, convenience store, and general merchandise retailer. Despite the devaluation of the peso, general economic unrest, challenging bureaucracies, and NAFTA implementation issues, Walmex—as it is often called—is a front-runner in the retail sector. The company purchased controlling shares of Cifra in 1998, increasing its ownership stake in the Mexican venture.[14] Another hurdle confronted Walmart when Walmex officials were accused of allegedly bribing a government administrator so that permits for store construction could be hastened. The Mexico attorney general began an investigation into the matter, although no complaint had been made against Walmex as of April 2012.[15]

- **United Kingdom**—Competitive retailing in the United Kingdom accelerated when Walmart purchased the Asda Group in 1999. At the time, Tesco, J. Sainsbury, Safeway, and Asda dominated British food retailing. Asda operated on a pricing strategy similar to Walmart's, and also employed customer greeters—an idea copied from Walmart.[16] The move has been a profitable one for Walmart and serves as a model of a successful acquisition strategy. In 2011 Walmart acquired 147 Netto stores in the United Kingdom from Dansk Supermarket. Most of these stores now bear the Asda name, as Walmart continues to build that brand.[17]

- **Brazil**—Walmart entered the market in São Paulo, Brazil with an abbreviated Sam's Club format in 1995. The company initially owned 60 percent of the operation; Lojas Americanas, Brazil's largest discount chain, owned the remainder. The operation faced intense competition and price wars from Carrefour and local retailer Pão de Açúcar. In 2001 the first Todo Dia store and a distribution center outside São Paulo opened. Todo Dia means *everyday* in Portuguese.[18] In 2011 Walmart Brazil infused more than $750 million into the company to build 80 new stores and renovate others.[19]

- **Japan**—In 2002, Walmart bought a small stake in the Seiyu supermarket chain, gradually increasing its ownership to 95.1 percent in 2007.[20] The company utilized lessons learned from a failed joint venture with Ito-Yokado in the mid-1990s and benefited from growing positive reactions from consumers toward discounters during Japan's prolonged recession.[21]

- **China**—In 1996 Walmart operated three Value Clubs in China in joint venture with a Hong Kong subsidiary of Bangkok-based C.P. Pokphard Company. The partnership ended 3 years later. The stores were not high performers for the company, but the experience served as a springboard to future expansion in China. The first Sam's Club opened in Shenzhen, China in 1996, followed by several more units.[22] In 2009 Walmart opened three Smart Choice convenience stores in Shenzhen, Guandong province, and closed them in 2012.[23] As this chronology emphasizes, Walmart had the foresight to wait for the standard of living to rise there and in other Asian countries and to recognize that not every acquisition is a keeper.

- **South Africa**—After a long and intense negotiation, the South African government paved the way for Walmart to enter the retail community in that country in 2011. Approval to merge with Massmart Holdings, Ltd. hinged on Walmart's acquisition of an initial 51 percent stake in the African company and adherence to several conditions, including keeping management and staff in place, respecting union agreements for 3 years, and providing a supply-train training program for local industries.[24] A price of $2.5 billion was agreed to in 2011, but as of January 2012 allocation of the purchase price to the fair value of assets and liabilities was still provisional.[25]

- **Canada**—Walmart entered the Canadian market in 1994 with its acquisition of 122 Woolco stores, purchased from Woolworth, Canada, Inc.[26] The company holds a significant share of the Canadian discount market. Canadian customers were not familiar with pricing strategies practiced by Walmart in its stateside stores and needed to be educated. It took several years to accomplish this and bring the stores to profitability.

- **Chile**—When Walmart acquired Chile's largest retail chain, Distribución y Servicia (D&S), in 2009, the arrangement included the provision that managers, workers, and store brands remain in their positions in the 250-plus stores. Despite the global economic downturn, Chile generally is regarded as a healthy investment climate. Ironically Carrefour, one of Walmart's biggest competitors worldwide, sold its stores to D&S when the French retailer pulled out of Chile.[27]

- **Germany**—Not all international ventures have proved fruitful for Walmart. When it acquired German retailer Wertkauf in 1998, the company departed from its customary joint venture entry strategy. Wertkauf operated 21 hypermarkets and gave Walmart its introduction to retailing in Europe. The following year, 74 Interspar stores were acquired from Metro AG, the major German retailer. The process of merging Interspar and Wertkauf offices, revitalizing stores, and extending its distribution system did not go smoothly.[28] In a strange twist of fate, Walmart sold the operation back to Metro in 2007, having concluded that the venture was not profitable. Walmart realized that customer expectations were different in Germany than in the United States and has subsequently adopted a conservative stance. The company has not ventured into Germany since. Walmart was still dealing with the financial fallout when it received a $1 billion tax benefit in 2011, followed by a $67 million dollar charge for tax and interest expenses in 2012 related to the termination of the German operation.[29] Sometimes volatile and complex, international dealings are simply business as usual for Walmart.

Walmart U.S.A.

Because of its size, healthy cash position, formidable expertise, and diversified formats and global position, Walmart weathered the recession better than most retailers. It experienced slower growth, made human resource cuts at headquarters, brought in third-party workers, took on new trading partners, adapted its pricing strategy, restructured its operations, and chose a new CEO—to name only a few changes that were made during the economic crisis. Identifying a few of the tactics implemented by Walmart lends another dimension of respect for the company and it innovative yet homegrown spirit.

- In early 2010, with a goal of increasing sales, the company reorganized its U.S. operations into three regional divisions in order to give more decision-making power to regional executives. The more autonomous structure is much like that of Walmart's international division. Functional areas, including real estate, store operations, and logistics, were combined into one unit, as was store planning and customer experience. In implementing the plan, Walmart laid off 300 of its 12,000 employees at headquarters; it was expected that up to 3,000 more layoffs would follow.[30]
- Concurrently, Sam's Club cut 11,000 positions—10,000 of which were part-time product demonstrators in the warehouse club division. In-store demonstrations and the handing out of samples have been outsourced to an independent marketing firm to help improve profit margins and differentiate the warehouse club from Costco Warehouse, its biggest rival.[31]
- Facing slow growth, the company proposed a host of measures meant to improve sluggish sales. One was in the area of private label development. Private label products comprise a growing percentage of goods in all grocery stores. By expanding its private label products Walmart hopes to keep the postrecession business of middle-class consumers who had adjusted their shopping habits by embracing these lower priced goods during the economic downturn.
- At the merchandise sourcing and procurement level, the industry giant has also made major changes. An agreement with Hong Kong manufacturer Li & Fung stipulated that Walmart target an initial $2 billion of its $300 billion product budget to the firm, which is one of the largest in the world. Cost reduction and improved quality are two of the major reasons for the move.[32]
- Twenty-four of Walmart's 371 stores and 43 deli outlets were damaged by the earthquake and tsunami in Japan in March 2011. Most belonged to its Seiyu chain, including two which were inundated with mud. Most were up and running within hours, ready and able to supply free bottled water and noodles to those in need. According to Scott Price, president and CEO of Walmart Asia, the company's valuable experiences dealing with disasters, including earthquakes in Chile and hurricanes in the United States, made it possible to activate Walmart's emergency operations center in Bentonville within minutes of the disaster in Japan.[33]

- After years of court battles beginning in 2001, a gender discrimination suit against Walmart was closed by the U.S. Supreme Court. The dispute was a class action presented on behalf of the estimated 1.5 million women employed by the company since 1998. Although the Supreme Court ruled that the number was too large to constitute a viable class and that commonality between women was hard to determine, court battles continue at the circuit and district level in California and Texas, respectively. In early 2012 Walmart filed Motions to Dismiss in both courts; only time will tell the ultimate disposition of these cases.[34]
- Competing with grocery chains like Kroger and Safeway, Walmart is ready to build its first Neighborhood Market in Los Angeles in 2012. Located on the outskirts of Chinatown, the 33,000-square-foot store is on the first floor of a senior housing complex. Although detractors have argued that the giant retailer would take business from small local retailers and perpetuate a cycle of poverty in the neighborhood by offering low-paying jobs, Walmart believes that its presence will encourage economic growth in the area and that its wages and benefits are competitive.[35] Sales of food and grocery products comprise about half of Walmart's revenue.

Sam Walton was a colorful and compelling figure, and retail analysts questioned whether the company would thrive after his death in 1992. More recently, some wondered how the planned succession of Mike Duke to the position of CEO would progress after the retirement of charismatic leader H. Lee Scott, who served from 2000 to 2009. Prognosticators will continue to monitor the strategies of the world's most successful retailer. Meanwhile, Walton's legacy will live on, and Walmart's mission and quest for dominance of the world retail market will continue unabated. And what is Walmart's mission statement? "We save people money so they can live better."[36]

Profile Discussion Questions
1. What tactics is Walmart using to maintain its position as the world's largest retail company?
2. What gives Walmart a competitive advantage? Utilizing situation analysis, examine the strengths and weaknesses of the company.
3. What are the main reasons Walmart decided to open stores outside the United States? How important to total company revenue is the international division?
4. When is it more advantageous for Walmart to purchase or merge with an existing retail company in another country rather than open new stores?
5. What kinds of challenges does Walmart face when it opens stores outside the United States? Of the countries mentioned in the profile, which do you believe holds the most opportunity for Walmart?
6. Walmart reached its goal of more than $443 billion in sales in 2012 despite the global recession. What were the main reasons for its success?

Profile Notes

1. Walmart Presentation. Corporate Headquarters. Bentonville, Arkansas, American Collegiate Spring Conference and Study Tour, April 8, 2006.
2. Walmart Stores. Bentonville, AR. Investor Relations. Financial News Release. "Walmart Releases 2012 Annual Shareholders' Meeting Materials. April 16, 2012. http:investors.walmartstores.com/phoenix.zhtml?c=112761&p-irol-newsArticle_pf&ID=
3. Stephanie Clifford. Unexpected Ally Helps Walmart Cut Waste." New York Times. April 13, 2012. www.nytimes.com/2012/04/14/business/wal-mart-and-environmental-fund-team-up-to-cut-waste/
4. Julie Cart. "Finding Shelter on the Open Road," Boston Globe, March 15, 2001, A2.
5. Walmart Stores. Walmart 2012 Annual Report, "Unit Count and Square Footage." Fourth Quarter, Fiscal Year 2012. http://walmartstores.com/sites/annual-report/2012/WalMart_AR.pdf.
6. Ibid. Extrapolated from: "To Our Shareholders, Associates and Customers." 3.
7. David Moin. "Walmart Set to Open Its First LA Store," Women's Wear Daily, February 14, 2000, 2,16.
8. Walmart Presentation. Walmart Neighborhood Market, Rogers, Arkansas, American Collegiate Spring Conference and Study Tour, April 7, 2006.
9. Internet Retailer. "Wal-Mart Puts E-commerce Growth Among its Top Priorities." April 17, 2012. www.top500Guide.com/wal-mart-puts=e-commerce-growth-among-its-top-priorities/

10. Sharon Edelson. "Wal-Mart's Mea Culpa on Apparel." *Women's Wear Daily.* June 6, 2011.

11. *Internet Retailer.* Email newsletter. "Mobile Commerce Top 300: Here Are This Year's Leaders in M-Commerce." November 8, 2012. Source: *2012 Mobile Commerce Top 300 Guide.* http://webmail.earthlink .net/wam/msg.jsp?msgrid=1937&x=1887642373.

12. Stephanie Clifford. "Wal-Mart Has a Web Plan to Bolster In-Store Sales." *New York Times.* March 10, 2011. www.nytimes.com/2011/03/11/business/11shop.html

13. Walmart Stores. "Data Sheet-Worldwide Unit Details," January 2, 2012. http://walmartstores.com/ Pressroom/news/10812.aspx.

14. www.walmartstores.com Annual Report 2009

15. David Luhnow and Anthony Harrup. "Mexico Attorney General Probes Bribery Allegations." *Wall Street Journal.* Corporate Watch. April 27, 2012. B5.

16. Emily Nelson and Ernest Beck. "Walmart Seeks UK Supermarket Firm," *Wall Street Journal,* June 15, 1999, A 3–4.

17. www.walmartstores.com Annual Report 2009

18. Miriam Jordan. "Walmart Gets Aggressive About Brazil," *Wall Street Journal,* May 25, 2001, A8,12.

19. Kantar Retail IQ. "Walmart Brazil to Invest USD 755 Million in 2011." May 4, 2011. www.kantarretailiq .com/ContentIndex/NewsDisplayLW.aspx?id=332718.

20. Walmart Corporate. "History Timeline," 2006 and 2007, 4. http://walmartstores.com/PrintContent.sapx? id=7603

21. Yumiko Ono and Ann Zimmerman. "Walmart Enters Japan with Seiyu Stake," *Wall Street Journal.* March 15, 2002, B5.

22. *Wall Street Journal.* "Retailer Expects to Open Six New Stores in China," June 4, 1998, B10.

23. Kantar Retail IQ. "Walmart Shuts Smart Choice." February 27, 2012. www.kantarretailiq.com/Content Index/NewsdisplayLW.aspx?id=467071.

24. Devon Maylie. "Wal-Mart Gets Nod in Africa." *Wall Street Journal.* June 1, 2011, B9.

25. Walmart Stores. *Walmart 2012 Annual Report,* "Notes to Consolidated Financial Statements." Number 14 Acquisitions, Investments and Disposals. 51. http://walmartstores.com/sites/annual-report/2012/ WalMart_AR.pdf.

26. Walmart Stores. "History Timeline," 1994, 3. http://walmartstores.com/PrintContent.sapx?id=7603.

27. Miguel Bustillo. "Walmart Offers to Acquire Chile's Largest Grocery Chain," *Wall Street Journal,* December 22, 2008, B3.

28. Mike Troy. "Walmart Goes Shopping for Next Acquisition," *Discount Store News,* June 7, 1999, 90,127.

29. Walmart Stores. *Walmart 2012 Annual Report,* "Notes to Consolidated Financial Statements." 51. http:// walmartstores.com/sites/annual-report/2012/WalMart_AR.pdf.

30. Sharon Edelson and Evan Clark. "Big Walmart Changes: Inks $2B Li & Fung Deal, Shakes Up U.S. Stores," *Women's Wear Daily,* January 29, 2010, 1, 11.

31. Stephanie Simon. "Walmart's Sam's Club Farms Out 10,000 Jobs," *Wall Street Journal,* January 25, 2010, B1.

32. Edelson and Clark, 11.

33. Reuters. "Wal-Mart to Reopen 12 Quake-hit Stores in Japan." March 28, 2011. www.reuters.com/assets/ print?aid_USTRE72R07320110328

34. Walmart Stores. *Walmart 2012 Annual Report,* "Notes to Consolidated Financial Statements." Number 11 Legal Proceedings. 49–50. http://walmartstores.com/sites/annual-report/2012/WalMart_AR.pdf.

35. Reuters. Business and Financial News. "Wal-Mart Inks Deal for First L.A. Neighborhood Market." February 24, 2012. www.reuters.com/assets/Print?aid=USTRE81o03J20120225.

36. Walmart Stores. Investor relations. "Frequently Asked Questions." http://investors/walmartstores.com/ phoenix.zhtml?c=11276&p=irolfaq_pf.

Unit Two

Retail Structures and Multichannel Strategies

The retail industry is in a state of flux. As you begin Unit Two you already are aware of major changes in the global business environment. Retailers that did not exist a decade ago are now commonplace; those that supposedly withstood the test of time are no longer with us. A stroll through any U.S. shopping mall or downtown area confirms this fact. Gone are Linens 'n Things and Circuit City; here today are Apple and Zara. Embracing these burgeoning elements of change and devising new strategies to manage unprecedented turmoil in the economy, society, and in the retail industry are mandated.

Most large retailers sell through more than one channel and do so globally. Forming new ventures, selecting business partners, and adapting brand strategies are some of the transformations occurring worldwide. Woolworth's, once a well-known "5-and-10-cent" variety store, closed its doors in the United States in the 1980s, but the brand found a second life internationally. Woolworth's Group plc closed more than 800 stores in the United Kingdom in 2009 and was soon reincarnated as www.wool worths.co.uk. Their new owner, Shop Direct Group Ltd., a catalogue and online company, set up the Web site that sells toys, children's wear, and candy.[1] The German store division also ceased operations in 2009; however, Woolworth's Ltd. of Australia continues to serve that country and

New Zealand. The latest upturn has Lowe's partnering with Woolworths in Australia to create Masters, a giant home improvement chain that you will read more about in Chapter 8.[2]

Characteristics, strengths, and challenges of brick-and-mortar retailers are addressed in Chapter 5. Strategic initiatives are echoed in many examples. Chapters 6 and 7 highlight direct marketers and electronic retailers, respectively. The online option has added new dimensions to multichannel retailing as catalogues and direct sellers jostle for their share of retail sales via the Web. Mobile commerce combines customer convenience, smartphone technology, and the unbridled power of the Internet. To further augment retail options, most multichannel companies also have a global presence; most global retailers, the focus of Chapter 8, also are multichannel retailers.

Multichannel retailing has evolved far beyond simply being an attractive tactic for companies to contemplate. Cross-channel synergies enable a retailer to operate more efficiently and profitably. In some cases each channel develops its own stamp of identity as retailers compete domestically and globally.

Endnotes
1. Lilly Vitorovich. "Woolworths Sees Rebirth Online." *Wall Street Journal.* June 26, 2009: B6.
2. *Financial Times.* "Lowe's Enters Joint Venture to Develop Home Improvement Stores in Australia." August 24, 2009. www.ft.com/intl/cms/c392db7e-916a-11de-879d-00144feabdc0.pdf.

Chapter 5

Brick-and-Mortar Retailing

Learning Objectives

After completing this chapter you should be able to:

- Describe key characteristics of retail stores, including size, physical facilities, target market, merchandise, image, pricing, and operational considerations.
- Contrast department, specialty, and discount stores.
- Examine several kinds of food retailing.
- Identify major players and trends in brick-and-mortar retailing across all categories.
- Review the strengths of brick-and-mortar retailing, and consider their impact on multichannel retailing.

Figure 5.1
Macy's department store has a strong presence at Victoria Gardens, a lifestyle center in Rancho Cucamonga, California.

Every retail store has its own distinct form and personality, but the same or similar functions are performed in each. The six universal functions of all retail businesses—merchandising, operations, promotion, finance, human resource management, and information technology—were introduced in Chapter 1. Because of similarities in organization, product orientation, and customer focus, retailers are classified into a few major types. In this chapter we consider classic brick-and-mortar stores that have walls and roofs.

Brick-and-mortar stores are broadly categorized as department stores, specialty stores, discount retailers, and food retailers. For each kind of store, typical characteristics—including size, target market, merchandise, image, pricing policy, turnover, and gross margin—are considered. Tracking how fast merchandise sells, and how much it costs a company to sell goods, are aspects commonly discussed by comparing turnover and gross margin. **Turnover** is the number of times inventory is sold and replenished in a year. It is also referred to as turn or stock turn. Gross margin was defined in Chapter 3. Where appropriate, characteristics such as organizational structure, site selection policies, and operational procedures are included in the sections that follow. Let's investigate the many facets of department stores, specialty stores, discounters, and food retailers.

Department Stores

Department stores, introduced in Chapter 1, are large-scale operations that carry broad assortments of goods and offer depth in most merchandise classifications and a wide variety of services. From an organizational standpoint, each department is operated as a separate unit, and merchandise is grouped according to similarity. Department stores differentiate themselves in several ways, although all carry national and private-label brands and operate stores large enough to be shopping-center anchors. Most department stores operate on turns of four to five annually. In this section, we begin by identifying key characteristics of the genre, and then look at problems facing department stores.

Department stores are described in terms of the markets they serve: value-driven, mid-market, and luxury. Target markets for all three types are derived from demographic, lifestyle, and psychographic criteria. Pricing strategies are designed to meet the needs of customers and fulfill the financial goals of retailers. Physical facilities vary along with operational tactics and the countries in which they operate.

Types of Department Stores

Using gross margin, image, price, and consumer orientation, we can identify several differences among the three categories of department stores.

- **Value-driven department stores** operate on lower gross margins, provide modest but pleasant facilities, and offer lower prices to budget-conscious consumers.
- **Mid-market department stores** operate on higher gross margins, provide more impressive facilities, and offer moderate prices to middle-class consumers.
- **Luxury department stores** operate on high gross margins, provide opulent facilities, and offer high prices to high-income customers who are more fashion-forward.

Merchandise quality, price, and target markets for value-driven department stores like JCPenney and Sears vary significantly when compared with mid-market department stores like Macy's and Dillard's and luxury department store retailers like Nordstrom and Saks Fifth Avenue. Macy's, featured in Figure 5.1, anchors a central portion of the Victoria Gardens lifestyle center located in Rancho Cucamonga, California. Sears and JCPenney are in the same center, but are on the outside edge of the development. Since there are no luxury department store or specialty store tenants at Victorian Gardens, we can presume that Macy's serves as the prime department store for this upper-mid-market shopping center.

Organizational and Operational Differences

Department stores are the showplaces of retailing. Whether located downtown, in shopping centers, or in freestanding locations, most have multiple floors on which to display their wares. They usually feature main stores and many branches, some in geographically dispersed locations. The buying and selling functions are designed for maximum efficiency.

Flagship and Multiunit Stores

Flagship stores are generally larger and have more character than other units of a department store company. A **flagship store** is the main store in a retail group, usually located in a city and often on the site of the original store. Suburban stores may be somewhat smaller and frequently more contemporary in design. As more accoutrements are added to new locations and renovated sites, many satellite stores seem as embellished as their flagships.

The flagship store or a corporate-headquarters building is the hub of merchandising, promotional, operational, financial planning, and information technology activity. The functions are the same in large multiunit department stores and smaller single-unit department stores. A department store organization consisting of a flagship store and two or more stores is considered a **multiunit department store**. The difference is that in large, multiunit organizations, a team of specialists performs each function. In smaller, family-owned department stores, fewer people perform multiple functions.

Separation of Buying and Selling Functions

More complex retail systems necessitate the separation of buying and selling. Buyers purchase merchandise for the entire company and work closely with vendors, store managers, and department sales managers, who are responsible for selling. This method allows economies of scale to be realized and makes for a more efficient and profitable organization. Because merchandise floor space is so valuable, most large retailers have moved their buying staffs to corporate headquarters or other locations off the store premises.

Comparative Target Market and Pricing Strategies

Department stores provide merchandise for consumers from newborns to centenarians, but that does not mean their target markets are defined as broadly. Demographics, especially age, income, and ethnic background, play a large role. Geographic locations and customer lifestyles are also important. A closer look at two major retailers, Bloomingdale's and JCPenney, illustrates the differences in the markets they serve and how they differ from limited-line department stores.

Bloomingdale's   The primary target market for Bloomingdale's New York City flagship store is women of about 50 years old. The average household income for Bloomie's shoppers is over $100,000. Price points on merchandise are higher than one would expect in a less cosmopolitan area, where the taste level is not as rarefied. These factors combine to influence merchandise and service choices made by this luxury retailer. Bloomingdale's is a division of Macy's.

Its newer SoHo store on Broadway was designed for a more youthful market. Bloomingdale's expects to open several more of the SoHo concept stores in Phoenix, Santa Monica, and the Georgetown section of Washington, D.C. The SoHo-type stores average 80,000 to 90,000 square feet compared with about 200,000 square feet for a full-size Bloomingdale's.[1]

The company opened its first two international stores in Dubai in early 2010. The units are licensed to Al Tayer Group LLC, a leading luxury retailer and distributor. Both stores—one for men's and women's apparel and accessories, and one for home goods— are in the Dubai Mall.[2]

JCPenney   Directing its merchandising efforts to a middle-class market, JCPenney finds its customers want name brands and fashion as much as their Bloomingdale's counterparts, but their average household income is significantly lower. Prices at JCPenney are thereby lower, and merchandise selections are made for less urbane customers.

A closer look at JCPenney alerts us to image shifts that have been successfully executed. JCPenney was known as a general merchandise chain until the mid-1980s, when the company repositioned itself and adopted a department-store image. The company's new value-driven concepts and top-notch online store may change customer perceptions once again. By adding in-store Sephora shops and a plethora of new private-label brands, Penney's is well poised to capture a younger market. Its first store in New York City opened in 2009 and was designed to compete with Macy's flagship store.

JCPenney is a high-volume department store in the United States, and a significant catalogue and online retailer. The company operates stores only in the United States and Puerto Rico and is listed at #22 in *Stores*' 2011 top-100 list of U.S. retailers.[3] Competition comes from other department stores, specialty stores, and discounters like Target.

Limited-Line Department Stores   Target markets of limited-line stores—such as Nordstrom and Neiman Marcus in the United States and Holt Renfrew in Canada, as well as Saks Fifth Avenue and Lord & Taylor—are more narrowly defined and price levels typically are higher than those in full-line department stores. Limited-line department stores are steeped in first-class contemporary fixtures and sumptuous décor. Aisles are wide and everywhere the focus is on the apex of fashion

Did You Know?
Bloomingdale's received a royal welcome when it opened its first international stores—one for fashion and one for home goods—at the Dubai Mall. Cutting the ceremonial ribbon was His Highness Sheikh Mansour bin Mohhammed bin Rashid Al Maktoum, son of Dubai's ruler. The vast Dubai Mall is adjacent to the Burj Khalifa, the tallest building in the world.
Source: Ritu Upadhyay, "Bloomingdale's Dubai Bash," *Women's Wear Daily*, February 2, 2010, 3.

Figure 5.2
Saks Fifth Avenue offers spacious store layout, opulent décor, and select merchandise lines befitting an upscale retailer.

brands and top-of-the-line cosmetics. Customer service usually exceeds expectations. For these reasons these companies are considered luxury retailers. Saks Fifth Avenue's interior is illustrated in Figure 5.2.

Global Examples: The Grand Magasins

In addition to the many fine U.S. department stores described in this section, awe-inspiring department stores exist worldwide. Department stores of this stature are called *grand magasins*, derived from the French word for storehouse. A few examples from Asia and Europe highlight their structures and their draw:

- Japanese department stores like Takashimaya and Isetan are famous for their lavish surroundings and extensive services. It is not unusual to have four or five sales associates help complete a sale with total finesse.
- Many department stores in Europe operate in buildings of historical significance. Magazin du Nord's flagship is an impressive Beaux-Arts building in Copenhagen, Denmark.
- Selfridges commands a full block on Oxford Street, one of the busiest shopping streets in London. In the past decade, an extensive renovation, along with highly creative services and promotions, heralded the company's shift toward an upwardly mobile, hip, young, and professional market. Combining sculpture and contemporary artwork with rare but highly sought luxury products, Selfridges' Wonder Room is designed for customers seeking a rare backgammon set, exclusive Hermes' Birkin handbag, or Rolex watch. Customers have the option of shopping in private rooms within the collection of boutiques and exquisite showcases.[4]
- Harrods in London is impressive with its one million square feet of selling space. The building is protected by a historical preservation order. Even if Harrods wanted to change its architectural features, including the mosaic ceiling on one of its seven food halls, it could not, under British law.

Figure 5.3
The Printemps flagship store is located near Galeries Lafayette on Boulevard Haussmann, a major shopping street in Paris.

- Two of France's leading department stores are Galeries Lafayette and Printemps. Printemps is known for its Art Nouveau building and in 2008 undertook a $50 million four-year renovation project. The top 10 percent of Printemps' customers spend on average $2,000 per month.[5] During the summer sale period both retailers advertise with huge outdoor signs, as illustrated in Figure 5.3. Galeries Lafayette is shown in Figure 17.1.

All retailers, whether domestic or international, are influenced by changes that emanate from multiple sectors. We'll look next at some of the pressures that confront the department store sector.

Department Store Challenges

Over time, a series of social changes, performance pressures, economic concerns, and perhaps poor decisions changed the nature of department store retailing. The number of major department store companies declined in the United States for many reasons, including economic recession, shifts in the competitive environment, the influence of the "sameness syndrome," and industry consolidation. Department stores in other countries relate similar obstacles and opportunities. A deeper look into each of these aspects will help clarify this complex issue.

Influence of Economic Recession

Department stores' share of total retail sales had been slipping since the 1980s. During the height of the recession that began in 2007, department stores reported significant declines each month between April 2008 and February 2009.[6] Hardest-hit were the upmarket, limited-line department stores including Saks Fifth Avenue and Nordstrom that had previously been relatively immune to steep declines. For much of this time, declines were in the double digits, showing that customers were shopping only for necessities, following sales closely, or not shopping at all.

Incremental Shifts in the Competitive Environment

Three areas of change that have led to problems for department stores are major shifts in merchandise focus, customer demands for value at lower prices, and competition from other retail sectors. Such problems did not arise overnight but were the product of 30 or more years of change and challenge.

Changes in Merchandise Focus   Determined to survive, some department stores concentrated on higher-margin apparel and dropped merchandise such as furniture, major appliances, home electronics, music, and sporting goods. Restaurants were scaled down or discontinued in many department stores. These decisions left retailers vulnerable because they were no longer providing the full range of merchandise and services their customers had come to expect. Image erosion and increased competition were the result.

Changes in Customers   Value more than status become more important to customers. Famous brands that formed the bulk of department store business were still important, but some customers preferred to sacrifice branded merchandise for lower prices. This shift in ideology was apparent in department stores as well as other retail organizations.

Changes in Competition   While department stores were busy competing against one another and adjusting their merchandise assortments, specialty and discount stores quickly filled the void. Specialty stores are extremely focused and bring a narrow variety of merchandise to their more highly defined markets. This directly opposes department store policy. Discounters offered hard lines that department stores were dropping, along with lower-priced soft goods. Off-price discounters, category killers, catalogues, and online retailers eventually added competitive pressure. Efforts to provide everything customers wanted, maintain merchandising leadership, and remain profitable could not be sustained.

Influence of Sameness Syndrome on Merchandise Buying

The large size of department stores implies a heavy investment in inventory. Not all items selected by merchandise buyers become bestsellers, so risk is high and the ability to identify precisely what customers want is always difficult. This, and the need to keep stockholders happy in good economic times and bad, impels department store buyers to be conservative in their selection of merchandise. When merchandise lacks differentiation, assortments become staid and redundant in the eyes of customers. The tendency of some retailers to offer the same or similar goods as their competition is called the **sameness syndrome**. Innovation is the lifeblood of department stores. Fearing big losses, however, merchants may seem paralyzed and unwilling to take risks on exciting but unproved merchandise. Consequently, customers who look for unique merchandise are disappointed and shop elsewhere.

Competitive pressures also contribute to ultraconservative attitudes toward merchandise buying. For example, most department stores purchase the bulk of their merchandise from a select group of large vendors that have proved satisfactory over time. Although it is good business to cultivate relationships with reliable vendors, this practice also contributes to uninspired merchandising, since other department stores are buying from the same sources. Many buyers are unable to seek out smaller vendors for unique merchandise that could bring new life to their stores because they are instructed to purchase goods only from approved companies. **Preferred vendor lists** identify prescreened manufacturers that are chosen to do business with large retail companies. The practice often closes out smaller vendors. This problem exists in other large retailing organizations, as well as department stores.

Effects of Industry Consolidation

The past decade saw many mergers and acquisitions in the department store sector. This concept was introduced in Chapter 3. Industry consolidation may also trigger the sameness syndrome. Larger organizations achieve economies of scale because of the quantities of merchandise they purchase, but this benefit does not spark creative merchandise planning. Inadequate training may also influence a lack of creativity at the merchandising level. Some retailers believe that effective merchants are not being developed at the store level as they once were. Disruption in human resources—including layoffs, job-hopping within the industry, and loss of talented employees lured into other fields—is another by-product of consolidation. Situations such as the worldwide economic downturn accelerate consolidation.

The saga of the German retail group Arcandor helps to illustrate the turmoil in this sector. In June 2009, Arcandor filed for insolvency—the equivalent of Chapter 11 bankruptcy protection in the United States. Arcandor owned 120 Karstadt department stores, considered comparable to other major retail groups in Europe and the United States; Primondo, a mail order company; Quelle, a large catalogue operation; and other holdings.[7] Metro AG, another large retail group that owns department stores as well as other retail formats, offered to purchase 60 Karstadt stores to add to its Kaufhof chain. However, because the company was not interested in buying the entire chain, as specified by the insolvency administrators, Metro was not among the six companies eventually named as potential buyers. By early September 2010, Nicholas Berggruen emerged as the victor, vowing to save the Karstadt name and 25,000 jobs within the company if rent-reduction proposals on real estate could be successfully negotiated. It appeared the initial talks with the landlord, Highstreet, were successful.[8] However, Karstadt announced in 2012 that it was restructuring and would most likely lay off 2,000 employees. It may shed 10% of its workforce by 2014.[9]

As this example illustrates, the problems associated with consolidation are global in nature. Let's investigate how other department store challenges are met.

Devising Turnaround Tactics

The nature of department stores is to bring a wide variety of goods to an expanded market. We've seen that some stores, trying to be all things to all people, diluted their merchandise assortments resulting in loss of focus. Department stores cut prices and promoted sales incessantly, thereby eroding store image, gross margin, and profits. It is certainly possible that the indecisive nature of customers and changing taste levels were also involved. Most analysts agree that the combination of these factors contributed to problems experienced by department stores.

At times, department stores have been described as being about as agile and timely as a Tyrannosaurus rex, taking longer to get goods to market than other types of retailers. Specialty stores turn merchandise faster, replace stock more rapidly, and identify hot new resources more quickly than department stores. Sluggish response times have greatly improved, but the recession that began in 2007 curtailed many of the improvements that were in progress. Proactive retailers closed stores, opened smaller stores, cut costs, improved services, and reduced staff. Retailers also used the downturn to rethink policies that no longer served their companies well, reviewing strategic policies and invoking many tactics to return their companies to their former glory.

Remarkably, department stores have been winning back market share in several ways. Some are looking to develop new demographic or geographic markets using creative marketing strategies. Product development advocates are launching new private-label lines so that their apparel and home goods lines are more exclusive. Many are adding concept shops. More companies are reemphasizing the experiential nature of their businesses and adding dazzling new opportunities and services for customers. By opening online stores, most have become full-fledged multichannel retailers.

These tactics are all working. The intricate merchandise procurement process and broad assortments that left department stores vulnerable now work in their favor. Large companies are better poised to source new products to meet changing customer demands because they have a broad network from which to draw. Department stores are reclaiming the market share they lost over the last decade. Mid-market companies are benefiting most from these changes.[10] Industry hopes are high that gains will be more pronounced across all sectors as the economy heals and strategic directions remain dynamic.

Marketing Strategies

Major retailers are attracting new demographic segments, reviving former formats, spinning off existing departments or emerging concepts into new stores, localizing merchandise assortments, and opening online stores. Market development and market penetration are key strategies used.

Reaching Age and Lifestyle Markets   Department stores are reaching out to underserved markets. To attract teenage shoppers they are bringing in brands such as Seven for All Mankind, Quicksilver, Baby Phat, and Ed Hardy. Some are bringing back lifestyle concepts like restaurants, cafes, and in-store candy shops that had been previously discarded. Food services, such as Nordstrom's in-store bistro and espresso bar, are once again appearing in department stores that are trying to reconnect with shoppers.

Spin-Off Departments and Stores   The practice of establishing new brands to meet the needs of new markets is growing in popularity. Some retailers have taken entire departments out of existing stores and opened freestanding stores. JCPenney did this with its Home Stores. Neiman Marcus developed Cusp—small, stylish boutiques geared toward women aged 21–45. The first four Cusp stores opened in 2006–2007. Nordstrom is reaching the off-price customer through its Rack stores, and Saks Fifth Avenue via its Saks Off 5th outlets. Macy's, Inc. announced that its Bloomingdale's division would open four Bloomingdale's Outlet stores by fall 2010. The first stores were planned for New Jersey, Virginia, and Florida, with others opening in 2011.[11]

Localizing Merchandising Assortments   As department store companies grow larger and cover more geographic regions, retailers lose some of their ability to connect with customers' tastes and preferences. Regional differences in consumer behavior have long been recognized. However, dealing with them can be complicated when a retailer has hundreds or thousands of stores domestically or internationally. Consolidation in the department store sphere comes at the cost of intimacy with the customer. This can be alleviated with programs that adjust merchandise assortments more intricately. Macy's instituted its "My Macy's" localization program in 20 areas of the United States in 2008. The initiative tailored product selections to the needs and wants of customers in several locales.[12]

Another way merchandise assortments are localized is through leased departments. Leased departments are often the provenance of gift-wrapping, jewelry, cosmetics, and shoe departments. As more manufacturers take on merchandising responsibilities and create stronger partnerships with retailers, this trend is expected to grow. Using leased departments, department stores can identify local businesses and vendors that customize regional products for sale in their stores.

Building Online Stores   Integrating brick-and-mortar stores with their cyber counterparts is a natural extension of retailing in the 21st century. Online stores not only serve regular store customers more effectively, they often draw new markets. Both JCPenney and Macy's have effective Web sites that are constantly being reevaluated and upgraded. Macy's online sales grew 38 percent for the first quarter of 2011, while its brick-and-mortar comparable store sales were up 5.4 percent.[13] According to chief executive officer (CEO) Terry Lundgren, Macys.com earned $30,000 in 1996, the first year the Web site was launched. Online sales now account for $1 billion in annual revenue.[14] Sears is known for driving traffic online and to its stores through its virtual social shopping activities. Its Web page is shown in Figure 5.4.

Product Development

Retailers are finding ways to compete using product development as a strategy. Some are using private labeling to add unique merchandise in a cost-effective way, while others are buying or licensing brands from manufacturers. Other department stores are adding branded concept shops to enhance their merchandise assortments.

Private and Exclusive Label Emphasis   Department stores are achieving higher margins by developing their own private-label programs and by purchasing or licensing manufacturers' brands for exclusive use. Several examples of department store branding initiatives illustrate the quest for differentiation.

- JCPenney's classic private label Arizona brand jeans are so well known they sell better than some manufacturers' brands. Its Worthington women's apparel label was launched in 1986 and is still a favorite of conservative female shoppers. JCPenney's keeps up with fashion trends as well. "She Said," a career sportswear line for women, was introduced prior to a holiday selling season. Private brands like these make up 50 percent of JCPenney's business, according to a spokeswoman.[15] JCPenney's invests in brand partnerships with companies

Did You Know?
Speaking at the 2011 National Retail Federation conference, Macy's CEO Terry Lundgren shared an anecdote about Stanley Marcus, of Neiman Marcus fame. Many years ago, after acquiring some spare change, the Marcus family had two opportunities: To build and run a store in Dallas, or invest in a fledgling soda company named Coca-Cola in Atlanta. As Marcus related: "Neiman Marcus was founded on a bad business decision!" Lundgren once served as CEO of Neiman Marcus and considered Stanley Marcus a mentor. (Source: Laura Gunderson, "Macy's CEO Moderates Last Session at National Retail Federation," *The Oregonian*, January 13, 2011, http://blog.oregonlive.com/windowshop/2011/01/Macys+ceo_moderates_last_sessi.html.

that fill unmet needs. Its exclusive arrangement with the Liz Claiborne brand and the entry of men's Big and Tall shops in its stores and online attest to this strategy.[16]

- Success with its INC and Alfani private label apparel lines, Hotel Collection of fine linens and bedding, and universal brand Charter Club, which covers multiple product categories, preceded Macy's foray into exclusive arrangements with manufacturers. The Martha Stewart Collection brings home textiles for bed and bath, kitchen gadgets, and furniture to Macy's.
- Kohl's has spent less time developing its own brands, opting to purchase and refine brands that have been in the marketplace, while licensing others. The company has introduced numerous exclusive and celebrity-driven apparel lines to round out its stable of brands. In 2008, Kohl's private-label and exclusive brands

Figure 5.4
Sears has been cultivating a more youthful market through its Web site. The virtual social shopping feature builds the Sears brand and increases traffic to its online and brick-and-mortar stores.

were expected to comprise about 41 percent of sales.[17] Among the exclusive lines at Kohl's are Simply Vera Vera Wang and Daisy Fuentes. The company also holds a licensing agreement to revive an older casual apparel brand, Hang Ten. Although sold in 40 countries, the brand hasn't had a presence in the United States since 2003.[18] The Avril Lavigne label, appropriately called Abbey Dawn after the singer's childhood nickname, was designed to enchant teens that shop at Kohl's. In 2011, the retailer added new lines by Jennifer Lopez and former husband Marc Anthony, expecting that the couple's untimely breakup would not taint the power of their brands, and in 2012 designer Narciso Rodriguez introduced a line.

Branded Concept Shops   In an effort to create more sales, higher margins, and increased focus, most department stores welcome branded concept shops. **Branded concept shops** are store-within-in-a-store departments featuring internationally known merchandise. Many carve out small specialty areas for the sale of apparel, brand-name linens and bedding, food, or lifestyle merchandise. Highly specialized merchandise with high brand recognition, such as Jo Malone or Bobbi Brown cosmetics and Tommy Hilfiger or Laura Ashley apparel, bring new profit centers to traditional retailers through branded concept shops. Bloomingdale's has teamed with high-end British skin care and cosmetics retailer Space NK, opening shops in all locations. The shops average 1,000 square feet and carry about 60 brands of cosmetic and fragrance products, many of them emerging brands unlikely to be duplicated in other department stores.[19]

This format also allows participating companies to expand on a broad scale without the high overhead of chain store expansion. For example, Fauchon, the French retailer of gourmet foods, expanded internationally by locating shops in department stores and airports. The Fauchon flagship store in Paris illustrated in Figure 5.5 features an extensive assortment of delicacies along with fine wines, candies and pastry, fresh vegetables, caviar, and more types of mustard than most of us have ever seen in one place.

Customer Service Initiatives
The concentration on customer services can only intensify as department stores seek to soothe busy shoppers, offer extensive personal service, and deal effectively with customers from around the world.

Enhanced Amenities   Some department stores have concierges on duty, much like those in better hotels. Also expected and appreciated by customers are convenient play areas for children and seating sections for seniors. Proactive stores alleviate problems that contribute to a frustrating shopping experience for many people. Some department stores use centralized, rather than departmentalized, checkout options to quell impatience on the part of time-starved consumers. Others bring their personal shopping services to a broader range of customers.

Personalized Service   Limited-line department stores are renowned for their service, a benefit to which many customers can attest. A customer buying a St. John knit suit at Nordstrom can expect service that lasts for the life of the garment. She can bring the garment back for free alterations if her size changes—within reason, of course!—and if the customer does not live in the immediate area or does not wish to pick up her altered suit at the store, the goods are shipped to her home free of charge. Follow-up telephone calls by Nordstrom staff are personalized and welcome when impeccable services have been rendered. After learning more about the customer's tastes, the sales associate will contact the customer when a new season starts or when there is a special sale. This is the essence of personalized service that never goes out of style. More department stores are considering the impact of high-level personal service as they plot future strategies.

International Customer Focus   Many stores have added multilingual signs in addition to bilingual associates; department stores around the globe attract a cross-section of foreign tourists and some experience greater ethnic diversity within their domestic markets. Stores in major cities already employ associates that collectively speak 50 different languages. Sales from international customers are significant. New York City hosted 9.7 million international visitors in 2010;[20] overseas shoppers spent approximately $7.5 billion while visiting the city.

Department stores will continue to face intense competition in a volatile economy. They will also contend with price adjustments, overdependence on promotion, and further consolidation within the industry. Despite the special problems they face, many will rise to the challenge admirably and continue to be recognized as truly exciting places to shop. Writer David Moin sums up the ideal department store: "What's the ultimate vision? Department stores as huge upscale carnivals with demonstrations, technology, interactive displays, parades, fashion shows, music, celebrities, and great restaurants. A little bit of what they have now, what they used to have, and more."[21]

Specialty Stores

Specialty stores may be as small as a single-unit sole proprietorship or as large as a several-thousand-unit corporate chain. In general, to be considered a chain, a company must operate more than ten stores. Specialists are known for being on top of trends, delivering excellent customer service, turning merchandise faster, and adapting to change more quickly than department stores.

Single-unit boutiques and gift shops and other sole proprietorships also belong in this category. Exclusivity and originality pervade merchandise assortments of small and large specialty retailers, although operationally, they are run differently.

Types of Specialty Retailers

There are specialty stores for all imaginable merchandise categories—apparel, shoes, accessories, food, appliances, automotive supplies, home electronics, furniture, toys, home furnishings, jewelry, and pharmaceuticals—and then some.

The smallest specialty store in London is Twinings, whose store in Fulham sells only tea. The American chains Lids sells only hats and Everything But Water only swimwear. The retailer Oxygen, featured in Figure 5.6, sells only streams of invigorating air, treated with aromatherapy fragrances if desired. These examples give dimension to the term single-line specialty store. To add a global flavor, Table 5.1 lists the top fashion retailers in Europe. How many of these companies are familiar to you?

Figure 5.6
When the product is oxygen, a single-line specialty store can bring clarity to both its product line and its customers. This Oxygen Bar is located in Tokyo, Japan, where the concept is very popular.

Table 5.1 Top Fashion Retailers in Europe

Rank	Company	2011 Turnover (sales in billions of euros)	Country of Origin/Headquarters
1	Inditex (owns Zara and Mango)	13.1	Spain
2	H&M	12.1	Sweden
3	Marks & Spencer	11.2	United Kingdom
4	C&A	6.5	Germany/Belgium
5	Next	3.9	United Kingdom
6	Primark	3.5	United Kingdom
7	Arcadia Group	3.0	United Kingdom
8	Debenhams	2.7e	United Kingdom
9	Benetton	2.7	Italy
10	Esprit	2.5	Germany

Source: "Fashion and Clothing Retailers in Europe," Veraart Research Group, 2011, www.retail-index.com/HomeSearch/RetailersinEuropedatabasebysector/English/FashionClothingRetailersinEurope.aspx.

Specialty chains cater to many consumer tastes and whims. Wellness-related stores such as General Nutrition Company (GNC) and Lululemon, the yoga and fitness apparel chain, contrast sharply with Marlboro shops and Godiva Chocolatier. Apparel specialty stores such as Guess and Gap are as popular in Europe and Asia as they are in the United States.

Proactive retail chains and single-unit proprietors work hard to create and maintain a competitive edge. Several important directions are considered here. Designer boutiques elevate apparel retailing to new levels and price points, serving as specialists to the stars. Some apparel retailers find strength in narrowing their customer focus and merchandise assortments. Others tighten their bonds with customers by creating environments or providing customer services that cannot be easily duplicated. Some specialty stores refine their target markets through spin-off and pop-up stores. The diversity of specialty stores gives structure to some of the classic formats like designer boutiques and destination stores, reveals emerging trends including spin-off and pop-up stores, and highlights the growing fascination with fast-fashion hot spots.

Designer Boutiques

In a class by themselves are standalone specialty stores, called **collection shops,** featuring merchandise by international designers such as Chanel, Prada, Versace, or Giorgio Armani. Some also operate within department stores. Collection shops are closely related to branded concept shops but are driven primarily by European designers-turned-retailers rather than mass-marketed brands. Perhaps a bit of import snobbery is at work when the likes of Max Mara, Louis Vuitton, or Hermes move into an area. American designer/retailers such as Donna Karan and Marc Jacobs also fit this category and thrive in international markets.

The designer connotation is the defining element in the expansion of collection shops. Price points and taste levels also play roles in shoppers' ability to discern differences between designer and nondesigner fashions. Some individuals perceive higher quality levels in designer apparel. Others do not see or care if there are differences, as long as the label is right.

Most designers produce merchandise in two or more price categories and sell their apparel in separate stores. Designer collections exemplify higher-priced merchandise. **Diffusion lines** are groups of merchandise that are produced and sold at lower prices than designer collections. Examples include Armani A/X and Versace's Versus.

Many designers are building flagship stores that acknowledge their importance in the retailing community. Twenty-thousand-square-foot monuments are located in major cities including London, Paris, Tokyo, and New York. Some industry observers feel this is another indication that power has shifted from department to specialty stores.

Destination Stores

There are a host of apparel retailers in the global marketplace; many are directed toward young people, but one size does not fit all customers. American Apparel, featured in Figure 5.7, departs from the norm by injecting fresh color and urban-hip styles with a club-dancer vibe. Apparel with an edge is displayed for young men, women, and children. Retail operations like this are considered **destination stores**—stores that have drawing power because they offer unique merchandise, cater to a specific lifestyle, or have strong brand identification. Destination stores offer goods that customers will go out of their way to purchase. Well-known retailers such as Apple, Tiffany, and L.L. Bean hold this distinction. Lesser-known small retailers that cultivate customers who refuse to accept substitutes for the products carried or gravitate to the ambiance of the store also are considered destination stores.

Spin-Off Stores

Spin-off stores are new chains launched by a retailer for the purpose of filling a market need or reaching a new target market. When American Eagle decided to open two new chains, beginning in 2006, it did so because of perceived needs in the market. The first spin-off, Martin + Osa, featured sportswear directed to men and women aged 28–40.[22] Martin + Osa styles were casual-chic rather then the basic jeans, tees, and jackets available at American Eagle. The second spin-off, Aerie, is a lingerie specialty store that carries bras, camisoles, and robes for young women 15–25. Initially,

Figure 5.7
American Apparel is a destination store because of its hip, edgy, and colorful fashion apparel. In order to draw customers in the highly competitive apparel market, specialty stores develop differential advantages.

Aerie was a sub brand within American Eagle stores before it was spun off to its own premises—usually next door to American Eagle.[23]

Enter the recession: Although Aerie was holding its own, Martin + Osa was having a difficult time finding and pleasing its market. The subsequent lackluster financial performance led to re-evaluation of these spinoffs in early 2010.[24] However, another twist to this saga had been added in 2008, when American Eagle launched its 77kids online store. 77kids offers apparel for infants through preteens—just like P.S. by Aeropostale and abercrombie by Abercrombie & Fitch.[25] By 2011, the company had opened its first brick-and-mortar stores, with 20 additional units expected to open by the end of the year. However, in 2012 American Eagle decided to discontinue its children's apparel business and was exploring exit options.[26]

As this example illustrates, an established retail presence doesn't necessarily translate into successful spin-offs. Pacific Sunwear of California opened over 200 street-fashion-inspired D.e.m.o. stores, but by January 2008 all had been shuttered.[27] Launched in 2005, Gap's Forth & Towne lasted only 18 months despite showing promise as a concept that generation X and younger baby boomers might embrace.[28] Many industry observers believe there is a dearth of fashion specialty stores geared to older markets; however, neither concept lived up to the company's expectations and both fell short of return on investment forecasts.

Occasionally spin-offs are simply smaller versions of a retailer's main stores with a different twist. In 2008, Tiffany opened a Tiffany & Co. concept shop in Glendale, California. The 2,600-square-foot store is devoted to contemporary fashion jewelry "in an atmosphere of easy elegance and accessibility."[29] This initiative may reflect the retailer's response to the fact that Tiffany stores are expanding faster in Europe than they are in the United States. The company's store in London, for example, is currently its most profitable in that geographic area.[30]

Pop-Up Stores

Introduced in Chapter 2, pop-up stores are a tactic used by specialists of many types. Although all types of retailers are capable of using this strategy, specialty stores appear to have an inside track. According to the Web site Trendwatching.com, the concept began in 2003 when a U.S. designer outlet called Vacant opened in empty stores in New York, London, Paris, and Berlin. The business model called for stints of one month in each city.[31] Testing the feasibility of opening brick-and-mortar stores, onine retailer Bluefly set up temporary quarters in New York City. Others use the tactic to move excess inventory during seasonal or crucial clearance periods.

Kiehl's features its lines of natural beauty and wellness products in a pop-up store on the University of Colorado campus. The retailer was looking to develop brand loyalty among college students. Another popular pop-up is Pink, Limited Brands' spinoff apparel brand that became a store chain. Pink stores opened in 12 college markets during one back-to-school rush. These pop-ups are considered brand-building tools but they also generate sales.[32]

Pop-up stores have come to the rescue as a way to move merchandise in a dire economy, and to build brand or test new products in better times. For the 2009 holiday season, Toys "R" Us set up 350 temporary sites, often taking over empty stores in shopping centers from October to January. Some opened as temporary toy departments in the company's Babies "R" Us stores.[33]

Unfortunately, the quarters available for rental on a temporary basis by pop-up stores are usually not in the best locations or in high-traffic areas. However, the draw of a bargain or a new experience can be electrifying when spread by word-of-mouth and alternative media to the customer.

Fast-Fashion Influence

The arrival and development of specialty apparel stores that sell well-designed, trendy fashion in high volume and at prices affordable to their young target market has had a great impact on the specialty-store genre. European specialists that practice this tactic include H&M from Sweden, Topshop from England, and Mango and Zara from Spain. U.S.-based Forever 21 and Charlotte Russe also fit this category. These stores have entranced fashion mavens and stolen market share from former favorites like Old Navy. In 2009, Zara became the largest fashion retailer in the world, topping Gap for the first time.[34]

The Japanese chain Uniqlo, owned by Fast Retailing, has expanded aggressively internationally and experienced consistent growth in the last several years despite the economy. The first U.S. store opened in 2007 in New York City to throngs of people anxious to get a glimpse of the Japanese version of fast fashion. Uniqlo is the topic of a Global Retail Profile at the end of Unit Five.

Market Segmentation and Operational Strategies   Unlike many other types of retailers, specialty stores zero in on one particular market instead of trying to create broad acceptance. There are also differences in their approach to the buying and selling functions.

Target Market Tactics

Age, interests, gender, income level, and ethnic origin—in fact, most any demographic or behavioral dimension—can be used to define specialty store market segments. For example, the chain Anthropologie attracts a young individualist with bohemian inclinations, while Gap seeks conservative 30-somethings and younger baby boomers who covet classic jeans and tees and can afford to pay a bit more for what are unquestionably very basic pieces.

The NHL Powered by Reebok flagship store in New York City carries men's, women's, and children's apparel as well as footwear and hockey equipment, commemorating all 30 of the National Hockey League's teams. Although the sport is played and enjoyed by both sexes, we might expect that the target market is somewhat skewed toward males and youngsters on sports teams. The lifestyle orientation is distinctly hockey fans.

Market segmentation will continue to be one of the most important strategies of the 21st century as specialty retailers become more precise in their selection of markets. The basis for segmentation might be unusual characteristics that make the store a destination highly sought after by shoppers in the know. When specialty stores identify an unmet need in the marketplace and then create a new concept, the spin-off usually is geared to a different market segment than that of the original store.

Buying and Selling Differences

You've learned that there are specialists who work in each functional area in department stores. In specialty stores, a few generalists within the store usually perform all the major functions. Of course this arrangement depends on the size of the operation and whether it is part of an independently held small business or a major chain. For example, in a small boutique, buyers—who are often owners—spend more time on the selling floor than do buyers in specialty store chains like H&M and Old Navy. Like department store buyers, specialty store buyers purchase merchandise to be sold in multiple locations, often work from central headquarters, and are not attached to one specific store.

Policies and procedures are determined centrally and one individual on the buying staff purchases merchandise. The responsibility for selling and servicing customers remains with local store management under the tight control of regional managers. This structure is typical of the Limited Brand's various specialty store divisions, which are housed in central headquarters in Columbus, Ohio.

Characterized by their limited lines of merchandise, specialty stores are changing in several ways. They must, because in many ways they have succumbed to the sameness syndrome, discussed earlier in the context of department stores. Many specialty stores appear interchangeable, and the trends they aspire to keep up with are often mass merchandised and copied to such an extent that they no longer count as trends. Are specialty stores, too, blending in with the retail pack? When you visit a shopping center, how many specialty retailers really stand out? Is their merchandise distinctive, or can you find the same general styles, trends, and colors at similar price points in multiple stores? The answers to these questions are invaluable as retailers aspire to compete effectively.

Drugstores   Traditional drugstores are also specialists that are fully adapting to changing market conditions. The 1980s saw many small, independent pharmacies close as national chains such as Walgreens, Rite Aid, and CVS expanded. In the 1990s, price wars, location maneuvering, and industry consolidation changed drugstore retailing. The millennium has witnessed further consolidation, added services, and broader outreach to customers.

Major Players   The top three drug retailers in the United States are Walgreens, CVS Caremark, and Rite Aid.[35] A host of mergers and acquisitions in the 1990s and early 2000s led to major ownership changes and consolidation in the industry. Some maneuverings were quite complex and convoluted. For example, JCPenney, in a departure from its usual department store business, acquired Eckerd's in 1996. Florida-based Eckerd's was then one of the top drugstore retailers in the United States. Brooks and Osco merged in 2001 and Penney's sold Eckerd's to the Canadian Jean Coutu Group in 2004. Rite Aid took over Brooks, which now included not only Osco but Jean Coutu, in 2008.

CVS merged with Caremark in 2007, making CVS not only a drug retailer but also a prescription benefits manager—a first in the industry. One result: customers can pick up 90-day maintenance prescriptions at stores rather than only through mail order as was the policy prior to the merger.[36]

Walgreens, although somewhat less affected by the major repositioning in drugstore retailing, was involved with acquisitions earlier in its history. More recently, in an attempt to build market share, the company acquired Duane Reade, a strong presence in New York City. Although Walgreens already had 70 stores in New York City, 60 percent of Duane Reade's 257 locations are in Manhattan, where Walgreens had only 13 stores. The move increased Walgreens' store count to 7,400 and is in line with the company's strategy to grow by acquisition, as well as organically.[37]

Location and Operational Strategies

As drugstores grow to accommodate their broader merchandise selections, many are forced to seek larger facilities. Freestanding locations more frequently are selected for new construction. Rite Aid and Walgreens favor corner sites. Several mergers and acquisitions magnified intense competition for prime locations from other chains.

The saga regarding cross-border prescription-filling by U.S. citizens in Canada continues to affect the industry. Canadian pharmacies offer significantly lower prices on many common and expensive drugs, and families that live near the border often make "drug runs" to save money. U.S. pharmacies assert that they are losing business, but customers retort that they are the ones that have to pay, challenging U.S. drug companies as to why they can't be more competitive. Many doctors in border towns are licensed to write prescriptions in both countries.

Merchandising and Service Tactics

Enhancing existing merchandise assortments and adding more unexpected surprises bodes well for drugstores looking to compete in an increasingly difficult marketplace. Services have been expanded as more customer-friendly, time-saving, and educational additions are made.

Several new services typify the new breed of drugstores, including drive-up prescription windows, in-store health clinics, and new product lines that go well beyond the limitations of prescription drugs and over-the-counter medications.

Scrambled Merchandising   Some drugstores are using scrambled merchandising to increase sales, test products, and amplify their role as purveyors of items that go far beyond their original service of providing prescriptions and over-the-counter remedies. Enter a drugstore today to pick up a prescription and you may find a new lounge chair, pet food, greeting cards, flip-flops, and apparel, as well as a range of snacks vying for your attention.

Walgreens partnered with Marvel entertainment to produce lines of superhero toys and food products. The merchandise featured Spider-Man, Iron Man, and the Hulk and was destined for stores in 2010.[38] The company introduced a private label named, simply, Nice!. Early development in the food, snack, and paper products areas yielded 400 items that will be distributed through Walgreens and Duane Reade drugstores by early 2012.[39]

Drive-up and Mail-Order Prescriptions   Services such as drive-up prescription windows help drugstores remain solvent in the face of strong competition from supermarkets, superstores, and warehouse clubs. The opportunities for customers to obtain their prescription drugs by mail order has added convenience for older customers and those living in rural areas.

In-Store Health Clinics   Working through and with corporations and government agencies, Walgreens is advancing a concept that will allow it to have in-store clinics and company health centers. Employees at participating companies would be able to obtain basic services—and even dentistry and eye care—under Walgreens' "Complete Care and Well-Being" program. Participants would also be given a discount on Walgreens private-label products such as toothpaste and child-care items.[40]

When the H1N1 swine flu threatened Americans' well-being in the winter of 2009–2010, CVS announced that it would administer the inoculation at its network of stores. Being proactive in this regard communicated a contemporary consumer viewpoint: a drugstore should be more than just a place to pick up prescriptions.

By concentrating on one kind of customer and one or a few types of products, specialty chains reduce risk. The flip side is that these retailers must be vigilant about keeping up with their customers' changing needs. If they do not, they risk losing those customers and market share. However, it is more efficient to stock merchandise for stores when customers have the same tastes and buying power, even if the stores are geographically dispersed. The high visibility that accompanies intense saturation of the marketplace is another major reason for the success of specialty stores.

Discount Retailers

Discount stores became the darlings of many consumer groups in the United States during the recession of 2008–2009 and in the years that followed, when the term "double-dip recession" was often heard. Prices in discount stores are much lower than those in department and specialty stores. The quality of goods reflects the reduced price levels, but as families tighten their belts and trade down during periods of economic decline, discount department stores often become the retail venue of choice at least for basic commodities.

Types of Discount Retailers

From discount department stores to huge, highly focused category killers, there are options galore when it comes to saving money. Off-price discounters usually focus on soft goods and have gained a coveted position as the place to go for name-brand bargains. Deep discounters like warehouse clubs work on low prices but offer products in bulk—sometimes too large for smaller families. Companies like Big Lots present some goods with defects and little consistency in stocking, but great bargains can be found. A **deep discounter** is a discount store that operates on much lower markups and gross margins than other discount retailers. "Dollar stores," including Family Dollar, Dollar Tree, and Dollar General, are also in this category. Factory outlet stores round out our selection of discounters. Nuances of size, pricing strategies, and physical facilities, as well as comparisons with other brick-and-mortar retailers are explored here.

Discount Department Stores

Discounters differ radically from traditional department stores. Décor at Kmart is minimal compared with Macy's but nonetheless effective for its purposes. Big-box discounters usually do business on only one floor, although this trend has changed as major discounters have entered urban areas where space is at a premium and expansion occurs vertically. Discounters continue to progress, assuming strategic directions originally attributed to department stores. These initiatives will benefit discounters in their respective domestic and global markets after the recession that made them indispensable to many consumers is only a memory.

Big-Box Designation   Discounters are known collectively as big-box retailers because of their tendency to operate from huge buildings. The term **big box** identifies a broad spectrum of discount and other retailers that operate out of large, utilitarian stores. Discounters seek competitive advantages as intensely as specialty and department stores. Continued domination by the top three—Walmart, Target, and Kmart—tends to obscure other players. Kmart is owned by Sears Holdings, the tenth largest retailer by revenue in the United States. Regional chains in this category include Stein Mart and ShopKo. The following vignettes contrast the top big-box discount department stores.

- *Walmart.* An excellent example of an astutely managed, profitable, and well-positioned retail operation, Walmart dominates large rural communities of 25,000 or fewer people in an ever-widening tier of stores throughout the world. Known for maintaining low prices, motivating store personnel, and operating in a cost-conscious manner, Walmart is acknowledged as being more technologically advanced than many retailers, and having a world-class distribution system.
- *Target.* Initially this upscale discounter reached for total market coverage in the United States but voiced no international expansion plans. It did reach beyond the continental United States with the opening of its first two stores in Hawaii in 2009.[41] This strategy changed when Target announced that it would assume leases for approximately 220 Zeller's discount stores in Canada. Target intends to open 100–150 stores under its own banner by 2014.[42] With its recent emphasis on enlarged food departments, some wonder if the company is losing its original upscale "Tarzhay" image.
- *Kmart.* Intense competition in this sector is underscored by the filing for bankruptcy protection by Kmart in early 2002 and its subsequent folding into Sears Holdings in 2005. The weakest of the three leading discounters, it is still a presence in many markets. Kmart operates some stores internationally but has curtailed expansion.

Walmart outperforms all other discounters, and Target attracts a younger, more affluent clientele than the others. Being caught in the nebulous middle may have contributed to Kmart's problems. Some retailers have successfully changed their images in order to carve out a more precise market niche. Progressive retailers will develop new formats and the assimilation of traits typical of department and specialty stores is expected to continue in the discount sector.

Trait Assimilation by Discounters   Many characteristics of specialty and department stores have been adopted by discounters, including the development of private-label programs, redesign of

selling floors to encourage more lifestyle departments, and use of cross-merchandising. Décor is less utilitarian as discounters recreate space, refurbish their stores, and add amenities.

Walmart made its own fashion impact with private labels like George and exclusive brands like surfer wear by OP and sportswear by White Stag. Miley Cyrus, well known for her role as Hannah Montana, partnered with designer Max Azria in 2009 to produce a line of casual wear for Walmart.[43] A visit to one of Walmart's prototype stores might reveal displays of throw pillows and home décor items similar to those sold in Target or Home Goods.

Target has popularized international designers like Italy's Missoni and Liberty of London in its focal point departments. It also excels at private labeling. People interested in basic fashion at a reasonable price seek its Xhilaration and Merona apparel lines. Its Archer Farms brand extends to grocery products and water, while the Choxie line proffers irresistible candies. A display of Xhilaration apparel is shown in Figure 5.8.

Upgraded Physical Facilities   Lighting in discount stores is bold rather than subtle, materials are more utilitarian than aesthetic, floor plans are structured in appearance, and almost every square foot is taken up with merchandise. However, as the format evolves, more discount department stores are raising their ceilings, widening aisles, and adding numerous amenities for their customers. National fast-food restaurants such as Pizza Hut now take the place of hot dog counters and celebrity-endorsed lines supplant no-name products in discount stores. Discount department stores usually seek locations in community shopping centers or in freestanding locations on the periphery of cities. This tendency is changing as key players assume anchor positions in regional shopping malls and move into city locations.

Category Killers

Category killers, introduced in Chapter 1, are immense specialty stores with strong discount overtones. Some of these chains are implementing tactics similar to those of department stores. The acquisition in 2009 of the foundering FAO Schwartz upscale toy stores by Toys "R" Us is one example. Conditions of the sale included ending the relationship initiated previously between FAO and Macy's, which had resulted in 260 FAO boutiques in Macy's department stores.[44]

For the 2012 holiday season Macy's and Toys "R" Us partnered to set up leased toy departments in 24 Macy's from coast to coast. The selling space averaged about 1,500 square feet and was to be open for three months.[45]

Types of Category Killers The Sports Authority is a leader in sporting goods. Home Depot and Lowe's represent home centers and do-it-yourself (DIY) stores. Office Depot, OfficeMax, and Staples provide office supply products to businesses and individuals. All three operate globally. Barnes & Noble represents the book market and Best Buy, the home electronics trade. Household pets are not ignored and shop with their families at Petco or Petsmart. Bass Pro Shops and Cabela's provide a plethora of goods for those who like to hunt, fish, or explore the outdoors. Category killers in the music industry have not fared as well due to the changing habits of shoppers and competition from online sellers. Both Tower Records and Virgin Megastores have closed stores in the United States, although Virgin still operates stores in Europe. Category killers share the superstore and big-box descriptors.

Strategic Directions These giants are experimenting with new strategies dictated by changing market dynamics. Three vignettes show the directions in which category killers are heading.

- *Sports Authority.* Sports Authority operates over 400 stores in 45 states and carries sports apparel for men and women, footwear, sporting equipment, and team sports provisions. After a series of mergers—and being owned by Kmart from 1990 to 1995—the company now is headquartered in Colorado. The company Web site carries more products than are available in stores.[46]
- *Home Depot.* Home Depot entered the home improvement business in 1978 and decided to reach a higher-end market when it opened its Expo stores in 2002. The units carried top-of-the-line appliances, lighting fixtures, and floor coverings in a stylish showroom environment. To cope with the economic downtrend, the company closed Expo in 2009.[47] Departing from its tradition of locating in suburban shopping centers, Home Depot opened in the heart of New York City in 2003, renovating what had once been B. Altman's, a well-known department store. The city store caters to residents of Manhattan, as well as commuters and visitors, with a merchandise mix tempered to suit this market. A large plant department—rather than the full-blown nursery expected at its suburban stores—offers a plant-and-deliver service to apartment-dwellers for whom it is too difficult to carry heavy plants and soil home. The store also features a larger-than-usual area of closet fittings, rugs, and fixtures meant for smaller homes. The New York store is featured in Figure 5.9. Home Depot is an international retailer through acquisition of stores in Canada, Mexico, and China.

Cyberscoop
Sports Authority says it offers more products on its Web site than it does through its stores. Go to www.sportsauthority.com and see for yourself. If convenient, check the store locator and visit the store nearest you. Scrutinize how the merchandise mix compares with the category killer's online assortment.

Figure 5.9
Home Depot defied tradition when it entered urban markets. Its store in New York City is housed in a former Altman's department store (a). Merchandise is adapted to the specific demands of urban customers. This in-store garden center offers a potting service for people who are apartment dwellers, and contrasts dramatically with the huge outdoor garden centers at its suburban locations (b).

a

b

- *Office Supply Retailers.* In sharp contrast to the larger markets they once sought, Staples, Office Depot, and OfficeMax are expanding to smaller towns. Some of these rural markets are underserved, but in other instances the arrival of category killers effectively eradicates small independent competitors. Staples relies on smaller express stores to reach customers in transportation terminals and other high-traffic locations such as malls. More discounters are expected to create such express-type units and focus on specific market segments.

Competitive Impact   Some category killers have been lost in the wake of the recession. Circuit City closed its doors, giving Best Buy and other home-electronics retailers an edge. The regional company hhgregg operates 173 stores in the United States—most in the Midwest. In 2011 it announced plans to open ten stores in Florida, providing 600 new positions.[48] Somewhat paradoxically, hhgregg leased several locations vacated by Circuit City, benefiting from less-expensive rents during the recession.

The competitive cycle goes on, with challenges emanating from Germany. Metro AG, Germany's largest retailer and the fourth-largest in the world, owns Media Saturn, its consumer electronic division. Metro's CEO made the bold statement that it would overtake Best Buy in terms of annual sales in the future. Metro already has stores in 32 countries and plans to enter China, while Best Buy presently has stores in only three countries, including China.[49] Time will tell whether this prediction will come true, but the possibility illustrates the highly competitive and global nature of retailing at this level.

Off-Price Discounters

Off-price fashion discounters bring famous-brand goods to shoppers at much lower prices than conventional department and specialty stores. Off-price stores have had a great impact on both customers and other retailers since their inception in the 1980s.

The philosophy of off-price fashion discounting is based on high volume gained through lower markup and faster inventory turnover—12 or 13 times per year. Many traditional retailers, especially department stores, are trying to emulate this off-price tactic. Considering that department store gross margins are higher and merchandise turns more slowly, it is not an easy task.

Types of Off-Price Retailers   This sector relies on selling high-volume merchandise in the tight off-price market. Key players include T.J. Maxx, HomeGoods, Marshalls, Shoe Megashop by Marshalls, and AJ Wright (all owned by TJX); Ross; and Dress Barn (now Ascenza Retail Group) in the mainline off-price group. Comprising a slightly more fashion-forward approach to off-price retailing are Nordstrom's Rack, Neiman Marcus' Last Call, and Saks Off 5th.

T.J. Maxx is the only U.S. chain that presently runs international off-price stores. The company operates in Canada, Germany, and Poland, and as T.K. Maxx in the United Kingdom. A brief look at the demise of Filene's Basement highlights several aspects of the closely competitive off-price sector.

Focus on Filene's Basement   The term *off-price* was not yet in use in 1909 when Filene's Basement opened in Boston. Originally, Filene's Department Store intended to sell slow-moving items from its upstairs store in its automatic bargain basement. It later added closeouts from manufacturers or other retailers to its inventory. Filene's Basement is not to be confused with Filene's Department Store, which was owned by May Company before Federated Department Stores acquired May (Federated is now called Macy's). The Filene's Basement store underwent a management buyout in 1988 but was forced to file for bankruptcy protection in 1999. It subsequently closed many of its underperforming suburban stores when it was acquired by Retail Ventures. The Boston flagship store was temporarily closed in 2007 to await redevelopment of its downtown Boston site.

In 2009, the economic decline forced a hiatus in downtown Boston's redevelopment plans. Declining sales forced Filene's Basement to file for Chapter 11 bankruptcy protection once again. The Buxbaum Group of California, a liquidator, purchased it in April 2009.[50] By June, several companies were bidding on the ailing off-pricer, including Crown Acquisitions, Syms, and Men's Wearhouse. Filene's Basement cited several reasons for its decision to refile for Chapter 11: poor performance in its suburban stores, the recession, tight credit markets, and the loss of the downtown Boston flagship store.[51] Ultimately, Syms acquired the chain. However, the acquisition in 2009 hurt Syms financially, and by the end of 2011, both it and Filene's Basement went out of business.

It is essential for off-price retailers to attain high sales per square foot. Yet with every new element of competition, this becomes more difficult. Competition is now coming from all sides: department, specialty, and discount stores; catalogues; and online retailers. Companies like Bluefly.com and other discount-shopping Web sites have changed the discount sector. Shakedown is inevitable.

Warehouse Clubs

The mission of warehouse clubs is to merge wholesale and retail audiences and bring a diverse product mix in bulk quantities at competitive prices to their members. Individuals and businesses pay nominal annual membership fees to shop at stores like Costco Wholesale, Sam's Club, and East Coast–regional firm B.J.'s Wholesalers.

Major Players

Brief overviews of the two top warehouse clubs follow:

- *Costco Wholesale.* Based in Issaquah, Washington, Costco merged with Price Club in 1993. Listed as the sixth-largest retailer in the United States, and the seventh-largest globally, Costco operated 412 warehouse clubs in 2010.[52] Approximately 60 percent of sales are generated by individuals and 40 percent by local businesses in an average Costco store. Well-known brands, offered at approximately 20 percent less than at conventional retailers, intermingle with Costco's own Kirkland brand. Its private label extends to everything from soda, shampoo, and socks to bakery goods. This technique is also practiced in other warehouse clubs.
- *Sam's Club.* A wholly owned division of Walmart, Sam's Club positioned itself as the upscale warehouse club as it experimented with a host of high-priced merchandise categories—everything from top-of-the-line big-screen TVs to an emerald ring for over $100,000. There were 609 Sam's Clubs operating in the United States and 100 in Brazil, China, Puerto Rico and Mexico collectively in 2011.[53] A typical Sam's Club display is illustrated in Figure 5.10.

Walmart opened the first Más Club unit in Houston in 2009. The warehouse club, geared to Hispanic shoppers, features a greater selection of products from Mexico. Among noteworthy services are a money center, pharmacy, clinic, in-store bakery that makes fresh tortillas daily, fuel station, and outdoor market area for special events. Some of the Hispanic delicacies offered include empanadas, tres leche cakes, chorizo sausages, carnitas, cactus leaves, tomatillos, and guacamole.[54]

Figure 5.10
On this visit to Sam's Club, the main feature was big-screen TVs. Warehouse clubs offer a broad assortment of goods that change regularly to meet the demands of the marketplace.

Key Characteristics   For warehouse clubs, volume is the key to profitability as it is in all discount operations. Warehouse clubs operate on very low gross margins, and markups average 8 to 10 percent on most products, putting them into the deep-discount category as well. Specializing in high-volume merchandise, warehouse clubs generate higher stock turns than other discounters.

Fewer stock keeping units are represented in most warehouse clubs. **Stock keeping units (SKUs)** are identified by the individual inventory control numbers—indicated on bar codes—which distinguish one product from another. Despite having more limited choices within individual merchandise categories, customers are treated to an array of merchandise such as fresh meat, bakery goods, fine wines, canned goods, apparel for the family, health and beauty aids, books, computers, and car tires. Also available are sporting goods, office supplies, jewelry, tools, and the occasional hot tub or Oriental rug. In-house pharmacies, decorating centers, gas pumps, and eye-care facilities have been added as warehouse clubs seek further competitive advantages. Many products are displayed on wooden pallets. During peak traffic periods, product demonstrators hand out samples of new foods or beverages to create excitement in an otherwise stark environment.

Usually located on the fringes of cities, warehouse clubs are rapidly working their way into high-traffic urban locations. Sales of home electronics in warehouse clubs and general merchandise discounters increased during the 2008–2009 recession—an example of how the misfortunes of some retailers create opportunities for others.

Factory Outlets

Factory outlets are clustered together in outlet malls that are destinations for countless shoppers. In the past, they were located very near production facilities and were called mill or company stores. This image is deceiving, since today's factory outlet stores have become chains themselves. They no longer possess a down-home image and most are not located near a manufacturing facility.

Major Players   Prime Outlets and Tanger are two outlet-mall developers in the United States. In late 2009, Simon Properties Group acquired Prime Outlets for $700 million, demonstrating further consolidation in this segment of the industry. Simon has significant investment capital available and is using the economic slump to purchase ailing properties. In this case, Lightstone Group LLC had already sacrificed four other malls to its lenders and was coping with huge debt on a hotel property that it owned. Prime Outlets was an advantageous buy for Simon since the properties operate at 92 percent occupancy and sales per square foot are $370.[55]

Key Characteristics   Manufacturers sell closeouts, seconds, and discontinued items through their factory outlet stores. Expect pared-down décor, facilities, and prices in true outlet stores. As outlet shopping strips and malls add upmarket retailers like Brooks Brothers, as well as amenities, prices ultimately increase. Other popular tenants include Nike, Puma, Barneys New York Outlet, Banana Republic Factory Store, Kenneth Cole, and Ugg.

Pricing in outlet stores has come under close scrutiny. Prices on comparable merchandise may be lower than those in department or specialty stores. However, customers have to work hard and be knowledgeable to find the rock-bottom prices that were customary in early, authentic factory stores.

Global Outlook   Outlet stores and malls are becoming more popular throughout the world. Levi Strauss is a universally recognized brand that successfully brought its outlet concept to the United Kingdom. Outlet malls now exist in Japan, a country that did not embrace the discount concept until it, too, encountered economic hard times.

Food Retailers

Traditional categories of food retailers—convenience stores, supermarkets, and restaurants—no longer adequately describe this aspect of retailing. Distinctions are less clear as grocery retailers add general merchandise and discounters become grocery retailers in return. Hypermarkets, a European innovation, have become almost synonymous with U.S. superstores. Both formats combine the best of grocery retailing with the sale of hard and soft goods.

Convenience Stores

You drive to On-the-Run; grab a power drink, bag of chips, and a sub from the in-store deli; fill up your SUV and pay at the pump; and you're out of there in five minutes and home in plenty of time for the evening news or the big game. That's why we love convenience stores. They have become a part of our lifestyles, keeping pace with us as we scramble to do more in what feels like less time.

Convenience stores seek innovative partnerships and are always scouting the next upgrade in services. You may be surprised by the home country of some chains or the types of businesses that have become convenience-store retailers.

Major Players

With more than 35,000 stores, the world's leading convenience store chain is 7-Eleven, owned by Japan's Seven and i Holdings Co. (#16 on the Top 250 Global Retailers list).[56] The company intends to expand its base in the United States by increasing the number of stores in heavily populated areas and by adding more fresh food selections.

7-Eleven operated approximately 6,727 stores in the United States in 2011, making it the largest convenience store chain by store count in the country. Major oil companies, including Shell, BP, Chevron, and Exxon Mobil, round out the top five convenience-store companies in the United States. Most operate stores through franchise or licensing agreements. BP North America generated the highest revenue at $15.9 billion in 2011. An international retailer based in Canada, Alimentation Couche-Tard, ranked sixth with 3,480 convenience stores in the United States. Another distinction: 2,916 of the total are company-operated units and bear the Circle K logo.[57]

One of the newer entries in this competitive sphere is Fresh & Easy Neighborhood Markets, developed by Tesco, the largest food retailer in the United Kingdom. The chain opened its first food markets in the United States in 2007, on the cusp of the recession. The larger-format stores had difficulty turning a profit for the British retailer, and it left the U.S. market in 2013. Worldwide, however, Tesco operates more than 1,200 stores. Design, layout, and merchandising tactics for the Fresh & Easy Express stores draw inspiration from the successful Tesco Express units.[58] A typical Fresh & Easy market is shown in Figure 5.11.

By 2012 Tesco operated 184 stores in Arizona, California, and Nevada. The company began testing smaller express stores of 3,000–5,000 square feet, opening five stores in Sacramento, California, in March 2012.[59] By early 2013, Tesco ended its experiment and announced the plan to close all its U.S. stores.

Figure 5.11
Tesco—England's largest supermarket company—owns the Fresh & Easy Neighborhood Market chain of convenience stores.

Key Characteristics

Convenience stores are characterized by their location: close to residential areas, places of business, or commuting routes. Quick-stops or c-stores, as they are often called, are small in size when compared with other food retailers, generally 1,000–4,000 square feet. Long hours—often 24 hours per day—are typical. Convenience stores carry limited food and nonfood items, from milk to motor oil, but there are always recognizable brands. Fast-food and deli components expand the c-store concept. The primary market is a shopper looking for quick-picks or emergency items. Prices are higher than in supermarkets but customers accept this because the stores are in the right place at the right time with the right products.

Most convenience-store ownership occurs through franchising and licensing. The number of company-operated establishments is declining as the major oil companies gain power and position in the industry.

Service Orientation

Banking, postal, and dry-cleaning services have become commonplace. Prepared food concessions—many with in-store seating—have grown in popularity. Considered an evolution of the corner mom-and-pop grocery store and neighborhood market, c-stores offer plenty of parking. Combining quick-pick foods and other sundries with gas stations is the norm in many areas, and more combination facilities are expected to dot the landscape. Companies tend to work on gaining a foothold in a geographic region before expanding further. For example, Alimentation Couche-Tard operated about 250 convenience stores in New England and on the Eastern seaboard for Irving Oil Company before expanding more intensely.

Supermarkets

Many supermarkets, responding to competition from convenience stores, are staying open 24 hours per day. Lower prices, express checkouts, electronic self-checkouts, and special entrances for time-pressured customers are strategies that supermarkets use to keep pace with convenience stores.

Supermarkets are self-service food stores with grocery, meat, and produce departments, and usually an element of scrambled merchandising. They operate on very low profit margins, and most sell generic and private-label brands in an attempt to increase their margins. Private-label products account for 15–20 percent of sales in most supermarkets. This helps keep customers interested and also increases sales and profits.

Major Players and Expansion

You guessed it: Walmart sells more food than any other retailer in the world through its Supercenters, Neighborhood Markets, and Marketside divisions. With headquarters in Cincinnati, Kroger is the second largest supermarket retailer in the United States, and the world's sixth largest retail company.[60] Ralphs and Fred Meyer are other supermarkets within the Kroger family. The top 10 North American food retailers are listed in Table 5.2.

Consolidation has affected the supermarket industry as it has all others. Companies seeking stronger, sometimes international stature have consumed other regional chains. Some of the largest supermarket companies in the world are based in countries other than the United States. Delhaize Group of France owns Food Lion, Hannaford, and Sweetbay Supermarket in the United States. Royal Ahold of the Netherlands is an aggressive supermarket retailer acquiring strong regional companies in other countries. Ahold's U.S. division owns Stop & Shop and Giant supermarkets.[61] Albert Heijn is the flagship brand of Ahold; one of its supermarkets in Amsterdam is illustrated in Figure 5.12.

Figure 5.12
Albert Heijn is the flagship brand of Royal Ahold. Located in the heart of Amsterdam, this supermarket is housed in a multistory building—not a common sight in the United States. In 2011, for the first time in its 124-year history, Albert Heijn opened a store outside the Netherlands. The lucky country? Nearby Belgium.

Cyberscoop
Visit the largest retailer in the world at www.walmartstores.com/press/news and look for the current Walmart Data Sheet featuring Worldwide Unit Details. You'll not only find the number of stores in all U.S. divisions, but also a summary of global units. Which country other than the United States has the most stores? Does this location surprise you?

Table 5.2 Top 10 North American Supermarkets

Rank	Company; Headquarters	Total Corporate and Franchised Stores	Food Sales in billions FY 2011–2012	Top Banner Names
1	Walmart Stores (all formats); Bentonville, AK	4,750	$264.2	Walmart Supercenter, Walmart Discount Stores, Sam's Club
2	Kroger Co.; Cincinnati, OH	2,435	$90.4	Kroger, Ralph's, Fred Meyer, and Pay Less supermarkets
3	Costco Wholesale Corp. (Warehouse Club); Issaquah, WA	592	$88.9	Warehouse club sells to consumers as well as businesses. Food accounts for $64 billion
4	Target Corp.; Minneapolis, MN	1,767	$70.0	Food accounts for $13.3 billion
5	Safeway, Inc.; Pleasanton, CA	1,678	$43.6	Safeway, Vons, Randalls, Tom Thumb, Hold 49% of 185 store chains in Mexico
6	Supervalue; Minneapolis, MN	2,434	$36.1	Albertson's, Jewel-Osco, Shaw's, Save-A-Lot, Shop'n Save
7	Loblaw Cos.; Toronto, Canada	1,027	$30.6 (est)	
8	Publix Super Markets; Lakeland, FL	1,045	$29.9 (est)	
9	Ahold USA; Quincy, MA	759	$25.1	Stop & Shop, Giant Foods & Peapod; Parent company located in the Netherlands
10	Delhaize America, Inc.	1,627	$19.2*	Food Lion, Hannaford, Sweetbay Supermarkets

Source: "Top 75 Retailers & Wholesalers 2012," http://supermarketnews.com/top-75-retailers-wholesalers-2012. (Data adapted to exclude wholesale grocers.)
*Fiscal 2011

Some supermarket and superstore companies have developed smaller grocery store formats for select locations. Walmart's Neighborhood Markets are similar to a superette. A **superette** is a small grocery store that is larger than a mom-and-pop store but smaller than a supermarket.

Specialty-Food Supermarkets

Making their mark on the industry are companies such as Whole Foods Market and Trader Joe's, which use engaging themes and emphasize healthier eating. Whole Foods draws an upper-income clientele and offers high-quality foods at higher prices than typical supermarkets. The company has chidingly been called "Whole Paycheck" because of its high-price strategy. If you are looking for scores of different types of sausages, each one looking more appetizing than the next, Whole Foods is the place to shop. The company has 288 stores in the United States, Canada, and the United Kingdom. Although the pace of expansion slowed during the recession, sales grew 11.9 percent in 2010 as the retailer's lower-priced products helped counter the downturn.[62]

Trader Joe's more than 350 stores focus on healthy, earth-friendly, international foods and a raft of private label items displayed in a friendly atmosphere with subtle island décor. The company is based in California and owned by the German retailer Aldi Nord, the eighth-largest global retailer.[63] Read more about Trader Joe's in From the Field 5.1.

Superstores and Hypermarkets

Some retailing experts point to superstores as U.S. versions of European hypermarkets, although true hypermarkets can be even larger stores. Perhaps the real differences between them are in the merchandise mix, the proportions of food and general merchandise, and consumer habits and perceptions.

Did You Know?
A little socializing in a grocery store's wine department might be OK for business. Whole Foods is testing 12 beer and wine bars in its stores and expects to open seven more if all goes well. If you're of age and near selected Whole Foods markets in Texas, Arizona, Illinois, or California, you can sample local wines and beers—and then stock up on kitchen necessities! (Source: Kantar Retail IQ, "Whole Foods Testing In-Store Bars," March 28, 2011. www.kantarretailiq.com/ContentIndex/NewsDisplayLW.aspx?id=326446&key=Vpab.)

From the Field 5.1 Trader Joe's Recipe for Success

It began with plain, "Greek-style" yogurt, which has a somewhat sharper taste than the traditional American kind. Then came the nonfat version and one mixed with honey. Soon a cornucopia of new flavors appeared. Strawberry, fig, and a yummy apricot/mango blend. The cost: $1.29 for an 8 oz. container,which is a little larger than a typical yogurt serving. That's how it is at Trader Joe's, where a trip to the supermarket is a sort of culinary adventure, a chance to discover something new, like apricot/mango Greek-style yogurt.

There are lots of ways to demonstrate customer service. Trader Joe's excels at one of the basics: delivering unique products at reasonable prices. From its earliest days, the chain has tried to bring unusual goods to a clientele ranging from gourmands to starving artists. The strategy helped Trader Joe's rack up an impressive 359 stores and $6.8 billion in U.S. sales in 2010.*

Sandy Skrovan, who heads food store research for a major consulting company, figures Trader Joe's generates sales in the neighborhood of $1,300 per square foot, which is double the supermarket industry average. "When you think of Trader Joe's, you think of innovative products," she says. "That's what drives their model—return patronage and quality products at a fair price."

In 1967, Joseph Coulombe owned a small chain of convenience stores in Los Angeles that were struggling to compete against 7-Eleven. Coulombe decided to add an assortment of 17 brands of California wine—very innovative at that time—and target yuppies, a newly coined demographic group. In the 1970s, he was among the first to offer treats such as brie, wild rice, Dijon mustard, and Vermont maple syrup. "We adopted a policy of not carrying anything we could not be outstanding in, in terms of price," Coulombe said. He added that the company encouraged small businesses as vendors.

Today, Trader Joe's carries about 2,000 products, versus 30,000 in a typical supermarket. Stores are on the small side, less than 15,000 square feet compared with 50,000 square feet for a small supermarket. About 80 percent of Trader Joe's goods are private label, compared with about 16 percent for the rest of the supermarket industry. The chain doesn't carry familiar mass-market brands like Coca-Cola, Budweiser, or Pampers.

Testing for many new products is done at company headquarters in Monrovia, CA. Staffers in the test kitchen ring a bell when new products are available so an employee tasting panel can sample. Beyond that, the company does not share information about its private label suppliers; likewise the suppliers do not talk about Trader Joe's.

Another distinctive feature of Trader Joe's is its cheerful employees. Inspired by a trip to the Caribbean, the book *Trader Horn*, and the dawning of the jet age, Coulombe sought to make a shopping excursion resemble a vacation. Employees wear Hawaiian shirts, hand out food and drink samples from tasting huts, and use nautical terminology. Store managers are called captains and assistant mangers are known as first mates, and all perform their tasks in stores that look rustic—replete with hand-lettered signs.

Ask a Trader Joe's employee about a product and he or she will sprint down the aisle, grab the item, answer your questions, and sometimes offer a taste test. No-questions-asked returns are the norm.

Coulombe treated his employees fairly by instituting a policy in the 1960s that full-time employees had to make at least the median household income for their communities. Store captains can make six figures annually. Part-timers can earn health-care benefits, a feature that makes the stores a haven for artists, musicians, and other creative types who wouldn't normally seek supermarket work.

Now 81 and retired, Coulombe sold Trader Joe's in 1979 to privately held German supermarket giant Aldi. The German owners have let the company run more or less autonomously, keeping many of the original strategies in place. Trader Joe's doesn't accept coupons, but maintains its everyday low-price strategy. At Trader Joe's, Coloumbe says, customers can entertain themselves by "actually talking" to employees.

Adapted and condensed from Christopher Palmeri, *Business Week*, www.businessweek.com/print/magazine/content/08_09/b4073058455307.htm
*Author's update: Source: "2011 Hot 100 Retailers," *Stores*, www.stores.org/2011/Hot-100-Retailers.

Superstores

Although they require a substantial investment, superstores permeate the retail scene, especially in heavily populated urban and suburban areas. They have a much broader profit base than smaller supermarkets. Walmart and Target operate superstores in the United States.

When superstores enter a new market, many small food stores are put at risk; some go out of business. Other retailers retaliate by refining their marketing strategies and continuing to compete. There will always be a place for large and small food retailers, depending on the needs of consumers. When you are in a hurry to go from school to work, wouldn't you rather shop at a 7-Eleven than a 150,000-square-foot superstore?

Hypermarkets

In Europe, Asia, and South America, the hypermarket is a way of life for most people, but it did not achieve the same status in the United States until superstores became closer in size and merchandising emphasis. **Hypermarkets** are stores of 150,000 square feet or more, 70 percent of which is devoted to general merchandise and 30 percent to food products. Approximately the same merchandise-to-food ratio is found in superstores. Hypermarkets carry fewer products than conventional supermarkets but great quantities of the products they do carry. Wielding their own brand of entertainment, hypermarkets feature employees wearing colorful uniforms, and balloons and banners swaying above cash registers or hanging from ceilings. In almost every aisle a demonstrator is cooking or serving anything from chocolate chip cookies to chicken-to-go.

Retail history chronicles several attempts of hypermarkets to find their niche in U.S. markets. Walmart's Hypermart USA, Kmart's American Fare, and French-owned Carrefour all entered the United States during the 1990s. None remains intact today. The Walmart and Kmart ventures evolved into superstore formats. Reasons for Carrefour's demise in the United States are included in the Global Retail Profile at the end of Unit Three.

Hypermarkets, like superstores, offer many store-within-a-store concepts. Dry cleaners, shoe-repair shops, banks, and pharmacies are expected in most large-format stores. Extended services, such as travel, ticket, and insurance agencies (and in one instance a marriage bureau) make hypermarkets special. Hypermarkets need great population density—more than one million people within a 30-minute drive radius—to make the concept work. The challenge is to sell enough higher-margin general merchandise in addition to food to make a profit. In countries where habits differ, people need convincing that hypermarkets are viable shopping alternatives.

Whether superstores or hypermarkets, the current global leaders are Walmart of the United States, Carrefour of France, Metro of Germany, and Tesco of the United Kingdom. The attractions at stores like these include innovative atmospheres and prices that are 10 percent below market prices for peak-demand merchandise. Where else would stock clerks zip around on in-line skates to fill shelves or service the needs of consumers?

As the distinction between superstores and hypermarkets fades, it will be interesting to see if both descriptors remain for retail formats that are more similar than disparate.

Full-Service and Quick-Service Restaurants

The restaurant industry employs 12.8 million people in 960,000 food-service establishments in the United States. Sales from all types of food-service business in the United States reached more than $600 billion in 2011. Included in this figure are sales from full-service restaurants, other eating and drinking establishments, vending and mobile sales, and quick-service restaurants. The National Restaurant Association uses the term *quick-service restaurant* (QSR), rather than the older designation fast-food restaurant, to refer to rapid-serve establishments.[64] Speaking of fast service, In-and-Out-Burgers, featured in Figure 5.13, caters to customers who want drive-through only convenience.

Figure 5.13
Speedy service is important to customers and efficiency is essential for quick-serve establishments. That's why the order-taker at In-and-Out Burger approaches customers waiting in the car line. The vast number of people with no time to cook is typical of the clientele of the famous California-based drive-through. Although some In-and-Out Burger outlets have indoor seating, most cater exclusively to customers who order on the go.

Entertainment and Merchandise-Focused Restaurants   Many food-service operators are also merchandisers and entertainers. Companies like Planet Hollywood and Hard Rock Café illustrate this point. Signature merchandise may comprise one-third of sales in theme restaurants like these. Logo jackets, T-shirts, key rings, and posters add to the excitement for the consumer and to profits for the businesses. Access to the Hard Rock Café in Miami is from either the Bayside Shopping Center or the marina—enticing both landlubbers and seafarers.

Quick-Service Restaurants   Quick service is an intensely competitive segment of retailing. Where one restaurant locates, others follow. It is not at all unusual to find four or five food retailers within a few yards of each other. Many U.S. restaurants are well known worldwide. QSRs were among the first to expand internationally and adapt their menus accordingly. The omnipresent Ronald McDonald, flanked by a banner advertising samurai burgers, was once spotted in front of a McDonald's in Kuala Lumpur, Malaysia. And Ronald showed up near Toys "R" Us in a shopping center outside Paris.

These low-priced, convenient family eateries have survived buy-outs, spin-offs, and global expansion. Pizza Hut, Taco Bell, and Kentucky Fried Chicken (KFC) are three QSR chains owned by Yum! Brands. Because of saturated home markets, all restaurant divisions have expanded globally. In late 2011, Yum! announced that it would sell its Long John Silver's seafood restaurants to LJS Partners LLC and the A&W All American Food Restaurants to A Great American Brand LLC. Yum! Brands indicated that it did not believe the two chains had significant international growth potential and that it would concentrate on its core businesses.[65] Yum! Brands operates more than 37,000 restaurants worldwide and plans to expand further in China, India, South Africa, and Russia.[66]

Leaving its parent company Baskin-Robbins, Dunkin' Brands went public in 2011. Dunkin' Donuts is opening units rapidly in Asia, although it has had a presence there for decades. In the second quarter of 2011, the company's international sales rose 17.3 percent compared with 6.3 percent for its stores in the United States.[67] Menus in Asian countries differ somewhat from those in American stores. Customers in South Korea can order sweet soybean doughnuts, 12-grain lattes, or red grapefruit coolatas, for example.[68]

Food Service Trends   According to the National Restaurant Association, customers want restaurants that provide value, convenience, and healthier options. Responses to a 2011 survey convey both the intentions of restaurateurs and the expectations of consumers:

- The restaurant industry expects to add 1.3 million positions in the next decade.
- Restaurant industry sales on a typical day in 2011 were $1.7 billion.
- Seventy-one percent of adults try to eat healthier fare at restaurants than they did two years ago.
- Sixty-nine percent of adults are more likely to visit a restaurant that offers food grown or raised in an organic or environmentally friendly way.
- Sixty-nine percent of adults are more likely to patronize a restaurant that offers locally produced food items.[69]

Restaurant chains worldwide usually are owned through joint ventures or master franchise agreements. Price-cutting tactics, new product development, and promotional campaigns are designed to encourage frequent repeat business. Most chains try to reduce operating expenses and improve productivity as they continue their quests for market share. Yum! Brands defrayed expenses by co-branding its restaurants. Seeing KFC and Taco Bell sharing one facility and parking area, as illustrated in Figure 5.14, is not unusual.

New Directions for Brick-and-Mortar Retailers

Chapter 2 mentioned many changes in the retail community and consumer sector created by the unparalleled economic slump in U.S. and global markets. In the face of dire economic indicators, retailers have shown they are a resilient lot. Some brick-and-mortar retailers are reducing selling space while others are growing larger or reallocating the space they have. Others have put expansion plans on hold until the global economy adjusts and becomes more amenable to growth. Some smaller retailers are encouraging customers to shop locally and help their communities while saving time and money. If they haven't already done so, most large and small brick-and-mortar retail-

Figure 5.14
Kentucky Fried Chicken and Taco Bell, both divisions of Yum! Brands, might share a common storefront, parking, and seating for customers at some locations. Co-branding saves money for the retailer and provides more options for customers.

ers have opened online stores. Some supermarkets and drugstores report cutting down on the number of options within some of their product lines, adjusting container sizes, and developing less costly private label options. All use technology to the fullest extent and focus on their customers as they seek competitive niches.

A few concluding examples highlight the retail modification and innovation occurring in the brick-and-mortar sector:

- Henri Bendel, the luxury boutique division of Limited Brands, ceased selling apparel and closed one of its three floors at its Fifth Avenue flagship store to focus on accessories, beauty products, and unique gifts. The New York City landmark was founded as a department store in 1895, but with the decline in apparel sales, a new vision was necessary. Bringing a wealth of experience from Coach, Gap, and American Eagle, Chris Fiore joined Bendel as president in early 2011.[70] By the end of 2011, the company expects to operate 19 stores in the United States, including the New York City flagship.[71] Taking the concept globally would be a possible next step.

- Several retailers adopted lower-price strategies to counter declining sales. Neiman Marcus introduced lower-priced merchandise into its designer collections to strengthen its range of middle-priced goods.[72] For the 2012 holiday season, the company plans to partner with Target by launching an exclusive collection from 24 American fashion designers. Items will be labeled with a joint NM logo and Target bullseye.[73] In radically different product categories, but employing the same general tactic, Pottery Barn Kids added new value lines of children's furniture, bedding, and clothing.[74]

- Pawnshops and consignment shops have gained a larger foothold in the world of brick-and-mortar retailing as a result of the recession and rising unemployment, which has made it difficult for many families to make ends meet. Several pawnshops reported increased sales and noted that their clientele has changed. Instead of drawing low-income customers looking to take loans of $75 on inexpensive jewelry or electronic goods, an influx of upper-income people has become the norm. One shop owner noticed that individuals were arriving in BMWs and Cadillacs. Some were looking for loans of $2,500 or more on watches that were

Cyberscoop

Henri Bendel was the first retailer to introduce a young French designer to fashionistas in the United States. Go to www.henribendel.com/about/henri-bendel-since-1895 and identify this historic person, who was destined to become famous in the world of fashion.

not worth that much money. Another shop owner cited a woman who wanted to pawn her $9,000 fur coat so that she could buy private school uniforms for her child.[75]

- Nontraditional mall tenants are claiming shopping center locations. The economy forced developers to reduce prices on mall stores that would have otherwise gone empty, making it possible for new, and sometimes unexpected, tenants to lease space. Tattoo parlors and antique shops are two brick-and-mortar retailers that are finding new locations in which to do business.

Some entrepreneurs flourish even during dismal economic times. The vulnerability of others is also apparent as in the case of high-end retailers that cope by lowering prices—something they never expected to do. Certain types of retailers are experiencing growth due to the unfortunate circumstances of other people and retailers.

Changes in the National Retail Federation (NRF) membership reflect many general retail trends presented in this chapter. The trade organization has noticed more small stores and fewer mid-sized stores joining its ranks. It has also observed that department-store membership has declined because of substantial consolidation in that sector. More hard-line retailers have joined NRF, as have food-service organizations, airport mall retailers, catalogues, and online stores. Global retailers are also well represented. In the next chapter, we'll look at the dynamics of retailers that practice direct marketing and direct selling.

Strengths of Brick-and-Mortar Retailers

In concluding this chapter and moving on to explore other retail channels, we'll highlight the strengths of each format. Brick-and-mortar stores hold these advantages in common:

- Their physical presence contributes to strong brand-building and high visibility.
- They depend on window displays, commanding store design and floor plans, and in-store visual merchandising to entice the customer.
- Experiential retailing is at its best when events, demonstrations, and other excitement are brought to customers on the premises.
- The personal touch, when delivered expertly, is not easily duplicated through other channels.
- Brick-and-mortar retailers command the greatest share of sales across all channels.

Summary

If you experience a degree of confusion in categorizing retailers, you are not alone. Defining brick-and-mortar stores is not an exact science. Even people in the industry blur distinctions as retailing theory and practice are rewritten.

There are different categories of brick-and-mortar retail stores, but the basic functions carried out in each are similar. Whether hidden behind the stairs in the stockroom in a small family operation, or located on the top floor of a major retail company's headquarters, those who direct operations share similar viewpoints. Profit through customer satisfaction is a universal goal.

There are department stores, specialty stores, discount stores, and food retailers of all descriptions. Stores may operate as small single-unit businesses or large multiunit chains. Department stores usually have a flagship store or corporate headquarters in or near a city, and store branches in other cities and suburbs. Locating branded concept shops within department stores is one way that manufacturers and retailers extend their reach. Brick-and-mortar stores expand their merchandise offerings through private-label programs, market development, localization, and online stores.

Specialty stores are growing their markets by spinning off departments into new chains or developing concepts that they perceive are lacking in the marketplace. Designer boutiques join with many other destination stores in the specialty realm. Scores of product categories and services form the core of brick-and-mortar specialty retailing

Discounters include companies that provide a wide selection of goods and services for diverse populations at low prices. Discount department stores, category killers, off-price retailers, warehouse clubs, and factory outlet stores belong to this sector.

Supermarkets are becoming superstores, while discount stores are emulating department stores or opening supermarkets themselves. Specialty supermarkets identify target markets that share similar lifestyles, with an emphasis on healthier eating, freshness, or unique delicacies. Hypermarkets have historically been stronger in Europe and other parts of the world than they are in the United States, but the distinction between hypermarkets and superstores continues to diminish. Theme restaurants are also entertainment specialists and sellers of merchandise. Quick-service restaurants continue to answer the general public's need for immediate gratification and an inexpensive meal, and are patronized frequently during economic downturns. Global retailers like Britain's Tesco and Seven and i Holdings in Japan own many convenience stores. Most offer finely honed product mixes and conveniences that suit today's busy lifestyles.

Brick-and-mortar retailers have several advantages, including strong physical presence and branding, visual appeal, and personalized customer service, and have a larger share of sales than other selling channels.

To counter the downturn in the economy retailers are taking many corrective actions, including reducing prices and costs, closing or opening stores, consolidating, putting some expansion plans on hold, and redefining merchandise assortments. Major supportive trade associations like the National Retail Federation (NRF) ensure a strong lobbying presence in Washington, D.C.

In the best of times and the worst of times, it is important to recognize the nuances that make retailing a most dynamic and fascinating industry.

Key Terms

Big box	Mid-market department stores
Branded concept shops	Multiunit department store
Collection shops	Preferred vendor lists
Deep discounter	Sameness syndrome
Destination stores	Spin-off stores
Diffusion lines	Stock keeping units (SKUs)
Flagship store	Superette
Hypermarkets	Turnover
Luxury department stores	Value-driven department stores

Questions for Discussion

1. Discuss two major strengths and two major weaknesses of department stores. What are department stores doing to regain or enhance competitive advantages?
2. Why are specialty stores considered experts at market segmentation? Give examples of stores in your area that support your answer.
3. How are off-price discounters different from other discounters? What new directions are off-price stores taking?
4. Why do we call category killers overgrown specialty stores? Does the comparison end there? In what merchandise categories do category killers appear to be most successful?
5. What are the similarities and differences between superstores and hypermarkets? In what circumstances do hypermarkets flourish? Will hypermarkets become as popular in the United States as they are in Europe and other parts of the world?
6. Why do restaurants like Hard Rock Café combine merchandise and entertainment with food? Are merchandise sales a significant part of revenue for theme restaurants?
7. To what degree are quick-service restaurants global retailers? Give several examples to support your answer. What trends are becoming more important to full-service and quick-service restaurants?
8. Brick-and-mortar retailing is one aspect of multichannel retailing. What special qualities give brick-and-mortar retailers advantages in the marketplace?
9. How are brick-and-mortar retailers modifying their practices to better ride out difficult economic conditions?

Endnotes

1. David Moin, "In Expansion Mode: Bloomingdale's Sets Rollout of SoHo Unit," *Women's Wear Daily*, September 11, 2008, 28.

2. David Moin, "The First Global Step: Bloomingdale's Opens Pair of Stores in Dubai," *Women's Wear Daily*, February 1, 2010, 1, 12.

3. "2011 Top 100 Retailers," *Stores*, July 2011, 1. www.stores.org/2011/Top-100-Retailers.

4. Nina Jones, "Selfridges' Room of Wonder," *Women's Wear Daily*, September 5, 2005, 26.

5. Jennifer Weil, "Printemps Courting Luxury Consumer," *Women's Wear Daily*, May 30, 2008, 12.

6. Maria Halkias, "Shoppers Departing Department Stores—and May Not Be Back," *Dallas Morning News*, February 20, 2009,,www.dallasnews.com/sharedcontent/dws/bus/stories/021909.

7. "Germany's Arcandor in Bankruptcy," *BBC News*, June 9, 2009, http://news.bbc.co.uk/go/pr/fr/-/2/hi/business/8091298.stm.

8. "Deal to Keep Karstadt Alive Moves Closer," *The Local*, September 3, 2010, www.thelocal.de/article.php?ID=29583&print-true.

9. "Neckermann, Karstadt to Shed More Than 3,000 Jobs." July 25, 2012. Top Story. www.catalogues catalogues.com. © Synergy Partnership Ltd 2012. (United Kingdom)

10. Elizabeth Holmes and Ann Zimmerman, "Shedding Dowdy for Cool, Department Stores Revive," *Wall Street Journal*. August 4, 2011, B1–2.

11. "Macy's, Inc. to Open Bloomingdale's Outlet Stores," *Yahoo! Finance*, January 21, 2010, http://finance.yahoo.com/news/Macys-Inc-to-Open-bw-784126564.html/print?x+0.

12. David Moin and Sharon Edelson, "Seeing a Ray of Hope: Fed's Outlook, Macy's Spark Retail Stock Rally," *Women's Wear Daily*, February 25, 2009, 1, 14.

13. Karen Talley, "Macy's Net Sets Bar for Retailers," *Wall Street Journal*. May 12, 2011, B4.

14. Hubble Smith, "Macy's Chief Addresses Power of E-Commerce," *Las Vegas Review-Journal*, September 23, 2009, www.lvrj.com/business/Macys-chief-addresses-power-of-e-commerce-60601962.html.

15. "Update 1—JCPenney Unveils Own Line of Women's Clothes," *Reuters*, September 11, 2009, www.reuters.com/articlePrint?ArticleId=USN1144449320090911.

16. "Is JCP a Buy, Sell or Hold?" *Forbes*, September 16, 2011, http://finapps.forbes.com/finapps/BuyHold SellAnalysis.do?tkr=JCP.

17. Doris Hajewski, "Putting on the Brakes: Kohl's Latest Retailer To Cut Back Expansion," *Women's Wear Daily*, May 1, 2008, 11.

18. Cheryl Lu-Lien Tan, "Kohl's to Bring Back Old Brand," *Wall Street Journal*, June 12, 2008, B4.

19. Sharon Edelson, "A New Makeup: Bloomingdale's to Open Space NK Shops," *Women's Wear Daily*, July 25, 2008, 1,10.

20. "International Visitors to NYC 2000-2010," NYC & Company, http://www.nycgo.com/articles/nyc-statistics-page.

21. David Moin, "The Department Store Saga," *Women's Wear Daily*, June 1997, 10.

22. Alexandra Steigrad, "Specialty Store Spin-offs Face Uphill Climb in Struggling Sector," *Women's Wear Daily*, February 9, 2009, 16-17.

23. Debra Hazel, "American Eagle Expands Chains," *GSR*, January 12, 2007, www.remedianetwork.com.

24. Alexandra Steigrad, "Martin + Osa Future in Question," *Women's Wear Daily*, January 15, 2010, 3.

25. Jaclyn Trop, "American Eagle's New 77kids Store Puts Focus on Younger Kids," *Detroit News*, April 14, 2011, http://detnews.com/article/20110414/BIZ/104140385.

26. Bloomberg News, "American Eagle Looks to Sell Children's Apparel Unit, *New York Times,* May 18, 2012, www.nytimes.com/2012/05/19/business/american-eagle-looks-to-sell-childrens-apparel-unit.

27. Alexandra Steigrad, "Specialty Store Spin-offs Face Uphill Climb in Struggling Sector," *Women's Wear Daily*, February 9, 2009, 16-17.

28. David Moin, "Gap Punts on Forth & Towne," *Women's Wear Daily*, February 27, 2007, 11.

29. "Tiffany & Co. to Open First New Concept Store in Glendale, California," Tiffany & Co., February 28, 2008, http://investor.tiffany.com/releasedetail.cfm?ReleaseID=296663.

30. Sophia Chabbott.,"Tiffany's Goal: Smaller Stores, Affordable Jewels," *Women's Wear Daily*, October 18, 2007, 3.

31. Matt Cowan and Mark Potter, "RPT-FEATURE: Temporary Shops That Are Here to Stay," *Reuters*, May 1, 2009, www.reuters.com/articlePrint?articleID=INLO50849520090501.

32. Jennifer Saranow, "Retailers Give It the Old College Try," *Wall Street Journal*, August 28, 2008, B8.

33. Joseph Pereira and Ann Zimmerman, "For Toys 'R' Us, Holidays Are Open and Shut," *Wall Street Journal*, September 15, 2009, B8.

34. "The Misnomer of Specialty Apparel," *Chain Store Age*, February 2009, 9A. (Source: "The Most Valuable U.S. Retail Brands 2009," InterbrandDesign Forum.)

35. "2011 Top 100 Retailers." *Stores*, July 2011, www.stores.org/2011/top-100-Retailers.

36. Kelly Nolan, "Analysts Split on CVS Plan," *Wall Street Journal*, June 10, 2009, B7A.

37. Greg Jacobson, "With Duane Reade Buy, Walgreens Gains on Many Fronts," *Chain Drug Review*, March 1, 2010, www.chaindrugreview.com/print_page.php?pg-inside-this-issue&sub+news&article.

38. Sandra M. Jones, "Walgreen's, Marvel Look to Form a Super-Team," *Chicago Tribune*, May 15, 2009, http://archives.chigagotribune.com/2009/may/15/business/chi-fri-retail-notebook-may15.

39. Sandra M. Jones, "Nicol Touch Comes to Walgreens Shelves as Store Brands Get Makeover," *Chicago Tribune*, August 18, 2011, wwwchicagotribune.com/business/ct-biz-0818-walgreens-label-20110818,0,4427808,print.story.

40. Amy Merrick, "Walgreen Broadens Its Health-Care Reach," *Wall Street Journal*, January 14, 2009, B3.

41. "Target to Open Twenty-Seven New Stores," *Yahoo! Finance*, March 3, 2009, http://bis.yahoo.com/bw/090303/200903030508.html?.v=1&printer=1.

42. S. John Tilak, "Bay Street—Target Entry Won't Affect Canada Retailers Equally," *Reuters*, March 7, 2011, www.reuters.com/assets/print?aid?=USN0424135920110307.

43. Ann Zimmerman, "Retailer Is Set to Launch Miley Cyrus Clothing Line," *Wall Street Journal*, June 4, 2009, B3.

44. Lisa Biank Fasig, "Toy's "R" Us Deal Means No More FAO Schwartz in Macy's," *Business Courier*, May 28, 2009, www.bizjournals.com/cincinnati/stories/2009/05/25/daily29.html?s=print.

45. Shaina Zucker, "Macy's, Toys 'R' Us to Partner at Memorial City Mall," *Houston Business Journal*, October 12, 2012. www.bizjournals.com/houston/morning_call/2012/10/macys_to_partner_with_toysrus_in.html.

46. "2008 Top 500 Guide," *Internet Retailer*, 258.

47. Rachel Tobin Ramos, "Home Depot to Pull Plug on Expo Stores," *Atlanta Journal-Constitution*, January 27, 2009, www.ajc.com/services/content/printedition/2009/01/27/depot0127.html.

48. Kantar Retail IQ, "hhgregg to Expand in South Florida," May 10, 2011, www.kantarretailiq.com/ContentIndex/NewsDisplayLW.aspx?id=332903.

49. Cecilie Rohwedder, "Metro Plots to Overtake Best Buy by Closing the Gap in China," *Wall Street Journal*, May 6, 2009, B2B.

50. Jenn Abelson, "Last Markdown for Filene's Basement," *Boston Sunday Globe*, May 24, 2009, A1, A14.

51. Jenn Abelson, "Rivals Enter Bids for the Basement," *Boston Globe*. June 4, 2009, B7, B11.

52. "2011 Top 100 Retailers." *Stores*, July 2011, www.stores.org/2011/Top-100-Retailers.

53. "Data Sheet: Worldwide Unit Details," Wal-Mart Stores, Inc., August 2011, http://walmartstores.com/pressroom/news/10690.aspx.

54. "Más Club Opens August 6 in Houston," Wal-Mart Stores, Inc., July 21, 2009, http://walmartstores.com/PrintContent.aspx?id=9323.

55. Kris Hudson, "Simon to Buy Outlet Landlord," *Wall Street Journal*, December 9, 2009, B3.

56. "2010 Top 250 Global Retailers." *Stores*, January 2011, www.stores.org/2010/Top-250-List.

57. "Top 100 Convenience Stores," *Convenience Store News*, May 23, 2011, www.csnews.com/userfiles/May232011-top100.pdf.

58. "Fresh and Easy Express to Hit California," *Convenience Store Decisions*, August 4, 2011, www.csdecisions.com/2011/08/04/fresh-easy-express-to-hit-california.

59. Shan Li. "Fresh & Easy to Close 7 Stores in California." Los Angeles Times. January 11, 2012. http://articles.latimes.com/2012/jan/11/business/la-fi-fresh-and-easy-20120111.

60. "2010 Top 250 Global Retailers." *Stores*, January 2011, www.stores.org/2010/Top-250-List; "2011 Top 100 Retailers." *Stores*, July 2011, www.stores.org/2011/Top-100-Retailers.

61. "SN's Top 25 Worldwide Food Retailers for 2011," *Supermarket News*, www.supermarketnews.com/profiles/top25-2011/index.html.

62. "2011 Hot 100 Retailers," *Stores*, August 2011, www.stores.org/2011/Hot-100-Retailers. (Statistics based on Kantar Retail research and company reports.)

63. *Stores*. Ibid.

64. "2011 Restaurant Industry Pocket Factbook," National Restaurant Association, www.restaurant.org/research/facts.

65. Leslie Patton, "Yum! Brands Sells A & W, Long John Silver's Chains Separately," *Bloomberg BusinessWeek*, September 22, 2011, www.businessweek.com/news/2011-09-22/yum-brands-sells-a-w-long-john-silver-s-chains-separately.html.

66. Annie Gasparro, "Restaurant Operator to Sell Long John Silver's, A & W," *Wall Street Journal*, January 19, 2011, B6.

67. Annie Gasparro, "Dunkin' Brands Profit Dips," *Wall Street Journal*, August 4, 2011, B4.

68. Julie Jargon and SungHa Park, "Dunkin' Brands Eyes Asian Expansion," *Wall Street Journal*, June 4, 2009, B6.

69. "2011 Restaurant Industry Forecast," National Restaurant Association, www.restaurant.org/research/facts.

70. Adrianne Pasquarelli, "Henri Bendel Gets a New Leader," *Crain's New York Business*, January 20, 2011, www.crainsnewyork.com/article/20110120/FREE/110129988&template=printart.
71. Henri Bendel, www.henribendel.com.
72. Tess Stynes, "Neiman Plans Lower-Priced Strategy," *Wall Street Journal*, June 11, 2009, B2.
73. Ann Zimmermann and Dana Mattioli. "Retail's New Odd Couple." *Wall Streen Journal*. July 11, 2012, B1.
74. Mary Ellen Lloyd, "Pottery Barn Kids Brand to Expand Value Lineup," *Wall Street Journal*, June 10, 2009, B7B.
75. Gary Fields, "People Pulling Up to Pawnshops Today Are Driving Cadillacs and BMWs," *Wall Street Journal*, December 30, 2008, A1, A6.

Chapter 6

Direct Marketing and Selling

Learning Objectives

After completing this chapter you should be able to:

- Discern several significant attributes of direct marketing and direct selling in multichannel and global contexts.
- Evaluate the impact of the economy on direct-marketing initiatives.
- List the advantages and disadvantages of catalogue retailing, direct selling, and telemarketing from both retail and customer perspectives.
- Explain other nonstore methods of retailing, including flea markets, auctions, mobile retailing, vending, and marketplace carts.

Figure 6.1

A direct-mail piece from Costco (a), an ad for J. Olson jewelers in a local shopping newspaper (b), and the highly specialized catalogue for Drs. Foster and Smith (c) show the versatility of direct marketing.

a

Previous chapters stressed how brick-and-mortar retail stores have changed along with the customers they serve. This chapter looks at retailers that do business through direct marketing and direct selling. Direct marketing uses catalogues, direct mail, telemarketing, and on-line selling to reach customers. Direct selling uses personal methods as well as online selling. Most direct marketers and direct sellers are multichannel retailers. Other aspects of retailing considered in this chapter are flea markets and swap meets, auctions, mobile retailers, marketplace carts, and the vending industry. All reach customers through nonstore retailing methods.

b

Direct Marketing

Just as brick-and-mortar retailers have become multichannel retailers, so have direct marketers. Customers' expectations are high and retailers of all types recognize that moving beyond their levels of original expertise helps companies develop new ways to reach and satisfy their customers.

Key Characteristics of Direct Marketing

We'll begin by focusing on the distinctions between direct marketing and direct selling, and then survey the process and identify key performance statistics associated with direct marketing.

Distinctions between Direct Marketing and Direct Selling
Although the terms were introduced in Chapter 3, the distinction between direct marketing and direct selling deserves further explanation. Direct marketing

c

involves direct communication to a consumer or business recipient, which is designed to generate an order (direct order), a request for further information (lead generation), or a visit to a store or other location to purchase specific products or services (traffic generation). Direct marketing advertising pieces are characterized by the sense of immediacy and urgency that they convey to the customer. Many brick-and-mortar retailers use direct marketing techniques to reach their customers.

Direct selling, in contrast to direct marketing, is a personal form of selling that involves meeting with the customer face to face. Depending on the company, its salespeople may be called distributors, representatives, or consultants. Products are sold primarily through in-home product demonstrations, parties, and one-on-one selling. Direct selling occurs in the workplace when representatives set up displays during coffee or lunch breaks or after work. Direct sellers also go online to communicate with their customers.

The Process of Direct Marketing

Direct marketing encompasses several key steps as put forth by the Direct Marketing Association:

- Collecting data for identifying and addressing categories of new or existing customers. Maintaining customer lists and database infrastructure is essential to this process.
- Analyzing data and developing relevant product offers and communications between the marketer and customer.
- Utilizing appropriate media to produce, deliver, and receive communications or exchanges of value including products, services, and payments between marketers and customers.
- Tracking and measuring communications and transactions between marketers and customers using market segmentation and optimization.
- Judging effectiveness by testing new communications against past communications and using results to improve future interactions between marketers and customers with the goal of building long-term relationships.[1]

State of the Industry

Changes are occurring in the global economy that affect direct marketers. Despite the recession and the subsequent pressure put on all companies to react, direct marketers have performed well in the United States. Many became leaner, instituted cost controls, and deployed more innovative marketing tactics in order to remain solvent.

The Direct Marketing Association (DMA) predicted that U.S. sales would reach close to $2 trillion in 2012, a slight increase over the previous year. Direct marketers were expected to spend $168.5 billion on advertising in 2012, accounting for about half of total advertising spending in the United States.[2] Total global advertising expenditures were approximately $466 billion in 2011.[3] Analysts believe that although global growth is modest, it may indicate that the market is stabilizing.

Direct marketing accounted for 8.7 percent of the GDP in 2012. The industry employs 1.3 million people and supports another 7.9 million other jobs within the supply chain and service sectors in the United States.[4] The number of print catalogues with online editions has increased exponentially as customers, increasingly comfortable with the digital format, are stimulated by the increased number of products they can browse online.

To better understand the process of direct marketing we need to look at the language of direct marketing—particularly those terms that address database marketing and mailing-list development.

Terminology and Tools

Like all specialized business areas, direct marketing has its own vocabulary and ways of operating. *Database* and *mailing list* are familiar terms to observers both inside and outside the industry. Other terms, such as *customer resource management* and *fulfillment,* introduce attributes that form the core of direct marketing. For example, **customer relationship management (CRM)** is the total company effort directed at satisfying the needs of all customers. **Fulfillment** is the practice of using physical and electronic distribution systems efficiently to deliver products to customers in a timely manner. By the time brick-and-mortar and online stores become multichannel retailers, they usually have adopted direct marketing terminology.

Database Marketing

The core of direct marketing revolves around information and the ability to capture and use it. Understanding how this works entails learning the language of direct marketing and the tools it uses to reach its mark.

Database marketing is the process of capturing and using observable and quantifiable information regarding customer behavior and aspirations. Computer technology has made sophisticated data collection possible. **Data mining** involves probing a database for pertinent information that can be used to target future offers to customers.

Most direct marketers begin with the premise that future customers are very much like present customers. Thus, in identifying new prospects, they follow a birds-of-a-feather-flock-together way of thinking. **Prospecting** involves seeking qualified potential customers through screening and analysis of database information.

The use of database marketing has made it possible to develop more intimate relationships with customers in many ways:

- More efficient market segmentation and market targeting is possible when more information is known about customers.
- Customers' needs are met more accurately when direct marketers merge the characteristics of their customers with the database information they have accumulated.
- Personalized offers are easier to develop when retailers can access more detailed information about their customers.
- Tapping into databases at the point-of-sale lets retailers match customer purchases with coupons representing other products that might be useful to them or those that are bought regularly.
- Shopping patterns can be detected over time that might not have been detected without database information.

Many other specialized terms are encapsulated in Table 6.1. This vocabulary provides a framework for understanding the unique operations that involve lists and databases.

List Development

Contact information for present and potential customers is essential to all retailers, but even more so for direct marketers and other direct-contact providers. Brick-and-mortar retailers send promotional material to customers primarily through their in-house lists. A **mailing list** is a collection of names, addresses, and contact information of present or potential customers compiled, from sources of significance, to direct marketers. Direct marketers rely heavily on mailing lists, which are the mainstay of their business.

Types of Lists   Lists of names come from a variety of sources:

- *House lists.* Often the first resource to tap when compiling a list, **house lists** are drawn from companies' own charge-account records or credit-card transactions.
- *Compiled lists.* Lists of potential customers' names and addresses that are prepared by commercial firms are called **compiled lists**. Magazine subscribers, club members, and census and other public data are typical sources. Many catalogue retailers, direct mailers, direct sellers, and online retailers also sell or barter their own lists to other companies. Many use cooperative databases rather than traditional databases. One study showed that the use of co-ops declined in 2010, but of the retailers that do use the shared service, more than half said they would rely more on co-op databases in the future. The most popular provider, used by 40.5 percent of respondents, is Epsilon/Abacus.[5]
- *E-mail lists.* Of increasing importance but hard to obtain are e-mail lists. The best lists are derived when customers opt in to direct marketers' programs because they trust the company or brand.
- *Cell phone lists.* Opportunities to communicate with customers via texting or social networking are becoming increasingly important. Lists can be formulated in this way.

Table 6.1 Specialized Terminology Used in List and Database Marketing

Term	Definition
Co-op databases	When two or more owners share and combine their lists so that each participant can access the combined information.
Co-op mailing	When a mail piece includes an offer from two or more mailers instead of just one.
CPM list pricing	Cost per thousand records from a list universe. For example, a list price of $100/M means that it would cost $100 to obtain 1,000 units from a given list universe (the total number of prospects on a list).
Data warehouse	A combination of a single organization's many different databases and electrically stored data; allows organizations to analyze customer information and demographics to help create targeted lists.
Hotline	The most current mailing list update available; typically priced at a premium.
List cleaning	The process of improving a list by updating the information and keeping data current and well maintained.
List select	These are repeated and notable categories contained within a list. Common selects include state, age, profession, and gender.
Merge/purge	The process of combining two or more lists or databases and then getting rid of duplicates in the created master file, reducing printing and mailing costs.
NCOA	The National Change of Address database maintained by the United States Postal Service; it allows mailers to update addresses, maintain accuracy, lower mailing costs, and lower the possibility of useless prospects (also called "nixies").
Response rate	Usually represented as a percentage, the response rate is the ratio of the number of people who responded to an offer divided by the number of people who were sent that offer.
RFM models	Short for recency, frequency, and monetary value measurements; these are used in predictive modeling, especially for consumer mailers and offers.
Suppression	The process through which addresses are taken off a mailing list. Senders of commercial e-mails must provide an opt-out option to comply with the CAN-SPAM Act. People who opt out are placed on a suppressed list to avoid future contact.

Source: Condensed and adapted from Jonathan Mack, "Lists and Databases 101," *DMNews Essential Guide Lists, Database Marketing and Data Services*, 2009, 14–15.

Advantages of Lists   Lists serve many purposes for direct marketers, including:

- Contacting existing customers more frequently.
- Expanding the customer base.
- Segmenting specialty markets.

Identifying lists appropriate for specialty markets can be particularly tricky. Suppose a direct marketer of cell phones wishes to reach a core Hispanic market in the United States. Marketers have learned that just because people are Latino does not mean they behave similarly when making purchasing decisions. Specific culture, language, and degree of assimilation into mainstream American culture all have a bearing on customer behavior. Therefore, care is taken to select the lists that best match the criteria and goals of the direct marketer.

Purchasing Lists   List purchasing is handled by facilitating firms that own, manage, and broker names and addresses to direct marketers. A **list broker** is a company or individual that acts as a middleman between list buyers and sellers. For example, a chain of fitness clubs (the buyer) might be interested in renting a list of names from a publisher of fitness magazines (the list owner). The list broker would handle the transaction. A **list manager** is a company that is responsible for organizing and keeping a list up to date for an owner.

Available lists might specialize in certain types of industries or cover a range of business types. Examples taken from the listings in *DMNews* give an idea of the breadth and scope of available lists and the number of names available:

- Arts and Crafts Enthusiasts, offered by eTargetMedia.com Inc.—459,475
- Extreme Sports Enthusiasts, offered by Walter Karl—21,703,974
- Bella Clear Product Buyers, offered by List Services Corporation—120,000 (60-percent female list of those who buy skin care products in hopes of improving their appearance)
- Wine Enthusiasts, offered by Lighthouse List—600,000 (70-percent male list of those who love wine, have joined clubs or gone to wine tastings, travel, and have incomes of $100,000)
- *Essence* Magazine E-mail Names, offered by Millard Group—153,115 (62-percent female list of African Americans who are subscribers to the magazine)[6]

A comprehensive list of people in Hong Kong who are family-conscious, household item shoppers, and e-mail users—as well as engaged to be married—gives insight into international markets. The list is broken down into four parts:

- Mail—222,644
- Fax—111
- E-mail—14,024
- Telephone—26,594[7]

A list is only as good as its accuracy. The degree to which members of a list possess the demographic, psychographic, or behavioral characteristics sought by direct marketers is also critical. The list is not useful if customers and prospects cannot relate to the offer.

Economic Impact   List value is based on cost per mille (CPM)—that is, cost per thousand impressions—in this case, names and addresses of potential customers. Most list brokers have experienced a drop in rental prices; a strong case can be made that the downturn in the economy and the influx of many new lists forced prices down. Average business-to-consumer (B2C) lists cost around $100–120 per thousand to rent. E-mail lists are more costly, at $250–400 per thousand names, but they are also considered more reliable.[8]

Factors That Encourage Direct Marketing Growth

Many factors have influenced the popularity of direct marketing. Customers' needs for convenience, reduced stress, and safety; desire for lifestyle enhancement; and quest for value all contribute to the popularity of direct marketing. Advanced technology plays a major role in the expansion of direct marketing and selling formats. Despite indications of shifts from one marketing channel to another, as well as economic woes, the predicted growth rate of direct marketing affirms its importance in the future. The following points prepare us for the discussion of direct marketing and its significance to retailers and consumers.

Changes in Consumer Needs and Values

Direct marketing reflects the social and economic fiber of a society together with the lifestyles of its members. The past decade has witnessed several subtle shifts in behavior that are linked to a change in values; desire for personalization, increased vigilance, concern for the environment, and the desire to reduce stress from various parts of their lives pave the way for the services that direct marketers can provide.

Customer Convenience and Comfort   Whether an individual is looking for an epicurean selection of foods, a yoga mat, or the latest version of the Guitar Hero video game, the physical process of shopping is made easier by direct marketing. If customers want to experiment with new cosmetics in the privacy of their homes, direct selling may be the answer. Sometimes, salespeople in retail stores are not helpful, knowledgeable, or available. Stores may not be open at the moment a person perceives the need to buy. In stores and direct selling, the retail process influences and somewhat controls the customer. In direct marketing, however, the customer controls the process to a large degree. For some, the flexibility of direct marketing is an attractive alternative to the relatively inflexible process of store shopping. Examples illustrating these nuances appear in this chapter.

Direct-to-customer selling is more convenient for elderly or disabled shoppers, who may not be able to access traditional stores. Families living in rural areas also benefit from direct marketing. Most people think twice about taking extra hours out of a normally hectic day to drive to a shopping center if the nearest one is 50 miles away. And since parking can be a hassle for most customers, saved time is worth money.

Reduced Stress   Some customers are finding that patronizing direct marketing firms diminishes stress in their lives. Not all individuals were born to shop, and for those that find mall shopping neither exciting nor therapeutic, nonstore methods are enticing. Parents who do not wish to cart children on extensive shopping expeditions also embrace direct marketing.

Many cities of the world experience intense traffic congestion. Customers who experience gridlock on highways may benefit from less-stressful options if they do not have to sit on a freeway for hours waiting to go five miles to their local mall. Environmentalists may also concur on this point, as some forms of direct marketing contribute less to transportation emission pollution and wasted energy. In parts of some cities, crime retards retail patronage. Direct marketing in particular is attractive to customers who are not comfortable on the streets or in malls at night. For consumers who feel threatened by criminal activity, direct marketing is a viable alternative to large, heavily populated shopping centers.

Advances in Communication Technology

When Steve Jobs, charismatic founder and leader of Apple, died in 2011, many tributes were written outlining his contributions to the digital age. One of these pieces addressed the profound impact he had on catalogue development as well as the e-commerce industry. For a brief look at the influence Jobs wielded—from Apple's inception to the recent iPad—read From the Field 6.1.

Many important developments were catalysts in the growth of direct marketing:

- The United States Postal Service (USPS) introduced ZIP codes in the 1960s, which enabled direct marketers to reach target markets residing in specific geographic areas more easily.
- Universal credit cards were also developed in the 1960s, and credit-card companies' mailing lists made the first large-scale database marketing possible.
- Advanced database systems help direct marketers reach, understand, and satisfy their customers.
- Media growth brings more opportunities for customer contact through network, cable, satellite, and Internet television, and interactive digital technology.
- Advances in fulfillment tactics, logistics, transportation, and postal delivery facilitate the movement of goods from source to consumer. One of the essential transportation services offered by DHL Global is illustrated in Figure 6.2.

Online retailing provides new avenues for retailers that choose to sell direct. Because of its importance as a direct marketing channel, electronic retailing is discussed in the next chapter.

Direct Marketing Challenges

An assortment of customer- and retailer-oriented issues compromise the ability of direct marketers and other sellers to maintain sales levels, much less grow their businesses. The recession's economic impact on business will, we hope, be old news by the time you read this. Changes in customer behavior, direct-marketing infrastructure, and the direct marketers that will reshape their operations (whether out of desire or necessity) are discussed next.

Customer-Oriented Challenges

Several attributes of customers today have been shaped by the recession and a subsequent reevaluation of financial and family values. We'll examine a few that are of interest to retailers.

Reticence to Spend The prolonged recession created vast uncertainty in consumers. It is no wonder sales are down for many direct marketers. Families facing shrinking pension funds, foreclosure, unemployment, and the other issues discussed in Chapter 2 clearly have had more important issues to deal with than shopping. It is not surprising when these customers cut discretionary expenditures; however, when those not as deeply disrupted by economic distress stop or scale back spending, there is more to consider. Some people perhaps reined in their spending out of guilt or deference to those who had lost much more. Others may have cut back after reevaluating core values that affected their families' moral and ethical decisions. Many simply decided that in uncertain times, a more cautious approach to managing finances was in order. As the recession progressed, even luxury-goods sellers felt the pressure to cut prices and encourage customers to shop. The reticence to spend is influenced as much by psychological factors as by financial position.

Figure 6.2
Deutsche Post DHL maintains fleets of delivery vehicles and state-of-the-art facilities to move products between direct marketers and customers. Motorcycles are most efficient when making deliveries in congested cities.

Information Overload Customers have more choices than ever, but this also means being bombarded with product options, media pitches, social networking, and the vast retail research benefits of the Internet. People experiencing information overload often compensate for feeling overwhelmed by withdrawing from tasks at hand, communication, or social interaction. With so many catalogues to choose from, some potential customers might respond, if asked about their behavior, that they like to look but become too stimulated by the options to place an order.

Rising Expectations of Quality A general trend across all selling channels is that customers expect a lot from retailers before and after they make a purchase. Not only do customers want quality—in the materials used, the make of a garment, the durability of an automotive part—but they also expect full treatment regarding shipping options, return policies, and other post-purchase services. Direct marketers that do not have a physical product to show compensate by exceptional photography, detailed and descriptive copy in mail pieces, and samples or fabric swatches accompanying a catalogue.

Receptiveness to Contact An always-touchy subject for direct marketers and customers is the fact that some people simply do not want catalogue companies, direct mailers, or telemarketers to contact them personally by any means. This is understandably distressing to direct markers, since sales are lost before they even begin. It is helpful when customers have the option to initiate contact with a company; thus, opt-in programs have proved to be a more effective way to turn prospects into customers. Many people, however, will volunteer personal information and are delighted to receive unsolicited contact from direct marketers—if there is something relevant, highly desirable, and fairly priced behind the offer.

Privacy Issues Progress has been made in the area of respecting customer privacy. Data breaches have been resolved, perpetrators brought to trial and convicted, and protections put in place to deter criminal activity. Payment systems that rely on the use of credit-card numbers are more secure. Do-not-call and do-not-mail programs are available to individuals who do not want their privacy invaded. This may sound like an ideal business world, but it is not. At the risk of sounding less than optimistic, wherever there are unscrupulous individuals and mistakes made due to human error, there will be invasions of privacy, identity and monetary theft, and yet-to-be-named infringements. Crimes affect not only customers, but also direct marketers—perhaps to a greater degree. Interruption of the flow of customer contact, inhibited sales, diminished credibility, and financial loss may lead to permanent business malfunction.

Retailer-Oriented Challenges

The costs of doing business, the promise and concerns of ownership change, horizontal and vertical competition, and the threat of cannibalism of sales are issues that confront direct marketers.

Increasing Costs Escalating postal rates and the high costs of paper and printing are of concern to catalogue and direct mail companies, since a significant proportion of expenses revolve around these items. For several years, as use of the postal service by the general public declines, the USPS has had to raise its rates for both consumer and business mailings to compensate for falling revenue.

Mergers and Acquisitions As in the rest of the retail world, changes of company ownership are evident in the direct marketing sector. For some companies, merging with or acquiring another firm is a way to grow the business and share expertise and resources. To the company being acquired, this can also mean layoffs and disruption in management. Recent ownership changes involving major brick-and-mortar, catalogue, and online companies have distinct global overtones. For example, the French conglomerate Pineault Printemps Redoute (PPR) divested itself of Conforama, a multichannel retailer of discount home furnishings, in order to concentrate on its fashion, jewelry, and lifestyle businesses. The division was sold in 2011 to South African household goods company Steinhoff International Holdings Ltd. Conforama has stores in France, Switzerland, Luxembourg, Spain, Portugal, Italy, and Croatia. PPR owns Redcats.com (United States), Puma.com (Italy), Gucci.com (Italy), Boucheron.com (France), YvesSaintLaurent.com (France), and StellaMcCartney.com (United Kingdom), among other internationally known brands.[9] PPR had earlier sold off its U.S. Redcats apparel catalogue division.

Speculation regarding mergers and acquisitions, as well as divestitures, is often highly charged with emotion since the disposition of human assets is at stake. Although many companies are forced to sell due to impending bankruptcy, acquisitions are also strategic growth initiatives. The ailing economy forces others to sell out to private-equity firms as revenue declines. These pressures will continue to challenge direct marketing and other businesses.

Competitive Environment For a catalogue company, competition comes from other catalogues, as well as brick-and-mortar stores, other direct marketers and sellers, and online retailers. It's a tough and ever-changing arena in which to entice customers to buy merchandise. Some multichannel retailers face diminishing returns from one selling channel when they add others. Cross-channel cannibalism is a form of internal competition in which sales from one channel decline when another selling format is initiated. For example, when the first wave of brick-and-mortar stores began to set up transactional Web sites, some observers feared that online sales would take away from store sales. In most cases, however, this did not occur. In a similar vein, catalogue retailers might have concerns about whether the opening of stores would diminish sales from print catalogues.

As more retailers use direct marketing and direct selling, they are finding that the methods are not competitive with retail stores but, rather are complementary to them. Let's see how retailers are using direct marketing separately and in conjunction with online methods.

Catalogue Retailing

Major brick-and-mortar retailers like Bloomingdale's, Neiman Marcus, Sears, JCPenney, and Harrods of London have all established thriving catalogue operations at one or more times in their history. But the history of catalogue retailers is as volatile as that of their brick-and-mortar relatives. Bloomingdale's discontinued its fashion catalogues in 2009; Montgomery Ward revived its general merchandise print catalogue—and initiated an online catalogue—in 2008 when it was acquired by Colony Brands.

Did You Know?
After folding its "Big Book" in 2009, JCPenney announced in late 2010 that it would discontinue its remaining specialty print catalogues in 2011. Are the major department stores on a trend curve, or will their Web sites adequately meet the needs of old and new catalogue shoppers?
(Source: Adam Dewitz, "JCPenney to Quit Catalogs," September 27, 2010, http://whattheythink.com/articles/53654-jcpenney-catalogs/?printmode.)

Otto Versand, a German catalogue company, purchased Spiegel in 1982. At one point, Spiegel owned Eddie Bauer, Newport News, Carabella, and AB Lambden catalogues, bringing grand-scale retailing to the industry. In 2004, Spiegel declared bankruptcy and was purchased by Golden Gate Capital; in late 2008 the company was sold again, to investor group Granite Creek Partners.[10]

Never before have catalogue shoppers had so much merchandise from which to choose. Catalogue companies offer everything from expensive writing instruments to environmentally kind vacuum cleaners, apparel for tall men and petite women, animal beds, and paraphernalia for ice climbing. Table 6.2 lists sales figures for the top 25 U.S. multichannel merchants. This compilation includes several retailers as well as manufacturers and suppliers. Some companies own multiple brands that are listed when appropriate.

Table 6.2   Top 25 U.S. Multichannel Merchants*

Rank	Companies	2010 Direct Sales	2009 Direct Sales	Market Segment
1	Dell	$52,161.0	$44,966.7	Computers
2	Thermo Fisher Scientific	$10,790.0	$10,110.0	Laboratory and research supplies
3	IBM	$10,496.0*	$9,500.0*	Computer hardware, software services
4	Staples—includes Corporate Express, Medical Arts Press, Quill Corp., and Smilemakers	$9,849.2	$9,640.3	Office supplies
5	CDW Corp.	$8,800.0	$7,700.0	Computers
6	Harry Schein	$7,530.0	$6,538.0	Dental, medical, and veterinary supplies
7	Wesco International	$5,060.8	$4,634.5	Electrical and industrial maintenance supplies
8	United Stationers	$4,830.0	$4,710.3	Office and facility supplies
9	OfficeMax	$3,766.0	$3,656.7	Office supplies
10	Hewlett-Packard Co.	$3,671.0*	$3,528.0*	Computers
11	VWR International	$3,600.0	$3,561.2	Laboratory and science education supplies
12	Systemax—includes Circuit City, CompUSA, and TigerDirect	$3,590.0*	$3,100.0	Computers, industrial supplies
13	Patterson Companies	$3,420.0	$3,204.5	Medical, dental, and veterinary supplies
14	Office Depot	$3,290.0	$3,483.7	Office supplies
15	Sears Holdings Corp.—includes Lands' End apparel and Sears.com	$3,107.0*	$2,875.0*	General merchandise
16	Sigma-Aldrich Corp.	$2,271.0	$2,146.7	Biochemicals and laboratory supplies
17	PC Connection	$1,970.0	$1,569.7	Computers
18	W.W. Grainger	$1,800.0	$1,500.0	Industrial supplies
19	MSC Industrial Direct Co.	$1,652.0	$1,441.3	Industrial supplies
20	HSNI—includes Garnet Hill, The Territory Ahead, and Frontgate	$1,500.0*	$1,310.0*	General merchandise
21	Limited Brands	$1,500.0	$1,388.0	Apparel
22	JCPenney Co.	$1,500.0*	$1,500.0*	General merchandise
23	Williams-Sonoma—includes Pottery Barn, West Elm, and Williams-Sonoma Home	$1,454.2	$1,224.7	Home décor, kitchenware
24	L.L. Bean	$1,440.0*	$1,400.0*	Apparel, outdoor gear, home furnishings
25	Deluxe Corp.	$1,400.0	$948.0	Business stationery and supplies

Includes B2B and B2C companies; direct sales expressed in millions.
*Indicates estimate.
Source: "19th Annual Ranking of the Top-100 Multichannel Merchants as Ranked by Sales," *Multichannel Merchant*, September 2011, 26–28, www.multichannelmerchant.com.

Types of Catalogue Retailers

Three distinct categories in catalogue retailing exist:

- *Pure catalogue companies.* Businesses that operate catalogue businesses only, with no (or few) stores. Between 2005 and 2010, the numbers of print-only catalogues declined from 3,836 to 1,158.[11] That number was expected to decline further as catalogues produced in both print and digital formats grow.
- *Multichannel retailers.* Brick-and-mortar retail stores that have catalogue operations and online stores. Examples include department and specialty store retailers such as Neiman-Marcus, Brookstone, Victoria's Secret, Delia's, and L.L. Bean.
- *Nonretail companies.* Businesses that previously did not operate retail ventures but have chosen to enter the catalogue field. Airlines, museums, and media companies are prime examples. Airline travelers are familiar with the Sky Mall catalogues that feature diverse retailers. Many museums depend on catalogues for additional revenue, and *National Geographic* magazine publishes a gift catalogue, featured in Figure 6.3, that calls attention to this nontraditional retailer.

Figure 6.3
National Geographic is a nontraditional catalogue retailer since it is primarily known for its magazine and television presence, as well as a Web site. Strong branding and reputation ensure a positive reaction from catalog recipients.

Catalogue and Store Comparisons

A comparison of several differences between brick-and-mortar stores and catalogue retailing illuminates the many advantages of catalogue retailing. We'll look first at the high points and then survey the disadvantages of catalogue retailing.

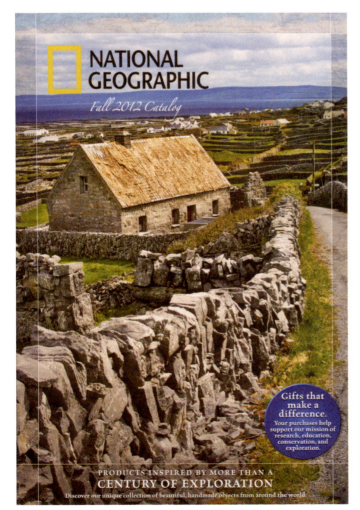

Catalogues have a longer carryover time than item advertising done by stores. **Carryover** is the period of time between a person's receipt of a catalogue or advertisement and the actual sale. Stores depend on foot traffic, whereas catalogue retailers aim for repeat sales from a captive audience in their homes. Stores rely on a continuous influx of new merchandise, while catalogues are able to present a significant percentage of repeat items. Companies sometimes send the same catalogue under different covers at closely timed intervals to different customers, a subtle change designed to test the strength of cover merchandise.

In terms of inventory management, a store can sell comparable items or suggest a switch to another item when something is out of stock. Direct marketers must backorder or cancel the order. In stores, inventory levels are planned in relation to overall sales and stock turn desired, while in direct marketing, commitments are made to fulfill each item's projected demand. If catalogue sales expectations are not met, merchants may choose to sell overstocked items to off-price stores and clearance specialists, or publish sale catalogues themselves.

Another difference is that catalogues create mood through size, design, layout, photography, and paper quality, while retail stores rely on store layout, décor, lighting, music, and other elements to create ambiance and draw attention to merchandise. Different sensory stimulation is used. Catalogue retailers work hard to differentiate their offerings from those of other retailers, particularly in the period leading up to Christmas—an intensely competitive time of year. Figure 6.4 illustrates one retailer's approach.

Finally, measures of productivity differ. Many catalogue retailers analyze sales per square inch of catalogue page, while most stores measure sales per square foot of floor space.

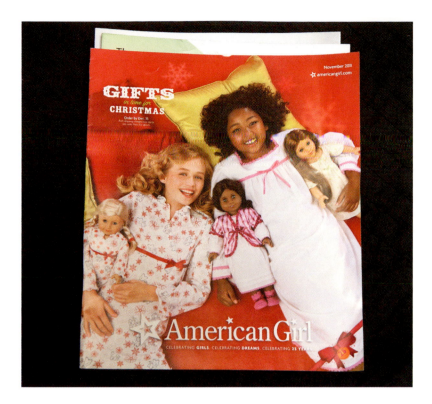

Figure 6.4
The American Girl
Christmas catalogue
appeals to girls who covet
American Girl dolls; it is
designed to stand out
among many other holiday
offers.

Disadvantages of Catalogue Retailing

Customers state several reasons why they may not order twice from the same company:

- Disappointment with product fit, color, or tactile quality.
- Merchandise damaged in transit.
- Motivation to purchase limited to a one-time sale or free offer.
- Slow service, backorders, goods permanently out of stock.
- Excessively expensive shipping.
- Rude or poorly skilled telemarketers.
- Too little or too much follow-up.
- Infringement of privacy.
- Unnecessary fouling of the environment.

Uncertainties of fit and inability to examine materials have been two of the major drawbacks of catalogue selling. Tactile and other sensory abilities are of concern to customers intending to purchase apparel and other soft goods. Some catalogue retailers have attempted to counter both problems by providing fabric swatches, liberal return policies, and postage-paid return mailing labels. Catalogue retailers that also have brick-and-mortar stores usually provide return-to-store options.

Catalogue retailers have seen print production costs rise, which increases their overhead. Despite the further expense, many set up Web sites. Some see this as a supplement to their printed catalogues, while others view online selling as a way to extend the breadth and depth of their merchandise assortments.

The Direct Marketing Association (DMA) has taken a proactive stance on the privacy issue. Direct marketing companies, by subscribing to the DMA Mail Preference Service (MPS) and maintaining in-house name removal lists, ensure that the public does not receive unwanted materials.

Trends and Strategies in Catalogue Retailing

The largest merchandise category in the catalogue industry is books—1,248 book catalogues were published in 2010. Apparel holds the second position, with automotive-products catalogues next in popularity.[12]

Williams-Sonoma earned $1.5 billion in direct sales in 2010 and is considered the major multi-channel company in the home goods market.[13] To refine its competitive position, Williams-Sonoma focused on value for its customers and chose to move advertising dollars from its catalogue to its online stores. The company also reduced the number of catalogues it mailed to its core customers—aged 35 to 50—because it found that they preferred the brick-and-mortar channel. The gourmet food, tableware, and kitchen-gadget company also owns Pottery Barn and West Elm. The Pottery Barn division reduced prices and engaged in more promotions. Similar strategies are evidenced through the catalogue industry.

Direct Mail

Another way direct marketers reach out to customers is through governmental postal services or other private carriers. Personalized print communication that arrives in the mail, provides relevant information on products, and elicits a direct response is called **direct mail**.

In the United States, direct mail accounts for 52 percent of total mail volume. Comparative sales statistics between catalogues and noncatalogue direct-mail pieces point out the importance of direct-mail marketing. Although the recession adversely affected the number of mailings and revenue generation, direct sales grew from $457 billion in 2010 to $477 billion in 2011. Catalogue sales grew from $114 billion to $199 billion in the same time frame.[14]

Characteristics of Direct Mail

Direct mail is a significant contributor to the direct marketing repertoire since it reaches people when they are more likely relaxed and ready to peruse eye-catching pieces. Retailers employ several different forms of direct-mail pieces, as well as other direct-response tactics, to remain strong in an uncertain economy.

Types of Print Pieces   Direct-mail pieces come in many shapes and forms. Some look like obvious promotional pieces while others resemble more intimate personal letters. Most capitalize on the power of tangibility and personalization, capturing attention on the envelope or enclosures by using customers' first or full names. Unusual graphics, colors, or themes also help set mailers apart from the deluge of postal clutter. Coupons and sweepstakes are a popular form of direct-response mailer. A study by the DMA showed that 52.4 percent of recipients read direct mail from merchants.[15] From the Field 6.2 speaks to the evolution of sensory-linked direct mail. Read about how taste and smell add pizzazz to a mailer.

Insert media also is a part of direct-mail promotional packages. Direct mail that reaches customers by riding along with newspapers or envelope mailers containing several offers from businesses is called **insert media**. The company 1-800-Flowers.com has found success using insert media to promote not only its sister brands but also other compatible offers from other direct marketers. For example, the company uses cross-promotional inserts for its Cheryl & Co. cookies, Fannie May candy, and Popcorn Factory goodies catalogues. Lisa Hendrickson, director of marketing for 1-800-Flowers.com, indicated that most inserts are simple and include a direct call to action as well as an expiration date. She says: "It's either a promotion code or an offer of good value like an arrangement with a free vase. Particularly in the current market, people are looking for value."[16] Figure 6.1 displays a direct-mail piece for Costco along with a front-page ad on a shopping newspaper mailed to local consumers and a catalogue for a specialized retailer. What's your choice of promotional material?

Market Impact   In the past, direct mail often got a bad rap. All too often it was dismissed as "junk mail"—a handle that conscientious direct mailers neither want nor deserve to hear. Direct mail today is slick, personalized, creative, and much more likely to target defined groups rather than mass markets. People look forward to getting their mail: 98 percent bring their mail into their homes the day it is delivered and 77 percent sort through it soon after.[17] This is the good news for direct mailers.

Growth of Digital Mail   As more direct mailers choose to personalize their offers to customers and integrate their campaigns with Web sites and e-mail, more flexible digital mail will be used. Presently, the volume of print produced on digital presses is expected to grow only 2–3 percent per year until 2013.[18] The benefits of classic offset printing are being combined with digital printing using high-speed inkjet equipment in a technique called **variable data printing (VDP)**. The advanced technology is expected to improve response rates in the future as the economy improves.[19]

Coping with Recession

Direct marketers and multichannel retailers have revised strategic plans and adapted customer contact methods to counter the downturn in the economy. The changes made by two companies—Dell and Bare Necessities—illustrate the importance of direct mail and catalogues in their plans.

Dell Computers Economizes   Changing its strategy away from catalogues and more toward direct-mail pieces during the recession gave Dell the option to use less expensive vehicles to reach its customers. The company used smaller pieces such as postcards to inform customers about new products that would benefit them based on prior purchases. It also increased the number of mailings to its best customers. Dell sends 200 million mail pieces per year, focusing on its active customers, as well as hand raisers.[20] In direct marketing lingo, **hand raisers** are customers or prospects who initiate contact with a direct marketer after receiving a targeted direct-mail piece with a special offer.

Bare Necessities Embraces Catalogue and Direct Mail   A pure-play online seller of underwear, sleepwear, and shapewear for 10 years, Bare Necessities published its first catalogue in 2009. The company uses postcard mailers as well as four-page and eight-page mini catalogues; shortly after delivery, it follows up with customers by e-mail. According to Dan Sackrowitz, vice president of marketing, Bare Necessities "views catalogs and direct mail as a great way to stay in front of customers during a recession."[21]

Many users of direct mail believe that companies should make more contact with customers during a recession, not less.

Challenges Facing Direct Mailers

Beyond economic concerns, several challenges face direct mailers:

- Obtaining measurable results from marketing efforts using appropriate metrics is one directive shared with all retailers.
- Do-not-mail list legislation is pending in several states with intended restrictions placed on commercial marketing. The DMA and the Federal Trade Commission maintain national opt-out programs for consumers. E-mail is now included in do-not-mail initiatives.
- Postal rate increases were enacted in 2007, 2008, 2009, and 2012. Several new postal regulations will affect mailers.

In the past, when the cost of a first-class stamp has risen, consumers have generally shrugged. Will they continue to do so as postal costs rise incrementally? Perhaps. Direct mailers are less accepting of rate increases because of the high volume of printed matter that they generate.

When average postal rates increased by 2.1 percent and flat shipping rates by 2.4–2.8 percent in January 2012, merchants reacted in various ways. Some felt strongly that postal increases should not be passed on to customers. With many other shopping choices, would they remain loyal if prices escalated? Others believed the increase might motivate businesses to research other digital options. Many announced their intention to cut down on the amount of mail pieces they send.[22] These are examples of strategic directions that direct mailers must reevaluate on a regular basis.

Despite an expected loss of $10 billion in 2011, the USPS is still a significant contributor to the economy, responsible for over $1 trillion in sales annually. The USPS has forecasted that it will continue to deliver approximately 150 billion pieces of mail in 2020.[23] Despite shifts in volume, marketing formats, the economy, and consumer choice, direct mail should secure its niche in collaborative multichannel initiatives.

Telemarketing

The telephone can provide retailers with a cost-effective means of generating incremental revenue and expanding market penetration. Telemarketing in the United States generated $18.5 billion in 2008 utilizing over 17,000 call centers.[24] The U.S. call center and telemarketing sector revenue is expected to reach $23 billion in 2012.[25] The industry had lost ground because of changing consumer sentiments; overaggressive call centers; fraud; competition from online, print, and store retailers; and the effects of the volatile economy. Direct marketers follow low labor rates and availability of skilled personnel, and many call centers have moved abroad—particularly to India and other offshore locations.

However, in 2012 there was significant job growth in the industry, due largely to retraining incentive programs and The U.S. Call Center and Consumer Protection Act, which aims to restore outsourced cell center jobs.

Still, telemarketers remain equipped to satisfy the needs of specific groups of consumers. For working people who have little free time and those who are disabled, catalogue shopping and teleshopping can be effective and enticing options. Several advantages of selling and shopping by telephone reinforce the convenience factor.

Advantages of Telemarketing

The telephone is a unique medium. A summary of its major strengths illustrates its effectiveness:

- *Person-to-person.* Although the medium is not a face-to-face means of contact, well-trained telemarketers can achieve high sales rates and recoup the missing personal touch through knowledgeable, friendly telephone service. Talking with a real person is important to many telephone shoppers.
- *Immediately responsive.* Telemarketing, when properly structured and controlled, permits immediate statistical feedback as well as meaningful market information from customers.
- *Incremental.* The phone can be used alone, but when used in tandem with other media, it increases the overall effectiveness of both media. Emphasizing toll-free telephone numbers and Web site addresses in sales literature may further improve mail response. The imme-

diacy of response is attractive to many retailers as a means of taking orders, encouraging multiple purchases, upgrading initial selections, cross-selling, and supporting online sales.

- *Cost-effective.* Like mail, the telephone is a cost-accountable medium, enabling the user to track multiple performance variables such as cost per name, cost per call, cost per lead, and cost per order.
- *Carefully targeted.* Prospective customers are selected on the basis of special interests, past sales behavior, and geography with relative ease via the telephone. The importance of mailing lists and databases cannot be understated.
- *Inbound and outbound capabilities.* Retailers utilizing telephone communications have flexibility. Phone calls from customers primed to order are handled efficiently and provide opportunity to encourage multiple sales. **Inbound calls** are those initiated by customers to companies or call centers. When the urge to shop strikes, a call can be initiated from just about anywhere on a landline or cell phone. **Outbound calls** are those initiated by the direct marketer to customers or prospects. Outbound calls allow the retailer to solicit new business, follow up on orders, and provide caring customer service and positive public relations.

While some retailers employ in-house telemarketers, the trend is to outsource this aspect of customer contact. Several concerns of call-center executives are listed in Table 6.3.

Disadvantages of Telemarketing

Like all other types of business, telemarketing poses its own challenges to retailers and customers:

- *Customer reticence.* Many people do not want their schedules interrupted with unsolicited calls. Others feel stressed and are inattentive. Effective training of telemarketers can overcome these obstacles. Omaha Steaks' customer-service representatives are skilled at relationship-building and use the information on their databases to encourage repeat purchases.
- *Constrained contact periods.* The Telephone Consumer Protection Act of 1991 includes guidelines for telemarketing companies to follow regarding socially acceptable hours during which calls can be made. Standard practice from ethical telemarketing companies is to call customers only between 9:00 a.m. and 9:00 p.m. Many people work long hours and find it difficult to place outbound calls and may not have the flexibility or desire to accept inbound calls. Customers who are not interested in using the telephone to contact retailers can easily opt out using do-not-call options.
- *Other prohibitions.* Also prohibited is the use of fax machines for unsolicited advertising, and use of artificial voice—also called robocalling—and automatic dialing systems for commercial purposes.
- *Inability to examine products.* Similar to other direct marketing methods, it is impossible to view a product or judge quality over the phone.
- *Inconsistent global infrastructures.* Using the telephone to reach consumers poses other problems as companies extend their reach globally. For example, in some Asian countries, up-to-date directories are virtually nonexistent, making telemarketing difficult. In less-developed countries, telephones are not prevalent, much less directories.

Table 6.3   Main Concerns Facing Call Center Executives in 2012

1. Empowering and engaging employees to drive business results.
2. Profiting from a multichannel/multimedia contact center.
3. Leveraging technology for efficiency and automation.
4. Positioning the contact center as a driver of business imperatives
5. Creating a culture based on continuous improvement.

Source: 2012 Call Center Summit—Survey Results, Call Center Week, www.callcenterevent.com/uploaded Files/EventRedesign/USA/2012/January/10622006/Assets/Survey_Results_Call_Center_Summit_2012.pdf.

The Federal Trade Commission implemented a free *do-not-call* registry in 2003 that was updated in 2007. Using this system, consumers call a toll-free number or sign up online indicating that they do not want to be called—either on landlines or cell phones—by telemarketers. Many states have set up similar programs independently. The government ensures fewer telemarketing calls within 31 days once a phone number is registered.[26]

Global Direct Marketing

Direct marketing is practiced worldwide. In fact, some of the largest direct-mail companies are European. The ease with which customers can be reached, response rates, and attitudes toward privacy differ dramatically around the world. In this section we'll look at two methods of global expansion used by direct marketers, as well as the economic impact of international direct marketing and some cultural differences in business practices.

Types of Global Direct Marketing Expansion

Direct marketing companies may choose to expand their companies globally in one of two ways. **Waterfall** is the international entry tactic by which companies enter several countries or markets concurrently. **Sprinkler** is the international entry tactic by which companies enter each country or market consecutively. The two strategies are graphed in Figure 6.5.

There are advantages and disadvantages to each method. Advantages of the waterfall method include lower financial risk and better control of revenue cycles, as well as better use of company resources due to advantageous timing of openings. Disadvantages include the possibility of competition entering the marketplace before the company has a strong foothold.

In contrast, the sprinkler strategy capitalizes on the recouping of high development costs sooner and offers the opportunity to build a brand over a broader market more rapidly, thus warding off competition. Of course, the downside is that all resources are committed simultaneously, putting the company at greater risk financially. In addition, setting up all countries at the same time compounds the task of building relationships and communications across markets.[27]

International Direct Marketing Expenditures and Revenue

Following the United States, the five markets that spend the most money on direct marketing advertising are Japan, Germany, the United Kingdom, France, and Italy.[28] Fascinating contrasts become apparent when we examine global direct marketing practices.

Waterfall Strategy

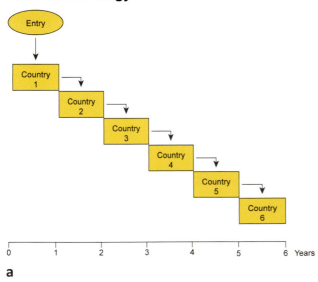

a

Sprinkler Strategy

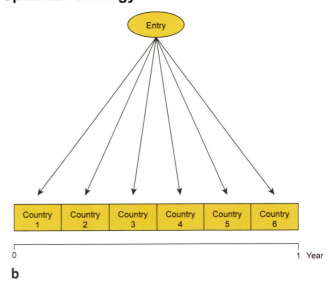

b

Figure 6.5
International Direct Marketing Entry Strategies. Using the waterfall strategy, companies enter each new country one after the other (a). Using the sprinkler strategy, companies enter several countries at the same time (b).

International Direct Marketing Practices

Direct mail companies face challenges as they expand their networks internationally. Several examples illustrate problems faced by direct mail companies and situations that may be more similar than dissimilar as direct marketers go global.

Receptiveness to Direct Marketing   Direct marketing companies receive high response rates from customers in many parts of the world. For instance, because households in developing countries like Malaysia have not been deluged with direct mail pieces, recipients view mailings as a novelty and take an interest in them.

In another example, German consumers are considered more receptive to direct marketing because they are well acclimated to catalogue shopping and have embraced online options. About 80 percent of German businesses use direct marketing to reach their customers. The most popular types of direct marketing and usage rates are listed:

- E-mail and Internet marketing—65 percent.
- Telephone marketing—31 percent.
- Direct mail—24 percent.
- Insert media—18 percent.

Direct marketers have challenges to meet as they access customers. Privacy and data protection laws are very strict in Germany as are regulations affecting unfair competition and rebates.[29]

Businesses looking to expand internationally judge receptiveness, affinity, response rates, as well as attitudes toward price, quality, and branding, as they plan direct marketing campaigns and meet local compliance standards.

Creative Adaptation and Cultural Sensitivity   Copywriting for direct marketing pieces needs to be suitable for the target country. For example, a written advertising piece might need to be changed to reflect different usages and spellings in various markets—a case in point being Malaysia, Hong Kong, Japan, and the Philippines, which are all targets for English-language marketers. A direct marketer creating a piece for Malaysia or Hong Kong would use British spelling, which is the norm in those countries. The same piece created for Japan or the Philippines would use American spelling. Despite higher costs, many direct marketing firms use local copywriters to translate copy into country-appropriate language and print separate versions of a catalogue.

Also important to identify are cultural responses to certain products. A gourmet food and beverage catalogue containing offers of pork or wine would be considered offensive by recipients in Saudi Arabia or Malaysia, two countries whose societies follow the dictates of Islam. For a company not to realize that Muslims do not eat pork or drink alcohol reflects inadequate research on the market and an insensitivity to the culture.

More Similarities Than Differences?   One expert in telephone services found that call-center problems may be universal. From his experience at global trade events, several problems mirrored those experienced in the United States:

- Offshoring call centers is a concern of businesses from Australia to Europe who complain about "foreigners" answering incoming calls regarding their products and services.
- Not only implementing technology, but training in its use and application is needed to ensure customer satisfaction.
- Customers worldwide are adopting government sponsored do-not-call lists.
- Telecommunication standards vary among countries, making it difficult to move into new regions.
- Customers everywhere want personal service more than self-service, and a well-trained person is still the best option when it comes to solving customers' problems.[30]

There are many benefits to using direct marketing internationally. For some retailers, it is an ideal way to introduce products into a new territory. When domestic economies are performing poorly, having offshore business in more robust areas buffers revenue loss. The key to success lies in the ability of practitioners to allocate the resources they need, employ them effectively, and adapt to local business practices as they go global.

Did You Know?
The catalogue industry is getting more personal. Almost 56 percent of catalogue executives surveyed said they would create customized catalogues for targeted customer groups in 2011. About 38 percent said they would use variable printing—the technology that is used to add "Hi, Gabrielle!" to the front page of a catalogue, or to create other personalized messages.
(Source: *Multichannel Merchant.* "Outlook 2011: Catalogs.")

Industry consultant Lois Geller proposes this rule of thumb for the success of direct marketing programs: Forty percent is due to the offer—the product itself. Another 40 percent is due to the adequacy of list. The final 20 percent is a result of the creative strategy used to reach the consumer.[31]

Direct Selling

Home and family-care products lead the field in direct selling, followed closely by wellness and personal care products. Although most direct sellers are women, many men and couples are also involved. Sales reached $30 billion in the United States and $132 billion worldwide in 2011.[32]

More workers have been trying direct sales as a result of the recession and subsequent lay-offs. Avon aggressively recruited sales representatives despite the downturn. Picture an Avon recruiting spot in which a middle-aged, well-groomed woman says, "I can't get laid off; it's my business." Encouraging power, control, and financial gain for reps, former CEO Andrea Jung embarked on what she called "the biggest recruiting drive in our history." During the first quarter of 2009, Avon added approximately 200,000 new representatives[33] and by 2010, it had a total of 6.5 million active independent representatives. Sales were $11.3 billion in 2011 with 11 percent of revenue attributed to Latin American operations.[34] However, several quarters of poor performance followed, coupled with major problems implementing a technology system in Brazil and a government inquiry into alleged bribery of foreign officials. In 2012 Sherilyn McCoy replaced Ms. Jung as CEO although Ms. Jung remains chairman of Avon.[35] Avon deals with the dynamics of global business just as all retailers must. Let this vignette set the tone for learning more about direct selling.

Types of Direct Selling

The two basic types of direct selling situations are person-to-person and group. We'll look at each method here.

Person-to-Person Contact

When a salesperson calls on a customer at home or at the customer's place of business, this is considered **person-to-person selling**. Contact is made by personal appointment or through other face-to-face contact methods. This approach accounts for 80.1 percent of all direct sales.[36]

One form of person-to-person selling, consultative selling, puts the customer in a position of greater power than in many store environments, although the salesperson still controls the direction of interaction. **Consultative selling** is in-home or in-office selling by specialists whose expertise the customer values. Consultants who work for home-furnishing businesses, as well as shop-at-home apparel, kitchen-tool, and cosmetics companies use this method. A look at Cutco Cutlery illustrates how direct sellers operate.

A division of Alcas Corporation of Olean, New York, Cutco sells high-quality knives and utensils through its wholly owned global marketing arm, Vector Marketing Corporation. Vector promotes Cutco sales in the United States and Canada. College students make up about 95 percent of Vector's independent contractor sales force in North America. Through initial family and friend contacts, sales are developed on a referral basis. An extensive support network and high-spirited motivational programs keep these commission salespeople committed to their work.

Cutco formed an international division in 1994. It entered the global market with the same mix of high-end products but gradually changed its marketing strategies to serve customers from different cultures better. When the company entered Korea, it assumed that college students would form the core of the sales organization as they did in North America. However, the company soon learned that slightly older women had a better affinity for the Korean customer and switched to that pool when seeking sales representatives. The ability to adapt has been a major factor in Cutco's success.

Group Direct Selling

The party-plan salesperson enlists the aid of one customer to assist in selling to others within a community. The **group direct selling** method encourages in-home or in-office selling to groups hosted by a sales representative who is also a customer. Individuals working from homes or offices become sales representatives and invite friends or co-workers to a gathering for demonstrations of the products in a party-like setting. Party-plan/group sales accounted for about 28 percent of all direct sales in 2010, focused primarily on female consumers.[37] Since so many women work, party-plan dealers more frequently bring their wares to places of business. The shop-at-home format is expected to persist since for many target customers, it serves the needs for social interaction as well as shopping. Tupperware, Party Lite, Magic Chef, and Mary Kay Cosmetics are direct selling firms that use the party plan as a primary means of reaching their customers.

Some of the newer party-plan direct-sellers include those that sell gently used gold or cherished chocolate. Gold parties generate money for those without jobs and individuals who want to clean out their jewelry boxes and have some fun. Participants receive 65 to 75 percent of what the gold is worth to a company that melts it down for resale.[38] Another direct-selling company is Dove Chocolate Discoveries. According to the Direct Selling Association (DSA), it's for people who want a direct-selling "sweet experience."[39]

The DSA, in Washington, D.C., is the leading trade organization for the industry; it not only serves the interests of manufacturers and distributors of products but is also a consumer advocate agency since it enforces high standards of ethics. For most direct sellers, the Internet is the next frontier. The top 10 global direct selling companies are listed in Table 6.4.

Cyberscoop
Attention chocoholics: Visit the official Dove Chocolate Discovery Web site at www.dove-chocolate-discovery.com, where you can set up a chocolate party and earn money by becoming a direct seller. Or, meet your friends on the official Facebook Fan Page, www.facebook.com/dovediscoveries—direct selling at its most scrumptious.

Table 6.4 Top 10 Global Direct Selling Companies

Rank	Company and Country	2011 Net Sales or Revenue (in billions of dollars)	Products, Marketing Style, Global Presence
1	Avon Products, Inc., United States	11.3 Net Sales	Beauty, jewelry, apparel; person-to-person; more than 100 markets
2	Amway, United States	9.2	Nutrition, personal and home care, beauty; person-to-person; more than 80 markets
3	Herbalife Ltd., United States	3.5 Revenue	Nutritional supplements, weight management, wellness, and personal care; Person-to-person in markets
4	Natura Cosmeticos SA, Brazil	3 Revenue	Personal-care products and fragrances; person-to-person and retail; operates in seven South and Central American countries and in France
5	Vorwerk & Co. KG, Germany	3.0 Net Sales	Household appliances and JAFRA cosmetics; person-to-person and party plan; 76 markets
6	Mary Kay Inc., United States	2.9 Revenue	Skin care and color cosmetics; person-to-person and party plan; operates in 35 countries
7	Tupperware Brands Corp., United States	2.6 Net Sales	Preparation, storage, and serving solutions for the home, and personal-care products; person-to-person and party plan; 2.6 million distributors in 100 markets
8	Oriflame Cosmetics, S.A., Sweden	2.1 Net Sales	Beauty; person-to-person; operates in 67 countries (but not in the United States)
9	Nu Skin Enterprises, Inc., USA	1.7 Net Sales	Sells more than 200 products through Nu Skin, Pharmanex and Big Planet brands; person-to-person in 52 international markets
10	Belcorp Peru	1.6 Net Sales	Beauty and lifestyle products; more than 938,000 beauty consultants serve in 16 international markets

Source: Adapted from "DSN Global 100," *Direct Selling News*, Special Supplement to the *Wall Street Journal* "The Equity in Social Selling, Financial, Personal, Global." June 2012, pp. 18, 20.

Multilevel Marketing Companies

Many direct selling companies are considered multilevel marketing companies. **Multilevel marketing** (MLM) refers to direct selling by firms that are set up in a pyramid-style hierarchy. Salespeople pay commission on sales they generate to the leader who has recruited them. Amway, Nu Skin, and Arbonne are examples of companies that are organized in this manner. Independent contractors—also referred to as pyramid leaders—recruit friends, relatives, and acquaintances to work for them. Recruits, in turn, recruit their own friends, relatives, and acquaintances. Recruiters earn commission on sales generated by each of their recruits, and pyramid leaders' commissions are based on sales from all levels of the pyramid. Monetary returns to the leader are significant if the sales organization is large and highly motivated. Amway, the world's largest multilevel marketer, sells everything from its signature household cleaning products to cars and telephone service.

Critics of this form of direct selling argue that only a few top producers make a good living. For most salespeople, incomes are not high. Some people object to the near-religious fervor that is part of the corporate culture. Others complain of unscrupulous recruitment techniques and pressure placed on recruits to purchase large inventories.

Advocates stress the unlimited opportunities for independent contractors to run a small business, the strong work ethic that many multilevel sellers develop, and the many business contacts sellers are able to generate as positive reasons to join these organizations. For many, it is the essence of free enterprise.

Types of Nonstore Retailing

Although not as frequently discussed, there are many areas of nonstore retailing that bring zest to direct-to-customer retailing. Vending machines, flea markets and swap meets, auctions, carts, various forms of mobile retailing, and temporary retail sites are all institutions that do not need formal or permanent stores in order to do business. Some provide opportunities for entrepreneurs to gain a foothold in retailing.

Figure 6.6
Optimal placement is important for vending machines. Dove ice-cream bars are available directly adjacent to a hotel pool, where, for a potential customer, convenience is high and impulse-purchasing likely.

The Vending Industry

Today, vending machines sell a variety of products and services from pantyhose to photocopying, coffee to condoms. It was not always the case. A brief look at the history of the vending industry, its current status, the advantages and disadvantages of the business, and sales and merchandise trends follows.

History and Present Status
Early in their history, vending machines dispensed small quantities of nuts, candy, or gum that sold for a penny. The devices were placed close to cashiers so that customers could easily get change. Vending machines helped retailers minimize the problem of collecting money and recording transactions for many impulse items purchased at the point of sale. Enterprising retailers in tourist areas took advantage of developing technology and installed binoculars and pay telescopes. Advances in refrigeration soon made it possible to dispense cold soft drinks in bottles.

As technology evolved, so did the lines of products sold in vending machines as well as locations for machines. Installations now exist in stores, airports, entertainment centers, hospitals, offices, industrial plants, highway rest areas, hotels, and probably your dormitory. A poolside vending machine is illustrated in Figure 6.6.

Advantages and Disadvantages
Vending machines are often accessible around the clock, eliminate the need for sales personnel, and are located indoors or outdoors. These advantages, however, are offset by some disad-

vantages. Theft, vandalism, high costs of purchasing and digitally updating equipment, breakdowns of machines, stock-outs, and low-quality image are among the most worrisome.

Vending and Store Retailing Comparisons

In traditional stores, if customers have a complaint or need service, they can ask sales associates or go to the customer-service desk for assistance. This is obviously not possible when dealing with a machine. Vending companies cope with the psychology of dealing with a nonperson in several ways. In a large, in-plant location, a full-service assortment of vending machines may take the place of a manually operated cafeteria. Vending companies may choose to have an attendant on the premises to greet customers, service machines, and make change. Even though change-making machines are readily available, the personal touch goes a long way in establishing good customer relations and preventing damage to machines. If a product has not been dispensed after money has been inserted, a customer might be provoked enough to abuse a machine physically. One would hope a customer would not respond in a similar fashion to a human sales associate.

Sales and Merchandise Trends

Traditionally, cold drinks, candy, coffee, and cigarettes (the four Cs) were the biggest sellers from vending machines. Food and beverages still garner the most sales but changes in other areas are apparent. Cigarette sales declined, reflecting a growing concern for wellness and laws banning sales to minors, while sales of products reflecting leisure pursuits increased.

When trends shift, the vending industry responds accordingly. The flexibility of vending and its links to advanced technology are obvious. Several examples illustrate new directions within the vending industry and the adaptive nature of nonstore retailing.

- Best Buy launched vending machines called *Best Buy Express* at eight U.S. airports. The units dispense cell phone and computer gear, digital cameras, headphones, travel adapters, and other electronic gadgets.[40]
- Disappointed that you forgot to pack a swimsuit? Purchase a pair of board shorts or a bikini from vending machines poolside at Standard Hotels in Los Angeles, Hollywood, Miami, and New York. Co-branded with Quicksilver, the hotel sees the vending machines as a convenience for guests—especially those wanting to take a late-night swim.[41]
- PepsiCo introduced its Social Vending System at a National Automatic Merchandising Association trade show in 2011. A full touch-screen vending machine lets customers interact with others at the point of purchase. The unit boasts digital technology enabling users to select a beverage and gift a friend by entering mobile numbers, then texting a message or creating a video at the machine to send to the recipient.[42]

The underlying principle illustrated by these examples is: if it can be sold, it can be vended—at any hour of the day and almost any place. Although there are an estimated four to six million vending machines in the United States, vending revenue suffered during the recession and in 2010 experienced one of its worst years since 1994. Industry sales in the United States that year were just under $20 billion.[43]

Once a cash-only business, the industry is embracing new wireless technologies and alternative payment methods—some are calling it v-commerce. The emphasis now is on health foods and gourmet items, apparel, digital cameras, mobile devices, and more—well beyond the traditional market of snacks and food service.

Indoor and Outdoor Nonstore Retailers

Looking for a Pokémon or a Harry Potter trading card? Visit a flea market. Want a quick cup of espresso? Try a marketplace cart in a shopping center. Opportunities for nonstore retailing abound and take many different forms.

Flea Markets

Visit a flea market and you will find everything from great-grandmother's silverware to pre-packs of athletic socks, fine furniture to "junque." Flea markets are called *swap meets* on the West Coast of the United States. Both are usually open only on weekends and are held indoors or outdoors. An outdoor

Did You Know?
Ice cream sales from vending machines have grown steadily since 2008, the start of the economic downturn, with average prices increasing from $1.20 in 2008 to $1.31 by 2010. Trivia fact: There were almost 41,000 dedicated ice cream machines on location in 2010. A point to ponder: Was sales growth triggered by the psychological stress accompanying recent economic uncertainty, turning us to the comfort of an ice cream sandwich? Or was the growth organic, caused simply by the price increase of the product? (Source: Elliot Maras, "State of the Vending Industry Report: Recession Softens, Giving a Better Top Line, Ice Cream Revives." *Automatic Merchandiser*, 30, http://media.cygnus.com/files/ctgnus/document/AUTM/2011/aug/1839_soivendingreport emf_10343108.pdf.)

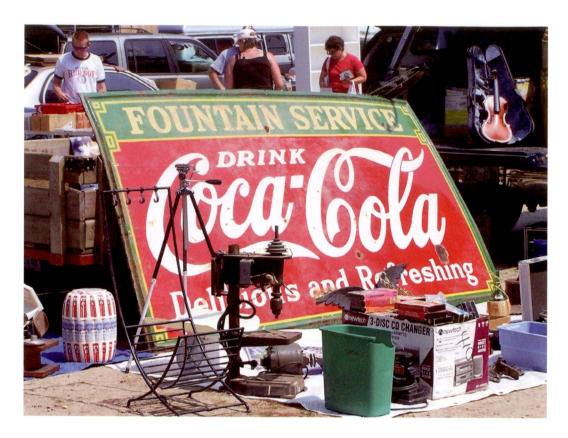

flea market is illustrated in Figure 6.7. Here anything from vintage apparel to used tools or perhaps a parakeet can be found. Flea markets are popular throughout Europe and much of the world.

Mobile Retailing

The chimes of an ice cream truck bring back fond childhood memories to most of us. Other foods, jewelry, imported leather goods—virtually anything—may be sold legitimately from the back of a truck or van, provided operators comply with local laws and have the appropriate permits. Equipped to go where the action is, catering trucks routinely bring food service to smaller factories and businesses whose employees do not have immediate access to restaurants and stores. Some mobile food service retailers have developed specialties.

The newest trend in L.A. is mobile gourmet bistro trucks. A Korean taco truck gained fame by advertising route stops on Twitter.com. The driver tweets where the truck will be in 20 minutes, and hundreds of people have been known to show up.[44] Customers line up patiently to order fine take-away food and to spot celebrities waiting alongside everyone else.

Auctions

Indoors, outdoors, or online, attending an auction is a fine way to observe supply and demand in action. Everything from livestock to cars, or simple household items to fine paintings and 19th-century claw-foot bathtubs are sold at auction. Sometimes the contents of an entire house go on the auction block. Called estate sales, these auctions can be fun, educational, and sometimes just a bit too enticing. The auctioneer in charge of selling goods rattles off information and solicits bids from spectators in rapid succession. It's easy to get caught up in the excitement and bid far more money than an item is worth. Despite this temptation, good values can often be found.

Auctions serve both retail and wholesale needs. Bidders can be antique dealers who are purchasing goods for resale in their shops. Some travel thousands of miles annually to get the best buys. Others are individuals purchasing items for their own homes or as gifts. Some attendees never give up the hope of finding an unexpected treasure: say, a $50 lamp that turns out to be a vintage Tiffany worth $50,000.

Marketplace Carts

Popular in downtown sites, tourist areas, and shopping malls, as seen in Figure 6.8, cart retailing has become a less risky way for many entrepreneurs to gain a foothold in the retail industry. After a few seasons of exposure, some cart retailers expand their businesses into stores. Some retailers operate carts on a larger scale and form chains. Having carts in 20 or more shopping centers is not unusual. Cart leasing can be expensive, especially during holiday seasons when a premium is placed on all available space. In a typical regional mall, during off-season periods, a simple mall cart leases for approximately $1,500 per month. Cart retailers tend to offer trendy products such as crafts, jewelry, souvenir items, snack foods, accessories, and T-shirts. Special interest groups like cat lovers, musicians, or candle devotees are easily reached through marketplace carts. Even popular direct sellers like Avon and Tupperware have sold through mall carts, further expanding their multichannel presence.

Temporary Retail Sites

Enterprising retailers are known for setting up shop in temporary sites where the "store" may be a makeshift booth, a patch of grass, or an available table. Craft shows, harvest fairs, carnivals, and community events create opportunities to sell products and services in short periods to people who are often primed to have fun and spend money. Some retailers make it their business to move with the events, and actually spend months on the road each year offering customers their wares. During the 2008 Olympics in Beijing, retailers were at their entrepreneurial best. Many global retailers of brand-name athletic wear and sporting gear set up temporary sites. In an interesting twist, the Beijing government set up temporary façades in front of small retailers in less-popular and perhaps more impoverished areas of the city, in order to put on a good face for tourists attending the games.

Preparing for the 2012 summer games in London, Locog, the Olympic organizing committee, opened a pop-up store in Hyde Park in early July. With a 1 billion pound goal. Simon Lilly, head of retail said, "If you've got $5.00 or $500.00, there's something for you." Anyone for a faux-gold miniature Olympic torch? It's supposed to be a top seller.[45]

Whether nonstore retailing occurs indoors or outdoors, is permanent or temporary, operates part-time or full-time, one truth is evident: retailing occurs just about anywhere products and consumers meet.

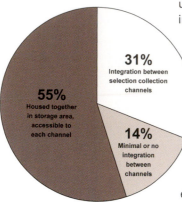

Levels of Multichannel Data Integration

55% Housed together in storage area, accessible to each channel

31% Integration between selection collection channels

14% Minimal or no integration between channels

Figure 6.9
Level of Multichannel Data Integration. Direct-marketing respondents were asked: "Which of the following best describes the integration among your data-collection channels?" (Source: *DMNews*)

Multichannel Integration

Retailers recognize that customers who often shop at their stores sometimes will want to shop by mail, phone, or computer. All retailers have gained a new respect for direct marketing methods and use them because they increase sales. Direct mail and catalogues once dominated direct marketing methods. Catalogues continue to be an important element in apparel marketers' multichannel strategies. The National Hockey League has found that when customers have a good catalogue experience, sales of team-related apparel sold on Shop.NHL.com increase.[46] Telephone contact works well when used in tandem with other direct marketing and multichannel methods. Adding new-generation mobile devices to the mix takes the best of telephone marketing and sets it spinning with access to new shopping channels and thousands of apps. Online selling has exceeded our expectations and continues to evolve. Consider the marriage of online and catalogue selling, then couple it with the iPad to fully appreciate the blossoming new avenues of e-commerce.

Here is the key for future direct marketing initiatives. For a true and harmonious multichannel environment to flourish, data will be integrated across all channels so that customer and operational information is readily available to retailers and all supply chain members. A graph illustrating the state of cross-channel data integration for multichannel retailers is shown in Figure 6.9.

Strengths of Direct Marketing, Direct Selling, and Nonstore Retailing

To refresh your knowledge of direct marketing, direct selling, and nonstore retailing, let's review some of the key attributes and strengths of each method as it reaches customers effectively. The significance of brick-and-mortar retailers, direct marketers, and direct sellers to multichannel retailing will become more apparent as we move on to Chapter 7, Electronic Retailing.

- Direct marketing's strength lies in its ability to reach customers expediently and with measurable results, using catalogues, direct mail, and telemarketing.
- Direct marketers may lack a physical storefront but they persuade customers to buy through personalized offers, well-crafted design, and the use of color and graphics on their catalogues and direct-mail pieces.
- Direct selling brings a distinct personal touch to customers through comfortable, sociable, nonthreatening, face-to-face situations for groups and individuals.
- Nonstore methods of contacting customers add other facets to retailing. Vending machines may seem cold and mechanical but offer convenience and incentives that make up for the lack of personal contact. (Think free-vend days at a company cafeteria.)
- The strengths of indoor and outdoor nonstore sites are that they provide entertainment, escape, fun, and—did we forget?—viable permanent and temporary locations for retail trade.

The cross-channel direction is reinforced by collaboration between supply chain members and is emblematic of future integrative directions for retailers and consumers. Never underestimate the power of retailing in all of its facets. It is limited only by the degree of inventiveness of retailers and entrepreneurs.

Summary

Because of dramatic breakthroughs in communications, distribution, and technology, more and more retailers are choosing to sell directly to consumers. As consumers have less time for shopping, seek more time for leisure activities, and demand value and service, they are becoming more responsive to direct marketing and direct selling methods. They are shopping in their homes and workplaces, by mail, telephone, the Web, and through personal consultants and party plans.

Direct marketing and selling are among the ways in which companies expand their retail business internationally. Although sales attributed to direct marketing traditionally came from catalogues, direct mail, and telemarketing, this direction is changing rapidly as more companies put their catalogues, flyers, and chat options online.

Brick-and-mortar retailers and other businesses are using direct marketing and direct selling methods as a way to integrate and supplement distribution strategies domestically and internationally and also as a survival tactic. Companies are delivering more solutions to their customers.

Flexibility is important as direct marketers face unprecedented changes in the economy, shifts in company ownership, postal and printing cost increases, and privacy laws that limit contact with customers and prospects.

In the vending industry, technology and convenience merge to bring many interesting nonstore retailing options to customers. Auctions, flea markets, carts, mobile retailing, and temporary sites round out the nonstore sector.

Multichannel integration is the directive for direct marketers, direct sellers, and all retailers. Sharing information across channels helps ensure smooth-flowing operations and may well lead to higher productivity. Most direct marketers are or will become multichannel retailers.

Key Terms

Carryover

Compiled lists

Consultative selling

Customer relationship management (CRM)

Database marketing

Data mining

Direct mail

Fulfillment

Group direct selling

Hand raisers

House lists

Inbound calls

Insert media

List broker

List manager

Mailing list

Multilevel marketing

Outbound calls

Person-to-person selling

Prospecting

Sprinkler strategy

Variable data printing (VDP)

Waterfall strategy

Questions for Review and Discussion

1. Why are direct marketing, direct selling, and other nonstore methods of retailing preferred by many consumers?
2. What are the differences between direct marketing and direct selling? How does each method reach customers?
3. Why have many brick-and-mortar retailers added print and online catalogues?
4. What are the special advantages of direct mail as a method of customer contact and promotion?
5. What are the principal benefits to retailers of telemarketing? In what situations is it most productive to use outbound calling?
6. How did the vending industry begin and what is its status today? Discuss the problems associated with the "psychology of dealing with the nonperson."
7. What role do flea markets, auctions, and other mobile or temporary site retailers play in the world of retailing?
8. Explain the importance of adopting multichannel initiatives as direct marketers and direct sellers strive to become more productive.

Endnotes

1. The Power of Direct Marketing: 2009-2010, Direct Marketing Association, Accessed October 18, 2011, www.the-dma.org/aboutdma/whatisthedma.shtml.
2. "DMA Releases 2012 Response Rate Report." General Direct Marketing and Mail Order Submitted by John Schulte. July 18, 2012. Direct Marketing Association. www.directmarketingnewswire.com/content/general-direct-marketing-mailorder/dma-releases-2012-response-rate-report-/4/12718.
3. Tony Case, "ZenithOptimedia Revises Down 2011 Global Ad Spending Forecast," *DMNEWS*, October 5, 2011, www.dmnews.com/zenithoptimedia-revises-down-2011-global-ad-spending-forecast.
4. Ibid. "DMA Releases 2012 Response Rate Report."
5. Melissa Dowling, "Outlook 2011: Catalogs," *Multichannel Merchant*, http://multichannelmerchant.com/outlook2011/outlook%20201Catalogs.pdf.
6. "Lists and Databases," *DMNEWS*, March 16, 2009, 15, and May 4, 2009.
7. "Special List," DMA Mailing List Service, July 24, 2009, www.dmasia.com/en/services/traditionaldm/directmailing/index.php.
8. "Mailing List Broker Costs," Marketing Comparison, www.marketingcomparison.com/mailinglist-costs.jsp?marketingId=1178119736704003027.
9. Mark Brohan, "French Retailer PPR Sells Off a Major Multichannel Brand," *Internet Retailer*, www.internetretailer.com/2011/02/02/french-retailer-ppr-sells-major-multichannel-brand.

10. Dianna Dilworth, "Catalog Holdings Sells its Spiegel Brands Unit," *DMNEWS*, September 22, 2008, 1.

11. "Gift, Home and Online-Only Catalogs Jump in Number from 2005 to 2010," Mediafinder, April 12, 2010, http://mediafinder.com/public.cfm?page+pressReleases/GiftHomeandOnline-OnlyCatalogsJumpinNumber from2005to2010.

12. Ibid.

13. "MCM 100 Power Players: Top 10: Home Décor/Furnishings." *Multichannel Merchant*, September 2011, 31.

14. "Deliverables," *Deliver*, August 2011, 2. (Source: *2011 DMA Statistical Fact Book*.)

15. Ibid. 5.

16. David Ward, "An Insert for Every Occasion," *DMNEWS*, June 9, 2009, 17.

17. "Statistically Speaking, Direct Mail Soars to New Heights," *Deliver*, July 1, 2011, www.delivermagazine.com/2011/07/statistically-speaking-direct-mail-soars-to-new-heights. (Source: United States Postal Service.)

18. Chantal Todé, "Digital Mail is Likely to See Yearly Growth," *DMNEWS*, February 16, 2009, 1.

19. Pamela Oldham, "The Changing Mail Game," *DMNEWS*, 2008, 04–05.

20. U.S. Postal Service, "Results-Driven Marketing in a Down Economy," DVD presentation by John Klemets, Dell and Nancy Gifford, Merkel Agency, 2009.

21. Ibid. DVD Presentation by Dan Sackrowitz, Bare Necessities.

22. Jim Tierney, "Merchants Say 2012 Postal Rate Increase Means Less Catalogs Mailed," *Multichannel Merchant*, October 20, 2011. www.multichannelmerchant.com/catalog/average-postal-rate-increase-2012-1020jt1imw=Y.

23. Kurt Ruppel, Marketing Services Manager, USPS, "Default, Insolvency, Shutdown...Oh, My!" October 5, 2011. www.iwco.com/blog.

24. "Telemarketing and Call Centers" U.S. Industry Report.," IBISWorld, May 15, 2009, www.ibisworld.com/industry/retail.aspx?indid=1468&chid=1.

25. Fred Coté. "Predictions on the Cloud Age: 2012." www.kunnect.com/resources/gspredictions.pdf. Source: Global Services. January 2012. www.globalservicesmedia.com.

26. FTC Consumer Alert, "Unsolicited Mail, Telemarketing and Email: Where to Go to 'Just Say No.'" Federal Trade Commission, August 10, 2011, www.ftc.gov/edu/pubs/consumer/alerts/alt063.shtm.

27. "International Direct Marketing—Internationalization Strategies," DHL Global Mail, www.dhl-global mail.com/dpgm?tab=1&skin=lo&check=no&lang=en&xmlFile=5002395. (Source: Backhaus/Büschken/Voeth, *Internationales Marketing*, Stuttgart 2003, 173.)

28. "Comparative Development of DM Expenditure," DHL Global Mail, 2008, www.dhlglobalmail.com/dpgm?tab=1&skin=lo&check=no&lang=en&xml1File=5002404#6214.

29. "Direct Marketing," *CCG 2011 Selling U.S. Products and Services*, Export.gov, http://export.gov/germany/MarketResearchonGermany/Country CommercialGuide/SellingU.S.ProductsandServices/index.asp#P33_9740.

30. Tim Searcy, "Call Center Problems Go Global," *DMNews*, June 18, 2007, 14.

31. Lois Geller, "Branding," Presentation to the Advanced Direct/Interactive Marketing Institute, Direct Marketing Educational Foundation, New York, June 6, 2000.

32. Scott Van Winkle, CFA. "The View from Wall Street-An Analyst's Perspective." A Special Supplement to the *Wall Street Journal* by Direct Selling News. "The Equity in Social Selling. Financial, Personal, Global." June 2012. p. 10–11.

33. Ram Charan, "The New (Recovery) Playbook," CNN Money.com, August 13, 2009, http://money.cnn.com/2009/08/11/news/economy/new_rules_recovery.fortune/index.htm. (Source: *Fortune* magazine.)

34. Hakki Ozmorali. "Biggies We Know What You Did Last Year." © The World of Direct Selling. February 27, 2012. www.worldofdirectselling.com/2012/02/

35. Serena Ng and Justin Baer. "Buffet Bats for Coty on Avon Offer." *Wall Street Journal*. May 11, 2012. B1.

36. "Direct Selling by the Numbers Calendar Year 2010." *Industry Statistics: Location of Sales* (reported as a percentage of sales dollars), 6. www.dsa.org/research/industry-statistics.

37. Ibid, "Sales Strategy," 7.

38. Kelly Evans, "Gold is the New Tupperware, And You're Invited to the Party," *Wall Street Journal*, December 19–20, 2009, A1, A10.

39. "Dove Chocolate Discoveries," Direct Selling Association, accessed February 16, 2010, www.dsa.org.

40. The Associated Press, "Best Buy to Launch Gadget Vending Machines," *Business Week*, August 11, 2008, http://business week.com/ap/financialnews/D92FRPSO1.htm.

41. "Quicksilver Goes Poolside With Vending Machines," *Women's Wear Daily*, July 30, 2009, 8.

42. "PepsiCo Introduces Social Vending System, the Next Generation in Interactive Vend Technology." *Internet Retailer*, May 11, 2011, www.internetretailer.com/2011/05/11/pepsico-introduces-social-vending-system.

43. Ilan Brat, "Restocking the Snack Machine," *Wall Street Journal*, August 3, 2010, B5.

44. Erik Sass, "Tweeters Use Twitter for Business," *MediaPost News*, February 26, 2009, www.mediapost.com/publications/?fa=Articles.printFriendly&art_aid=101018.

45. Alice Speri. "It's Not Gold; It's Olympic Schlock." *Wall Street Journal*. July 26, 2012 B1.

46. Nathan Golia, "Mail's Multichannel Power," *DMNEWS*, July 27, 2009, 12.

Chapter 7

Electronic Retailing

Learning Objectives

After completing this chapter you should be able to:

- Evaluate the scope and status of electronic retailing.
- Identify strategies used by top-ranked retail Web sites.
- Compare the advantages and disadvantages of electronic retailing from both retail and customer perspectives.
- Discern what constitutes an effective Web site in terms of design and technological development.
- Illuminate the ways online retailers are addressing the expectations of online shoppers.
- Identify key trends and strategies in online selling.
- Highlight other methods of electronic retailing including the rise of m-commerce.

Figure 7.1
Apple and Target made digital history when the companies partnered to sell iPads and other electronic wonders yet to come to Target stores.

Online stores are the youngest members of the retail world, but they have already become an inviting shopping option for multitudes. Other methods of electronic retailing give customers the convenience of shopping at home, or in some cases, wherever they may be. Home shopping channels and their online counterparts provide a shopping alternative for television devotees. Through infomercials that both entertain and educate, direct response television (DRTV) softens the impact of a sales pitch. **Infomercials** are television commercials that combine detailed product information, demonstration, and excitement with a call to action. **Direct response television (DRTV)** is an advertising medium used by direct marketers with the intention of eliciting an immediate response from consumers.

To supplement their marketing efforts, many retailers use electronic kiosks. **Electronic kiosks** are small computer displays or vending units in stores or other locations that help generate sales or provide extended customer services.

Although elements of design remain the same for most creative expression, Web design and development have their own language and distinctions. The use of digitally enhanced graphics, navigational software, interactive features, and transactional capabilities draw customers. Sales performance and customer contact metrics make online selling both an art and a science.

Advanced Internet technologies help all supply chain members and customers do business more efficiently and expediently. Using search to reach relevant customers is the objective of all online retailers. Payment options in the world of e-retailing are as varied as they are in the brick-and-mortar world, and privacy and security issues are concerns of all online shoppers. The fastest growing aspect of e-retailing is shopping by mobile phone, anytime, anywhere, any place. All aspects are discussed in this chapter.

Online Retailing: Overview and Impact

It is difficult to keep abreast of technological changes, much less implement or use them. Retailers must do both to remain competitive. While continuing to do business through conventional channels, multichannel retailers—introduced in Chapter 1—operate online stores. For many companies that value a global presence, one of the most effective ways to expand is through online retailing.

Terminology and Tools

Although embedded in our vernacular, definitions of frequently used terms bear clarification. The **Internet** is a vast system of interconnected computer networks that allows computers worldwide to access and exchange information. **Intranets** are internal computer communication systems within a business or institution. Secured computer links between business partners such as retailers and suppliers are called **extranets**.

The **World Wide Web** (often shortened to "the Web") refers to the totally integrated informational and commercial electronic services accessible via global computer networks and wireless technology. A **Web site** is a specific location of a business, organization, or person on the World Wide Web. A **universal resource locator (URL)** is the complete Web site address, which includes an access protocol and the domain name. The **domain name** is the portion of a Web address that contains the company or other unique name and the identifier, such as .com, .net, or .biz. **Internet service providers (ISPs)** are national or regional companies that provide access to the Internet for a monthly fee.

The Internet Corporation for Assigned Names and Numbers (ICANN) is the organization that oversees Internet addresses. In 2008, it approved changes that would enable businesses to obtain nontraditional suffixes beyond the standard .com, .net, and .org. With this change, businesses can personalize their URLs to make them more marketable; however, the costs are high to obtain a nontraditional suffix. The suffix .biz was approved in 2001, and .travel in 2005, but neither has reached widespread use.[1] There are 94.5 million domain names in use. ICANN expects that the first custom names will be online by late 2012. A company or individual must pay $185,000 to apply for a custom name and suffix.[2]

Search engines are computer programs used to find and index all the information that is available on the Web. They provide the mode of transportation to specific Web sites on the Internet. Companies such as Google (the largest search engine), Microsoft Network's Bing, Yahoo, and Ask.com are in this category. Some advertise extensively through conventional as well as electronic media.

Browsers are software programs that facilitate Web navigation, the search for information, or access to a site. They allow us to turn on and tune in to the Internet.

Types of Online Business

Several abbreviated terms are used to describe the various dimensions of business conducted online. **E-commerce** includes all goods and services sold on the Internet and through other electronic means, including business-to-business (B2B) and business-to-consumer (B2C) transactions. It is the all-encompassing term for business conducted on the Web.

Recall from Chapter 1 that manufacturers selling to retailers and producers of raw materials selling to manufacturers are examples of B2B transactions. When we go online to score a bargain at Bluefly.com or download a song by Beyoncé in iTunes, we are participating in a B2C transaction. **Consumer-to-consumer (C2C)** transactions are those completed by individuals selling to one another. A person who sells goods on eBay or Craigslist, or through independent social networking sites is participating in C2C transactions.

E-retailing includes online and other electronic transactions involving goods and services for personal, nonbusiness use. **M-commerce** is business conducted using wireless devices such as cell phones, smartphones, or tablets—in other words, iPhones, Androids, iPads, and iPad Minis.

The next sections review the current state of online retailing, including worldwide usage of the Web and advantages and disadvantages of online retailing.

Ups, Downs, and Current Status of E-Commerce

In the 1990s, the information superhighway grew rapidly to encompass wholesale and retail superstores in cyberspace. E-commerce boomed, the numbers of retail and B2B users mushroomed, and technology companies flourished. Then came the dot-com crash. The volatility of the economy and the resultant failure of many online retail and other technology-driven businesses compromised progress. Early forecasts, which predicted that electronic commerce would soon overtake brick-and-mortar stores as the major form of retailing, soon abated.

The economy rebounded in the years after the millennium only to experience deep and global recession later that decade. Online stores have weathered the most recent economic downturn better than many brick-and-mortar retailers. Multichannel retailers are better equipped to deal with economic crises, since they benefit from having more than one method of reaching customers and are able to spread the financial risk across the channels in which they operate. E-retailing remains a strong option for consumers, if not the only answer to their shopping needs.

Worldwide Internet Usage and Sales Trends

Growth in online access has been explosive. Worldwide, there were in excess of 2.1 billion Internet users in 2011, almost six times the number of people who were online in 2000.[3] Figure 7.2 ranks the top 15 countries in Internet usage.

In 2008, Internet usage by consumers in China topped usage in the United States for the first time.[4] By 2011, China had 23 percent of the world's users while the United States claimed 11.6 percent. Countries that were slower to adopt Internet technologies are rapidly making up for lost time. Russia had 42.8 percent of its population online in 2011. In the Middle East, Iran's usage rate has grown substantially; in Africa, Nigeria is experiencing a growth phase.[5] The penetration rate is climbing as the technological infrastructure improves and customers gain access to computers.

E-retailing sales in the United States reached approximately $197 billion in 2011, with annual sales expected to reach $279 billion in 2015.[6] Worldwide e-commerce sales reached $575.5 billion in 2010, and predictions indicated that more than $1 trillion would be realized by 2013.[7] If these forecasts prove accurate, the Web will influence half of all retail sales in the United States through direct online sales and those influenced by the Web.

Spain is considered the top e-commerce market for sales increases with an estimated growth rate of 37 percent. Brazil, China, Russia, and Mexico follow with growth percentages in the mid-to-high 20th percentile.[8]

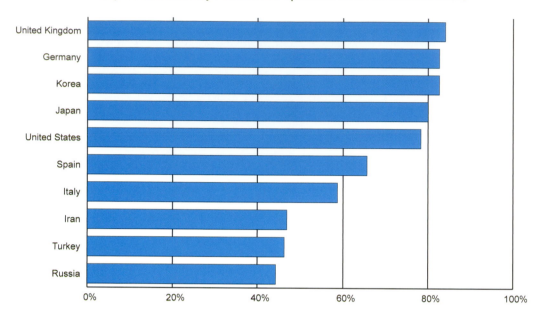

Top 10 Countries by Percent of Population Who Are Internet Users

Figure 7.2

Top Ten Countries Ranked by Percentage of Their Population Using the Internet. (Source: Based on data from Internet World Stats, Miniwatts Marketing Group. http://www.internetworldstats.com/top20htm.)

Impact of the Economic Downturn

Several aspects of online retailing were affected by the recession that began in late 2007. Cost savings, expansion, and discounting were the objectives of many retailers over the ensuing years.

For some online retailers, lean times spurred them to practice forms of cost cutting. About 88 percent indicated that they intended to reduce the size of their staffs or alter hiring plans, and 56 percent said they would spend less on search advertising.[9] Others sought to refine marketing efforts, and substantial numbers intended to increase e-mail contact with customers.

The French supermarket company Casino Group launched a discount Web site geared to customers affected by the economic downturn. Called CDiscount, a new version of the site designed for the United Kingdom competes with Amazon and Tesco. Selling home electronics, apparel, wine, and much more, the online retailer expects to lure customers with intensive promotions every day and customer-friendly payment plans.[10] This action could be the first step toward further international expansion in Europe and other markets. The top retail Web sites in Europe—including the three companies mentioned above—are listed in Table 7.1.

Regardless of the recession, one study showed that 70 percent of U.S. retailers planned to invest as much or more in e-commerce updates in 2009 than they did the previous year.[11] A 2011 study found that 73 percent of respondents intended to budget for Web site design upgrades, while 82 percent planned to execute these enhancements within 12 months.[12]

Popular Product Categories

Several retail product and service categories are widely sought after on the Web. Apparel and accessories were the top merchandise category on the Web in 2010, followed by housewares and home furnishings, and then sporting goods, according to the industry publication *Internet Retailer*. Online apparel sales initially grew more slowly due to issues with fit and the inability to inspect merchandise prior to purchase. However, by 2010, apparel and accessories were one of the biggest growth categories.[13]

Books are always a good seller on the Internet, but the shape and form have greatly affected consumer response to this once-traditional product. In the spring of 2011, for the first time, sales of e-books at Amazon.com were greater than those of print books.

Table 7.1 Europe's Top Online Merchants

Rank	Company	Home Country	2010 Sales (in US$ billions)
1	Amazon.com, Inc. (Europe)	United States	80.35
2	Otto Group	Germany	5.34
3	Tesco Stores	United Kingdom	4.40*
4	Staples, Inc. (Europe)	United States	3.95*
5	PPR SA (Pinault, Printemps, Redoute; primary URL: LaRedoute.fr)	France	3.21
6	Home Retail Group (primary URL: Argos.co.uk)	United Kingdom	1.41*
7	3 Suisses	France	1.64*
8	CDiscount.com	France	1.64*
9	Neckermann Gruppe	Germany	1.55
10	Dixons Stores	United Kingdom	1.52*

Internet Retailer estimates.

Source: "2011 Top 300 Europe," adapted from Mark Brohan, "Europe's Top 10," *Internet Retailer*, March 15, 2011, www.internet retailer.com/2011/03/15/europes-top-10.

Annual sales and performance metrics for major merchandise categories are graphed in Table 7.2. Figures are based on the *Internet Retailer 2011 Second 500 Guide*: indeed, so great has the growth of online sellers been that the trade publication found it necessary to cover sites ranked 501–1000. Total sales for this group topped $2.5 billion, and many of the second 500 are the

Table 7.2 Annual Online Sales by Merchandise Category

Merchandise Category	2010 Web Sales	Increase over 2009 Sales	Share of 2010 Second Top 500 Retailers
Apparel/Accessories	$572,145,959	21.29%	23.17%
Automotive Parts/Accessories	$ 78,657,087	13.18%	3.18%
Books/Music/Video	$ 93,341,377	5.65%	3.78%
Computers/Electronics	$152,317,071	14.24%	6.17%
Flowers/Gifts	$116,953,539	9.76%	4.74%
Food/Drug	$116,656,060	11.08%	4.72%
Hardware/Home Improvement	$149,565,037	17.41%	6.06%
Health/Beauty	$144,779,606	20.18%	5.86%
Housewares/Home Furnishings	$341,712,591	16.81%	13.84%
Jewelry	$105,892,567	15.61%	4.29%
Mass Merchant	$ 81,737,944	51.14%	3.31%
Office Supplies	$135,498,245	9.47%	5.49%
Pet Care	$ 30,212,164	6.61%	1.22%
Sporting Goods	$264,727,914	14.19%	10.72%
Toys/Hobbies	$ 85,512,498	12.38%	3.46%

Source: Mark Brohan, "Know Thy Customer," excerpted from graph "Who's Up and Who's Down (By Merchandise Category)," *Internet Retailer*, August 2011, 47. (Based on results of *The Internet Retailer 2011 Second 500 Guide*, an annual survey addressing sales and growth of second group of 500 online retailers [#501–1000] in the United States.)

Figure 7.3
Rue La La is a discount fashion Web site whose customers are "members" of an elite shopping group. Its Web page shows how members register for a private event—perhaps a flash sale that runs for only 36 hours. The message: Act fast!

up-and-coming online powerhouses of the future. The first 500 online retailers accounted for $129.4 billion, or 78.2 percent of the top 500 sales.[14]

Discount fashion sites, including those that can only be accessed through exclusive memberships, top the trend list for the shop-till-you-drop crowd. True to the mission of bringing designer fashion to the online masses, these sites have mastered the flash sale. Selling peak demand, special promotion, or designer's overstocks for a brief period announced with very little customer notification is called a **flash sale**.

Since 2008, RueLaLa.com has been selling designer handbags, shoes, and apparel for approximately 35–70 percent off regular prices. The U.S.-based company received much coverage in the trade and consumer publications for its exclusive "members-only" sales, time-limited promotions, and dependence on word-of-mouth advertising. Rue La La also sells spa packages and yoga sessions. It was the first of the discount designer sites to engage in mobile commerce.[15] A Rue La La Web page is seen in Figure 7.3.

The Japanese site Glamour-sales.com operates similarly to Rue La La and other private sale Web sites, with a few unique twists. Although operating in Japan, the company is owned by a group of French investors. Sixty fashion brands comprise about half of its sales, and the company also offers luxury hotel packages, Peugeot cars, and gourmet foods. U.S.-based Gilt Groupe Inc. also operates a Japanese version of its Web site. Since its launch, the site has attracted more than 20 million members and anticipates sales of 50 billion yen ($508.7 million) by 2014.[16] The Japanese market for luxury goods has always been strong, but this new thrust toward private discount fashion sales during a global economic downturn is all the more fascinating.

Structures of Online and Multichannel Retailers

Almost 100 percent of major retailers sell online. With that said, retailers fall into one or more of the following categories:

1. *Pure-play retailers.* Companies that do not operate retail stores or engage in other nonstore distribution, and do business exclusively online. Amazon.com and Newegg.com are examples.
2. *Dual-channel retailers.* Companies that operate primarily from brick-and-mortar stores but also engage in business online. Companies like Walmart, Macy's, and Home Depot fit this description.
3. *Multichannel retailers.* Retail companies that sell through more than two marketing channels. Retailers in this category, including The Territory Ahead, L.L. Bean, and Victoria's Secret, sell through stores, catalogues, and online.
4. *Electronic spin-offs.* Retailers that originally traded by means other than online. As examples, the television shopping channel QVC operates QVC.com and the NBC network runs ShopNBC.com online.
5. *Nontransactional sites.* Retailers that maintain Web sites and provide company information but do not sell online. Many small retailers have nontransactional sites and use them to provide information and education to their customers. They keep in touch by e-mail, phone, Twitter, and social networking sites like Facebook.

As the online sector matures, many nontransactional sites will likely add online shopping services. Some pure-play sites have failed, yet Amazon.com—the top-grossing retail site with about $48 billion in 2011—is a pure-play. Brick-and-mortar retailers have taken a proactive approach, adding catalogues and online stores to become multichannel retailers. Expect these directions to continue as the multichannel label becomes commonplace.

Optional Selling Formats

Other e-retailing strategies include several models that parallel existing institutions in the real world. They include online malls and auction sites.

Online Shopping Malls

Major providers present numerous opportunities for customers to visit scores of retailers by a simple click of the mouse. Sponsored by search engines, sites like Bing Shopping are outmaneuvering comparison-shopping site malls like Shop.com and Best-Price.com through aggressive promotions. For example, Bing Shopping offered twice the usual amount of cash back if shoppers registered for its Cashback program. Dedicated marathon shoppers could save 15 percent shopping at BarnesandNoble.com and 22–40 percent at eBags.com during such limited-time promotions.[17]

International shopping experiences are cultivated by visiting myriad malls emanating from other countries. Many luxury-goods retailers first found online homes at eLuxury.com, a subsidiary of Louis Vuitton Moet Hennessy (LVMH), the French conglomerate. These sites bring extensive exposure to many designer retailers—including Dior, Celine, Marc Jacobs, and Dolce & Gabbana—and defy the common assumption that customers do not like to shop for posh merchandise online. However, even luxury-goods malls were affected by the recent recession. LVMH discontinued eLuxury.com late in 2009. Although the designer site experienced consistent sales growth, the decision was made to convert the site into an online magazine targeting people with an interest in fine leather goods, jewelry, cars, yachts, and services. Many of the designer brands featured on eLuxury.com now have their own sites, which also contributed to the decision to change the format.[18]

Online Auctions

Electronic auctions are opportunities for customers to be entertained and perhaps obtain a great buy in a reasonably secure environment. Most auction sites charge sellers a listing fee and percentage of the selling price. eBay.com, the online marketplace operates in this way, specializing in collectibles such as Pokémon and Hello Kitty, antiques, vehicles, and products that appeal to special-interest groups. Celebrity memorabilia of all types have become hot properties for online sellers. eBay also offers fixed-price sales and is moving more in that tactical direction. It also has ramped up its apparel sales by introducing a special section devoted to flash sales of designer goods and, at the other end of the pricing spectrum, an online outlet mall.[19]

Online auctions are not without their problems. Bogus bids that drive up prices, product misrepresentation, nondelivery of goods, and other instances of fraud compromise their reputations. To ensure safe transactions, eBay.com developed rules for online buyers and sellers. Sellers are prohibited from bidding on their own merchandise, and buyers are given free insurance against fraud or mislabeled goods by eBay. These safeguards greatly improve the image of online auctions.

eBay was considered one of the top e-commerce sites in terms of sales and profits in 2002, but by the end of the decade it had declined significantly. One of the key strengths of the company is its PayPal online payment system, which continues to perform well. In 2011 eBay acquired Zong, a service that accepts payment using cell-phone carriers, giving eBay's 100 million users the option of charging online physical and virtual purchases to their cell-phone bills. Zong has affiliations with approximately 250 mobile operators in 45 countries.[20]

eBay operates globally, in North America, Europe, and Asia, and is looking to expand farther. To enhance its core retail marketplace business, eBay acquired Gmarket, a South Korean e-commerce company, for $1.2 billion in 2009.[21]

Retailer and Customer Perspectives on E-Retailing

Identifying elements that help and hinder online retailers and customers provides essential knowledge that can be used to improve the retail transaction. This process sets the stage for further discussion of online customers.

Advantages and Disadvantages of Online Retailing

Online retailing offers several advantages to both retailers and customers, as well as some disadvantages.

Did You Know?
Every month, eBay sells three to four Ferraris through its mobile apps. Luxury jewelry, watches, and handbags are favorite holiday purchases on the site. In 2010, eBay reached almost $2 billion in m-commerce sales. (Source: Bill Siwicki, "eBay Hits Nearly $2 billion in M-Commerce Sales Worldwide in 2010," *Internet Retailer*, January 5, 2011, www.internet retailer.com/2011/01/05/ebay-hits-nearly-2-billion-mobile-sales-worldwide-in-2010.)

Advantages to Retailers

1. Online stores are always open. Online stores and shopping malls provide access around the clock, every day—24/7/365.
2. Web retailers reach mass markets; niche markets also are easily accessed.
3. Online selling is still relatively new, and the great potential of this channel offers businesses ample opportunities for growth.
4. An online presence extends brand awareness both locally and globally.
5. Brick-and-mortar stores and direct marketing businesses are enhanced when online stores are added.
6. Database development and data mining facilitates awareness of customer behavior and helps create more personalized programs for customers.
7. Online selling may make cost reductions in store leasing, staffing, operations, and data collection possible.
8. Setting up a Web site is less expensive than setting up a store—especially for small retailers.
9. Web sites greatly expand geographic and demographic markets for large or small retailers.
10. E-mail provides excellent promotional and customer service contact.

Disadvantages to Retailers

1. Customers lack the opportunity to touch, examine, smell, and interact physically with products.
2. The technology is still evolving and some customers do not embrace the technological aspects of online shopping.
3. Customers are concerned about privacy and security, and some are reticent to shop online.
4. Product misrepresentation due to poor-quality or inconsistent graphics is possible.
5. Without an efficient search engine, customers may have difficulty finding retailers' sites.
6. Currency exchange, taxes, tariffs, and shipping are challenges, especially in emerging international markets.
7. Channel conflicts can occur as manufacturers and suppliers set up their own sites and bypass retailers.

Advantages to Customers

1. The convenience of shopping from the home or office 24/7/365 is compelling to many people.
2. Customers save time shopping online and some experience greater savings on purchases.
3. Customers can easily research products, compare prices, read peer and retailer reports, and socialize and shop with friends.
4. Customers report fewer shopping-related hassles. As many have said, it is easier to shop online than it is to find a parking spot at a mall, and online shoppers are not exposed to problems such as traffic, crowds, and street crime that may be associated with shopping at brick-and-mortar retailers.
5. Increased access to a broader array of products and services is available online.
6. Customers expand their trading area by shopping internationally.

Disadvantages to Customers

1. Perceived and actual relinquished privacy regarding disclosure of financial and other personal information.
2. Possibility of credit-card fraud or account-number theft through data breaches.
3. Inability to authenticate online retailers since any company or person can set up a site.
4. Problems with technology, such as slow or sporadic transmission; too many clicks to find what is needed can irritate customers.
5. Distribution hassles, including untimely delivery and inconvenient return policies.
6. The inability to physically examine products, try on apparel, or smell an aroma.
7. Vast time commitment when searching sites; it might take less time to drive to a mall!
8. Feeling overwhelmed by the myriad choices available online compared with stores or catalogues.

Shoppers who frequent traditional retail establishments voice some of these same disadvantages. For example, "too much to choose from" is mentioned by reluctant mall shoppers as one reason why they do not like to shop. Online shoppers may also have difficulty picturing themselves in a digitally rendered garment. This problem with Web page illustration is similar to reports by catalogue shoppers who cite dissatisfaction with goods ordered from catalogue photographs.

To help customers discover new fashion directions, JCPenney formed a partnership with People StyleWatch, an offshoot of *People* magazine. On a specially flagged section of JCPenney.com and through in-store promotions, customers can browse young women's apparel, shoes, and accessories that the magazine considers the trendiest items from the exclusive designer lines produced for Penney.[22] On one visit to the Web site, several Olsenboye items—designed by Mary-Kate and Ashley Olsen—were spotted.

The Online Shopper

Who is the online customer? Elusive, ageless, hip, easy to please, or impossible to predict? Maybe a digital diva, introduced in Table 4.1? Any and all of the above describe this customer of the 21st century. Many studies have examined the intricacies of customer behavior online. The generalities mentioned above are not sufficient as we explore the nuances of customer behavior and the propensity for shopping online or not. E-retailing may be most appealing to individuals who view traditional shopping as torturous.

Gender Differences in Internet Usage

According to the U.S. Census Bureau, 51.26 percent of Internet users were female and 48.36 percent male in 2010.[23] Although these statistics do not indicate online shopping habits, they do alert us to some gender-related differences.

When it comes to purchasing apparel, accessories, and jewelry online, according to one source, women transact 71 percent of sales and men 29 percent. Despite this apparent imbalance, Natalie Massenet, founder of Net-a-Porter for women, believes there is demand for her spin-off site for men, Mr. Porter. She believes a successful online retailer needs to understand and appreciate the way men want to shop.[24]

In other countries such as France and Turkey, more men than women are Internet users. Culture, gender roles, and access to technology affect these differences. From the Field 7.1 describes a French luxury Web site for men and explores some of the differences between men's and women's behavior online.

Multichannel Shopping Affinity

Online shoppers are more likely than non-online shoppers to shop by phone, from catalogues, via television, and at brick-and-mortar stores. When shoppers frequent more than one marketing channel, they are also likely to spend more money annually. The results of a survey on cross-channel shopping showed that 55 percent of respondents had purchased a product online for in-store pickup. This indicates the growing importance of Web-to-store options for customers. Comfort with the integration of selling channels is fundamental to the receptiveness of customers to online service initiatives.

Age-Relevant Distinctions

The technology-oriented customer of any age is more open to new technology, innovation, and change. Younger shoppers who have grown up with the Internet are likely to purchase products online. Research findings show that in the United States, 4 million young women between the ages of 12 and 17 years, representing 52.6 percent of the total teen online market, purchased products online in 2010.[25] Other studies indicate that older baby boomers and silver seniors are among the fastest growing groups of Internet users.

Although age, income, and reaction to the economic downturn may be interrelated, interpreting the results of consumer surveys when these variables are in play is difficult and findings may run counter to expectations. One study conducted in the first quarter of 2009 found that individuals over 45 living in households with incomes of $50,000 to $100,000 cut back on their

Cyberscoop
Go to www.jcpenney.com and click "People StyleWatch" to see what's sizzling in the retailer's fashion departments— perhaps something irresistible from Mary-Kate and Ashley Olsen's Olsenboye line. Penney's also has a Facebook page, a JCPTeen Facebook page, and a Twitter handle that promotes many brands. (Source: Lisa Lockwood, "The Social Swirl," *Women's Wear Daily*, May 31, 2011, 14.)

online spending by 11 percent; at the same time, people aged 18–44 increased their spending by 15 percent.[26] Could these findings mean that younger online customers were less affected by the economic downturn than older consumers? Could they signify that younger people perceived the economy was improving at the time of the study and therefore felt justified in increasing their expenditures? Or were younger buyers simply more willing to risk their cash on self-gratification? Results of such studies cannot give observers the full picture but do give rise to speculation.

Gender, age, multichannel shopping tendencies, and tendency to adopt new technologies are not the only relevant attributes of Internet users. However, they seem to surpass all other demographic and psychographic characteristics in importance.

Elements of Web Site Development: Turning Surfers into Shoppers

For modest costs, retailers can set up simple Web sites. The picture changes as transactional capabilities and arrangements with search engines are broached and advanced applications and designs are planned. As retailing options change, so does the demand for prime locations and attractive facilities, whether it is a shopping mall or an online store that is under construction.

Fledgling online retailers face many challenges including optimizing brands, financing the operation, choosing workable strategies, designing an appealing site, optimizing search, convincing customers to shop electronically, and keeping them coming back.

Challenges to Retail Start-Ups

Starting a retail business online poses unique challenges. It's not easy to design a store when that store is intangible. Image transfer is important as retailers look to recreate their successful brick-and-mortar formats without the help of walls, windows, or floor plans. Retailers must create not only user-friendly Web sites, but also those that have the ability to become familiar destinations. If you are a regular Gap shopper, the Gap online store should exude the same product quality, selection, and superior customer service as its store and catalogue operations.

Financing a Web Site

There are two principal ways to set up a Web site—own or rent. If these options sound similar to owning or renting a conventional store, they are. Large retailers may prefer setting up dedicated sites, called nodes, which can cost several hundred thousand to over a million dollars. Special software, design services, and connection fees become part of set-up costs and frequent updates increase maintenance costs. Smaller retailers usually prefer to rent a Web page, called a hosted site, from a service provider. A modest fee per month and an outlay for design and updates are all that is necessary to open a store online.

Characteristics of Effective Online Retailers

Reports indicate that online retailing may work best for certain types of retailers including those that:

- Use their online store to offer more breadth and depth of merchandise than is possible in stores with limited square footage, or carry narrow and deep assortments like many specialty stores.
- Target highly defined market segments.
- Use vast creativity to sell.
- Sell products that do not require close inspection or handling.

Individuals interested in purchasing parts for vintage automobiles, gothic tattoo patterns, or shoes made from vegetable products can quickly identify specialty sites featuring such items. Retail formats that lend themselves to high creativity also attract attention. Formats that delight the masses like Amazon or Sears, or specialty sites like Best Buy, provide significant extensions to brand appeal and retail sales. The top 25 customer-favorite online retailers as determined by *Stores* magazine, are listed in Table 7.3.

Setting Up Online Stores

Attracting customers to your Web site, creating in them a strong desire for your products or services, and effecting an action to purchase may sound like simple goals. In fact, it is the synergy of many design and technological elements that forges an appealing and effective Web site. The attractiveness of the Web site is certainly a product of superior design, but for customers to become fully engaged the navigation tools that make the site work are equally important. Since most sites are set up to sell, transaction mechanisms must be available. Advanced technologies that enable high-level user interaction as well as offer rich media, heightened graphics, and 3D capabilities are considered **Web 2.0** features. These extra features delight our senses, give us better views of products, and amplify our emotions. **Web 3.0** features are technically advanced systems that mesh online shopping and offline services. The site-to-store programs that require newer, more complex cross-channel platforms are an example.

Other capabilities ensure better communication, education, and information than in the early

Table 7.3   Customers' Top 25 Favorite Internet Retailers

Rank	Retailer	Main Product
1	Amazon.com	General merchandise
2	Walmart.com	General merchandise
3	eBay.com	Online marketplace
4	BestBuy.com	Electronics
5	Kohls.com	Apparel
6	JCPenney.com	Apparel
7	Target.com	General merchandise
8	Macys.com	Apparel
9	Sears.com	General merchandise
10	Google.com	Information
11	Old Navy.com	Apparel
12	Overstock.com	General merchandise
13	QVC.com	General merchandise
14	Kmart.com	General merchandise
15	LandsEnd.com	Apparel
16	Lowes.com	Hardware
17	WomanWithin.com	Apparel
18	Forever21.com	Apparel
19	Yahoo.com	Information
20	HomeDepot.com	Hardware
21	LLBean.com	Apparel
22	Blair.com	Apparel
23	Gap.com	Apparel
24	Zappos.com	Footwear
25	Nordstrom.com	Apparel

Source: "2012 Favorite 50," *Stores,* September 2012, www.stores.org/2012/Favorite-50-List.

days of the Web. Customer services and opportunities to communicate with the retailer help ensure a transition from visitor to customer.

Web site Design
A Web site's home page must convey a retail image in such a way that potential customers are encouraged to peruse the site. Since the home page is the first screen that appears to the user, it becomes the equivalent of a store window. Advertising graphics on Web site pages are called **banners**. As with most forms of advertising, banner ads did not necessarily precipitate immediate sales, but they did build brand awareness. Newer digital tactics have mostly supplanted banners. Advanced search ads, widgets, pop-ups, rotating images, and other attention-getters are the tools wielded by contemporary Web designers.

Aesthethics of Design Strong graphics, brand-enhancing color choices, appropriate typography, and interactive features must lead prospective customers through the site logically and expediently. These elements become the "store fixtures" and "visual merchandising" of online retailing. Merchandise presented graphically with great care or shown via streaming video compensates somewhat for the inability of customers to touch and examine the merchandise.

Whether a design is being developed for a Web site, catalogue, or magazine advertisement, basic rules apply. Flow, balance, proportion, and selection of typography all convey an image and are carefully considered. Many sites use a popular two-thirds/one-third page breakdown tactic, placing key information and graphics in a two-column configuration and collateral material in the third column, and saving ample room at the top for a logo, search boxes, and "gotcha" elements.

Web 2.0 Features The technology that brings us flash, zoom, and 360-degree product rotation adds zip and zing to our online experience. Known collectively as Web 2.0, these special features enhance Web site design and make the visit to a site more interactive. These technologies are fun to use and, more importantly, increases sales.

The company 3DVO makes software that creates 3D views of products used by many worldwide companies including outdoor outfitter REI, Overstock.com, and Amazon.com. According to Troy Sheen, chief executive officer (CEO) of 3DVO, customers of Web sites that offer this technology spend more time at the sites, return more frequently, and spend more. He said: "We know we increase all three of those to the tune of 33 percent more time spent on their Web sites, three times as many people coming back to the site, and about a 20 percent uplift in sales. So, it's not small."[27] An example of 360-degree rotation is shown in Figure 7.4.

Other Web 2.0 applications include:

- Alternate views of a product.
- Personalized features.
- Color swatches.
- Online video.
- User ratings and rankings.
- Microsites.
- Widgets.

Web 3.0 is not far behind, with more integrative options than those developed under the Web 2.0 umbrella. Web 3.0 merges advanced customer-oriented interactive capabilities with artificial intelligence. Drawing from the wealth of information found on social networking, mobile, and other sites, Web 3.0–enabled sites are more pointed in their ability to correlate customer behaviors with product and service sales efforts.

Use of Avatars Some media sites feature avatars that entertain or take visitors shopping; others let you create one that looks like you! An **avatar** is an animated digital form that portrays a person. Avatars have become regular features of many online stores. Kohls.com gives 'tweens and teens the chance to create their own avatars and then dress them in outfits purchased inexpensively in "stardollars" from Stardoll.com. The enormous potential of this approach was highlighted when the Web site featured virtual versions of Kohl's Abbey Dawn apparel collection, designed by per-

////////////////////////////////////
Cyberscoop
To add some international flavor, visit www.mirapodo.de, a German online footwear store that's known for its excellent internal search capabilities. Shoppers can interact with deep inventory of merchandise, rotate shoes without clicking, choose from several zoom options, and narrow search results by material, size, color, and special product attributes. Don't let the language difference faze you—the icons and graphics speak a universal language. (Source: "Top 10 Tips for Optimizing ROI With Dynamic Content Guide," Adobe Scene7, March 2011, 6, www.adobe.com.)

former Avril Lavigne. The grand plan was to have visitors to the Stardoll site click through to Kohl's site, which they did by the thousands.[28]

Another version of an avatar is My Virtual Model, a virtual service that lets individuals create replicas of themselves that can be used to try on apparel from the host site. Lands' End, H&M, Sears, and Speedo swimwear all use this service. OneStopPlus.com, billed as the first and only Web mall for plus-sized women and big-and-tall men, also uses My Virtual Model. Shoppers can mix and match up to 30,000 outfits on their personal avatars using this advanced technology.[29]

Navigation and Transaction Capabilities

In addition to aesthetics and digital graphics, navigational tools must be top rate and transactions easy to complete. For example, shopping cart and checkout features must be clearly identified and easily accessed. **Shopping carts** are special software features that online shoppers use to collect products and park them electronically until they are ready to check out. Included in the many navigation and transaction tools that form the infrastructure of all commercial Web sites are:

- Site maps that are clear and concise.
- Drop-down menus that are logical, functional, and appropriate to the content.
- Sidebars that include pertinent links to microsites or other relevant information.
- Smooth, preferably one-page checkout options.
- Choice of payment plans.
- Guided, visual search capabilities.
- Easy-to-access contact points such as e-mail, chat, store location services, and links to social media sites.

In addition to functional Web site platforms, graphics, product presentation excellence, and sound and video enhancement, a range of communication tools further enhance the underpinnings of a site and the level of engagement for its visitors.

Figure 7.4
An action-oriented Web 2.0 tool is 360-degree product rotation.

Customer Communication Tools

Never before have there been so many ways for retailers to contact customers and vice versa. Let's compare some of the contemporary contact methods, interactive options, and e-mail.

Blogs, Vlogs, and Pods

As customers we revel in the opportunity to share our responses; see and hear commentary about retailers, customers, or celebrities; and rapidly access the sites we savor.

Blogs are written narratives that convey opinions and solicit reader feedback online. Topics might range from child-rearing practices to political viewpoints, social faux pas, reiki and reflexology, applying makeup, piercing one's navel, baking bread or panforte, or one's experience at a retail store. The diversity of opinions exchanged is the key to positive and negative feedback for retailers, and is sometimes great satisfaction for blog writers who learn that yes, they do have a voice. Profiles of bloggers differ by region, discussion topics presented, and levels of expertise; retailers seeking to incorporate blogs into their marketing efforts in countries other than their own are advised to research cultural and colloquial differences before they decide to pursue this approach.

An offshoot of blogging, **product reviews** are communications generated by customers or retailers that seek input on merchandise performance, pricing, customer service, or other topics. Those that are peer-initiated generate a high level of credibility, since the opinions given are from people just like us.

Closely related, **vlogs** are blogs that have a video component. A **podcast** is an audio file used to lend credence, opinion, or detail to Web-based content. On an e-commerce site, podcasts might include commentary about a company, its merchandise lines, or its stance on environmental concerns.

Most retailers value input from customers—whether positive or negative. Some retailers have started their own forums to encourage customers to share their shopping experience with the company and other customers. This version works more like a social networking experience: participants share not only opinions but also constructive criticism regarding the company. Retailers also benefit from increased brand visibility, publicity, and the opportunity for further interaction with customers. In a way, this functions as unpaid consulting for the retailer.

Widgets and Microsites

Online merchants, looking to personalize their online content, deliver advertising messages in an engaging way through the use of widgets. **Widgets** are embedded code that users insert into Web sites, blogs, or social-networking pages to provide information, interactive activities, and items for sale. Messages that are enjoyable for the recipient are much more likely to be passed on to peers, which is the objective for the companies that use widgets. For example, a Dell advertising campaign called "Regeneration" used a widget to ask consumers, "What does it mean to be green?" Respondents on Facebook were able to post their answers on their wall for friends to see, thanks to the Graffiti widget application.[30]

Widgets can be categorized as lifestyle (those based on entertainment or self-expression) or functional (those designed to inform or add utility to the user's online experience). A widget that calls up an image of a celebrity with whom the viewer can relate, or one that presents a game or video is a lifestyle version. One that uses a currency converter, map, or other option to interact with the company's brand would be a functional widget.[31]

Microsites are Web sites run independently from a primary URL that provide value-added information, activities, or new concepts that enhance the user's experience. For example, JCPenney runs Arizona jeans as a microsite. The Arizona brand targets a younger, more active audience than its parent brand and benefits from the exclusivity brought by the microsite concept.

Chat and Tweet

Web-based communications include various types of online chat, as well as the short (and sometimes-sweet) tweet. Let's consider both options.

Click-to-call customer-service functions have been available for several years. With **click-to-call,** online customers seeking information can request that customer-service representatives call them rather than placing the call themselves. Using this form of contact, online customers with questions on a product or service insert their telephone numbers in the appropriate field and state when they would like to be called by a customer service representative. Amazon.com was one of the first online retailers to offer click-to-call to its U.S. customers and subsequently rolled out the service through its sites in Germany, France, and the United Kingdom.[32]

Click-to-chat takes click-to-call online contact a step further by offering live chat to customers. In **live chat,** customers make contact with a real person through telephone or instant messaging while simultaneously using a Web site. Inventive software lets customers and retailers enjoy speedy response via online dialog. Using live chat, customers ask questions about products or delivery and receive answers in real time.

Some companies have developed multimedia software that allows customers to use text, graphics, audio, and video to answer questions about their orders. Using some of the newer live chat software, customer-service representatives can interact with six or more customers simultaneously. In one survey, 54 percent of e-retailers said that customers who engaged with retailers using live chat converted to a lead or sale 20 percent or more of the time. Approximately 25 percent of companies offered live chat in 2011.[33]

Twitter.com began as a Web site where laconic individuals could pop off a quick message to friends, family, or associates. The currency of such microblogging, a **tweet** is a short message of no more than 140 characters that is sent via computer, tablet, or smartphone.

Twitter's user growth rate fell significantly during the waning months of the recession. Despite the decrease, Twitter has improved in other measurement categories, notably in the number of profiles followed by average users. Twitter believes the slowdown in growth and increase in user-ship are attributed to more engaged and enthusiastic users. This shift may be positive for retailers as they tap further into the technology.

Retailers see the microblogging site as a combination of selling, servicing, communicating with customers, and brand-building. Online shoe retailer Zappo's has been using Twitter since 2007 and the firm's CEO, Tony Hsieh, finds it useful for communicating with customers. Zappo's also runs @Zapposinsights as its membership site and offers Twitter followers tips on how to create a strong company culture.[34]

Apple communicates with both customers and employees via six Twitter accounts. One is for general announcements and apps, while others are for special interests, such as @iTunesMovies and @iTunesPodcasts.[35]

Retailers use Twitter because it offers a snapshot view of what their customers are thinking. More than 90 percent of Twitter mentions come from consumers. Of these, only 12 percent of tweets name a brand.[36] Expect that many retailers will be onboard tweeting their next sale by the time you read this, and that consumers will be reading and acting upon them.

E-mail Communication

Promotional offers work best for merchants when they can reach loyal customers regularly. In the past, customer queries on some sites were not answered for several days, but that changed positively with improved systems and better staffing practices. Most e-mail messages sent by re-tailers are for promotional and transactional purposes, but increasingly, they are being used for the retention of current customers. E-mail used in conjunction with other marketing is meaningful to customers and effective for retailers. Figure 7.5 shows the types of e-mails sent by marketers.

Companies use e-mail because it is a relatively low-cost method of reaching customers in a semi-personal way. The use of e-mail is growing: in 2011 approximately $1.5 billion was spent on e-mail marketing; by 2016, expenditures in the United States are expected to reach $2.5 billion.[37]

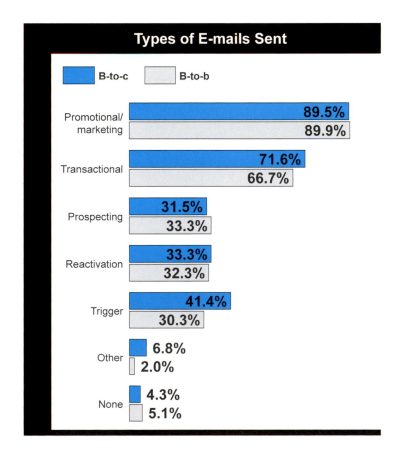

Figure 7.5
Types of e-mails sent by marketers (Source: Sherry Chiger and Lisa Santo, "Multichannel Merchant Outlook 2011: Marketing," Multichannel Retailer, www.multichannelretailer .com.)

E-mail newsletters are popular; at the same time, traditional newspapers have been losing readers as more people turn to the Internet as a source of news. Shorter bursts of news along with reader-directed advertising may signal a new era for the delivery of national and local news and editorial opinions.[38] Advocates of this approach believe that delivery of news will become more personal and interactive, which will benefit both newspapers and readers.

As online and other retailers develop e-mail programs, they are cognizant of possible problem areas involving customer reception. For example, many Internet users consider all unsolicited e-mail spam. Sometimes these very same people have given permission for a company to send e-mails regarding new merchandise, sales, or special offers. Permission-based e-mail is most effective. Retailers should be explicit about the amount of e-mail delivered, the frequency with which it will be sent, and the purpose of the e-mail at the time new or existing customers are approached for their e-mail addresses and other personal information. Age also is a factor in receptiveness of messages. E-mail is the preferred method of contact for people aged 55 to 64 years, but the least preferred by individuals 15 to 17. Teens would much rather text.[39] A 2010 study concluded that 51.1 percent of 18- to 34-year-olds want a cell phone with e-mail access, and that older adults are following this trend. Nearly 43 percent of adults want e-mail capabilities on their cell phones—almost double the percentage recorded 4 years earlier.[40]

Customer Service Expectations

From accessing company information to finding a location or receiving advance notification of a sale via e-mail, services available on retail Web sites run the gamut from basic to sublime. The following examples show what customers expect:

- Product reviews and recommendations; blogging opportunities.
- E-mail and chat services.
- Online versions of printed catalogues.
- Cross-channel services, including loyalty programs, ordering and pickup options, promotional offers.
- Personalization, such as the option to customize apparel and shoes, having your name appear when you log on, and tailored promotions.
- Private-event retailing featuring exclusive sales or invitation-only events.
- Fan networks that operate as online social communities sponsored by the retailer.

Customer-Oriented Initiatives to Improve Sites

Retailers are constantly at work, refining their online tactics to discover what customers want and using that information to build a Web infrastructure that not only supports but also exceeds those expectations. Aberdeen Group identified several customer-centric online retailing tactics that proactive companies are using to improve their Web sites, including:

- Personalized loyalty and service offerings.
- Drag-and-drop comparison shopping tools.
- Mobile shopping carts.
- Cross-channel access to wish lists.
- Coordinated promotion, shipping, payment options, and fulfillment practices among online, store, catalogue, and mobile channels.
- Customer rating and feedback options.[41]

When it comes to providing crucial services that keep customers coming back for more, retailers and customers are like-minded. This is important to acknowledge as online strategies and policies are developed, implemented, and evaluated.

Online Strategies and Policies

What are online retailers doing to stay on top of the competition, draw new customers while keeping the loyal ones happy, and fulfill the whole gamut of hopes, dreams, and schemes? Several examples of online retail tactics are highlighted in this section, as well as the role search plays in bringing online retailers closer to their goals. The relationship between social networking and retail selling is also examined, as are the specifics of cross-channel integration.

Highlights of Online Strategies

Online retailers are carving out niches for their operations that are innovative, cost-conscious, socially apt, and growth-centered. The following examples highlight the strategies used by top online retailers to set the tone for excellence.

- *Target.* The second-largest discounter in the United States left its online partnership with Amazon to strike out on its own. By setting up its own site, Target gained more control over its Web platform, branding initiatives, and the consistency of the multichannel experience it provides for its guests. Speaking of Target partnerships, its decision to team-up with Apple, selling products that make the ultimate links to multichannel shopping easier for customers in their stores, was worthy of illustration in Figure 7.1.
- *Michaels.* The arts-and-crafts specialty retailer, with 1,047 stores in the United States and Canada, has stayed true to its "Where Creativity Happens" motto. Through public demand and Web site traffic, the company learned that its customers wanted more online projects as a way to both save money and enjoy the experience with their families. Its series of how-to videos features creative craft expert Jo Pearson leading workshops in everything from jewelry-making to holiday tree–decorating. Some segments, called craft-a-thons, also feature live chat.[42]
- *Victoria's Secret.* Setting up an online social environment came naturally to this retailer when it saw that much of its online traffic was coming from Facebook. By early 2011, more than 12 million "likes" were recorded on the intimate-apparel retailer's page. It is not surprising that Victoria's Secret is the most popular retail site on Facebook, followed by the company's Pink brand in second position.[43]
- *Newegg.* Social responsibility is a keynote for growing numbers of online retailers. Newegg made its Web site easily accessible to blind people, becoming the first online retailer to reach certification standards put forth by the National Federation for the Blind. The initiative required special software used by blind people to convert text and images into audio files so that they can complete the basic processes involved in making a purchase online.[44]

Charlotte Russe, the apparel chain, successfully overhauled its Web site and developed programs to please its young, fashion-oriented customers. Read about the technologies the company implemented in From the Field 7.2. These examples are indicative of the lengths to which online retailers go to fully engage their customers. In the next section, we'll look at how search drives potential customers to Web sites.

The Power of Search

Search engine optimization is as critical for online retailers as intense promotion is for brick-and-mortar stores and lists are for catalogue retailers. The goal is the same: to effectively engage customers. The industry term for harnessing ways to increase the number of visitors to a site by increasing the site's ranking within the search engine is called **search engine optimization**. Distinguishing between natural and paid search is the first step to understanding the process. Both are necessary to optimize the numbers of potential customers driven to a retail Web site.

Natural search is used to look up a topic of general interest or to do research. It is also called organic search or natural-search marketing, and requires no monetary compensation. **Paid search** involves the advertisements located in the sponsored link boxes at the top of a Web page, which are purchased by online retailers. Prime position helps capture the attention of viewers, and retailers pay premium prices to be at the top of the list. This is also called pay-per-click advertising. Both are types of **external search,** which uses search engines such as Google to locate Web sites of interest.

Internal search is used within a Web site to allow visitors to locate information or items easily. For example, you might do an internal search on the Sports Authority Web site by typing into the search box "Merrell hiking boots" to see if the retailer carries your favorite brand.

More retail sites are implementing programs to encourage deeper internal searches by customers. The percentages of Web sites where customers select merchandise using several criteria are:

- 42 percent—color.
- 29 percent—size.
- 23 percent—customer ratings.
- 22 percent—new merchandise arrivals.
- 16 percent—sales or specials.[45]

Whether directed at paid or natural search, the objective of retailers is to harness the power of search and get relevant key words working for them. Key words are chosen carefully to avoid being too generic but reflect the business, name, mission, merchandise, and other unique qualities that will make a retailer's site stand out from the competition.

Internet Retailer ranks online retailers on the basis of their effective use of both natural and paid search. To be considered a top retailer in this dimension of online retailing, companies are assigned points every time their name and key words appear in the first five paid and natural search results in each merchandise segment. In 2010, the top company in paid search was Amazon.[46] Spending on search marketing in the United States was expected to reach $18.8 billion in 2011 and $33.3 billion by 2016.[47] Google Inc. dominates the bulk of paid search spending in the United States. In the third quarter of 2011, 81.6 percent of paid search spending was attributed to Google.[48]

Almost all online marketers use paid search advertising and search engine optimization, and this trend is expected to continue. However, the growing tendency toward the use of rich media display advertising will gradually reapportion online retailers' advertising budgets away from search.

Social Networking and Online Selling

Once social interaction met the online customer head on, it was only a matter of time before retailers followed, establishing a presence in online communities. Whether on social sites like Facebook, Pinterest, MySpace, Linked In, Twitter, and YouTube or coupon sites like Groupon and LivingSocial, users communicate with each other, the social sites with which they resonate, and the retailers they follow and friend. Read more about LivingSocial and Groupon in the article in From the Field 7.3.

Founded in 2004, Facebook has become a giant in the social networking community with an estimated 800 million users globally—and about 100 million in the United States alone. Retail applications quickly became part of Facebook's game plan. By the end of 2009, 56.8 percent of the top 500 e-retailers had Facebook pages,[49] and as of 2011, 86 percent were a part of the social network.[50]

Social sites are a requisite for major brands because of the customer interaction and potential word-of-mouth advertising that is possible. For example, becoming Facebook "friends" with

From the Field 7.3   LivingSocial Bags a Deal with Whole Foods Market

In September 2011, LivingSocial sent a nationwide offer of $20 worth of groceries for $10 at Whole Foods Market to each of the daily deal operator's more than 32 million U.S. members. The deal, which went live at 5 a.m. Eastern time and was available for 24 hours, sold more than 900,000 vouchers by 5:30 p.m. The offer approached LivingSocial's record deal of 1.3 million Amazon.com discount vouchers sold the previous January. LivingSocial and Whole Foods hoped to sell 1 million vouchers.

To further entice shoppers to purchase the voucher, 5 percent of the proceeds from the deal was slated to go to the Whole Foods' Whole Kids Foundation, whose goal is to educate and inspire families to improve children's nutrition and well-being. The foundation's Facebook page allows customers to vote to disburse funds to either healthy cooking classes aimed at educating teachers on nutrition, or to grants for school gardens.

Demand for the vouchers slowed down LivingSocial.com, which sparked comments on Twitter, such as "Is everyone trying 2 buy @WholeFoods deal on @LivingSocial? Their site is not working" and "Haven't tweeted in like 20 odd days but had to say that @Living

Social's customer service is non-existent. Will never buy from again!!!" The spokesperson acknowledged the slowdown and said LivingSocial's technical team was working to resolve the issue.

The offer could prop up LivingSocial's revenue, which in August had dropped to $45 million. In that month, Groupon's revenue rose to $120 million, according to daily deal aggregator Yipit, marking the second consecutive month that Groupon gained and LivingSocial lost revenue.

Moreover, in its first full month, Groupon Getaways, the daily deal leader's travel offering, outperformed LivingSocial Escapes in the travel deals segment. Groupon's offering generated 42 percent more revenue than LivingSocial Escapes and averaged 78 percent more revenue per deal, according to Yipit. (Data are estimates based on its tracking of daily deal companies throughout North America, and exclude mobile offerings such as Groupon Now and LivingSocial Instant Deals.)

Adapted from: Zak Stambor, "LivingSocial Bags a Deal With Whole Foods Market," *Internet Retailer*, September 13, 2011, www.internetretailer.com/2011/09/13/livingsocial-bags-deal-whole=foods-market.

Sephora means being able to participate in exclusive promotions, receive in-store event notices, see videos, and take part in polls and discussion boards. The participatory nature of Facebook lends itself well to building loyalty with retail customers and finding new customer "friends."

Facebook opened its site to direct retailing of products after conducting tests with a few virtual and physical merchants on its Facebook Gift Shop. One of the participants was American Greetings Interactive, the card and gift company, which sold virtual goods including video postcards and animated icons.[51] Facebook realized that selling merchandise in addition to selling advertising increases its revenue sources. Other networking sites have followed suit.

Having customers who opt to "like" them on Facebook contributes significantly to sales for Walmart. The discounter found that its Facebook fans are 40 percent more likely to purchase items from Walmart than the average shopper who is not affiliated with Facebook.[52]

Equally valid is the objective for retailers to build brand awareness and develop stronger relationships with customers through social networking sites. For many customers, intimacy on a vast scale is preferable to getting lost in the mass-merchandised shuffle. Social networking with retail overtones delivers the personal touch that many customers seek as they affirm their sense of belonging through cyber communities. The opportunity for social networking sites to partner with retailers is compelling as it ensures additional users and lucrative returns for both parties.

Cross-Channel Strategies

Retailers actively seeking Internet shoppers go to great lengths to dramatize the pleasures of online retailing. Web shopping is often positioned as a supplement or alternative to conventional store shopping. For example, store retailers are using point-of-purchase (POP) counter cards and other signage to advertise their Web-to-store merchandise pickup services. Some retailers outfit store personnel in T-shirts bearing the Web site address or use the shirts as giveaways. Other tactics include cross-channel promotion and push and pull methods.

Cross-Channel Promotion

Businesses intending to grow sales online often use cross-channel promotion. **Cross-channel promotion** is the practice of using multimedia to promote retail Web sites or other channels used by a retailer. Retailers hope that sales in their primary distribution channels are not cannibalized as a result of online store growth. Retailers make press kits and press releases available on their Web sites for editorial departments of magazines, newspapers, and other online business to help generate publicity for their Web sites. Fashion retailers, in particular, set up Web links between their Web

Did You Know?
Shoppers that visit American Eagle's e-retailing site via Facebook spend 58 percent more than those who are referred from other sites and sources—a perfect example of f-commerce at work. (Source: Josh Constine, "Mounting Evidence Shows Potential of Social Ecommerce, Contradicting Recent Reports," *Inside Facebook*, April 7, 2011, 2, www.insidefacebook .com/2011/04/07/potential-of-social-commerce.)

sites and those of fashion magazines such as *InStyle, Elle,* or *Glamour.* Many companies run online shopping incentives in catalogues or via e-mail advertisements to keep their Web site addresses highly visible.

Product-placement advertising is increasingly seen on TV and in the cinema. Breakthroughs in interactive technology allow items seen on some TV shows to be purchased online. Using this technology, viewers can order an outfit worn by a favorite performer on the latest episode of *Dancing With the Stars* while the show is still in progress.

In this arena, as in others, Facebook has become the place to see and be seen. Soft Surroundings published an interactive version of its apparel catalogue at the site, including a direct link to its commerce site so fans could make purchases. Visitors to Brooks Brothers' Facebook page benefit from a totally integrated shopping experience and can place their orders directly from that page. The merger of social networking and retailing is one of the most significant developments in the evolution of e-commerce.

Push and Pull Effects

Push and pull strategies were introduced in Chapter 1. Using pull strategies, the customer activates the selling process, perhaps by requesting further information from a retailer. The push strategy occurs when the retailer initiates activity to put forth saleable merchandise to the customer. This may involve sending promotional messages to a broad spectrum of potential customers. The practice serves a function as retailers test new products on their Web sites. Early online retailers tended to push information onto the viewer rather than let the customer pull information from the site. However, most retailers discovered the benefits of letting customers extract information based on their specific interests and needs. The shotgun approach implied by a push strategy is less effective than a pull strategy.

The implications of push or pull strategies for merchandising, sales promotion, and customer service are vast. Some retailers include gift directories that allow customers visiting a toy site to retrieve information on what a four-year-old boy might like for a birthday gift. Cosmetic companies elicit detailed information about skin types and product preferences, and shoppers benefit from product counseling via live chat. Customers make better product choices and may purchase more products when a pull rather than a push strategy is used.

Payment, Privacy, and Security Issues

Retailers that sell online encourage customers to share pertinent personal information in order to build and use databases. Several strategies are used to ensure the accuracy and security of the information retailers collect. Some involve secure payment options; others address protection against identity theft and fraudulent use of personal data. Sadly, the use of malware, a type of software used to access computers with criminal intent, is rising. Retailers and consumers must remain vigilant as they seek solutions to various affronts.

Payment Methods

PayPal, a familiar payment option on the Internet, is no longer the only game in town. Many customers pay using credit cards. Others prefer cash-loaded smart cards. Some like pay-me-later options. Several options are surveyed here and the most popular methods are graphed in Figure 7.6.

Most retailers agree that at some point, there should be a standardization of payment options. As online retailers seek more international sales, the added hassle of dealing with many foreign currencies compounds the multiple payment options. For customers, trust, security, and ease of use are the important factors that influence choice of payment plan.

Credit Cards   Conventional credit cards are the most popular form of payment online. The risk to retailers is higher when taking credit cards online because actual signatures are not readily captured; thus, the percentage fee charged by credit card companies is higher than what is charged to brick-and-mortar retailers. Despite the additional costs, credit card transactions are considered the most ubiquitous form of payment in the United States. In 2011 $123.5 billion worth of online transactions were paid by major credit card; by 2016 that number is expected to grow to $200.8 billion.[53]

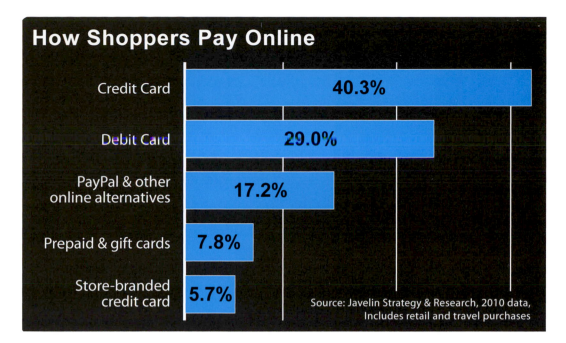

How Shoppers Pay Online

Payment Method	Percentage
Credit Card	40.3%
Debit Card	29.0%
PayPal & other online alternatives	17.2%
Prepaid & gift cards	7.8%
Store-branded credit card	5.7%

Source: Javelin Strategy & Research, 2010 data,
Includes retail and travel purchases

Figure 7.6
Most popular online payment methods (Source: Don Davis, "Online Retailers Stand to Profit From Lower Debit Card Fees," *Internet Retailer,* July 2011, Statistics: Javelin Strategy and Research, 2010. Data include retail and travel purchases.)

Third-Party Payment Plans   Several payment services fit into this category. PayPal is a third-party service since it operates as a link between retailer and consumer. PayPal's digital payment system is owned by eBay, but works independently of the company. Mobile payment services, another intermediary, add the cost of products purchased to a person's monthly cell phone bill.

Some inroads have been made with e-mail payment plans from retailers. The facilitator Bill Me Later, owned by PayPal, works like this: customers are e-mailed an invoice from the retailer and then have the option of paying electronically through partner banks or by mailing a paper check. The system is less expensive for retailers than other methods of payment and is easy for online shoppers. If invoices are not paid in full, customers have the option of extending their terms. However, some consumers have found the interest rates exorbitant.

Only 14 percent of online transactions emanating from international customers are processed through PayPal. The company considers this low percentage an opportunity to refine and further develop its policies on currency conversions, international shipping costs, customs regulations, return policies, and language barriers. Most of these international sales are from Hong Kong and elsewhere in China.[54]

Smart Cards   Customers and retailers benefited from smart card technology when loyalty programs were brought online. Smart cards, also called *prepaid cards,* can be conveniently reloaded with currency via telephone. Most retail stores, catalogues, malls, restaurants, and Web sites offer smart card gift certificates. However, because smart cards require a special reader, the cost of upgrading existing payment systems is prohibitive for some retailers.

Smart cards have been more popular in Europe than in the United States, where credit cards are deeply embedded in customer habits and have saturated the payment market. Smart cards are useful for small purchases and ensure the privacy of customers since they contain no personal data, only monetary funds.

Methods of Reducing Fraud

As in all other forms of commerce where currency—hard or electronic—is concerned, misuse and fraud are omnipresent online. However, it is expected that innovations such as the secure electronic transaction protocol will help guard Internet transactions. **Secure electronic transmission protocol (SET)** is a type of software designed to make transactions between buyers and sellers safer. Major credit card companies developed the technology, and industry support garnered from other credit card companies, banks, and computer software companies has given momentum to the cause.

Did You Know?
Customers who don't have a bank account, credit cards, or debit cards—or who simply like to pay with cash—can use PayNearMe to make purchases, pay utility bills, or transfer money on e-commerce or e-retailing sites. More than 6,000 7-Eleven stores in the United States honor customers' purchases—through partners PayNearMe and money transfer company Ria—that are subsequently paid for in cash at 7-Eleven. Many transactions are completed via mobile phone and finalized at a 7-Eleven register.
(Source: Leena Rao, "PayNearMe's Cash Payments Product Can Now Be Used For Money Transfers, Bill Pay And More," TechCrunch, May 10, 2011, http://techcrunch .com/2011/05/10/paynearmes-cash-payments-product-can-now-be-used-for-money-transfers-bill-pay-and-more.)

Most Web sites are adequately protected from the basic kinds of criminal intent. Companies such as Symantec, which owns and has adapted the VeriSign symbol, ensure that sites are secure and advertise this fact through use of a logo icon—often placed on home pages for easy recognition by visitors to a site.

Some companies are developing devices that can scan the irises of eyes to tighten security at ATM machines. Voice, face, and fingerprint scanners that verify identification at the point of sale involve technologies that are expected to transfer well to the Internet and mobile devices. Google and Facebook have each invested in face-recognition technology that will improve security. As systems become more sophisticated and widespread, it is expected that risks to retailers and customers will be reduced.

Privacy and Security Safeguards

Moving from a cash-based society—where a degree of anonymity is experienced—to one where personal details are divulged in order to do business is upsetting to some customers. People are understandably apprehensive about the type and amount of personal information that is readily available on the Internet. It is quite possible that records of everything from our birth to the last box of cereal we purchased are accessible to outside sources. Privacy safeguards are in a state of flux as industry self-regulation and governmental legislation continue to evolve.

Protecting Privacy   The line between information considered private and proprietary and that which people are willing to share isn't always clear. One person may not think twice about providing a name, address, telephone number, and credit-card number over the phone to a catalogue retailer. Another may hesitate before sharing that information online, concerned about the possibility that it will be sold or bartered to other businesses, or even stolen by unscrupulous individuals in either circumstance. Those that volunteer information may be more susceptible to unsolicited e-mail or advertisements directed to them via the Internet—in other words, spam. Despite possible risks, online shoppers eager to receive the next great deal may not hesitate to divulge basic personal data as well as more sensitive information. For most of us, the greater the perceived gain, the more personal information we will share.

Public and Private Information   It is easy for anyone to find out matters of public record including births, deaths, marriages, divorces, mortgage transfers, bankruptcies, corporate acquisitions, and initial public stock offerings (IPOs). It may be a bit more difficult, but not impossible, to dig up past employment and medical records and information on personal behavior. Medical records are increasingly available online as healthcare professionals make the transition to Web-based record-keeping. You have probably observed a physician reviewing your medical history from a laptop, or have ordered a prescription from your neighborhood pharmacy over the Internet. Credit card use, telephone activity, and the number of hits on a Web site are all pieces of information that are readily available to the professional marketer and the talented amateur detective.

Adopting Privacy Measures   Some Internet providers do not sell the telephone numbers of their subscribers to telephone marketers, although they may use them to do telemarketing on behalf of the companies with which they partner. With retailer and provider partnerships on an upswing, this decision is a mixed blessing for shoppers.

Pin codes and passwords set up by providers for customers help maintain privacy and security standards. Encryption codes prevent hackers from breaking into systems and stealing sensitive data. **Encryption codes** are computer programs that prevent unauthorized users from committing crimes such as fraud and access of personal information. **Hackers** are individuals who break into computer systems with criminal intent. In recent years, retailers ranging from supermarkets to off-price specialty chains have incurred data breaches.

Data Breaches   When hackers enter a commercial or other Web site for the purpose of stealing customer information or sales transaction records, this is called a **data breach.** Hackers represent the darker side of computer savvy. TJX, the parent company of several off-price stores, settled a suit in 2009 that resulted from a 2005 data breach. The parties involved settled for $45 million in damages.[55] The court also mandated that TJX report annually to federal authorities on its updating of systems and implementation of further precautions to prevent another breach from affecting millions of customers.

As postscripts to this incident, hacker-informant Albert Gonzalez, perpetrator of the crimes against TJX (as well as OfficeMax, Barnes & Noble, and restaurant chain Dave & Busters) pleaded guilty in late 2009 to several counts of hacking into computer systems, identity theft, and wire fraud.[56]

Gonzalez' sentencing for the TJX-based breach took place in March 2010. Earlier he had entered into an agreement with the government that he would be imprisoned for 15–25 years.[57] As part of a plea bargain for another case involving Heartland Payment Systems, 7-11, and Hannaford Brothers supermarkets, Gonzalez agreed to pay back $2.7 million in restitution.[58]

Stiff law enforcement efforts should cut down on the amount and intensity of data breaches and other cybercrime that cost both retailers and customers time, money, and peace of mind. However, there is no shortage of devious minds when subterfuge is linked to monetary gain, and both retailers and customers need to remain vigilant.

Government Regulation of the Internet

Upholders of the U.S. Constitution's First Amendment are at odds with parents and others seeking to implement provisions that would guard against indecent materials being seen by or sold to children online. Struck down by legislators in 1997, the Communications Decency Act would have been a provision of the 1996 Telecommunication Act, making it a crime to transmit indecent material to minors via the Internet. The industry responded with software blocking systems to make discretion a parental responsibility.

Several bills passed or pending in Congress and state legislatures affect Internet use. Many of these have serious implications for retailers and other practitioners of e-commerce. For example, the deluge of printed privacy policies delivered along with credit card bills in 2001 was a direct consequence of the Gramm-Leach-Bliley Act of 1999. The ways companies might use customers' private information was explicitly stated. In addition, account holders were given the option of sharing—or not sharing—their personal information with third-party companies.[59]

A similar focus is evident internationally. The European Union's new General Data Protection Regulation is an update of an earlier directive setting out new enforcement powers for privacy agencies aimed at protecting the vast amount of personal data that flows between Europe and the United States by means of cloud service providers.[60] In this usage, "cloud" refers to **cloud computing**, which involves software applications that are accessed on the Internet rather than from the hard drives of computers, tablets, or other mobile devices. Popular applications include e-mail access; data, photo, and video storage; and Web hosting.

In the United States, proposed anti-piracy legislation including the Stop Online Piracy Act (SOPA) and the related Protect IP Act (PIPA) met with mixed levels of enthusiasm. SOPA was designed to block access and funding for foreign and domestic Web sites offering films, TV shows, and music stolen from rightful copyright holders. Although the entertainment industry supported the bill, online media moguls believed the government had overstepped its boundaries. PIPA pertained to only foreign Web sites. Both initiatives stalled in the legislature in late 2011.[61] The Cyber Intelligence Sharing and Protection Act (CISPA) met with greater acceptance in April 2012, when the U.S. House of Representatives approved the bill. It would allow Internet companies to share confidential customer data with the National Security Agency and other pertinent government offices.[62]

Online businesses contend that a light hand concerning government regulation will allow the Internet to grow. Most e-commerce participants advocate self-regulation as a way to monitor Internet activity that may compromise customer privacy and security. In that way, the industry—not government—will control the medium and protect its ability to generate sales. Controversy is inevitable when customers' rights to privacy are violated.

Internet Taxation

Another key issue for online retailing involves sales tax on Internet purchases. The United States does not have a governmental policy regarding Internet taxation, although recent legislative actions at the state level have affected companies doing business online. Internet purchases were exempt from taxation in the early years of the Internet. However, states have become more inclined to levy taxes on consumer purchases just as they do on sales from brick-and-mortar retailers.

Amazon, Overstock, and Blue Nile were some of the online retailers that have refused to collect taxes from customers in certain states and, as a result, discontinued affiliate programs in those states or threatened to do so. Some states contend they need the tax revenue from out-of-state sellers. In mid-2009, New York, Rhode Island, Hawaii, and North Carolina passed laws requiring e-retailers doing business through in-state online marketing affiliates to collect sales tax. Since the sales agents have a physical presence, the states consider affiliates nonexempt. E-retailers maintain that the affiliate arrangements simply facilitate advertising for the online companies.[63] Only five states in the United States do not have sales taxes and are therefore somewhat immune to governmental intervention.

Acutely aware of the inevitable, by 2011 Amazon was collecting taxes in five states and had made agreements with seven others to begin implementing collection starting in 2012 through 2016. In Texas, Amazon agreed to start collecting taxes in exchange for building new warehouses in the state that will help reduce shipping costs and delivery time to customers.[64]

Brick-and-mortar retailers have long argued that online sellers should be taxed at the same rate as conventional stores. Estimates of lost taxes from online sellers range from $10 to $13 billion annually.[65] The U.S. Congress will press for legislation that will standardize collection across all states and e-retailers.

Web Analytics

Measuring the outcome of online initiatives is another necessary function performed by Web retailers. As they quantify certain customer behaviors, retailers use a variety of analytical tools. Among the major metrics charted and used to evaluate performance and return on investment are the following:

- Traffic counts—numbers of people who access a Web site.
- Conversion—numbers of visitors to a site who make a purchase.
- Average order size—calculated in terms of dollars and units.
- Shopping cart abandonment rates.
- Return visitors—how many people become loyal customers; retailers may also record recency and frequency of visits and purchases.
- Effectiveness of customer service.
- Level of brand-awareness.
- Receptiveness of customers to new features on the Web site.[66]

More information on the use of major metrics to chart financial performance is given in Chapter 14.

Monitoring tools enable retailers to research customer behavior as it happens. Opinion is divided as to whether tracking devices perform a valuable service or result in excessive invasion of customer privacy. Many retailers and customers believe that having more information about customer shopping habits allows retailers to better select and personalize promotional messages and merchandise directed to the individual consumer.

Customer-Tracking Programs

Customer-tracking software alerts retailers to why some customers avoid certain Web pages. It can also determine why customers, after filling their shopping carts, exit a site before selecting a payment option. Companies that track customers' online behavior and use the information to personalize ads or information that will later be sent to them are engaging in **behavioral targeting**. Using relevant information, retailers are able to upgrade their sites, remerchandise their online stores, and bring better value to their online customers.

When customers are clearly informed about the degree of surveillance of their online activities and the depth of information sought they are usually more amenable to monitoring. In 2009, Sears came under the scrutiny of the Federal Trade Commission, which charged that the company did not adequately inform customers of the full scope of its monitoring practices. A settlement was reached.[67] The key to successful tracking appears to be full disclosure of the retailers' intentions in a prominent Web page location. Customers can then decide whether the program is the right option for them.

Types of Assessment Tools

Online retailers can choose among a bevy of tools—both performance-based and predictive—that measure Web performance and other selected attributes. These assessment tools include:

- *Results-oriented metrics*—Used to measure highly quantifiable measurements such as customer conversion rates, Web site hits, and branding impressions.
- *Split testing*—Used to compare the results of two related variables such as the use of two different color schemes on the same Web page.
- *Multivariate testing*—Used to test several variables concurrently such as different headlines, illustrations, and sources of traffic generated by search engines.
- *Cognitive measures*—Based on human reaction to different marketing stimuli. Studying a person's pattern of clicks on a Web site, finding out what types of people are more likely to read a retailer-generated blog, and discerning what types of imagery are preferred by men and women are examples.

Online retailers need constant real-time data to answer many of the questions they have about customer behavior and ultimately to determine the most effective tools for their Web sites. Pressure to perform comes not in accumulating the most visitors to a site, but in serving repeat visitors and providing a virtual environment that suits the customer and encourages sales. The use of Web analytics provides rich information for retailers that are ready to implement high-level evaluative measures. Top analytics technologies used in e-commerce are graphed in Figure 7.7.

Online stores and malls are the most ubiquitous forms of e-retailing, but not the only ones. The next section explores more technologically driven nonstore retailing options.

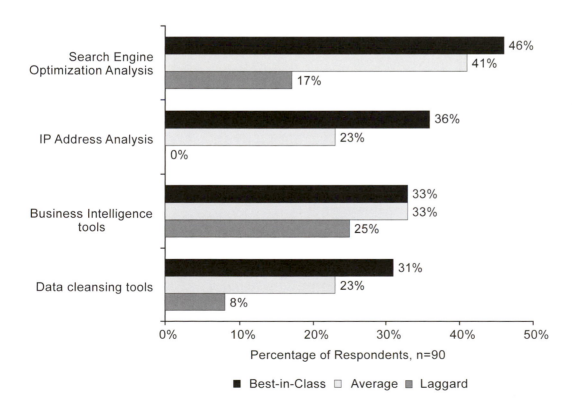

Figure 7.7
Top E-Commerce Analytics Technologies Currently in Place (Source: Greg Belkin,"Retail E-Commerce Analytics. Cornerstone of the Complete Customer Profile," Aberdeen Group, February 2010, 18.)

Electronic Retailing Options

Electronic kiosks, television retailing, and online videos are other ways in which retailers are reaching customers through technology. Each aspect is considered in this section.

Electronic Kiosks

Not a new innovation, kiosks have been in use for as long as ATMs. Robotic units that sell DVDs, computer accessories, flowers, tickets, and emergency supplies without human intervention are now in common use. Information kiosks provide store and local-area highlights, and sometimes Internet access to customers. Kiosks take up little space and are located anywhere people are in transit, shopping, or seeking services at odd hours. Airports are popular locations for these devices. In 2011, approximately 2 million kiosks were installed worldwide; about half of them are in North America.[68]

Electronic kiosks are extensions to conventional businesses. Many brick-and-mortar retailers use kiosks to extend their store inventories. Some retailers use the technology to provide better customer service. Customers can swipe their loyalty card at a kiosk to update or redeem points when the conventional store is closed, or to access information online. These are three applications that indicate the great potential of kiosk retailing. Other examples illustrate the options open to creative retailers:

- Growth of Macy's online sales is frequently higher than in-store sales. The company carries more than 50,000 SKUs online and offers cross-channel access to inventory through in-store kiosks.[69]
- Redbox had approximately 33,000 DVD kiosks in place in 2011, serving the needs of avid movie viewers. To address the needs of gamers, it added game rentals to 21,000 kiosk locations. At the $1-per-night rental fee, revenue soared.[70]
- In-store kiosks help supplement sales of hard-to-stock items. Using this approach, a multiscreen kiosk was set up to educate customers and sell lawn and garden products in some Carrefour hypermarkets in France.
- Kiosks are frequently used for human resource purposes. McDonald's uses them to recruit employees in many of its restaurants.
- Gap encourages customers to shop for out-of-stock items using in-store terminals. Either on their own or with the assistance of a sales associate, customers can easily locate the jeans they fell in love with but couldn't find in their size in another store and have them sent to their home or to the local store for pickup.
- Telecommunication companies and banks find multiple uses for kiosks, as shown in Figure 7.8.

The North American kiosk market is expected to reach $1.1 trillion by 2015.[71] As momentum builds, along with shoppers' expectation of self-service, kiosks will bring more options to customers and more sales to retailers.

Television Retailing

There you are, sitting in front of your 52-inch LCD HDTV, zapping. You pause for a moment as a sleek model in spandex appears, demonstrating the latest exercise techniques on sparkling equipment. You become more intrigued as you learn how to combat flabby gluteal muscles, and before you know it, a half hour has passed. You are experiencing a 30-minute infomercial. Then comes the call to action: "Dial our 800 number—operators are standing by—or visit our Web site at www.goglutes.com." Zap again to see what HSN or QVC have to offer. It might be jewelry, apparel, cosmetics, or exercise equipment.

What could be better selling tools than big screen presentation, stereo sound, excellent visuals, brilliant color, and action? These tools power the sales growth of home shopping channels, infomercials, direct response television (DRTV), interactive television shopping, and online video.

Home Shopping Channels

Once considered the principal pastime of senior citizens and kooky collectors, home shopping channels have crossed geographic, demographic, and psychographic thresholds as more people shop electronically.

Figure 7.8
Kiosks used by Verizon and Sovereign Bank are technologically advanced and eye-catching. Both are in a retail megaplex in Wakefield, Massachusetts, where Jordan's Furniture and an IMAX theater are housed.

Two major channels compete in the United States and both also have an international presence. The first to enter the interactive electronic market was Home Shopping Network Interactive (HSNI), with ordering and fulfillment centers located in St. Petersburg, Florida. The second was QVC, headquartered in West Chester, Pennsylvania. Its acronym stands for "Quality, Value, and Convenience." Networks NBC and HGTV also have retail Web sites. In contrast, Home Shopping Europe (HSE24), a German-based shopping channel, serves customers whose tastes are distinctly different than those of Americans.

Certain product classifications sell better than others on U.S. shopping channels. Jewelry, dolls, and other collectibles have fared well. Apparel sales have not met expectations of U.S television retailers for two main reasons. Customers do not find that fashions are adequately portrayed on TV, and items cannot be touched or tried on. Lower-priced apparel sells well because the perceived risk to consumers is lower, but television shoppers voice the same complaints as those who frequent online store and print catalogues. Scheduling television segments according to audience preferences is also a challenge.

Spotlight on HSN HSN carries items ranging from $20 jeans to $200 handbags and built a business using celebrities such as Ivana Trump and Susan Lucci. HSN is part of IAC/InterActive Corp. The shopping channel was also involved in international television shopping ventures in Japan and Germany. HSN offers simultaneous online shopping so that family and friends can enjoy the experience together. A "Shop by Remote" service encourages subscribers to purchase items viewed onscreen by clicking an icon. Customers who have preregistered their credit card can purchase the desired item immediately using their TV remote control.[72]

HSN is bringing more digital changes to its customers through a multichannel format. It includes video regularly on its Web site, and an iPhone app lets users watch live-streaming TV in high definition. The company has a major presence on YouTube as well.[73]

Spotlight on QVC Founded in 1986, QVC is considered more sophisticated than HSN and has partnered with retailers such as Saks Fifth Avenue and designers such as Diane von Furstenberg to sell fashion items. In joint venture with BSkyB, QVC operates globally.

Employing a cross-promotion strategy, QVC maintains a Web site, QVC.com. The ability to order online rather than enduring an hour-long TV promotion appeals to many contemporary shoppers.

At the company's headquarters, computer kiosks in the lobby grant both guests and employees access to the Web site. A retail store and marketplace carts on the premise add to QVC's presence as a multichannel retailer.

The company leads cable shopping channels in revenue, holding a 69 percent share of the market, and earned close to $9 billion in 2010. E-commerce accounts for 36 percent of its business. QVC is owned by Liberty Media Interactive, which in turn owns a 32 percent share in HSN[74]—a fact that invites us to ponder what the future will hold for both shopping channels.

Spotlight on HSE24   Germans are known for being the most aggressive mail-order and catalogue shoppers in the world, and their tendency to shop nonstore retailers was expected to carry over to the e-retailing sector.[75] However, when Home Order Television (HOT) went on the air in 1995, those involved learned that it was not easy to transfer an American concept to Germany.

Initially, the programming was not as exciting and fast paced as that on U.S. shopping channels. German shoppers perceived TV shopping as tacky and also displayed different product tastes. For example, customers liked to shop for wine via TV and looked for more expensive jewelry than their U.S. counterparts. Since then, attitudes have changed, as well as ownership.

In 1996, Home Shopping Network (HSN) purchased a 10 percent share in HOT and eventually changed its name to Home Shopping Europe (HSE24). Between 2005 and 2007, HSN was the sole owner; the network was subsequently sold to a German corporation.

HSE24 operates from Munich and also serves Austria and Switzerland. It offers a variety of products ranging from popular brands like Krups and Bosch to items from medium-sized companies and even family-run ventures. As on American shopping channels, several of the regular presenters have become familiar faces. Among HSE24's customers, 66 percent of shoppers are over 50 years old, part of a demographic known as "woopies" (short for well-off older people). Seventy-nine percent of the customer base is female.[76]

The language on the television shopping screen is difficult to interpret unless you can read German, but the format is remarkably similar to that of U.S. shopping channels. Figure 7.9 shows a celebrity marketer promoting skin care products during an HSE24 teleshopping segment.

Figure 7.9
Home Shopping Europe (HSE24) beams satellite and cable channels to households in Germany, Austria, and Switzerland. Left: German cosmetics marketer Judith Williams promotes her line during prime time for teleshoppers. Right: Show moderator is Andrea Lutz. Beauty and wellness products account for 30 percent of sales at HSE24.

Direct Response Television (DRTV)

Thirty-minute infomercials that entertain as well as sell are another form of e-commerce that is used by manufacturers and retailers to reach consumers. Direct response television is the advertising medium of choice for direct marketing companies that present their products via infomercials and short spots. It is easy to become hooked by the energetic, sincere-sounding pitch of the host. With 30 minutes or more in which to sell, much detail can be given about a product. For the retailer, however, production and airtime costs can be prohibitive. Companies that choose this format have all the tools of professional delivery at their disposal. No wonder many of us do not realize we are watching an infomercial until well into the presentation.

NordicTrack is a heavy user of DRTV during primetime on A&E or ABC Family channels. Snuggie blankets are promoted during evening hours, and the PedEgg debuted on CNN. During the recession, many companies sought a shorter spot format to unload excess inventory. Conversely, for some retailers time segments of 1–2 hours are becoming popular. The wellness products company Gaiam uses longer time periods to show its Wave Speed Slimming System.[77]

Internet Video and Interactive Television

The backbone of true interactive retailing is video datacasting. **Video datacasting** is a technology that sends Internet data using digital television. An early application of the technology was WebTV, developed by Microsoft. With an Internet connection and a TV tuner card, viewers could watch regular TV, cable, or satellite broadcasts on their computer screen. Much like using a TiVo system, individuals can receive data from any of these sources 24 hours per day and store them for future use if desired. In 1998, Microsoft entered into an agreement with the cable company TCI to allow the marriage of cable and Internet technology to take place.[78] This direction has changed the face of retailing.

Many retailers have integrated video into their Web sites regularly. As examples, Nike featured Kobe Bryant jumping over a sports car and OfficeMax used dancing elves for a holiday promotion. With many social networking options, videos of all types spread around the Web as fast as a virus. Online video campaigns featuring appealing brands that are shared with friends and family are called **viral video**. Viral video usually includes action, humor, how-to features, or educational components. The dramatic and expressive qualities of video are predicted to shake up digital advertising. Online video marketing expenditures were expected to reach $7 billion by 2012.[79]

As cable providers begin to carry more interactive portions of programming and broadband high-speed connections become fully utilized, digital options will intensify. Using this technology, students might access a special reading list or supplemental video while watching a program on a history channel. Watching TV programming is one thing; serious shopping is another. However, the potential of this medium is compelling to retailers. Other benefits of television include being able to reach exclusive target markets while people are more relaxed at home. This is also a pull system, since viewers initiate programming and ultimately product choices.

Mobile Commerce

Since their inception in the early 1990s, cell phones have become an additional body appendage for many. However, the mobile device–as–shopping vehicle was not mainstreamed until the mid-2000s. It is the fastest growing wireless segment, with technology barely keeping up with demand for more options, services, and products.

The m-customer is younger, more in tune with social networking, and eagerly anticipates the expanding capabilities of his or her cell phone. Because mobile device–users form a social networking and blogging stronghold, iTrackr.com has set up a free service to help mobile Web users find what they want. Let's examine the factors that have brought us to this point and see how retailers are using mobile retailing to enhance their ability to reach customers.

Worldwide Mobile Usage and Sales Trends

The growth curve for m-commerce is following the same rapid-rise pattern as the Internet did in its early stages. The good news for retailers is that the number of people in the United States using their mobile devices to access the Internet is rising proportionately. Mobile device–users in European

////////////////////////////////

Cyberscoop

Go to amazon.com and check out the Amazon Flow app (released in November 2011), which provides information about popular products like books, music, film, and household products, and allows users to purchase them *using image recognition*. Point that smartphone and see for yourself.
(Source: "12 Crucial Consumer Trends for 2012: Section 12. Point and Know," Trendwatching, http://trendwatching.com/trends/12trends2012.)

and Asian countries began accessing the Internet in this way earlier than Americans, and more people in Japan now access the Web via cell phones than PCs.[80] *Internet Retailer* surveys brick-and-mortar chains, online and catalogue retailers, and manufacturers regarding m-commerce adoption and status annually. Their 2012 report showed that only 24.1 percent of merchants operate a mobile commerce site and only 16.4 percent have both an m-commerce site and mobile apps for a variety of smartphones and tablet devices. Almost 58 percent of respondents said they were not yet equipped for m-commerce, but about 68 percent they were prepared to increase spending.[81]

Deloitte forecast that *M*-commerce sales in the United States would reach $158 billion in 2012.

Technology and the Customer

Setting up shop on a mobile device is not quite as easy for a retailer as texting a friend is for us. Proactive retailers have invested in mobile commercial sites for which shoppers must use a mobile Web browser. The conversion from PC monitor to cell-phone screen challenged retailers to simplify graphics, minimize copy, and adapt screen designs to suit the smaller format. Privacy and security features also are considered in a mobile and wireless context.

Ralph Lauren Polo Corp. was one of the first retailers to use quick response (QR) technology, which facilitates entry to its mobile site. **Quick response codes** are two-dimensional barcodes—usually black-and-white squares with pixels (short for picture element)—that are scanned and downloaded by smartphones. Users scan QR codes in advertisements, mailers, posters, store windows, or on TV to get discounts on products or obtain free apps for their mobile devices, among other options. According to David Lauren, senior vice president of advertising, marketing and corporate communications for Polo Ralph Lauren, "Consumers want flexible and convenient services that are accessible on-demand. M-commerce is so appealing because you can shop anywhere, anytime." He added: "With our mobile site the consumer can shop the U.S. Open collection, watch tennis videos, locate a store and fully experience the brand—all in the palm of their hand."[82]

As technology advances, mobile networks are working to keep pace with the demands of multiple applications and the transitions needed to bring online stores to customers via m-commerce. One study determined that 51 percent of customers are more likely to shop with retailers that have mobile-equipped Web sites.[83] So grab your iPhone or your Android and start shopping. There are even mobile apps to help you spend wisely!

Strengths of Electronic Retailing

As we conclude our focus on retail structures and multichannel strategies, let's review the strengths of online, television, and mobile forms of e-retailing.

- Online stores give more customers access to more merchandise (and more retailers access to more shoppers) than either party could have anticipated two decades ago.
- Retailers grow their existing brick-and-mortar and direct marketing businesses exponentially when they include online selling channels.
- Customers benefit from 24/7/365 access to their favorite online retailers when they are inspired to access them through their computers, smartphones, and tablets.
- Online retailers utilizing rapidly changing technologies are surmounting the early problems of examining or trying on merchandise and connecting with customers in a personal way.
- Digital video communications and interactive shopping are being perfected, taking merchandise selections and the retail experience literally to the big screen and into the third dimension.
- Mobile retailing extends the reach of the online store to more shoppers, more frequently, and with an instant exuberance that suits many shoppers today.

This chapter has explored many new options for retailers. The rapid evolution of technology, as well as lingering fallout from the recent recession, has offered challenges to many in e-commerce. The next wave of development will provide new, exciting, and, it is hoped, more stable paths to profitability. Optimizing search, evaluating sales, judging promotion effectiveness, and measuring customer response have progressed substantially as Web metrics have become more sophisticat-

Did You Know?

QR codes were expected to be the principal technology used to facilitate mobile sales during the 2012 holiday period.
(Source: Rimma Katz, "QR Codes Key Driver in 2012 Holiday Marketing Efforts," *Mobile Marketer.* October 22, 2012. www.mobilemarketer. com/cms/news/software-technology/14039.print)

Cyberscoop

Visit www.target.com's Target Mobile site to see what every smartphone user needs to know. All information about technical and navigational essentials is on one page. You'll find links to the mobile Web; Android, iPhone, and iPad apps; and text alerts on top, and a barcode scanner, shopping lists, gift cards, and coupons on the bottom. Who could possibly want more than this enticing merchandise?
(Sources: Target and The E-tailing Group, Inc., "Online Merchandising and Mobile Engagement (Edition 2 of 2)," *4th Quarter 2010 Annual Mystery Shopping Study,* February 11, 2011, 5.)

ed. The message is in the medium: e-commerce, e-retailing, m-commerce, and other digital and wireless wonders have changed the face of retailing.

Summary

E-retailing is to many people the most exciting form of nonstore retailing and a significant aspect of multichannel retailing. Doing business online, via electronic kiosks, television shopping channels, direct response TV, interactive television, online video, and mobile commerce will inspire retailers and tempt consumers. Online retailing is expected to grow, although the growth rate will slow as the industry matures. Some retail Web sites may transcend the financial performance of some brick-and-mortar retailers, but more likely, online retailing will become a part of an integrated, multichannel approach that provides convenient shopping choices for all customers.

There are many advantages and disadvantages to retailers and customers who choose to participate in online retailing. The principal advantage to retailers is the opportunity to grow their businesses. Another is the option to increase their customer base by expanding globally. Retailers reach customers in their homes where access is possible 24/7/365. The key customer advantages of online retailing are convenience and timesavings. Major concerns are the inability to physically examine products, privacy issues, and security breaches. The rewards will outnumber the risks.

Online shoppers vary greatly by country and are changing rapidly as people from diverse geographic, demographic, and psychographic backgrounds gain access to the Internet. Online retailers may be structured in any of the following ways: pure-play, dual-channel, multichannel, electronic spin-offs, or nontransactional sites.

Designing Web sites that sell requires both art and science. Effective sites must capture the customer's attention on the homepage and present exciting graphics, product descriptions, and merchandise in a safe, user-friendly environment. Customer interaction is greatly enhanced by technologically advanced Web 2.0 and 3.0 tools. Search engine optimization and marketing communication are keys to finding and keeping customers. To assess productivity and customer usage, online retailers utilize Web analytics.

The use of electronic kiosks is growing. Home shopping networks operate worldwide and also run companion Web sites. Web-linked interactive television, DRTV, and viral video are delivering new options to consumers.

E-retailing is here to stay, providing innovation and promise for retailers and customers in the 21st century.

Key Terms

Avatar

Banners

Behavioral targeting

Blog

Browsers

Click-to-call

Click-to-chat

Cloud computing

Consumer-to-consumer (C2C)

Cross-channel promotion

Data breach

Direct response television (DRTV)

Domain name

E-commerce

E-retailing

Electronic kiosks

Encryption codes

External search

Extranets

Flash sale

Hackers

Infomercials

Internal search

Internet

Internet Corporation for Assigned Names and Numbers (ICANN)

Internet service providers (ISPs)

Intranets

Live chat

M-commerce

Microsites

Natural search

Paid search

Podcast

Product reviews

Quick response codes

Search engine	Viral video
Search engine optimization	Vlog
Secure electronic transmission protocol (SET)	Web 2.0
Shopping carts	Web 3.0
Tweet	Web site
Universal resource locator (URL)	Widgets
Video datacasting	World Wide Web

Questions for Review and Discussion

1. What is the status of e-retailing today? What impact do online stores have on brick-and-mortar retailers and catalogue retailing?
2. Who is the typical Web shopper? How are demographics and psychographics of the typical shopper changing?
3. What are two possible disadvantages to retailers that sell online? How can these obstacles be overcome?
4. What are two advantages to customers who shop online? How can online retailers use these advantages to provide better customer service?
5. What constitutes an effective retail Web site? Of those you have visited, which do you believe are the most compelling? Why?
6. How are electronic kiosks used by retailers to expand their businesses and better serve their customers?
7. What types of shoppers do home shopping channels attract? How widespread is the concept? What is the relationship between home shopping networks?
8. What is the status of mobile commerce? What technological challenges have been overcome to better serve m-commerce customers?

Endnotes

1. Charisse Jones, "New Web Address Endings Could Be Start of Turf Wars," *USA TODAY*, April 6, 2009, www.usatoday.co/money/industries/technology/2009-04-06-web-site-domain-names_N.htm.
2. Sam Holmes and Christopher Rhoads, "Web Addresses Enter New Era," *Wall Street Journal*, June 21, 2011, B8.
3. Internet World Stats, "Internet Usage Statistics: The Internet Big Picture," March 31, 2011, www.internetworldstats.com/stats2.htm. (Sources: Nielsen Online, International Telecommunications Union, and other regional sources.)
4. eMarketer, "A Billion Internet Users, and Counting," February 17, 2009, www.emarketer.com/Articles/Print.aspx?id=1006899.
5. Internet World Stats, "Top 20 Countries With the Highest Number of Internet Users," June 30, 2011, www.internetworldstats,com/top20.htm. (Sources: Nielsen Online and International Telecommunications.)
6. "U.S. E-Retail Sales 2009-2015," *Internet Retailer*, www.internetretailer.com/trends/sales. (Source: Goldman Sachs.)
7. "Global E-Commerce Sales 2010-2013," *Internet Retailer*, www.internetretailer.com/trend/sales. (Source: Goldman Sachs.)
8. Zak Stambor, "Retailers Open Their Virtual Doors to International Web Shoppers," *Internet Retailer*. July 2011, 36. (Source: Cisco systems, Inc.)
9. "As Economy Impacts Online Retail, Companies Shift Marketing Focus," Shop.org, May 5, 2009, www.shop.org/c/journal_articles/view_article_content?groupId=1&articleId=979&ve. (Source: Shop.org/Forrester survey, *The State of Retailing Online 2009*.)
10. Marcus Leroux, "France's Cdiscount to Launch in UK," *Times Online,* March 27, 2009, www.business.timesonline.co.uk/tol/business/industry_sectors/retailing/article5989598.ece.
11. "Online Retailers Are Investing More in E-Commerce Despite the Bad Economy," *Internet Retailer*, July 21, 2009, www.internet retailer.com/printArticle.asp?id=31200. (Source: E-tailing Group.)
12. "Key Findings and Conclusions," *Adobe Scene7 2011 Survey: Digital Marketing in the Next Decade*, 3. Adobe Scene7.
13. "Top 500," *The Internet Retailer Top 500 Guide, Internet Retailer*, June 2009, 36.
14. Mark Brohan, "Know Thy Customer," *Internet Retailer*. August 2011, 45.
15. Cate T. Corcoran, "Rushing Into the Club: Private Sale Websites New Boom in E-tailing," *Women's Wear Daily*, August 11, 2009, 13.

16. Amanda Kaiser, "New Luxury Site Targets Japan as Online Sales Gain," *Women's Wear Daily*, August 27, 2009, 5.

17. "Online Shoppers Flock to Bing's Double-Cashback Offer, Hitwise Says," *Internet Retailer*, August 18, 2009, www.internetretailer.com/printArticle.asp?id=31520.

18. Julee Kaplan, "ELuxury Ceasing Retail Operations," *Women's Wear Daily*, January 9, 2009, 4.

19. David Moin, "eBay's Apparel Push: New Selling Formats, More Brands in Wings," *Women's Wear Daily*, February 22, 2010, 10.

20. Tess Stynes and Stu Woo, "eBay Set to Buy Payments Firm," *Wall Street Journal*, July 8, 2011, B7.

21. U.S. Securities and Exchange Commission, Washington, DC, Form 10-Q, eBay, Inc., Note 3 Business Combination, Acquisition of Gmarket. Filed July 19, 2009. http://investor.ebay.com.secfiling.cfm?filingID= 1193125-09-157212.bay.com.

22. David Moin, "People StyleWatch to Flag Penney's Trends," *Women's Wear Daily*, April 19, 2010, 5.

23. "Internet Access by Selected Characteristics, 2010: Table 1157," U.S. Census Bureau, www.us.census.gov/compendia/statab/2012/tables/12s1157.pdf.

24. Ray A Smith and Paul Sonne, "Mr. Porter to Test Men's Urge to Shop Online," *Wall Street Journal*, February 10, 2011, D6.

25. " Graph: U.S. Teen Female Online Buyers, 2005-2010. Media Usage and Shopping Habits of Teens," *eMarketer*, March 4, 2011, www.emarketer.tv/Articles/Print.aspx?1008263. (Source: GfK MRI, "Teenmark.")

26. Don Davis, "Here Today, Here Tomorrow: Internet Retailer 2009 Conference Report," *Internet Retailer*, August 2009, 30. (Source: comScore, Inc.)

27. "3-D Technology Increasing Sales on Retailers' Websites," Ksl.com, February 26, 2009, www.ksl.com/index.php?nid=481&sid=5708057.

28. Cheryl Lu and Lien Tan, "Retailers 'Sell' to Young Virtually," *Wall Street Journal*, August 19, 2008, B8.

29. PR Newswire, "OneStopPlus.com Launches Technologically Advanced 'Virtual Model,'" *Market Watch*, October 17, 2011, www.marketwatch.com/story/onestoppluscom-launches-technologically-advanced-virtual-model-2011-10-17.

30. Dianna Dilworth, "Widgets Enter the Limelight," *DMNEWS*, September 8, 2008, 1, 30.

31. Michael Raisanen, "Widgets: What Are They Good For?" IMedia Connection, August, 15, 2008, www.imediaconnection.com/printpage.aspx?id=20187.

32. Jessica E. Vascellaro, "Online Stores Adopt Click-to-Call Customer Service," *Wall Street Journal*, March 15, 2006.

33. Zak Stambor, "Video and Chat Help E-Retailers Get Personal with Customers," *Internet Retailer*, July 2011, 28. (Sources: Retail effectiveness, The E-tailing Group Inc., Percentage offering chat, Datamonitor.)

34. Matt Ferner, "20 Popular Feeds From Retail Companies," Practical Ecommerce, May 2, 2011, www.practicalecommerce.com/articles/2753-20-Popular-Twitter-Feeds-from-Retail-Companies.

35. Ibid.

36. "Data Bank, The Week in Stats: Marketers' tweets can be organized in the following categories..." *DMNEWS*, August 9, 2010, 8. (Source: 360i.)

37. "Interactive Marketing Spending to Hit $76.6 Billion in 2016," *Advertising Age*, August 24, 2011, http://adage.com/print/229444. (Source: Forrester Research Interactive Marketing Forecasts, 2011-2016 (US).)

38. Dianna Dilworth, "Newspapers Engage With E-mail," *DMNEWS*, June 1, 2009, 11.

39. "Data Bank Messaging Preferences by Age Group," *DMNEWS*, October 27, 2008, 8. (Source: ExactTarget.)

40. "Nine of 10 Americans Have Cell Phones, but Talking Isn't All That Matters; Internet, Email, Important Attributes." National Retail Federation, June 17, 2010, www.nrf.com/modules.php?name=News&sp_id=948&op=printfriendly&txt=National-Retail-Federation. (Source: NRF/BIGresearch Consumer Intentions & Actions (CIA).)

41. Sahir Anand and Chris Cunnane, "New Age Multi-Channel Retailing: Prospects for Digital Revolution and Avenues for Better Integration," Aberdeen Group, January 2009, 14-15.

42. "Michaels 2010 Annual Report," Michaels, March 2011, 2. www.michaels.com.

43. Laura Heller, "The Future of Online Shopping: 10 Trends to Watch," *Forbes*. April 20, 2011, www.forbes.com/sites/lauraheller/2011/04/20/the-future-of-online-shopping-10-trends-to-watch.

44. "Newegg Takes the Lead in Making Its Website Accessible to Blind People," *Internet Retailer*, August 6, 2009, www.internetretailer.com/printArticle.asp?id=31393.

45. Nesli Karakus, "Retailers Find Rich Insights in Their Site Search Data," *Internet Retailer*, July 2001, 51. (Source: The E-tailing Group, Q4 2010 data.)

46. Mark Brohan, "The Big Boys Dominate Paid Search," *Internet Retailer*, July 21, 2010, www.internetretailer.com/2010/07/21/big-boys-dominate-paid-search. (Source: The Search Marketing Guide, 2011 Edition.)

47. Shar VanBoskirk for Interactive Marketing Professionals, *U.S. Interactive Marketing Forecast, 2011 to 2016*. August 24, 2011, 3. (Source: Forrester Research Inc.)

48. Thad Rueter, "Paid Search Spending Increases 7% in Q3," *Internet Retailer*, October 17, 2011, www
.internetretailer.com/2011/10/17/paid-search-spending-increases-7-q3.

49. Bill Siwicki, "Facebook: The New King of Social Networks Reinvents Itself for Brands." *Internet Retailer*,
August 2009, 48.

50. Bill Briggs, "Top 500 Retailers Take a Liking to Social Networks," *Internet Retailer*, May 21, 2011, www
.internetretailer.com/2011/05/31/top-500-retailers-take-liking-social-networks.

51. "Facebook Finds a Friend in E-Retailers-and Added Revenue, One Expert Says," *Internet Retailer*, August
20, 2009, www.internetretailer.com/printArticle.asp?id=31549.

52. Allison Enright, "Facebook Friends are Friends Indeed," *Internet Retailer*, November 16, 2011, www
.internetretailer.com/2011/11/16/facebook-friends-are-friends-indeed.

53. Internet Retailer. "Credit Cards Make a Comeback in Online Shopping." Growth of Online Payment Methods (Graph). Source: "4th Annual Retail Payments Forecast 2011–2016." Javelin Strategy & Research. January
2012, 64.

54. Allison Enright, "U.S. E-Retailers Miss Out On Selling to Global Shoppers, PayPal Says," *Internet Retailer*,
January 11, 2011, www.internetretailer.com/2011/01/11/us-e-retailers-miss-out-selling-global-shoppers-
paypal-says.

55. Joseph Pereira, "How Credit-Card Data Went Out Wireless Door," *Wall Street Journal*, May 7, 2007,
A1, A12.

56. Keith J. Winstein, "Major Cyber-Theft Suspect to Plead Guilty," *Wall Street Journal*," August 29-30, 2009, A3.

57. United States District Court District of Massachusetts. Government Sentencing Memorandum. United
States of America v. Albert Gonzales. March 18, 2010, 1, www.wired.com/images_blogs/threatlevel/2010/03/
gonzales_gov_sent_memo.pdf.

58. Elinor Mills, "Hacker Gonzalez Pleads Guilty in Heartland Breach," December 30, 2009, http://news.cnet
.com/security/?keyword=TJX. (Source: InSecurity Complex.)

59. John Schwartz, "Privacy Policy Notices are Called Too Common and Too Confusing," *New York Times*, May
7, 2001, www.nytimes.com/2001/05/07business/07PRIV.html.

60. "EU Justice Minister Warns US on 'Self-Regulation,' Draft European Privacy Law Now Available," Privacy.
org, December 7, 2011.

61. Luke Johnson. "What is SOPA? Anti-Piracy Bill Explained." *Huffington Post*. January 9, 2012. 1. www
.huffingtonpost.com/2012/01/19/what-is-sopa_n_1216725.html.

62. Declan McCullagh. "House Approves CISPA Despite Last-Minute Push by Opponents." April 26, 2012.
Source: Privacy Inc.-CNET News. http://news.cnet.com/8301-31921_3-57422567-281/house-approves-cispa-
despite-last-minute-push-by-opponents/

63. Geoffrey A Fowler and Erica Alini, "States Plot New Path to Tax Online Retailers," *Wall Street Journal*, July
3–5, 2009, B1.

64. Stuart Woo. "Amazon Softens Stance on Taxes." *Wall Street Journal*. April 28–29, 2012. B3.

65. Joanna Ramey and David Moin, "Pressure Mounting For Taxes on E-tail," *Women's Wear Daily*, June 20,
2011, 7.

66. Optaros, "Step 1 Determine Key Metric to Improve," in *Social Ecommerce 2009 Planning Guide*, 3.
(Excerpted and embellished by author.)

67. Emily Steel, "Web Privacy Efforts Targeted," *Wall Street Journal*, June 25, 2009, B10.

68. "Worldwide Installed Base and Projections 2011," in *Kiosks and Interactive Technology*, Summit Research
Associates, Inc., www.summit-res.com/kanditreport.html.

69. "At Mid-Year, Web Sales Trump Store Sales at Macy's," *Internet Retailer*, July 15, 2009, www.internet
retailer.com/printArticle.asp?id=31136.

70. Ben Fritz, "Redbox Revenue, Operating Income Soar," *Los Angeles Times*, July 28, 2011, http://latimes
blogs.latimes.com/entertainmentnewsbuxx/2011/07/redbox-revenue-operating-income-soar.

71. North American Self-Service Kiosks Market Study, IHL Group, 2011, www.inlservices.com/ihl/product_
detail.cfm?page=&ProductID=5.

72. Jessica E. Vascellaro, "HSN Eyes 'Remote' Shopping," *Wall Street Journal*, May 24, 2007, D3.

73. Sharon Edelson, "HSN's Digital Transformation," *Women's Wear Daily*, June 15, 2011, 9.

74. Christopher C. Williams, "Make Tracks for Liberty Interactive," *Barrons*, March 26, 2011, http://online
.barrons.com/article/SB50001424052970204728104576216651658705370.html.

75. Michelle Penz, "Teleshopping Gets a Tryout in Europe," *Wall Street Journal*, September 9, 1996, B10A.

76. Ibid. "Customers, HSE24Customers: An Affluent Target Group With a Big Potential," www.hse24.net/en/
wirueberuns/unternehmensportrait/kunden.

77. Mary Elizabeth Hurn, "Deals Abound for DRTV," *DMNEWS*, March 2, 2009, 11.

78. Rob Fixmer, "Personal Computers; Windows 98 Feature Combines TV, Terminal, and the Internet," *New
York Times*, November 18, 1998, 5.

79. Vicki Powers, "Video Stars," *DMNEWS*, November 24, 2008, 13.

80. Jessica E. Vascellaro and Emily Steel, "Something New Gains With Something Borrowed," *Wall Street Journal*, June 5, 2009, B6. (Source: J.P. Morgan.)

81. Mark Brohan, "Retailers Diving Into Mobile Commerce Are Coming Up With Significant Sales," in *The Internet Retailer Survey: Mobile Commerce, Internet Retailer*, October 2011, 27-30.

82. Marc Karimzadeh, "Ralph Lauren Taps Into M-Commerce," *Women's Wear Daily*, August 15, 2008, 2.

83. *Adobe Scene7 Mobile Commerce Survey: Mobile Shopper Insights for 2011*, Adobe Scene7, February 2011, www.scene7.com/report/AdobeScene7_Mobile_Shoppers_Insights.pdf.

Chapter 8

Global Retailing

Learning Objectives

After completing this chapter you should be able to:

- Summarize the dynamics of global expansion and the reasons why it occurs.
- Identify factors critical to the success of global retailers.
- Discern the advantages and disadvantages of the many types of global retail involvement.
- Explain the impact that the balance of trade has on the global economy and retailing.
- Relate how culture affects retailing practices in various countries.
- Highlight the global flow of retail expansion.

a

b

c

Figure 8.1
Marketplaces evoke the true essence of retailing—a plethora of products, haggling for the best price, and social interaction. Worldwide, vendors present spices and shoes, silks and saris, carpets and cell phones. Some have been in business for centuries. (a) At this Moroccan souk, elders pass the time of day, talk, and observe the shoppers in action. (b) Independent merchants and often their families sell their wares, which range from household staples to propane tanks sold from motorcycles. (c) For the locals, this is a way of life; for the tourists, a glimpse of the roots of retailing. Access to the souk is by two-footed, four-footed, or four-wheeled transportation, and participants seem to enjoy the pace.
(Photos courtesy of Gordon Lothrop.)

All but the most pessimistic observers recognize opportunities for retailers to expand globally. To appreciate the impact of global retail expansion, consider that McDonald's has more than 33,500 restaurants in 119 countries, and that almost 70 percent of its sales come from outside the United States.[1] On one hand, volatility in the Middle East may retard international retail development; on the other, the rise of China as an economic power may hasten it.

There is much to weigh in the global marketplace. You have learned that changes in technology, trade laws, competition, product sourcing, brand recognition, and customer behavior all affect retailing. This chapter examines the impetus for global expansion, the pros and cons of expansion, factors critical for success, the intricacies of global trade, and the ins and outs of global expansion. Cultural differences are considered, with retailing in China as the topic of the Global Retail Profile at the end of this unit.

Global Retailing: Overview and Impact

As in earlier chapters, by way of introduction, we'll survey terminology that applies to international trade and retailing. We'll look next at the financial impact of global retailing and identify countries that are the most involved in internationalization.

Terminology

Terms that are specific to the international sector lay the groundwork for the content of this chapter. To begin, we need to clarify the distinctions between industrialized and emerging countries, since each provides an important expansion base for retailers seeking to expand operations.

Industrialized countries are those that have reached full production capabilities with well-developed infrastructures and technologies. Countries that are presently developing their infrastructures and economies are called **emerging countries**. The status of each offers retailers unique opportunities to launch operations.

Retailers that operate domestically can choose to expand on two levels beyond their own national borders. **Domestic retailers** are companies that do business only in their home countries. **International retailers** include companies that operate in their home countries and in countries within their own or one other trading bloc. **Global retailers** are companies that do business in their home countries and in more than one other trading bloc. Walmart, a global retailer, is based in the United States but also does business in the Asia/Pacific region, North and South America, and Europe.

Top Countries and Regions for Retail Expansion

For fiscal year 2010–2011 the top 250 global retailers accounted for $3.94 trillion of total retail sales, slightly higher than the previous year. Analysis of the top retailers shows that 41.7 percent of sales of the top 250 global companies are attributed to the United States. European retailers including the UK, account for a 38.7 percent share of sales of the top 250.[2] The Asia/Pacific and Africa/Middle East regions are growing rapidly as a way to counter foreign competition. A ranking of the top emerging countries for retail development appears in Table 8.1.

Because many retail chains do not operate under the names of their parent companies, it is sometimes difficult to discern country of origin or ownership. For example, European powerhouses own some of the largest supermarket chains in the United States. In an effort to dominate East Coast supermarket retailing, the U.S. division of Netherlands-based Royal Ahold acquired several companies including Giant-Landover, Giant-Carlisle, Stop & Shop, and the Peapod online supermarket. Ahold generates 60 percent of its revenue from its U.S. divisions and competes directly with Walmart.[3] To further emphasize the complexity of international holdings, Walmart owns the chain Asda in the United Kingdom. Liz Claiborne owned the international apparel chain Mexx, but sold that to a private equity firm in 2010.

Not surprisingly, the larger the company in terms of sales volume, the more likely it is to be a global retailer. Also of interest is that over half of the top 250 retailers sell food and fast-moving consumer goods.[4] Walmart, Carrefour, and Tesco are prime examples. The top 20 global retailers are listed in Chapter 3, Table 3.1.

Did You Know?

After using its famous founder's name as its corporation's signature for more than three decades, Liz Claiborne got a new moniker. As of May 2012, the well-known fashion retailer changed its name to Fifth & Pacific Cos. The change better reflects its key brands—Juicy Couture, kate spade, and Lucky Brand. The Liz Claiborne brand was sold to JCPenney.

"Liz Claiborne Inc. Officially Fifth & Pacific Companies, Inc." Press Release. Liz Claiborne, Inc. May 15, 2012. http://finance.yahoo.com/news/liz-claiborne-inc-officially-fifth-113103366.html

Table 8.1   The 2011 Global Retail Development Index

2011 Rank	2010 Rank	Country	Region	GRDI Score
1	5	Brazil	Latin America	71.5
2	8	Uruguay	Latin America	65.5
3	6	Chile	Latin America	64.7
4	3	India	Asia	63.0
5	2	Kuwait	MENA	61.3
6	1	China	MENA	61.2
7	4	Saudi Arabia	MENA	59.5
8	9	Peru	Latin America	58.2
9	7	United Arab Emirates	MENA	58.0
10	18	Turkey	MENA	37.0

Rankings are based on an equally weighted index of four measures: (1) market attractiveness, (2) country risk, (3) market saturation, and (4) time pressure.

GRDI = Global Retail Development Index; MENA = Middle East/North Africa.

Excerpted from A.T. Kearney, Figure 1, "The 2011 Global Retail Development Index," in *Retail Global Expansion: A Portfolio of Opportunities*, 1.

(Source: A.T. Kearney analysis. Data compiled from Euromoney, Population Reference Bureau, International Monetary Fund, World Bank, World Economic Forum, Economist Intelligence Unit, and Planet Retail.)

Dynamics of Global Expansion

The environmental factors introduced in Chapter 2 provide a context within which to explore the dynamics of retailing on a world stage, because many of these factors affect global expansion. Changes in consumer behavior also precipitate expansion in some areas. This information provides insight into the optimal conditions under which expansion occurs.

Setting the Stage for Global Expansion

Economic indicators, saturated domestic markets, emerging markets, global brand awareness, technological advances, global sourcing, trade alliances, and available capital all contribute significantly to changes in the global environment.

Economic Indicators

The recession of 2008–2010 influenced retail markets in much of the world—particularly in the United States, Europe, and Asia. Despite the economic upheaval, many emerging regions and countries are ripe for retail expansion. Individuals in emerging countries, including many in Latin America and Africa, are faced with the dilemma of having money but not enough stores in which to spend it, or not enough products to buy. Growing numbers of middle-class families with new-found discretionary incomes are ready to purchase retail products, and will, when the effects of the recession subside worldwide.

Saturated Markets

Retailers in many industrialized countries are experiencing the pains of sustained growth in saturated markets. This was a key factor in the expansion of quick-serve restaurants decades ago and is the motivation for many mass merchandisers and fashion apparel chains now.

Emerging Markets

Several geographic areas have been identified as prime targets for retail development. Criteria used to determine these countries or regions include gross domestic product (GDP), population statistics, mean household income, retail sales per capita, stage of industrial development, and degree of political stability. The fast-growing BRIC economies—Brazil, Russia, India, and China—accounted for 17 percent of global GDP in 2010. However, consulting firm PricewaterhouseCoopers (PwC) expected to see 40 percent GDP growth over 2011 and 2012.[5]

Two BRIC countries—China at 9.1 percent and India at 6.9 percent—top the list of major countries with high GDP growth rates.[6] In comparison, the United States has the largest economy in the world as measured by GDP, but a low GDP growth rate. However, if China's rapid growth continues, by approximately 2050, it will surpass the United States to become the largest economy.[7] Fashionistas will appreciate learning about the top emerging countries for retail apparel expansion in Table 8.2.

Global Brand Recognition

The relative ease of global travel, improved communications, and more effective marketing have contributed to brand awareness. It's no wonder that Gap jeans find a home in Bangkok, Chanel handbags in Japan, or Fortnum and Mason tea in the United States. Many students participate in study-abroad programs at universities worldwide. Employees of global corporations are assigned overseas, and trips overseas are a popular form of vacation travel. Travelers integrate their new-found products into their lives and often find that their taste levels change as well.

The consulting group Interbrand annually ranks the most valuable brands of global retailers using three primary criteria:

- Financial performance.
- Role of brand.
- Brand strength.

Table 8.2 Top 10 Emerging Countries for Global Retail Apparel Expansion

2011 Rank	2009 Rank	Country	Comments
1	3	China	The broad array of retailers, from discount to luxury apparel, makes China appealing to all markets. China's move to the top ranking is precipitated by its huge population and rising incomes. Many global players, like IZOD (the U.S. apparel and accessories retailer for women and men), which intends to open 3,000 stores within 5 years, will continue to expand.
2	–	United Arab Emirates (UAE)	The profusion of wealth in this region and the fashion-consciousness of its residents and tourists propelled the UAE to second position. Prada (Italy); Bloomingdale's, Saks Fifth Avenue, and Victoria's Secret (United States); and Hugo Boss (Germany) are among the retailers in UAE luxury malls.
3	–	Kuwait	Another haven for those with high discretionary income and a zest for fashion merchandise, Kuwait is poised for long-term retail growth. Gross leasable space more than quadrupled between 2006 and 2010. Look for American Eagle, Versace, Cartier, and Hong Kong's Shanghai Tang.
4	8	Russia	The recession, risk of political instability, and lots of red tape made Russia's retail growth more risky but also opportunistic for retailers seeking to expand. IKEA (Sweden), Metro (Germany), and Auchan (France) have a presence. Growing retail sales per capita helps propel fashion retailers in the market.
5	9	Saudi Arabia	Gap, Banana Republic, and Cole Haan sell in this conservative Muslim country where women wear fashions under their full-coverage traditional dress. The King Abdullah Economic City, under development near the Red Sea, has earmarked 8.7 million square meters for retail use that will eventually house 50,000 shops.
6	4	India	India is an appealing market because of its population of 1.2 billion and the growth in its middle and upper classes. At the mall Select Citywalk, tenants include Mango, Guess, Body Shop, and Nike. However a protectionist movement has soured the plans of big-box retailers like Walmart (United States) and Tesco (United Kingdom) from entering the market by disallowing 51 percent direct investment. Single-brand retailers like Nike fare better as they can invest on a 100 percent basis.
7	1	Brazil	Predicting GDP growth through 2013, bolstered by the tourist draw expected for two global sporting events, and a pro-business government, Brazil's retail market is hot. International retailers presently in the country include Zara, Timberland, Louis Vuitton, and Hermés. The 30 new malls planned for 2012 will surely attract many more fashion retailers.
8	10	Turkey	Brand-conscious and young, the Turkish market welcomed retailers like Benetton and Ralph Lauren. Growing numbers of women in the workforce, more mall construction, and a reprieve from a recession should further benefit apparel retailers.
9	–	Vietnam	Moving up in economic influence due to a heightened apparel manufacturing base and opening the retail sector to 100 percent foreign capital investments, the Vietnamese market is growing. Traditional retailers still prevail, but modern formats like the United Kingdom's Tesco are emerging.
10	7	Chile	Considered the most stable economy in Latin America, Chile is becoming a draw for retailers like Walmart and apparel chains. Gap opened the first of 25 South American franchised stores in Santiago in 2011.

(Source: Adapted from A.T. Kearney, "The 2011 GRDI Findings," Global Retail Apparel Index, in *Retail Global Expansion: A Portfolio of Opportunities.* 2011, 1_11; and multiple trade sources and press releases.)

In researching these areas, Interbrand considers both earnings attributed to sales, as well as companies' estimated profits for the next five years.[8] Table 8.3 documents the top three retailers in each of seven countries or regions.

To many Americans abroad who are a bit homesick, spotting a Dunkin' Donuts in Kuala Lumpur or a Pizzeria Uno in Seoul is comforting. The same could be said for non-American travelers who gravitate toward restaurants that serve goods from their home countries.

Major shifts in targeted markets, shrinking financial resources, and pressures to bring more tourists—and potential shoppers—into U.S. cities are addressed in the following microcosmic example. Philadelphia, Pennsylvania typically draws in excess of 600,000 visitors to its historic and cultural sites, a number far below nearby New York's 8.5 million annual visitors. The Philadelphia Convention & Visitors Bureau marketing budget was a mere $900,000 in 2011, compared to a high of $2.5 million in 2005. In past years, the majority of visitors hailed from western Europe; however, the European debt crisis put a damper on travel for many. The key for Philadelphia was not to ignore its European visitors but to partner with tour-group operators and advertise in Brazil. Many Brazilians already visit New York City and shop for brands including Apple, Burberry, Coach,

---

Table 8.3 Interbrand Rankings by Retail Brand Value for 2011

Country or Region	Top 3 Retail Brands Including Primary Products/Formats
United States	1. Walmart (food and general merchandise)
	2. Target (general merchandise and food)
	3. Home Depot (do-it-yourself)
Canada	1. Shoppers Drug Mart (drugstores, general merchandise)
	2. Canadian Tire (automotive products)
	3. lululemon athletica (yoga and fitness apparel)
United Kingdom	1. Tesco (food and general merchandise)
	2. Marks & Spencer (department store)
	3. Boots (drugs, health, and beauty)
France	1. Carrefour (food and general merchandise)
	2. Auchan (food and general merchandise)
	3. Leroy Merlin (do-it-yourself)
Germany	1. Aldi (food and general merchandise)
	2. Media Mart (electronics)
	3. Edeka (food and multiple formats))
Spain	1. Zara (apparel)
	2. El Corté Ingles (department store)
	3. Mango (apparel)
Asia-Pacific	1. Woolworths (Australia; food and general merchandise)
	2. Uniqlo (Japan; apparel)
	3. Harvey Norman (Australia; electronics and appliances)

Rankings are based on: (1) financial performance, (2) role of brand, (3) brand strength, and (4) companies' profit estimations for the next 5 years.

Adapted from "Store of the Future," InterbrandDesignForum, 2011,

http:// issuu.com/interbrand/docs/thestoreofthefuture?mode=embed&viewmode=presentation&layout=http%3A%2F%skin.issuu .com%Fv2Flayout.xml&showFlipBtn=true.

From the Field 8.1   Web Site Advocates Hand-Made Crafts, Giving to Others

Whether they sell beaded earrings, painted flowerpots, or homemade soaps, Web sites that offer an alternative to chain stores are popping up and growing in popularity. One of them, MadeitMyself.com, is similar in concept to eBay. Shoppers buy items from sellers who post them on the site and ship directly to the buyer. Many of the craft sites—including Etsy, one of the best known, focus on handmade goods, art, or specialty items.

Creators of the sites and retail experts say the companies are growing in number, popularity, and sales because customers are increasingly looking for unique items they can't find in chain stores. The rise of the Internet has made it easier for shoppers to find and buy those items.

MadeitMyself.com was launched in November 2008 with 5,500 sellers signed up, and 2,200 listing products on the site. It's the brainchild of Ray Victors, who hatched the idea while traveling the world with his brother, who does missionary work. His brother's program, Rick Alonzo Missionaries, spreads gospel through multimedia art presentations, including live painting performances.

Victors found that artists in places like Guam and the Philippines didn't have a way of selling their work outside their neighborhoods. He told a man in Fresno, California, about his idea, and over breakfast one day the man handed him a check for a large amount. Victors declined to give the man's name or the dollar amount of his investment.

National Retail Federation spokesman Scott Krugman said such sites are proliferating as more people seek affordable, unique items. "The Internet provided a tremendous opportunity to create a mainstream marketplace. There's so many more ways of shopping and it only makes sense entrepreneurs would try to make that experience easier for shoppers."

Victors of MadeitMyself believes that people like communicating with the sellers and reading their bios on the site. He said, "They want to have something personalized that they can tell stories about."

Nina Seyedabadi of Fresno regularly shops MadeitMyself.com. She's bought soap in the shape and scent of cupcakes, a handmade wood truck for her two-year old nephew, and clay polymer charms for a bracelet. Mushroom pizza is her favorite food, so she requested a seller to make her a charm in the shape of a tiny slice of mushroom pizza. The pair collaborated on the designs through the site's messaging system before Seyedabadi bought the charm. She said: "It's so affordable."

Products at such sites are often affordable because sellers don't have overhead like marketing costs, Krugman added.

MadeitMyself.com, based in Fresno, California, only sells handmade items, giving it a competitive advantage over other firms that sell vintage and commercially made merchandise in addition to handmade pieces. A special "giving back" section featured on the site allows users to donate to charities using PayPal.

Condensed and adapted from Bethany Clough, *The Fresno Bee*, July 21, 2009, Distributed by McClatchy-Tribune Information Services, www.philly.com/philly/business/technology/072109_made_it_myself.html.

Author's Update: A review done by Small Business Trends in October 2011 reinforced that MadeitMyself.com remains a free marketplace. T.J. McCue said, ". . . It looks to be a rapidly growing community and handmade artisan service."

Other investigation showed that MadeitMyself.com receives 9,374 unique visitors every month and that the majority come from the United States.

Sources: T.J. McCue. "You Made It Yourself: Now What? 29 Places to Sell Your Handmade Creations. October 7, 2011. http://smallbiztrends.com/2011/10/29-places-sell-handmade-creations.html

SiteTrail.com "Visitor Analysis" June 5, 2011. http://www.sitetrail.com/madeitmyself.com.

---

and Kenneth Cole in the suburbs, and Philly's Bureau hopes to lure some of these visitors, perhaps through its Web site—which is geared to international shoppers—TaxFreePhilly.com. India is also a country of interest, since many visitors already come to the city for education and business, as well as shopping.[9]

International shopping festivals are a draw for tourists and generate revenue for retailers. In particular Dubai, China, Japan, Thailand, and Singapore are famous for staging gala shopping promotions.

Advanced Technology

As emphasized throughout this text, technology is changing the way business is done domestically and globally. Retailers and customers can have what they want, both where and when they want it. The Internet facilitates global trade for both small and large retailers. Sourcing products from around the globe as well as locally, members of a craft collaborative discuss selling online and giving back to the community in From the Field 8.1.

It is critical for international retailers to share information with their stores and the members of the supply chain that support sourcing, manufacturing, distribution, and fulfillment. Online tools greatly enhance communication initiatives.

Global Sourcing

Companies that purchase raw products, manufacture goods, maintain sound quality control, and ship merchandise to their intended end users efficiently have long held dominant positions in the marketplace. Integrated computer networks are a necessary component of global retailing. Hypothetically, they could facilitate the movement of goods from a factory in Slovakia to a consolidator in London, and ultimately to brick-and-mortar stores or an Amazon.com warehouse in the United States.

Retailers that move merchandise efficiently are well positioned to expand globally. When a company seeks global dominance, it goes where labor rates are favorable, well-trained workforces are available, local governments are open to foreign investment, and products and services are obtained at a good value. In their respective ways, Tesco, Costco, and Bata are masters of these techniques. Bata was included in this example because it is the largest shoe company in the world, even though most American shoppers are not familiar with the brand. The company is headquartered in Toronto, Canada, and is a multinational company. A Bata shoe store is illustrated in Figure 8.2.

a

Trade Alliances

EU, NAFTA, CAFTA, ASEAN, MERCOSUR, and WTO are acronyms familiar to the international business community. NAFTA, CAFTA, EU, and WTO were introduced in Chapter 2. The European Union (EU) is one of the largest trading blocs in the world with 27 member nations. Details on the eurozone and its common currency appear later in this chapter. The **Association of Southeast Asian Nations (ASEAN)** is a trade alliance set up in 1967 with backing from the United States to benefit countries including Brunei, Indonesia, Malaysia, the Philippines, Singapore, Thailand, and later, Vietnam.

MERCOSUR is a trade bloc that promotes free trade among several South American countries, including full members Argentina, Brazil, Paraguay, and Uruguay, and associate members Chile, Peru, Bolivia, Colombia, and Ecuador. Venezuela's request to become a full member began in 2004. Due to

b

Figure 8.2
Bata has shoe factories in developing countries and retail stores worldwide, including one in France (a). The company also maintains a shoe museum in Toronto, its home base (b).

differences in ideologies among some member nations, it was not until 2012 that full membership was granted. Paraguay was ousted from MERCOSUR after the impeachment of its president, but membership will be reconsidered after the 2013 presidential elections.[10]

The end of the 20th century saw fewer barriers and less bureaucratic turmoil related to trade, although there is still much room for improvement. **Free trade,** the practice of conducting business without boundaries or taxation, is emerging as the global norm. Adherence to this approach means better products, lower prices, and greater selection.

During downturns in the economy, many individuals and countries that do not support free trade adopt a protective stance. Boycotting foreign-made products in order to support domestic manufacturers is called **protectionism**. According to the World Trade Organization (WTO), the United States, China, India, Argentina, Brazil, Germany, the United Kingdom, and Japan have come under scrutiny regarding the imposition of restrictions against other countries. A few examples highlight common concerns relating to free trade:

- Argentina accused China of exporting inexpensive denim fabrics that compromised production in Argentina.
- Brazil had a similar complaint regarding synthethic fibers coming from China.
- The increase in value-added tax rebates on exports of textiles and apparel and export subsidies by India also came before the WTO.[11]

The first two cases involved anti-dumping inquiries. **Dumping** is the practice of exporting goods that are priced lower than the same goods manufactured in the country that imports the merchandise, thus creating unfair advantage.

The "Buy American" provision in the 2009 U.S. economic stimulus package was challenged by Canada. The northern neighbor deemed the program protectionist, particularly disturbing since Canada is the largest trading partner of the United States.[12]

Trade conflicts between the United States and China have been reciprocal. The United States threatened to place high tariffs on tires from China that it believed were hurting the U.S. domestic tire industry. China countered that it would cease importing chicken and auto parts from the United States if the tariffs on tires were imposed. In retaliation for duties on Chinese seamless steel pipe imposed by the United States in 2009, China set punitive duties on large cars and SUVs exported from the United States in 2011.[13] An extra 22 percent tax on vehicles would surely deter Chinese customers from "buying American." As if this weren't enough, in the last quarter of 2012, major Japanese car manufacturers reported significant decline in their sales to China. The escalating territorial dispute between the two countries was cited as a reason.[14] Retaliatory measures between countries may seem strange and superficial by our standards, but the process is part of a vast history of trade discrepancies and policy modifications.

Availability of Capital

As in other vital areas of business, global expansion demands that capital and credit be readily available. The development of truly global banking institutions, investment firms, and currency markets makes this possible. The global recession slowed business expansion in many parts of the world but also precipitated the beginnings of a new world financial order. Ultimately, the changes that result will facilitate global investment and encourage retail expansion.

By the end of 2011, recovery was underway; however, many analysts cautioned that the return to economic health would be slow. Global stock markets were at best unstable. The EU struggled with debt crises involving several of its member countries, and the United States coped with widespread unemployment and housing market declines. This climate was not amenable to growth.

Global economic output was expected to grow by 3.2 percent in 2012. Forecasts indicated that GDP growth would rise to 3.5 percent from 2013 to 2016, and then slow to 2.7 percent from 2017 to 2025—for an average 3 percent growth rate. Fully developed economies are predicted to grow at a slower pace during the 2013–2016 period, while many of the fast-paced emerging markets are expected to slow from a 6.4 percent rate in 2012 to a 1.3 percent rate in the same interim period. In the 2017–2025 period, both fully developed and emerging countries are projected to grow at 3.4 percent.[15]

The daunting task of revising guidelines and sustaining financial systems must be undertaken before world markets can respond. This is only one facet of a highly complex, but not necessarily highly evolved, global economy. The slowing growth of global GDP is less of a risk than the slowdown in average output per capita. It is promising to know that the future of the world economy is significantly affected by each and every worker on our planet: Retailers that intend to grow their businesses will eventually evaluate safer, more readily available options for funding global expansion.

Changes in Customer Buying Patterns

Branding plays a big role in generating customer awareness globally. Exposure to new cultures, ideas, media, and products increases the likelihood that existing tastes will change. This applies to Americans' taste for foreign goods and conversely, the tastes of people elsewhere for U.S. products. Certain countries are known for producing top-quality products in one or more categories. As examples, a high-performance automobile made in Korea may not be as highly prized as one from Japan. One would not expect to find sophisticated knit designer fashions in India but would in Italy. Taste levels and value consciousness are particularly important dimensions of customer behavior.

Taste Levels

Taste in products varies greatly by country—particularly those attributes of taste involving style, color, packaging, and dietary preference. However, one constant remains. Throughout the world, taste levels are homogenizing, becoming more alike than different from one global neighbor to another. This phenomenon is caused by a variety of factors, including intensive exposure to world media, greater access to the Internet, and increased frequency of global business and personal travel.

Import snobbery—a preference for imported goods—was introduced in Chapter 3. Certain individuals perceive a greater value in imported products, perhaps reveling in remarks like "my lingerie comes from Paris," or "I purchased that hand-tooled leather saddle in Ecuador." Graff, a luxury

jeweler on London's Bond Street, is illustrated in Figure 8.3. The jeweler was ranked number one in a survey of wealthy customers. "When you want something truly rare, you go to Graff," said Milton Pedraza, chief executive officer of the Luxury Institute, the company that completed the study. The appeal of imported goods from luxury retailers lends credence to import snobbery. Perhaps we all sometimes share these sentiments.

Value Consciousness

The quest to obtain value for money spent is important to people worldwide. Attaining higher levels of education in both an academic and a consumer sense makes people more sophisticated and wary. Periods of recession and other economic unrest make individuals more cautious about how, where, or whether they should spend their money. Changes in spiritual values make some people question whether so many "things" are needed in the first place. Such caution is a common and important part of the consumer experience.

Well-educated consumers demand better products. Wariness challenges retailers to become more conscious of consumers' wants and needs and more creative in developing marketing strategies. As discussed in Chapter 4, Customer Behavior, living well, providing for one's children, and desiring a safe and comfortable home are universal desires. These aspirations continue to bolster retail sales.

In addition to monitoring changes in the global retail environment and in consumers, it is imperative for retailers to explore the many reasons why international expansion is occurring. Those who do will be better poised to open stores abroad—a growth strategy that many analysts believe is as important today as online retailing, and a tactic used by many multichannel retailers.

Advantages and Disadvantages of Global Expansion

Although it may appear that global retailing is a contemporary movement, the seeds for expansion were sown long ago (see Figure 8.1). Quick-serve food restaurant chains such as McDonald's and Kentucky Fried Chicken (KFC) were among the first to identify global opportunities. Producers of consumer goods like Coca-Cola and Pepsi, along with designer brands like Chanel and Burberry, have traded internationally for decades and are highly visible. Many pluses and minuses are considered when retailers expand globally.

Facilitating Factors

There are many reasons why retailers look to other countries for expansion.

- Many retailers have saturated or nearly saturated domestic markets. For continued growth, those operating in mature markets must look abroad. This is why retailers are aggressive internationally. Mergers and acquisitions have created huge retail companies, contributing to market saturation.
- Higher sales and profits may be experienced globally. Many retailers report higher growth rates in international divisions than in domestic holdings. For example, Avon—a multichannel and global retailer—attributes about 80 percent of revenues to sales from outside the United States. Brazil is Avon's largest market, with sales of $2.2 billion in 2010. Sales in all of Latin America account for 40 percent of total sales.[16]
- High labor costs in fully industrialized, mature markets impel many retailers to produce goods offshore. The logical extension is to retail goods in the foreign countries where they are being manufactured. For example, Walmart sourced products from China for decades before it opened stores in that country.
- Reduced trade restrictions in some parts of the world pave the way for easier entry and operations.
- Improved technology and communication systems, infrastructure, and logistics help advance world trade.
- Lower costs of land and buildings in foreign markets—especially those in emerging countries—are attractive to retailers.
- Market potential is greater in fully industrialized countries where disposable incomes are growing. Despite the most recent recession, this is one reason why many foreign companies expand to the United States, where the standard of living is high.
- When the economy is strong, private equity capital for investment is available to retailers.

Potential Problems

Expansion abroad also presents potential problems including the following:

- Some international transactions involve extensive red tape. Receiving governmental approval in foreign countries is often difficult, time-consuming, bureaucratic, and prone to bribery.
- Finding adequate retail space for large-format stores is often difficult or too expensive in countries with limited landmass.
- The possibility of devaluation of domestic against foreign currencies makes investment outside a retailer's home country more risky.
- Many retailers that struggle to be profitable in their home markets are reluctant to take on the responsibilities of foreign expansion.
- Qualified employees are difficult to recruit in some foreign countries.
- Political instability, wars, and terrorist acts in certain regions deter retail expansion.
- Infrastructures may not be sufficiently developed to support retail expansion in some emerging markets.
- Access to high-speed Internet is essential for online retailing and is not available in all regions.

When the pros and cons are compared, it is apparent that global expansion is a logical, compelling, and potentially lucrative direction to take.

Trade-Related Issues

It is becoming easier to do business nearly everywhere in the world. Fewer tariffs and diminished quotas mean freer movement of goods. Bureaucracies in the past made starting a business time-consuming and paper intensive. As governments recognize the value of increased trade, they have removed barriers to business openings.

Antiquated laws, protectionist policies, and cultural biases also retard development. Progressive nations of all sizes in all stages of industrial development agree that to promote a workable global economy, all parties involved must be flexible. To expedite global expansion, local governments, chambers of commerce, financial institutions, trade associations, and ministries of trade work with retailers as facilitators. **Ministries of trade** are government offices able to assist businesses with importing and exporting activities. The common goals of these organizations are job creation, sales, profits, and good will.

Several trade preference programs offer duty-free status or reduced import taxes on U.S. imports from emerging countries in Central America, the Caribbean, Africa, and Asia. One of these programs is the Generalized System of Preferences, which covers 129 countries and allows duty-free status for up to 4,800 products. Another is the Andean Free Trade Preference Act (AIPA), which was enacted to help Bolivia, Columbia, Ecuador, and Peru fight drug production and trafficking by enhancing economic alternatives such as duty-free status on products imported from selected countries, as well as the United States. Both programs were scheduled to expire at the end of 2009, but were extended through July 2013.[17] The National Retail Federation supported these continuances.

Criteria for Global Success

Global and international retailers face the same challenges domestic retailers face, and then some. The need for quality management, prime locations, adequate financing, astute merchandising, and good customer service does not change substantially by country. However, the desire to go global requires a new mindset for retailers that believe they can rely on their domestic experience exclusively. Strategies for global success vary greatly depending on the type of retailer, country of expansion, and market receptiveness. Respect for diverse cultures and ways of doing business, as well as empathy with partners and employees are personal adjustments that help ensure a fruitful venture

Critical Decision Areas

Companies contemplating international expansion examine several criteria before doing so. Ten critical decision areas are:

1. *Type of ownership.* Should the operation stand alone or be part of a joint venture, partnership, or licensing or franchise arrangement? In most cases, it is advantageous—and sometimes mandatory—to set up some type of local partnership.
2. *Management logistics.* Decisions are made on whether the company will be run from the home country, either by expatriates or local management.
3. *Degree of cultural integration.* Retailers should fully acclimate to the countries and local communities in which they operate. A successful global retailer is one that can walk the fine line between adapting totally to a culture and encouraging change within that culture in a non-threatening way.
4. *Strategic planning direction.* Incomplete planning and faulty marketing do not work internationally any more than they do domestically. All retail projects require a long-term approach, keen insight regarding the strengths and weaknesses of a situation, and the ability to foresee the unexpected. Being alert to new opportunities as they unfold is another crucial element, as is thinking globally on all levels of an organization.
5. *Operational flexibility.* Learning how business and social practices differ from those in the home country is crucial. Several examples clarify this point. Functioning in a region where modern technology is lacking but goods still have to be moved efficiently is exasperating. Operating a business in a country where religious activities impact Fridays, rather than Saturdays or Sundays, requires adaptability. Bribes may not be a part of our business practice but it is customary in many countries to give monetary or gift "incentives" to expedite shipment or to grant access to the "right" person in customs.
6. *Research orientation.* Retailers conduct research before entering new markets. Population trends and buying habits are two areas that need to be identified and studied. Awareness of the developmental stage of countries is integral to expansion plans. Fully industrialized countries such as Germany require different types of stores than countries like Malaysia, which will

not reach full industrialization until well into the 21st century. Disposable household income and GDP growth by country and per capita help retailers determine consumers' spending levels.

7. *Product sourcing efficiencies.* The ability to procure products globally is another variable in the formula for success. Setting up an efficient supply chain and trusting partnerships with vendors and contractors is vital.

8. *Technological expertise.* Using technology that streamlines manufacturing, movement of goods, merchandise management, database development, and communication is essential to retailers with global outlooks. Online business intelligence—including data capture and analysis and the selection of appropriate performance metrics—is fundamental to success.

9. *Business focus.* "Know yourself and to your own self be true" may be the overriding theme of global retailers. They must know what business they are in and how they are perceived by their customers. The more markets entered the more likely it is that customers will possess vastly different attributes and have different needs. Maintaining a clear focus becomes more challenging under these conditions.

10. *Flexibility and sensitivity.* Entry into a new market may take less time if the right partnership is formed in the first place. Learning to be flexible and sensitive to the nuances of a culture that is unlike your own can be daunting. Flexibility in management practices, employee training, and development of customer service standards is essential.

Other Success Factors

Other success factors are worth noting at this juncture. Retailers considering expansion first try to do business in countries that speak the same language. For example, retailers in Spain are wise to enter other Spanish-speaking countries first. In this case, cultural similarity is more important than geographic proximity. This concept is particularly important for companies contemplating entry strategies. For Spanish companies entering non–Spanish-speaking countries, it may be wise to wholesale goods first. Using local employees to manage the distribution operation and then gradually moving into retail sales is less risky. The trendy apparel company Zara, a division of the Spanish company Inditex, requires that all of its store managers outside Spain speak Spanish.

Many luxury retailers have entered Spanish-speaking countries. Read about how famous Italian footwear retailer Salvatore Ferragamo competes in Latin American markets and gain insight into the Latino luxury customer in From the Field 8.2.

It may be more sensible, and ultimately more cost-effective, for a retailer to expand within its own trading bloc. For example, Japanese department stores expanded first to Hong Kong, Singapore, and other Southeast Asian countries before making significant strides elsewhere. Keeping a low initial investment helps ensure staying power in the marketplace, future growth plans, and eventual profitability.

On a similar note, when conducting business in another country, discussions may begin in English but soon lapse into the local vernacular. Decisive points, innuendo, and basic understanding are frequently lost. It is wise to use translators in these situations.

Foreign language ability gives an executive an edge when dealing in international markets. Schooling, family background, and proximity to neighboring countries where a different language is spoken all influence a person's foreign language abilities. Individuals desiring careers in global retailing should be fluent in at least one language other than their own. The most frequently spoken languages in the world are graphed in Figure 8.4. Is it time to brush up your Arabic, Hindi, Bengali, or Portuguese, or to sign up for a class to boost your marketability abroad?

Acknowledging all sides of the expansion issue, some analysts believe that a backlash movement could occur. More retail expansion could cause national boundaries to diminish in importance, taste levels to become interwoven, and philosophies to merge. If so, customers caught in these crosswinds may choose to reemphasize national pride and buy products only from their own countries. Global retailing requires executives to carefully study and adapt to the cultural climate wherever they intend to do business.

From the Field 8.2 Salvatore Ferragamo's Head of Latin America Shares Expert Understanding on Luxury

Diego Stecchi, president of Latin America & Caribbean at Salvatore Ferragamo, one of the most experienced luxury professionals in the region, shares his understanding of the potential of the luxury market and the exceptional performance of Ferragamo in Latin America.

Salvatore Ferragamo is one of the international luxury brand pioneers in Latin America. What is Ferragamo's main competitive advantage in comparison with other international luxury brands?

Ferragamo's competitive advantage is its heritage, design and quality of products, and "made in Italy" process. It is one of the world's main players in the luxury goods sector, whose origins date back to 1927. Salvatore Ferragamo is active in the creation, production, and sales of shoes, leather goods, clothing, silk products, and other accessories, as well as fragrances, eyewear, watches, and jewelry. Attention to uniqueness and exclusivity; uniting style, creativity, and innovation; and Italian quality and craftsmanship have always been the hallmark of the brand's products.

Your company has the most extensive retail presence among major international luxury brands in Latin America. How is your retail network currently operating and what is your future development strategy?

Currently, we have 84 points of sale in Latin America, of which 28 are directly owned and 56 are non-direct franchises and wholesale clients. The directly operated stores are based in countries such as Mexico, Argentina, Chile, and the island of St. Thomas. Non-direct operations are in Brazil, Colombia, Peru, Panama, Costa Rica, the Dominican Republic, and others. We are planning further development in Chile, Brazil, and Mexico.

Are Latin Americans more drawn to Italian or French luxury brands?

It is difficult to determine given that Italian brands are now owned by French companies and vice versa. However, Italian brands are mostly known for their expertise in leather goods including shoes and bags, and French brands are known for their expertise in cosmetics, fragrances, and jewelry.

What is the best-performing country in Latin America in terms of sales results?

Mexico is our primary market in terms of sales performance, followed by Brazil.

What are, in your view, the most important differences between the profiles of U.S. and Latin American luxury customers?

In Latin America, consumers can be divided into two groups: classical luxury and aspiring. "Classical luxury" consumers are more conservative and always have been surrounded by luxury goods, and therefore do not believe the brand name they wear defines their status. On the other hand, "aspiring" customers buy a luxury product because they believe it defines their status. They are less conservative and more inclined to spend significant amounts of money. In the United States, consumers are more mature in terms of the fashion world and rather than focus on the brand, their choices are led by the trends and latest collections.

Adapted and condensed from CPP-LUXURY.COM, December 15, 2011, www.cpp-luxury .com/en/salvatore-ferragamo-s-head-of-latin-america-shares-expert-understanding-on-luxury_1933.html.

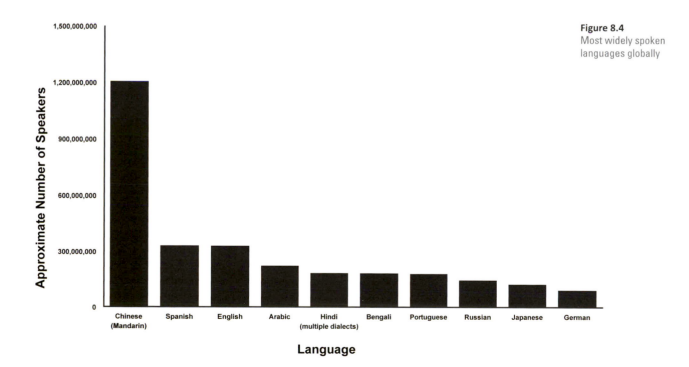

Figure 8.4
Most widely spoken languages globally

Entry Strategies for Global Retailers

Each of the several entry strategies retailers use to do business globally has advantages and disadvantages. The type of involvement selected depends on the objectives of the retailer, degree of control desired, availability of management, intercultural expertise, and budget. Modes of entry include:

1. *Wholly owned acquisitions.* With this approach, growth is organic. Retail ownership, control, and fiscal responsibility remain solely in the hands of the single proprietor, partnership, or corporation involved in global expansion. No local venture partners are sought, although local management might be employed. This is considered a low-risk, high-reward mode of entry.

2. *Joint venture.* Commonly called a JV, this type of involvement is an agreement between the retail company doing the expansion and a compatible company in the host country. Under this arrangement, the two parties agree upon some portion of actual ownership, control, and fiscal responsibility. Companies such as Walmart, Carrefour, and Pier 1 have operated on this basis. Risk is shared, but so are profits.

3. *Franchising.* Expansion is less risky when dealing with a proven name and format. Setting up effective master franchise systems is essential when working internationally. A **master franchise** is an ownership arrangement in which one company buys the rights to a large region of a country, setting up scores of individual stores. Strong brand recognition and economies of scale due to group purchasing are the benefits of this option.

4. *Licensing.* This arrangement occurs when a manufacturer or retailer agrees to pay for the right to use a brand or store name to gain entry and awareness for a product or service in a marketplace. Products are made and sold under the name of the licensor. For example, the Italian eyewear company Luxottica licenses several designer lines of eyewear including Burberry, Dolce & Gabbana, Donna Karan, Prada, Tiffany, and Versace.[18] Company kate spade moved from handbags to china tableware through licensing. This is considered a moderate-risk method of expansion.

5. *Consignment.* Merchandise from a manufacturer or distributor is placed in a retail store, but revenue is not remitted to the vendor until the goods are actually sold. The risk is clearly on the manufacturer or distributor under this arrangement. Many Japanese department stores work on this basis with their vendors, and many global and domestic retailers are experimenting with this format.

6. *Concession.* This is similar to a leased department within a retail store, in-store shop, or mall site. The manufacturer or distributor pays rent for square footage in a store directly to the retailer. In some cases, concessionaires also pay a percentage of sales or profits to the retailer. For example, the U.K. fashion apparel brand Lipsy has found it advantageous to sell to companies such as Topshop, but also runs concessions independently in department stores including Selfridges and House of Fraser.[19] Square footage in the concession area may expand as sales grow.

7. *Agents and consultants.* Companies interested in starting international operations often seek agents in the countries they wish to explore. These individuals or firms are familiar with their local markets and have experience sourcing and marketing similar products. They operate on a fee or commission basis. Agents are also used to scout locations, find partners and contractors, and consult on local business practices.

8. *Exporters.* Exporting products from one country to another is less risky than other types of involvement. The responsibility of a manufacturer or retailer for selling and shipping products usually ends once the goods have been received by the retailer. Since many retailers now manufacture the goods they sell, this has become an initial mode of entry for some vertically integrated companies.

9. *Online stores.* One of the more popular forms of global expansion is opening an online store. Usually this makes the company a multichannel retailer as well. Amazon has many international Web sites and distribution centers to support sales fast and efficiently.

On a high-risk to low-risk spectrum, it is much more difficult to stand alone in a global marketplace. However, it is at this level that the most control over an operation is exercised in terms of direction, store image, operations, and financial planning.

Table 8.4 Advantages and Disadvantages of Select Types of International Retailing Engagement

Type of Involvement	Advantages	Disadvantages
Wholly-Owned Acquisitions	• Supply-chain expertise and contacts in place • International and domestic management utilization • Existing infrastructure • Local knowledge of market utilized • Maximum control	• High initial cost • Difficulty finding and integrating compatible stores • High financial risk
Joint Ventures	• Strengths of two partners • Local presence in the market • Local contacts • Local management • Less financial risk	• Difficulty finding the right partner • Communication problems between partners • Possible erosion of store image
Franchising	• Consistent image • High brand recognition • Established operational procedures	• Risk of too-rapid growth • Risk of oversaturation
Licensing	• Immediate access to market • Opportunity to build brand equity • Lower risk	• Lack of control over brand quality • Communications problems with licensees • May erode perception of brand if done excessively

Often it is necessary to trade off some control in order to minimize risk. This is the main reason many joint ventures are solidified around the world. Local expertise provides better security services and business perspective. Learning ways to do business in the community, circumvent red tape, motivate employees, and understand local laws and customers is accomplished best with the aid of a well-chosen partner. The advantages and disadvantages of selected types of involvement are summarized in Table 8.4.

International Trade Issues

In the arena of international trade, many factors encourage or retard the movement of goods. The balance of trade is affected by trade alliances, agreements, and disputes.

Balance of Trade

The **balance of trade** is the difference between a country's imports and exports over a period of time, such as a year. For example, the U.S. trade deficit increased in 2009 even though overall trade was down during the recession. Although the world trade volume increased by an encouraging 2.5 percent in June 2009, the WTO predicted that total world trade would be down 10 percent for the year.[20] All countries are to some extent connected with one another; thus, what happens at this level of trade economically impacts the flow of retail goods globally. Retailers monitor economic indicators regularly because their business depends on it.

When trading partners do not agree on import or export practices, restrictions on trade may occur. **Trade sanctions** are penalties imposed on one country by another in an attempt to curb unfair trade practices. Governing bodies, such as the WTO, administer import and export laws and mediate disputes.

Factors Facilitating Trade Development

Currently, many industrialized countries receive more products from foreign countries than they market to them. For example, China exports more goods to the United States than the United States ships to China. To restore a favorable balance of trade, countries in this predicament need to export more domestic products. Factors that encourage trade include favorable currency exchanges, high-level marketing skills, efficient transportation systems, low-wage labor, quality control standards, trade alliances, and trade policies that minimize protectionism. We'll look briefly at each of these factors.

When currency is overvalued in the international exchange markets, each currency unit may buy more overseas than domestically—depending on the country. A weak dollar makes U.S. exports less expensive on the world market. During the recent recession, the worth of the dollar plummeted against the euro, making it cheaper for firms in the eurozone to buy U.S exports. As sales of U.S. exports rise, this helps reduce the trade deficit. To clarify this point, consider the effects of currency valuations on international travel. When the pound sterling is strong against the dollar, travel to London is very expensive for American tourists and students studying abroad. In response, some opt to postpone their travel plans. On the flip side, European visitors flocked to the United States because the euro was worth much more than the dollar, making U.S. hotel stays, meals, and shopping significantly less expensive.

Manufacturers and retailers in many emerging areas of the globe now have more savvy: they've learned marketing skills that were once privy to marketers in the United States and other fully developed countries. More efficient transportation has lessened logistical problems in many parts of the world. Lower manufacturing wage scales in some parts of the world—particularly Asia—translate to lower prices on products exported from those areas.

In the past, less stringent quality control standards meant that products from some countries failed to gain acceptance among consumers elsewhere in the world. This situation paved the way for higher-quality goods to be imported from other areas. Quality control is a more pressing issue in emerging countries. As retailers and manufacturers become more experienced in developing standards and training employees, this problem becomes less apparent.

Regional trade alliances in several parts of the world have made importing easier and more cost effective. Fewer protectionist policies exist once nations embrace the benefits of free trade.

Importing is risky in part because of the possibility of change to international politics. Retailers search for resources in stable countries that produce quality goods at a low price. Organizations like Target, Limited Brands, Pier 1, Macy's, and Forever 21 are masters at foreign sourcing.

Trade Sanctions

If it's not bananas, it's wine and cheese—or handbags! Imposing tariffs or placing bans on the importation of products are examples of trade sanctions. A "banana dispute" between the EU and the United States began when bananas marketed by U.S. companies were shunned in favor of fruit imported from Africa and the Caribbean. Products from these areas were preferred in the EU because tariffs were lower. The EU contended that it had abided by guidelines imposed in 1997 by the WTO that were designed to encourage fair trade.[21] By 1999, the problem had escalated, and the United States imposed WTO-approved trade sanctions on the EU. Included on the list of European products that would be taxed at 100 percent rates were designer handbags, electric coffee makers, bed linens, and bath salts.[22]

In 2009 the United States threatened to levy taxes on French cheese and wine exports in retaliation for EU restrictions on imports of American beef that had been treated with hormones. U.S customers and retailers who buy imported gourmet products, including French wine, cheese, chocolate, and jam, were understandably concerned that prices would escalate if the tariff went into effect.[23] In this case, an agreement was reached before that happened.

Trade sanctions drive up retail prices considerably for large and small retailers alike, making it difficult to purchase stock and placing products out of reach of most customers.

Focus on the European Union

Many organizations, countries, trading blocs, and individuals create the mechanisms that foster and regulate international trade. For more than 50 years, Europe conceived of an integrated economy that would incorporate elements of free trade, harmonization, and standardization. This did not come easily for the European Economic Community (EEC), which officially became the EU in 1992, nor has it always been a smooth existence. **Harmonization** occurs when tax rates across several countries are brought into equilibrium. **Standardization** refers to the establishment of uniform operational, environmental, and monetary systems across several countries.

Membership and Objectives

As of 2012, the EU comprised 27 countries. The map in Figure 8.5 shows the current membership. Many former Eastern European countries are provisional members and must build their GDP and financial status before becoming full members; Bosnia, for example, is not expected to join the EU

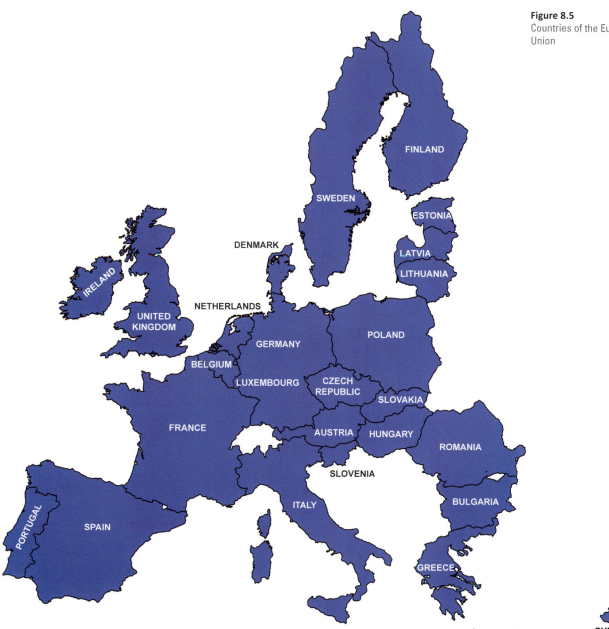

Figure 8.5
Countries of the European Union

before 2015.[24] The European market includes more than 800 million people who, under the guidelines of the EU, trade across geographic borders without restrictions. Citizens are free to travel or work in other EU countries.

According to the Annual Growth Survey, the EU made progress in the following areas during 2011:

- *Financial consolidation and macroeconomic stability.* Improvement occurred, but challenges caused by worsening economic conditions made modifications difficult to implement.
- *Labor market reforms.* Policy changes, skills training, and lifelong education initiatives saw some improvement; wage reforms were met with modest success, albeit in very few countries.
- *Growth-enhancing measures.* Slow progress was reported in research, development and innovation, transport, and energy; however, obstacles associated with competition, services, and networking industries continued to frustrate.

The EU put forth an aggressive agenda for 2012 and beyond. Many initiatives revolve around returning to normal lending practices within the membership, building the digital economy as well as foreign trade, coping with unemployment and the resultant social problems, and facilitating startups for new businesses.[25]

Background

As early as 1952, six countries—Belgium, France, Italy, Luxembourg, the Netherlands, and the Federal Republic of Germany—banded together to do less-restrictive business in the coal and steel industries. In 1958, the Treaty of Rome established the EEC. The Single European Act of 1986 initiated the drive to reach unity by 1993. By this time, the United Kingdom, Ireland, Denmark, Greece, Spain, and Portugal had become members. On the last day of 1992, the Maastrict Treaty ensured that the 12 member countries would work together to create economic and institutional efficiencies.[26] Later, Finland, Sweden, and Austria joined.

Provisions of the Agreement

Operational and policy changes in several areas were implemented. Reverberations are still being felt in the EU and around the world as a result. These changes include:

- *Free trade.* Previous bilateral trade agreements between European countries were terminated, opening the borders to the free flow of goods and services. Tariffs were eliminated.
- *Harmonization.* The leveling off of value-added taxes among member nations is an ongoing goal—the issue has been under discussion since the inception of the EU. A **value-added tax (VAT)** is a tax levied at each stage of processing for a raw material or of production and distribution for a commodity or retail product. VAT is used in EU countries and is similar to a sales tax in the United States except that it is collected at each stage of production. VATs vary greatly by country. For example, the standard rate in Luxembourg is 15 percent and has remained constant since 1992. In Sweden, the rate has been 25 percent since 1990. Italy, undergoing its own debt crisis, raised its VAT from 20 to 21 percent in September 2011 and increased it again from 21 to 23 percent in early 2012 in order to raise money.[27] Eventual harmonization at about 17 percent is anticipated, which will facilitate business between EU countries and be less confusing for customers.
- *Standardization.* Uniform quality controls, health and safety standards, and weights and measures were introduced. Standardization was difficult to achieve for some EU countries. For example, changing the unit of measure for many supermarket products from pounds to kilograms was a challenge for many retailers in the United Kingdom.

Currency and Monetary Policy

Another provision of the Maastrict Treaty was the establishment of a central bank. The **European Central Bank (ECB)** is the financial institution that administers currency policy for the EU. One of the objectives of the ECB is to encourage intra-European trade.

The common currency used by the EU is the **euro**. The system set up to facilitate the adoption and use of the euro for participating members is the **Economic and Monetary Union (EMU)**. Individual country currencies remained in effect alongside the euro until the official euro adoption date, January 1, 2002. The debate over the new currency was heated. As of 2012, the **eurozone** (countries within the EU that have adopted the euro) comprised 17 countries: Austria, Belgium, Cyprus, Estonia, Finland, France, Germany, Greece, Ireland, Italy, Luxembourg, Malta, the Netherlands, Portugal, Slovenia, Slovakia, and Spain.[28] The United Kingdom, Sweden, and Denmark are among those countries that have not adopted the euro.

For the record, although rates change every day, on September 1, 2011, the euro was worth $1.45 against the dollar, its peak for the year beginning August 4, 2011, to August 3, 2012. On January 13, 2012 the euro had dropped to $1.28 and then to $1.21 on July 24, 2012—a record low for the time period charted.[29]

Influence on Retailers and Consumers

The transition to the euro required adaptations by businesses and consumers alike.

- Catalogue companies adjusted pricing on merchandise, reprinted catalogues, and altered packaging.
- Computer systems in Italy and Spain were reconfigured to accept decimals for prices written in euros. In the local currencies of these countries, decimals had not been used.
- ATMs needed to be refitted.
- Vending machines required adaptation to accept the new currency.

The adoption of the euro also discouraged cross-border bargain hunting. Before the transition, shoppers traveled from country to country to find the best prices. One could say standardization of the common currency spoiled their fun!

The EU levied a tax on products and services ordered online by customers within the EU in 2003. This affected U.S. suppliers of music, DVDs, software, and computer games delivered over the Web. For example, if a customer in the Netherlands ordered a download from a music site in the United States, the retailer was expected to charge the customer the current VAT rate in effect in the Netherlands. Intra-European transactions are also taxed.[30] Imagine the time, money, confusion, and legal obligations involved when dealing with so many different taxation policies in the 27-member EU.

In October 2011, the European Commission released its proposal for a Common European Sales Law. If passed, the law would allow online businesses to tax sales under a single rate throughout the EU. Proponents believe that this option would give customers more convenience and a wider range of products from which to choose. Although the United Kingdom is not a member, it does ample trade with the EU. The director of the British Retail Consortium said that a common tax base would make it easier for U.K. retailers to expand into more countries.[31] This is a prime example of how decisions made in one region affect business policy in others.

The economic downturn adversely affected the financial solvency of several EU members. Plagued by debt, several countries came under close scrutiny by EU officials in late 2009. Concern escalated when Greece, Portugal, and Spain were deemed at risk of being unable to pay their debts, despite safeguards written into the eurozone regulations. Although EU member nations are expected to cap their debt at 60 percent of GDP and carry budget deficits no greater than 3 percent, some countries were accused of hiding the true size of their debts and indulging in sophisticated financial maneuvers to remain members in good standing.[32]

Some analysts believe the crisis underscores the reality of the EU: there is one common currency in the eurozone but its 17 different economies comprise members with radically different viewpoints.[33] When Italy made headlines in later 2011 because of its escalating debt crisis, and shortly after Greece announced its impending insolvency, the news sent tremors of concern worldwide.

EU members, the European Central Bank, and Greek governmental officials worked diligently to mend the Greek economy and prevent the country from dropping out of the 17-country common currency bloc. All parties involved had mixed feelings about the dilemma, but the general consensus was to keep Greece solvent. The ECB sold bonds as part of its monetary policy to raise funds for its emergency-lending program, called ELA, and later to back loans to Greece and other nations in need.

In exchange for assistance from the ECB, officials stipulated that Greece complete an intensive review of its finances, implement austerity programs to reduce government costs, raise taxes, and ultimately lower its debt. Greek voters represent two parties; Syriza, made up of left-wing austerity advocates, and the New Democracy, which favored a conservative bailout package. At a special election, citizens supported the bailout platform of the New Democracy.

ELA stands at €100 billion as of May, 2012. Greece appears to be on track, but should the bailout plan fail, contingency plans are under consideration.[34]

As this book went to press, the crux of the EU's problems did not appear to have been fully grasped or articulated by some of the countries most involved. Various proposals have been put forward in an attempt to resolve the financial crisis, and a long grueling process has commenced.

Agreements make world trade more fluid, but knowledge of cultural differences is equally imperative. By learning about the values and habits of other societies, retailers smooth their entry into countries where ideologies differ from those at home.

Cultural Influences and Issues

Customer perspectives on pricing, frequency of shopping visits, gift-giving, store loyalty, and customer service; perceptions of status goods; and responsiveness to sales promotion differ around the globe. Retailers' days of operation and merchandise for sale may be affected by the religious beliefs of the prevailing culture. Examples of cultural differences that affect retailing follow.

Religious Factors

Whether a store closes to observe the Sabbath—and the day on which it does—depends on the population's adherence to prevailing religious tenets. In the United States, stores usually are open seven days a week. If they are closed at all, shorter hours may be in effect on Sundays in this predominantly Christian nation. In Hassidic neighborhoods of New York City, stores are closed on Friday night and Saturday—the Jewish Sabbath.

Friday is the Sabbath day for Muslims, necessitating store closings in most Muslim-majority countries; Sundays are simply another business day. In Malaysia, however, attitudes are changing. Although stores in small cities and towns in this Muslim nation adhere to custom, stores in large metropolitan areas tend to straddle the issue. Shopping malls in Kuala Lumpur are open every day, much like those in cities around the world, but smaller retail stores are more likely to be closed on Fridays.

Food and beverage consumption is also affected by religious beliefs. Observers of Islam and Judaism do not eat pork or consume alcohol; Hindus do not eat beef.

Local ordinances called *blue laws* in some U.S. cities and states forbid the sale of alcoholic beverages or certain business activities on Sundays. For example, lobster fishermen in Maine can reposition or set bait in their lobster traps on Sundays but cannot haul in the traps—even if they are full—and sell their catch. They have to wait until Monday to get the lobsters to market.

When France approved store openings on Sunday, the decision had more to do with lifestyle than with religious obligations, but there were opposing viewpoints. Many French people consider Sunday a day of rest, and value this time spent with families. Retailers, for their part, expressed concerns about productivity and job growth.[35]

As these examples illustrate, retailers must be aware of how religious beliefs and taboos affect retail selling, and recognize that change usually occurs slowly when tradition and lifestyle conflict with retail progress.

Shopping Frequency

Cultural inclinations and infrastructure combine to influence consumer behavior. For example, Londoners tend to shop frequently due largely to habit, but the transportation system also plays a role. The public bus and underground systems are convenient and well used, but not meant for the transport of a week's worth of groceries. Rather than make one main grocery expedition per week,

Figure 8.6
It appears there are more bicycles than cars in many areas of Europe. Customers in the Netherlands adapt their shopping habits accordingly by shopping more frequently but buying less per trip. Blokker, an electronics chain is visible on the right. Imagine carrying your new 60″ TV screen home on your bike or back.

as many suburban U.S. families do, London shoppers—like most metropolitan Europeans—make several trips, purchasing only what they can carry home easily.

In Denmark and the Netherlands, shopping is done in smaller increments because so many people ride bicycles to work or school. It's not unusual to see rows of bikes parked in busy downtown areas or public venues. Figure 8.6 illustrates typical transportation in the Netherlands; we'll infer the accommodations one has to make when shopping by bicycle or on foot.

Attitudes Toward Gift Giving

Customs related to gift giving also differ in different parts of the world. When scholars from the University of Arizona studied the practice of gift giving in Japan, they noticed the rituals surrounding gifts of fruit during special holiday periods. Fruits such as oranges and grapefruit are considered luxuries in Japanese households, not part of the regular diet as they are in the United States. Therefore, in a country where gift-giving is an art, they are well received. The process is governed by complex cultural parameters. The source of the product—in this case the retail store—and packaging are as important as the fruit itself. Only perfect fruit, first individually wrapped then gift wrapped in carefully chosen, fine paper is appropriate. Price is not a major consideration since a small box of fruit can cost about $100 and a large basket around $600.[36] This tradition affects many types of retailers, because fruits are sold at specialty and department stores as well as food stores during the holiday season.

Status and Brand Consciousness

The acquisition of products—materialism—is not limited to the United States. Status-oriented products, brands, and even malls are received with different degrees of enthusiasm around the world.

Retailers with strong brand equity do well in Japan, where status and prestige are important commodities. American brand names are not quite as prestigious as European ones, but American style and culture do exert great influence. For example, apparel from the Gap and Ralph Lauren—as well as American music—are particularly well received. Young Japanese women in particular are fond of designer brands and spend huge sums acquiring fashion. Chanel handbags and Prada sportswear seem more significant to them than to most American women of the same age.

Figure 8.7
Vivo City in Singapore
typifies future-tech design
in a shopping mall for a
sophisticated city.

The blatant modernity of Vivo City, the largest retail and lifestyle mall in Singapore, suits shoppers who seek status. The curvilinear design of the center, illustrated in Figure 8.7, appeals to fashion customers and those who want to enjoy its harborside location.

Joe Camel may be dead in the United States, but he is alive and well in Asia. Although cigarette advertising is banned on TV in some Asian countries, tobacco companies find ways around that restriction. Camel and Dunhill produced lines of upmarket men's apparel in order to increase visibility of their brands in Asia. A significantly greater percentage of the Asian population smokes compared with the U.S. population. Marlboro menswear shops are evident in many European cities. Customers respond well to branding initiatives of this type. Labels and merchandise are valued differently, and cultures have a strong influence on the formations of those values.

Responsiveness to Promotions

Internationally, differences in customer responsiveness to sales-promotion events are significant. A month-long promotion at Metrojaya department store in Kuala Lumpur, Malaysia, featured a variety of western-style merchandise—shirts, cowboy hats, denim apparel, and giftware—displayed in fixtures inspired by covered wagons. Part of the extravaganza included a performance by clog dancers from an American university. What was most impressive was the support and enthusiasm shown by spectators. Crowds began forming more than an hour before each scheduled performance, the display floor was swarming, and cash registers were ringing. Although advertising for the promotion was intense, most malls in the United States would have to work twice as hard to bring in as many motivated shoppers—even in good economic times. Customers in the United States are inured to the number of promotions staged in countless, easily accessed malls. For the Malaysian shopper, however, the events were fresh and appealing. Fascination with the American Wild West was also apparent in the Chinese store illustrated in Figure 8.8.

Walmart observed similar receptiveness at some of its grand openings in South America. Customers there seem to be intrigued by giveaways and festivities, and frequently bring their entire families to store celebrations.

There is no aspect of life—shopping behavior included—that is untouched by culture. Business decisions that have the potential to affect religious beliefs, deep-rooted customs, and habits of all types are therefore best approached with sensitivity.

Figure 8.8
Asian fascination with the American Wild West is manifested in this cowby-hatted shopper leaving a menswear store in China.

Expansion: The Flow of Global Retailers

U.S. retailers are converging on almost all continents and global retailers are landing on American shores as well. Some retailers are bypassing the United States but expanding aggressively in other regions. No selling formats are immune. The following examples highlight movement within the retail community from a variety of geographic and strategic directions. Many topics in the preceding sections such as selecting a mode of entry, mitigating economic downturns, choosing timing, and finding the right partner are reinforced through multiple examples.

U. S. Retailers Reach Out

Designers, fast-fashion chains, specialty formats, and experiential retailers are branching out. Our first example, U.S.-based Build-A-Bear Workshop, introduced in Chapter 1, with its high level of customer engagement and participation, is an experiential retailer.

- *Build-A-Bear Workshop reduces U.K prices.* The retailer has 346 company-owned stores in the United States, Puerto Rico, Canada, the United Kingdom, Ireland, and France, and 62 franchised stores in Europe, Asia, Australia, and Africa.[37] To counter the downturn in the global economy, Build-A-Bear adjusted its prices in the United Kingdom to make the customized toy experience more accessible to customers. The lowest initial price point was reduced from £12 to £8.[38]

- *Forever 21 reconsiders European expansion.* This U.S.-based fast-fashion chain is rapidly becoming a global presence, having opened stores in several European countries, as well as the CentralWorld shopping complex in Bangkok, Thailand.[39] Forever 21's apparel could very well be universal in its appeal; however, the apparel retailer is reviewing its expansion plans in Europe due to consumer uncertainty and the effects of the debt crisis.[40]

- *Ralph Lauren expands in Turkey and Europe.* Opening in a luxury mall in Turkey during a recession isn't for every company, but for Ralph Lauren Corp., the time was right. In its Istinye

Park mall store in Istanbul, 75 percent of the merchandise mix is Collection, Purple Label, and Black Label goods, the company's upmarket apparel lines. Ralph Lauren had tested the Istanbul market by running a branded concept shop in the Harvey Nichols' department store for two years prior to the launch.[41] The company changed its name from Polo Ralph Lauren to Ralph Lauren in 2011, and then revealed plans to open 100 of its Club Monaco specialty apparel stores for men and women in Europe.[42]

- *Marc Jacobs targets Madrid and children.* Striking up a regional partnership, the designer opened his Marc by Marc Jacobs store in a glass-enclosed corner location in downtown Madrid. Each of the company's stores is merchandised to suit its location; for example, Madrid sells more clothing for children and the Athens store carries more menswear.[43] Speaking of children, Little Marc Jacobs children's apparel is to be launched in 2012 in the United States. The line is produced by Children Worldwide Fashion (CWF), considered the European leader in children's luxury fashions. Import and distribution expert Jamari International Limited has been engaged to probe the U.S. market for department and specialty stores to sell the collection.[44] Marc Jacobs markets apparel lines for men and women worldwide.

- *Williams-Sonoma selects a franchise model.* To expand in the Middle East, Williams-Sonoma entered into a franchise agreement with partner M.H. Alshaya Company. The company opened Pottery Barn and Pottery Barn Kids divisions in Dubai and Kuwait in 2010, and in 2011 added five more franchised stores in the Middle East. The company is taking a long-term position regarding global expansion. By late 2011, retail revenues were being driven by Pottery Barn, West Elm—a new home-goods division—and international franchise operations.[45] The franchise model is less risky for retailers entering vastly different cultures.

- *Best Buy in-and-out of the United Kingdom.* The major electronics retailer in the United States opened 11 megastores in the United Kingdom with partner Carphone Warehouse in April 2010, and then abruptly announced their early 2012 closure in November 2011.[46] Bob Willett, head of Best Buy's international unit, said in 2009 that his main concerns about expanding to the United Kingdom were the maturity of the market and competing with Tesco.[47] As it turned out, Best Buy Europe withdrew because of dire economic conditions and unmet profit expectations. Timing is of the essence when committing to a significant real estate transaction, whether domestically or globally.

- *Kitson tests Japan but chooses U.S. expansion.* Licensing is another way to test a market for receptiveness to new stores, brands, and merchandise lines. Trendy Los Angeles–based retailer-to-the-stars Kitson explored entering Japan in 2008 under a licensing agreement with Itochu Corp. to operate three Kitson stores in Tokyo. The company had tentative plans to open stores in China, South Korea, and Singapore in 2010, intending to use revenue from international licensing to help fund store expansion in the United States.[48] By 2011, no international stores had opened, but Kitson had expanded its small chain of exclusive boutiques in California, adding a 15,000-square-foot flagship store in Glendale as well as new format stores Kitson Men, Kitson Kids, and Kitson Studio. Other signature stores were opened, including those on L.A.'s legendary Melrose Avenue and in Malibu—and a Kitson Kids at Downtown Disney in Anaheim.[49]

- *Lowe's heads down under.* Home improvement retailer Lowe's formed a joint venture with Woolworths Ltd., Australia's largest retailer. Lowe's first international store, named Masters, opened in a suburb of Melbourne in September 2011, and 150 more stores are planned over the next five years. Major competition in the hardware sector comes from market leader Bunnings.[50] A joint venture is a sound solution when opening a first store internationally. Read more about Masters' competitive advantages in From the Field 8.3.

Other U.S. retailers, from American Apparel to Home Depot, T.J. Maxx to Starbucks, are circling the globe looking for opportunities to present their products in ways that satisfy local tastes and perhaps change them just a bit. Growing demand for their merchandise may help retailers develop their customer bases faster. It's a small world, word travels fast over the Internet, and many brands are highly visible even before retailers arrive on terra firma.

From the Field 8.3   Woolworth's and Lowe's Launch Hardware Giant Masters in Australia: 10 Strategy Lessons from the Competition's New Rival

Australia is on the brink of a war—for the hearts and minds of "tradies" (contractors and tradesmen), DIY-ers, and sausage-sizzle-loving hardware consumers around the country. On September 1, 2011 in the Melbourne suburb of Braybrook, supermarket giant Woolworths and its joint venture partner, U.S. hardware giant Lowe's, opened the first of what promises to be a 150-strong chain of Masters stores.

The move is designed to break the dominance of market leader Bunnings, which is owned by conglomerate Wasfamers, the owner of Woolworths' other great rival, Coles. There were signs that the war won't only be fought on the shelves: Masters chief executive, Texan Don Stallings, has already fired a shot at his rival over suggestions that some hardware suppliers refused to deal with the new kid on the block. While Stallings was careful not to name Bunnings, the market leader dismissed the allegations as being "palpably untrue." This is unlikely to be the last skirmish between Bunnings and Masters.

Here are 10 ways Masters will differentiate itself:

1. *For whom the bells toll.* If you've ever wandered around a big box retailer trying to find a staff member to help you, then you will appreciate the Masters' bell system—ring the call bells located around the store and a staff member will be with you in 45 seconds.
2. *Trained to the hilt.* When staff members arrive, they should be able to answer all your queries—Masters says it will pour 100 hours of training into staff to make them experts and lift customer service levels.
3. *Gender targeting.* To prevent the store from becoming a haven only for men, Masters has tried hard to create a female-friendly environment. The new store features a mother's room, a playground and even shelves in the paint section where handbags can be rested.
4. *Out of the warehouse.* Bunnings is the king of the warehouse model—Masters is promising something different with better lighting and air-conditioning features in stores.
5. *Upmarket push.* To match the more upscale décor, Masters is focusing on more upmarket product lines, with designer brands such as Marc and Laura Ashley featured in the paint and wallpaper section. While the chain promises to beat competitors' prices by 10 percent, chief Stallings describes the product range as "aspirational."
6. *Bringing something new to market.* The partnership with Lowe's has allowed Woolworths to tap the U.S. giant's buying power and bring some products to Australia that haven't been seen here before. These include Char-Broil barbeques, Troy-Bilt lawnmowers, and even truffle trees so Australians can grow their own gourmet produce.
7. *Smart sourcing.* The buying power of Lowe's will also allow Masters to source product directly from factories all over the world. This will leave Masters well placed when the hardware battle becomes a price war, as it looks very likely to do.
8. *Partner up.* Masters realized that taking on Bunnings won't be easy to do by itself. As well as the partnership between Woolworths and Lowe's, Masters will partner with financial service providers American Express and HSBC to provide finance for big purchases (say, a complete kitchen) and for tradies.
9. *Drive "buy."* Masters will offer drive-through facilities for tradies and a dedicated trade office to get these customers in and out quickly. It is expected that trade accounts will represent up to 50 percent of revenue, which is likely to be more than $23 million per store.
10. *Bring in the Golden Arches.* One of the most controversial aspects of Masters is that its new store includes a McDonald's outlet inside and the traditional sausage sizzle (a Bunnings mainstay) will only be allowed during limited periods. Controversy aside, it looks like a smart move—there's nothing like a Maccas (Australian slang for McDonald's) to build foot traffic.

Adapted and condensed from James Thomson, "Woolworths to Launch Hardware Giant Masters Tomorrow—10 Strategy Lessons from Bunnings' New Rival." *Smart Company*, August 31, 2011, www.smartcompany.com.au/retail/20110831-woolworths-to-launch-hardware-giant-masters-tomorrow-strategy-lessons-from-bunnings-new-rival.html.

Fast-Fashion Retailers Warm to the United States

International fast-fashion apparel retailers are at the head of the class when it comes to foreign expansion. Several entered the U.S. market in the last decade. The formats are vital, attractive, stylish, and centered on young men and women who value fashion in their lives. The following examples focus on the apparel sector exclusively.

- *Inditex leads global apparel retailers.* Named the "International Retailer of the Year" by the World Retail Congress held in Berlin in 2011, it's no surprise that Inditex, based in Spain, is also the largest global fashion retailer.[51] With 5,618 stores in 84 markets, the company reported 15 percent higher sales in the first quarter of 2012 than it did in the comparable period in 2011. A division of Inditex, Zara will have approximately 2,000 stores by the end of 2012.[52] For fiscal year 2011–2012, Inditex net sales were €13.8 million. The original Zara store opened in 1975, its first foray outside Spain was to Portugal in 1988, and its initial store in New York City opened in 1989.[53] In 2011, Zara launched its e-commerce site in the United States and in late 2012 it will open an online store in China where the apparel

retailer already has 100 brick-and-mortar stores.[54] A Zara store in Marrakech is illustrated in Figure 8.9.

- *Uniqlo tests the U.S. market.* The Japanese company Fast Retailing Co., Ltd. achieves just that with its Uniqlo division. Launching its first U.S. store in New York City in late 2006 with much verve, the company was well on its path to global domination as a fast-fashion retailer. In 2011, it opened not one but two flagship stores in Manhattan—one in Herald Square and another on Fifth Avenue.[55] Uniqlo is open to the demands of the marketplace and changes its format to suit the clientele in each area it enters. In 2009, Uniqlo opened a new 1,000-square-foot men's store in Selfridges' London store on Oxford Street, where it has had a presence since 2007. Uniqlo also has two other freestanding stores on Oxford Street;[56] this is not unusual since the street is one of the most heavily trafficked shopping streets in the world. Other retailers also have multiple locations. In recognition of its aggressive expansion, high performance, and transcendent merchandise presentation, Uniqlo is the topic of the Global Retail Profile following Unit Five.

- *Mango defies recession.* The second-largest Spanish apparel company, Mango has 2,400 stores in over 100 countries worldwide, including one in Sri Lanka. An independently held company operating as MNG Holding S.L. Consolidated Group,[57] it is a leading competitor to Zara and H&M. Operating as MNG in the United States, Mango operates several freestanding stores but is best known for its in-store boutiques in JCPenney department stores. Rafael Ayash, Mango's U.S. director, said this about opening in difficult economic times: "In Chinese, recession means opportunity."[58] Clearly a positive attitude goes a long way for Mango.

- *H&M covers the world.* In business since 1947, Swedish company H&M entered the United States in 2000 and initially opened stores very aggressively on the East Coast. One of the first of the "cheap chic" retailers, its lines inspire fashion-conscious, thrifty shoppers from teens to baby-boomer men and women.[59] H&M now has expanded cross-country. Including company-owned and franchised stores, the company had over 2,300 units in about 40 countries in mid-2011. Recent additions are first stores in Romania, Croatia, and Singapore, with major expansion planned for China and the United States.[60] When the company launches a new collection by a famous designer such as Karl Lagerfeld or Roberto Cavalli, customers line up well before the store's opening time to get first pick of the apparel. Donatella Versace designed limited-edition lines of women's, men's, and children's wear scheduled for 300 stores worldwide and online in late 2011.[61] Get to H&M early when one of these events is imminent. H&M is profiled following Unit Four.

- *Topshop comes to New York.* The much-awaited opening of Topshop's first flagship store in the SoHo district of New York City took place in 2009. According to Sir Phillip Green, who co-owns parent company Arcadia Group with his wife, "This is genuinely the best store we have ever built." Long a fixture on London's high streets, Topshop's SoHo store is the first international store that is owned by the company, not franchised. It features a Topman menswear floor, and Topshop women's apparel departments on the main level. A photo of Topshop's New York store is featured in Figure 8.10.

Notice that all of the retailers mentioned in the previous section began their U.S. expansion in New York City. It's understandable that the U.S. fashion capital lures fashion retailers, as well

Figure 8.9
Spain's Zara, the star of parent company Inditex, is venturing to all corners of the globe. The apparel chain sells to fashion-conscious customers in New York as well as exotic locales like Marrakesh, as documented in this photo. (Source:www.inditex.com/en/press/photo_gallery/our_stores.)

//////////////////////////////////

Cyberscoop
Sweet Mango MNG . . . Love that look! Pull out your smartphone and download a Mango app at www.itunes.apple.com/us/app/mangomng/id372216941?mt=8.

as multitudes of customers daily to see what's new. If a retailer can make it there, it can make it anywhere!

Other Latitudes and Attitudes

As global expansion progresses, East meets West (and visa versa), nontraditional retailers contemplate their next big move abroad, and designers open multiple flagship stores. For many global retailers that target luxury as well as younger markets, the move to Asia and beyond is being considered.

- *Stella McCartney opens in Asia.* London designer Stella McCartney has been in a 50/50 partnership with French conglomerate Pineault, Printemps, Redoute (PPR) luxury-brands division since 2001. In addition to selling to about 600 wholesale accounts in 50 countries worldwide, McCartney has 15 stores in major cities including London, Paris, New York, Los Angeles, and Hong Kong. As creative director for the Adidas Team GB, she is designing athletic as well as fan apparel for the 2012 Olympics in London.[62]

- *Ermenegildo Zegna's retail roots in China.* We often think of China as a relatively new market for fine goods from around the world, so it may come as a surprise that Italy-based Ermenegildo Zegna celebrated its 20th anniversary in China in 2011. More than 30 years ago, Zegna was sourcing raw materials and fabric in Inner Mongolia for his menswear business before opening his first store in Beijing in 1991. The company now has a presence in more than 35 cities with approximately 80 points of sale in China.[63] Having global aspirations, Zegna built flagship stores in Milan, New York, Tokyo, Hong Kong, and other major cities. In 2012, the menswear specialty store opened in Riyadh, Saudi Arabia, in collaboration with luxury retailer Rubaiyat.[64]

- *South Korean brand hits the United States.* Competing with stores like Abercrombie & Fitch, Hollister, and American Eagle Outfitters can be daunting, but South Korean retailer Who.A.U. (text-talk for "Who are you?") has penetrated the U.S. fashion scene. The company's first stores opened in Connecticut and New Jersey in 2007, and it scored a prime location on Manhattan's 34th Street in 2010. As Daniel Pang, North American president of Who.A.U., said: "You need a lot of courage to cross over from the East to the West."[65] The company's quirky California designs, executed by South Korean designers, show the increasingly borderless dimensions of fashion.

- *Tommy Hilfiger's global brand.* Not long ago, customers would have never expected a quintessential American brand like Tommy Hilfiger to expand worldwide and move its headquarters to the Netherlands. The company distributes its diverse product lines to specialty and department stores in the United States, Canada, Mexico, Central and South America, Europe, South Africa, and throughout the Far East.[66] In India, Hilfiger works with the Murjani Group, which will open 500 franchised Hilfiger accessories stores and double the number of wholesale accounts—from 1,000 to 2,000—by 2015.[67] Hilfiger's international interests are diverse and emblematic of global brand recognition and acceptance.

- *U.S. ice cream in Egypt.* Cold Stone Creamery operates more than 1,500 locations in 19 countries including China, Korea, Canada, Denmark, and the United Arab Emirates—a rather vast geographic representation. Arizona-based parent company Kahala Corp. opened its first international store in Tokyo in 2005. The company has set up master franchise agreements with partners in a dozen countries or regions including Brazil, Sweden,

Did You Know?
Sir Philip Green was named "Retailer of the Year" by the National Retail Federation in 2011. The trade association honored the top man at Arcadia Group, which includes Topshop, Topman, British Home Stores (BHS), and others. Supermodels Naomi Campbell and Kate Moss refer to him as "Uncle Phil." (Source: Samantha Conti, "Topshop's Top Man on Being Sir Philip." *Women's Wear Daily*, January 11, 2011, 1, 4.)

Figure 8.10
A tribute to fast fashion, Topshop's flagship store in New York City is the London-based company's first in the United States.

Nigeria, the Caribbean and Egypt. The company signed a 10-year agreement with the conglomerate Squadra, to open eight Egyptian stores by 2016.[68] Other specialty food retailers are looking to bring their treats to receptive markets as they internationalize. Most are acutely aware of legal, language, and customer-preference differences as they refine their business models.

Global Retailing in a Multichannel World

There is a considerable amount of traffic between countries on our Earth, and not necessarily vehicular, either. Retailers are identifying new options, opening brick-and-mortar stores, revamping catalogues for international delivery, opening new direct selling channels, and establishing online stores in places that once sounded exotic or untouchable. These vignettes have offered a taste of what is happening in the world of retailing.

Gregarious, tenacious, and indefatigable all describe the kinds of men and women who take the stage in international business. Those that enjoy a challenge will savor the chance to work for a global company. Does this describe you? If so, the rewards can be great. Opportunities loom for those who have polished their retail skills as well as their compassion for people they have yet to meet, understand, and value.

As we bring Unit Two to closure, remember that global retailing is the pinnacle for retailers that have already incorporated multichannel operations—and vice versa. When retailers expand globally, cross-channel synergies become essential. Fulfillment systems become more taxed, and customer contact more difficult to deliver in multiple languages, once the domestic border is breached. No one ever said retailing was easy, but many maintain there is no other business like it in the world.

Summary

Major retailers think globally. There are advantages and disadvantages to retail expansion abroad, most stemming from economic and cultural factors. Saturation of domestic markets is a principal reason why retailers seek alternative markets. Growth is a major motivator.

Better communication, media usage, international travel, more educated customers, higher perceived value of foreign goods, and greater access to online retailers everywhere have precipitated interest in global retailing.

To be successful, international retailers adapt to the countries in which they do business. This is not always easy. Cultural disparities and differing business practices pose major challenges for retailers.

The role of importing and exporting in a world economy is complex and prone to change due to economic and political volatility. In order to counter trade imbalances, imports and exports are carefully monitored. Trade organizations and agreements benefit countries engaged in international trade. The formation of the European Union in 1992 changed trade expectations in and outside of the region.

Retailing practices differ by country. Location strategies, sale periods, display techniques, merchandise, branding, as well as the balance of brick-and-mortar stores and online retailing, may vary. But serving customers to the best of their ability is a universal focus of retailers worldwide.

Key Terms

Association of Southeast Asian Nations (ASEAN)
Balance of trade
Domestic retailers
Dumping
Economic and Monetary Union (EMU)
Emerging countries
Euro
European Central Bank (ECB)
Eurozone
Free trade

Global retailers
Harmonization
Industrialized countries
International retailers
Master franchise
MERCOSUR
Ministries of trade
Protectionism
Standardization
Trade sanctions
Value-added tax (VAT)

Questions for Review and Discussion

1. What are the distinctions among domestic, international, and global retailers?
2. Discuss some of the key reasons for the increase in global retail expansion. Which countries are the most internationalized when it comes to global retail expansion?
3. What are the advantages and disadvantages to retailers that choose to expand abroad?
4. Discuss critical success factors for global retailers. Which factors do you believe are most important?
5. Identify one high-risk and one low-risk type of global retail involvement. What are the advantages of each? If your 250-store fashion chain is exploring global expansion, which mode of entry would you use? Justify your decision.
6. What do we mean by a "favorable balance of trade?" What factors affect global trade positively and negatively?
7. In what ways should global retailers be alert to cultural differences? Discuss several examples.
8. Choose one or more retailers that have expanded globally from the many examples in the last sections of this chapter. Research the company throughout the semester and use your material and updates as the basis for class discussions.

Endnotes

1. McDonald's 2011 Annual Report. "Managements' Discussion and Anaysis of Financial Condition and Results of Operations." Overview. Description of the Business. p. 9 www.abcutmcdonalds.com/content/dam/AboutMcDonalds/Investors/Investors%202012/2011%20Annual%20Report%20Final.pdf.
2. "Global Powers of Retailing Geographical Analysis," in *Global Powers of Retailing 2012*, Deloitte, January 2012, www.deloitte.com/consumerbusiness.
3. Robin van Daalen, "Dutch Grocer Bests U.S. Rivals," *Wall Street Journal*, August 21, 2009, B2.
4. Deloitte, January 2012. www.deloitte.com/consumerbusiness.
5. "BRIC Economies are Expected to Account for 40% of world GDP Growth Over 2011 and 2012, Says PwC Economists," PricewaterhouseCoopers Media Center, August 4, 2011, www.ukmediacentre.pwc.com/News-Releases/BRIC-economies-are-expected-to-account-for-40%-of-world-gdp-growth-over-2011-and-2012-says-pwc-economist.
6. "GDP Growth Rates, List By Country," Trading Economics, accessed December 21, 2011, www.trading economics.com/gdp-growth-rates-list-by-country.
7. Ibid.
8. "Interbrand Rankings by Brand Value for 2011," in *Best Retail Brands for 2011*, 1–3, InterbrandDesignForum, www.interbrand.com/en/BestRetailBrands/2011.aspx.
9. Peter Van Allen, "Budget for Attracting Foreign Tourists Is Sharply Curtailed," *Philadelphia Business Journal*, October 21, 2011, www.bizjournals.com/philadelphia/print-edition/2001/10/21/budget-for-attracting-foreign-tourists.html.
10. Tamara Pearson. "Venezuela's Full Membership of Mercosur Converts the Bloc into 'Fifth World Power.' August 1, 2012. p. 1 http://venezuelananalysis.com/news/7142.
11. John Zarocostas, "WTO Warns Protectionism on the Rise," *Women's Wear Daily,* July 7, 2009, 13.
12. Phred Dvorak, "U.S., Canada Dismiss 'Buy American' Spat," *Wall Street Journal*, September 17, 2009, A15.
13. Reuters, "Factbox: China-U.S. Trade disputes Pile Up," *MSNBC*, December 15, 2011, www.msnbc.msn.com/id/45680616/ns/business/t/factbox-china-us-trade-disputes-pile-up.
14. Rose Yu, Colum Murphy and Yajun Zhang, "Boycott Hits Japan Car Sales," *Wall Street Journal,* November 10–11, 2012, B4.
15. *Global Economic Outlook 2012*, 1, The Conference Board, www.conference-board.org/data/globaloutlook.cfm. (Sources: International Monetary Fund (IMF) and Organization for Economic Cooperation and Development (OECD).)
16. Erin Lash, "Ten Things Potential Avon Investors Should Know," Morningstar, September 19, 2011, www.morningstar.ca/gobalhome/industry/news.asp?.
17. "Andean Trade Preference Act (ATPA)—Expiration of Duty-Free Treatment," and "Generalized System of Preferences (GSP)," U.S. Customs & Border Protection, CBP INFO Center, https://help.cbp.gov/app/answers/detail/a_id/266 and https://help.cbp.gov/app/answers/detail/a_id/325.
18. "Luxottica Group to Distribute €0.22 Dividend Per Share," Luxottica, September 18, 2009, www.luxottica.com/export/sites/defalt/shared/files/press_release/2009_09_18_dividend.
19. Julian Goldsmith, "Fashionista Gives Supply chain a BT Makeover," *Silicon.com*, June 25, 2007, www.silicon.com/retailandleisure/0,3800011848,39167639,00.htm.

20. Paul Hannon and John W. Miller, "World Trade Volume Climbs 2.5%," *Wall Street Journal*, August 27, 2009, A7.

21. Julie Wolf, "Banana Dispute with US, EU Hits New Stage," *Wall Street Journal*, December 14, 1999, B7A.

22. John Simons, "Handbags, Bed Linens Included in List of Goods Covered by Trade Sanctions," *Wall Street Journal*, April 12, 1999, A24.

23. Juliet Chung, "Looming Tariffs Whet Appetite for Delicacies," *Wall Street Journal*, March 31, 2009, "A3.

24. "EU Enlargement: The Next Eight." BBC News Europe. July 4, 2012. p. 2 www.bbc.co.uk/news/world-europe-11283616?print=true.

25. European Central Bank, "The 2012 Annual Growth Survey: Frequently Asked Questions," 2–3, Europa, November 23, 2011, http://europa.eu/rapid/pressReleasesAction.do?reference=MEMO/11/821&format= HTML&aged=0&language=EN&guiLanguage=en.

26. Commission of the European Communities, "The European Single Act: Countdown to December 1992" and "The European Community," Directorate-General for Information, Communication and Culture, Brussels, Belgium, October 1990.

27. International VAT Services, "EU VAT Rates 2012," TMF Group, accessed December 31, 2011, www.tmf-vat .com/vat/eu-rates.html.

28. European Commission. The Euro. Which Countries Have Adopted the Euro—and When? p. 1. http:// ec.europa.eu/economy_finance/euro/index_en.htm (accessed August 3, 2012).

29. "US Dollar to Euro Exchange Rate Graph—Aug. 4, 2011 to Aug. 3, 2012. p. 1 Source: United States Federal Reserve Bank of New York. www.indexmundi.com/xrates/graph.aspx?c1=USDollars=365.

30. Associated Press. "European Union to Tax Internet Sales," *MSNBC*, April 7, 2002, www.msnbc.com/news.

31. "Plan for Single EU Online Shopping Law Good for Customers and UK Retailers," British Retail Consortium, October 11, 2011, www.brc.org.uk/brc_news_detail.asp?id=2060.

32. Charles Forelle and Susanne Craig, "Debt Deals Haunt Europe," *Wall Street Journal*, February 22, 2010, A1–A2.

33. Ruth Sunderkand, "The Eurozone's Troubles Hurt Us Too," *The Observer*, February 14, 2010, www.guardian .co.uk/business/2010/feb/14/eurozone-crisis-Greece.

34. William Boston, Brian Blackstone and Matthew Dalton. "Europe Plans for Greece Exit." *Wall Street Journal*. May 24, 2012. A-1, A-10.

35. David Gauthier-Villars, "Mon Dieu! Sunday Work Hours Upset French Devotion to Rest," *Wall Street Journal*, July 24, 2009, A11.

36. Soyeon Shim and Ken Gehrt, "Japanese Gift Giving," Presentation, Global Retail Symposium, University of Arizona, Tucson, March 1997.

37. "Company Profile," Build-A-Bear Workshop, accessed December 27, 2011, http://phx.corporate-ir.net/ phoenix.zhtml?c=182478&p=irol-homeProfile.

38. Nicola Harrison, "Build-A-Bear Lowers its Entry Price Point," *Retail Week*, March 6, 2009, www.retail-week .com/printPage.html?pageid=2002597.

39. Pitsinee Jitpleecheep, "Forever 21 Store Launches," *Bangkok Post*, October 10, 2008, www.bangkokpost .com/printthis.php.

40. Alexandra Biesada, "US Retailers Review European Expansion Plans," Hoover's, December 9, 2011, http:// bizmology.hoovers.com/2011/12/09/us-retailers-review-european-expansion-plans.

41. Suna Erdem, "Lauren Opens First Store in Turkey," *Women's Wear Daily*, October 14, 2008, 2.

42. Olivier Guyot, "Club Monaco Plans to Open 100 Stores in Europe," Fashionmag.com, September 5, 2011, http://uk.fashionmag.com/news-199424-Club-Monaco-plans-to-open-100-stores-in-Europe.

43. Barbara Barker, "Marc by Marc Jacobs Opens in Madrid," *Women's Wear Daily*, October 20, 2008, 5.

44. "Launch in the US," Children Worldwide Fashion Group, December 1, 2011. www.groupecwf.com/actualite .php?language=4change=1&id_menu=53.

45. *Williams Sonoma Inc. Form 10-Q Filing*, Securities and Exchange Commission, December 9, 2011, 15, 16. www.faqs.org/sec-filings/111209/WILLIAMS-SONOMA-INC_10-Q.

46. John Clark, "Best Buy Closes UK Stores," ZDNet, November 7, 2011, www.zdnet.co.uk/news/business-of-it/2011/11/07/best-buy-closes-uk-stores-40094372.

47. "Update 1—Best Buy Delays UK Launch to Spring 2010," *Reuters*, March 18, 2009, www.reuters.com/article Print?articleId=INLI72568420090318.

48. Anne Riley-Katz, "Kitson's Global Move," *Women's Wear Daily*, June 23, 2009, 3.

49. "About Us," Kitson, http://shopkitson.com/index.php?page=about.

50. James Thomson, "Woolworths to Launch Hardware Giant Masters Tomorrow—Strategy Lessons From Bunning's New Rival," *Smart Company*, August 31, 2011, www.smartcompany.com.au/20110831-woolworths-to-launch-hardware-giant-masters-tomorrow-10-strategy-lessons-from-bunnings-new-rival/print.html.

51. "Inditex Recognized as International Retailer of the Year at the World Retail Congress," Inditex Group, October 3, 2011, www.inditex.com/en/press/other_news/extend/00000884.

52. Press Release. "Inditex's Net Sales Rose by 15% to 3.4 Billion Euros in the First Quarter of 2012." Inditex Group. June 13, 2012. p. 1. press_releases/extend/00000923.

53. Graham Keeley and Andrew Clark, "Zara Overtakes Gap to Become World's Largest Clothing Retailer," *The Guardian*, August 11, 2008, www.guardian.co.uk/business/2008/aug/11/zara.gap.fashion/print.

54. Inditex Group Press Release June 13, 2012. p. 3.

55. Elaine Misonzhnik, "Uniqlo Makes Splash With Two Giant NY Stores as International Retailers Continue to Eye U.S.," *Retail Traffic*, October 13, 2011, www.printthis.clickability.com/pt/cpt?expire=&title=Uniqlo+Makes +Splash+With=Two+Giant+Stores+as+International+Retailers+Continue+to+Eye+US.

56. Koji Hirano, "Uniqlo to Open at Selfridges," *Women's Wear Daily*, January 15, 2000, 3.

57. "Mango Opens its First Store in Sri Lanka," *Daily Financial Times*, December 22, 2011, www.ft.lk/2011/12/22/ mango-opens-its-first-store-in-sri-lanka.

58. Jean E. Palmieri, "Mango Forging Ahead with Expansion in U.S.," *Women's Wear Daily*, February 27, 2009, www.wwd.com/retail-news/mass-off-price/mango-forging-ahead-with-expansion-in-us-2035180.

59. Lauren Sherman, "America's Favorite Foreign Retailers," *Forbes.com*, March 24, 2009, www.forbes.com/ 2009/03/24/foreign-retailer-favorites-lifestyle-style-foreign-retailer_slide.html.

60. Joelle Diderich, "H&M Profit Drops 18%," *Women's Wear Daily*, June 23, 2011, 2.

61. Allessandra Ilari, "H&M Goes Va-Va-Voom With Versace," *Women's Wear Daily*, June 22, 2011, 1, 8.

62. "Stella McCartney Celebrates London," StellaMcCartney, November 22, 2011, www.stellamccartney.com.

63. "China: Zegna Family Celebrates 20 Years in China," Fibre2Fashion, September 27, 2011, www.fibre2 fashion.com/news/printstorey.asp?news_id=103601.

64. "Saudi Arabia: Ermenegildo Zegna Opens New Flagship Store in Saudi Arabia," Fibre2Fashion, January 4, 2012, www.fibre2fashion.com/news/printstorey.asp?news_id=106856.

65. Eric Wilson, "Who Are they, Indeed," *New York Times*, May 16, 2010, www.nytimes.com/2010/05/20/ fashion/20ROW.html?pagewanted=print.

66. "Textiles, Apparel and Luxury Goods: Tommy Hilfiger B.V. Company Overview," *Businessweek*, January 5, 2012, http://investing.businessweek.com/research/stocks/private/snapshot.asp?privcapId=319534.

67. Malavika Sharma and Saikat Chatterjee, "Tommy Hilfiger India Franchise to Open 500 Accessories Stores," *Businessweek*, June 30, 2010, www.businessweek.com/news/2010-06-30/tommy-hilfiger-india-franchisee-to-open-500-accessories-stores.

68. "Cold Stone Creamery Enters Continent of Africa with Egypt Expansion Plans. Cold Stone Creamery. June 5, 2012. www.businesswire.com/news/home/20120605006456/en/Cold_Stone_Creamery_Enters_Continent_ Africa_Egypt.

Unit Two: Global Retail Profile
Retailing in China

The glass façade of the Apple Store in Shanghai reflects the Gap logo across the street, reminding us that we live in a global marketplace. Throngs of Chinese customers visit Apple daily, reflecting an interest in American products and growing buying power.

Retailers who choose to operate globally face unfamiliar environments. It is to their advantage to learn all they can about countries in which they intend to do business. Nothing has captured our attention more than China's meteoric rise to economic heights. This profile offers glimpses into the status of retailing in China, addressing divergent viewpoints, cultural issues, and business practices. Look for similarities and differences with methods of retailing in your home countries.

Emerging China

It seems odd to speak of the People's Republic of China (PRC) as an emerging nation when you examine its strong economic position and the overwhelming tenacity the Chinese have demonstrated in attaining that goal. The retail community is ripe for expansion, and that is exactly what China is promoting.

Looking briefly at the background of the country sets the tone for its retail industry today. Chinese civilization dates back more than 4,000 years. The vast population is 92 percent Han Chinese with 56 minorities, and the major dialect is Mandarin Chinese. The unit of currency is the yuan (worth about 6.3 to the U.S. dollar in mid-2012). The longevity of this civilization, its tumultuous history, and recent rise to economic power underlie cultural differences that challenge those companies that would enter the retail community. China's industrial and economic rise was rapid but the cultural and ethical changes that are necessary to compete effectively in the world of retailing have been slower to evolve.

China today faces several problems tied to its explosive economic growth, including more recent signs of deceleration. Economic development is concentrated in coastal areas, creating tension between urban wealth and inland poverty. The recent worldwide recession cut consumer demand for Chinese products, slowing industrial production and giving impetus to a reverse migration of workers from coastal factories back to the countryside. Massive environmental problems and the unsettling presence of human rights issues are only beginning to be addressed. Although viewers were impressed by the televised pageantry of the Olympics in 2008, human rights violations continue to dampen the attitude of many westerners toward China. The country's push to achieve industrialization has placed great demands on the world's resources such as oil.

With a population of 1.3 billion people, one would expect a raucous, unrestrained scramble by global retailers to grab a piece of the action in China. In fact, companies began making overtures to enter the China trade long before the World Trade Organization (WTO) listed China as a preferred trading partner. Many global retailers have had a foothold in China for a decade or more.

When we consider China we must also consider Hong Kong, which was returned to China in 1998 after many years as a British Crown Colony. Taiwan, the Republic of China (ROC), adds another dimension to this vast, yet fragmented culture. The economies of these three entities are as different as the taste levels and buying habits.

Economic Indicators and Reverberations

The slowdown of exports to the United States and other chief trading partners restrained the growth of China's economy during the height of the downturn in 2007–2009. Its cash reserves, in excess of 3 trillion in U.S. dollars, sheltered the country somewhat from the depths of recession experienced elsewhere in the world.[1] By 2011, China's purchases of U.S. products—everything from seafood to chemicals and electronics—had increased 13.1 percent to more than $100 billion. But, of course, the United States purchased even more goods—from apparel, accessories, and leather goods to computer parts—from China, creating a $272 billion trade imbalance in 2011.[2]

Although China's GDP growth rate was the highest in the world at 9.2 percent, and per capita GDP was estimated at $8,400 for 2011, a slowdown in GDP growth was predicted for 2012. In 2011 China's top three export trading partners were the United States, Japan, and Hong Kong.[3]

China is the second largest retail market in the world after the United States, but according to Chinese researchers that position may not be sustainable. Retail sales in China are expected to reach $4.3 trillion by 2015, an increase of more than two-thirds over 2010 levels.[4]

The socioeconomic dichotomy that exists today in China is difficult to articulate. Many of the affluent live in the urban coastal areas. The middle class is expected to grow in numbers and ability to spend. Personal household disposable income is expected to double between 2010 and 2020.[5] Chinese households have been categorized using four descriptors; the percentage share of urban household income in real 2010 dollars and forecasted dollars for 2020 for each category are outlined below:

Households	2010 Share	2020 Share	2020 Annual Income Forecast
1. Affluent	2 percent	6 percent:	> $34,000
2. Mainstream	6 percent	51 percent	$16,000 to $34,000
3. Value	82 percent	36 percent	$6,000 to $15,999
4. Poor	10 percent.	7 percent	< $6,000

The astounding anticipated growth in the number of Mainstream households, and decreasing share of the Value group, presents a challenge to retailers who are identifying target markets and making decisions about merchandise assortments. Whether they should select the currently large Value group or align with future predictions of a significantly larger Mainstream market will be given thoughtful judgment.[6]

The economies of China and the United States are inexorably linked. The balance is changing as China grows and labor costs of manufacturing rise, forcing price increases on exported goods. For example, Nike's revenue grew 16 percent from sales in China in its fiscal fourth quarter, which ended in early 2011. However, gross margin declined about 3 percent due to increases in product costs.[7] Nike manufactures much of its footwear in China.

Ethical issues that impede social understanding among the two countries and much of the developed world remain. More on Nike follows in the next section.

Human Rights and Ethical Concerns

The use of child and prisoner labor, presence of sweatshops, unsafe manufacturing plants, environmental violations, unethical practices, improper use of production materials, disrespect for copyrights, and lack of quality control regarding children's toys are some of the issues that China and its trading partners are discussing. Issues regarding food additives, Internet censorship, and religious intolerance also appear on Chinese and WTO dockets.

Nike is considered an industry leader in dealing with alleged violations of human rights and unethical practices in China. The company reported that underage workers, improperly paid workers, and faulty documentation are widespread problems in China. More than 200,000 workers representing 180 manufacturers are under contract to Nike and produce about one-third of all athletic footwear sold by Nike, as well as apparel and equipment.[8]

Facebook explored extending its social networking service to China in 2011 and expects to contend with the issues of free expression and assembly online in a country that is known for rigidity concerning those rights. Earlier, Google moved its Chinese operations to Hong Kong when the ROC would not stop censoring online searches.[9]

Problems like these are widespread; affect the supply chain, and more importantly, compromise the well being of workers and the rights of citizens.

Top Chinese Retailers

The Chinese retail community is a bubbling caldron of activity. Mergers and acquisitions are becoming as commonplace in China as elsewhere in the world. Chinese retailers are bulking up to counter the influx of retail competition from around the world, and some are setting their sights on expansion into global markets, to compete directly with established western brands. For example, Li Ning, China's leading maker of athletic shoes and sportswear opened a flagship store in Portland, Oregon, not far from Nike's home town of Beaverton. Meanwhile international retailers have been setting up shop in the major cities in China for the last decade, and the openings continue.

Several Chinese retailers are large enough to make the Top 250 Global Retailers listing. The three companies listed below are the major retail revenue drivers in China and among the top 100 retailers globally. Notice that appliances, electronics, and food dominate the merchandise offerings of these retailers.

1. **Bailian Group**—Earning $13.3 billion in sales in 2010, the company operates predominantly supermarkets, but only in China.
2. **Gome Home Appliance Group**—Based in Beijing, Gome generated $12 billion in sales in 2010. The company operates in mainland China and Hong Kong.
3. **Suning Appliance Co. Ltd.**—This company, an electronics specialist, generated $11.1 billion in sales in 2010 while operating only in China.[10]

Other strong domestic retailers also merit discussion. Noteworthy companies in mainland China include:

- **Dalian Dashang Group**—Like many other Chinese retailers, Dalian began as a supermarket and is known by the city from which it emanates. The company has diversified its holdings and today is considered primarily a department store.
- **Wumart Group, Beijing**—Not to be confused with Walmart, the company says the roots of its name are the words *wu mei,* which mean "beautiful products" in English. Wumart is Beijing's largest supermarket retailer. The company has made several acquisitions as it gears up to compete with foreign retailers. Consolidation in the supermarket sector is anticipated.
- **Jiuguang Department Store**—Hong Kong company Lifestyle International Holdings Ltd. opened its first Jiuguang department store in Shanghai in 2004. It was followed by the largest individual department store in China, the Jiuguang in Suzhou, in 2009. A smaller Juiguang opened in Dalian a few months later. The 170,000-square-meter Suzhou facility, located at the Harmony Times Square, combines Chinese and international luxury fashion goods with food, business, and entertainment options.[11] (High-tech visuals include a 500-meter-long LED screen, believed to be the largest in the world.[12]) Two more Jiuguang stores are planned for 2011–2013. Lifestyle International also owns the SOGO department stores in Hong Kong. In 2011, the group's total sales were up 22.6 percent over the prior year.[13] Perhaps bigger really is better.

China's retailers are growing at a rapid pace. Whether it's regional, national, or international supremacy they seek, strategies are in place for supermarkets, superstores, electronics and appliance specialists, and fine department stores to flourish.

Retail Ownership and Expansion Strategies

China differs from much of the industrialized world because of its continued state ownership and control of key industries, but this is expected to change as ownership shifts from government-held enterprises and partnerships to independent and foreign ownership. We'll look at current ownership practices before examining the influx of global retailers to China and initiatives by Chinese retailers to expand outside their country.

True to the roots of this communist country, about half of all retail companies are state-owned enterprises. As the term implies **state-owned enterprises (SOEs)** are companies that are owned by the Chinese government. They comprise almost 50 percent of firms. About 11 percent are former SOEs turned privatized state-owned enterprises. **Privatized state-owned enterprises (PSOEs)** are companies that were formerly SOEs but are now owned by private Chinese firms. **Foreign joint ventures (FJVs)** are companies that are funded by foreign direct investment. **Organic firms (ORGs)** are newly developed domestic Chinese companies. Together they account for approximately 35 percent of companies in China.[14] Organic firms that are funded by foreign resources use the abbreviation **FJV/ORG**.

Many mergers and acquisitions are in progress as the Chinese retail industry builds. Much negotiation is expected as global retailers enter the market. The use of *guanxi* is of greater importance in situations where FJVs or organic growth is anticipated. **Guanxi** is the use of personal connections to do business. This involves giving gifts, sharing meals, granting favors, and building a relationship over time. Some observers consider it very similar to networking.

Global Retailers in China

Many significant global retailers currently operate in China. They include Carrefour of France; IKEA of Sweden; Aeon of Japan; Tesco of the United Kingdom; many fast-fashion retailers, including H&M, Zara, and Topshop; and a plethora of retail companies from the United States, including Starbucks. A few examples of their tactics follow.

Carrefour (France) The largest foreign retailer in China is Carrefour. The hypermarket company operated 184 stores in China in 2011 and plans to open more. Carrefour faces intensifying competition from Walmart and a joint venture between Ruentex Group of Taiwan and Groupe Auchan—long a major competitor of Carrefour in France. Called Sun Art Retail Group Ltd., the partnership has 197 superstores in China under the banners of Auchan and RT-Mart.[17] Carrefour is looking for national coverage as it continues its expansion from large cities to smaller ones. The profile that follows Unit III provides additional details about this global retailer.

IKEA (Sweden) The Scandinavian furniture and home furnishings retailer opened its first Chinese store in Shanghai in 1998. By 2012 it had 11 stores, with sales of approximately $775 million.[18] IKEA stores are huge buildings in which some merchandise areas are laid out showroom style so that consumers can see how goods will look in their homes. At the Beijing store serious shopping often seems secondary to the pursuit of fun; the store has become a destination in which to browse, eat, escape from the heat, spend time with family, and, on occasion, nap. Locals call the store "Yi Jia"[19]—an auditory connection to IKEA. As younger customers enter the Chinese market in larger numbers, values are changing. The growth of the middle class has meant that more people are setting up their own homes. IKEA is willing to wait until more customers with the same sentiment are ready to shop rather then nap.

Aeon Company (Japan) Expansion in China has not happened as rapidly for many international retailers as they once predicted. The giant conglomerate Aeon delayed the planned opening of 100 stores in China from 2011 until 2013. This hesitation was attributed to the slowdown in retail sales during the period between the summer Olympics in Beijing in 2008, when sales growth was between 15 and 18 percent, and the end of that year, when growth had dipped to 5 to10 percent.[20] To improve its business in China, in 2012 Aeon announced that it would open headquarters in Beijing and bring its TOPVALUE private-label products to Chinese customers.[21] Although primarily a supermarket retailer, Aeon has diversified retail divisions. Number 18 in the *2012 Top 250 Global Retailers,* it earned $54.1 billion in revenues in 2012.[22]

U.S. Retailers in China Big-box retailers like Best Buy and Home Depot; luxury retailers like Saks Fifth Avenue and Coach; specialists such as L.L. Bean, Timberland, Dockers, and Forever 21; many quick-serve restaurants, including McDonald's, Yum! Group, and Starbucks; and, of course,

Walmart, have opened in China or in one case left the market. Focusing on the efforts of a few of these retailers broadens our understanding of the variety of retail formats that are expanding in China. The profile that follows Unit I summarizes Walmart's experience in China. Let's look at the status of some of the others:

- **Yum! Brands**—KFC and Pizza Hut are the top quick-serve and casual dining restaurants in China. Two Asian-only brands, also owned by Yum!, are East Dawning and Little Sheep Group. Further expansion plans include locating in transportation hubs and hypermarkets in new and growing cities.[23] As the market leader, Yum! entered China in 1987 and by 2011 had approximately 4,000 restaurants, compared to McDonald's 1,500 units. Fast food is well accepted in China; Yum! Brands announced in 2011 that operating profit from China accounts for more than 40 percent of total corporate profit.[24]
- **Coach**—In mid-2008, Lew Frankfort, chairman and chief executive officer (CEO) of Coach, announced plans to add 50 stores to its 15 in China. Eight of the company's stores are in Hong Kong, including a 9,400-square-foot flagship with a riveting steel and glass facade.[25] By 2011 the chairman's prediction had been modestly exceeded. There were 66 Coach stores, with 30 more in the works. That year, Coach China represented 5 percent of worldwide sales, which were $ 4.1 billion. The company operates through department store shop-in-shops, flagship, retail, and factory store formats.[26]
- **L.L. Bean**—Quintessential American retailer L.L. Bean opened its first store in China in 2008 with partner Youngone Corp. of Korea. In both layout and design the 3,000-square-foot Beijing store, located at the open-air Solana Mall, evokes the company's Freeport, Maine, flagship.[27] By 2011 62 stores were operating in China.[28] Revenues for fiscal 2011 were $1.52 billion for the privately held company.[29] L.L. Bean expects that Chinese outdoor enthusiasts will prove to be very similar to its U.S. customers. In time the company may identify differences in taste, design preferences, and usage and adapt its merchandise assortment accordingly.

To this point we've examined several types of ownership and partnership arrangements that are prominent in China and highlighted the influx of domestic and global retailers now doing business in China. Next we'll look at the merchandise buying process and dispel some manufacturing myths.

Buying and Manufacturing Trends

Comparisons between retailers from around the world are always illuminating. Although differences in actual business practices are waning, methods of doing business can be surprising in countries such as China where basic ideologies diverge from those held in other parts of the world. Merchandise buying is quite standard, while gathering talent to improve and expedite the design process for both in-country manufacturing and international contracting is under development. Many manufacturing facilities in China are modern, brightly lit, and hygienic—perhaps not what many outsiders would expect.

Although Chinese industry is often criticized for its working conditions, many manufacturers go to great lengths to provide a comfortable and safe environment, as well as housing, for their workers, many of whom come from remote parts of the country. In a campus-like setting, workers live and work at the Tsai Chaio Company, Ltd., which has facilities in Shenzhen and Donguan. The company manufactures woodenware, including small pieces of furniture and poly-resin crafts. Products include attractive acrylic figures, decorative pieces, and Christmas items, 90 percent of which are exported to U.S. distributors and retailers.[30]

According to the Department of Commerce, Chinese manufacturers supply the U.S. with 78 percent of its footwear, 71 percent of neckties, approximately half of all dresses and baby clothing, and 90 percent of house slippers.[31] At these rates it is evident the main source of goods for many large U.S. retailers is China.

The Chinese Consumer

The Chinese consumer is presently among the most important in the world in terms of numbers, pent-up demand for merchandise, and growing opportunities to earn and spend money. Retailers learn about characteristics of Chinese consumers through various reports. Highlights of one study done annually by researchers follow:

- Chinese customers were more confident about their financial status in 2011 than they were in 2010.
- Fifty-eight percent of respondents said they anticipated higher incomes in 2012. In the previous study only 39 percent had high expectations.
- Customers bought in greater quantities, more frequently, and purchased more expensive items in a specific merchandise category in 2011 than in 2010.
- The number of first-time buyers in urban areas declined. In the past this group has contributed significantly to merchandise sales growth.
- Customers in some of the newly developed city areas like Chengdu purchased personal care products for the very first time in the previous year.
- Shoppers whose purchases involved choices among two or three brands 2 years ago now are selecting from among three to five brands.
- Shoppers are increasingly brand consciousness but not necessarily brand loyal.
- Rising inflation rates may be contributing to price sensitivity and disloyalty to brands. Some customers blamed inflation for their higher annual expenditures.[32]

The global recession affected many retailers in China. However, the Chinese penchant for luxury goods is world renowned, and customers were not stymied during the economic slowdown. The French luxury goods company Louis Vuitton Moet Hennessy (LVMH) found that Chinese customers were purchasing more Louis Vuitton apparel and handbags—and Hennessy cognac—than both Japanese and American counterparts. To meet increasing demand, LVMH opened 15 additional Louis Vuitton stores in 2009 and increased the number of Sephora stores (its cosmetics and fragrance division) to 70.[33]

Bulgari, another LVMH company, increased its advertising budget from less than $1 million in 2009 to $3.3 million in 2010. If we use the LVMH experience as a benchmark, the Chinese economy was certainly in recovery by the beginning of 2010. China's market for luxury goods, including jewelry, leather goods, and designer apparel, is expected to be the largest worldwide by 2020.[34]

In an initial public offering Prada, the Italian fashion house, was listed on the Hong Kong stock exchange in mid-2011. According to Miuccia Prada, president and head designer, the company plans to open 10 to 12 stores annually to add to its existing 14 Prada stores on the Chinese mainland.[35] International retailers are indisputably answering the demands of Chinese customers.

Profiling the typical Chinese consumer is not a simple task because of the diverse population, geographic expanse of the country, decreasing gap between rich and poor, and rapid changes in lifestyles that have occurred over the past two decades. There is much interest in delving deeper into the behaviors of Chinese shoppers and also looking at them comparatively. Shopping preferences have changed radically in less than 20 years, and online and mobile influences add additional dimensions to our framework of understanding.

Profile Discussion Questions

1. Review the household breakdown and consider which strategic direction you would support if you were a retailer doing business in China. Would you choose the Mainstream or the Value group as your target market? What factors will be considered in your decision?
2. Several human rights issues and ethical concerns mentioned in the profile are bound to affect our impression of China. How should retailers from abroad doing business in China handle situations that could potentially compromise their ethics or damage their company's image or sales?
3. How does retail ownership in China compare to owning stores in the United States or your home country?
4. Judging from the many examples given in this profile and your text, what retail characteristics and strengths do you believe are most necessary for conducting business in China successfully?
5. The standard of living is rising in China. How is this factor affecting consumers' perception of brands and their financial status?
6. How well are luxury retailers performing in China? Were they affected by the downturn in the global economy?

Profile Notes

1. Bob Davis. "IMF Urges Boosting of Yuan." *Wall Street Journal*. July 21, 2011. A12.

2. Dexter Roberts. "China's Surprising U.S. Buying Spree." *Business Week*. March 27, 2012. www.business week.com/printer/articles/15540-chinas-surprising-u-dot-s-dot-buying-spree.

3. *The World Factbook*. China."Economic Overview." www.cia.gov/library/publications/the-world-factbook/geos.ch.htm/ (Available April 22, 2012.)

4. Laurie Burkitt and Loretta Chao. "Made in China: Fake Stores." *Wall Street Journal*. August 3, 2011. B1.

5. Yuval Atsmon and Max Magni. "Meet the Chinese Consumer of 2020." Changing Demographics. *McKinsey Quarterly*. March 2012. 2. www.mckinsey.com.

6. Yuval Atsmon and Max Magni. "Meet the Chinese Consumer of 2020." Exhibit 1. "The Share of Chinese Households in Each Income Level Will Shift Dramatically by 2010." *McKinsey Quarterly*. March 2012. 3. www.mckinsey.com.

7. Maxwell Murphy. "Nike Sales Power Profit Rise." *Wall Street Journal*. June 28, 2011, B4.

8. Reuters. Nike Press Release. "Nike Reports Persistent Problems at China Factories," March 14, 2008. www.reuters.com/articlePrint?articleId=CNTHK26912020080314.

9. John Bussey. "Facebook's Test in China: What Price Free Speech?" *Wall Street Journal*. June 10, 2011, B1–B2.

10. *Stores*. "Global Powers of Retailing 2010," The Top 250 Global Retailers, #63, #153, #167, January 2011.

11. Lifestyle International Holdings, Ltd. About Us. Corporate Milestones. www.lifestylehk.com.hk/eng/about_us/milestones.htm. (Available April 25, 2012)

12. *China Retail News*. "China's Largest Department Store Opens in Suzhou." February 16, 2009. www.china retail.org/shownews.asp?id=566.

13. Lifestyle International Holdings, Ltd. Press release. "Lifestyle International Announces 2011 Annual Results." February 27, 2012. www.lifestylehk.com.hk/mediacenter/

14. Brenda Sternquist. *International Retailing*. Chapter 17. "Retailing in the People's Republic of China." Second Edition. Fairchild Publications. New York. 2007. 466,468.

15. Gerrit Wiesmann and Kathrin Hille. "Metro Sets Sights on Chinese Market," *Financial Times*, March 24, 2009. www.ft.com/cms/s/0a094f6e-1955-11de-bec8-0000779fd2ac,dwp_uuid=dc15438a-a

16. Kantar Retail IQ. "Metro Plans to Double Stores in China." May 15, 2012. www.kantarretail.com/Content Index/NewsDisplayLW.aspx?id=474194.

17. Laurie Burkitt. "Big Retail In China To Grow Still Hotter." *Wall Street Journal*. July 8, 2011. B8

18. *China Observer*. "IKEA China: Build a Loyal Following Through Customer Engagement Online." March 22, 2012. http://thechinaobserver.com/2012/03/22/ikea-china-build-a-loyal-following-through-customer-engagement-online.

19. David Pierson. "Beijing Ikea is More a Destination Than a Store," *Boston Globe*, August 27, 2009, A8.

20. Mei Fong. "Retailers Still Expanding in China." *Wall Street Journal*. January 22, 2009. A8. 2009.

21. Kanter Retail IQ. "AEON to Establish Headquarters in China." February 29, 2012. www.kantarretailiq.com/ContentIndex/NewsDisplayLW.aspx?id=467326.

22. *Stores*. "2012 Top 250 Global Retailers." www.stores.org/2012/Top-250-List (Available January 17, 2012)

23. *Asian Business Daily*. "KFC Owner Yum Says Its Future Is In Asia." December, 2011. 9. http://asianbusiness daily.com/2011.12/kfc-owner-yum-says-its-future-is-in-asia/

24. *China Beverage News*. "China: A Look at Strategies from McDonald's, Yum! Brands." September 17, 2011. Source: Mark Brandau in *Restaurant News*. http://chinabevnews.worldpress.com/category/mcdonalds-china/

25. Constance Haisma-Kwok. "Coach's Gateway to Growth in China," *Women's Wear Daily*, May 30, 2008, 3.

26. U.S. Securities and Exchange Commission. "Coach, Inc. Form 10-K Annual Report." August 19, 2011. 5. http://COH_081911_Form10K[1].pdf

27. Chantal Todé. L.L. Bean to Open First Store in China This Month." *DMNEWS*, September 17, 2008. www.dmnews.com/LL-Bean-to-open-first-store-in-china-this-month/Print/article/11

28. L.L. Bean. "2011 Company Fact Sheet." www.llbean.com. (Accessed April 25, 2012.)

29. CBS News. Portland, Maine. "LL Bean Sales Grow Despite Weak Economy." March 9, 2012. www.cbsnews.com/2102-505245_162-57394523.html?tag=contentMain;contentBody.

30. Fu Hung Wang. Tsai Chaio Company brochure. Interview. Birmingham, Alabama, March, 2006.

31. Jon Hilsenrath, Laurie Burkitt and Elizabeth Holmes. "Change in China Hits U.S. Purse." *Wall Street Journal*. June 21, 2011, A1–A12.

32. Yuval Atsmon and Max Magni. "China's Confident Consumers." McKinsey Quarterly. November 2011. www.mckinseyquarterly.com/article_print.aspx?L2=20&L3=73&ar=2879.

33. Matthew Curtin. "China's Taste for Luxury," *Wall Street Journal*," October 21, 2009, C16.

34. Laurie Burkitt. "In China, Women Begin Splurging." *Wall Street Journal*. June 13, 2011, B1–B6.

35. Alison Tudor. "Prada Sees Future in Asia." *Wall Street Journal*. June 18, 2011. C3.

Unit Three

Store Location and Planning

Retail expansion was rampant during the last half of the 20th century. In the early years of the 21st century, it has become more difficult to find locations that will provide a profitable return on investment. The recession that began in 2008 dampened the prospects for retail development. The economic downturn affected mall developers, construction companies, lenders and insurers, and retailers themselves. The industry still was grappling with change as this book was going to press.

The art and science of site selection relies on careful monitoring of available real estate, researching the trading area to determine the right fit for a prospective retail development or store, as well as negotiating the sale or lease with terms that are affordable so that retailers will profit from the sale of merchandise.

Retail development has spawned malls and shopping centers of all sizes, shapes, themes, designs, amenities, tenant mixes, community intentions, and even degrees of environmental "greenness." In their carefully chosen geographic areas, shopping centers are designed to reach a specific target market, in the same way that individual retail stores or chains are.

The layout and design of the retail store or mall is artistically engineered, merging merchandise, visual display, and other sensory aspects to create a compelling environment for the customer. It should be welcoming, easy to navigate, safe, and spotless. And that's just for starters. This unit will explore the many factors that make a selling environment in the right location an effective one.

Chapter 9

Site Selection

Learning Objectives

After completing this chapter you should be able to:

- List the key factors involved in choosing a specific retail site.
- Explain what a trading area is and how it is determined.
- Discuss how optimal locations are selected using research and analysis based on geographic information systems.
- Identify the principal types of commercial locations used for retail development.
- Delineate various alternative locations that have grown in popularity.
- Compare the advantages and disadvantages of owning retail property versus leasing it.
- Discuss how retail leasing costs are derived and what affects different rates.
- Assess trends in leasing strategy during an economic downturn and examine the role of real estate investment trusts in retail development.

Figure 9.1
An ideal site for a lifestyle center is this one in Rancho Cucamonga, California. Views of the mountains and the warm climate add to the enjoyment of shoppers frequenting the broad array of trendy retailers at Victoria Gardens, where a trolley bus for transportation within the multi-acre shopping center lends an experiential touch.

As customers, we probably give little thought to how and why shopping centers and individual stores appear in certain spots as if by magic. Retailers that intend to grow domestically and globally evaluate potential business locations scientifically, using technology-driven tools and lifestyle, demographic, and geographic analysis.

Most large retail organizations confront overstored situations as markets mature; this is one reason why retailers expand internationally. Other companies develop new stores in sites previously considered unprofitable, unimportant, or unattractive, or those vacated by a retailer that went out of business.

This chapter addresses site-selection criteria, common research practices, standard types of retail locations, and ownership/leasing arrangements, adding a new dimension to your study of retailing.

Criteria for Site Selection

Choice of location is perhaps the most important decision that retailers make. A good location allows easy access and attracts large numbers of customers. Even minor variations in location can have an impact on market share and profitability. Since many retail outlets have nearly identical product offerings, this point becomes more significant. Location represents a long-term investment; a poor location decision is extremely difficult to overcome. Matching retail offerings with potential customers in the right location requires skill and imagination.

The specifics of the trading area are gathered in order to determine a customer profile. A **trading area** is the geographic area from which a retailer draws its customers. Many examples of demographic information, included earlier in Chapters 2 and 4, are useful to review in this context. Details such as household income, whether residents are homeowners or renters, the market value of homes in the area, and levels of fashion consciousness provide a deeper look at customers.

In order to determine an appropriate site, retailers need information on city population dynamics, national and local economic trends, the competition, and local media. Some knowledge of the history of the city or town, including its reason for existence, is also important. Knowing that Detroit, Michigan, has been an automotive manufacturing city for 100 years and has sustained a deeper economic crisis than many other U.S. cities obviously imparts information crucial to housing and commercial development in the area. Criteria used when selecting a specific site include the following:

- *Pedestrian traffic.* The number of people who pass by a location is important to chart, but should be qualified as to shoppers and nonshoppers. Pedestrian traffic is monitored by time of day and the age and sex of people in transit. Checklists stating minimum requirements are often used in this context. For example, a prospective retailer evaluating a location in a seaside resort shopping center as a site for a candy shop might need to confirm that 100 people enter the area hourly before considering that location for the store. More about checklists is included in the section on research techniques later in this chapter. If a more qualitative study is sought, individuals could be questioned as to destination, shopping habits, and retail preferences.
- *Vehicular traffic.* An analysis of traffic patterns, congestion times, and road conditions is needed. This information is particularly important for retailers such as convenience stores, quick-serve restaurants, gasoline stations, and shopping centers. Software programs are available to help retailers with this task. Retailers might see that alternative means of transportation are needed to safely and effectively move shoppers around the premises. The trolley bus featured in Figure 9.1 is a solution for visitors to a large lifestyle center that is spread out over several acres.
- *Parking.* The number and quality of parking spots, their distance from the store or mall site, and the availability of employee parking should be evaluated. Parking lot size should be judged on the ability to service customers not just on average shopping days, but also during peak traffic periods such as holidays. Convenient, inexpensive, and safe parking should be easily accessible for customers who drive to urban sites. Extremely large facilities plan for shuttle services to convey customers from their cars to the door. Some upscale stores and malls offer complimentary valet parking.
- *Infrastructure.* Both customer vehicles and delivery trucks require access from major highway networks to retail stores and malls. Many public highways are open to passenger car traffic but not to large commercial vehicles. Infrastructure analysis allows retailers to evaluate how public and private conveyances may affect their location. Physical facilities and services that support a specific area—and include highway and transportation systems,

Figure 9.2
Corner locations are highly desired by brick-and-mortar retailers because they present two faces to the public and capitalize on heavy foot traffic. Apparel retailer H&M selected this site under development at a California shopping center.

Figure 9.3
BCBGMAXAZRIA and Juicy Couture draw similar customers at The Summit, an upscale lifestyle center in Alabama. Retailers frequently look for compatible neighbors when they choose locations.

communication networks, and public and private utilities—are examples of **infrastructure.** Stores in central business districts need proximity to mass transportation. Customers are occasionally perplexed when they see two identical gas stations or quick-serve restaurants across the highway from one another. Most likely, traffic pattern studies have indicated commuting patterns that justify two units. When the highway is physically divided, the reasoning is more apparent. At that point, infrastructure criteria are as important as vehicular traffic issues. Infrastructure decisions have an impact on safety, customer convenience, and business efficiency. A few yards or meters can make all the difference in retail.

- *Placement and visibility.* Specific location on a street or in a shopping center is carefully studied. Corner locations are important to high-volume retailers. Although rent is higher for street corner sites, larger sales volumes justify the choice. Companies like Starbucks and Walgreens seek corner spots as part of their location strategies. As illustrated in Figure 9.2, fast-fashion retailers like H&M also benefit from corner locations. Some retail companies look for spots that are near compatible retailers. That paradigm suggests that a group of strong retailers increases the draw of an area. For example, Bob's Stores, a retailer of casual men's and women's apparel, seeks sites near Marshalls, the off-price retailer. BCBGMAXAZRIA and Juicy Couture also select companion locations when available, as illustrated in Figure 9.3. It is the cumulative attraction that benefits both retailers.

Macroenvironmental factors surrounding the selection of a mall are complex, but so are the microenvironmental decisions on specific store placement within the mall. For example, some chain stores seek spots directly adjacent to anchor stores; others look to be near food courts in order to benefit from the increased traffic in those areas. Apparel stores prefer not to be next to food operations, due to the intense aromas, and many retailers do not like corner locations in the "L" of a community shopping center. More on this topic appears in Chapter 10.

Researching the Trading Area

Sophisticated marketing research methods have replaced traditional manual methods, but the goals remain the same: to learn everything possible about people who are shopping in an existing store, or who will be shopping in the future when a new concept is presented, or both. We'll begin with a review of the types of information that should be assembled as the site selection process unfolds. Then the three standard types of trading areas will be described before moving on to simple research tools and more complex mapping methods.

Sources of Information

Several secondary and primary sources of information are used to evaluate a potential retail site. Information that comes from previously published sources is considered **secondary data**. To answer specific questions pertinent to a site, primary data also are used. Information compiled to address specific research issues is called **primary data**. Research techniques vary depending on whether an area has already been developed or will involve new construction. Most research begins with a survey of secondary data.

Using Secondary Data

Retailers can obtain much existing data from the U.S. Census Bureau and other governmental agencies. Included in population data is information on age, gender, marital status, race, occupation, and educational background. Chambers of commerce, local municipalities, and trade associations are also respected sources of information. The International Council of Shopping Centers (ICSC) and the National Retail Federation, referenced frequently in this text, update a wealth of statistics annually.

The Nielsen Company is well known for its demographic estimating services and market sales potential analysis in conjunction with its Claritas division. Much of the data extends to the city and zip code level, making it particularly useful for specific site selection applications. More on Nielsen Claritas trading area analysis methods appears in the geographic information systems discussion later in this section.

Retail sales trends by product lines, an effective buying income figure, and a buying power index are useful research tools. **Effective buying income (EBI)** is a statistic that measures the availability of personal disposable income in an area. The **buying power index (BPI)** is a weighted value that measures the purchasing ability of households in a trading area. The higher the index, the more likely it is that the area will be able to sustain retail sales.

The formula used for calculating BPI is shown conceptually below:

BPI = Effective buying income of an area · 0.5
+ Retail sales of an area · 0.3
+ Population of an area · 0.2

Weighted components are used to calculate the percentage of BPI, retail sales, and population in a specific area of the United States. The weights reflect the importance of each of the three components.

Retailers also determine whether a population is expected to grow, decline, or remain constant. This information is directly correlated with sales. Information on occupations and income levels of potential customers within the trading area assists retailers in placing the right kind of store in a particular locale. Tiffany & Co. would probably not find success locating on a college campus, but the Gap and Domino's Pizza would.

Dwelling types are analyzed, as is the composition of homeowners versus apartment dwellers. Residential analysis will illuminate customer groups based on ethnicity, religion, disability, or age that need specific kinds of merchandise.

Collecting Primary Data

When fresh input is needed, primary data are sought. Administering exit interviews to a random group of customers at a mall is an example of primary research because it generates new information. Timely, detailed demographic data, including family income, family size, age of respondent, gender, number of children, educational background, occupation, and type of housing, are compared with secondary data published on the area. Interviewers might also record the amount spent during that particular visit to the mall. Finally, interviewers gather information regarding customers' attitudes toward the store and its competition.

Customers do not always go directly from their homes to shopping areas; in fact, many shop near their place of work. Commuting patterns are determined by capturing zip code information at the point of sale, through in-store surveys, or by using vehicle spotting techniques. Monitoring the license plates of automobiles entering shopping center parking lots is one way to further define commuting habits, trading areas, and target markets.

Types of Trading Areas

The immediate area surrounding an existing store or new geographic site is the best place to start gathering information. Three basic types of trading areas are classified according to the density of potential customers in a geographic area:

- **Primary trading area**—A geographic area that encompasses 50–80 percent of a store's potential customers. It also is referred to as the *primary service area* (PSA). It is the area closest to the store and possesses the highest density of customers in terms of population and per capita sales. Convenience stores draw well from this area, but poorly from the secondary trading area.
- **Secondary trading area**—A geographic area located just outside the primary trading area that contains an additional 20–25 percent of a store's potential customers.
- **Tertiary trading area**—A wide area located outside the primary and secondary trading areas, containing 5–25 percent of a store's potential customers. It is also called the *fringe* area.

As examples, a discount store might have a primary trading area of two miles, a secondary trading area of four miles, and a tertiary trading area of eight miles. Potential customers are more dispersed in the secondary and tertiary areas. Different store types also have an impact on the size of their trading areas. Furniture retailer Ikea may pull customers from a 250-mile radius and Starbucks from less than a one-mile radius in many locations.

Trading Area Analysis

Retailers of all sizes and levels of site selection expertise have many tools from which to choose. This section examines different methods from the simple to the more complex.

Determining a Trading Radius

To determine the geographic area from which a retailer will draw its customers, two methods are considered. Ring analysis and polygon analysis are appropriate to use when analyzing an existing store or considering a specific geographic point for possible construction.

Ring Analysis   Using an existing or potential retail site as the locus to determine a trading radius is called **ring analysis**. Also known as the *concentric circles method,* this type of analysis helps a retailer determine customer potential. For example, analysts might study an area using three-, five-, and ten-mile radius rings as shown on a map. Ring analysis is useful but does not fully describe an area. Studying consumers' driving times in tandem with ring analysis is a more effective measure.

Polygon Method   More often, a polygon method is used rather than the ring method. The **polygon method** is used when determining a trading area by considering natural and human-made phenomena that apportion the space into straight-sided geometric shapes. Polygon analysis, developed by Thiessen, does not presume that all customers are interspersed equally in the trading area. This method is useful when physical barriers, conservation land, or a body of water exists within the site being studied. For example, a swamp consisting of several acres is not habitable and therefore, equal-dispersion population estimates using a purely concentric model would not be valid. The polygon method allows the swamp to be considered when analyzing the area. Information on competition, supply and demand, and other pertinent data regarding the trading area can be included when using either method.

Market Share–Weighted Trade Areas   One of the more sophisticated and most accurate measures employed by site selectors involves creating market share–weighted trade areas. The technique involves taking the basic polygon approach two steps further. By adding components of market share and household income in a carefully constructed formula, much more detailed and accurate information on the trade area can be compiled. The importance of clearly defining a trading area cannot be overstated.

Determining Economic Feasibility

Retailers use several methods to determine the economic feasibility of new locations. Some consider the sales volume that could be expected from customers in a geographic area. More advanced measures consider the level of competition in an area and the degree of retail saturation.

Sales Potential   The total amount of possible sales that can be realized in a trading area is called **sales potential**. The sales potential of a trading area is determined by studying the number of households and the average household income in a trading area. It is calculated by multiplying the number of households in an area by the average household income in the area.

To estimate an individual retailer's potential share of sales, the amount spent for different types of products can be calculated using percentages derived from government or industry sources. Retailers also calculate the portion of the market that is not presently being served. Subtracting the actual sales from the potential sales in an area provides this number.

Estimating Competition   The degree to which a trading area is overstored or understored indicates its level of **retail saturation**. Saturation reflects the amount of competition in the marketplace. If an area is saturated, it means that the number of stores in the trading area is adequate to satisfy customers' needs and wants, but not so high that sales for all retailers in the area are diluted to the point that few turn a profit.

The **index of retail saturation (IRS)** is a measurement tool that allows retailers to determine the degree of competition in a trading area by calculating the total square feet of selling space devoted to each product line. The formula used to calculate IRS is shown conceptually below.

IRS = Households in trading area · Retail expenditures per household for product line

Information of this kind is used to help determine shopping-center size and tenant mix. This quantitative measure uses refined sales potential figures along with retail square footage numbers to create a ratio that helps site selection specialists compare potential sites. The sales per square foot number can be applied to specific retail formats based on product line such as shoe stores, drugstores, or home improvement centers. Sales potential figures are also tailored to the selected product line.

Finding the Optimal Site

Several methods are used to determine the optimal site for a store, ranging from the simple and inexpensive to the more complex and costly. Checklist and analog methods are considered fundamental, while regression analysis and use of gravity models are more substantive. Combining geographic information with descriptive consumer demographics is costly, but most productive for site selectors. We'll describe these methods and explore their uses in this section.

Fundamental Site Selection Methods

Checklists and analog methods are basic ways to collect information that is of use in the hunt for the perfect location. Although simple, they can be very effective when completed with skill and a fine eye for detail.

Checklists

When using checklists, retailers establish a list of criteria that are measured against specific attributes of potential sites. Criteria are chosen based on the needs of the retailer and might include traffic counts and proximity to highways. Income levels, housing types, and ages of residents in the trading area are types of data that could be important to site selectors. This manual method is inexpensive to implement but is somewhat subjective and lacks the rigor of more quantitative measures.[1]

Analog Method

The **analog method** is used to obtain a sales forecast by comparing potential new sites with existing sites. By plotting customers' home addresses on a map, marketing analysts can estimate how many sales dollars an existing store draws from each point. Sometimes pushpins are used to mark the map. Taken in aggregate, this information gives a picture of where the store's total sales volume comes from. By indicating a percentage of those sales dollars—typically 70 percent—the analyst establishes the store's trading area. Several software packages and Web-based tools enable this relatively simple form of analysis to be done. Using this method, the retailer then creates a model to which new sites can be compared. The retailer cannot determine whether a new site will be successful without a good idea of what has worked in existing units and what can be expected in terms of sales.

Advanced Site Selection Tools

The use of statistical measures to refine the site selection process is common and can generate reliable and valid data. Experienced statisticians who also understand site selection variables implement regression analysis and gravity models.

Regression Analysis

Multiple regression is a dominant method used to produce sales forecasts for new and existing stores. The statistical modeling method allows a retailer to include several variables in its analysis of a specific site. For example, square footage of the store, inventory turnover, and characteristics of the trading area are appropriate to use in the calculations. This method provides a high degree of objectivity, although considerable expertise is needed to construct the model.[2]

Gravity Models

Some retailers may ask the question, "What if we located a store here?" Others may want to determine the impact if a competitor opened a store nearby. Both scenarios suggest the need for **gravity models**, which are calculations used to identify the customer-drawing power of geographic areas. Supply and demand forms the basis for analysis using this method. Several types of pertinent data are combined to measure customer tendencies more accurately. Gravity models are based on the assumption that two cities draw customers from the surrounding towns in direct proportion to the square footage, attraction, and number of retailers in those cities. Another element involved is the distance between the cities and the outlying population: the larger the city, the greater the draw; the larger the distance, the less intense the pull. The point at which influence of one city or the other becomes stronger is calculated. These data are used to predict customer patronage.

One classic method is Reilly's Law of Retail Gravitation. Developed by William J. Reilly many decades ago, this method remains the basis for contemporary site selection research.[3] One version uses the formula shown below to determine the point at which two trading areas meet.

$$\text{Trading-area boundary of City A in relation to trading-area boundary of City B} = \frac{\text{Miles between Cities A and B}}{1+ \sqrt{\dfrac{\text{Population of City A}}{\text{Population of City B}}}}$$

Models like these go beyond traditional trade-area analysis because they acknowledge that customers cannot be defined only in terms of geographic boundaries. Newer versions utilize location and the characteristics of customers and sites, as well as competition in the area. For example, a site with excellent visibility, located on an interstate highway directly off the exit ramp, may be the perfect spot for a home-improvement store. Learning that the city also has an above-average number of homeowners with moderate household incomes adds to the knowledge base. If it is also determined that customers in the area have a strong desire to purchase do-it-yourself supplies and that there is no competition for their dollars in the area, then this site would rank high. The next step is to combine information found using gravity models with demographics and other hybrid platforms that make the site selection process even more accurate.

Geographic Information Systems

A look at several technology-inspired site-selection tools illustrates the level of sophistication now being brought to such research. Systems by which retailers can analyze and map potential sites on the basis of interrelated demographic, psychographic, and geographic data are called **geographic information systems (GIS)**. These readily available software programs enable retailers to learn more about customers than simply where they live. Users access information from various databases and business documents, superimposing it on a map. For example, since Starbucks usually has several locations in each city, the company uses GIS to determine the degree to which the trading areas of each unit overlap. When two or more types of data are overlaid to more accurately define the drawing power of a specific site, this is one form of **spatial analysis**. Spatial analysis also involves finding new information from old or incomplete data. Returning to the previous example, Starbucks might use spatial analysis to determine potentially strong new sites.

GIS is also used to identify cities that have high population density, specific types of housing in that city, and local transportation routes. By using spatial interaction models, retailers learn more about how customers find their ways to their stores. Database development figures prominently in GIS. More retailers are using GIS systems than ever before because they are effective and they make many mapping applications possible.

Geodemographic Marketing Tools

The marriage of geography and demography has resulted in a variety of innovative solutions for retailers that are seeking not only the perfect location, but also a wealth of information about their customers. **Geodemographics** refers to the combination of geographic information with demographic attributes that describe a population. **Geodemographic marketing tools** use computer-based mapping to identify consumer segments in specific geographic locations. The premise of geodemographics is based on the old adage: "birds of a feather flock together." Most such tools use some form of **cluster analysis**, which is a method used to group people according to their attributes and behaviors. Clusters are used to determine market segments and define target markets, allowing retailers to recognize opportunities in geographic regions they previously bypassed. One of the major companies involved with geodemographic research and market segmentation is Nielsen Claritas, mentioned earlier in the chapter. Two of the company's applications that are of interest to retailers are explained here.

PRIZM Segmentation Nielsen Claritas provides a lifestyle and behavior segmentation tool called PRIZM that is based on geodemographics. PRIZM is an acronym for Postal Residences in Zip Markets. This neighborhood classification technique blends demographics, psychographics, and geography, allowing marketers to identify specific customer groups. Groups are then pinpointed by region, state, city, zip code area, neighborhood, city block, and ultimately, specific address.

U.S. households are assigned to one of 66 groups through factor and cluster analysis. Governmental data as well as information from private sources are used in the process. PRIZM clusters are based on dozens of key census variables, plus customer purchase records. Each cluster represents a distinct social group and/or lifestyle stage and indicates predictable patterns of buying behavior. Specific segments have catchy names, such as *Young Digerati, Kids & Cul-de-Sacs,* and *Heartlanders.* Knowing that members of the *Heartlanders* group may be keen on fishing but not on clothing boutiques may be of considerable importance to retail developers. And if you were Bass Pro Shops, you'd like to know where people who love to fish are located.

Because PRIZM is linked to many marketing and direct-mail provider databases in the country, the system can effectively target consumer segments based on most types of purchase and media behaviors.[4] Three PRIZM clusters are illustrated and described in Table 9.1.

Identifying High-Growth Areas Mapping strategy starts with an analysis of the larger geographic area in contention for a new retail store or mall. To identify high-growth communities, Nielsen Claritas works with core-based statistical areas. **Core-based statistical areas (CBSAs)** are geographic areas of both metropolitan and micropolitan communities. Approximately 85 percent of the U.S. population lives within a CBSA. **Metropolitan areas** have a population of at least 50,000 people. Populations that range from 10,000 to 50,000 are considered **micropolitan areas**.[5]

Using CBSA tools, research and geodemographic experts at Nielsen Claritas identified seven population growth factors that are linked with fast-growing geographic markets:

1. Large land areas.
2. Booming suburban rings.
3. Widespread affluence.
4. An increasing Hispanic population.

Table 9.1   Sample PRIZM Social Groups

Cluster Identification	Description
URBAN U1 Urban Uptown #04 Young Digerati	The Young Digerati are the nation's tech-savvy singles and couples living in fashionable neighborhoods on the urban fringe. Affluent, highly educated, and ethnically mixed, Young Digerati communities are typically filled with trendy apartments and condos, fitness clubs, clothing boutiques, casual restaurants, and all types of bars—from juice to coffee to microbrew.
SUBURBAN S2 The Affluentials #18 Kids & Cul-de-Sacs	Upscale, suburban, married couples with children—that's the skinny on Kids & Cul-de-Sacs, a lifestyle of large families in recently built subdivisions. With a high rate of Hispanic and Asian Americans, this segment is a refuge for college-educated, white-collar professionals with administrative jobs and upper-middle-class incomes. Their nexus of education, affluence, and children translates into large outlays for child-centered products and services.
TOWN & COUNTRY T3 Middle America #43 Heartlanders	America was once a land of small middle-class towns, which can still be found today among Heartlanders. This widespread segment consists of older couples with working-class jobs living in sturdy, unpretentious homes. In these communities of small families and empty-nest couples, Heartlanders pursue a rustic lifestyle where hunting and fishing remain prime leisure activities along with cooking, sewing, camping, and boating.

Source: Excerpted from Nielsen Claritas. PRIZM and its segmentation explanations from The Nielsen Company 2011.

5. Diversified employment.
6. Long commutes.
7. The presence of lifestyle shopping centers.[6]

The combination of population growth and demographic projections creates rich data that help retailers identify areas ripe for expansion. Using CBSA information, Nielsen Claritas created 15 markets characterized by select demographic and growth rates and sorted them into three main population-sized groups named Metro Cities, Metro Towns, and Micro Towns. Their findings suggest future directions for domestic retail expansion.[7]

A related approach is used by a major consulting group, which examines retailer presence and expansion plans by surveying over 300 international retailers in over 70 countries annually. In the 2011 study, the top ten cities most targeted as a retail destination were Dubai and London (tied for first place), followed by New York, Paris, Madrid, Hong Kong, Moscow, Los Angeles, Singapore, and Barcelona. Almost half the retailers surveyed had a brick-and-mortar store presence in major global regions, including the Americas, Europe, the Middle East and Africa, and the Asia/Pacific region. American retailers had the greatest global presence, with 73 percent operating in all regions.[8] Site-selection specialists consider information like this when they firm up expansion plans.

Mapping Techniques
The company Environmental Systems Research Institute (ESRI) provides a wealth of business services for retailing and other industries. One of the applications is the Retail MarketPlace Profile, which assembles information on a particular address or locale. For example, a full report summarizes demographics, including population, households, and income data, and provides a tally of total retail sales figures for the area by industry group in terms of supply, demand, and retail gap in an area. It also accounts for aberrations that would skew research findings at several radius levels, for example, 0.75 miles, 1.5 miles, and 3.0 miles.[9]

Another service for a mall developer or retail company is the Major Shopping Center Locator. Using ring analysis, it lists and plots major shopping areas within selected miles from a proposed site. Information on distance from site, year opened, and leasable area in square feet is included.

Figure 9.4
Rich Web 2.0 features make ESRI's interactive mapping techniques state of the art. This example shows the expenditures for retail goods by zip code areas of Chicago. (Source: ESRI)

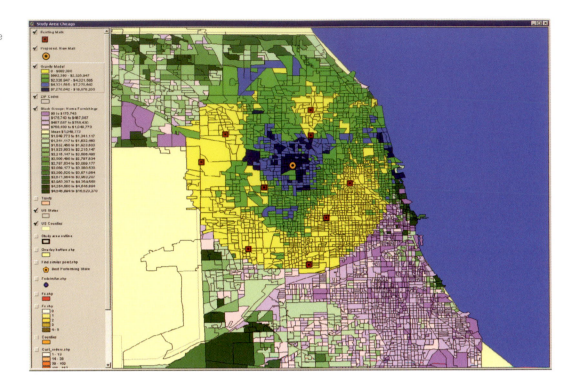

ESRI is also renowned for producing gravity models at different informational levels. Many of its products are Web-based and can be adapted in real time depending on the application. Maps from ESRI's Business Analyst Online showing expenditures in retail goods by zip code appear in Figure 9.4.

In addition to the companies mentioned in this section, a wealth of other resources exists at all retail budget levels. Many companies with different strengths in location intelligence are bringing products to the marketplace. For example, Pitney Bowes offers MapInfo Professional, a Microsoft Windows–based mapping and geographic analysis tool. Although no retailer should be without access to the most sophisticated site tools in the market, most experts agree that there is still a place for instinct and experience in site selection.

Types of Retail Locations

Finding the optimal location is another consideration in the site-selection process. Each geographic region or city consists of a variety of commercial areas that incorporate retail operations. As with all decisions relating to location, each choice has inherent benefits and disadvantages.

Commercial Areas

Although there are many hybrids, three types of commercial real estate form the core of options for retailers that are not affiliated with shopping centers: freestanding stores, central business districts, and string streets. Shopping centers and malls are other forms of commercial districts. Because of their impact on retail trade, shopping centers are discussed separately in Chapter 10.

Freestanding Stores

A **freestanding store** is a self-contained building often located on the periphery of a shopping center or city. Freestanding buildings also are constructed in downtown areas. Easy parking, flexible hours, lower rent, and ease of one-stop shopping characterize units located on the outskirts. Toys "R" Us uses this strategy in most of its U.S. locations and many of its international sites, as illustrated in Figure 9.5.

Figure 9.5
Toys "R" Us often seeks
freestanding locations
like this one, near a Tesco
supermarket at the Brent
Cross Shopping Center,
north of London, where
parking is plentiful and
access is easy for families.

Retailers dominating a city block also are considered freestanding even though they may be located in busy downtown areas with limited parking and high rents. Macy's and Saks Fifth Avenue's flagship stores in New York City and Harrods' London site bear this distinction. Flagship stores of specialty retailers like Ralph Lauren often stand alone. Some occupy opulent restored mansions and other architectural wonders. Because drawing clientele is expensive, small independent stores usually cannot afford freestanding locations such as these. Instead they develop sites in former homes and historic buildings, in tourist or smaller trading areas.

Areas in which numerous freestanding stores are located are called power nodes. A **power node** consists of a grouping of big-box stores—including at least one power center—located at or near a major highway intersection.[10] The term power node should not be confused with shopping centers that are called *power centers,* which are discussed in the next chapter. The importance of power nodes accelerated in the 1990s, although the tendency of big-box retailers to locate in specific areas was noticed decades earlier.

Central Business Districts

Central business districts are downtown commercial areas in large and small cities where many businesses including retailers tend to congregate. They offer a broad range of specialty, convenience, department, and, increasingly, discount stores. Usually within easy reach of financial and other commercial buildings, retailers in central business districts depend on foot traffic as well as private and public transportation to bring in business. **High streets** are busy retail thoroughfares where many retailers locate in large cities of the United Kingdom and other countries. They best compare to main streets in the United States where many storefront retailers congregate. Downtown in the United States equates to *city centre* in the United Kingdom. Some high streets, like London's Bond Street and Sloane Street, have become magnets for designer and other luxury goods retailers.

The popularity of central business districts in the United States vacillated in the last century. Downtown districts that faded in the 1970s experienced renewal in the 1980s and 1990s and remain strong today.

Did You Know?
London's incomparable
Harrods department store
was sold to Qatar Holdings
in 2010 for $2.2 billion—
roughly twice the retailer's
annual revenue. The
freestanding department
store, which occupies
an entire city block on
Brompton Road, was owned
for 25 years by Mohamed
Al Fayed, who also owns
the Ritz Hotel in Paris. It is
said that Al Fayed rescued
the aging department
store and turned it into "an
unapologetically opulent
retail experience."
(Source: Samantha Conti, "Al
Fayed Says Farewell: Qatar
Holding Acquires Harrods for
$2.2 Billion," *Women's Wear
Daily,* May 10, 2010, 1, 12.)

Downtown Revitalization Redevelopment projects have created prime sites for many retailers. Stores such as the Gap, Talbots, and Williams-Sonoma, operating primarily as mall retailers, have opened in downtowns large and small. Several reasons precipitated the move to city centers. Many customers perceive in-town shopping as slower-paced compared to stressful mall visits. This perception varies greatly depending on the size of the city; shoppers in New York, Hong Kong, or London might not agree. Retailers find rents in many downtown locations more palatable than in shopping centers. They also welcome city support for snow removal, outdoor electricity, and parking. Many downtown retailers serve upper-income families living in cities and those that prefer to avoid the redundancy of malls.

A new urban renewal movement draws retailers to refurbished downtowns in many parts of the United States. The South Beach section of Miami showcases restored art deco–style hotels, restaurants, and retail stores in a section of the city that had been neglected for decades.

Discounters: Urban or Suburban? The movement of suburban discounters to major metropolitan cities began in the 1990s and has not subsided. Kmart opened in New York City on 34th Street near Penn Station in 1996 and also has a store on Broadway near Union Square.[11] Target joined the parade to Manhattan in 2010, when it opened its first store in East Harlem.[12] Now most discounters have a presence in major urban areas like New York City, except Walmart. In 2010, the company announced plans to open a SuperCenter in East New York, Brooklyn; 2 years later, plans had not come to fruition. However, Walmart pressed on with plans for several smaller Express Stores in the greater New York City area.[13]

Figure 9.6
Off-price stores like Marshalls have been departing from their usual mall locations to situate in central business districts like this one in Minneapolis.

Suburban centers are also drawing discount retailers. Massachusetts-based TJX Company, parent of off-price retailers T.J. Maxx, HomeGoods, and Marshalls, has many units in smaller community centers. Minneapolis is home to Target, and its headquarters and flagship store are located downtown. Marshalls also seeks downtown areas, including Minneapolis, as illustrated in Figure 9.6. What sounds like an incongruity is really a strategy: retailers are moving to where their target customers are, whether that is in urban or suburban locations.

String Streets
Retail thoroughfares located away from central business districts that retain thriving clusters of retail shops in or near residential neighborhoods are called **string streets**. Independent stores often find homes in these areas, which may become a locus for innovative specialty retailing. Intermingled with national chains, these shopping areas retain unique characteristics that make them destination points for local residents and workers, as well as tourists. Melrose Avenue and Melrose Place in Hollywood, and Spring and Wooster Streets in New York's SoHo, are prime examples. At one time, SoHo (the New York City area so-named for its location *south of Hou*ston Street) was home to art galleries and idiosyncratic shops that exuded a bohemian flavor. Now it has designer shops, global retailers, and gourmet restaurants while retaining its quirkiness.

Rodeo Drive was named the number-one best shopping street in America for holiday shopping by *U.S. News and World Report*.[14] The notoriously pricey string street in Beverly Hills has continued to draw millions of people annually, even during the economic downturn. By the end of 2011, stores on Rodeo were expected to be 98 percent occupied with asking rents of approximately $500 per square-foot per year.[15] From the Field 9.1 highlights other rents that are escalating in luxury markets in several global locations. The Beverly Hills address is so popular globally that a street in Seoul, Korea, was named in its honor. Stores on Rodeo-Gil are as trendy as those on its California counterpart. *Gil* means street in Korean.

Outside Philadelphia is a revitalized small downtown that has many attributes of a string street. Located on the Schuylkill River, Manayunk has a boardwalk, casual dining, and a combination of local shops peppered with a few national chains in renovated older buildings. See them in Figure 9.7.

Alternative Retail Sites

A rash of locations gained popularity in the last few decades and continue to influence site selection decisions. Going where the customers are—even if that means to hospitals, museums, zoos, hotels, resort towns, train stations, airports, or underground—is changing the location strategies of many retailers.

Transportation Terminals

Travelers to London's Heathrow Airport have enjoyed shopping while waiting for international flights for years, but airports as sought-after retail destinations have been slower to evolve. Now large and small retailers have joined the fray, and duty-free shops are no longer the major tenants. Futuristic urban developments designed around airport hubs are becoming sites for residential, commercial, entertainment, and retail use. Some may call such a mega project—like those in Dubai; Honduras; and Chongqing, China—an "aerotropolis."[16]

Heathrow's Terminal 5   Owned by BAA (the acronym for British Airports Authority), Terminal 5 opened in early 2008 and defies imagination—or at least our perception of airport retailing. Restaurants range from Krispy Kreme to fine-dining establishments where champagne is the norm. The terminal has a galactic look, with huge open expanses, over 300 giant billboards, and 200 flat-screen TVs; it reportedly has more advertising than any other airport in the world.[17]

Some of the 48 retail brands at Terminal 5 include Harrods' 11,000-square-foot department store and Tiffany, which opened its first-ever airport store at Heathrow. Fashion mavens are drawn to Prada, Dior, and Coach, as well as Bulgari and Cartier jewelers. Other United Kingdom–based retailers include Mulberry apparel, Dixons electronics, and WHSmith books.[18]

///////////////////////////////////
Cyberscoop
JCDecaux of France is a premier supplier of electronic signage used in shopping centers, airports, and other commercial venues worldwide. See the glitz and powerful imagery the company has installed at Heathrow airport outside London by going to www.JCDecauxairport.co.uk and clicking on "Profiles." Or visit www.jcdecauxairport.co.uk/site/profiles%20Book%202012.pdf.

a

Figure 9.7
Located on the outskirts of Philadelphia, Manayunk has successfully blended local enterprises with national chains like Banana Republic on this string street. It fits in so well you can barely see the store sign on the old stone building (a). Independently owned boutiques and restaurants make Manayunk a destination for both locals and tourists (b).

b

Atlanta Airport's Global Retailers   Hartsfield-Jackson Atlanta International airport is considered one of the world's busiest airports—and that counts only air traffic. The airport might want to add a category for shoppers, who pour through its 90 retail stores, 114 food and beverage locations, two duty free shops, and 56 service outlets daily. The airport shops attract many luxury retailers, including the international jeweler Bulgari, designers Salvatore Ferragamo and Ermenegildo Zegna, as well as Brooks Brothers.[19] Airport retailing is a conduit to customers worldwide. For this reason many international retailers select these sites.

Post-9/11 Changes   As travelers and airline officials grappled with new rules in the post-9/11 era, shopping habits and passengers' use of time in airports also changed. People spent more time in airports due to more intense screening of both travelers and luggage. Airline regulations and budget cutbacks meant travelers needed to allocate time to shop for carry-on food. Limitations on the types of items that could be carried onboard were strict. Needs had changed.

Airport retailers have heard customers' requests for more conveniences and new ways to spend extra time and money. Here are a few examples of what travelers want:

- More full-service restaurants with a broader choice of quality meals, as well as those that provide nutritious and affordable take-out and take-on meals.
- Personal services, including nail and hair salons; mini massages.
- Quiet alcoves to read or nap as well as business centers with computer access
- A variety of retail shops in which to browse and shop.

Trains: Above and Below Ground   Retailers also play a major role in the popularity of Union Station in Washington, D.C., and Grand Central Terminal in New York City. Not only can you board a train from these facilities, but you can also dine or shop while you wait. Underground transportation systems also provide opportunities to reach customers on the run. Retail shops are part of the British underground network, fondly called "the tube." Subway stops and above-ground access points in major cities such as Montreal and Chicago grant access to vast underground retail offerings. When space limitations or climate are issues, malls go underground. It's hard to believe that the five-level mall illustrated in Figure 9.8 is under the city of Montreal. Collectively the malls are called "La Ville Souterraine," in French, or "The subterranean city."

Tourist and Historical Sites

Customers in resort areas are usually relaxed and more susceptible to retail temptations. For this reason, tourist destinations are often desirable targets for retail development. Shopping sites that appeal exclusively to tourists have also been well received.

Sites with Historical Precedence   Rising from cactus-strewn land close to the Mexican border, Tubac, Arizona, is the location for a well-planned complex of gift shops, restaurants, antique stores, jewelry, and pottery specialists. On the periphery of the village sit the ruins of the historic Presidio, part of the network of colonial-era Spanish forts that once dominated the southwestern United States. History buffs are welcome to tour the facility, but the village exists primarily as a tourist stop for travelers heading to Tucson or Nogales. A performing-arts center and art galleries also draw traffic.

Some historical restoration areas have become retail destinations in themselves. Williamsburg, Virginia, for example, has much more to offer tourists than just tours of historic homes and reenactments of colonial life. The city is a magnet for retail development.

Resort-Centered Retail   Tourism's reach extends to hotels and resorts, many of which have installed retail shopping centers. Hotels in Hong Kong and Bangkok include shopping malls as an integral part of their facilities. Casinos in Las Vegas and elsewhere link shopping facilities to their operations in increasing numbers.

A popular shopping destination in Las Vegas is the Forum Shops at Caesars Palace. The development has been so successful that it has had three additions since it opened in the late 1990s.

Figure 9.8
Montreal's many underground malls, like Cours Mont-Royal, are routine to residents but an adventure for tourists. It makes sense to locate below the surface in a country where the winters are long and hard and the summers are short.

The architecture of the complex is meant to replicate that of ancient Rome—complete with statues, interior store façades inspired by several historic periods. The shops and restaurants are top-notch, and many of the entrances and exits are conduits designed to move shoppers right into the casino. Careful planning has premeditated every nuance of customer access and traffic flow. Before the recession, the Forum Shops generated sales of about $1,400 per square foot. By 2008, sales had diminished to about $1,200 per square foot, still three times that of average shopping centers.[20] A photo of the Forum Shops appears in Chapter 3; see Figure 3.5 on page 79.

Club Méditerranée SA—better known as Club Med—is moving up in the world as it adjusts its brand image from mid-market fun to upmarket luxury. This shift is seen in the number of new retailers it has brought to its four- and five-star resorts, now called "villages." Guests can choose from global apparel brands like Armani and Ralph Lauren as well as Swarovski jewelry. The company is looking to Asia for further expansion, and says that of its 60 million potential guests worldwide, 26 million are from Asia.[21]

Tourist Attractions   Who can resist a stuffed panda if you've met a real one at the San Diego Zoo? Zoos and wild animal parks serve as hosts to retailers as well as the animals that are the main draw. The Wild Animal Park outside San Diego has added numerous marketplace carts in addition to the gift shops that are located strategically over its sprawling property.

Seaside villages like Rockport, Massachusetts, have lured visitors seeking surf, sun, and shopping for over 100 years. Gift and souvenir shops blend with breakfast nooks, seafood restaurants, candy shops, a music performance hall and pricey bistros in Bearskin Neck, located on the harbor. Art galleries dot the streets and the piers, one of which is the site of the brick-red, much-painted wharf shack "Motif #1." Boat tours and kayak rentals attract active participants, as seen in Figure 9.9. Many areas like this are partially—if not completely—seasonal, so retailers must earn their revenue between Memorial Day and Columbus Day.

Hospitals

Hospitals have expanded, while making their facilities more amenable to visitors, patients, and employees. Gift shops have gained visibility as a result. One study showed that more than 77 percent of hospital gift shops are located in the main lobby. More than two-thirds of gift shop custom-

a

b

Figure 9.9
Resort towns like Rockport, Massachusetts, provide plenty of options for vacationers, including this kayak rental service located directly on the dock (a). Keeping inventory dry is a goal for many retailers, but not for North Shore Kayak; its kayaks are stocked on the other side of the jetty (b).

ers are employees and about 20 percent are visitors, which goes against the common perception that most shoppers buy goods for patients they are visiting.[22] The addition of services such as hair salons, better merchandising practices, and perhaps a Dunkin' Donuts or two adds to the draw of these choice locations.

Retailers are more committed than ever before to bringing their goods to the places where people congregate. Transportation facilities, tourist areas, hospitals, and schools are all appropriate sites.

Owning and Leasing Retail Property

Deciding whether to buy or lease a store, build from scratch, or acquire an existing property are other aspects of the site-selection process. Negotiating the transaction requires time, expertise, and determination.

Buying Versus Leasing Property

There are advantages and disadvantages to purchasing as opposed to leasing property. Evaluating all possibilities is imperative before a place of business is chosen.

Owning the Premises

Benefits   By owning the premises, retailers benefit because they:

- Do not have to worry about a lease expiring or having to renegotiate a complex lease.
- Can alter or repair the store without landlord approval, as long as changes conform to local zoning laws.
- May be able to lease space to other retailers either as leased departments or stores as space permits.
- Benefit from increases in real-estate evaluation. In periods when real estate values appreciate, return on investment (ROI) on the property may outweigh ROI on the retail business.

Disadvantages   On the other hand, there are negative aspects to owning because retailers:

- May tie up capital that might be better invested in inventory. Small retailers, in particular, may not have enough capital to both purchase and stock a store.
- May not want to be landlords or property managers.
- Have sole responsibility for paying tax and maintenance charges.
- May face decreases in property values in periods of economic downturn.

Leasing Retail Space

Benefits   By far the more common method of acquiring retail space, leasing may benefit retailers in several ways:

- The location available for lease may be in the highest traffic area—usually in a mall.
- Owners may lack capital for purchasing property; leasing may be the only alternative.
- The ROI may be greater if available funds are invested in inventory rather than in real estate.
- The additional responsibilities of owning real estate are avoided, allowing the owner to concentrate on running the retail business.

Disadvantages   Retailers that lease space may face these drawbacks:

- Leases are complex, all-encompassing, and binding.
- Restrictions, policies, and procedures specified in a lease must be adhered to, although sometimes impractical or difficult to endure. Usually store hours, signage, and renovation are regulated in a lease.
- Because of high costs of space in prime locations, smaller retailers may have difficulty breaking even, let alone profiting.

Zoning Restrictions

Whether a property is owned or leased, retailers are expected to adhere to local regulations. Zoning laws are designed to protect community image by restricting certain kinds of development, the size of retail structures, or some outside signage, for example. Other types of ordinances might involve hours of store operation or whether a commercial establishment is allowed to do business at a specific location.

Some zoning laws adversely affect retailers and appear to be unjust, as highlighted by the following example. A fitness center was located off a secondary road in a small industrial park behind a stand of trees. The facility could not be seen from the highway. After a complaint from a nearby residential property owner, the center was forced to remove its roadside sign, which had been in place for several years. Heated discussion ensued, and the town zoning board ruled that the sign was illegal and could not be replaced. Despite appeals and the signing of petitions by local residents who supported the fitness center, less than a year later it was out of business. Incongruously, less than 500 feet from the entrance to the industrial park the zoning laws differed, and an unattractive hand-painted sign promoting an in-home business still stands. The legal system is often slow to change even when positive community response supports it. Retailers contend with issues such as this quite often.

Negotiating with a Developer

Once the decision is made to lease a property, considerable time and effort go into negotiating the transaction with a property developer. A lease is a contract covering land, buildings, selling space, or a combination of these features, in which rights are described between the property owner (lessor) and the company or individual renting space (lessee). There are as many varieties of leases as there are stores in a shopping area. A typical lease runs 50 pages or more and covers everything from basic rental rates per square foot to escape clauses should either party choose to terminate the agreement before the lease expires. Several leasing technicalities deserve attention.

Bases for Establishing Rates

Most retailers lease space on the basis of square footage, assessed annually but paid in a variety of increments. **Base rent** is a fixed payment determined by the square footage used that is due monthly or annually. **Percentage rent** is a percentage of annual sales above a threshold volume paid by the retailer to the lessor. Often both methods are used in tandem so that retailers pay a fixed payment per square foot plus a percentage of sales above a certain volume stipulated by the lessor.

Retailers may negotiate with the developer or landlord to spread payments in proportion to typical retail sales cycles. Under this arrangement, retailers pay more rent in the busy months of November and December and less in the slower months of February and March. Others may negotiate to make payments in ascending increments over the period of time of the lease. This practice is beneficial to new retailers that need time to establish themselves in the marketplace.

Derivation of Charges

Cost per square foot is largely determined by type of location, dynamics of the trading area, geographic area, and type of store. Size of the organization also affects the ability to negotiate rental rates. Chains belonging to major companies like Limited Brands (United States), Inditex (Spain), and Louis Vuitton (France) are in a much better bargaining position than small independent retailers.

In the case of mall stores, merchandise category and position within the mall affect rental costs. For example, fine jewelry stores are usually charged more rent than apparel retailers because jewelry stores are expected to generate higher volume.

Comparative regional leasing costs are difficult to identify because rents vary greatly by city, region, and country. It is possible to lease space in a strip mall on the outskirts of a small city for approximately $10 to $15 per square foot. However, retailers hoping to rent a store on posh Fifth Avenue in New York City could expect to pay as much as $1,631 per square foot in 2009. (Due to the recession, that amount was down 17 percent from the 2008 rate of $1,958 per square foot.)[23]

Did You Know?
Asking rents on Fifth Avenue between 50th and 59th streets in New York City took a leap to $2,750 per square foot in May 2012—22 percent more than in 2011. The "gilded stretch," as it's called, houses Saks Fifth Avenue, Louis Vuitton, Tiffany & Co., and Apple, among other top retailers in the world. (Source: Ilaina Jonas and Phil Wahba. "Retail Rent on Manhattan's Fifth Avenue Soars." May 18, 2012. © Thomson Reuters. www.reuters.com/assets/print?aid=USL1E8G1C6020120518)

Additional Leasing Costs

In a typical retail lease, several other items are referred to as triple net charges. **Triple net** is a leasing term that describes a retailer's responsibility for paying insurance, utilities, and internal upkeep. The term gradually evolved to include other items, inclusion of which may depend on the retailer's ability to negotiate. These charges include:

- *Common area maintenance.* Charges assessed on retailers to fund general mall upkeep internally and externally are called **common area maintenance (CAM)**. Examples include contributions for general mall upkeep, housekeeping, snow plowing, window washing, and outside refurbishment. Similar to "condo fees" in their intent, CAM charges are usually expressed in dollar amounts tied to the amount of square footage leased. The fees may range from $2 to $10 or more, depending on the property.

- *Promotional funds.* Sometimes called association charges, these fees are collected to fund shopping center activities such as fashion shows, special sale circulars, community activities, or the presence of special guests for holiday celebrations.

- *Taxes and insurance.* These charges are usually prorated for each retailer on the basis of gross leasable area. **Gross leasable area (GLA)** is the amount of square footage available for lease in a shopping center, excluding common areas such as walkways, offices, and parking areas. In 2011, shopping center GLA represented 7.3 billion square feet in the United States. California, Florida, and Texas led the country in GLA in 2010, accounting for 29.3 percent of the total.[24]

- *Utilities.* Although most large malls provide central heating, ventilation, and air conditioning (HVAC) as part of the lease, retailers are expected to pay their own electric and communications bills. In some circumstances, even these payments are negotiable.

During downturns in the economy, it is common for retailers to ask for concessions from their landlords. For example, reduced rents, longer time to pay, delayed payments, or frozen CAM charges were negotiated during the worst part of the 2007–2010 recession. As the recession persisted, however, many landlords became less willing to negotiate.

Peripheral Locations

Tracts of land on the periphery of a shopping center or other commercial site that are often owned by the developer of the property, are called **outparcels**. Proper marketing and merchandising of adjacent land maximizes investment for developers. Most major retail companies have separate departments that handle peripheral land development.

In addition to shopping and living complexes, hotels are often partners in peripheral developments. Recreational and entertainment facilities might include theaters, ice-skating rinks, and other sports facilities. Restaurants with a variety of themes and price points may enrich the retail mix. Office buildings, medical complexes, and financial institutions may also be included in the plan.

After the decision to launch a peripheral land project has been made and prime uses determined, other issues might arise. Easement agreements drawn up between the developer and key retailers have a tremendous impact on what the developer can and cannot do with the peripheral land. An agreement that allows limited use of land owned by someone else is called an **easement agreement**. For example, easement agreements might prohibit competing stores, limit parking to certain areas, or specify infrastructure improvements. The developer is placed in a crucial spot among the planner, retailers, and other businesses that want control over land development. Regardless of the many potential logistical and planning problems, land surrounding major developments is fertile soil for many retailers.

Trends in Leasing and Property Acquisition

Amid the prolonged deleterious effects of the recession in 2008–2009, optimists expected that the economy would rebound in 2010. However, global repercussions were still being felt in 2012. Several changes in leasing practices and retail acquisitions occurred during this period of uncertainty,

From the Field 9.2   Increasing Globalization Drives International Brands to Enter U.S. Market

Broader economic warning signs, including a persistently high unemployment rate, have yet to slow down the recovery in retail sales. As a result, demand for retail space continues to grow and new concepts, of which there were few to be found at the depths of the recession, have reemerged.

Unlike in years past, however, when established U.S. companies drove most of the growth by launching new brands that targeted different age ranges or price points than their established lines, creativity now is being driven by international retailers that have saturated their home markets. To be certain, there are some new domestic concepts as well, but to a lesser degree than foreign transplants, according to retail tenant brokers.

Most established retail chains have little room to grow within their own countries, says Matt Winn, senior managing director of U.S. retail services with brokerage firm Cushman & Wakefield. That means if they want to continue growing, they have to look for opportunities overseas. That's why U.S. retailers like J. Crew and Target have been looking for sites in Canada, while the U.S. market has in turn welcomed a string of Canadian chains, in addition to brands from Australia, the United Kingdom, France, Poland, Mexico, and Chile. "They need new eyeballs and new people to buy the brand," Winn says.

Canadian apparel companies made a strong push into the United States in 2011. Toronto-based fast-fashion retailer Joe Fresh signed two leases in New York, while upscale Vancouver-based chain Aritzia picked up speed by opening new locations after lying low through the recession

years. Both retailers have the potential to eventually operate stores in multiple malls stateside.

Latin American chains have also made inroads here and range from Chilean home furnishings seller Casaideas to Uruguayan swimsuit chain Zungara to Mexican children's entertainment venue KidZania, which seeks large chunks of space in class-A malls around the country.

Among U.S.-based newcomers, the emphasis is on experiential retailing. Make Meaning is a New York–based do-it-yourself crafts venue that executives believe has the potential to grow to 100 stores over the next few years. At Make Meaning, people exercise their creativity by learning glass blowing or jewelry design.

Overall, after a few years of very tepid growth, both retail property owners and leasing brokers say there has been a pickup in the number of new players, whether coming from the heartland or from far-off lands. "It's just starting to ramp up," says Michael P. Glimcher, chairman of the board with Glimcher Realty Trust, a Columbus, Ohio–based regional mall REIT. "No one was even thinking about new concepts for a long time. But when I am on the West Coast, I see a number of apparel retailers who have two, three, four stores and are growing. We are clearly not where we were at the peak, but over the next few years, you'll see a ramp-up."

Adapted and condensed from: Elaine Misonzhnik, "Increasing Globalization Drives International Brands to Enter the U.S. Market," *Retail Traffic*, July 29, 2011, www.printthis.clickability.com/pt/cpt?expire=&title=Increasing+Globalization+Drives+International+Brands+to+Enter+US+Market.

---

encouraging retailers to make more effective property acquisition and management decisions. The following realities suggest elements of constant turbulence, instability, and discordance:

- Retail vacancy rates are low in some areas and high in others.
- Cost of space continues to rise in some areas and decline in others.
- Some retailers sublease their facilities to compatible businesses.
- In other circumstances, retailers practice multibrand strategies by sharing space, signage, and other resources.
- Still others reduce the sizes of new stores in order to reduce their leasing costs.
- Many more international retailers are entering the United States market. Read about some of the location decisions being made and the retailers that are changing the face of retailing in From the Field 9.2.

Vacancy rates, temporary tenancy, legal changes in bankruptcy filings, and the role played by real estate investment trusts influence retailers and occasionally radically change their business goals and objectives. A **real estate investment trust (REIT)** is a legal and financial arrangement by which substantial property is owned and large-scale real estate transactions are masterminded. An overview of the state of retail development in the United States follows.

Status of U.S. Retail Development

Real estate research firm Reis indicated that there were tentative but positive signs of improvement in early 2012, but that the retail real estate industry was still not ready to say "economic turnaround." Vacancies remained at their highest levels since 1991, and rents were inching higher.[25] The lowest and the highest retail vacancy rates expected for 2011, by metropolitan area, are listed in Table 9.2.

//////////////////////////////

Cyberscoop

To spot "America's Best Shopping Streets," visit U.S. News Travel at http://travel.usnews.com/features/Americas_Best_Shopping_Streets.

Reis found that retail rents were up slightly in the fourth quarter of 2011 compared to previous quarters. Average rents were $19.04 per square foot for strip centers and $38.18 for malls. Very little new store construction is occurring; 4.5 million square feet of new shopping center space was available in 2010 and only 4.9 million square feet in 2011. For existing malls, this is an advantage, since there is less competition for new tenants.[26]

The retail real estate industry expected to tabulate fewer store closings in 2011 (2,196 in the first three quarters when all the numbers are in) than in all of 2010 (5,572). Some industry experts posited the optimistic view that 2012 would see about a 30 percent lower figure. This reinforces the premise that retail chains already have implemented many cost-saving tactics that make them less vulnerable to closure. Others believe that store closings will reach 5,000 largely due to the vulnerability of small specialty stores and the continued liquidation and restructuring undertaken by some of the larger chains.[27]

Temporary Tenants

Retailers testing new formats or locations favor short-term leasing. Shopping centers with available space benefit from leasing to temporary tenants in several ways:

- First, the positive psychological aspect of shopping in a mall that has no vacancies is apparent.
- Second, temporary tenants often become permanent if their experiment at the site has been successful.
- Third, retailers running seasonal businesses may benefit from a temporary site.

Some shopping centers with big-box vacancies are shifting the use of these large spaces to feature entertainment options, childcare facilities, and other opportunities for customers and retailers. When Borders bookstore filed for bankruptcy, the company identified almost 300 stores that might become available. Site selectors and brokers identified several retailers that would be suitable to fill the empty spaces. Some of their choices included Whole Foods, Planet Fitness, Barnes & Noble, hhgregg, Forever 21, furniture stores, and bowling alleys—something for everyone.[28]

Bankruptcy Laws Affecting Leasing

Changes in the legal environment have an impact on leasing decisions. In 2005, the U.S. Congress passed the Bankruptcy Abuse Prevention and Consumer Protection Act (BAPCPA), which made it more difficult for retailers in Chapter 11 reorganization to break leases. An amended section required debtors to keep or reject their property leases within 120 days of filing. An added provision allowed for 90-day court-approved extensions.

Supporters of this law contended that too many retailers in the past had used Chapter 11 reorganization unfairly, solely for the purpose of vacating unprofitable locations. Opponents argued that when hundreds of stores are involved, reorganization of retail companies is difficult; the near impossibility of adhering to rigid timeframes might thus force retailers to liquidate prematurely. However, they conceded that many other variables were involved in the financial woes experienced by many retailers, including the scarcity of available capital due to the credit crisis, the overleveraged capital structure of some companies as they entered Chapter 11, the competitive dominance of discount retailers, and the growth of online sales. Compounding the retailers' plight were several amendments to BAPCPA that protect creditors; these would have made it difficult for retailers to reorganize whether or not the national and international economies had remained strong.[29]

At times the plight of one retailer is a golden opportunity for another. When several retailers invoked Chapter 7 either directly or indirectly related to the recession, their actions paved the way for other retailers to take over their leases. Several such takeovers occurred in the food and beverage sector. The parent company of Bennigan's restaurant chain filed for Chapter 7 bankruptcy liquidation, and subsequently, Panera Bread Company negotiated with landlords to move into several vacated locations. After Outback Steakhouse pulled out of its Canadian locations, Chili's Grill & Bar in Ontario, Canada, inquired about moving into the former Outback slots.[30] In these cases, the companies were not in reorganization, which meant the timeframe legalities did not apply and the lease transitions were less difficult to accomplish.

Influence of Real Estate Investment Trusts

Huge financial entities control most of the activity in large-scale retail real estate transactions. REITs are involved in acquisitions of land and shopping centers. Many firms, like the mall owner and developer Simon Properties, have evolved into REITs in order to control more aspects of retail development. REITs have great monetary power and marketing thrust. Three examples offer strategic highlights:

- Simon Property Group—Simon either owns or has a share in 400 properties worldwide and is the largest developer in the United States. In 2011, the company upped its share in the King of Prussia Mall in Pennsylvania from 12.4 percent to 96 percent. The mall's average annual sales are $750 per square foot, while the industry average is about $350 to $450.[31] Simon is considered capital-strong and better equipped to weather the economic downturn.
- General Growth Properties—After successfully repelling the wolves of Chapter 11, General Growth Properties' strategic plan centers on the company's key properties. The company reconciled 30 less-desirable malls by forming a new REIT, Rouse Properties, Inc. Some of the key properties in General Growth's 137 mall portfolio include Tysons Galleria in Virginia, Water Tower Place in Chicago, and Ala Moana Center in Honolulu.[32] The company intends to raise rents in some upmarket malls, increase occupancy, and sell some office buildings and strip malls.[33]
- DDR Corp. (formerly Developers Diversified Realty)—This company owns and manages approximately 570 properties in 41 states, Canada, Puerto Rico, and Brazil. Best known for open-air strip malls in the United States, the company is the largest retail landlord in Puerto Rico. It plans to increase long-term growth and value by concentrating on prime property acquisitions.[34]

REITs will continue to play significant roles in shopping center development globally. Power comes from vast holdings, deep pockets, and the ability to raise funds for domestic and global projects. These vignettes have acquainted you with some of the strategies REITs are using to ride out the recession while also pursuing new opportunities.

Using site selection tools and adequately analyzing trading areas is a valuable aspect of store location and planning since the right location contributes substantially to retail success. Business-to-business use of the Internet for buying and leasing commercial property is growing. This practice will reshape the ways retailers approach real estate transactions involving land, individual stores, and shopping centers. The next chapter examines shopping centers and malls as eminent retail sites.

Summary

Choosing appropriate locations is one of the more crucial decisions retailers make. Factors considered when selecting a site include pedestrian and vehicular traffic patterns, parking availability, infrastructure, placement, and visibility. The principal types of trading areas are primary, secondary, and tertiary.

Primary and secondary research help determine the optimum location for a store or shopping center. Simple and advanced geographic information systems bring analytical tools to site selection research. Geodemographic marketing tools combine geographic, demographic, and lifestyle aspects for a more complete look at potential retail sites.

Main types of commercial sites excluding malls are freestanding locations, central business districts, and string streets. Growing emphasis is placed on newer sites such as transportation terminals, tourist and historic areas, hotels, and hospitals.

There are several advantages and disadvantages of owning and leasing space. Leases include base rate per square foot plus a percentage of sales. In addition, costs including common area maintenance, promotion fees, taxes, insurance, and utilities are usually included in a lease.

Peripheral land surrounding a key location also is considered when developing retail space. Leasing to temporary tenants, remaining informed about changes in legislation that affect retail leasing, and looking for opportunities in the face of economic crises are tactics used by major retailers and developers.

REITs are important because as major owners or investors in retail real estate and companies, they set the tone for financial stability within the industry.

Just as many GIS tools utilize the Internet, many retail real estate transactions are now conducted online. Said another way, the three classic principles of retailing remain: location, location, location.

Key Terms

Analog method
Base rent
Buying power index (BPI)
Central business districts
Cluster analysis
Common area maintenance (CAM)
Core-based statistical areas (CBSAs)
Easement agreement
Effective buying income (EBI)
Freestanding store
Geodemographic marketing tools
Geodemographics
Geographic information systems (GIS)
Gravity models
Gross leasable area (GLA)
High streets
Index of retail saturation (IRS)
Infrastructure
Metropolitan areas

Micropolitan areas
Outparcels
Percentage rent
Polygon method
Power node
Primary data
Primary trading area
Real estate investment trust (REIT)
Retail saturation
Ring analysis
Sales potential
Secondary data
Secondary trading area
Spatial analysis
String streets
Tertiary trading area
Trading area
Triple net

Questions for Review and Discussion

1. How do infrastructure, placement, and visibility affect retail site selection decisions?
2. Define the terms primary trading area, secondary trading area, and tertiary trading area. How is sales potential calculated for a trading area?
3. How do retailers use geographic information systems during the site evaluation process?
4. What are the advantages and disadvantages of a central business district as a retail location?
5. What types of retailers prefer a freestanding location? Why?

6. Why are some retail companies aggressively seeking nontraditional locations such as airports and tourist areas? Why are some sites better able to attract international customers?

7. If you were going to open a store, would you choose to own or lease? Justify your decision.

8. How is a typical retail lease calculated? What additional costs are usually included?

9. What trends in leasing and property development are retailers embracing as they ride out the recession and plan for economic recovery?

10. What is the purpose of a REIT? What function do REITs serve in retail business development?

Endnotes

1. Tony Hernandez and David Bennison, "The Art and Science of Retail Location Decisions," *International Journal of Retail and Distribution Management* 28 (2000): 360.

2. Ibid.

3. William J. Reill,.*Methods for the Study of Retail Relationships*, Monograph Number 4, (Austin: University of Texas Press,1929), 16.

4. "Prizm Social Groups," in *SRDS LMAA: PRIZM Social and Lifestage Groups*, The Nielsen Company, 2011, www.srds.com. (Also available at: www.my bestsegments.com.)

5. Terry Muñoz and Mike Mancini, "Finding Growth in Challenging Times," *Research Review* 16 (2002): 4.

6. Ibid, 8.

7. Ibid, 9.

8. "2011 Global Rankings Top 20 Cities," in *How Global is the Business of Retail?* CB Richard Ellis, 2011 6, www.cbre.com.

9. Brent Roderick, "Discover Retail Opportunities with ESRI's Retail MarketPlace Data," ESRI. www.esri.com/news/arcwatch/0809/retail-marketplace-data.html.

10. Maurice Yeates, "Big-Boxes, Power Centers, and Power Nodes," in The GTA @Y2K The Dynamics of Change in the Commercial Structure of the Greater Toronto Area, Chapter 4 (Toronto: Centre for the Study of Commercial Activity, 1999), 45.

11. John Holusha. "Kmart Coming to Manhattan with 34th Street Store." *New York Times.* Archives. August 25, 1996. pp. 1–2. www.nytimes.com/1996/08/25/realestate/kmart-coming-to-manhattan-with-34th-street-store.

12. Laura Heller. "Target Takes Manhattan, Chicago and Malvern, Penn." July 23, 2010. Aol Original. www.dailyfinance.com/2010/07/23/target-takes-manhattan-chicago-and-malvern-penna/.

13. Nancy Scola. "Inside Walmart's Slow, Quiet Campaign to Crack New York City." April 25, 2012. pp. 1, 4. Capital New York. www.capitalnewyork.com/article/culture/2012/04/5773123/inside-walmarts-slow-quiet-campaign-crack-new-york-city.

14. Marie Cunningham, "Rodeo Drive is Named One of 'America's Best Shopping Streets,'" *Beverly Hills Patch.* December 2, 2011, http://beverlyhills.patch/articles/rodeo-drive-is-named-one-of-america-s-best-shopping-streets.

15. "Top Retail Districts Show Strength in First Half," *Los Angeles Times*, August 24, 2011, http://latimesblogs.latimes.com/money_co/2011/08/top-retail-districts-show-strength-in-first-half.html.

16. Greg Lindsay, Cities of the Sky," *Wall Street Journal*, February 26-27, 2011, C1–C2.

17. Aaron O. Patrick, "Mass of Messages Lands at Heathrow," *Wall Street Journal*, February 15, 2008, B3.

18. Heathrow Airport Shopping, "A List of All Shopping Stores at Heathrow," Heathrow Terminal Five Shops. accessed 2011, www.holidayextras.com.

19. Janet Jones Kendall, "Airports New Retail Concepts Taking Off," *Atlanta Business Chronicle*, February 25, 2011, www.bizjournals.com/atlanta/print-edition/2011/02/25/airports-new-retail-concepts-taking-off.html.

20. Anne Riley-Katz and Rachel Brown, "Fear and Closings: Once-Booming Vegas Hits Economic Wall," *Women's Wear Daily*, April 1, 2009, 12.

21. Max Colchester, "Club Med Looks for Balance," *Wall Street Journal*, December 8, 2008, B8.

22. John Donnellan, "Hospital Gift Shops as Retail Enterprises," Paper presentation, American Collegiate Retailing Association, Spring Conference, Washington, D.C., April 1998.

23. "The Price is Right," *Women's Wear Daily*. June 25, 2009, 11. (Source: Real Estate Board of New York's Spring 2009 Report.)

24. "Did You Know? Facts Sheet," and "The Shopping Center Industry-National Impact," in *2011 Economic Impact of Shopping Centers*, International Council of Shopping Centers (ICSC), accessed May 12, 2011, www.icsc.org.

25. Ben Berkowitz, "U.S. Retail Vacancies Stuck at 20-Year Highs," *Reuters*. January 9, 2012, http://uk.reuters.com/assets/print?aid-UKL1E8C6A8820120109.

26. Kris Hudson, "For Malls, Occupancy Firms Up," *Wall Street Journal*, January 9, 2012, B1, B2.

27. Elaine Misonzhnik, "Store Closings Likely to top 5,000 in 2012," *Retail Traffic*, November 10, 2011, www
.printthis.clickability.com/pt/cpt?expire=&title=Store+Closings+Likely+to+Top+5000+in+2012.

28. "10 Ideas for Filling Vacant Borders Stores," *Retail Traffic*, January 4, 2012, http://retailtrafficmag.com/
retailing/expansionplans/10_ideas_for_Filling_vacant_borders_stores.

29. Lawrence C. Gottlieb, Michael Klein, and Ronald R. Sussman, "BAPCPA's Effects on Retail Chapter 11s
Are Profound," Turnaround Management Association, February 19, 2009, www.turnaround.org/Publications/
Articles.aspx?objectID=10643.

30. Paul Ziobro, "Expanding Eateries Target Shuttered Sites," *Wall Street Journal*, March 31, 2009, B1.

31. Kris Hudson, "Ownership Rises to 96% Of King of Prussia Mall," *Wall Street Journal*, September 15, 2011, D5.

32. Kris Hudson, "General Growth Starts Year With a Gamble," *Wall Street Journal*, January 4, 2012, C9.

33. Ilaina Jonas, "Update 2-General Growth CEO Maps Out Recovery Plan," *Reuters*, March 1, 2011, www
.reuters.com/assets/print?aid=USN0111822820110301.

34. "Developers Diversified Completes $123 Million of Strategic Transactions in the First Quarter of 2011,"
DDR Corp., March 31, 2011, http://ir.ddr.com/releasedetail.cfm?ReleaseID=561047.

Chapter 10

Shopping Centers and Malls

Learning Objectives
After completing this chapter you should be able to:
- Describe the basic types of shopping centers.
- Discuss several trends in shopping center development.
- List several examples of centers that provide experiential retailing and acknowledge why they are successful.
- Document how older malls are adjusting to competition from newer facilities.
- Explain how developers work with their management teams to achieve profitability.

Figure 10.1
The Dubai Mall is the largest mall in the world— for the moment. It is located in Downtown Burj Dubai (UAE), a neighborhood described as the "new heart of the city."

The type of retail site that has had the most impact on the way we live is the shopping center. There we look for entertainment, socialization, exercise, education, and fast or fine dining in addition to sartorial sustenance—better known as retail therapy.

Shopping center construction slowed in the early 1990s and has continued on a downward trajectory, reflecting changes in the retail environment mentioned throughout this text. The economic slowdown that began in late 2007 placed constraints on mall development as customers became scarce and many retailers struggled to survive. There were 107,833 shopping centers of all sizes in the United States in 2011—a number that has remained fairly constant since 2009. California has more than 14,000, the most of any state.[1]

In early 2012, there were 2,972 Canadian shopping centers, with at least 25,000 square feet of gross leasable area. Ontario claims 1,251 of them, the most of any Canadian province.[2] In Europe, there are in excess of 5,000 shopping centers. The countries earmarked in 2011 as having the highest growth potential of their prime properties were Sweden, France, and Finland.[3]

Trends in mall development parallel the turmoil in the economy, the changing sentiments of customers, the need to revitalize older sites, and the effects of retail saturation. In some instances, new construction is replacing outdated malls. In others, older structures are being converted to new retail formats. Malls that offer experiential retailing have proliferated as developers recognize customers' desires to play as well as shop. Outlet centers remain important as people continue to seek more for their money. Many developers combine trends to create hybrid malls.

Major shopping center developers are committed to building brand awareness of their properties through new products and services directed to customers. These and other contemporary issues are explained in this chapter.

Classification of Shopping Centers and Malls

The first wave of shopping centers consisted of groups of freestanding stores in suburban locations where ample free parking was available. A **shopping center** is "a group of retail and other commercial establishments that is planned, developed, owned, and managed as a single property." A central roof—like that seen in some contemporary shopping malls—did not cover early shopping centers. A **mall** is "a climate-controlled structure in which retail stores are architecturally connected."[4] Shopping malls are planned for maximum accessibility, designed either horizontally or vertically, and positioned above or below the ground. If not enclosed and climate-controlled, a shopping venue is a shopping center, not a mall. However, the terms are often used interchangeably.

Shopping centers are described by concept, size, trading area, presence and type of anchor stores, and tenant mix. This section contrasts basic types of shopping centers, and considers trends and changes in the basic formats, including hybrid developments. A **hybrid center** is a shopping area of mixed composition that combines the qualities of two or more basic shopping center configurations with contemporary additions. The evolution of the shopping center format is no more complete than that of store, nonstore, and online forms of retailing.

Shopping Center Types

Several basic types of shopping centers, categorized as "open-air centers" or "malls" by the International Council of Shopping Centers (ICSC), are differentiated in the next few pages.[5]

Open-Air Centers

Many shopping centers, whether large or small, bear the distinction of operating in the great outdoors. Smaller strip/convenience centers and neighborhood configurations are included in this category. Larger community, theme/festival, lifestyle, power, and outlet centers also operate in the open air.

Strip/Convenience Center   Strip centers are constructed on main roads that carry substantial traffic in predominantly residential areas. A **strip center** is "an attached row of stores or service outlets managed as a coherent retail entity."[6] Main tenants are usually small supermarkets, drugstores, or convenience stores positioned next to five to ten other small retailers. Strip centers are configured in straight line, "L," or "U" shapes. Often they are anchorless and the trading radius is only about a mile.

Neighborhood Center   A convenience center, usually with a supermarket anchor, that occupies 30,000 to 150,000 square feet of gross leasable area (GLA) is called a **neighborhood center**. Usually development of neighborhood centers follows upturns in the housing market. New apartment complexes or a rise in single-family homes within a 3-mile radius mean new opportunities for food and convenience retailers. Figure 10.2 shows a neighborhood center in Florida with an atypical roof design.

Community Center   A neighborhood center that has been expanded to serve people in a three- to six-mile radius is called a **community center**. It requires 100,000–350,000 square feet of GLA and is anchored by large tenants such as supermarkets or discounters, or both, as well as a greater emphasis on toys, books, electronics, apparel, and other soft-goods retailers. The trading area is slightly larger than that of a neighborhood center.

Theme/Festival Center   A shopping venue oriented toward entertainment as well as shopping is called a **theme/festival center**. Socializing and dining are key pursuits for people who frequent these centers, which are also called festival marketplaces. The first to launch the concept in 1976

Figure 10.2
The Pompano Shopping Center qualifies as a neighborhood mall, with Publix Supermarket as its anchor and approximately a dozen specialty stores, services, and restaurants. Its planet-like dome provides visibility and uniqueness.

was the Faneuil Hall/Quincy Market project in Boston, followed closely by Harborplace in Baltimore, Union Station in St. Louis, Bayside in Miami, and Riverwalk in New Orleans. Riverwalk was opened in 1986 and was damaged during Hurricane Katrina in 2005. The marketplace will be revitalized by the Howard Hughes Corp. and become the Outlet Collection at Riverwalk, with a reopening planned for 2013.[7] Most theme/festival centers are located in historic districts, near seaports, or in revived downtown areas that serve as destination spots for visitors. These centers require 80,000–250,000 square feet of GLA and have a trading area of 25–75 miles.

Lifestyle Center   A shopping center that focuses on a lifestyle cluster, upscale specialty merchandise, and food and entertainment in an outdoor setting is called a **lifestyle center**. Featuring a cadre of retailers, these centers are suited to high-traffic, bustling locations in urban or suburban areas. Lifestyle malls target upper-income people with refined fashion tastes, particular lifestyles, or those on vacation, to name only a few possibilities. Lifestyle centers require 150,000–500,000 square feet of GLA and may draw customers from a radius of 8–12 miles. Many have plazas, town squares, or other common spaces for customers to enjoy.

The Marina Village is a lifestyle center at the posh Atlantis resort on Paradise Island in the Bahamas. It features open spaces where entertainers perform and meandering walkways that encircle the marina, where luxury yachts are moored. Marketplace carts sell local crafts and sunglasses and brilliantly colored buildings house fine jewelry stores, apparel boutiques, an art gallery, and restaurants ranging from Johnny Rockets' family fare to ultra-pricy French cuisine. Figure 10.3 illustrates the quaint Bahamian-style retail stores, including a favorite U.S.-based ice cream company that has been owned since 2000 by Unilever Group, a British company.[8]

Power Center   A shopping center that has as many as seven anchor stores—usually discounters, warehouse clubs, or category killers—is known as a **power center**. Originating in the mid-1990s, power centers have 250,000–600,000 square feet of GLA. Although they resemble oversized strip malls or older regional malls, the similarity ends there. Category-dominant retailers like Best Buy or Home Depot and discount and off-price stores are familiar tenants. The trading radius for a power center is five to ten miles.

a

b

Figure 10.3
The Marina Village at Atlantis, in the Bahamas (a), encourages guests to enjoy the pace of shopping by providing lots of open and casual seating areas among its stores and restaurants, including Ben & Jerry's (b), in this upscale, tropical wonderland of a lifestyle center.

Outlet Center   The original intent of factory outlet stores (as a place for manufacturers to sell their excess stock) has been surpassed by today's outlet malls. A shopping center composed mainly of stores owned by manufacturers or retailers selling popular brands at a discount is called an **outlet center**. They range from 50,000 to 400,000 square feet of GLA and draw from the surrounding 25- to 75-mile area. Although manufacturers or their representatives still own the majority of stores in a factory outlet mall, customer focus and retail mix has changed radically.

Shopping Malls

Climate-controlled with lots of parking and many amenities, indoor shopping centers include regional and super regional malls.

Regional Mall   A center consisting of at least two anchor stores and 40–80 smaller stores serving a minimum of 100,000 people is called a **regional mall**. Major mall tenants occupying large, usually corner or end stores are called **anchor stores**. Regional malls require anywhere from 400,000–800,000 square feet of GLA and draw customers from a five- to 15-mile radius. Chain stores are well represented. Most malls are built by developers that lease stores to retailers, occasionally building out the peripheral areas with restaurants, big-box concepts, and entertainment or service businesses. The number and types of stores are controlled in order to limit competition within the shopping center.

Super Regional Mall   A shopping center consisting of three or more anchor stores and hundreds of specialty and service retailers, with more than 800,000 square feet of leasable area is called a **super regional mall**. It has more of everything that a regional mall has and frequently includes hotels, office buildings, and recreation centers. Discounters are also common sights in centers that may cover 120 acres. Super regional centers often serve a population of one million or more and draw from a radius of 5–15 miles. Draw is affected by competition in an area, as discussed in Chapter 9.

The next sections examine how these basic configurations have evolved into new breeds of shopping centers.

Trends in Shopping Centers and Malls

Outlet centers are in the throes of further evolution in the United States and other parts of the world. Demographics, lifestyles, and unifying themes set the tone for more lifestyle and specialty developments. The following discussion illuminates trends and diversity in specialty and outlet centers.

Focused Specialty Centers

Shopping centers are assuming a variety of different guises. Shopping centers with themes that are often theatrical or cultural bring new dimensions to specialty malls. These highly stylized centers share common characteristics although locations and architecture are quite diverse. The inspiration comes from foreign cities, ethnic groups, enlightened lifestyles, and historic buildings or places, to name only a few sources.

Venice in Vegas The Venetian Hotel in Las Vegas is home to The Grand Canal Shoppes. Top retailers and restaurants abound, but it is the experiential details that impress the public. When strolling the mall, it's not unusual to see a wedding in progress—perhaps on one of the bridges that pass for the Rialto. Outside cafés are replicated indoors, and designer names tempt you from every available nook. Figure 10.4 shows a gondola departing from a row of retail shops on the indoor canal.

Ethnicity Inspires The chief factor in the development of a mall in Koreatown, a part of Los Angeles, California, is the strong Asian demographic surrounding its location. Ma Dang the Courtyard, a 100,000-square-foot specialty mall, opened in June 2010. Designed in Seoul, South Korea, the stone structure features Korean-style architecture and symbolic Asian design. Its name, Ma Dang, means "courtyard" in Korean. Among the tenants are several Korean, Chinese, Japanese, Italian, and fusion restaurants; approximately 40 retail specialty stores; and a three-screen movie theater that can seat 650 people. The developer's intent is to draw Korean, other Asian, and American customers to its stores, food operations, and cultural activities.[9]

Figure 10.4
Is this location Venice, Italy or Las Vegas, Nevada? The Grand Canal Shoppes at the Venetian Hotel assemble many extra touches that make them a shoppertainment destination. Don't be surprised if there's a wedding in progress when you visit. Only in Vegas!

Lifestyle Magnets Several small strip centers and sections of the downtown area in Sedona, Arizona, attract customers interested in exploring their psychic selves. Many residents and visitors interested in spiritual renewal believe Sedona is home to vortexes of energy that emanate from the red rock geology. Retailers capitalize on this interest, selling books on meditation and self-study, crystals, new age music, and astrological artifacts. Visitors can have their auras cleansed or photographed, Tarot cards read, and futures told by individuals who provide these special services. Yoga and Reiki classes are readily available. Lifestyle and curiosity are the components that drive sales in these specialty centers.

Historic Buildings The Philadelphia Bourse, historically a financial and trade center in downtown Philly, is now the Bourse Food Court and Specialty Shops. The focus is on breakfast and lunch for local workers and tourists—especially history buffs, who can peruse old photographs of the building in its "before" stage. The Bourse interior is featured in Figure 10.5.

Market selectivity and unique merchandise describe specialty malls. It is not the intent of specialty centers to fill all customer needs as most regional malls attempt to do.

Outlet Centers Revitalize

The number of U.S. outlet malls began to decline in the mid-1990s. The drop in popularity was attributed to several factors. Customers had become more sophisticated and recognized good values when they found them. Not all merchandise in all outlet centers was significantly less expensive than that found in other retail centers. Competition had intensified across all retail formats and shopping centers. Subsequently, expansion of manufacturer's outlets diminished and companies were forced to close underperforming units during the economic crisis.

Countering this decline, top developers have opened successful upmarket outlet malls. And, compared with outlet malls in general, classic outlet villages have maintained their popularity over time. In difficult economic times, outlet centers tend to do better than mainstream retailers.

Did You Know?
U.S. developer Tanger Outlet Centers and its Canadian counterpart RioCan Real Estate Investment Trust are bringing more outlet centers to Canada. Their first task is to upgrade an existing outlet mall north of Toronto by doubling its size and bringing in more prestigious brands like Hilfiger and J. Crew in addition to Coach and Michael Kors, which are already ensconced. Long-range plans include developing an outlet mall network across Canada. The partnership also provides opportunities for U.S. retailers that are already in Canada to open discount divisions. (Source: Dana Flavelle, "U.S. Outlet Mall Operator Crosses Into Canada," *The Star,* November 21, 2011, www.thestar.com/printarticle/1090399.)

Outlet Malls Go Upscale   High-end retailers like Gucci, Saks Off 5th, Coach, Ferragamo, kate spade, Brooks Brothers, and Ralph Lauren are finding it pays to locate in upmarket discount malls. Many retailers have discarded antiquated assumptions that outlet malls are no more than places to move old stock. According to Steve Sadove, chairman and chief executive officer (CEO) of Saks Fifth Avenue, "Outlets have become more of a distribution channel than just a sell-off channel."[10] The realization that cash-cautious customers are just as brand-oriented as their upscale counterparts helps fuel the demand for high-end outlets.

Outlet Destination Centers   Outlet centers that thrive answer more consumer needs than simply thrift. Vacations once meant going to lakes, mountains, or the seashore. Now, getaway weekends spent at outlet malls vie with traditional leisure pursuits. Outlet stores in Freeport, Maine, are a destination for shoppers year-round. During the peak summer season, hotels within a 100-mile radius of Freeport often are booked. The once-quiet resort town, best known as the home of L.L. Bean, has become outlet city. Although development is monitored and most new stores fit the town's colonial flavor, Freeport's Main Street now evokes a much different image. What was once a typical small town center is now a succession of freestanding stores and strip malls, and development has spilled over to many of the side streets. Stately homes have become quick-service restaurants and the former library is now home to the Vermont Teddy Bear store. Though most businesses close at night, L.L. Bean remains open 24 hours a day. At 11:00 p.m. it still does a brisk trade. Not all local residents are happy about the changes, despite the increase in real estate values and jobs. Most leave the area on weekends to avoid the heavy traffic that now snakes through the town, which once housed shoe manufacturing and shipbuilding industries.

International Outlet Malls   Outlet mall developers and customers in other parts of the world also experience resistance to change. Japanese shoppers were much slower than U.S. consumers to embrace outlet malls. In the past, the Japanese taste for top-quality items and distaste for anything labeled "discount" precluded their acceptance of outlet stores. Times have changed along with the economy and customers. Simon Property Group has brought their trademarked concept of Premium Outlets to properties in 27 states in the U.S., Puerto Rico, as well as joint ventures in Malaysia, Mexico, South Korea, and Japan. The company has eight centers in Japan, as well as an interest in Kobe-Sanda Premium Outlets.[11] One of its outlet centers is featured in Figure 10.6.

Hybrid Shopping Centers
Many variations on basic types of shopping centers are evolving as lifestyles, business practices, competition, and economies change. Providing shopping experiences that satisfy several needs simultaneously is crucial to the success of newer formats. Mixed-use centers, vertical malls, and underground malls serve customers in a variety of locations worldwide. Discount malls cultivate customers who are price-conscious, huge shopping arenas draw the multitudes, and malls that focus on experiential retailing bring out the need for the hedonistic expression that exists in most of us.

Figure 10.6
Simon Property Group owns Premium Outlet Centers in the United States and international markets. The architecture in this high-end Japanese outlet center, Kobe-Sanda Premium Outlets, bespeaks wealth so shoppers will feel comfortable in an atmosphere that addresses their need for luxury while providing value.

Value Centers

The general construction slowdown in U.S. mall development greatly affected power centers. When companies like Steve and Barry's, Circuit City, and Linens & Things go out of business, voids are left. Value centers have evolved in an attempt to fill these gaps. A **value center** is a cross between a power center and an outlet mall. Discounters, warehouse clubs, category killers, and scores of factory outlet stores comprise the tenancy. Very often targeted to a tourist market, these centers need a concentration of about 1.5 million customers to be successful.

Megamalls

Although there are not many examples of true megamalls, those that exist are noteworthy. A **megamall** is a mall of well over 2 million square feet, drawing from a trading area of over 100 miles and, in some cases, several states or provinces. A megamall houses 500–800 stores, service businesses, restaurants, and entertainment facilities. Extensive acreage and tremendous draw is required, limiting the number of potential sites.

West Edmonton Mall in Alberta, Canada; Mall of America in Bloomington, Minnesota; Woodfield Shopping Center in Schaumburg, Illinois; and South Coast Plaza in Costa Mesa, California are examples. In terms of GLA, they are the four largest malls in North America, and they offer visitors a multitude of shopping and entertainment experiences:

- West Edmonton Mall has 5.3 million square feet of GLA and over 500 stores. Among its amenities, Edmonton has a five-acre water park, ice rink, 18-hole miniature golf courses, amusement park, and a casino. [12]
- Mall of America has 4.2 million square feet of GLA including retail and entertainment businesses: 520 stores, eight nightclubs, and 14 movie screens.[13] Mall of America also holds unique promotions like Multiple Matrimony, at which dozens of couples are married in the mall simultaneously.
- Woodfield Shopping Center has 2.7 million square feet of GLA and a plethora of shopping delights.
- South Coast Plaza, with 2.7 million square feet of GLA, boasts more upscale designer shops than most malls and considers its premises among the "most luxurious shopping destinations in California."[14]

Cyberscoop
At your leisure and with
your eyes wide open, visit
the Dubai Mall Web site
at www.thedubaimall.
com. Check out the global
retail tenants and the
glamour and glitz of the
neighborhood, next door
to the Burj Khalifa. At 2,717
feet, the Burj is the tallest
building in the world. For
now, that is: Saudi Arabia
has a 3,281-foot tower in
the works.
(Source: Summer Said, "Saudis
Plan World's Tallest Building,"
Wall Street Journal, August 3,
2011, C10. Statistics: Council
on Tall Buildings and Urban
Habitat.)

These malls are tourist destinations, not only for Americans but for travelers worldwide. But none qualifies as the largest in the world. That distinction belongs to the Dubai Mall, which opened in November 2008 in the UAE. Its 5.6 million square feet of retail space include 1,000 stores, 165 of which are new to the region. Bloomingdale's, representing the United States; Galeries Lafayette, the famous French department store; and the United Kingdom's Marks & Spencer and Debenhams share one of 10 mini-malls inside the gigantic building with other retailers. Another mini-mall houses the Gold Souk. The mall's Fashion Avenue has 440,000 square feet of luxury brands including Chanel, Calvin Klein, Gucci, Jean Paul Gaultier, and Roberto Cavalli. The Dubai Aquarium and Discovery Centre is prominently featured, as is an attached five-star hotel and an Olympic-sized ice rink—a major draw in this hot, arid nation.[15] The Dubai Mall is illustrated in Figure 10.1.

Megamalls have not yet been fully accepted in China, largely due to overdevelopment during the country's recent boom years coupled with less-than-expected enthusiasm on the part of Chinese consumers.

A **value megamall** is a large hybrid mall containing elements of power, value, and outlet centers, with added entertainment components. Value to customers is redefined by the intense retail mix in these centers, which range from one to two million square feet. National specialty chains and designer outlets may coexist with category killers, off-price stores, discounters, food, and entertainment retailers. More of everything appears to be the main theme. Value megamalls generate three times more volume than traditional malls.

This conglomeration of stores providing fun for all was the brainchild of Mills Corp., developer of outlet centers throughout the United States. At one time Mills owned 42 malls and took the concept global by opening value megamalls in Spain, Singapore, and Scotland. By 2005, however, the company was in financial trouble due to accounting issues, write-offs of ten projects, lawsuits, and overinvesting.[16]

Mills' involvement with what became the controversial Meadowlands Xanadu complex in New Jersey may also have precipitated the company's acquisition by Simon Property Group Inc. and Farallon Capital Management LLC in 2007.[17] Begun in 2004 and originally scheduled to open in 2008, the Xanadu project was beset with problems from the start. The economic downturn, tightening of capital markets, and partnership shuffles collectively forced a construction halt in early 2009.[18]

In May 2011, Triple Five, the owner of the Mall of America and West Edmonton Mall, took control of the empty complex. A name change, to American Dream @ The Meadowlands, paved the way for expansion and completion of the long-struggling complex. Triple Five intends to invest more money into the project, which has already absorbed $1.9 billion. New amenities will include a water park, ice rink, and more retail space. The Ghermezian family, who owns Triple Five, is confident that their investment will pay off.[19] Triple Five received a $700 million loan in 2012 to move forward with the project and take control of the site. The company anticipates securing another $1.7 million in financing to complete the project.[20] Considered a major coup for the developer, DreamWorks Animation SKG, Inc. is scheduled to open the first North American theme park at the complex in late 2013. Look for characters from *Shrek, Puss in Boots, How to Train Your Dragon,* and many more DreamWorks favorites.[21]

Mixed-Use Centers

A shopping center with two or more uses, such as an office building with a retail mall and residential areas, is called a **mixed-use center**. Many of these centers include a combination of shopping, living, working, transportation, and entertainment facilities. Some started as regional centers and grew by adding services and facilities. Mixed-use centers may locate in renovated public buildings or develop separate, totally planned communities.

Union Station, a landmark mixed-use complex, is featured in Figure 10.7. It houses the Amtrak terminal for Washington, D.C., a theater complex, several restaurants and cafes, a huge food court, and 160,000 square feet of retail space. The restored Beaux Arts décor made Union Station the perfect setting for two Presidential Inaugural Balls in the 1990s.[22]

Val d'Europe, a short train ride from Paris, is an example of a planned community. Shopping areas are open, living space is in use, and industrial space has been developed, but Euro Disney

Figure 10.7
Union Station in Washington, D.C., is the epitome of a mixed-use center. Travelers can purchase their Amtrak tickets, then enjoy shopping and dining while waiting for their trains. Both locals and tourists find sustenance at the large food court on the lower level.

estimates that the town will not be complete until 2030.[23] As of 2005, about 20,000 residents of a planned 50,000 called the development home. Buses and trains convey customers among the theme park, hotels, residences, and shopping centers; and Disneyland Paris is one train stop away. Val d'Europe village has 130 shops and a food court, as well as a Sea Life Aquarium that draws visitors. Nearby is an Auchan hypermarket and a discount mall. Nostalgia buffs will appreciate the buildings, which resemble 19th-century Parisian architecture.[24]

Vertical Malls

A shopping center in a high-rise building, usually in an urban location, is called a **vertical mall**. Renovation of downtown areas, scarcity of land, and concentration of customers in urban areas paved the way for vertical malls. Water Tower Place in Chicago, the Nordstrom-anchored San Francisco Centre, the Manhattan Mall in New York City, and Les Ailes du Mode in Montreal are examples of vertical malls.

The benefits of high-traffic, urban locations do not exempt vertical malls from problems. The evolution of one vertical mall provides a useful case history. Merger and acquisition activity in the 1990s spurred changes at the eight-story Manhattan Mall on 6th Avenue between 32nd and 33rd Streets in New York City. The home of Gimbel's Department Store from 1910 to 1986, the center was originally called A&S Plaza when it opened in the late 1980s. Abraham and Straus (A&S) department store, the first anchor tenant, evolved into Stern's after Macy's and A&S merged in 1995. That same year, the space was renamed Manhattan Mall. Poor performance necessitated the closing of this and other Stern's stores in 2001.[25] Several plans under consideration at that time included transforming the vacated space into smaller specialty store units or leasing the space to a big-box store and other smaller retailers.

Owned by Vornado Realty Trust since 2006, the center is now a 14-story atrium-style mall with an eclectic tenant mix. From Express and Charlotte Russe to Top Gun Leather Clothing and Hype Outfitters, there is much to attract trendy shoppers. There is even a Kitty Kastle that carries Hello Kitty products and a Starbucks in the food court on the top floor.[26] In 2009, JCPenney made a rare urban appearance when it opened on two floors of the Manhattan Mall. Penney's had operated stores in New York City for 75 of its 107 years in business, but had not done so

Cyberscoop
Next time you're flying to Paris or are on any long flights, bring your iPad and shop in the air. SkyMall is granting free access to www.SkyMall.com on WiFi-equipped planes. Don't get too carried away—currency conversion rates are higher in flight. For now, just visit the site and see how far Sky Mall has come since offering its first in-flight catalog.
(Source: "Internet Retailer 2012 Hot 100 Web Sites (Specialty/Non-Apparel)," *IRNewslink*, December 1, 2011, 7.)

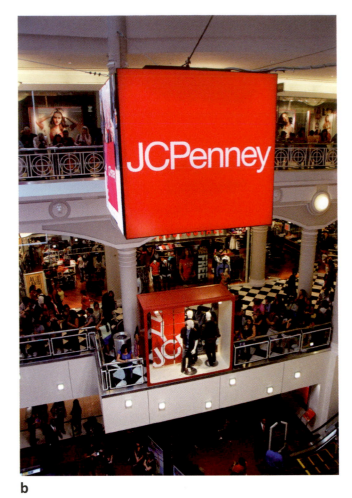

a

b

Figure 10.8
The Manhattan Mall (a) has a rich history. In the 1980s it was called the A&S Plaza when the famous department store was the anchor tenant. In the 1990s, the business climate precipitated change. Stern's became the principal department store when A&S and Macy's merged. After a decade in which specialty stores dominated the space, JCPenney opened on the main level, bringing the department store format back to the building in 2009 (b).

recently.[27] And so the saga continues. The structure as it appeared in the atrium and current anchor of JCPenney is shown in Figure 10.8.

Where department stores have retrenched, vertical malls have blossomed, bringing a fresh approach to urban retailing. Despite the high costs of real estate in select urban areas, most vertical malls appear to withstand the test of time.

Underground Malls

As noted in Chapter 9, some shopping centers bear the distinction of being located underground. Although such malls originated in cities such as Montreal and Toronto, where long, cold winters curtailed trade, there are other reasons for their existence. Shopping malls make sense at underground transportation stops. In several cities worldwide, malls make shopping more convenient for subway commuters. Lack of available land and congested shopping areas also precipitate underground developments.

Crystal City Mall This complex and underground center in Arlington, Virginia, is a place where, in theory, people need never feel the rays of the sun. Residents, many of whom are government employees, live in high-rise apartment buildings and might take an elevator to the lower level in the morning, stop in the underground mall for breakfast, and scurry to work in other skyscrapers via several underground concourses. After work, they can spend more time in the Crystal City

Shopping Arcade, do grocery shopping, stop at the dry cleaners, and have dinner before returning to their dwellings. This lifestyle may be extreme for some tastes, but it is possible in this mixed-use center. There are now street-side restaurants and shops in the promenade section, and the entire area continues to undergo vast urban planning and development.

Le Carrousels du Louvre   Tourists can't help noticing this mall on the Rue de Rivoli, under the famous Louvre museum in Paris. Museum exits funnel patrons right into the shopping arcade. Tenants include Sephora, Esprit, Lalique, Hertz Car Rental, Apple, and a gourmet food court. The mall supports local and international retailers, not simply museum-sponsored gift shops, as is common in other museums.

Chelsea Market   Located in New York City's meatpacking district, the Chelsea Market is also partly subterranean. As seen in Figure 10.9, the mall is carved out of old factory buildings and presently serves as both wholesale and retail headquarters for many vendors. The meatpacking district is becoming a retail hot spot in New York City, as hipster and designer boutiques, as well as restaurants, move into the neighborhood.

Climate, limited space in large cities, and conservation and preservation issues in others have brought shopping centers underground around the world. The move has not darkened the enthusiasm of customers.

Experiential Retailing Influences Malls

Malls that appeal to multiple senses and needs are present throughout the world. Some shopping enthusiasts and retailers use the term *shoppertainment* to describe a type of experiential retailing that was introduced earlier in Chapter 3. (The term is attributed to Larry Siegel.) **Shoppertainment** occurs when retail shopping is combined with many forms of entertainment in stores and malls. Centers are designed to amuse customers, encourage longer stays, present new activities, and—almost as an afterthought—generate retail sales. They encourage the total retail experience. Several examples illustrate how developers are addressing the experiential needs of growing numbers of people. In the first example, notice how the purpose of the Metreon changed with time and customer preferences.

The Metreon   Sony opened its Metreon, billed as "an entertainment megaplex," in San Francisco in 1999. The 360,000-square-foot extravaganza encompasses an entire city block and houses the AMC

Figure 10.9
You'll find Chelsea Market in the lower level of a former factory in New York City's meatpacking district. Visitors can buy fresh foods, bakery goods, freshly butchered meat, and a seasonal pumpkin or two at this site, which is designed to serve both wholesale buyers and retail shoppers.

Theater and IMAX; restaurants, amusements, and retail stores round out the tenant mix. Microsoft's first retail unit was located in the Metreon, along with Sony's PlayStation video game venture.[28] Online competition was a key factor in the decision of Sony and others to create huge experiential retailing complexes. However, times change. The Metreon itself did not succeed in the marketplace. Some analysts believed the complex was only built as a theme park for the Sony brand.

In 2006, the property was sold to Westfield Group and Forest City Enterprises, which planned to reimage the site as a restaurant and community-oriented center. The companies' redevelopment plan was approved by the city, and the first restaurants were recruited, including Buckhorn Grill and Jillian's. The original four-story mall was sold, but the developers retained the profitable cinema complex and TILT Arcade. The flagship PlayStation space and the Sony store closed, and some retail shops and restaurants opened on the ground level.[29]

Revamping continued in 2011 when Mayor Edwin M. Lee, together with Westfield Group (which bought out Forest City's share in 2010) and Target, broke ground on an 85,000-square-foot CityTarget store, scheduled to open in late 2012. The store is located on the second level and will be accessible through a two-story glass entrance that engineers the flow of customers directly up to CityTarget. Also included in the renovation is a 470-seat dining terrace and a new retail and food service promenade on the first floor. Among the retail and restaurant tenants are La Boulange Bakery, Massage Envy, Chipotle, and Chronicle Books. Major improvements to the AMC Theaters and IMAX on the third floor, and the City View event center on the fourth floor round out the latest phase of development.[30] In another turn of events, Starwood Capital will buy a 90 percent share of seven U.S. malls from Westfield Group in 2012. The transaction includes the Metreon Mall project.[31] As one era ends, another begins, exemplifying the cycle of retail development.

Carnaby Street Tucked behind the famous department store Liberty of London, and running parallel to Regent Street in London is Carnaby Street. Only a few blocks long, it has served as a gathering spot for young locals and tourists for decades. In the 1960s, it was considered the heart of the Mod movement. Since then, its popularity and retail tenants have waned, but the echo of a time when risk was rewarded survives. The area was reclaimed in the 1980s and once again has recharged itself during this century, attracting many familiar and eclectic retailers.

Despite worldwide economic doldrums, sales in the Carnaby Street area have been strong. The locals attribute this in part to the influx of denim and streetwear retailers from all over the globe, and the expansion of the retail concept to the many side streets in the area.

Italy's Diesel, Japan's Muji, Hilfiger Denim, Boss Orange, and Levi's are well-known global retailers on Carnaby. The Swedish brands Monki and Cheap Monday, both owned by H&M, draw a youthful target market.[32] Carnaby Street is a place to see and be seen—if you're young, hip, and perhaps a bit quirky. That's how it is and has always been.

Lotte World The largest multiuse shopping center in Korea includes an amusement park, global as well as local retailers, and an ice rink. The upscale Lotte World center in Seoul is so large that during New Year celebrations a parade is held indoors, featuring traditional floats and people dressed in folkloric Korean apparel. The company operates department stores, hypermarkets, supermarkets, and convenience stores as part of the Lotte Shopping division that generated $23 billion in 2012 and projected revenue of $35 billion by 2014.[33]

Whatever the setting, entertainment is an important concept in mall retailing. The need to experience the environment, relax, and have fun may be as strong as the need to acquire material goods. When developers acknowledge these human needs and respond creatively, the result is sales and profits.

Shopping Center Challenges and Strategies

When slick new centers enter established trading areas, competition flares. Some centers built in the late 1960s and early 1970s aged gracefully, others did not. Retailers and shopping center management were challenged to devise new strategies, including renovation and reimaging. Customer fascination with old-fashioned lifestyles and downtowns sparked another direction for tired malls and undeveloped areas. Another technique used by retailers and developers as they adjust to pressures in the marketplace involves breaking up older malls into freestanding or other configurations. Adaptive renewal is the theme.

Town Center Development

New open-air shopping centers, or renovated old ones, are being developed as town centers. **Town centers** are retail urban villages located outdoors and consisting of buildings with nostalgic architectural features or theme designs. Sometimes older malls are converted to open-air centers. In other instances brand-new malls are constructed. Unlike a lifestyle center, a town center has a residential component as well as business services.

The Easton Town Center on the outskirts of Columbus, Ohio, is an example of a town center project that was developed from scratch. On land owned by Limited Brands, the complex covers more than 150 acres and is a tribute to the ingenuity of Leslie Wexner, CEO of Limited Brands, and Steiner Company, the developer. Strolling the traffic-controlled streets of the downtown center may give visitors the impression of being on a film set because it evokes a near-perfect community. Easton Center capitalizes on this perfection in a customer-friendly, enticing way. Retailers include a variety of restaurants such as Cheesecake Factory and upmarket home décor stores like Restoration Hardware. Store façades are reminiscent of those in older downtowns—with the exception of a few superstores like Barnes & Noble. During later phases of development, residential areas and a fashion mall anchored by Nordstrom were added.

Other luxury brands, including Burberry, Coach, Tiffany and Co., and Henri Bendel, were joined in the North District by Sephora and Michael Kors in 2012.[34] The award-winning Easton Town Center received recognition for design and development by the ICSC in 2000. It was named one of the "five most innovative malls in the world" in 2011 by a prominent trade publication.[35]

Complexes like these rely heavily on architectural details to convey the village image. Walkways are often paved with cobblestones to capture a vintage spirit. Building materials are carefully chosen to reflect the theme. Developers direct their efforts toward customers who are bored by the sameness syndrome that often besets traditional shopping centers. Projects of this magnitude must achieve critical mass so that consumers instinctively consider town centers their first choices when selecting shopping venues.

Lifestyle Center Growth

Less dependent on nostalgic downtown themes than town centers, lifestyle centers are becoming destinations of choice for retailers and consumers in the 21st century. Designed for easy access, convenience, and the ultimate in ambiance and abundance, these centers primarily serve active, young, affluent families. Retailers such as Williams-Sonoma, Pottery Barn, Ulta, Ecco, Anthropologie, Urban Outfitters, lululemon, and Abercrombie & Fitch—as well as department stores, high-end children's stores, and service and entertainment businesses—comprise the tenant mix.

There are over 400 lifestyle malls in the United States.[36] Some have already enlarged and updated their facilities in order to keep pace with their customers and the competition.

Demalling

The term *malling* is used to describe the expansion of the shopping center movement. Now demalling is finding its voice in mall development. **Demalling** occurs when older enclosed malls are broken up into open-concept clusters of stores and other multiuse construction. Circumstances— usually aging—occasionally warrant the conversion of enclosed mall space to open-concept shopping centers. The following examples illustrate this point.

The Cottonwood Mall, a traditional enclosed mall near Salt Lake City, Utah, was demalled in 2008, supposedly to be remalled in 2010. The plan was to add offices and residential units, providing a mixed-use format that would offer the requisite shops, cafés, and restaurants, a cinema, condos, cottages, and single-family homes. Plenty of room for streets, walking trails, and a public plaza was anticipated.[37]

However, by 2011 the 57-acre site remained near-vacant. The only notable exception was the presence of Macy's department store. The troubled economic times had claimed yet another victim. General Growth Properties, then-owner of the property, staved off bankruptcy and split the development company into two separate units. The spin-off, Howard Hughes Corp., is preparing the site and soliciting tenants with an anticipated completion date of 2014 for the first phase and 2015 for the second. After a three-year delay, all parties involved were cautiously optimistic about the future of Cottonwood.[38]

Demalling serves a valuable purpose in shopping center growth and redevelopment. However, some early outdoor centers have withstood several cycles of development as they morphed from clusters of stores to enclosed malls and back again to a collection of freestanding big-box stores. Concepts are rarely finite.

Expansion

While some centers are contracting or reconfiguring, others are expanding. Some add new levels and extended parking while others construct entire wings designed to reach new markets.

The Somerset Collection—once too luxurious to be called a mere mall—is located in Troy, Michigan. In the early 1990s, the atmosphere was cultivated and quiet, with not a McDonald's in sight. The elite market segment was shrinking, however, and new tactics had to be implemented.

To reach an expanded market, the center added a new wing in the mid-1990s. In addition to Saks and Neiman Marcus, Macy's and Nordstrom now anchor the 1.5-million-square-foot center. Although still upscale by most standards, the expanded center includes newer specialty retailers that appeal to a broader cross-section of customers. Adding logistical interest, the center's new section is connected to the old by a 700-foot-long enclosed moving skywalk that spans a major highway.[39]

Although the mall movement moved later and more slowly to other areas of the globe, many early centers also are ripe for renovation. Expansion works best when centers are ripe for renovation due to age, when increased competition tips the balance, or when new viable markets initiate change.

Spatial Reconfiguration

Another area of mall development that is receiving attention is the layout and tenant allocation within centers. Faced with changing customer expectations and increasing competition, including the threat of online shopping, mall owners are reconsidering layout strategy. When Borders exited a shopping center on the outskirts of Boston, the developer turned it into a free community ice skating pavilion called "Freeskate at Mansfield Crossing" in 2012. Repurposing a mall is another tactic used to fill vacated retail space in a positive way.[40] Some malls position competing stores in clusters rather than interspersing them throughout the mall, previously a common tactic. The rationale behind this shift is customer-driven. Many shoppers requested that malls situate all stores that carry children's products in the same general area, making it more convenient for parents and children. Some centers are catering to department store customers by positioning anchors in close proximity to each other. Other developers that were holdouts in encouraging discounters now welcome stores such as Target as anchors.

Lot 10, a shopping center in Kuala Lumpur, Malaysia, blends East and West by offering brands with global flair. The Japanese-owned mall is anchored by the Isetan department store. When the mall first opened in the 1980s, it adopted an unusual pricing policy. Retailers carrying lower-priced merchandise were located on the bottom floors—with food products on the basement level—and as customers rode up the escalators, prices got steeper, too. Designers including Hugo Boss and Armani were located on the top floor; Benetton was near the middle.

As competition became more intense in the mid-1990s, mall officials reconfigured the space, inviting more moderately priced retailers to lease space. Many more services such as beauty spas and hair salons were added. Although the emphasis on high-priced designers may have been minimized, the emphasis on fashion was not. Lot 10 has six levels of stores and services and is located in the Bintang Walk shopping and entertainment district. Today the British department store Debenhams, along with Body Shop, Ed Hardy, Zara, Timberland, Haagen Daz, and a National Geographic store, share space with myriad Asian brands including the designer Zang Toi.[41] Fortunately, the Delifrance café was spared, as it is a perfect people-watching spot. Lot 10 on Jalan Sultan Ismail is illustrated in Figure 10.10.

Strategies used by developers to extend the lives of malls are both innovative and discordant. In one setting, the outdoors is moved inside to create a new reality. In other circumstances, the outside shopping experience popular on the main streets of days past is revived. In some centers, major renovation efforts are needed to keep up with burgeoning populations. The contrast in approaches indicates the complexity of shopping center development, the need to carefully interpret customer demand, and the ingenuity of those dedicated to building profitable businesses.

Figure 10.10
Lot 10, an urban vertical mall in the heart of Kuala Lumpur, Malaysia, has reflected evolving visions of the mall since its inception in the 1980s. The mixture of stores presently reaches out to local retailers and designers, as well as global brands. This view shows Debenhams, a branch of the well-known London department store.

Shopping Center Management Trends

Mall management involves much more than collecting rents and seeing that the mall opens on time. Professionalism sets the tone for the shopping center industry as management assumes responsibility for marketing and productivity as well as operations. Developers and owners are increasingly concerned about brand equity and are promoting their names at every opportunity. These and many other issues affect shopping center operations. The top 10 owners of retail real estate are listed in Table 10.1.

Table 10.1   Top 10 Retail Property Owners in United States

Rank	Company	Headquarters	U.S. Properties	International Properties
1	Simon Property Group	Indianapolis, IN	338	65
2	General Growth Properties	Chicago, IL	195	–
3	Developers Diversified Realty	Beachwood, OH	525	24
4	Kimco Realty	New Hyde Park, NY	816	942
5	Centro Properties Group*	New York, NY	588	–
6	The Inland Real Estate Group of Cos.	Oak Brook, IL	1,308	–
7	CBL & Associates Properties	Chattanooga, TN	148	–
8	Macerich[†]	Santa Monica, CA	65	–
9	Westfield[‡]	Los Angeles, CA	55	64
10	Weingarten Reality	Houston TX	312	–

Source: Excerpted from "2011 Top Owners (1 through 10)," Retail Traffic, May 11, 2011, http://retailtrafficmag.com/research/rankings/2011_top_owners_1_10_05112011. Ownership status as of December 31, 2010, unless otherwise noted.

*Private equity firm Blackstone Group acquired Centro's U.S. properties in March 2011; Centro Properties Group's home office is in Australia (Reuters, March 1, 2011).

[†]Properties updated January 31, 2012 (www.macerich.com).

[‡]Westfield's home office is in Australia; its U.S. division is based in Los Angeles.

Stronger Marketing Orientation

On behalf of the owners, one of mall management's chief responsibilities is to plan and implement projects to increase their tenants' sales. Motivation is strong because profit for the mall is made on percentage rent, not on base rent. Therefore, if stores do well, the mall does well.

Mall marketing 20 years ago meant simply having a craft, car, or fashion show. Now the focus is on stronger promotions that involve most merchants and show measurable sales results. Mall loyalty programs, one-day sales, bonus bucks, birthday clubs, community-partnered programs and those that target specific lifestyle clusters are more effective.

Mall management maintains good relations with anchor stores but is not as involved in their marketing efforts, working more directly with individual line stores. Mall managers receive weekly sales reports and can help retailers tailor promotions to help increase sales. Most malls offer customer service and sales training for store staffs. Adept at visual merchandising and other sales promotion strategies, mall management can also offer assistance in these areas.

Promoting Malls as Brands

As consolidation in the industry intensifies, developers are concerned with positioning their shopping centers competitively. Like many retailers, major mall developers are establishing their companies as brands. Some are undertaking promotional campaigns to make their ownership status more visible to customers. Prime and Tanger outlet malls feature their logos prominently on all properties in tandem with the mall's local name. Mall management is responsible for implementing programs that edify the differential advantage of each center. Prime Outlets has been owned by Simon Property Group since 2010. Simon formed a partnership with its rival, Tanger Factory Outlet Centers, to build a center in Texas for a scheduled 2012 opening.[42] It appears the brands are merging as they work in tandem.

Simon Property Group believes that customers want to know who owns the shopping centers that they patronize. The company embarked on a nationwide campaign to promote the Simon name as a brand a decade ago. Using television and radio commercials, parking lot signs, new lettering on doors, and posters in its malls, the Simon brand was brandished wherever customers gathered.

The Forbes Companies, a real estate development company, relies on a formula when beginning a mall development project. Nathan Forbes, the company's managing partner, believes these guidelines encourage good branding:

- When acquiring a department store anchor, at least one of the anchors should be new to the geographic area.
- 40 percent of small specialty store tenants must be exclusive to the immediate marketplace.
- Restaurants are expected to be national chains with sit-down formats and different food themes and menus.
- The mall must be clutter-free and unique, and the architecture impressive.[43]

Forbes also prefers no kiosks or marketplace carts in his malls, nor does he offer temporary leasing. He believes the focus should be on the stores.

These examples show the extent to which mall owners are promoting their brands, which also benefits the retailers that do business in their centers. Whether customers care if their favorite shopping center bears a developer's brand name is inconclusive. It may hold true that location, tenant mix, experiential opportunities, customer value, and need satisfaction remain the chief factors for selecting a mall.

Coping With Lost Revenue

During the recession, occupied retail space dwindled as companies curtailed expansion plans, went out of business, or made business decisions to close some of their stores or shrink the square footage they occupied. Vacancy at shopping centers in the United States averaged 11 percent by the fourth quarter of 2011.[44] Nearly 3,300 store closings took place in 2011 due to strategic initiatives such as downsizing or liquidating the business and approximately the same amount was expected in 2012.[45] Although landlords reported that retail leasing conditions were improving, in the first half of 2012, store closings increased by 34 percent over the same time period in

Did You Know?
In the category of offbeat news: Hungary has temporarily banned shopping malls. The government halted construction of centers larger than 300 square meters in order to protect smaller businesses, which make up 99 percent of all retail enterprises but earn only 31 percent of revenues. That means large, often international, corporations receive 69 percent of retail turnover and account for only 1 percent of all retail businesses. What are the pros and cons of this decision?
(Source: "Hungary Bans New Shopping Malls," *Wall Street Journal*, November 11, 2011, http://blogs.wsj.com/emergingeurope/2011/11/11/hungary-bans-new-shopping-malls/tab/print.)

2011. Many of the closures were a result of positive paring-down of unprofitable units, others from online competition, some as necessary strategic moves, and a few from bankruptcy filings. As examples, Betsy Johnson store closings were due to bankruptcy proceedings and American Eagle Outfitters closure of its 77 kids division was a strategic decision to refocus on its core brand.[46] To counter the lost revenue and fill space, mall owners consider several options.

Retenanting the Shopping Center

Mall management, working on behalf of the developer, needs successful releasing programs in order to maintain an optimum tenant mix. Finding new retailers to replace those that have gone out of business or otherwise vacated the premises is called **retenanting**. Retailers that are not generating adequate revenues and those that have gone out of business need to be replaced with others that will fill the gap as soon as possible.

Retenanting involves analyzing the existing retail mix, revitalizing some of the large older stores, and subdividing others into more efficient retail space. Attracting innovative retailers is another option. One revival tactic that emerged during the economic slump was to recruit smaller retail chains to lease unoccupied mall space. Another tactic is to bring former freestanding big-box stores into the mall. These initiatives are good for both mall and retailer.

- For the developer, it means spaces are filled and rent revenue streams resume.
- For the mall, it means an infusion of new brands to combat the sameness syndrome. Rather than abiding by safe yet boring stores, more innovative developers seek to add offbeat and independent retailers to their centers.
- For the small retailer, it means high visibility and possible expansion at a lower cost per square foot than was available a few years earlier.
- For customers, it means the excitement of new merchandise assortments and shops to explore.

Among the retailers being recruited by malls with available space are Kohls, Dick's Sporting Goods, Costco, Crate and Barrel, The Container Store, DSW shoe stores, Best Buy, H&M, and many others. Read more about trends in retenanting in From the Field 10.1.

Bumpbacks Restore Image

Occasionally bumpbacks are used to create an appearance of unity when a large mall tenant moves out. Locating a smaller, usually temporary tenant, in the front portion of a space vacated by a larger retailer is called a **bumpback**. Bumpbacks utilize square footage only in the portion of a vacant site that faces out to the mall. A temporary tenant moves in and the mall appears to be full until a permanent replacement is found. Pop-up stores that are seasonal or testing customer response to their products in the shopping center are prime candidates for bumpback areas. Pop-up stores were introduced in Chapter 2.

The tenant mix in a shopping center is adjusted to accommodate changes in the economy or trading area demographics as leased space becomes available.

Reducing Mall Hours

To cut operational costs, some shopping centers reduce the number of hours they are open. When developers like General Growth, Simon Property Group, and Westfield Group cut hours, it is usually at the beginning and the end of the day and, in some instances, only temporarily. This is only one small way that malls are economizing. Operating expenses for super regional malls have been decreasing steadily since the crest of the recession.

Presence of Service Retailers

Tenants that sell services rather than tangible products round out the retail mix in most 21st-century shopping centers. Health clubs, hair and nail salons, photo studios, cellular phone service providers, and myriad financial services are commonplace. Newer entrants are medical clinics, day-care programs, eyebrow grooming salons, and teeth-brightening services. Not only do services dilute the sameness syndrome, they also provide customers with more opportunities to attend to personal and family needs at one stop.

From the Field 10.1 — Regional Mall Owners Seize Power, Lifestyle Center Tenants

As other retail formats struggle to keep vacancies in check, regional mall owners aim to take advantage of market conditions to siphon off tenants. Retailers that have traditionally operated freestanding stores or taken locations in power and lifestyle centers have increasingly signed leases at enclosed regional malls, say property owners and consultants interviewed by *Retail Traffic*. If the trend continues, it could help regional malls remain mainstays in their trade areas, these sources say.

In 2011, for example, CBL & Associates Properties Inc., a Chattanooga, Tennessee–based REIT, welcomed a 46,500-square-foot Dick's Sporting Goods store to its Layton Hills Mall in Layton, Utah. The retailer took over space vacated by Mervyn's in December 2008. Meanwhile, Bed Bath & Beyond was hiring people for its new store at the Rogue Valley Mall in Medford, Oregon, owned by General Growth Properties. And Simon Property Group opened a 23,000-square-foot Container Store at its SouthPark Mall in Charlotte, N.C.

All of these retailers have operated in malls before, but typically have preferred freestanding locations or spots in neighborhood and power centers. A unique combination of market forces created an opportune time to expand into regional malls. To begin with, there was available space. In the first quarter of 2011, the vacancy rate at regional malls reached 9.1 percent, according to Reis Inc., a New York City–based research firm. Vacancy for anchor stores stood at 4.8 percent and was 11 percent for in-line spaces. That means that where previously there were few opportunities for users of large spaces to build at malls, in 2011 the market had plenty of empty department stores to accommodate their needs, said Anthony Cafaro, Jr., co-president of Cafaro Co., a Youngstown, Ohio–based privately held mall owner. It also made the idea of bringing in power centers and lifestyle center tenants more palatable to mall managers and landlords.

Some tenants, meanwhile, concentrated on shrinking their square footage, a trend that made it more challenging for them to find appropriately sized boxes at power centers, says Gerry Mason, executive managing director with the New York City office of Savills, a real estate services provider. For example, before the recession, Dick's Sporting Goods would often open stores as large as 70,000 square feet. In the aftermath, most large tenants preferred going smaller, and enclosed malls offered a greater range of store sizes from which to choose.

Finally, the change in market conditions coincided with the end of many 10- and 15-year power center leases signed in the mid and late 1990s, notes Jeff Green, president of Jeff Green Partners, a Phoenix, Arizona–based real estate consulting firm. So at the precise moment that big-box retailers began looking at smaller prototypes, many of them found themselves unencumbered by previous lease agreements.

As for the regional mall owners, power center and lifestyle tenants presented a twofold opportunity. At a time when many of them struggled to fill holes left over by failed department store anchors such as Mervyn's, tenants that looked to lease tens of thousands of square feet could help drive down vacancy rates. "More importantly, however, bringing in stores normally associated with other retail formats helps regional malls to regain their footing as the dominant shopping destination in their trade area," said Richard S. Sokolov, president and COO of Simon Property Group. "We are constantly trying to upgrade the mix of our tenants to enable us to maximize our market share," Sokolov noted. In the past, "the mall just didn't have the square footage to accommodate those users. But as there was an increasing number of department-store boxes that ceased to be, that opened up a new opportunity," he continued. "Then, as those tenants opened in the malls, they found their stores were productive and that encouraged them to pursue more opportunities [of that kind]."

Although the trend is still in its infancy, regional mall owners are working to expand their tenant lists. "What we are seeing is a lot of discussion, a lot of back and forth," says Mason. "If you can take someone like PetSmart or GolfGalaxy, which traditionally went into 30,000-square-foot or 40,000-square-foot boxes and put them into a 20,000-square-foot space at the regional mall, it's a real win for the mall."

"Every negotiation is different, but obviously we are able to strike financial deals that we think work for us and the tenant thinks work for them," Sokolov notes. "The nature of the deal is a function of the quality of the location, and the quality of the property and the business the tenant thinks they can do at that location."

Adapted and condensed from Elaine Misonzhnik, *Retail Traffic*, April 20, 2011, www.printthis.clickability.com/pt/cpt?expire=&title=Regional+Mall+Owners+Seize+Power+Lifestyle+Center+Tenants.)

It is expected that most malls will make a concerted effort to bring more service tenants and community-centered conveniences to their malls.

Management Training Programs

Participating in continuing education and professional development programs are ways in which managers advance their skills. Training programs conducted by trade associations provide certification in many areas of mall management. The ICSC operates the University of Shopping Centers. Its curriculum covers a wide range of topics including retailing, finance, lease administration, development, design, architecture, construction, law, technology, marketing, management, leasing, loss prevention, and security. More information on security is covered in Chapter 11. The ICSC also holds meetings annually at which industry trends and workshops are presented.

Programs such as these ensure that mall managers are well versed in the workings of shopping centers.

The mall movement ebbs and resurges, but it is far from over as new variations and opportunities present themselves. Customers may be fickle, value-conscious, status-oriented, or time-starved, but they are still drawn to malls. Experiential retailing, revamped discount centers, and invigorated lifestyle complexes are playing more important roles in shopping center development throughout the world. These trends are expected to continue well into the 21st century. Customers that become weary of traditional shopping centers can, and will, go online.

Summary

Economic downturns and retail saturation affect mall development. Fewer malls are being built this decade, but those that are constructed will answer modified needs. Facilities will not only serve customers' basic needs, but also provide satisfying life experiences.

Shopping centers take several basic forms. Open-air varieties include strip/convenience, neighborhood, community, theme/festival, lifestyle, power, and outlet centers. Regional and super regional malls are considered climate-controlled indoor malls.

Hybrid developments have taken on many new shapes, sizes, and characteristics. Some of these formats include megamalls, mixed-use centers, vertical and underground malls, and those that encourage experiential retailing or shoppertainment.

Adaptive renewal of existing malls is an important issue. To compete with newer facilities, many malls built more than 25 years ago have been renovated. Others are becoming town or lifestyle centers, demalling, or expanding as market changes dictate. Lifestyle centers have reconfigured property designs this decade.

Major developers and mall management companies throughout the world give marketing high priority. Most promote their properties as brands. Developers extend customer choices by providing innovative services in their shopping centers. Mall developers and management also are involved with leasing and retenanting, operations, finance, construction, security, and other business functions. The pressure to compete with online retailers for customers' dollars is ongoing. Shopping center industry members value ongoing professional development as they maintain and surpass industry standards.

Key Terms

Anchor stores	Regional mall
Bumpback	Retenanting
Community center	Shoppertainment
Demalling	Shopping center
Hybrid center	Strip center
Lifestyle center	Super regional mall
Mall	Theme/festival center
Megamall	Town centers
Mixed-use center	Value center
Neighborhood center	Value megamall
Outlet center	Vertical mall
Power center	

Questions for Review and Discussion

1. How do the basic types of shopping centers differ in terms of size and draw?
2. What are the purposes of a mixed-use center? Give an example of one that you have visited or read about.
3. In what geographic areas do vertical malls thrive? What customer groups do they usually serve?
4. How is the lifestyle center trend compatible with changes in customer demographics?
5. Give an example of a mall that combines value, factory outlet shopping, and entertainment. Does this hybrid format appeal to you? Why or why not?
6. What happens to malls when they age? What adaptive renewal strategies are developers using to make shopping centers more competitive?
7. The tendency for developers to recruit retailers to fill vacated spaces is changing the tenant mix for the better at some malls. Give some examples of newcomers in shopping centers that illustrate this point.
8. Discuss how mall owners are branding their properties. Do you agree with this strategy? Why or why not?

Endnotes

1. "Did You Know? Facts Sheet," in *2011 Economic Impact of Shopping Centers*, International Council of Shopping Centers, May 12, 2011, www.icsc.org.

2. "Total Number of Listings in 2012 Edition," *Canadian Directory of Shopping Centers*, www.mondayreport.ca/mondayreport/cdsc.cfm.

3. "ING's Top Shopping Centre Markets in Continental Europe," in *European Retail View*, ING Real Estate Investment Management Europe BV, Spring 2010, 5, www.ingreim.com.

4. "U.S. Shopping Center Definitions," International Council of Shopping Centers, December 2010, www.icsc.org. (Sources: Appraisal Institute, CoStar, and the ICSC.)

5. Ibid.

6. Ibid.

7. "Howard Hughes Corp. to Redevelop Riverwalk Center in New Orleans." July 27, 2012. http://retailtraffic mag.com/management/leasing/Howard_hughes_redevelop_riverwalk_neworleans_07272012/ © 2012 Penton Media, Inc.

8. Unilever Group. "Brands in Action." Ben & Jerry's. www.unilever.com/brands_in_action/detail/ben-and-jerrys/291995/?wt.contenttype=view%20brands. © Unilever 2012.

9. Dakota Smith, "Ma Dang Opens, Shows Off Koreatown's Newest Theater," Curbed, June 6, 2010, http://la.curbed.com/archives/2010/06/ma_dang_opens_shows_off_koreatowns_newest_theater.

10. David Moin, "High-End Opportunity for Outlets," *Women's Wear Daily*, April 14, 2008, 10–11.

11. Ibid.

12. Terry Pristin, "Bringing the Mall of America Magic to New Jersey," *New York Times*, May 10, 2011, www.nytimes.com/2011/05/11/realestate/commercial/ghermezians-hope-to-bring-mall-of-america-magic-to-new-jersey.

13. Ibid.

14. "United States Country Fact Sheet," in *2011 Economic Impact of Shopping Centers*, International Council of Shopping Centers, May 12, 2011, www.icsc.org.

15. "Frequently Asked Questions," The Dubai Mall, accessed February 1, 2012, www.thedubaimall.com.

16. Ryan Chittum and Jennifer S. Forsythe, "Mills's Malls May Spark Interest," *Wall Street Journal*, February 17, 2006, B2.

17. Erika Murphy, "Simon/Farallon's $7.9 B Offer Wins Mills," *GSR*, February 16, 2007, www.globest.com/cgi-bin/udt/im.display.printable?client_id=gsr_archives&story_id.

18. A.D. Priutt and Lingling Wei, "Dreams of Retail 'Xanadu' Meet Harsh Reality," *Wall Street Journal*, February 10, 2010, C8.

19. Terry Pristin, "Bringing the Mall of America Magic to New Jersey," *New York Times*, May 10, 2011, www.nytimes.com/2011/05/11/realestate/commercial/ghermezians-hope-to-bring-mall-of-america-magic-to-new-jersey.html?pagewanted=all.

20. Elliot Brown. "American Dream Project Gets Reboot." *Wall Street Journal.* June 6, 2012. c12.

21. "Meadowlands Mall to House the First DreamWorks Theme Park in the Country." July 13, 2012. http://retailtrafficmag.com/management/leasing/meadowlands_signs_dreamworks_theme_park_07132012/ © 2012 Penton Media Inc.

22. Union Station Fact Sheet. Washington, D.C., 1998.

23. Euro Disney Associés, S.C.A., "Euro Disney: Val d'Europe Continues its Tertiary Development," November 23, 2011, www.4-traders.com/EURO-DISNEY-67837/news/EURO-DISNEY-Val-d-Europe-continues its-tertiary-development.

24. Edmund Mander, "Disneyland Paris to Get Grown-up Fun—a Mall," *Shopping Centers Today*, November 1998, 35. (Updated on www.valdeurope.com November 5, 2009.)

25. "Stern's Leaving Manhattan Mall," *Shopping Centers Today*, International Council of Shopping Centers, September 25, 2000, 1.

26. "Fact Sheet," Manhattan Mall, New York, accessed January 31, 2012, www.newyorkjourney.com/manhattan-mall.htm.

27. Sharon Edelson, "Penney's Launches With Pizzazz in Manhattan," *Women's Wear Daily*, August 3, 2009, 3.

28. Khanh T. L. Tran, "Sony Builds Big-Box Entertainment," *Wall Street Journal*, June 23, 1999, B12.

29. John Upton, "Revamped Metreon Slated to be Restaurant-Centric," *The Examiner*, March 4, 2009, www.sfexaminer.com/local/Revamped-Metreon-slated-to-be-restaurant-centric-40700262.html.

30. "Mayor Lee Breaks Ground on New Metreon and City's First Target Store," Office of the Mayor, San Francisco, May 5, 2011, www.sfmayor.org/index.aspx?page=380.

31. Kris Hudson. "Starwood Capital to Buy Malls." *Wall Street Journal.* April 18, 2012. c12.

32. "Monki and Cheap Monday Carnaby Street Stores Set to Open in February," Shoparazzi, January 24, 2012, www.shoparazzi.com/blog/2012/01/24/monki-and-cheap-monday-carnaby-street-stores-set-to-open-in-february.

33. "Lotte Shopping Earnings Momentum to Pick Up on HiMart Acquisition." August 9, 2012. Asia Pacific Equity Research. © 2012 JP Morgan Chase & Co. www.morganmarkets.com. Statistical source: Company data, Bloomberg, J.P. Morgan estimates.

34. "What's Hot. New at Easton: Additions for 2012," Easton Town Center, accessed January 25, 2012, www.eastontowncenter.com/whatshot/newateaston.aspx.

35. Tim Feran, "Easton Honored as Trendsetter," *Columbus Dispatch*, December 9, 2011, www.dispatch.com/content/stories/business/2011/12/09/easton-honored-as-trendsetter.html.

36. "Did You Know? Facts Sheet," in *2011 Economic Impact of Shopping Centers*, International Council of Shopping Centers, May 12, 2011, www.icsc.org.

37. David Moin, "No More Mall-ification: Developers Rejig Sites Rather Than Build Anew," *Women's Wear Daily*, June 9, 2008, 1, 10, 12.

38. "New Tax Deal May Speed Cottonwood Mall Revival," *Salt Lake Tribune*, June 2, 2011, 1–3, www.sltrib.com/sltrib/news/51832278-78/tax-cottonwood-project-holladay.html.csp.

39. David Moin, "Forbes' Formula for Branding the Mall," *Women's Wear Daily*, October 16, 2006, 12.

40. Susan Reda. "Vacant Space Repurposed." From Stores. May 12. www.stores.org/content/vacant-space-repurposed?adid=ST_weekly.

41. Lot 10, accessed January 25, 2012, www.lot10.com.my.

42. Elaine Misonzhnik. "To Avoid Conflict, Tanger and Simon Join Forces on Outlet Project in Texas." July 13, 2011. http://retailtrafficmag.com/development/newdevelopment/simon_tanger_join_forces_07122011/index.html. © 2012 Penton Media, Inc.

43. David Moin, "Forbes' Formula for Branding the Mall," *Women's Wear Daily*, October 16, 2006, 12.

44. Hui-yong Yu, "Shopping Center Leasing Increases in U.S. as Consumer Confidence Increases," *Bloomberg*, January 11, 2012. (As reported at www.reisreports.com/index.cfm/news.)

45. Barbara Farfan,"Roundup of 2011 U.S. Retail Stores Closing, Downsizing, or Going Out of Business," About.com. Retail Industry, accessed November 21, 2012, http://retailindustry.about.com/od/storeclosingsandopenings/a/2011-US-Industry-Stores-Closing-Liquidations-Roundup-Chains-Going-Out-Business_5.htm.

46. Elaine Misonzhnik. "Store Closings Are Up Compared to Last Year, but Store Openings Are Rising as Well." August 9, 2012. http://retailtrafficmag.com/management/leaisng/store_closings_up_store_openings_too_08092012/ © Penton Media, Inc.

Chapter 11

Store Design and Visual Merchandising

Learning Objectives

After completing this chapter you should be able to:

- Summarize the components of store image.
- Evaluate how retail store design is planned and implemented.
- Investigate how the elements of art and principles of design apply to visual merchandising.
- Identify the options available to the visual merchandiser in both exterior and interior display.
- Discern why safety and security are considered part of store planning and design.

Figure 11.1
Coach issues the invitation: the superb corner location, rounded façade infused with the company's logo, and dazzling entryway charm customers into coming inside to shop.

Interactive window displays, tantalizing racks of sale merchandise, your kind of tunes in the background, aromas that tempt and please your senses, electronic games, and giant digital signage—all are essentials of store design today. The combination of things seen and unseen is the force that draws customers into a store. It also is the reason they choose not to enter. Because many retailers carry the same or similar merchandise, retailers must create a differential advantage. One way to do that is to carefully consider the various components of store image.

Store planners create excitement through traffic flow, building materials, fixtures, technology, lighting, sound, and scent. Visual merchandisers use these tools plus artistic expression to create compelling places to shop.

Activity in the retail environment affects store design as it does every other aspect of retail. Customers are difficult to impress—largely due to stimulation from the media, intense retail competition, and changes in society. Mirroring the growing importance of technology in our lives, many stores of the 21st century are monuments to the electronic age. Some stores have interactive dressing room mirrors that allow friends to watch online from a remote location as you model new outfits for their approval. You can change clothes digitally if you like, or at least play with colors and silhouettes to see which look best on you. Other retailers provide electronic kiosks that allow you to order merchandise from a larger assortment than could possibly fit into a store.

Store design is the result of contemporary social influences. Enter a specialty store filled with candles, crystals, herbs, and books on yoga, Reiki, and spirituality. Notice the astrological theme in the rich blue-and-gold décor. Inhale the patchouli incense and enjoy the music of a sitar. Changes in lifestyles have made it possible for retail stores such as this to thrive.

There is a fine line between the architectural features of store design and the promotional aspect—visual merchandising. Because of this close relationship, both topics are covered in this chapter.

Components of Store Image

Retailers work hard to develop, refine, and maintain a distinct identity. **Store image** is the combination of concrete and esoteric factors that is the total impression of a retailer retained by its customers. The perceived image that retailers have of their stores should coincide with that experienced by customers. Store layout and design are important components of store image, but many other factors are involved:

- *Physical appearance of the store.* Interior and exterior architectural features, window displays, fixtures, and merchandise affect the appearance of the store. Traditionally, discount stores have been less compelled to trade from showplaces than from utilitarian big boxes, yet the trend toward higher ceilings, wider aisles, better lighting, and more attention to visual merchandising by discounters like Target has blurred the distinction. For lower price and service formats, it is appropriate to maximize the square footage with a tonnage of goods. On the other hand, an exclusive apparel boutique in a high-end location may use a minimalistic approach to store design. Having less merchandise on the floor sends a message of exclusivity to an upscale clientele. The fashion retailer illustrated in Figure 11.2 uses a pared-down approach to the amount of merchandise on the floor and the simple, but effective décor.

Figure 11.2
Minimalistic design is used in this high-end boutique in Old Montreal. Simplicity, clean lines, and a few select pieces of apparel typify this approach.

- *Merchandise quality and pricing policy.* Merchandise may be high-quality and high-priced, low-quality and low-priced, or any combination in between. All are valid tactics as long as the objectives of retailers and the expectations of customers mesh.
- *Ambiance.* **Ambiance** is a mood evoked by the use of tangible and intangible store design tools. It is the feeling brought forth by something as simple as a scent in the air, such as "Bomb-shell in Love," a concoction of pink grapefruit, luscious peony, and sensual sandalwood scents, or "Very Sexy"—for women or men—in Victoria's Secret stores. Ambiance also is projected by more complex factors such as subtle color variations in a carpet or the intensity of a light fixture. Ambiance is one reason why customers return to a store, or Web site, again and again.
- *Employee attitude and appearance.* The impressions made by sales associates, greeters, and managers reflect store image. Customers respond to employees who are dressed appropriately and share similar personal characteristics with them. Apparel stores in which employees are dressed in store merchandise sell more merchandise. Individuals who have multiple body piercings or green spiked hair may not encourage sales in a conservative store, but they surely would in Hot Topic.
- *Advertising.* The face that retailers put before the public is a powerful aspect of store image. One determinant of image is the use of white space in a print advertisement or Web page. **White space** is the portion of an advertisement that is not used for type or illustration. In general, the more white space used in an advertisement, the more upscale the store. Conversely, the less white space used in an advertisement, the more likely the store is a discount operation. Notice how this concept parallels the amount of merchandise displayed on the selling floor, which differs whether the store is upmarket or a discounter.
- *Customer service.* Retailers do not always compete solely on the basis of price, quality of merchandise, location, or physical features of their stores. Customer service also contributes to store image. Many customers return more often if they are assured of courteous, knowledgeable service and hassle-free transactions.

/////////////////////////////////
Cyberscoop
Go to the Costco Warehouse Club Web site at www.costco.com—or any other discounter's site with which you're familiar. Is the "white space" on the home page commensurate with the impression you get upon entering the company's brick-and-mortar store? It should be!

Once retailers have found an image that works for them, they usually stay with it. However, some stores have successfully changed their image in order to seek new markets or update their retail persona.

Dunkin' Donuts sells coffee, donuts, and other baked goods from almost 10,000 stores in 31 countries through franchise and licensing agreements. The company's image has changed appreciably in the decades during which it has been in business. When the first franchises opened in 1950, products were served from luncheonette counters by wait-staff, the menu was limited to coffee and donuts, and the décor was simple and utilitarian. Most stores were in downtown areas. By the 1990s, Dunkin' Donuts stores were more colorful and inviting, counters became self-service, and the menu had expanded to sandwiches, bagels, and the famous Coolattas. Today, many units are freestanding and most provide café-style tables and chairs. To compete with Starbucks, it began serving lattes and other espresso drinks. Healthier choices like flatbread egg-white breakfast sandwiches attracted a broader market. The company added more satellite centers and drive-up windows and expanded across the United States from its strong East Coast base. It has also added to its global presence.

Among other factors, image changes reflect shifts in customer lifestyles, competition, and company goals. Consistency of image also is important as retailers grapple with the forces of change.

Planning Store Design

Store planners give stores visual personality by thinking like customers. An honest answer to "What would make me want to shop here?" lends impetus to the process. The anticipated outcome of store design is to create an environment that customers want to visit more than once. Intensifying the "wow" factor doesn't hurt either.

Objectives of Store Design

Generating sales is a strong motivation behind effective store planning. Specific objectives of store design address many factors including financial goals, merchandise compatibility with image, operational efficiencies, aesthetic concerns, customer comfort, safety features, and competitive advantages. Three objectives are highlighted here.

Figure 11.3

You can't miss the message conveyed by the huge Toys "R" Us Ferris wheel that meets your eye as soon as you enter the Times Square store in New York City: shopping here is fun!

Increase Sales and Profits

The ultimate objective of store design is to increase sales and profits. Therefore all merchandise categories under consideration are carefully evaluated in the context of store image, target market, and accessibility. Store planners and designers work with management to determine prime floor positions for top-selling brands and merchandise classifications. Seasonal goods, special purchases, and slower-moving merchandise also require appropriate placement. Stock turnover rates influence selection and positioning of goods on the selling floor. All decisions and performance metrics affect sales and profits.

Increase Operational Efficiency

One of the reasons most national chains adopt common storefronts and layouts is to present a consistent image. This practice also increases operational efficiency by carefully delineating space requirements for each product classification or department. Usually planograms are used to guarantee adherence to store layout and merchandise presentation standards. Developed by central headquarters, or outsourced to specialists, **planograms** are detailed scale drawings that illustrate precisely where each fixture and piece of merchandise is to be placed in a store. Less is likely to go wrong when all stores in the chain follow established practices. Planograms are part of the science of store layout and merchandise placement. Operational efficiencies occur when space is well allocated to maximize traffic flow and placement of merchandise.

Oracle Corp. is among the companies that have developed space management software to help retailers optimize their shelf space and plan store layouts. Its Oracle Retail Macro Space Management solution offers valuable components, including store layout, fixture, and signage planning; planogramming (optimal merchandise assortment planning based on available space); and publishing and executing plans. Approximately 65 percent of retailers have space-management programs in place.[1]

Avert the Sameness Syndrome

Many shoppers in regional malls go from one specialty shop to another without knowing the names of the particular retailers they visit. Redundancies in merchandise and basic store designs make it difficult to articulate a clear identity for some individual stores—even though each company may believe it appeals to a distinct market segment. However, establishment of a differential advantage through innovative store and Web site design helps overcome the sameness syndrome and build the retail brand.

New directions in brick-and-mortar stores and their online counterparts are challenging retailers to adopt new paradigms. Read more about changing attitudes toward the merging of physical and virtual space and the future role of stores in From the Field 11.1.

Process of Store Design

Before creating a store design, retailers must identify their target market, store image, merchandise assortment, and philosophy of selling. Once that is accomplished, theme, space allocation, and implementation costs are addressed.

Set the Theme

In the context of a written work or a piece of music, a theme is a recurrent subject or melody. Applied to store design, it is the story the store tells, the song it sings to customers. Look at the Ferris wheel inside Toys "R" Us in Figure 11.3. It is easy to see that the store's theme is fun, fantasy, and adventure. In this case materials, color, lighting, motion, and size communicate the message. Who could miss it?

From the Field 11.1   Physical Space

The retail store is not dead and it's not going away. But it will evolve as the lines between the physical and the virtual worlds continue to blur. Retailers will need to think carefully about how their physical stores can and should change to offer the customer a compelling experience. They should also consider how technology could be seamlessly integrated into the physical space to support store operations and the customer.

Shifting to an Experiential Environment

The role of the physical space is shifting from a transactional model to an experiential one, in which customers have a personalized experience with the brand. In a study carried out by Deloitte, 85 percent of respondents indicated that in five years, providing customers with a compelling brand experience will become a primary role of the store, eclipsing traditional shopping, mentioned by 79 percent of respondents.

For retail executives, connecting with customers and building brand awareness are top priorities. And, while social and mobile channels provide avenues for retailers to be cutting edge, the consensus among the executives surveyed is that brick-and-mortar stores are still the leading format for providing higher service levels and building brand awareness.

Weaving the Virtual Store into the Physical Store

The physical store must evolve to include elements of the virtual world as customer demand for an integrated experience across channels grows. Retailers should consider how to connect with customers across channels to provide them with an immersive and meaningful brand experience. Social commerce—networking sites, blogs, and online forums—can be crucial to making this happen, especially as smartphones become ever-present. Today, customers are bringing their social networks to the store. Retailers need to make social commerce a core pillar of their future store strategy.

Take this a step further. Social commerce can instantly spread the word of a shopping experience—good or bad—to a network of millions.

Retailers should consider how to incorporate social media and commerce into their physical space to drive an immersive brand experience. Harnessing the connected customer experience can encourage customers to engage in conversation about products, experiences, and the brand.

In a separate Delloite study, 40 percent of consumers said they rely more on online recommendations from others when considering a purchase than on marketing messages from retailers; 25 percent said they use smartphones to read or view consumer-written reviews.

Reevaluating Future Store Counts and Footprints

Retailers should prepare now to quickly and effectively respond to future sales channel trends. In fact, survey respondents said they expected the percentage of sales generated by brick-and-mortar stores to significantly decline over the next five years, from 91 percent to 63 percent. Despite this finding, the majority of retail respondents said they anticipated an increase in their company's total store count in the future, while the total average sales floor size is expected to remain unchanged. In light of these findings, retailers need to reevaluate their future store counts and footprint strategy. They may consider smaller counts and footprints, especially when they factor in other variables, such as fuel prices and operating expenses.

As retailers look to increase revenues, some are planning to expand into international markets, while others are testing markets through e-commerce sites. The United States, Canada, and Latin America are the top three geographic areas where survey respondents anticipate building more stores over the next three to five years. Equally important to geographic expansion are other criteria, such as the store operating model, enabled technologies, and store formats—whether it'll be a traditional brick-and-mortar store or a store within a store, for example.

Condensed and adapted from: Lisa Gomez and Lisa Fritsch, "Deloitte's Store 3.0 Survey: The Next Evolution," *Physical Space*, September 2011, 7–8, www.deloitte.com/assets/Dcom-UnitedStates/Local%20Assets/Documents/us_consulting_thenextevolution_011312.pdf.

Configure the Space

The next step is to establish a comprehensive plan for the building space, with input not only from designers and planners, but also from merchandisers and managers. Configuration of the store is dependent on planned sales and merchandising objectives. For example, Jones New York is an important apparel brand for many department stores. Because sales volume is high and the business is profitable, prominent square footage is dedicated to the label. Return on investment relative to merchandise placement is important to retailers.

Seasonality also affects use of space. In many stores, an important holiday, the back-to-school period, or a change of weather initiates new allocations of selling space. Several measures that help retailers determine the proper amount of floor space for merchandise categories or departments are discussed later in the chapter.

Determine the Costs

In planning the store, costs must be anticipated. These cover architectural design, construction, and mechanical engineering systems; interior design, fixtures, and display elements; and all operational equipment. Planning and construction time schedules also affect cost estimates.

Store planners carefully consider buildout or retrofitting costs. **Buildout** refers to the process of implementing a design–build construction project. Retailers invest in stores and shopping centers that they expect will compete successfully for many years. Buildout and retrofitting can create discord. Designing a store requires constant evaluation of new techniques, styles, materials, and methods of fabrication and installation—all with an eye toward energy efficiency and sustainability. Incorporating green materials and construction processes and ensuring energy efficiency are the top priorities for builders early this century.

Details of the Physical Structure

Before the customer steps over the threshold, the store is selling. Every detail of the façade, display windows, parking areas, and entry canopies creates an impression, inviting us to enter. Much planning goes into this phase of store design.

The Invitation

The exterior design of freestanding buildings or shopping centers welcomes customers first. Elements such as signage, window display, entrances, protection from weather, and distinctive character are commonly combined in an arresting architectural form. At the same time, the form is influenced by the store's interior functional needs. The façade of a Coach store in Hong Kong, illustrated in Figure 11.1, is in tune with its image and location—opulent, fashion-forward, and brand-prominent.

Imaginative window displays also are an aspect of exterior design. Variations are based on location—whether in a central business district, shopping mall, or freestanding store—and depend on accepted standards of taste, use of materials, construction techniques, and security factors. Windows are often called the eyes of the store and, when used well, are important communicators of store image.

Floor Plans

The basic guidelines for laying out a retail selling floor are to (1) fully utilize all of the space available and (2) avoid sacrificing function for aesthetics. Reinforcing the point: the ultimate objective of store layout and design is to maximize sales. There are two basic floor plan designs and several alternative arrangements.

Grid Format   Linear geometric floor arrangements with aisles and fixtures parallel or perpendicular to walls are called **grid floor plans**. Such rigid spatial configurations, similar to the gridiron pattern of a football field, are common floor plans for discounters, category killers, supermarkets, superstores, and drugstores. Maximum available square footage is allotted for merchandise placement.

Freeform Pattern   Less structured floor arrangements with emphasis on engineered traffic flow are called **freeform floor plans**. Upscale department stores, specialty stores, and others tend to use freeform layouts. Although these plans are less rigid than grid plans, there is no less emphasis on traffic flow, placement of departments, merchandise, and fixtures. A freeform floor plan at Saks Fifth Avenue is illustrated in Figure 11.4.

Combinations and Variations   Retailers combine aspects of grid and freeform floor plans to achieve greater variety in layout and presentation of merchandise, and meet specific traffic flow objectives.

- *Racetrack.* Floor arrangements in which elements of grid and freeform plans are combined to direct customers around the entire store by means of oval-shaped walkways are called **racetrack floor plans**. Racetrack floor plans encourage customers to shop the entire store. Walkways are designated by the materials used in their construction. Macy's uses tile or wood flooring for its racetrack, which contrasts with other parts of the floor that are carpeted. The distinctive design of Target stores includes light-colored floor tiles and wall colors, and the signature red stripe that delineates the racetrack walkways. Many of Target's departments are set up in classic grid style, as seen in Figure 11.5. Smaller stores also benefit from this design. A small racetrack circling a central cashier station promotes excellent traffic flow and allows staff a 360-degree view of the store, which provides a measure of security.

Figure 11.4
The Louis Vuitton Collection shop in Saks Fifth Avenue articulates the elegance of a freeform floor plan with room to browse, relax, or complete the sale. The mannequin positioned next to an artful prop is the focal point.

Figure 11.5
Target stores use a racetrack floor plan with many areas set up in grid style, as in this music and movie section of the store.

- *Pathway plans.* Particularly suited to large, one-level stores, pathway plans are good architectural organizers. **Pathway floor plans** engineer traffic from the front of the store to the rear and back again by means of designated walkways. Stew Leonard's famous food markets, located in Connecticut and Yonkers, New York, use a floor plan that resembles a roadway. The pathway actually winds its way through the entire store, like the famed yellow brick road in the *Wizard of Oz.*
- *Diagonal plans.* For small, self-service stores, a diagonal plan is optimal. Aisles placed at 45-degree-angles to the side walls provide the cashier, who is usually near the front of the store, with sight lines to all areas. Drugstores and music stores sometimes use the diagonal plan since it maximizes visibility of the many small items on display.
- *Curved plans.* For boutiques, salons, or other high-quality stores, curved plans create inviting environments for customers. Graceful curved walls or counters encourage traffic flow and enhance eye appeal. Although these plans are more costly to construct than angular or square plans, the results can be dramatic when a focal point such as a water fountain or artful merchandise display is placed in the center.

Traffic Flow Variables

Traffic flow is closely related to type of floor plan, aisle width, lighting, merchandise and fixture placement, and other intangible factors. Traffic-flow engineering refers to the methods used to draw customers efficiently through the store. It is based on several assumptions. First, given an equal opportunity to go left or right, 85 percent of customers will turn right and do so at a 45-degree angle. This may happen because approximately the same percentage of the population is right handed. Second, many customers enter a store to browse and are not on a shopping mission that would take them directly to a specific area of the store. Third, studies show that male and female customers have different shopping habits and preferences regarding store access routes. For example, men prefer to access mall stores directly from the parking lot. Women prefer to enter through the mall's general entrances before visiting specific stores.[2]

Studies to determine natural traffic flow in frequently used areas can provide helpful information. Nonmovable elements such as escalators, elevators, stairways, and entrances also need to be accommodated when planning store layouts.

Space Allocation and Productivity

Once a general floor plan is designed, space is allocated to each product classification. Square footage is not assigned equally to all merchandise categories, and several factors influence prioritization.

Allocation by Performance

High-volume or high-margin goods deserve prime square footage, which is why jewelry, small leather goods, cosmetics, and fragrances frequently are positioned in high-traffic areas in department stores, often in the center core of a racetrack floor plan. This information is used by planners as they allocate appropriate square footage to departments based on contribution to store sales.

Personal Space Considerations

Aisle width and adequate personal space are other details to be considered. In hard-lines departments, about four feet of space is allowed between racks or displays. In soft-goods areas, width is often slightly less. Customers are uncomfortable if adequate space for viewing goods is not granted, and if they are forced to shop too close to other customers. Studies have shown that if a customer is brushed by a browsing shopper, he or she may choose to move on, rather than complete a purchase.

Retail behaviorist Paco Underhill has studied the effects of close quarters on shoppers. During one session, he filmed a group of shoppers examining neckties at Bloomingdale's in New York City. The display rack was positioned on a main aisle near the store entrance. After observing the interaction for a while, he noticed that a shopper would approach the rack and shop for a few minutes until another shopper bumped into them or jostled them slightly from behind. It was evident that female shoppers were more uncomfortable with this than male customers. Underhill calls this the "butt-brush" factor. Once the tie rack was moved to a quieter area, sales went up.[3]

Positioning Merchandise

Whether merchandise is put out at regular or sale price, for the convenience of the customer or the retailer, every detail is considered regarding optimal positioning of goods on the selling floor.

Attitudes toward Sale Goods

The positioning of sale merchandise varies according to the philosophy of the retailer. Some retailers believe that sale merchandise should be prominently positioned at the front of the store. Supporters of the opposite tactic prefer that sale merchandise be positioned at the rear of the store. They believe that customers will work a little harder to find sale items, and that exposure to higher margin and perhaps newer merchandise will distract them as they head for the bargains.

The Convenience Factor

Frequently purchased items like milk are often located at the back of grocery stores and impulse items like candy near the checkouts. The retailer's objective is twofold: to remind customers to purchase items they might otherwise have forgotten, and encourage them to gravitate to new products as they make their way to the milk. This is strategic positioning from the retailer's perspective, but is it convenient for the customer? If a customer only wants milk, he or she may choose a convenience store rather than a supermarket. Candy displays at the register reflect a similar disconnect between retailer and customer objectives. However, responding to requests from parents trying to keep high-calorie temptations away from their children and themselves, most supermarkets have now added "no candy" checkout lanes.

Space Productivity Metrics

Sales per square foot is the standard unit of measurement for productivity in most conventional stores used as examples throughout this text. However, sales per square meter is used in some foreign countries. Sales per linear foot is used to measure productivity in supermarkets and some other stores that rely on shelf or refrigerated space for merchandise presentation.

Simple sales per square foot figures are helpful in making decisions on space allocations. Average sales per square foot numbers vary greatly by type of store and merchandise category. For example, cosmetics departments generally earn greater sales per square foot than children's clothing departments. High-performing discount stores like Walmart typically earn more dollars per square foot than other similar discounters, but less than most grocery stores.

Many factors affect productivity, but comparing sales per square foot with retail industry averages is useful in the early stages of store layout planning. Of course, this method only considers sales, not contribution to gross margin or profitability. More sophisticated measures are used when more information is available and are discussed in Chapter 14.

When a new store opens, or an existing store adds a new merchandise category, it is impossible to use past sales figures to allocate space. Most trade associations, including the National Retail Federation, as well as specialized trade publications provide data on existing retail stores that are used as benchmarks for new ventures. Determination of return on investment relative to merchandise placement is an important productivity measure for retailers.

Cyberscoop
Retail store planning and space productivity require the help of cost-saving technologies, as do other elements of the retail mix. Visit Galleria Retail Technology Solutions at www.galleria-rts.com to learn about the company and the consumer-centric products they carry. Don't miss the retail case studies.

Tangibles and Intangibles of Store Design

Flexibility is the creative core of successful store designs. Tangible features include fixtures that are usually moveable. Concept shops and designer boutiques, constructed from modular wall units, are semi-permanent, allowing them to be reconfigured easily when the next important trend debuts. Intangible features are used to create atmosphere in a store. These include sound, lighting, and scent.

Selecting Fixtures

Fixtures have traditionally been subdivided into wall systems and floor fixtures. In each category, there are ample varieties from which to choose. Fixture manufacturers sell their wares at industry shows, through catalogs, and online.

Wall Systems

Full-height perimeter partitions and high partitions placed between departments are called **wall systems**. High wall systems house many mechanical subsystems of the building: lighting, heating, ventilating, and air conditioning. A full-height partition is attractive and creates a strong surface for merchandise placement. However, wall systems obstruct the line of sight and make it more difficult for sales associates to serve customers effectively. High walls also create more security concerns.

Slat wall is a building material often used on wall surfaces. Its tongue-and-groove construction simplifies merchandise display since a variety of hooks, shelves, and other hardware are easily hung from the grooves. The system is flexible and can accommodate many types of merchandise. A disadvantage is that slat wall is sometimes overused, making it seem less exclusive to some observers.

Floor Fixtures

Display units designed to house and present merchandise are considered **floor fixtures**. Included in this category are showcases, tables, gondolas, counters, platforms, pedestals, garment racks, and point-of-sale fixtures. **Gondolas** are moveable, bin-type display fixtures frequently used for promotional merchandise.

Fixtures are either custom designed or selected from manufacturers' stock catalogues. Floor fixtures are generally prefabricated and prefinished. Some stock fixtures are built of knockdown metal parts that allow for simple on-site fabrication.

Custom fixtures are used when retailers want to project an exclusive image. Although they are more expensive than stock fixtures, they convey brand image more powerfully.

Most floor fixtures are rotated seasonally or as merchandise emphasis changes. The forms, materials, and colors of fixtures should complement the merchandise and the store image. Floor fixtures often are positioned on an angle to encourage traffic flow, create more effective display areas, and add harmony to the overall aesthetics of the store.

Figure 11.6
This shirt display fixture at a Sam's Club may look primitive, but it sells.

In-house ingenuity sometimes produces the most effective fixtures. The men's shirt display illustrated in Figure 11.6 was built from wooden pallets and stray pieces of lumber by a Sam's Warehouse Club staff member. Previously, shirts had been displayed on tables; after the new fixture was introduced, sales increased significantly.

Creating Ambiance

As important to store design as the floor plan itself is the creation of ambiance. The intangibles of store design such as electronic imagery, sound, lighting, and aroma are used to create overall atmosphere. This aspect is often the first or second expression of image perceived by customers.

Sights and Sounds

Walk into Best Buy; what impresses you first? If you are like most customers, probably whatever show is playing on the big screens. The sounds and visual imagery are welcoming, pique interest, and ultimately encourage sales.

High Lights and Low Lights

Lighting is a significant intangible element of store design and a great evoker of mood. Bright lights usually signify task-oriented, methodical shopping environments. Discount and convenience stores, supermarkets, superstores, and category killers come to mind. Subtle lighting invites us to slow down and stay awhile, puts us in a relaxed mood, and makes our outing a sensory experience. Consider the ways Apple stores, Hot Topic, and many day spas use lighting to evoke specific moods in customers.

With the vast array of lighting options in today's market, care should be taken when deciding how to light entire floors or individual displays. Track lighting is used in many specialty stores because it is flexible, creates spotlight effects on merchandise, and lends a theatrical flair to store design. **Track lighting** is display lighting that consists of moveable units mounted on vertical or horizontal tracks.

For discount stores, overhead lighting is usually chosen. Long fluorescent tubes that cast consistent, bright light are installed in ceilings. Since intense light fatigues many customers, retailers should under-light rather than over-light, or risk defeating their purpose of encouraging sales. As retailers develop environmentally sound lighting plans, many increase their use of natural light by adding skylights. Others are experimenting with solar panels and photovoltaic systems. At the very least, energy-saving light bulbs are replacing older, less efficient ones.

The Scent of a ...

The aroma that permeates a store conveys image and may influence the amount of time customers spend in the store. Some retailers, including Abercrombie & Fitch, pipe the aroma of branded fragrances into the vestibules of their stores. Shopping malls also introduce pleasant scents into their common areas. Scents of fresh-brewed coffee and baked cinnamon buns draw customers to food courts; they are uplifting and add to the general pleasure of the shopping experience. The aroma of apple-spice candles may be all that is needed to lure customers into a Yankee Candle shop.

These are the tools of the trade. The fine line between science and art becomes more apparent when visually powerful merchandise presentations are designed and implemented.

Visual Merchandising

Successful music groups and successful stores have a lot in common. They both relate to the widest possible audience and attempt to convey messages to their ticket holders or customers. Both attributes contribute to their continuing popularity. Fans in concert arenas and customers in stores want action. They want assurances that they are experiencing the best show around. It is the true measure of worth for performers when customers share favorable experiences with their peers and purchase their favorite group's work. The same concept holds true for retailers—except in this case, the store is their performance hall.

The impact of superior visual merchandising is profound. However, retailers must contend with several potential obstacles:

- Much of the merchandise in directly competing stores is virtually identical.
- A customer's first contact with a retailer's goods may be online—barring influences from advertising or loyalty programs.
- There is an overabundance of retail selling space in most developed countries, and a plethora of goods.
- Many customers are dealing with the effects of the recession and the ensuing lack of confidence in spending.

In this environment, visual merchandising takes on even greater importance. Retailers that create engaging visual presentations in their stores encourage sales in ways that have yet to be duplicated online or in catalogs.

Visual merchandising is an art—integrating a palette of color, signage, mannequins, fixtures, lighting, ambiance, and merchandise. Visual merchandising communicates store image to customers whether that image stresses service, quality, prestige, or exclusivity.

Merchandise Presentation

When a customer approaches a store or department, featured merchandise is the first thing he or she sees, followed by displays on the back wall. Areas that show major sales potential are called thrust areas. **Thrust areas** are prime locations in stores used for the display of new, high-margin, or seasonal items. For instance, as prices come down and sales escalate prior to the holiday season, Walmart will position featured items, such as discounted big-screen TVs, in thrust areas near the store's entrance.

Merchandise placement influences traffic patterns. Customers will gravitate to faced-out merchandise that is positioned around a racetrack or other high-traffic part of the store. **Faced-out** placement occurs when merchandise is displayed on fixtures so customers can see the product head-on. Fixtures called four-ways or quads often are used for this purpose.

Key areas in stores that are used for rotating promotional displays or small temporary departments are called **swing areas**. The space used for a trim-a-tree shop in December may become a swimwear boutique in June. Swing areas capture attention and guide customers to other key areas of the store.

Customers want to be entertained, excited, and educated. Theatrical elements are used to lead customers to the merchandise and to encourage purchases. Effective presentation uses repeated patterns, angles that direct the eye to thrust areas, vibrant or soothing colors, and occasionally incongruities. Visual merchandisers who create action see the results of their efforts in the store's increased sales. An aura of theater is summoned in all kinds of retail stores, as illustrated throughout this text.

Other senses, in addition to visual, are not overlooked in merchandise presentation. For example, product information is communicated through touch. When Lord and Taylor positions its soft cashmere sweaters on display fixtures close to popular walkways, more than an attractive sale price is bringing customers to the registers.

Art Elements

Visual merchandising employs the same basic art elements used in all recognized art forms. The main difference is that visual merchandising creations are temporary in nature and have a commercial purpose rather than a purely aesthetic one. The success of any display is measured by the resulting sales. The artistic merit of the display itself is a qualitative measurement of image. Art elements refer to the building blocks of all art forms—line, texture, color, and weight. They are considered when creating displays and setting up departments.

Line

The lines that define the construction of the merchandise itself impart special meaning to the customer. The same principle holds true for window and in-store displays. Vertical lines produce feelings of precision, rigidity, and directness. Curved lines give feelings of flexibility and continuity. Horizontal lines represent calm, quiet, and restfulness, and may also give the impression of width. Diagonal lines indicate action and movement. When lines are joined together, they form two- and three-dimensional shapes in various geometric configurations that become the essence of fabric prints, props for displays, and backgrounds for window treatments.

Texture

Texture is the look or feel of an object's surface. Texture may be real or artificial. The element of texture is vital in a display, for it creates either harmony or contrast. Real texture is inherent in the merchandise itself; examples are the smoothness of silk or the coarseness of straw. Customers easily detect authentic texture by touch. Using artificial texture makes something appear different from what it really is, such as when faux marble is sponged or painted on a tabletop.

Color

Color is a dramatic and powerful tool in overall store design. Color can be used to identify shops within the store, to support a theme, to indicate a promotion, or to bring excitement to staple merchandise. It is used to create a specific mood. Visual merchandisers first consider the colors of the items that are being displayed. Then they build a color story that will complement the merchandise and incite interest. The color presentation should also be one to which customers will relate.

Colors have psychological overtones and evoke personal associations. The primary colors—red, blue, and yellow—have the most shelf appeal, which is why they are frequently seen in supermarket packaging. Blue is the most popular color in the United States, but not necessarily in all cultures. In some Hispanic cultures, lavender is a color of mourning, so retailers mounting a spring dress display might be wise to acknowledge this tradition. When illuminating merchandise, knowledge of color theory is used. Complementary colors, those that are opposites on the color wheel, spark strong color contrasts. Red and green are complementary colors, for example. If emerald green dresses are presented in a window display, putting red gel filters on track lights makes the green fabric appear more vibrant. Probably the most important element of visual merchandising, color is inherent in each piece of merchandise, prop, and fixture. Visual merchandisers try to elicit psychological reactions from consumers through an understanding of color.

Weight

Every piece of merchandise has an actual weight and an optical weight. **Optical weight** is the amount an object appears to weigh rather than what it actually weighs. A foam pillow covered with dark faux fur may look heavy because of the texture and color, for example, but in reality it is very lightweight because of the materials. The optical weight of an object is more important than its actual weight in terms of visual merchandising and balance in a display. Shape, color, and texture will determine the optical weight of an object, and this awareness will confirm its placement in a display. Lighting and shadows also affect the optical weight of an object.

Design Principles

Design principles refer to the methods used to manage space in order to create unity within a work of art, an advertisement, a Web page, or a display. The perception that all design elements belong together is called **unity**. Principles of design—balance, repetition, proportion, contrast, dominance, and rhythm—have their place in visual merchandising. If elements are placed with skill, unity is achieved in the display. These principles relate to two- or three-dimensional space.

Balance

Display artists choose either symmetrical or asymmetrical balance when creating visual arrangements. In either case, the display is divided in half by an imaginary line that serves as a central axis. **Symmetrical balance** involves positioning items on either side of a center line so that they are equally weighted optically. For example, merchandise can be centered horizontally or vertically. Equally weighted amounts are placed on each side of an imaginary line, but not necessarily exact duplicates of items in the display. Symmetrical balance also is called *formal balance*. **Asymmetrical balance** is the positioning of items on either side of a center line so that they are not equally weighted optically. The items on either side of the imaginary line are not identical but appear unified because they draw on other design principles such as proportion or contrast to create weight. Asymmetrical balance also is called *informal balance*.

Repetition

Repetition is the regular occurrence of an object throughout a display. Repetition is accomplished through the use of color and form. The shoe display in Figure 11.7 shows that using three identical hanging chairs on which elegant styles are presented may bring more recognition or meaning to viewers. Several mannequins positioned in a row create more impact than one. Using the same sun-and-surf background, but different swimsuits, in a series of window displays also creates repetition and a sense of continuity. Repetition helps customers register a theme and also reinforces purchasing behavior.

Proportion

Proportion acknowledges a harmonic relationship between objects—and the spaces between objects—in displays. Sometimes displays are purposely out of proportion. Oversized display elements create more attention than conventionally sized units. Consider the effects on consumers of a giant cup of coffee in neon colors on a café sign or a huge moose sculpture at the entrance of a Cabela's outdoor outfitters store.

Figure 11.7
The design principle of repetition relies on the premise that the more products on display, the more substantial the display appears to customers, who are then more likely to examine the products.

Contrast

Contrast occurs when tension is created between props and merchandise or between any of the elements of visual merchandising design. It must be dealt with carefully and skillfully. Contrast is used as an attention-getter. For example, stark white modular furniture displayed against an ink-black background uses color contrast to make the furniture stand out and arrest the eye of the customer.

Dominance

A focal point, also called dominance, is necessary if a display is to be entirely successful. This is the main point to which customers' eyes are drawn. Dominance is accomplished through placement of merchandise and is enhanced by eye movement, use of color, or lighting. In Figure 11.8, the focal point is the mannequin in the bikini. Rhythm is also apparent since the flying figures draw your eye upward and the colorful plasma screen draws your interest to the rear of the swimwear department.

Rhythm

Rhythm refers to the feeling of visual movement that brings the eye through all aspects of a display. It also transmits unity to the observer. Items in a display are positioned skillfully so that the eye is led from one piece of merchandise to another. Because most people in Western cultures read from left to right, visual merchandisers in Western countries use this inherent eye flow to create rhythm. This is not the case in some Eastern cultures, and rhythm elsewhere in the world may be established by creating a right-to-left flow.

Figure 11.8
This inventive swimwear display in a Montreal department store uses dominance, rhythm, and color to create visual appeal and unity.

Although technically not a principle of design, motion is used by visual merchandisers to attract attention. It is closely related to rhythm. Turntables in a window display, spinning pinwheels, jiggling signs, round-racks in perpetual motion—all are used to not only capture customers' attention, but also keep it for a longer time. A window display at a French Connection store on London's Kings Road featured three rotating black and red circles behind three well-placed mannequins dressed in black. All sidewalk traffic stopped and stared.

While art elements and design principles are the aesthetic backbone of the visual merchandising trade, windows are the surface features that attract attention, create interest, and urge customers into the store.

Window Displays

Window displays have only a few seconds to capture the attention of potential shoppers passing by. For customers who are already in the store, an interior display has more time to make its point.

Windows are not as common in conventional shopping centers as they are in downtown sites or newer town and lifestyle centers. Many older shopping malls were constructed with few or no outside windows; the emphasis was on interior display. Some anchor stores had outside windows, but it was not the norm for in-line stores. Non-anchor stores located along corridors of enclosed malls are called **in-line stores**. The movement toward outdoor centers is bringing back the importance of the outside window. Windows are branding tools and give credence to the character and the quality of merchandise carried.

Several different kinds and configurations of windows exist. Whether a store is freestanding, located on a downtown street, or in a shopping mall, these popular types are easy to spot:

- *Open-back.* Open-back windows combine the window and the selling floor itself through physical and visual unity. They are used by smaller stores because they create the illusion of more interior space than really exists. Glass panels sometimes are used to permit the customer to see through the window into the store while providing some protection for the merchandise on display.

- *Closed-back.* Closed-back windows are the favorite of creative window trimmers because they are like a stage. Since the back of the window is partitioned off from the store, customer focus is totally on the merchandise and without distraction. Proper lighting can turn a closed-back window into a magical display location.
- *Glass storefronts.* Some merchants consider modern glass storefronts, through which customers see directly into a store, more valuable than open-back or closed-back windows. The entire store interior becomes visible, and the interaction of customers, merchandise, and salespeople produces a lively setting by day and night.
- *Shadowboxes.* When the objective is to use little space but create a visual oasis, shadowboxes are used. **Shadowboxes** are small display windows located in-store or out, often used to display luxury items. Since they are closed off from distractions, shadowboxes are small but eye catching. Jewelry retailers find shadowboxes useful when displaying exquisite, expensive pieces. The use of an impressive shadowbox fixture in a Lalique crystal store is shown in Figure 11.9.

In-Store Displays

Window displays provide the initial attraction, but the store interior is where visual merchandising truly assists in selling. Increased emphasis on in-store display has prompted innovation on the part of visual merchandisers. Creative treatments make use of display arrangements and units, mannequins and forms, signage, and point-of-purchase displays.

Display Arrangements

The elements and principles of design combine in several practical spatial arrangements including step and pyramid displays. End-cap displays are another format used to attract customers in supermarkets, discount stores, and other retail venues that use a grid floor plan. Special techniques are

Figure 11.9
The first fixture customers see as they enter the elegant Lalique crystal store is the vertical shadowbox. Color and lighting call attention to the artfully displayed feature items.

used to maximize vertical merchandising opportunities. The following arrangements are used with almost any classification of merchandise and in many store settings.

Step Format   A **step format** begins at a low point on one side and climbs incrementally to a higher point in a diagonal arrangement. With this format merchandise and props may be either symmetrically or asymmetrically balanced, depending on the impact desired.

Pyramid Format   A three-dimensional step arrangement produces a **pyramid format**—a geometric display that follows the lines of a triangle, beginning at a broad base and progressing to an apex. Sometimes an additional prop or piece of merchandise is displayed on the apex.

End-Caps   Stores configured in a grid floor plan usually use end-caps. These crucial merchandising areas incorporate shelf, step, or pyramid display elements to enhance merchandise presentation in supermarkets and category killers. Customers rarely resist special promotion or sale merchandise in these high-traffic areas.

Striping   Retailers practice this technique when they want to impress customers with their great depth of stock. Striping is most effective in stores that have high ceilings. **Striping** is the practice of displaying merchandise in vertical formats to bring attention to deep assortments carried by the retailer. It is impossible for customers to reach baseball hats that are above eye level on a 20-foot "stripe" in Sports Authority stores, but that isn't the intent. **Eye-level merchandising** utilizes the line of vision in an approximate 18-inch range of eye level for optimal product placement. The point of striping is to show the vast assortment available, to warehouse stock, maximize store productivity, and create visual excitement. Apparel arranged using the striping technique is illustrated in Figure 11.10.

Display Units
Constructed units used to display merchandise include platforms, ledges, environmental settings, and showcases.

Figure 11.10
The striping technique is an impressive way to show color variety and depth of stock. No one expects customers to take products from the top shelf; the intent is to highlight the assortment.

Platforms and Islands   Displays created in a prominent area using temporary or permanent low-rising units are called **platform** or **island displays**. Usually square, rectangular, or round in design, platforms are available commercially or are constructed by the display department from wood and then covered with a variety of suitable materials. Islands tend to be more permanent and are placed near entrances to key departments, escalators, elevators, and other high-traffic areas. Spotlights installed above these areas maximize visibility.

Ledges   Ledges are used in a different manner from other display areas since they are often located above eye level. One type of ledge is found in main-floor selling areas such as a central cosmetics area. These are normally trimmed according to the store's current promotion or for holidays. This type of ledge is usually visible from all four sides and is designed accordingly. Other types of ledges may rest above traditional rack or shelving units or on staircase risers. They are commonly used for display of merchandise, theme-related props, or graphics and informational signage.

Environmental Settings   Simulated rooms with three walls used to display home furnishings and accessories in a coordinated group are called **environmental settings**. Adding appropriate wall covers and carpets allows customers to see how furniture will look in their own homes. Some department store retailers may cross-merchandise by placing apparel-garbed mannequins in the room setting.

Showcases   Showcases serve a triple purpose. First, they can be positioned to physically enclose space on the selling floor. Second, they can store merchandise directly on the floor. Third, they can be impressive pieces of furniture that contribute to store image. Cases should be simple and uncluttered and, as in all displays, the merchandise should dominate. Cosmetic showcases, positioned at a slight angle, allow maximum exposure of products and encourage traffic flow. Some are set so they cut off sharp corners, which allows easier access by customers and more faced-out space to display goods. The Godiva chocolate showcase, shown in Figure 11.11, demonstrates how showcase housing protects the product and ensures freshness.

   The key to any display is coordination and a unified presentation. Continuity of a display theme is necessary in related promotional materials, signage, and advertising.

Figure 11.11
Godiva chocolates are always appealing, and customers feel more compelled to purchase when candy is displayed in a clean glass-enclosed showcase.

Mannequins and Forms

Mannequins and forms are used by soft-goods retailers and are chosen to complement store image. When chosen well, customers identify with them easily. Mannequins may be very human-like or distinctly abstract—the choice depends on store image and target market. Some mannequins are constructed from advanced polymer and resin compounds; others are made from soft, pliable materials that allow more flexibility than older, rigid types.

Forms take varied shapes. Broomsticks may be used to display goods hanging from a horizontal bar, and wire sculptures to present a variety of soft goods. Soft sculptures are also used to display merchandise.

Signage

The use of signs can help or hinder merchandising efforts. External signs do more than announce a retailer's presence. They might herald a seasonal sale. Internal signs are used to draw attention to a specific department, special purchase, newly arrived merchandise, a sale, or service areas. Signs that are poorly designed, produced, or placed in a retail store can dilute a retailer's relationship with the customer.

Signage speaks its own language, judging by the aisle interrupters, danglers, and wobblers found in stores today. **Aisle interrupters** are signs, usually made from cardboard, that protrude into an aisle. **Danglers** are signs that are suspended from a shelf. **Wobblers** are signs on spring assemblies that jiggle to attract attention.[4] These types of signs are popular in supermarkets and drugstores. The principles of design are considered when creating signs because they convey not only information, but also store image.

Self-Service Displays

Simple display props or counter cards by cash registers have evolved into sophisticated point-of-purchase (POP) aids. POP display areas are expanding dramatically as manufacturers provide retailers with bigger, more complicated permanent displays. They do this to maintain a high level of brand awareness, for consistency, and to give them an edge on their competitors. The basic rule in POP design, however, is to put merchandise in as attractive a package as possible using as little space as possible.

As mentioned in Chapter 3, the use of interactive displays is growing among large retailers and shopping center operators. Interactive touch points are used on some street-side window displays. Increasingly, technological elements such as this are being integrated into store design.

Safety, Security, and Asset Protection

Safety and store security are addressed as part of store design. Aesthetics sometimes are sacrificed to make the shopping environment a safe one for customers and a secure one in which to do business. Safety factors are important to acknowledge in the early planning stages of store design, and are equally significant to visual merchandisers. Sprinkler systems, access for disabled people, stairwells, escalators, raised or lowered areas, and sensible material choices are all relevant to store design. Selecting and housing security systems is not the glamorous side of store design, but it is necessary. Some stores have incorporated security ports into their store design. Constructed from usual construction materials, ports can provide an unobtrusive area for electronic or human surveillance activities. Examples include two-way mirrors, decorative columns, or display props.

Video and Electronic Article Surveillance

Larger retailers usually use cameras to monitor traffic flow, employees, and customers. Surveillance systems are often housed in behind-the-scenes areas or a nook in the stockroom. Control centers allow security personnel to view various parts of the store on a continual basis.

Electronic article surveillance devices are integral parts of most retailers' security plans. **Electronic article surveillance (EAS)** is a system that uses various security devices, often triggered at store exits, to deter theft. The bulky, often unattractive equipment that houses the triggering devices has given way to a new breed of security apparatuses designed to blend in or enhance store décor as well as provide a security function. Hidden in vases, pedestals, or even "watch manne-quins," these new devices seem more like unique store fixtures than obtrusive security systems.

Dressing Room Security

About 32 percent of inventory shrinkage in retail stores is attributed to customer shoplifting.[5] A good part occurs in dressing rooms. Therefore, all retailers that provide fitting rooms plan for the positioning of them. Hiring security guards or attendants is not financially feasible for many retail-ers. Fitting rooms that are located where they are in direct view of employees on the selling floor are more effective than those that are built in clandestine areas of the store.

Other security techniques revolve around the type of fitting rooms incorporated into the floor plan. For example, many stores opt for the "barrel effect" when designing dressing rooms. Al-though privacy is granted, the customers' heads and feet are visible while they are in the cubicles. The psychological inference that customers are in less than total seclusion reduces shrinkage. Oth-er stores use lockable fitting rooms, while retailers that service large numbers of customers plan double rows of fitting rooms as modular units. In this way, some fitting rooms are put out-of-service during slower periods. Locating dressing rooms within close proximity to restrooms is discouraged since it encourages shoplifting.

Organized Retail Crime

Shoplifting and internal theft by employees increase every year, as does organized retail crime (ORC)—a topic that was introduced in Chapter 3. In 2012, 96 percent of retailers surveyed said that their companies were victims of ORC. That figure was up slightly over the previous year.[6] The prac-tice inhibits some of the finer points of display and store design, and decisions made on the basis of asset protection are as stringent as those that involve the aesthetics of visual merchandising.

Professional thieves often find it easy to enter a store and distract a sales associate while their partners in crime strip tables by scooping merchandise into bags and baby carriages, then rapidly exit the store. Stolen goods are then fenced; that is, resold to pawnshops, at swap meets, flea mar-kets, in temporary stores, and on the Internet. Retailers have identified their stolen merchandise at one or more of these fencing locations; 69.1 percent in physical locations, 73.4 percent through e-Fencing locations.[7]

Cargo theft is also a pressing problem, as is the increasing level of violence displayed by pre-meditated thieves. **Criminal "flash mobs"** are pre-established groups of people that enter stores for the purpose of raising havoc, harassing sales associates, and stealing merchandise. Assaults oc-casionally have been reported by retailers. Some groups have organized their rampages on social network sites, by texting or sending viral e-mails.

Sadly, knowledge of deviant behavior must be incorporated into store design, floor plan, posi-tioning of goods, selection of fixtures, and, of course, choice of security systems.

The scope of store design and visual merchandising is all-encompassing. Extensive strategic planning, knowledge of visual merchandising practices, availability of technological display tools, and implementation of appropriate security systems help create memorable retail emporiums. Most important, store design and buildout offer retailers an effective way of claiming a differential advantage over their competition.

Summary

Designing a store that welcomes customers is a goal of all retailers. Many factors contribute to store image, including physical appearance of the store, merchandise, ambiance, employee atti-tude and appearance, advertising, and customer services rendered.

Objectives of store design include increasing sales and profits, maximizing operational effi-ciency, and averting sameness. Creating a workable theme that conveys store image and creates a differential advantage is important. Using space effectively and anticipating realistic costs are equally important.

The façade of a store, including its outdoor display windows, invites customers in. Once over the threshold, floor plans encourage traffic flow. Two basic floor plans are grid and freeform. The racetrack floor plan is a popular one used by many large retailers and is a combination of both basic plans. There are many variations on both themes. Methods of assigning space to individual departments vary, but most are based on profitability and return on investment.

Fixture design and placement are important aspects of store planning. An amenable ambiance is created through the use of intangible aspects of design such as lighting, sound, and aromas.

Merchandise presentation is dependent on a working knowledge of art elements and principles of design. Art elements include line, texture, color, and weight. The principles of design include balance, repetition, proportion, contrast, dominance, and rhythm. The goal in using the elements and principles is to create unity, the sense that everything works in the visual perception of the display.

Exterior window displays bring customers into the store; interior displays convince them to buy. Windows may be open- or closed-back. Glass storefronts and shadowboxes are other options.

Common display arrangements include step and pyramid formats. End-caps and the striping technique are effective in-store display formats. In-store areas also utilize showcases, platforms and islands, ledges, and environmental settings.

Mannequins, forms, and signage project store image. Self-service displays and entertainment kiosks enhance the in-store experience by presenting easy access to merchandise and providing an element of fun that may keep visitors in the store longer.

Planning for safety and implementing effective security systems also influences store planning and design.

Key Terms

Aisle interrupters	Planograms
Ambiance	Platform displays
Asymmetrical balance	Pyramid format
Buildout	Racetrack floor plan
Criminal "flash mobs"	Shadowboxes
Danglers	Space productivity index
Electronic article surveillance (EAS)	Step format
Environmental settings	Store image
Eye-level merchandising	Striping
Faced-out	Swing areas
Floor fixtures	Symmetrical balance
Freeform floor plan	Thrust areas
Gondola	Track lighting
Grid floor plan	Unity
In-line stores	Wall systems
Island displays	White space
Optical weight	Wobblers
Pathway floor plan	

Questions for Review and Discussion

1. What are the key components of store image? Use these as criteria to evaluate stores in your area. What constitutes an effective store image?
2. What is the most important objective of store design?
3. Describe the two basic plans for a retail sales floor layout. Under what circumstances is each used? Give examples of retailers in your area that use each type.
4. What is space productivity? How is it measured? Do all categories of merchandise contribute to sales equally?
5. How does traffic flow in a store affect merchandise placement? What specific techniques do retailers use in thrust areas?
6. What is ambiance in store design? Give examples of retailers that are known for using ambiance to enhance image.

7. Why is a display that uses asymmetrical balance more visually exciting than one that uses symmetrical balance?
8. What is the difference between open-back and closed-back windows? When is each used? What are the main advantages of shadowboxes?
9. Explain how point-of-purchase (POP) displays have evolved in visual merchandising. Give an example of one such display that caught your eye in a store.
10. Why are safety and security considered store planning and visual merchandising issues? Explain what retailers are doing to discreetly prevent shrinkage.

Endnotes

1. "Managing Space as an Asset," in *Invigorate Operational Excellence: Enabling New Ways of Working,* 4–5, Oracle Retail, www.oracle.com/oms/retail/invigorate-op-excellence-072011-433045.pdf.

2. Cynthia Hall, Simon Property Group, Interview, Manchester, New Hampshire, October 2001.

3. Paco Underhill, *Why We Buy, The Science of Shopping* (New York: Simon & Schuster, 2000), 17–18.

4. Yumiko Ono, "'Wobblers' and 'Sidekicks' Clutter Stores, Irk Retailers," *Wall Street Journal*, September 8, 1998, B1.

5. "Shrinkage On The Rise. According To Preliminary National Retail Security Findings," National Retail Federation, June 14, 2011, www.nrf.com/modules.php?name+News&op=viewlive&sp_id=1136.

6. *Organized Retail Crime Survey 2012,* "Organized Retail Crime Levels at All-Time High." p. 7. www.nrf.com/organizedretailcrime. National Retail Federation.

7. Ibid.

Unit Three: Global Retail Profile
Carrefour, France

The number two retailer in the world—and one of the most internationalized—is Carrefour. At the Mall of the Emirates in Dubai, the emphasis is on value pricing—a preoccupation with many customers worldwide.

Walmart is the largest retailer in the world, but unless you are a retail aficionado, you may not be aware that Carrefour is the largest in Europe and the second-largest globally. Considered the inventor of the hypermarket, Carrefour operates big-box stores that carry a unique mix of food and general merchandise. But that's not all. Through development, mergers, and acquisitions, the company operates supermarkets, convenience, discount, and cash-and-carry stores to satisfy the needs of diverse global customers. Carrefour had 9,680 stores in 23 countries as of March 2012,[1] with sales revenue that reached approximately $111 billion in fiscal year 2011. Stores in France account for more than 43 percent of total group sales.[2]

History and Leadership

Carrefour was founded in 1959 by Marcel Fournier and Louis Defforey in Annecy, an industrial city in eastern France. The first store was located in the basement of what was then Fournier's department store, but soon moved to its own site. It was an immediate success. Shortly thereafter, the families Halley and Duval-Lemonnier established the original version of what became Carrefour's long-term competitor, Promodès. Carrefour's first hypermarket opened in 1963.[3] The company merged with Promodès in 2000.[4]

Daniel Bernard was the top executive at Carrefour from 1992 to 2005, a period of rapid growth for the company. Many auxiliary businesses were launched during that time, including insurance, travel, financial, pharmacy, and photo services, adding new dimensions to the company's hypermarkets. By 2005, sales had slipped; shareholders lost faith in Bernard and replaced him with two executives, Luc Vandevelde and Jose-Louis Duran. Vandevelde had been president of Promodès until the merger with Carrefour and was a member of the Carrefour board.[5]

Robert Halley, a descendent of one of the founders of Promodès, succeeded Vandervelde in 2007 following disagreements about strategy. By 2008, the internal disputes precipitated an action by the Halley family, who were majority shareholders. Approximately half of their shares, amounting to 10 percent of the total, were sold to Colony Capital's Blue Capital, the investment vehicle for

Louis Vuitton Moet Hennessy (LVMH). Under the leadership of Bernard Arnault, LVMH became the largest shareholder.[6] Arnault is considered France's richest man.

Like many retailers during this period, the company was affected by the global recession. Duran, now chief executive officer (CEO), was criticized by LVMH for his plan to change the name of the company's Champion supermarkets to the Carrefour Market brand. To his credit, he sold unprofitable operations in Switzerland and Portugal and expanded in Poland and China, both growth markets.[7]

Although sales picked up later in 2008, Lars Olofsson replaced Duran at the beginning of 2009. Olofsson, a key executive for three decades at the Nestlé Company, was one of the first officers to be appointed from outside the company in its history.[8] Joining the company at the height of a global recession challenged Olofsson's attempts at revitalization. One sign of the times during the holiday season: even champagne sales were sluggish at the hypermarkets.[9]

Olofsson embarked on a major shift in strategy. Rather than continue with its quality-based platform, Carrefour changed its emphasis to private label branding, ostensibly "making Carrefour to groceries what IKEA is to furniture."[10]

Competition

Visiting one of Carrefour's hypermarkets on an educator's study tour alerted my colleagues and me to the impressive size and internal workings of the company. It also gave us an opportunity to learn about the competitive sphere from executives at the Villabé store located south of Paris.

We learned that Carrefour considered Auchan its chief competitor in France. It believed Auchan offered a broader merchandise assortment, generated more fun, and encouraged better traffic flow. While Carrefour competed on the basis of quality, Auchan competed on the basis of price. Carrefour executives contended that its stores were better maintained than those of Auchan and that its customers recognized and appreciated this attribute. Globally, Carrefour recognized Casino Groupe of France, Tesco of the United Kingdom, Metro of Germany, Aeon of Japan, Ahold of the Netherlands, and Walmart of the United States as other competitors.

When CEO Olofsson joined the company, he became aware of two problems that his predecessors had failed to resolve. During the economic downturn, customers perceived that prices in the hypermarkets had become too expensive, although by Carrefour's standards they were not. To test strategies designed to restore customers' faith in Carrefour's low-price intentions, Olofsson initiated new tactics at the Villabé store. Larger, bolder store signage was introduced, and banners highlighting the company's familiar "Quality for All" slogan were replaced by stronger, price-oriented advertising. Olofsson, concerned about the image of hypermarkets in an age when people are living in smaller households and in need of more convenience, considered alternative tactics in 2010.[11]

A visit to a hypermarket is daunting to those with limited time, as we learned on our tour. Although a compelling format with many products to choose from, hypermarkets are not for everyone all of the time.

Numbers, Formats, and Sizes

Carrefour's retail empire encompasses more than hypermarkets, of course, and there is evidence that smaller venues are gaining momentum. The breakdown of store formats and numbers for 2012 follows:

- Hypermarkets—1,452
- Supermarkets—2,995
- Convenience—5,170
- Cash & Carry—154[12]

Although its typical hypermarket is 100,000 square feet, Carrefour has operated stores as small as 50,000 square feet and as large as 240,000 square feet. Sizes of hypermarkets are shrinking. Smaller supermarkets at 30,000 to 55,000 square feet and convenience stores are popular additions to the retailer's facilities repertoire.

Two convenience store formats are the 8,000-square-foot Carrefour Contact stores, which operate in small villages and towns, and 4,000- and 6,000-square-foot Carrefour City stores, located in densely populated urban areas. These stores are open from 7:00 a.m. to 11:00 p.m. to answer the needs of highly mobile city residents.[13]

At the end of 2010, Carrefour operated more than 6,300 "hard discount" Dia stores, about 2,000 of which were franchised. Hard discount stores carry 80 percent mass-market products and 20 percent perishable products. They are similar in merchandise mix and pricing strategies to deep discounters, mentioned in Chapter 5. Dia stores are located in France, Spain, Portugal, Turkey, Argentina, Brazil, and China.[14] The Dia concept originated in Spain in 1979 and came to Carrefour through the merger with Promodès in 1999. By mid-2011, after several quarters of disappointing sales, Carrefour shareholders approved a spin-off of Dia. The company is listed on the Madrid and other Spanish stock exchanges and each Carrefour shareholder received one Dia Group share for each Carrefour share held. This decision was another part of Olofsson's 3-year strategic plan.[15]

The company also operates Web sites in several countries, including France, Spain, Belgium, and Turkey. Online-based services vary by country but include home delivery and in-store or in-warehouse pickup options.[16]

Merchandise Brands and Policies

Basic merchandise assortments are similar in most Carrefour stores in France although they vary in the international locations. Key merchandise areas include electronics; textiles (soft goods such as apparel and home furnishings); produce, meat, and groceries; and bazaar, which features toys and seasonal items. The company individualizes the merchandise mix for local tastes.

Stores carry shallow merchandise assortments by supermarket standards, but do substantial volume in the products they carry. Carrefour's private-label programs cover most merchandise groups. About 20 major outside vendors contribute to 45 percent of sales and include consumer goods giant P & G and beverage firm Diagio. Part of Olofsson's hypermarket revitalization plan included reducing many of the non-food products since he believes the company cannot compete in all categories of goods.[17]

Food sales account for approximately 70 percent of the hypermarket business, with general merchandise making up the remaining 30 percent. The range of profit on items is staggering, with lower profits generated by nationally branded groceries and high profits recorded on in-house brands and bakery goods. The latter is considered a high-volume, high-turn, high-profit department for Carrefour. Merchandise turnover is called *turn of stock* in France.[18]

Store Design and Promotion

Light, bright, and scrupulously clean interiors typify Carrefour hypermarket stores. Wide aisles are prominent and a grid floor plan is used. Merchandise kiosks add interest to the spacious, customer-friendly stores. Visually, a "pile 'em high and watch 'em buy" strategy is used. The bottled water section covers at least 50 feet of linear shelf space and reaches nearly to the ceiling, creating impact if not easy reach.

A wealth of auxiliary services is often housed in retail space adjacent to a hypermarket. This creates a mall-within-a-mall appearance and adds to the store's definitive presence. Several kiosks and shops complement the main store at the 100,000-square-foot Villabé site. A pharmacy, optical shop, travel and insurance agency, photo and print shop, ticket bureau, and even a marriage license counter tempt one-stop shoppers. Carrefour is the owner and principal anchor in the mall where global retailers McDonald's and Toys "R" Us lease space, along with local and regional specialty stores and chains.

When Carrefour consummated the Dia Group spin-off, it also announced plans to sell 25 percent of its real estate division, Carrefour Properties. As well as serving as a vehicle for infusing cash into the business, perhaps this action moves Carrefour away from owning mall property and performing landlord duties.[19]

Global Expansion

Since global expansion began in 1973 when Carrefour opened in Spain, the company has become one of the most internationalized companies in the world. It operates in Europe, Asia, South

America, and the Middle East. Global stores are wholly owned, owned with partners, or are franchised. The following examples lend credence to the aggressive global strategies implemented by Carrefour:

- **Russia**—Carrefour opened its first hypermarket in Moscow in mid-2009, bucking trends set forth for the European stores. The sales area covered about 870,000 square feet on two floors and carried twice as much non-food compared to food items.[20] Shortly after the company opened a second hypermarket, it exited the market due to poor sales performance and pressures from its parent company—surely a surprise to customers.[21] Knowing when to fold is an important strategic decision that is not always welcome, but sometimes is necessary for long-term growth.

- **China**—Carrefour entered China in 1995 and by the end of 2011, had 203 hypermarkets in China.[22] A desire to "buy local" precipitated Carrefour's announcement to source more fresh produce in China rather than import. The company set up over 300 direct purchase locations, sourcing 30 percent of fresh produce from local farmers in 17 provinces or regions. Plans include increasing the fresh food percentage to 50 percent in large cities including Beijing and Shanghai.[23]

- **Poland**—Carrefour's focus is on franchising in Poland, where its stores are well received by Eastern European customers. The company intends to open many Carrefour Express stores in partnership with British Petroleum (BP).[24] By the end of 2011, the company had 84 hypermarkets, 176 supermarkets, and 164 convenience stores.[25]

- **India**—By law, a company can only participate in foreign direct investment in India if the business is a cash-and-carry wholesale operation. Under its Carrefour Wholesale Cash & Carry logo, the French retailer opened its first store in New Delhi in 2011.[26]

- **Brazil**—In 2010, Carrefour announced that it would invest heavily in rapidly growing Brazil by expanding its store base and initiating online selling.[27] While sales in France had slipped in recent quarters, sales in Brazil were growing. Pão de Açúcar and Walmart are Carrefour's main competition, and each company plans to open more stores. If this sounds to you like the beginnings of a turf war, you are correct. Pão de Açúcar is owned by Brasileira de Distribuição, or CBD. Casino owns shares in Pão de Açúcar, so it had already developed a partnership with the company. In early 2011, Carrefour and Casino were vying aggressively for control of Pão de Açúcar. Carrefour sought a merger with CBD that Casino viewed as "hostile."[28] By mid-summer, Carrefour's proposal had collapsed: in the end, the Brazilian bank that was supposed to finance the Carrefour-initiated merger withdrew its $3 billion financial support.[29] Strong sentiments like these hold the potential to adversely affect strategic moves from prospective retail suitors.

As interest shifted globally from hypermarkets to smaller retail big-box stores, Carrefour initiated successful hypermarket conversions in several countries, notably Spain and Belgium. Carrefour Planet stores, as they are called, generated double-digit growth and routinely outperform hypermarkets that have not yet been retrofitted.[30]

Carrefour in the United States

A look at Carrefour's experience in the United States offers many lessons about such global expansion efforts. Soon after opening a 330,000-square-foot store outside Philadelphia and a smaller one in New Jersey in 1988, Carrefour realized that it would have to adapt its ways of doing business to those preferred by U.S. shoppers. For example, Carrefour initially merchandised the store in the French style, placing paper goods in houseware departments rather than in grocery areas as is common in U.S. supermarkets. Newspaper advertising was used, although Carrefour rarely does so in France. Despite this, research later showed that 60 percent of customers learned of the stores by word of mouth. Customers complained that Carrefour carried too few items and that they could not complete their weekly food shopping in the store. Management responded by adding more merchandise to the assortment.

The organizational structure also differed from that of typical U.S. mass merchandisers. Rather than relying on a central buying office, each department manager at Carrefour was responsible for buying and pricing merchandise, dealing with human resource issues, planning profit, and setting gross margins.

Although the Philadelphia store eventually reached a sales volume of $1 million per week, the company's target had been $5 million per week. In the end, despite predicting the opening of 21 stores by 1992, the company pulled out of the United States in late 1993. Several reasons were cited, among them:

- The store format was too large for U.S. customers.
- Stores were mismanaged.
- Competition was too intense.
- The shopping experience was too time-consuming for customers.
- Customers were unaccustomed to shopping for food and general merchandise concurrently.
- Union boycotts and zoning problems in the Philadelphia area caused conflict.
- The company had overinvested in store construction.[31]

Since that experience, Carrefour has wisely shopped its global competition before setting up operations in a new country. As a result, today it is considered a seasoned global retailer. Some analysts believe Carrefour will eventually re-enter the U.S. market. Since Carrefour was once a minority shareholder in U.S. retailer Petsmart, this affiliation might indicate renewed interest when the economy stabilizes.

Public perception of Carrefour as a high-priced hypermarket may have contributed to sales declines during the recession as customers shopped more conservatively. As it polishes its global presence, the company has looked to implementation of cost savings, market share growth strategies, and an emphasis on smaller storefronts. The company will enter a new era in mid-2012 when Lars Olofsson steps down to make way for new CEO Georges Plassat. Plassat has strong credentials in retailing, most notably with Carrefour rival Casino. Look for the game of high-stakes global retailing to continue.

Profile Discussion Questions

1. What differentiates Carrefour stores from typical supermarkets or superstores? Why do customers like shopping at Carrefour?
2. Explain the advantages and disadvantages of a "pile 'em high and watch 'em buy" visual merchandising technique.
3. Carrefour's international experiences have many lessons to teach other retailers that expand abroad. Of the examples given in this profile, which issues do you believe are the most challenging and why?
4. What do you believe were the three main reasons for the demise of Carrefour in the United States? Do you think Carrefour would succeed if it opened stores in the United States in the future?
5. Carrefour has changed leaders three times in the past decade. What are the advantages and disadvantages of turnover of the chief executive? What did Lars Oloffson achieve in his 3-year tenure?
6. How do Carrefour's global expansion plans compare to Walmart's?

Profile Notes

1. "Carrefour Q1 2012 Sales Up 1.5% to €22.5bn, Resilience in Food, Continued Weakness in Non-Food Spending, Development of Store Network by Banners - Q1 2012," Carrefour Group, April 12, 1012, www.carrefour.com/cdc/group/current-news/q1-2012.html.
2. "2011 Results: Key 2011 Highlights," Carrefour Group, March 8, 2012, 1, www.carrefour.com/docroot/groupe/C4com/Pieces_joints/CA/2012/CA_T1_120412_UK.pdf.
3. "History," Carrefour Group, accessed April 30, 2012, www.carrefour.com/cdc/group/history.
4. Brandon Mitchener and David Woodruff, "French Merger of Hypermarkets Gets a Go-Ahead," *Wall Street Journal*, January 26, 2000, A19.
5. Robert Murphy, "Carrefour CEO Steps Down," *Women's Wear Daily*, February 4, 2005, 2.
6. Robert Murphy, "Shareholder Move at Carrefour," *Women's Wear Daily*, March 6, 2008, 17.

7. Robert Murphy, "Talk of Change Atop Carrefour," *Women's Wear Daily*, July 18, 2008, 11.

8. Robert Murphy, "Nestle's Olofsson Replacing José Luis Duran at Carrefour," *Women's Wear Daily*, November 19, 2008, 5.

9. Cecilie Rohwedder, "Carrefour Braces for More Global Retail Weakness," *Wall Street Journal*, January 16, 2009, B1.

10. Christina Passariello, "Carrefour's Makeover Plan: Become IKEA of Groceries," *Wall Street Journal*, September 16, 2010, B1-B2.

11. Cecilie Rohwedder, "Carrefour Restores Low-Prices Strategy," *Wall Street Journal*, June 30, 2009, B4.

12. "Carrefour Q1 2012 Sales Up 1.5% to €22.5bn, Resilience in Food, Continued Weakness in Non-Food Spending, Development of Store Network by Banners - Q1 2012" Carrefour Group, April 12, 1012, www .carrefour.com/cdc/group/current-news/q1-2012.html.

13. *Financial Report 2010*, 24, Carrefour Group, www.carrefour.com/docroot/groupe/C4com/Pieces-jointes/ RA/2011/Carrefour_Rapport_Financier_2010_72DPI_RVB_GB.pdf.

14. "DIA: A New Global Leader in Hard Discount, Q4 2010," Carrefour Group, accessed July 18, 2011, www .carrefour.com/cdc/finance/spin-off-of-100_-of-dia-project/dia—a-new-global-leader-in-hard-discount .html?com.carrefour.cdc.print.page.content=true.

15. Joelle Diderich, "Carrefour Shareholders Green-Light Dia Spin-Off," *Women's Wear Daily*, June 22, 2011, 2.

16. "E-Commerce," Carrefour Group, www.carrefour.com/cdc/group/our-business/our-stores/our-stores-folder/e-commerce-en.html.

17. Christina Passariello, "Carrefour Tries Diet, Cutting Food Choices," *Wall Street Journal*, June 28, 2010, B3.

18. Villabé Presentation.

19. "Carrefour to List Dia and Carrefour Property," Kantar Retail IQ, March 2, 2011, www.kantarretailiq.com/ ContentIndex/NewsDisplayLW.aspx?id=325420&key=Vpab.

20. Elena Berton, "Carrefour Opens First Moscow Store," *Women's Wear Daily*, June 19, 2009, 13.

21. Mimosa Spencer, "Carrefour, in Shift, to Exit Russia As It Reports 2.9% Drop in Sales," *Wall Street Journal*, September 16, 2009, B5.

22. "Store Network Consolidated, Hypermarkets, China. End of December 2011," Carrefour Group, www .carrefour.com/groupe/C4com/Groupe/Nos%20activités/Nos&20parcs%20de%20magasins/Parcmagintegre GB31122011.pdf.

23. "Carrefour China Increases Direct Sourcing," Kantar Retail IQ, April 22, 2011, www.kantarretailiq.com/ ContentIndex/NewsDisplayLW.aspx?id=332264&key=Vpab.

24. "Carrefour Express Stores Planned for BP Petrol Stations," *Retail Poland*, May 19, 2011, www.retailpoland .com/104508/Carrefour-Express-stores-planned-for-BP-petrol-stations.

25. "2011 Results: Key 2011 Highlights," Carrefour Group, March 8, 2012, 1, www.carrefour.com/docroot/ groupe/C4com/Pieces_joints/CA/2012/CA_T1_120412_UK.pdf.

26. Joelle Diderich, "Carrefour Opens First Store in India," *Women's Wear Daily*, January 3, 2011, 2.

27. Fabiola Moura and Ladka Bauerova, "Carrefour Plans $1.4 Billion Brazilian Investment," January 21, 2010, www.bloomberg.com/news?pid=2-670001&sid=aZCQf43eS08M.

28. Christina Passariello and John Lyons, "French Giants Vie in Brazil," *Wall Street Journal*, June 29, 2011, B5.

29. John Lyons with Luciana Magalhaes, "Carrefour's Brazilian Retail Merger Collapses," *Wall Street Journal*, July 13, 2011, B5.

30. "Q2 2011 Sales," Carrefour Group, July 13, 2011, www.carrefour.com/cdc/group/current-news/q2-2011-sales-en-1.html?com.carrefour.

31. Elliot Zweibach, "Carrefour Closing U.S. Stores: Two Hypermarkets in Northeast to Shut Within Two Months," *Supermarket News*, September 13, 1993, 1.

Unit Four

Retail Management

Whether it's communicating with customers, working with the community, or hiring and overseeing the individuals that run and support the enterprise, retailing is a people business. Store, catalogue, and online employees attend to the workflow as business objectives are met. But it is the role of management to ensure that the company's goals are accomplished expediently and within budget.

Every step of the way—whether buying products that will tantalize customers, setting up a selling floor, hiring sales associates who are in tune with today's customers, or analyzing performance data—humans are involved. Whether a shopper carefully researches a pending purchase online or, on the spur-of-the-moment, zips into a store and spends a fortune, for retailers it's all about satisfying the shopper. To accomplish this, those who work with employees, vendors, and customers synchronize the retail process.

We discuss management—of operations, finances, merchandise, and human resources—in this unit because all of these areas involve the human factor in retailing. Carefully chosen merchandise, exciting promotions, tight financial controls, or select locations cannot guarantee preeminence unless there are also talented people to execute directives and managers to organize, supervise, and mentor their staffs.

The success of all retail organizations depends on the ability to recruit, train, and retain human assets at every level. With more than 42 million retail jobs in the United States in 2011 alone, this is no small task.[1] Nurturing the entrepreneurial spirit is vital in large and small organizations. Employees adopt the mindset of ownership through the positions they hold within a company and the passion they exhibit while working. They treat their responsibilities as seriously as if they actually owned the business. Small business owners are intrinsically motivated to succeed and usually perform many of the key functions of store operations themselves. They employ fewer people but share with them an unbridled enthusiasm for the work they accomplish.

You've been reading about managers throughout the first chapters of this book, now it's time to learn what they actually do. By examining management, from general history, theory, and principles through specific job categories and activities, we'll gain a broader perspective of how managers perform their vital role in lubricating the wheel of retailing.

Endnote
1. "About NRF," National Retail Federation, Accessed February 2012, www.nrf.com.

Chapter 12

Principles of Management

Learning Objectives
After completing this chapter you should be able to:
- Survey the origins of the management concept and various definitions and types of management.
- Explain the process of management.
- Examine retail corporate and store hierarchies by surveying key positions and their placement on organizational charts.
- Discern responsibilities of key executives in retail operations.
- Assimilate the concept of organizational leadership by studying types of leaders and leadership skill-building tactics.
- Discuss characteristics of highly effective retail organizations.
- Identify tools used to assess personality style and affinity for management.

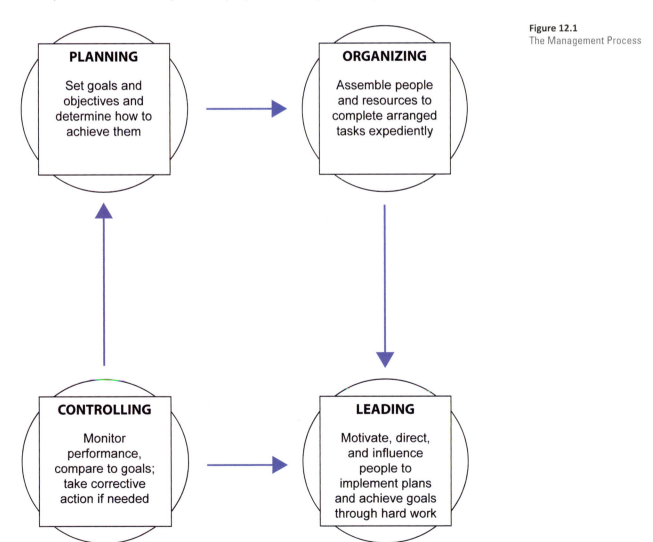

Figure 12.1
The Management Process

Like other aspects of retailing that you've studied, management is an art and a science. The practice melds sound skills for dealing with people with analytical tools that expedite quantitative decision-making. Spreadsheets provide numbers—the scientific components. To cultivate human resource finesse and organizational prowess, people are needed who are creative and exercise common sense when developing applications and solutions. This is the artful component. Team building, leadership, and accountability underscore the basis for management theory today. Let's begin by examining definitions of management within an historical context.

Definitions, History, and Structure

Depending on the era and the source, managers have been viewed as "the boss" and "the leader"—among other straightforward but undoubtedly gender-biased monikers. Phrases such as "the man in charge," "the man upstairs," or "boss man" do not meet today's standards for professional, nonbiased, or even casually accepted titles. The shift from "the boss" to "the manager" to "the leader" reflects the gradual change from an archaic, autonomist supervisory role of managers to the participatory, team-based model popular today. Examining several views of management illustrates how this swing occurred.

Management Defined

Consult a dictionary and you will learn that the word "manage" is derived from the Italian verb *maneggiare,* meaning to handle. The noun *management* emanated from the French word *mesnagement,* which later evolved into *ménagement.* A quick survey of Web sites, professional, and educational resources offers slightly different definitions of "management" and "manager"; what most have in common is the leadership dimension.

The Fairchild Dictionary of Retailing offers this summation on what management is: "Those activities involved in running a business . . . including planning, organizing, coordinating, implementing, directing and monitoring the program of an organization . . . [and] the individual or group of individuals responsible for directing an organization."[1]

Give the basic management definition a marketing skew and you have something like this: **Management** is the administration of a company by leaders who are responsible for setting goals and objectives, implementing business and marketing plans, fostering innovation, guiding and motivating staff, and earning a profit through satisfaction of customer needs and wants.

The person or persons who control, monitor, or direct a business are called **managers**. For example, managers supervise a workforce, deal with crises, and direct sales associates.

Types of Management

Although practitioners differ on the need for many types of management, most agree that several separate branches evolved to answer the needs of business. They include:

- Strategic management.
- Operations management.
- Human resource management.
- Marketing management.
- Financial management.
- Information technology management.
- Retail management.

Some business leaders believe that one general management discipline fits all needs and that the basic principles of managing people remain the same no matter what type of organization is being discussed. A brief history of the managerial concept follows, introducing several different ideologies, people who have influenced management theories and practices, and some of the current tools and beliefs.

History of the Managerial Concept

The origins of management as a method of expediting business-related activity are older than we might think. Although the use of Arabic numerals beginning in the fifth century and double-entry bookkeeping in 1494 paved the way for more sophisticated accounting tools used by managers today, strategies for optimizing human resources to achieve desired goals and outcomes have probably been developing since people began living collectively in groups.

Machiavelli's Contribution

Niccolò Machiavelli—the 16th-century diplomat, statesman, and writer—believed that political treachery was a common human fault and that it was acceptable to fight evil with evil when working with individuals or groups. In his famous historical tome on leadership, *The Prince,* he advised leaders to use fear to maintain control of the populace in the Italian city-state of Florence, where he lived. Published in 1532, the book was translated into English in 1602.[2] So forceful were his ideas that Machiavelli's name came to be equated with a type of leader or manager who is cunning and relentless in the pursuit of wealth and power, and who takes a hard-handed and heartless approach to the process. We'd like to believe that management has evolved from this rigid interpretation to a more humanistic one. However, despite the negative connotations associated with his name today, Machiavelli was considered a shrewd, powerful, but effective leader.

Eighteenth- and Nineteenth-Century Perspectives

Scottish economist and philosopher Adam Smith wrote on many topics including resource allocation, production, and pricing issues. His work, *Inquiry into the Nature and Causes of the Wealth of Nations,* was published in 1776.[3] These topics remain fresh today.

Heralding the shift from an agricultural economy to the beginnings of an industrial one, Eli Whitney, inventor of the cotton gin, and James Watt, of electric production and measurement fame, developed concepts of standardization, quality control, and work planning—some of the same issues that perplex managers today. Classic views of management were refined in the late 1800s as a result of the Industrial Revolution. As businesses expanded and organizations grew larger, it became necessary for managers to develop guidelines, processes, and new methods of finding help as well as deeper theoretical views and information. In 1881, Joseph Wharton founded the first higher-education course in management. The Wharton School of Business at the University of Pennsylvania is named after this early advocate.

Born in England in 1791, Charles Babbage, a mathematician, was another pioneer in the formation of management tools, notably calculating machinery that could perform several types of calculations rather than just one. Often called "the father of computing," he was not given due respect for his accomplishments in his lifetime. In 1991, to celebrate the bicentennial of his birth, the Science Museum in London constructed and successfully operated his calculating machine, called the Difference Engine, using Babbage's original designs. The machine consists of 4,000 parts and weighs over three metric tons.[4]

Before the turn of the century, an approach known as **closed management** was the norm. Using this approach, managers kept their focus strictly within the company, without soliciting outside considerations or input. Industry experts outside the company were not consulted, nor were customer or staff opinions of company practices solicited. The contemporary practice of openly sharing, within a company, knowledge of both internal systems and relevant external factors is called **open management**. This method advocates gathering business knowledge from all constituents, including boards of directors, staff, customers, outside consultants, trade associations, bankers, and shareholders.

Twentieth-Century Developments

Developments in management theory and practice drew from sociology and psychology. By the early 20th century, the work of Abraham Maslow, Douglas McGregor, Robert Owen, Mary Parker Follett, and others inspired a focus on behavioral management. Follett's definition of management, "the art of getting things done through people," underscored theoretical change and the influence of the social sciences.

In 1908, Harvard Business School offered the first Master of Business Administration (MBA) degree. The first program drew 33 regular students and 47 special students with a faculty of 15 academics.[5] Frederick W. Taylor and Frank and Lillian Gilbreth wrote from a scientific perspective in this era. The focus was on quality control, testing, and inspection of products. This concept was furthered by W. Edwards Deming and others who were largely responsible for bringing Japanese products up to world-class standards in the 1940s.[6]

As mid-century neared, Delbert J. Duncan of the University of California, Berkeley, and Stanley C. Hollander of Michigan State University wrote the first retail management book. Published in 1941 as *Retailing: Principles and Methods,* the work was later changed to *Modern Retailing Management.* The textbook remained a key resource for students and retailers for decades.[7] Peter Drucker, a prolific writer on applied management, went on to become famous in this genre and a familiar name to students of business. According to Drucker, the basic responsibilities of management are marketing and innovation.

From the middle to late 20th century, several developments debuted, including total quality management, management by objectives, and numerous information technology–centered programs. Cog's Ladder and Six Sigma exemplify management tools that were introduced at this time.

Cog's Ladder Group Development   In 1972, Procter and Gamble employee George Carrier first published his thoughts on group management. The paper, "Cog's Ladder: A Model of Group Growth," appeared in a company newsletter.[8] **Cog's Ladder** is a group management theory that uses five developmental stages to assess group interaction and effectiveness. The five stages are:

1. *Polite.* Group members become acquainted with each other and assess others' personalities, strengths, and weaknesses. Tone is light, simple, and noncontroversial.
2. *Why are we here?* Working with a moderator or group leader, members identify the reason for the group's existence. The group works on goal-setting, and individuals work on fitting in with other members.
3. *Bid for power.* Group members parry as individual ideas are discussed and examined for worth and usefulness to the group's mission. Leaders, contributors, and followers emerge.
4. *Constructive.* Members begin to weigh and value others' opinions and develop a team spirit. If new members are added to the group in this stage, group dynamics are reevaluated.
5. *Esprit.* Taken from the French phrase *esprit de corps,* interpreted as spirit of the team, the group evolves to the highest level of group interaction and effectiveness.[9]

All groups work through the five stages, although not necessarily in the same order. Individuals' personalities resonate differently in response to those of other group members, their role within their organization, and the task itself. According to advocates of Cog's Ladder, this process is necessary in order to work effectively and reach satisfactory completion of group tasks. More detail regarding the characteristics of each development stage, strategies for proceeding from one level to the next, and comments on what to expect from group participants appears in Table 12.1.

Six Sigma Initiative   Developed by Motorola, the **Six Sigma** initiative uses economic metrics (econometrics) to increase efficiency and quality in businesses.[10] (In manufacturing parlance, "six sigma" indicates a process that is nearly free of defects.)

Six Sigma uses quantitative measures to determine quality, enabling a company to prioritize programs for improving products that are of lowest quality.[11] The method is ongoing and can also be used with services, processes, and businesses. It is as much a mind-set as it is a quantitative tool. Usually groups of four to six people engineer the implementation of Six Sigma, which includes activities crucial to any project:

- Gathering product information.
- Identifying customers.
- Determining customer requirements.
- Formulating a plan of action to improve quality.
- Improving the product to Six Sigma standards.

//////////////////////////////
Cyberscoop
To learn more about Six Sigma and how managers earn their "black belt," go to www.isixsigma.com and click on the "New to Six Sigma" tab.

Table 12.1 Cog's Ladder: Group Development and Performance Guidelines

Development Stage	Characteristics	Strategies for Moving On	Comments
Polite	• Getting acquainted • Sharing values • Establishing group structure • Cliques are formed • Conflict usually absent • Disclosure at a minimum	• Use of ice-breakers to encourage participation • Agenda setting • Organized information sharing	• Some members will only share information that will later aid in their bid for power • Time is the most exploited resource • Focal point is self-disclosure versus embarrassment
Why We're Here	• Defining goals and objectives • Cliques grow • Begin risk taking • Sense hidden agendas	• Sharing and discussing individual and group expectations • Formally defining goals	• This step is often skipped, but must be returned to so that the group can move into constructive stage
Bid for Power	• Group members attempt to influence others' ideas, values, or opinions • Internal competition • Cliques assume power • Disclosure is cautious • Group-building important	• Understanding group dynamics and clear role differentiation of members • Sharing relevant skills and experience; developing plans to utilize talents	• Role, power, and definition issues in this stage • Power differential is necessary if there is to be leadership • Members may share meaningful expertise in this stage • Some groups never get past this stage
Constructive (Cooperative)	• Attitudes change • Active listening • Team spirit builds • Cliques dissolve • Leadership shared • Conflicts resolved • Effective use of resources and talent	• Adopt common approach to problem-solving • Decision-making process based on consensus	• Problem-solving stage • Group will find common model for problem solving • Some danger of "group think" • New members not easily accepted
Esprit	• Unity; high cohesiveness • High spirits and morale • Mutual acceptance • Intense loyalty • Cliques absent	• Dealing with new challenges • Expand risk taking • Team evaluates performance and sets new directions	• "Group think" may need to be dealt with • Complacency and sense of isolation may set in • New member would cause regression to an earlier stage

Source: D.L. Miersma, "Cog's Ladder: Group/Team Development Model," accessed January 6, 2011, http://componentleadership.pmi.org/tips/templates/COG's%20 Ladder%20a%20model20%for%20group-team-WindowsInternetExplorer.

Six Sigma was used in the 1990s to spur changes in corporate culture. Businesses today are more concerned with bottom-line results, and in pursuit of that goal many have deployed the newer Lean Six Sigma approach. **Lean Six Sigma** refers to initiatives that specifically produce cost-saving measures, also called *lean practices* in business. Several leading manufacturers and retailers have used Lean Six Sigma to shave expenses and implement sound financial practices.[12]

From the late 20th through the early 21st century, management theory and practices evolved quickly and vigorously. Changes in attitudes and human behavior irrevocably modified

Table 12.2 Behavioral Changes in Managerial Performance: 1990s to 2010s

FROM: 1990s	TO: 2010s
Individual accountability	Mutual support, joint accountability, and trust-based relationships in addition to individual accountability
Dividing those who think and decide from those who work and do	Expecting everyone to think, work, and do
Building functional excellence through each person executing a narrow set of tasks ever more efficiently	Encouraging people to play multiple roles and work together interchangeably on continuous improvement
Relying on managerial control	Getting people to buy into meaningful purpose, to help shape direction, and to learn
A fair day's pay for a fair day's work	Aspiring to personal growth that expands as well as exploits each person's capabilities

Source: Jon R. Katzenbach and Douglas K. Smith, Table 10.1, "Behavioral Changes Demanded by Performance in the 1990s and Beyond," in *The Wisdom of Teams* (New York: HarperBusiness, 1993), 211.

management style and strategies during this period. A synopsis of these changes is found in Table 12.2.

Twenty-first–Century Viewpoints

A growing need to conduct business skillfully in the brave new world that is the 21st century is apparent. The interactive nature of multifunctional teams in organizations today makes it impractical to slot management into specific cubbyholes. The individual is encouraged to innovate, but equally expected to be a team player. Accountability is expected at all stages of the management process. **Accountability** is a policy that ensures that job expectations are satisfactorily met by the person or persons held responsible for the action.

As more democratic and consensus-building models are implemented, the trend may return to more general management platforms. This may seem contradictory, or at least somewhat confusing. Follow business news reports and you will learn that old-style management practices are still used by some companies. When you read of layoffs in certain corporations and substantial bonuses given to the "big bosses" it remains clear that some things never change. Patriarchal hierarchies are slow to adopt new models. Going forward, firms that react to change first, fast, and fully will claim or retain their places as industry leaders.

The Management Process

Four stages in the management process apply to all businesses and organizations, from retail companies to digital advertising agencies, multinational companies to churches. They include—but are not limited to—planning, organizing, leading, and controlling. The management process is portrayed graphically in Figure 12.1. Types of planning used by managers are addressed first.

Planning

You learned about strategic planning, one of the principal visionary tools used by retailers, in Chapter 3. Company leaders and top-level managers execute strategic planning with input from many levels of the organization. Two other forms of planning are tactical and contingency planning. **Tactical planning** is very detailed short-term planning that is usually done in a narrow vein by middle and lower management. When original plans do not reach fruition, managers seek alternative methods for achieving goals—an action called **contingency planning**. This may take place at all levels within an organization, but often is spearheaded by employees who are privy to breaking news and information about the flow of merchandise.

Figure 12.2
Well-stocked departments are evidence of both tactical and contingency planning methods. Merchandise managers plan for selling seasons well in advance but always are on alert for extenuating circumstances that necessitate a change in strategy. If the kitty litter on the endcap advertised for $10.79 didn't arrive in time for the planned sale, then management would likely make a substitute.

For a departmental merchandise manager, planning might consist of ensuring that a full inventory of jeans would be available for customers shopping for back-to-school items in early August. This is a form of tactical planning. In contrast, the vice president of merchandising would be involved with planning at a higher level—setting sales goals for numerous departments, planning the flow of goods for a longer period of time, and scouting private-label manufacturers looking for the best deal on jeans that ultimately are sold for the back-to-school season. Continuing the example, if the company's contractor in Asia could not supply the goods in time for fall selling, the vice president might opt to use a manufacturer that could comply with the time-sensitive delivery date. This is an example of contingency planning. When you visit a store and notice its well-stocked and inviting merchandise assortments, like the one in Figure 12.2, you can be sure that both tactical and contingency planning were used by merchandise managers. Further aspects of merchandise planning and management are discussed in Chapter 15.

Organizing

The ability to organize all elements of an action so that it meets company goals is crucial when organizing a team or project, and directing its outcome. This is not a simple task. Whether the retailer is small or large, many factors intertwine and the performance of numerous people, materials, contractors, and others must be coordinated if actions are to be completed on time. Achieving organization in a business involves allocating resources, assigning tasks, confirming completion, and conducting follow-up communications as necessary. Coherence and consistency are equally relevant.

Leading

Choreographing, directing, supervising, and motivating employees to implement plans and complete assigned tasks effectively all sound more like the actions involved in preparing to stage a Broadway play than those required to lead a retail initiative. Actually, there are similarities when we address leadership in the context of the performance of retailing. Leaders today prefer to encourage employees to take ownership of the actions they are assigned. This is an essential component

Figure 12.3
Mentoring and promotion from within the organization are important considerations for Neiman Marcus. Read about the backgrounds and management styles of top executives outgoing & incoming CEO's, Burt Tansky and Karen Katz. (Source: Neiman Marcus executives photo from "The Key Players," *Women's Wear Daily,* April 27, 2010, 13.)

of **empowerment**—the act of enabling individuals to complete tasks by providing resources, instilling motivation, and expecting them to take responsibility for the outcome. Empowered employees usually work in teams to discuss, design, and carry out programs themselves. This is in stark contrast to earlier eras when managers essentially gave workers orders and criticism in about equal amounts. Empowering employees makes them feel as if they truly are important to the company; in turn, employees tend to feel a stronger sense of ownership in the outcome of the task or project, and are much more likely to want to communicate with their managers.

Another important aspect of leading is mentoring, which exists from initial management training programs to the upper echelon where senior-level managers are groomed to take over new positions. **Mentoring** is the informal training given to one employee by another who is of higher rank within an organization. It is said that good mentoring can pave the way to promotion for managers who are open to this type of communication and interaction. Optimally, not only expectations of the job are discussed but also the political climate that the employee will find in a new department or division and the interplay among executives. Mentors also are invaluable in providing introductions to other professions outside the company that may be beneficial to the person being mentored. The mentor then, is a coach, guide, and guru all wrapped into one.

The benefits of long-term mentoring became apparent when Burton Tansky, president and chief executive officer (CEO) of Neiman Marcus, announced his retirement in 2010 and new top leaders were selected. Karen Katz was named to succeed him. She had been with the company since 1985 and had held a variety of positions, most recently in the office of the chairman. There, she served as executive vice president of the group, taking on new responsibilities for strategic business development and marketing. To retail insiders, this move signified that she would most likely be Tansky's successor.[13]

Jim Gold had been president and CEO of Bergdorf Goodman (a division of The Neiman Marcus Group) since 2004, and in 2010 was promoted to president of specialty retail and store operations for Neiman Marcus's full-line stores as well. Gold and Tansky arrived at Neiman Marcus at about the same time, and Gold learned the importance of diversifying his management experiences within

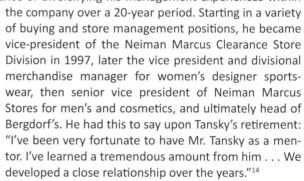

the company over a 20-year period. Starting in a variety of buying and store management positions, he became vice-president of the Neiman Marcus Clearance Store Division in 1997, later the vice president and divisional merchandise manager for women's designer sportswear, then senior vice president of Neiman Marcus Stores for men's and cosmetics, and ultimately head of Bergdorf's. He had this to say upon Tansky's retirement: "I've been very fortunate to have Mr. Tansky as a mentor. I've learned a tremendous amount from him . . . We developed a close relationship over the years."[14]

It is evident that the route to the top is long and challenging. Without mentors, most candidates never get off first base. Photos of top Neiman Marcus executives discussed in this section appear in Figure 12.3.

Controlling

Knowing what is happening in all facets of a business and pinpointing areas of strength and weakness are critical elements in management. Observing, communicating with managers and staff, seeking solutions to problems, and rewarding innovation are core concepts. Monitoring behavior and evaluating performance require subjective and objective measurement, as managers reach for excellence. Establishing parameters for decision making and reporting, and developing job descriptions for every position set the tone for effective supervision of employees. Comparing performance to goals, and then taking action if necessary, is at the heart of controlling.

Staffing, training employees, and assessing performance are functions of management that are carried out by human resource specialists. This aspect of retail management is discussed in detail in Chapter 13.

Organizational Structure

The size of a company usually dictates the number of executives, managers, and staff needed and the organizational structure. Specialty, discount, and department stores have different needs than online stores and catalogue retailers. Huge organizations such as Walmart, with three million employees worldwide, need more store general managers and staff than do specialty retailers selling custom apparel for dogs and cats. Online companies run by fewer people require less complex organizational charts than do multidivision department store groups.

Building Organizational Charts

Organizational charts are used to identify the chain of communication (formerly called command) and indicate the responsibility level of positions in the company hierarchy. Charts are usually prepared for the company as a whole, the board of directors, and separate divisions, right down to individual departments as needed. Discerning who reports to whom is one of the major uses of organizational charts. Employees are sometimes able to glean knowledge of the internal political structure once names are placed in their proper boxes on the chart.

Position titles may not be the same in every company. In fact, many businesses create a lexicon of their own as a way of asserting their individual corporate identity; for example, store managers are identified as "store team leaders" at Target stores. An organizational chart for Target's corporate executive management is illustrated in Figure 12.4.

A company either supports the mission and vision statements that were mentioned in Chapter 3, or if necessary, regroups and changes the formal authority schematic for the better. Clarity is called for as positions and responsibilities are adjusted. A store-level chart is quite different from a corporate one since the latter usually begins with the general manager.

There is no one template for constructing an organizational chart since most firms do not subscribe to a cookie-cutter method of defining their workforce and its potential for interaction. For instance, the home improvement retailer Lowe's places much more emphasis on the merchandise zones in its stores by allocating the bulk of its management to that sector.

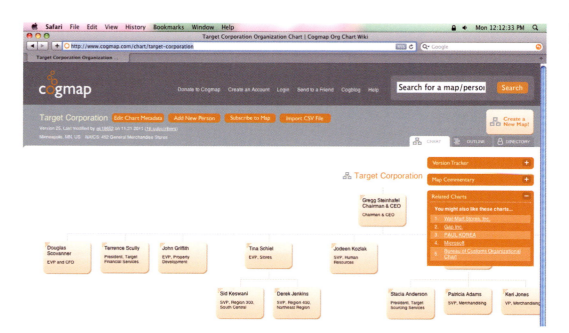

Figure 12.4
Organization chart for Target Corporation.

Executive, Managerial, and Staff Positions

In large retail organizations, many positions and levels of staff are appropriate, necessitated by the demands of time, space, merchandise, real estate, global divisions, and critical areas, which converge in the process of running the operation profitably. A few examples of positions at various levels of a retail company are listed below, along with the roles they play.

- *Chief executive officer (CEO).* Directs all activities planned to implement administrative policies and strategic planning for a corporation or large division of a firm. Reports to the chairman of the board. In foreign companies, the CEO is sometimes called a managing director.
- *President.* Oversees all operations of a corporation or large division of a firm. In many situations, the positions of CEO and president are held by the same person.
- *Chairman (or chairwoman) of the board.* Leader of the board of directors in publicly held companies. Wields a great deal of power regarding financial and other strategic planning.
- *Board of directors.* Serve as an advisory board to the firm. Individuals from inside and outside the company or conglomerate with specific expertise are selected. In family-held companies, often one or more family members sit on the board. In large firms, the board also assists with identifying, hiring, and developing executives to become future corporate leaders.
- *Senior management.* Take responsibility for strategic decision making for the company and their functional areas. Executives at vice presidential levels as well as high-ranking directors and heads of major areas such as merchandising, marketing, finance, stores, online, and human resources are included. Executive vice presidents (EVPs) hold positions of great authority and decision-making power in their respective functional areas. Senior vice presidents (SVPs) and vice presidents (VPs) head smaller segments of a functional area and report to an EVP. For example, in a multiunit department store, there would be an EVP of human resources, an SVP of human resources, and perhaps a VP for corporate recruiting. Directors within a specific area are included in this section in some organizations. Other members of top management include a chief financial officer (CFO), chief operations officer (COO), and perhaps a chief information officer (CIO). They are the firm's top executives and are future-oriented.
- *Middle management.* Report to senior managers who are in charge of their specific areas. Senior buyers, asset protection directors, and warehouse managers are examples. Ranks of salaried department or area managers supervise small or large staffs depending on the size of the company and the organization's structure. At the store level, general managers, district managers who oversee eight to ten specialty stores in a chain, and regional managers who are responsible for several states usually are in this category. Each of these managers would report to a director of stores or an SVP or EVP of stores, depending on the setup of the company. Having said that, some general managers of large retail chain stores may hold the dual distinction of being an SVP or EVP at the corporate level.
- *Lower management.* Responsible for executing the tasks and programs originated by senior and middle management. Employees at this level include assistant department managers, assistant buyers, and perhaps a visual merchandising team leader.
- *Supervisors.* Workers who have been given additional duties to fulfill, such as scheduling counter help, or overseeing warehouse staff or customer service associates. Head cashiers would also fit this category. Often, but not exclusively, people in these positions are hourly wage earners.
- *Staff.* Employees not covered in any of the above categories including front-line cashiers and sales associates in stores, and behind-the-scenes maintenance workers and security guards at either corporate headquarters or stores.

In sheer numbers, lower and midlevel staff far outnumber high-ranking executives in retail organizations. Through upswings and downturns in the economy, positions at this level have continued to offer opportunities for those just graduating from college.

As the 2008–2010 recession waned, many retailers began hiring more staff to fill slots previously vacated by layoffs. In early 2010, for example, Macy's announced that it would add 725 mid- and entry-level positions over a two-year period for its online stores, Macys.com and Bloomingdales.com. For the bulk of 2010, Macy's online sales were close to 30 percent higher than the previous year, justifying the hiring initiative. The company expects to add almost 3,500 online positions overall, including positions in merchandising, marketing, site development, and other technical areas, by 2013.[15] Industry pundits viewed this announcement as a positive indicator of growth in the retail industry.

Routinely made decisions that may seem contrary to those outside the retail industry add nuance to the cyclical nature of retailing. In early 2012, Macy's Inc. announced the closure of five Macy's and four Bloomingdale's stores. Collectively, more than 830 workers were affected by the decision, which was based on mediocre financial performance in certain locations, including the Mall of America. Earlier, the company had announced that five new Macy's stores and five new Bloomingdale's outlet stores would open by the end of the year. What appeared to be an equal trade was actually thoughtful decision making to help perpetuate a stable and profitable operation.[16]

Characteristics of Successful Managers

Effective retail managers possess a range of personal competencies and skill sets, which are highlighted next. Some of these attributes have greater relevance in particular settings, and no one person has all of the traits mentioned. As examples, a charismatic presence can be nurtured, but this trait is more likely inherent in certain individuals. Other individuals may be whizzes with data, having acquired significantly advanced accounting or information technology skills, but may not be as effective when dealing with human resource issues. It is the melding of various abilities, talents, passions, learned skills, and experience that make a manager.

Competencies of Effective Managers

An effective manager should possess both interpersonal and skills-based, task-oriented abilities. Most retailers agree that ideal managers are forward-thinking, results-oriented individuals with aptitudes for risk-taking and integrating solutions in a complex, multichannel, global environment. As if this weren't enough, high-level managers are expected to be prescient, skilled at identifying and recruiting talent that will fit the corporate culture and respond well to training and mentoring. Being alert to opportunities and threats—both inside and outside the organization—is another requirement of managers.

Of the various skills-based attributes expected of managers, written, oral, and technological competencies are among the most important because they relate to the ability to communicate with others. All human relations work relies on advanced communication skills, including the ability to express compassion, show empathy, and offer effective redirection or correction, when necessary. And, in a field where time is of the essence, time-management capabilities are essential in retailing.

Qualities of Lean Six Sigma Managers

Being a risk-taker and an insightful manager are admirable traits, but they are only two of the necessary qualities sought in candidates for managerial positions. Companies that use the Lean Six Sigma method, introduced earlier, have identified the following ten criteria in their ideal employee:

1. *"Fire in the belly"*—Possesses an intense desire to improve the way an organization operates.
2. *People skills*—Works well with others, both inside teams and outside groups.
3. *Project management*—Completes tasks successfully and expediently.
4. *Systems thinker*—Knows that processes enable work to be accomplished and that over time, processes need to be reevaluated and improved.
5. *Multitasker*—Can juggle many tasks concurrently.
6. *Unstructured environment manager*—Handles chaos well.
7. *Big-picture thinker*—Is goal-oriented and works to bring all constituents together to meet objectives.
8. *Organizational navigation skills*—Can work through problems without being overly dependent on higher management.
9. *Critical-thinking skills*—Able to conceptualize, analyze, synthesize, evaluate, and apply information from multiple sources; embraces innovation while integrating analytics in the decision-making process.
10. *Analytical skills*—Is comfortable and adept at using mathematics, logic, and reasoning.[17]

Lean Six Sigma methods are used across all types of organizations, and many retailers find that their companies operate more efficiently after implementing the program. The ten Lean Six Sigma traits mentioned here have much in common with other substantive programs used by proactive retail companies.

Traits of Future Leaders

At the Annual CEO Summit sponsored by *Women's Wear Daily,* 135 presidents and CEOs were surveyed to pinpoint the skills needed by tomorrow's business leaders. Their responses suggest that different skills are needed to succeed in the 21st century. The most compelling finding was the need for "leaders with a new perspective," with 74 percent of those surveyed indicating that they intend to recruit from outside the retail industry in the near future. Retailers also are looking for candidates who have an affinity for the newer methods of doing business and have talents not currently apparent in retail organizations.[18] The graphs in Figure 12.5 compare areas of expertise of the retail respondents (left) with the key specialty areas from which the next generation of leaders should arise (right). The most important leadership skills for those seeking success at an executive position are inferred in Figure 12.5.

By examining the fundamentals of business ideology and practice, we can better understand the dynamics of individual, team, and business interactions in any firm or nonprofit organization that employs people. The next section focuses on organizational leadership in retailing.

Organizational Leadership

There are as many types of leaders as there are individual personalities. Leading a retail organization requires strengths in many sectors since managers cannot predict what special skills are needed from day to unpredictable retail day. **Leadership** is the process of one person influencing another individual, team, or group of people to work toward common goals. **Organizational leadership** is the umbrella term for the cross-functional, team-oriented management models that encourage consensus-building and formulating solutions to problems. Several individual styles of leadership are explained next.

Types of Leaders

Examine the three types of leaders below. Do you or people you work with display any of these characteristics?

- *Autocratic leaders.* Make decisions independently, then inform employees or subordinates. A solo performer, the autocratic leader seeks little advice inside or outside the company.
- *Democratic leaders.* Involve others in the decision-making process by asking for employees' opinions, which are shared and evaluated before decisions are made. In some retail organizations, input is sought from sales associates as well as those in executive positions.
- *Transformational leaders.* Motivate employees to work for the greater good of the organization rather than exclusively for personal goals. Transformational leaders usually possess charismatic qualities as well as formidable management and team-building skills themselves.[19]

The concept of organizational leadership relies upon developing transformational leaders. This contemporary view is championed by many top retail companies such as CVS Caremark Corp. with over 7,300 retail drug stores in early 2012 and close to $60 billion in revenue in 2011.[20] Read about how the executive vice president of merchandising and supply chain helped develop the company's upmarket Beauty 360 concept stores and the factors that led to the closure of the 23 stores in May 2012 in From the Field 12.1.

Building Leadership Skills

You may have heard the axiom "leaders are born, not made" or, conversely, "leaders are made, not born." Which is it? Probably a bit of both, since many personality traits influence executive performance, and leadership skills are taught, ingrained, and perfected. Leadership, teamwork,

What were your primary areas of expertise prior to becoming a top executive? Select all that apply.

Discipline	%
Finance	23%
International Business	19%
Marketing	51%
Merchandising	42%
Operations	26%
Product Design/Development	33%
Sales	44%
Technology	6%
Other	13%

What discipline would be the most effective pipeline for the next generation of leaders in retail? Select one response.

Discipline	%
Finance	2%
International Business	11%
Marketing	21%
Merchandising	26%
Operations	6%
Product Design/Development	13%
Sales	6%
Technology	11%
Other	4%

Figure 12.5a
Most Effective Pipelines for Future Leaders based on executives' experience.

Why will your company recruit for leadership positions from outside the retail industry? Select all that apply.

	%
Want leaders with a new perspective.	69%
Want leaders who are better prepared for new ways business is conducted.	52%
Want leaders with skills/expertise that are not currently available in the industry.	45%
Talent pool in retail is limited.	43%
Other	11%

Figure 12.5b
Most Important leadership traits sought when recruiting executives from outside the retail industry.

entrepreneurism, best practices—all ring true. Organizations that demand high performance from their managers tend to nurture their leaders by identifying, mentoring, training, and giving them input at every juncture. As with all management models and practices, there are advantages and disadvantages to this endeavor. These are addressed next, along with the circumstances under which teams work most effectively.

From the Field 12.1   CVS Comes Calling

CVS Pharmacy spent several years readying its doors for prestige beauty brands, the chain's executive vice president of merchandising and supply chain, Mike Bloom, told attendees of the 2010 Beauty CEO Summit held in New York City. "We actually believe that we've earned the right to have a seat at this prestige beauty table," he said.

Bloom introduced the audience to the retailer's upscale beauty concept called Beauty 360, which were located adjacent to 25 CVS stores and stocks premium-price brands, ranging from Cargo cosmetics to Warren-Tricomi hair care. "The Beauty 360 concept was actually over ten years in the making," said Bloom. "We didn't just make this decision overnight. It was a logical next step for CVS." Addressing the prestige beauty executives in the room, he said, "Many of you here know we've been knocking on your doors for several years. We put a lot of time, a lot of energy, and a lot of resources into getting it right. We listened to our customers, we listened to industry experts—many of you in this room— and we continue to listen today."

Bloom clarified that CVS viewed Beauty 360 as an additional channel of distribution, not a replacement for existing prestige beauty channels. He noted that the company found that 40 percent of Beauty 360 customers were new to CVS and had not purchased beauty products at the chain before shopping Beauty 360.

Some five million customers a day stream through CVS's chain of more than 7,000 stores, which translates to 35 million a week, said Bloom. What's more, 80 percent of the chain's customers are female, and together they generate $4.5 billion in beauty sales at CVS, or 900 million beauty products a year.

"Our clear focus on health and beauty, our ability to reach millions and millions of customers each and every day, and our unparalleled real estate position makes Beauty 360 a natural extension to current distribution because it offers a controlled environment that protects your brand as well as offering superior customer service," said Bloom. "We believe this is, at minimum, a $2 billion opportunity for this industry. We believe there were somewhere in the neighborhood of 750 to 1,000 stores that are right for Beauty 360 throughout all the key markets in the United States."

Adapted from Molly Prior, "The Beauty CEO Summit 2010," *Women's Wear Daily*, June 11, 2010, 6.

Author's Update: Further expansion was not meant to be. In May 2012, CVS closed all 25 Beauty 360 stores as well as its online store. Most of the stores were located in California, with one each in Connecticut and Washington D.C. CVS officials addressed the closure:

CVS/pharmacy has made the decision to refocus our efforts on the growth and development of our core CVS/pharmacy beauty business in order to satisfy a wider group of our customers . . .

[The Beauty 360 stores] proved to be a tremendous learning experience for our organization . . . [M]any aspects of the Beauty 360 concept . . . were positive. In the past four years, we have learned a great deal about our beauty customer through our experience with Beauty 360 and plan to apply many of these learnings to future enhancements within our beauty department at CVS/pharmacy.

Source: http://www.bizjournals.com/sacramento/news/2012/03/27cvs-to-end-its-beauty-360-operations.html?s=print.

Advantages of Teams

Members of teams quickly become aware of the pros and cons of being part of a group. On the plus side is the satisfaction that comes from working together to achieve a goal—we are ecstatic when our soccer team wins the playoffs after working hard all season. Many parallels can be drawn between teamwork in the sporting sense and leadership and performance in retail management. Listing some of the advantages of teams is at the crux of this discussion:

- Many heads are better than one. Multiple viewpoints add dimension to discussions and aid brainstorming.
- Group members bring different skill sets to the table.
- Teams cover more ground in a shorter period of time and find more possible solutions to problems.
- Teams encourage cross-functional learning, thereby raising the bar of performance.
- Teams can better grasp the challenges facing all constituents, not just those in their own area.
- Teams have more fun on the job than off the field! Getting out of the cubbyhole and associating more closely with other colleagues is beneficial to both the individual and the company.[21] A team at work and obviously fully engaged in the process is illustrated in Figure 12.6.

The best teams are those that form around mutual interest in a topic or problem. This is more likely to occur when participants are in an environment where upper management provides clear performance standards and methods of assessment.

Disadvantages of Teams

Team members also know the frustration that can develop when working with others—for instance, classmates in a study group. Members may not share the workload equally, and personality

Figure 12.6
Organizational leadership is built on successful team interaction utilizing diverse skills and talents in a nonthreatening group atmosphere. Group leaders facilitate timely completion of tasks and encourage optimal quality work from members.

conflicts may make it difficult to engage in meaningful discussion. It doesn't get any easier when retail executives comprise the teams. When working in teams in a business setting, members may:

- Display lack of interest or a level of excitement for the task at hand.
- Convey feelings of futility.
- Believe time could be better spent.
- Engage in one-sided or nonconstructive discussions.
- Drift away from the point being made or task at hand.
- Voice negative attitudes toward teamwork before meetings or work activities begin.
- Initiate personal negative commentary by group members about other group members or colleagues who are not present.
- Blame top management or the company in general, or conduct meetings only to impress their supervisors, not to generate solutions.[22]

Conditions that Foster Successful Teamwork

Much has been said about the advantages of teams that perform well and find solutions to pressing problems. Cog's Ladder, mentioned earlier, symbolizes the importance placed on identifying and developing teams so that they function well in organizations.

The environment in which teams work most effectively, stay on task, and flourish is difficult to gauge since all organizations operate differently. However, a few commonalities can be identified. Effective teams:

- Develop a strong sense of purpose and direction.
- Encourage commitment on the part of team members.
- Recognize skill sets that need work within the team—technical competencies, decision-making, problem-solving, goal- and objective-setting, or interpersonal abilities—and seek outside professional trainers or facilitators if necessary to improve these skill sets.
- Break down tasks or decisions into small, manageable units, rather than trying to complete the project or visualize the "big picture" in one sitting.
- Positively reinforce performance.
- Select an effective team leader.

And, if all else fails, successful teams change the composition of the team. Next, let's look more closely at the role that highly motivated, magnetic leaders play in management circles.

Impact of Charismatic Leaders

Although the characteristics of teams, corporate cultures, and managers all merit scrutiny, it's the traits of effective leaders that generate unending fascination. When Terry Lundgren, president, chairman, and CEO of Macy's, takes the stage at a retail conference, all eyes and ears are upon him. A charismatic leader, immaculately attired and groomed, he conveys an ease of communication combined with a strong presence. Lundgren's indefinable ability to magnetize his audience—and employees—is noteworthy.

H. Lee Scott, former CEO of Walmart, could make an "intimate" audience of several hundred people feel as though he was speaking to each of them individually. This was my experience at one of the company's famous Saturday morning meetings, held at its headquarters in Bentonville, Arkansas. Standing onstage at the podium, Scott seemed a half-mile away as he introduced our group of 60 educators from the American Collegiate Retailing Association. Then, to our great surprise, he walked down the aisle of the large auditorium to our section and spent a few minutes answering questions, "up close and personal." We were in awe of this personable leader who never missed a beat as he worked the audience and promoted the Walmart brand. That day I learned firsthand the inestimable value of a charismatic leader.

Stellar leadership is not limited to large retail organizations that have the resources to train and empower executives. Small businesses and online startups benefit equally from the leadership guidelines introduced in this chapter. A leadership profile of Dany Levy, who created the online guide DailyCandy, is presented in From the Field 12.2.

Selected Job Profiles of Retail Managers

We can gain insight into what retail managers actually do to meet their goals and objectives by looking closely at two key positions in the retail hierarchy. First let's examine how a general manager oversees multiple sectors in a large retail store.

General Manager

The person or persons who manage an entire brick-and-mortar store or even an online store are responsible for overseeing the efficient operation of the retail venture. Day in and day out, working long hours (sometimes seven days a week, especially during holiday periods) for a general manager (GM), the pace is fast and ever-changing. Depending on the size and volume of the store, GMs earn from $35,000 to well over $100,000 annually. Here are some of the responsibilities of a GM:

- Oversees and participates in the many integrated processes that are needed to run a store. Included are sales and customer service, inventory, visual merchandising, financial controls, information technology, sales promotion, loss prevention, maintenance, human resources, and community relations.
- Hears and reads reports from all sector managers; oversight is broad and time-consuming.
- Motivates employees through meaningful incentives and by being a role model for staff.
- Approves workplace scheduling.
- Encourages and empowers sector managers to make decisions and initiate new programs.
- Identifies future store leaders by observing employees on the job and receiving feedback from reporting managers.
- Encourages planning for succession, a topic that is discussed more fully in Chapter 13.

Effective GMs are acutely aware of the overlap between pure management functions and the need to encourage and execute change on the job. The goal of most companies is to increase store sales and profits while providing optimal customer service to their customers. Some companies have found it effective to operate with co-managers. The specialty chain Express uses this approach in its larger stores that carry men's and women's fashion in adjacent areas.

Pivotal points of decision making for GMs stem from all aspects of the retail business. Let's delve further into the specific tasks carried out by managers of the operations area.

From the Field 12.2   Q&A: Dany Levy, The Incidental Leader

Dany Levy, founder of the online guide DailyCandy, discusses the evolving nature of her role as a female entrepreneur.

While she was working as a magazine journalist, Dany Levy dreamed up the concept for the curated online guide DailyCandy, and set out on her own to produce a free daily e-mail: a New York city–based insider's guide to what's hot, new, and undiscovered—from fashion and restaurant news to gadgets and travel. Ten years later, with three million subscribers, she is guiding her vision on a global scale with a new owner, and reflects on how her role as a leader has changed and evolved over time.

What was behind your decision to start your own business?

I majored in creative writing at college, and then went into journalism. As the Internet was fast becoming a mature medium, it was the realization that I could do something really interesting with my passion that made me decide to start a business. It wasn't a eureka moment; the idea kind of bubbled up. Over the years, I've often been asked whether the idea comes first, or the desire to be an entrepreneur. For me there's no doubt it's the idea. You can't just decide to be an entrepreneur. I identified an opportunity and committed to it; it was as simple—and completely life-changing—as that.

Do you think leadership is in your DNA, or have you learned it over time?

It's a combination of the two, of course. There are different types of leadership that are required for a company at different stages, and I tend to lead by inspiration, rather than through any particular management skill. Part of the reason that DailyCandy has done so well is that I was aware of what I was good at and what I was less good at, and I made sure to hire around my weaknesses. I found a great CEO early on, and he became the day-to-day management, enabling me to remain the visionary.

So then, are you saying you're more of a delegator or a hands-on leader?

Different employees need different things, so you need to be both. The skill is in reading the specific situation and responding to it well. I'm blessed with a phenomenal staff, and have taken care to pay close attention to every one of them, particularly as we've grown. You have to remain very aware of whom you're working with, and flexible enough to recognize that everyone's needs are different. But this doesn't mean being a doormat: you need to be firm and consistent, too.

How has the vision changed as DailyCandy has grown?

I think the core has stayed the same. DailyCandy is much more female than I originally thought it would be. That refocused the vision from producing a general city guide to concentrating around a female demographic. In the beginning, it was very much about the things that I like, but as we've grown, new people have had to communicate their understanding and expertise, so that's changed of course. I encourage all of our contributors to develop individually without imposing my taste, but at the same time, work hard to be sure that what they do falls within the overall brand and its tone and voice. Brand consistency is key.

What are the most difficult leadership decisions you face?

Some of the more difficult decisions are about disagreeing with people I respect, when I'm required to take a good look at the reality of the situation. Companies are like families, but keeping hold of the bigger picture is important. I know I'm facing a difficult decision when I feel myself working to preserve the family dynamic at the same time as making a hardheaded business decision.

What people or brands do you turn to for inspiration?

I'm always inspired by people who have created amazing brands from scratch—like Marcia Kilgore, who carefully built the Bliss brand from a one-room spa in SoHo to a worldwide brand. I admire Natalie Massenet, who created Net-a-Porter, which has been a whopping success, largely because of her keen eye, business savvy, and knack for quality and curation. I also admire Tina Brown, who executes any project she takes on with great competence and determination.

How will your role evolve?

I'm pleased with where I am. Managing both up and down is rewarding. I'm tuned into the business, and our owners (Comcast) take account of my opinions and input. But things are moving fast; I know what's coming tomorrow and maybe next week, but as for six months' time, I've no idea, except that I'll be ready for it. I'm very solution-oriented.

Is there a piece of advice you received in the course of the growth of DailyCandy that stands out?

It's important to keep mentors, and I know I wouldn't have survived without them. I've always been amazed by how many people are willing to help an entrepreneur.

Adapted and condensed from an interview by James Waite in *Open Book, A Practical Guide to Business Growth*, American Express, June 29, 2010, 5, www.openforum.com/idea-hub/topics/managing/article/open-book-leadership-open-book-leadership. (Edited and produced by Winkreative, New York.)

Store Operations Manager

Smooth retail operations involve more than just displaying designer apparel, selling hot new e-books, or recruiting on college campuses. Behind-the-scenes operations managers play important roles in ensuring that the physical plant is in top shape before, during, and after employees and customers are present. Operations include but are not limited to opening and closing the store, seeing that the store is clean and in good working order, conferring with maintenance, asset protection, shipping and receiving, customer service, peripheral departments, and warehousing.

Store Maintenance

The maintenance department is in charge of the interior and exterior of the store. Everything that relates to cleanliness—of floors, walls, ceilings, stock areas, and those all-important restrooms—falls under the manager's jurisdiction. The language of heating, ventilation, and air conditioning

(HVAC) is one in which maintenance is fluent. But this sector is not through with work yet. If the store is not located in a shopping center, management of the parking lot, as well as trash pickup, snowplowing, and grounds upkeep, also are responsibilities. We often take for granted the many details for which this team, and ultimately the operations manager, are responsible.

Stores that opt to locate in a mall soon learn that shopping center managers are sticklers for detail. If, for example, there are too many fingerprints on the interior doors of a retail tenant, the tenant—after a verbal warning—may be fined for cleanliness infractions.

Asset Protection

The team responsible for asset protection, also called loss prevention, is fully engaged in reducing shrinkage by monitoring the flow of traffic in and out of the store so that visitors with criminal intent are deterred from committing theft or apprehended if caught red-handed. Asset protection managers and staff work to make the store a safe and secure environment for customers and employees. Visual and virtual surveillance is part of their job description, as is dealing with shoplifters, employee theft, and organized retail crime (ORC). Many work with local, state, and federal law enforcement agencies in the quest to deter theft and capture perpetrators.

After examining the various contingencies that must be managed by retailers, we might wonder how they manage at all. Proactive retailers look to industrial, manufacturing, and marketing companies, as well as other retailers, for clues to successful operations. Those that use product management tactics find that they organize tasks and their workforce better, as you'll see in the next section.

The human element in retailing is a crucial and challenging one, with numerous areas of responsibility managed by human resource departments. The intense effort involved in identifying, selecting, training, mentoring, and assessing employees, and administering job-related benefits, makes the position of human resource manager worthy of mention here, setting the stage for the broader coverage of human resource management (HRM) in Chapter 13.

Characteristics of Highly Effective Organizations

We've reviewed key characteristics of effective managers. It is equally important to highlight some of the qualities of successful organizations. Retailers that use product management, solve problems diligently, embrace global differences, and grow healthy businesses with vigor are much more apt to meet their objectives than those that do not.

Practice Project Management

Notorious multitaskers, retail managers deal with the demands of customers, employees, and their own managers. Keeping the operation flowing smoothly is critical to the success of any manager. "We open at 9:30 am, not 9:35 am," is an example of the level of detail ensured by those in charge. Store managers give input regarding new merchandise, although they are not buyers. They deal with union problems, although they might not be legally or politically geared for such interaction. Most participate in human resource activities, although they have departments that specialize in training.

Project management allows managers to break down the essential activities that have an impact on their work and reorganize staff in meaningful ways to create reactionary teams. To better support their retail operations, managers should:

1. Ensure adequate staffing so they can delegate tasks and thereby prioritize their own work.
2. When implementing new ideas, try them out consecutively, not concurrently.
3. Avoid introducing a new concept unless they know how they will measure results.[23]

As an example, suppose you were considering featuring warm outdoor apparel on your retail Web site in August. Using a product management approach, you would first study regional climate patterns as you built your plan. It's customary to sell winter apparel in August in New England, but to market down jackets in temperate southern California might seem foolhardy—or not. Suppose that, along with a Web site, you operate a brick-and-mortar store located in an area close to mountains, and price the merchandise for aggressive promotion. California outdoor aficionados would likely respond by purchasing warm clothing, but probably not at the pace at which New Englanders would buy it.

In a similar vein, if you thought you might sell more cold beverages in your supermarket on hot days, you would want to recognize that it is humidity that increases people's thirst, not heat.[24] Thus, you could expect to benefit from a rush on ice-cold flavored waters if your store was located in steamy Florida, but in Arizona, sales might not be as robust when it was 106 degrees Fahrenheit with low humidity.

The project-management approach is one retailers should thoughtfully consider as they juggle the many small details of the business that require skillful coordination.

Deal Positively with Obstacles

There is an old adage that suggests: "if life deals you lemons, make lemonade!" Whether the obstacle is declining sales, a Chapter 11 bankruptcy filing, the loss of a key executive, a natural disaster, identity fraud on a retailer's Internet site, internal subterfuge, or unproductive teams, thoughtful action—rather than negative reaction—is called for. If plan A hasn't worked, it's time to put plan B into effect. Organizations that are responsive to changes such as these—and one can almost predict that management is dealing with more than one concern concurrently—expend great effort in a timely fashion using whatever tools are available.

When the retailer The Sharper Image filed for bankruptcy in 2008, sales plummeted and stores were closed—lemons! Camelot Venture Group bought the rights to the brand and, in 2009 brand transformation began. By Christmas 2010, evidence of the new Sharper Image was evident: The Web site was up and running, and catalogue sales were helping to boost the brand. Although the brick-and-mortar stores were gone, Sharper Image products were available through retail stores including Bed Bath & Beyond, Kohl's, Belk, Staples, and at The Bay in Canada.[25] Ah, lemonade!

Understand Global Differences

Management practices—and the effectiveness of those practices—differ depending on the part of the world or the country being studied. In general, companies that use monitoring, goal-setting, and incentives are associated with superior performance. This holds true whether they are located in the United States or elsewhere. Large multinational retail chains are the best managed and, on average, founder- and family-run firms are the worst managed. Researchers from Stanford and Toronto Universities surveyed 600 firms in Canada, the United Kingdom, and the United States to assess management's best practices. U.S. retail companies ranked first, with Canada second and the United Kingdom third. U.S.-based multinational chains doing business in Canada scored highest, showing that U.S. chains influence Canadian managers' performance significantly.[26]

Often societal and cultural differences, in both business practices and lifestyles, must be navigated by expatriate retail managers. Three examples—involving hours of operation, vacation time, and changes in retirement practices—highlight the kinds of seemingly small issues that can perplex expatriate managers who are not prepared for them.

Working hours vary somewhat internationally. Time spent on the job may be longer or shorter per day, week, or year. Vacation periods may be as meager as 1 week a year for full-time staff or nearing four to five weeks in certain countries. In Spain, for example, the workday stops at about noon so workers and shoppers can partake of traditional afternoon siestas. Stores reopen later in the afternoon and do not close until 9:00 p.m. or later.

Workers in France traditionally have taken four or five weeks of vacation, coinciding with the closure of manufacturing facilities during the midsummer period. Because retail stores remain open during this period, managers must juggle work schedules around employees' lengthy vacations. Recently, however, the effects of the new socialist government have begun to alter even entrenched labor practices. In 2012, under the new regime of President François Hollande, legislative action was passed that increased the minimum retirement age for French workers from 60 to 62 and the age to receive full pension from 65 to 67.[27] As might be expected, workers, outraged by the proposals, had demonstrated against the new policies. At least the long vacation period remains intact.

Adaptation is challenging, and the search for solutions affects management at all levels when companies expand abroad, underscoring the value of research before major decisions are made.

Retailers that plan global expansion have a responsibility to train their managers in the nuances of the global workplace.

Maintain a Healthy Organization

Maintaining a positive attitude regarding the many changes society and the business world face every day is no small task, but it is essential for managers to strike the right chord if they are to encourage a healthy attitude in their employees. At a workshop given by McKinsey & Company, 150 retail industry participants were asked to vote on their company's organizational health as measured by three factors: alignment, execution, and renewal. See From the Field 12.3 for the results of the exercise and a larger survey completed by McKinsey.

To attain and maintain a highly effective organization, most retailers strive for:

- A high level of trust between employees and management, and respect for the interchange of relevant information across all levels.
- Adequate numbers of highly skilled managers who are adaptable, cross-trained, and able to see the big picture.
- Well-designed organizational structures and systems that facilitate the capture and analysis of data so that managers can perform their jobs.
- Incentives for all employees to troubleshoot problems, as well as suggest and implement meaningful solutions.[28]

In addition, most publicly held retail companies prioritize the maintenance of good relations with their shareholders. All work to uphold the company's mission and vision statements, and to operate under well-conceived ethical and environmental platforms and at a high level of social consciousness. In this case, health and wealth go together, because highly effective companies also are the most profitable.

Assessing Your Management Style

Most of us enjoy learning about what makes us tick. Are we achievers or developers? Do we pride ourselves on being empathetic or see ourselves more as activators? Do we have what it takes to be a manager? Fortunately, there are many tools that can help aspiring retailers determine areas in which they excel and those that they do not embrace as heartily.

One particularly good resource is the StrengthsFinder Profile. The profile was developed by a psychologist and a vice president of the Gallup Organization and has been used by more than two million people, lending validity to the idea that is sought after by business leaders. The assessment is based on three tools that the authors of the profile believe are necessary to building a strong life:

1. Understanding how to distinguish your natural talents from things you can learn.
2. A system to identify your dominant talents.
3. A common language to describe your talents.[29]

The profile questionnaire is available through human resource departments, educational organizations, and employee assistance programs, and on the Internet via a unique access code included in each copy of *Now, Discover Your Strengths,* by Marcus Buckingham and Donald O. Clifton. The Web-based interview derives a person's five most powerful signature themes from a list of 34 descriptors. Sample results might be Responsibility, Strategic, Analytical, Self-assurance, and Futuristic. The process is more complex than this, but careful analysis and chart-building enable a user to identify his or her strengths, weaknesses, and affinity for management, and also lend insight into the success of the employee's organization.

Working with a group of university staff members, who were preparing for promotion or anxious to intensify their abilities in their current position, I was privileged to see the StrengthFinder tool in action. The facilitator of the group was trained to analyze the results, interpret the many questions posed by group members, and guide the discussion in ways that showed the participants how the new information could enhance their lives, enabling them to interact more effectively with their managers or become managers themselves. The results were illuminating and were reexamined repeatedly in discussions throughout the academic year.

"What Color Is My Personality" is another instrument that can be used to assess personality traits and how they relate to managing people. Self-discovery is often the first step to change, and therefore valuable both for personal growth and for improving interactions with fellow employees or managers. The questionnaire portion of the tool requires users to chose the terms that best fit their personalities from 24 sets of words and phrases. Results are tabulated and plotted on a personality indicator graph. Using color, individuals learn whether they are:

- Red—action-oriented.
- Yellow—precision-directed.
- Green—outer-directed and people-oriented.
- Blue—inner-directed.

Most people have tendencies toward all colors but are strongest in one or two.

The graph includes extrovert and introvert categories on the top-to-bottom axis, and task and process categories on the left-to-right axis, which further define an individual's qualities. Hypothetically, a person who scores high in both red and green is very extroverted. One who is high in both red and yellow is very task-oriented. Further analysis may indicate that a person is overly task oriented—the type of person that would not stay on a job very long. In organizations, productivity-oriented individuals tend to be red, and service-oriented people tend to be blue or green.

Individuals who score highest on opposite poles—red and blue or green and yellow—may find themselves confused by results that don't seem to be synchronized. As with all measurement tools, professional analysis is recommended to ensure that results are not misconstrued. While the results lend insight into human traits and behavior, they are neither infallible nor absolute. At best, they may clarify tendencies and perhaps a strength or skill we never knew we had. The main advantage to the color system is that it assesses behavior commonly used in the workplace.

This instrument is not unlike the widely applied psychologically based Myers-Briggs assessment tool, which uses descriptors to indicate personality tendencies. The test culminates in the following general extrovert and introvert tendencies, broken down to specific categories with their letter designations:

Extrovert (E)	Introvert (I)
Intuition (N)	Sensing (S)
Thinking (T)	Feeling (F)
Perceiving (P)	Judging (J)[30]

Cyberscoop

Go to www.StrengthsFinder.com to see how you can assess your special talents. How is this information helpful in identifying your management style? Will this help you manage others? From the home page click on "learn more" under the StrengthsFinder 2.0 information. Next, browse About the Book, History, What's New, and Research. Then read "Use Your Access Code" information and click on "enter access code" in the top right-hand corner. From that point, you will be asked to register and will be allowed to do a self-assessment. Good luck; there's lots to learn on the site even if you choose not to do the survey.

A plethora of similar self-assessment instruments is available on the Web. Not all are scientifically based, but many are fun to use and some present true insights that are valuable both to those interested in general self-improvement and prospective managers.

Management is put to the test in the fast-paced world of retailing, where margins and profits can be slim at best and particularly elusive during times of economic turmoil. Adherence to sound managerial principles and new ways of thinking, testing and executing converge to make a good company great. This is an ambitious framework, but one well worth implementing.

Summary

Management fuses both art and science when deriving appropriate strategies and systems to move people, products, and services in the same direction, so that retail goals and objectives are met while earning a profit. The concept of management lends itself to all functional areas of a company, including—but not limited to—operations, human resources, finance, marketing, information technology, e-commerce, and the retail organization itself.

Dig deeply into the history of management and you will find many colorful and astute theorists and practitioners. From Machiavelli, who "managed" the citizenry of Florence, Italy, in the 16th century, to Peter Drucker, who applied theory to management practices in the 20th century, the timeline is peppered with wit, intelligence, and hard work. Tools developed in the last part of the 20th century include Cog's Ladder, which deals with group management development stages, and Six Sigma, a quantitative method that uses econometrics to increase quality and efficiency in business.

The four phases of the management process are planning, organizing, leading, and controlling. These are used by many different kinds of businesses and not-for-profit organizations—anywhere people gather to do the work of the world.

Organizational charts graphically represent the many executive, management, and staff positions in a firm. Company positions such as supervisors and staff are usually not charted, since those positions are not considered managerial. Store chart hierarchies usually start with the general manager.

To be considered successful, a retail manager should possess aptitude for and high interest in the industry, as well as a variety of learned skills, inherent abilities, and personal qualities. Managerial candidates need to have time-management skills, an indefatigable nature, and the ability to multitask—while still finding humor in the day's work and worries.

Team spirit is at the core of management theories today. The ability to lead is one of the most valuable skills a retail manager develops. Organizational leadership celebrates cross-functional, team-oriented management models. There are many types of leaders, including autocratic, democratic, and transformational. An individual's personality type greatly affects leadership style, but leadership tactics are also learned.

Implementing a team approach has both advantages and disadvantages for retail organizations. Key advantages are the varied viewpoints and skills contributed by members, a possibly shorter path to solutions, and innovation when members are intensely interested in the topic. Disadvantages include possible lack of interest among team members, negativity expressed in views of the company or other group members, difficulty staying on point, and loss of productive time when irrelevant topics are allowed to sidetrack discussions. Teams work best when there is a joint sense of interest, purpose, and commitment.

Each managerial position in a company has a prescribed job description. While different companies have different needs, one commonality in retailing is the role of a general manager (GM). GMs have broad knowledge of the retail workplace, since they are in charge of all functional areas in a store or multichannel business. Sector or department managers report to the GM, who motivates and encourages them to take initiative in making decisions and implementing new procedures. Operations managers in stores are examples of managers who report to a GM. Their responsibilities are specific to the area they head and vary greatly from sector to sector.

Successful organizations share several qualities, just as successful managers do. High-performing retail companies use project-management methods, are able to cope with obstacles effectively, understand global differences, and place emphasis on building a healthy organization.

Individuals interested in learning more about their management aptitude or style can do so using varied educational and commercial instruments, consultants, and assessment specialists. Many tools are available online. Retailers who plan well, develop their employees, and continue to build skills in their forward-thinking managers will thrive in the 21st century.

Key Terms

Accountability
Autocratic leaders
Closed management
Cog's Ladder
Contingency planning
Democratic leaders
Empowerment
Leadership
Lean Six Sigma
Management

Manager
Mentoring
Open management
Organization charts
Organizational leadership
Project management
Six Sigma
Tactical planning
Transformational leaders

Questions for Discussion

1. What does the field of management encompass? State the argument for specialized management fields, such as retailing or human resources, as opposed to general management for all firms.
2. Is management an older practice than we think? Support that question by summarizing a key development in management theory or practice from each of the past five centuries.
3. Explain the five steps of Cog's Ladder. How is this information used to make group management more efficient?
4. Six Sigma is an econometric method of deriving efficiency and quality standards. What is the essence of this method? Identify companies that are using this tool.
5. There are four widely accepted elements of the management process. Chose the one you are most interested in or knowledgeable about and discuss its importance when managing a retail company.
6. Have you ever heard or seen a charismatic leader? Drawing from the examples in this text or from your own experience, discuss the special qualities these executives possess. How do they have an impact on their companies?
7. What are the essential differences between senior and middle management in a retail company?
8. List and elaborate on the three distinctive competencies that effective managers should possess.
9. An organizational leadership approach is used in most retail businesses today. What is at the core of this ideology and what are its key advantages and disadvantages?
10. Under what circumstance do teams work most effectively? State and elaborate on your point. Can you relate these circumstances to your own experiences in study or work groups?
11. Of all the responsibilities that fall to a general manager in a retail store, which three do you believe are the most difficult to carry out effectively?
12. The concept of product management had its roots in manufacturing and marketing firms. Why has it been adopted by retailers?
13. Several factors that are characteristic of highly effective organizations are presented in this chapter. Which one do you believe is of most consequence to retailers that expect to thrive in a challenging economy?
14. For those of you who are or hope to become managers, what benefits do you ascribe to the personality assessment tools that are used by business and other organizations?

Endnotes

1. Rona Ostrow, *The Fairchild Dictionary of Retailing,* Second Edition (New York: Fairchild Books, 2009), 237.

2. Niccolò Machiavelli, *The Prince* (1532), in *Three Renaissance Classics*, ed. Burton A. Milligan (New York: Charles Scribner's Sons, 1953). (Introduction and notes by Burton A. Milligan: iv.)

3. "About Adam Smith," International Adam Smith Society, accessed February 9, 2012, www.adamsmith society.net/about-adam-smith.html.

4. "Who Was Charles Babbage?" Charles Babbage Institute, University of Minnesota, accessed February 9, 2012, www.cbi.umn.edu/about/babbage.html.

5. "Our History," Harvard Business School, accessed February 9, 2012, www.hbs.edu/about/history.html.

6. "History of Quality: Inspection and Quality in Japan," Business Performance Improvement Resource, accessed February 9, 2012,. www.bpir.com/total-quality-management-history-of tqm-and-business-excellence-bpir.com.html.

7. Delbert J. Duncan and Stanley C. Hollander, *Modern Retailing Management, Basic Concepts and Practices*, 9th ed. (Homewood, Illinois: Richard D. Irwin Inc., 1977), Front matter.

8. "Stages of Team Development: Cog's Ladder," Evergreen Consulting, accessed January 6, 2011, www .evergreenconsulting.com/stages6b.htm.

9. Ibid.

10. Fred Reichheld, *The Ultimate Question: Driving Good Profits and True Growth* (Boston: Harvard Business School Press, 2006), 40.

11. Suzanne Turner, "Six Sigma," in *The Little Black Book on Management* (New York: McGraw-Hill, 2010), 154–155.

12. Brian Burnsed and Emily Thornton, "Six Sigma Makes a Comeback," *Businessweek*, September 10, 2009, 1, www.businessweek.com/print/magazine/content/09_38/b4147064137002.htm.

13. Ibid.

14. David Moin, "Big Changes at Neiman's. Burt Tansky to Step Down. Katz and Gold Move Up," *Women's Wear Daily*, April 27, 2010, 1, 12–13.

15. David Moin, "Macy's to Beef Up E-commerce Staff," *Women's Wear Daily*, January 5, 2011, 1, 9.

16. Associated Press, "Closing: 5 Macy's and 4 Bloomingdale's Stores," January 5, 2012. AZ Central, www .azcentral.com/business/articles/2012/01/01/20120105closing-macys=bloomingdales-stores.

17. Forrest W. Breyfogle III, "Start Small with New Lean Six Sigma Initiatives," iSixSigma, accessed January 6, 2011, www.isixsigma.com/index.php?option=com_k2&view+item&id=1218:&itemid=182.

18. Arnold J. Karr, "Future Leaders Need Different Skillset," *Women's Wear Daily*, November 1, 2010, 1, 3.

19. Michael Levy and Barton H. Weitz, "Leader Decision Making," in *Retailing Management*, 6th ed. (New York: McGraw-Hill/Irwin, 2007) 469–470.

20. Profile—CVS Caremark Corp. "Financial Summary." March 31, 2012. http://retailsails.com/monthly-sales-summary/cvs/ Source: The company; Retail Pharmacy segment only.

21. Jon R. Katzenbach and Douglas K. Smith, "Dealing With Obstacles," Excerpted from *The Wisdom of Teams* (New York: HarperBusiness, 1993), 2–18.

22. Ibid: 150–151.

23. Jeff Porten, "Project Management Techniques in Retail," E-How.com, April, 2010, www.ehow.com/ way_5364751_project-management-techniques-retail.html.

24. Ibid.

25. "About Us" and "Retail Locations," Sharper Image, accessed February 14, 2011, www.sharperimage.com/ si/company/about-u.jsp.

26. Nick Bloom and John Van Reenen, "Management Practices in Europe, the U.S. and Emerging Markets," Stanford University, Lecture 7, February 2010.

27. Cecile Brisson. "For Some, French Retirement Age Goes Down." Associated Press. June 6, 2012. http:// news.yahoo.com/french-retirement-age-goes-down-not-192959740--finance.html

28. Eliza G. C. Collins and Mary Anne Devanna, "How to think Like a Manager: The Art of Managing for the Long Run (Figure 1.3 Characteristics of a highly effective organization: A long-run point of view)," in *The Portable MBA* (New York: John Wiley & Sons, Inc., 1990), 7.

29. Marcus Buckingham and Donald O. Clifton, "Strong Lives," in *Now, Discover Your Strengths* (New York: The Free Press, 2001), 28–35.

30. Myers-Briggs™ is the registered trademark of Consulting Psychologists Press, Inc.

Chapter 13

Human Resource Management

Learning Objectives

After completing this chapter you should be able to:

- Discuss current challenges facing human resource management, including the impact of downsizing, displacement, and outplacement.
- Describe the primary responsibilities of the human resource department, including recruiting, placing, training, and retaining employees.
- Delineate the types of training programs used by contemporary retailers.
- Document the ways technology assists retail recruitment and training.
- Review key responsibilities of human resource managers.

Figure 13.1
It's all about the human assets! Students learn the ropes from the vice president of corporate recruiting as they explore the world of retailing at Saks, Inc.

This chapter examines human resource planning and management from different perspectives. Challenges retailers routinely face—regarding the labor pool, including fluctuating unemployment rates, part-time workers, shrinkage, motivation, and diversity in the workplace—are covered here. Amid economic recalibrations, the retail industry remains a desirable place to build a career, with opportunities that require a range of talented and skilled individuals. First let's look at the numbers.

Retail Employment Trends

In the United States, approximately one in four workers is employed in retailing.[1] The economy may be up, down, or flat, nationally or globally, but customers worldwide still need products and services. To appreciate the impact retailing has on the marketplace, it helps to focus on trends in three areas: job growth and salary expectations, employment fluctuations, and age and gender breakdown of the workforce.

Retail Job Growth and Salary Expectations

Despite the recent recession, job growth in the retail sector in the United States is expected to continue into the second decade of the millennium. Between 2006 and 2016, a 12 percent gain in the number of retail salespeople, as well as sales and marketing managers, is anticipated. Most retail positions are at the sales-associate level.[2]

The average hourly wage for all retail employees in early 2012 was just over $16.00.[3] The highest hourly earnings go to motor-vehicle dealers and employees of electronic shopping and mail-order houses, who average about $18.00 per hour.[4]

Little or no growth is predicted for retail buyers for the next several years. Average annual income for wholesale and retail buyers was $55,540 in 2008, the most recent year for which labor statistics were available. The top 10 percent earned about $90,000. The sales manager category of government data encompasses retail managers. This category is also expected to grow, and currently median salaries for managers are about $100,000.[5]

Employment Pool and Workforce Participation

In the period leading up to the millennium, the United States experienced one of the lowest unemployment rates in 30 years. Many retailers were hard pressed to find suitable employees, necessitating creative recruitment tactics. New hires were lured by lucrative bonuses, generous discounts on merchandise, and more money if they referred other suitable employees.

By 2008, the tables had abruptly turned as recession-linked unemployment soared. Many U.S. retailers were forced to displace employees at various times during the downturn. In the human resource context **displacement** means reducing the size of the workforce by laying off employees or granting early retirement. Early in 2010, some signs of improvement were seen. Unemployment fell slightly and retail trade employment rose by 42,000 jobs, distributed among food stores, clothing stores, and general merchandise retailers.[6] The increase was considered a tentative but positive direction for retailers. By early 2012, unemployment had continued to fall to 8.5 percent, but not fast enough for some families that had lost their homes or individuals who had been out of work for more than a year or two. The retail job market fared better than many, adding 390,000 jobs between the low point of December 2009 and January 2012.[7]

Age and Gender Diversity

Retailing continues to be a young person's business. In January 2012, 30.8 percent of the civilian labor force in the United States was between 16 and 19 years old.[8] (This is down from 32.6 percent in 2009.) At the opposite end of the age spectrum, approximately 16 percent of people over 65 were in the workforce, supporting the current trend of employing senior citizens in many businesses. Typically, many people in these age groups work in retail businesses.

Gender differences in the retail job market are apparent. Women make up slightly less than 50 percent of the U.S. workforce. A comparative look at women's participation in the workforces of several countries is shown in Table 13.1. Notice that France and Sweden have the highest percentage of women in the workforce and Italy has the lowest.

Layoffs in the recent recession have had an impact on gender rates in employment in the United States, as women retained jobs at a greater rate than men. For example, between December 2009 and January 2010, the civilian labor force lost 258,000 jobs—168,000 for men and 90,000 for women.[9] Several factors influenced this spread. Men have traditionally assumed jobs in construction, forestry, transportation, utilities, and some manufacturing sectors that were greatly affected by the downturn. Some women have taken over the role of economic breadwinner in their families, although many of their jobs are not high-paying. The reasons for this imbalance are deep and complex and affect some socioeconomic groups and geographic areas more than others.

In the recent recession, unemployment in other developed economies and the European Union increased by 4.9 million. Men accounted for 64 percent of the total of those unemployed. The International Labour Organization urged caution when attempting to analyze the reasons for

Table 13.1 Percentage of Women in the Labor Force

Year	United States	Canada	Australia	Japan	France	Germany	Italy	Netherlands	Sweden	United Kingdom
1977	41	37.9	36.1	37.7	39.5	39	31.4	28.6	43.8	39.2
1987	44.8	43.1	40	39.6	43.9	40.3	35.3	37.9*	47.8*	43
1997	46.2*	45.3	43.1	40.5	46.1	43.4	30.6	42.3	47.5	45.1
2007	46.4	47	45.1	41.3	47.6	45.6	40.6	45.6	47.6	45.9

Excerpted from "Percent of Women in the Civilian Labor Force 1960-2007," Bureau of Labor Statistics,

ftp://ftp.bls.gov/pub/special.requests/ForeignLabor/lfcompendiumt10.txt

* Indicates a break in series.

this phenomenon, noting that there is a "clear lack of gender equality in global labor markets and this situation can be easily confused with the gender impact of the current crises."[10] These conclusions are similar to gender-based workforce tendencies in the United States.

Typically, women in the United States have held a disproportionate share of positions in specific types of retailing. Women are overrepresented in department, general merchandise, drug, book, apparel, accessory, and jewelry stores, and underrepresented in auto dealers and service stations, building materials, furniture, home electronics, and sporting goods stores. Apparently old stereotypes die hard.

Human Resource Planning and Budgeting

Like goods and services, human resource assets are planned for and budgeted. To be productive, employees need to understand the company vision as well as the merchandise they will be offering and the customers they will serve. Effective orientation and training help staff acquire skills and balance their professional and personal lives. In the best situations, retailers lend ongoing support to their employees and reinforce what is taught. The trends in the previous section and the statements reflected here lay the groundwork for human resource planners.

Challenges to Human Resource Planning

Supplying properly trained people at the right time, in the right place to implement company objectives is at the core of human resource planning. Although the following challenges are germane to retailing, businesses in general voice many of the same areas of concern.

Low and High Unemployment

Retail employment in the United States fluctuates monthly. It is easy to understand that if the majority of sales are generated during holiday periods, extra personnel should be scheduled during that time. It is sometimes more difficult to anticipate whether layoffs will be necessary during an economic downturn. However, this was the case as retailers retrenched during the recent recession. Both situations imply that change is inevitable as retailers plan for coverage.

When unemployment rates are low, there are fewer eligible people to hire. Incentives increase and alternative labor pools are tapped. Retailers that find the job market diminished target senior citizens, disabled persons, and non–English speakers. Some retailers go to extreme measures offering monetary rewards to new hires and bonuses to current employees who recommend them. Signing bonuses and outright piracy become common. **Piracy** is the luring of personnel from other firms. Companies outside the retail industry are known for attracting top-notch staff and management to other fields.

During the tight labor markets that existed in the United States in the 1990s, retailers become creative in their recruitment techniques. In 2001 and 2007—years immediately preceding economic downturns—restaurants in summer resort areas offered various incentives to prospective

Did You Know?
Despite high unemployment rates in 2011, growing numbers of employers worldwide reported difficulty filling positions. In Japan, almost 80 percent of employers stated that finding qualified job candidates was not easy. India reported 66 percent and the United States 52 percent. Do the problems lie in training, retraining, fit, education, experience, or the economy? Your task is to find out what and why. (Source: Peter Cappelli, "Why Companies Aren't Getting the Employees They Need," *Wall Street Journal,* October 24, 2011, R1, R6. Statistics: ManpowerGroup.)

employees. College scholarships, $500 sign-on bonuses, free housing, and transportation were advertised as employers raced to staff their businesses.

When unemployment rates are high, the marketplace is flooded with job seekers but jobs are scarce and competition high for the few available positions. Despite recurring boom and bust cycles, competition for qualified people in high-level positions increased in the 1990s and 2000s and will continue to do so as the recession ebbs.

Lower Wages

Retail remuneration may not be competitive with other industries, particularly at the sales associate and lower operational staff levels. Although the minimum wage in the United States increased to $7.25 in 2009, it is evident that this level of compensation is not adequate for full-time workers. Wage rates also vary depending on the type of retail business. For example, Costco Wholesale is known to pay its front-end help more than double the minimum wage, which is also more than many other retailers are paying in areas where Costco is located. Retailing relies heavily on part-time employees who are usually minimum wage workers.

Internal Theft

Employee theft is a problem for retailers. Depending on the type of retail store, shrinkage as a percentage of sales varies from less than 1 percent to about 3 percent. Losses from employee theft are higher than those from shoplifting and undoubtedly a slap in the face to retailers who invest time and money into training individuals for positions and providing a pleasant environment in which to work. The 2011 Global Retail Theft Barometer showed that total North American shrinkage was $45.3 billion, and 44.1 percent of theft losses were attributable to employee theft.[11] A study involving 43 countries worldwide found that total shrinkage cost retailers $119 billion in 2011. Retailers surveyed indicated a 6.6 percent increase in employee crime over the previous year.[12] Sadly, in some cases employees also are involved in organized retail crime.

Internal theft is a growing concern that greatly affects human resources since some crimes enlist the support of employees within a business. Dealing with accomplices to a sweetheart deal is not one of the more appealing types of interaction for human resource professionals. **Sweethearting** occurs when retail employees add merchandise that has not been paid for to the shopping bags of relatives or friends.

Effective employee screening methods aid in reducing the number of dishonest employees. Retailers also use advanced surveillance systems that monitor both employees and customers to curb theft. Some implement 24-hour hot lines or Web sites on which employees can report infractions without fear of disclosure. Losses incurred through employee theft greatly affect profit and are one of many topics that should be addressed during the hiring process.

Unionization

After World War II, as both retailers and service industries grew at a fast pace, they became targets of union organizers. Then (as now) there were many low-paid, unskilled workers in large stores who wanted and needed bargaining power. Unions seemed the perfect answer, yet few inroads were made.

Since the 1950s, the union movement has progressed more slowly in retailing than most labor organizers expected. Only 13 percent of employees in the United States—approximately 5.9 million people—were members of unions in 2011.[13] This figure is low for three reasons:

1. Retail management has over time recognized the important role human resources play in the struggle for profit. As compensation plans and enrichment programs increase, there is less need for employees to organize.
2. Attitude of employees is pro-management in firms where promotion from within is advocated.
3. Part-timers make up the bulk of the employees in most retail organizations; usually only full-time workers belong to unions.

The three significant retail unions are the United Food and Commercial Workers International Union (UF&CWIU), an affiliate of the UFL-CIO; the United Store Workers, an affiliate of the Retail, Wholesale Distributive Services Union; and the Retail, Wholesale, and Department Store Workers

Union. The UF&CWIU has been fighting Walmart's advances into the freestanding supermarket business. Walmart has traditionally discouraged union intervention in its stores. However, more than half of all supermarkets in the United States employ unionized workers. As Walmart's expansion escalates, the play between this strong retailer and the unions intensifies.

Recently the UF&CWIU made overtures to organize 5,000 workers at 27 Target stores in New York City. Earlier in 2011, a group of employees at a Target store in Valley Stream, New York, had asked for union assistance, stating that they did not earn enough to support their families or afford health insurance. Target countered that its wages were competitive and that a union was not necessary.[14] Discussions like this typify a union's attempts to move into supermarkets.

In a dedicated attempt to develop national skill standards and certification for retail workers, the National Retail Federation (NRF) initially partnered with the UF&CWIU and DECA, a student marketing association, to provide training for retail sales and service personnel. DECA originally stood for Distributive Education Clubs of America, but the educational program is now known by its acronym. Using guidelines established by the National Skill Standards Board (NSSB), the first Retail Skills Center opened at the King of Prussia Mall outside Philadelphia in 1997.[15] Today, the National Retail Federation Foundation, the research and education division of the NRF, partners with skills centers throughout the country as it continues to advocate training for retail workers.

The centers target students, transitional workers, part-time workers, and current employees interested in upgrading their skills. Many are from lower-income, ethnically diverse families. Participants learn basic sales and customer service skills. Counseling, internships, placement services, and language development are all options in the program.

Rising Health Care Costs

One of the chief issues facing Americans as this book went to press was the state of health care. Rising costs, limited coverage, exclusionary insurance policies, and the question of who pays are serious issues for all families and businesses.

In expanding health care coverage to uninsured Americans, the question of whether the government should take on some or all of the costs was hotly debated in Washington, D.C. throughout the summer and fall of 2009. Retailers became involved as proposals were put forward mandating their responsibility for paying for more coverage for their employees. Benefits administration is a key area within the human resource department in all organizations, and the ongoing efforts to reform health care in the United States will affect staffers involved in that area.

Uncertainties surrounding federal legislation enacted in 2010 continue to confound big and small business and add to the complexity of budgeting for already financially burdened households. The Patient Protection and Affordable Care Act (PPACA), expected to be implemented in 2014, specifies that every American must have health insurance, although individuals and small businesses are required to have a less rigorous benefits package. Many retailers and their employees believe state-imposed coverage is too expensive and that retailers with stores in many states would find administration challenging.[16] Others advocate a country-wide health plan.

Many retailers, preempting edicts from Washington, initiated their own efforts to cut health care costs internally in the years leading up to the federal bill. Supermarket retailer Safeway developed its Healthy Measures program in 2005, after learning that 70 percent of health care costs were the direct result of behavior. The program focuses on preventability, susceptibility to major diseases, and individual behaviors. The four most prevalent chronic conditions are cardiovascular disease, cancer, diabetes, and obesity. Employees are screened for these health problems and are given discounts from $780 to $1,560 if they meet specified biometric goals. Preventative programs target reducing tobacco usage, maintaining healthy weight, and lowering blood pressure and cholesterol levels. Since its launch, Safeway has seen an increase in voluntary participation and greater ability to manage its health care costs.[17]

Burgerville is a chain of 38 restaurants, serving Oregon and southwest Washington since 1961. The company's experience with health insurance reform is exemplary in the retail trade and is widely reported in business publications. After surveying its employees, it learned that health care costs were one of their chief concerns. In 2006, Burgerville implemented a health care benefits package that includes full medical, dental, and vision coverage, and its 1,500 employees pay a $30 monthly premium for individual coverage as long as they work a minimum of 25 hours per week. (In 2006, the premium was $15.) The impact on employee morale and turnover was profound. The year after inception, turnover went from 128 percent to 55 percent. Jack Graves, the chief cultural officer, said, "We've got many more long-term employees." As the Affordable Care Act approaches, Graves said the company will continue to work "to interpret its potential impact."[18]

Expect health care discussions to continue as retailers, consumers, and the government refine the search for solutions. Minimum wage, working conditions, gender equity, sexual harassment, and diversity are other pressing issues, not only in the United States, but in many global markets. As emigration continues and families relocate, they assimilate to new cultures. Racial and ethnic diversity present new challenges and opportunities to employers around the globe. Legislation on these and other issues keeps retailers fully engaged in monitoring and influencing the passage of laws that affect the industry. Details of how retailers provide a better environment for workers, and improve the image of retailing, are presented throughout this chapter.

Human Resource Budgets

Staffing is planned far in advance and based on an analysis of the prior year's performance and following year's expectations. A human resource budget considers all fluctuations of retail sales on a yearly, monthly, weekly, and daily basis. Companies that develop a human resource budget may have less need to use executive search firms when a sudden opening occurs. Luring executives from competing firms, or cutting staff during a business downturn might also be avoided when planning is done with a cushion for unanticipated events.

Operating with a human resource budget allows companies to build in funds for college recruiting with the goal of identifying prospective interns who might join their executive training programs upon graduation. Figure 13.1 shows two university students shadowing a human resource executive at Saks, Inc. Students who participate in **shadowing** observe exactly what happens on the job and have the opportunity to discuss their career goals with executives. In turn, the company cultivates relationships with college students in hopes of recruiting the best and brightest for management training.

Six-Step Plan

The six basic steps involved in developing and implementing a human resource budget are:

1. *Forecasting personnel needs.* The forecast should begin at the lowest operating level and continue through to the highest executive level in the organization. It should include the number of people required and job descriptions for each position.
2. *Compiling an inventory of current employees.* A review of personnel records helps identify the skills and status of current personnel. This information helps identify the type of training needed if existing employees are promoted or transferred within the organization.
3. *Modifying existing data.* The budget is affected by both internal and external factors. For example, the rate of employee turnover or the acquisition of one retailer by another alters personnel needs. The condition of the economy also changes staffing requirements.
4. *Planning for succession.* Improved selection and training methods may lower employee attrition, whereas promotions and retirements may result in additional staffing needs. Introduced in Chapter 12, **planning for succession** is the process of identifying qualified internal talent who will be available for promotion when an executive change is anticipated. Candidates are considered in advance so that appropriate training, mentoring, skill enhancement, or transition activities can commence. Planning for succession is future-directed.
5. *Executing the budget.* This takes place after approval and support of top executives is secured. Without adequate financing, facilities, and staff to carry it out, the plan will not succeed.
6. *Evaluating accuracy.* Assessment substantiates the quantitative and qualitative aspects of human resource planning. Continuous monitoring and evaluation of the plan is essential.

Thorough, thoughtful, timely human resource planning reduces attrition and increases the likelihood that a retail organization will function smoothly. Read how Urban Outfitters is using a new budgeting system, including components that help the company manage staffing needs, in From the Field 13.1.

Human Resource Tools

Once the budget is set, these three tools help to match applicants to job requirements:

1. *Job analysis.* A **job analysis** determines the specific employment needs of a company. The analysis focuses on what needs to be done and who can do it. The job analysis is accomplished through observation, questionnaires, and personal interviews. From the data gathered, a meaningful job description is written.

2. *Job description.* A **job description** is a summary of the basic tasks expected of a person in a position. It includes work requirements, skills needed, and identification of an immediate supervisor. The section on work requirements indicates what, how, when, and why a task is done. A job description also serves as an assessment tool. If standards are established for each task, then employee performance can be measured against each standard. The job description makes an employee aware of performance expectations and the activities necessary for promotion.

3. *Job specification.* A **job specification** identifies the personal qualifications and educational background required for the position. This is prepared using the information provided in a job description with the addition of education level, years of experience, and personal attributes relevant to the position sought. Many companies only consider those who meet the desired qualifications before granting an interview.

Guidelines are helpful, but remaining flexible may lead employers to a candidate who displays exceptional qualities that surpass standard cutoff criteria. With these procedures and cautions in mind, retailers identify new assets and bring them into the organization.

Human Resource Components

Recruitment, placement, training, and assessment are key components of human resource management. People who are engaged in human resource work understand all areas and often become specialists in one.

Did You Know?

If you are wondering what area of retailing has shown the greatest growth, look no further than online operations. In 2011, Macy's announced that it would add 3,500 full time, part-time, and seasonal positions at macys.com and Bloomingdales.com over a two-year period. Other retailers are also revving up their online divisions, which for many have become leading revenue generators. (Source: David Moin, "Macy's to Beef Up E-commerce Staff," *Women's Wear Daily*, January 5, 2011, 1, 9.)

Recruitment

In retailing, the sources of employees are almost as varied as the positions. An electronic help-wanted sign might attract the right kind of part-time employee to a local pizza shop, but it would probably not bring the right prospective fashion director to a department store. An advertisement on Monster.com may reach entry-level sales associates or managers but not necessarily an executive vice president. Regardless of level, the search method is matched to the (1) job, (2) type of retail establishment, and (3) target market. The importance of this matching process cannot be stressed enough in an industry characterized by long hours, night and weekend work, part-time workers, low compensation, and a labor pool that often lacks experience and training. There's an adage in retail: "You gotta love it!" Identifying recruits that have a passion for the business is part of the matching process.

Filling positions effectively is critical because profit margins in retailing are small. Both money and time are wasted if recruiting is done in a haphazard manner. Methods of recruitment vary depending on whether staff or management is sought.

Methods for Recruiting Staff

Employees for non-managerial positions are recruited in several ways, both within the store and outside it.

Internal Sources   The internal sources for staff employees (which includes sales associates, stock clerks, and basic office and information technology help) are:

- *Current employees.* They are excellent candidates for transfers or promotion, and since they are in-house, are often available on short notice.
- *Past employees.* Former full-time or part-time help with good performance reviews are productive with minimal retraining. This option is useful when business cycles are erratic.
- *Employee recommendations.* Friends or relatives of employees who are looking for work and have the needed skills and training are often good risks.

External Sources   The external sources for staff employees are:

- *Online jobs sites.* Web sites like Monster.com, Careerbuilder.com, and, in the fashion industry, WWDcareers.com are good places to start for a wide array of available positions. Some also offer job-seekers resume-writing tips and information on how to handle a telephone or online interview.
- *Newspaper advertisements.* Advertisements work well when filling peak season needs. However, online advertising and other modes of recruitment are increasingly supplanting newspapers as sources of job information for young people.
- *Government employment agencies.* These are excellent places to post jobs for part-time or full-time entry-level help.
- *Private employment agencies.* Of limited use for entry-level employees, they have value in locating staff in technical areas, such as accounting and information technology.
- *Educational institutions.* High schools and two- or four-year colleges and universities are excellent sources for part-time or summer help. High schools that have DECA programs are particularly attuned to the needs of retailers. Postsecondary students from all majors are routinely sought. Business majors requiring internships or cooperative education experiences are particularly good candidates.
- *Unsolicited applicants.* Walk-in applicants often seek part-time or entry-level sales or stock clerk jobs and may be interviewed on the spot.

Effective retail recruitment advertising brings information to prospective employees where they are most likely to read it. Sometimes that's the electronic bulletin board in the campus food court and occasionally the flyer taped to the restroom mirror.

Methods for Recruiting Managers

The internal sources for managerial employees are similar to those used for recruiting staff positions, but differ in scope and intent.

Internal Sources Promotion from within is one of the best methods for securing new executives and is supported by human resource professionals. For example, Target uses several resources to identify talented employees and cultivate their skills. Leadership training, executive coaching, individual development plans, and opportunities to advance all serve to rapidly spark interest and encourage employees to stay with the company. The importance of mentoring managerial talent was mentioned in Chapter 12.

Often, a participant in a company's management training program will leave to work in management positions in other firms and then return, years later, to fill a vice presidential slot. Keeping in touch with former executives who left in good standing is always a good idea.

External Sources External sources for managerial employees include advertising and word of mouth, but take on a different guise than those geared toward staff personnel:

- *Referrals and networking.* Business insiders' acquaintances who might be potential employees are categorized as **referrals**. Suppliers, customers, and even competitors may suggest individuals as prospective executives. Because the skills developed in one retail organization are easily transferable, there is opportunity for movement within the industry. At trade industry conferences, retail executives have the opportunity to examine the job market and network with other business leaders. **Networking** is the process of mingling with groups and speaking with individuals who may be in a position to offer information, a referral, or a job. Many conversations may revolve around human resource needs, but the off-topic information may be just as useful as the listener learns about the business world and life in general. For those already employed, networking presents the opportunity to see and be seen—high visibility may inspire your next promotion if your skills and accomplishments shine through in a professional manner.

Figure 13.2
Fashion industry help-wanted ads appear in print and online editions of publications such as *Women's Wear Daily.*

- *Advertisements.* When seeking middle- and upper-level managers, retailers often advertise in metropolitan and trade papers such as the Sunday edition of *The New York Times, Wall Street Journal,* or *Women's Wear Daily.* Local newspapers and magazines are also used. A fashion industry recruitment advertisement is featured in Figure 13.2.
- *Executive search firms.* Some recruiters specialize in finding the right executives for their clients in particular industries. Individuals or agencies that are paid to find managers or executives for a client company are called **headhunters.** Many work regionally, maintaining detailed databases, getting to know retailers and their needs, prescreening potential employees, and saving time for human resource managers. Pirating from other retailers is one of their techniques.
- *College and university recruiting.* Educational institutions have long been primary sources for retail management trainees. College seniors with majors in the business disciplines, including marketing and retailing, are actively recruited. Merchandising students from programs in consumer science areas are prime candidates. Students from liberal arts curricula who have excellent communication skills and problem-solving abilities are also sought. Many retailers are involved in internship or cooperative education programs, which allow them to bring potential trainees into the company while they are still in school. Other retailers become guest lecturers in retailing classes or host field trips, exposing a new generation to the rewards of

Figure 13.3
Career Day panel discussions give students an overview of buying, marketing, store management, and human resources.

retail management. In Figure 13.3, panelists representing various retailing career paths address students gathered at a Career Day program at Saks, Inc.

- *Job fairs.* Colleges and independent agencies host job fairs at which scores of employers have the opportunity to meet students nearing the completion of undergraduate and graduate degrees.
- *Trade association Web sites.* Organizations like the National Retail Federation, International Council of Shopping Centers (ICSC), and others maintain job postings on their Web sites or via online newsletters and briefings. These listings are usually for positions at the middle management level or higher and require more experience than new graduates would be expected to have.
- *Unsolicited applicants.* Graduating seniors often send resumes to retailers in geographic areas where they hope to locate. Some retail managers who wish to relocate to another part of the country or the world also operate in this manner.
- *Unpaid internships.* Some highly qualified job applicants have found it difficult to resume a career after being displaced, particularly during economic downturns and periods of high unemployment. Many turn to unpaid internships with companies that need help but are not ready or able to commit to a full-time position. Those with experience in the field usually work for several months after which—if they are well received by the company and a position becomes available—they may receive an offer of full- or part-time employment. Increasingly, this has become a viable pathway back into the workforce.

Quality-of-life issues may be the biggest factors complicating recruitment. Retail's perceived image as a field characterized by long hours, weekend work, and comparatively lower wages is the main factor that turns prospective employees away from careers in retailing. Spending more time with family and friends, and achieving a better balance between life and work are goals expressed by many people. As a result, flexible scheduling and child-care options are sought by prospective employees.

Uses of Technology in Recruiting

Research has shown that, on average, companies spend $1,700 per employee, per year on human resource communication. Using employment and job application kiosks, these costs can be reduced. Kiosks are used externally for recruitment and internally for benefits administration. Walmart and Safeway supermarkets both use job-application kiosks. Internally, management of 401(k) plans, pay-stub distribution, employee scheduling, and posting of company news can all be handled through kiosks, saving time for staff and the human resources department.[19]

The Swiss company Adecco works with retail clients in North America, Europe, and Australia. Job-search kiosks are placed in shopping malls and on college campuses. Through kiosks, the company places millions of people in jobs annually.

As previously noted, online sites like Monster.com and Careerbuilder.com are useful recruiting tools for some retailers, particularly for staff positions. Rite Aid and Blockbuster use online recruiting for both staff and management positions. Technology intensifies the search process for both staff and management positions. Social networking sites like LinkedIn and Facebook are additional avenues contributing input to employee selection. More information about online job search is provided in the Appendix, Retail Career Directions.

Selection and Placement

The careful selection and matching of potential employees to existing openings results in greater productivity and lower attrition. They are also key factors in maintaining high company morale.

To select the best applicants, employers evaluate and rank each job-seeker on the basis of predetermined criteria. Evaluation and selection techniques vary widely from one retailer to another. Many companies rely on the rapport that builds during personal interviews in evaluating the applicant pool. Some rely mainly on applications and resumes. Others find interviews, testing, or simulated problem-solving situations effective in the selection process. When the final choice is made, most firms use a combination of both objective and subjective measures.

Application Forms

Almost all retailers require prospective employees to complete application forms that gather preliminary information used for further screening of candidates. Application forms are commonly completed online but many are written onsite. Questions that help employers distinguish between qualified applicants are used. It is a violation of the Equal Employment Opportunity Act to ask questions that could be discriminatory, such as those concerning race, religion, age, or sexual orientation. Even if no current openings match an applicant's skills, if he or she is deemed a good future prospect, his or her application may be kept in the company's database.

Resumes

The resume reflects a person's organizational and communications skills, both important in retailing. Almost everyone who applies for full-time work, especially those who are looking for jobs that require customer contact, should be required to submit a resume. Although resumes are expected from candidates who apply for executive management programs, they are not always used when evaluating staff personnel.

Interviews

A job candidate is interviewed once or even several times before being hired. The initial interview for staff personnel usually takes place at the time the application is filled out. It is generally conducted by an employment interviewer and lasts about 15 to 20 minutes. There are several purposes of an interview:

- To obtain additional information from the applicant.
- To verify the information on the application.
- To eliminate applicants who do not seem to qualify for the jobs available.
- To inform the applicant about the company.

Candidates who are under serious consideration, particularly for positions as managers or management trainees, are invited to return for follow-up interviews. These are more formal and intense than initial interviews. Stress interviews sometimes are used to see how a person reacts under pressure. A **stress interview** is a type of screening tool in which a panel of interviewers fires questions requiring quick, thoughtful answers and looks for evidence of problem-solving ability by the candidate.

Awareness of how people talk and behave during an interview may help in selecting, motivating, and managing them effectively. According to Lee J. Colan, a human resource consultant, interviewers should spend 80 percent of their time listening to prospective employees. Companies should prepare questions that will help identify candidates' ability to handle difficult situations.[20]

Using psycholinguistics, interviewers observe the correlation between language and behavior patterns. In some respects, everyone uses this technique to learn more about people. Suppose you were to talk with an individual who assumed a defensive posture with arms tightly crossed during an interview or a personal conversation. Most observers would correctly surmise that this person does not have an open attitude to whatever is being discussed.

Testing

During earlier eras of recruiting, some testing instruments were considered discriminatory when questions appeared to be biased toward a race or gender. Discerning potential problems, retailers investigated their testing programs and took remedial action when necessary. Some decided to eliminate tests except for those directly related to skills such as math and computers, for example. Larger retail companies use standardized psychological tests to predetermine aptitudes toward drug abuse or criminal activity. Small retailers rarely use extensive testing.

Applicants may be asked to take personality tests either in person or online. However, the efficacy of such testing came under close scrutiny during the recession when competition for too few jobs escalated the practice of cheating. The footwear retailer Finish Line discovered that answer keys for its in-store tests had been placed online and were being used by applicants seeking to pre-screen the expected answers.[21] Even tests administered online may not be properly monitored and are open to cheating, although companies that develop and administer the tests say that cheating is not widespread. Another concern is the degree to which personality tests accurately reflect the tendencies of the candidates.

Reference Checks

Toward the end of the selection process, the company checks references provided by prospective candidates. Reference checks are conducted by mail, e-mail, telephone, or personal contact. Checking references—professional, educational, or personal—gives the employer an opportunity to verify information that was obtained through the application and interviewing process. Most people will not list a person or company as a reference if they suspect the respondent will speak of them in anything other than glowing terms. This fact alone takes some of the objectivity and credibility out of references.

Physical Examinations

Some retailers may require applicants for full-time jobs to take physical examinations. Physical examinations are always required for those who handle food or drug products as part of their job. Drug testing is common, and some retailers require AIDS testing. Although applicants can refuse to take these tests, most people do not if they really want the job.

Final Selection

The candidate who successfully passes all steps in the selection process is hired. Human resource professionals do not make hiring decisions lightly. They spend a great deal of time reviewing applications, resumes, and tests of the candidates who have made the final cut. Sometimes all staff members who participated in the interview process make a group decision.

In special circumstances, companies may outsource the hiring process. For example, Hickory Farms, the specialty food retailer, does most of its business from temporary sites during the holiday season. It has to increase its sales force by hiring 5,000 people to staff 600 mall stores. To do this efficiently, it hired Headway Corporate Resources to implement its Adaptive Recruitment Process

Outsourcing (RPO) program. Headway takes care of recruiting, screening, background checks, on-boarding, and even payroll for Hickory Farms.[22] **On-boarding** includes the initial orientation activities and preparation sessions for new hires.

The best selection process does not always produce perfect employees. All human resource managers try to improve methodologies. Some candidates are asked to participate in role-playing exercises. **Role-playing** is a training exercise in which individuals experience a situation through dramatization, by participating as actors. Usually this approach is limited to candidates for management positions. Whatever system is used, objective criteria and testing, human resource management experience, and good personal judgment should go into the final decision.

On-Boarding and Training

Nothing produces more anxiety than a new beginning. Remember freshman orientation or the move to a new town? Starting a new job brings forth the same feelings even in those who have worked before. A new organization presents us with unfamiliar people, regulations, and duties. Even the most self-confident person needs to be eased into an organization and provided with proper training.

Orientation

An orientation program should be offered to every new employee in a retail organization, whether the new person is a full-time management trainee or a part-time sales associate. Familiarizing new workers with their roles, the company, its policies, and other employees are important aspects of on-boarding. Classroom activities, company manuals, DVDs, and online learning are used.

During its on-boarding program, Limited Brands goes to great lengths to help new employees get settled at its Columbus, Ohio, headquarters. Chief executive officer (CEO) Leslie Wexner greets all new recruits during their first day-and-a-half of meetings. The company also provides information and field trips to help acclimate participants to the Columbus area. Seminars with key department heads are held and mentoring is encouraged.[23]

Goals and Scope of Training

Training in all retail institutions has the same goal—to develop employees' ability to perform their jobs to the satisfaction of customers, management, and themselves. While appropriate for new employees, training programs also should be made available on a continuous basis to all employees.

New employees are trained in the basic skills required to do their jobs, but skills grow stale if not updated. Rapidly advancing technology has made it imperative to be on top of the knowledge tree in all retail sectors. Experienced personnel may need professional development sessions on new computer systems, leadership training, team building, merchandising techniques, advanced selling, stress management, or customer service skills.

Initial Staff Training   When new sales associates or support staff are hired, they may spend a few hours of their first day on the job filling out various company and government forms and then attend orientation sessions. The next few days are spent learning retail systems. The amount of training provided depends on the complexity of the job.

New sales associates are also taught selling techniques, which may be followed by a day or two of on-the-job training. **On-the-job training (OJT)** involves instructing employees during regular working hours while they also are doing productive work and are being paid regular wages. Initial training techniques may include lectures, role-playing, discussion, and case studies. In most large retail operations, self-paced computer learning modules are used. They are often housed on company file-sharing sites. Figure 13.4 depicts a Home Depot employee working on a training module in the store's learning lab. Home Depot believes that in addition to computer-based training designed to teach basic skills using simulations, an important aspect of training is personal mentoring. The company enlists the support of outside tradespeople to help educate sales associates who will be providing plumbing, painting, or construction advice to customers on the floor.[24]

Improvement of training programs and involvement of part-time as well as full-time employees benefits all retailers. The goal is to decrease attrition of sales associates and support staff.

Did You Know?
By 2014, about 70 percent of large companies will use elements of video games for at least one business process. "Gamification" tactics are used to motivate employees, build brand loyalty, train managers, and even improve data entry. Some are golf-themed or require building virtual cities; others simulate business situations in amusing ways. Companies have found that employees trained using video games learn more, retain more, and reach a higher skill level than those trained in less interactive environments—which makes one wonder: what could a company do with Angrybirds or Farmville? (Source: Rachel Emma Silverman, "Latest Game Theory Mixes Work and Play," *Wall Street Journal,* October 10, 2011, B11.)

Figure 13.4
Home Depot's e-learning
centers provide employees
with online modules to
enhance skills in several
areas.

Supervisory Training   Often, retail sales associates are promoted to supervisory positions. Some are experts in their job functions but not in human relations. Many find they are ill equipped to deal on a professional level with co-workers with whom they have socialized. All new supervisors should learn human relations skills. It is not easy to manage peers or people significantly younger or older than oneself, keep sales up, and motivate employees concurrently.

Management Training Programs   Designed to develop managerial talent, formal training programs are commonly found in large retail organizations. College graduates enter a company as management trainees and progress to higher-level positions by interspersing study of policies, procedures, and finance with increasingly demanding work assignments.

Training of line management tends to be more formal, longer, and in some respects more generalized. **Line management** are members of the management team who are directly involved with retail functions such as operations, customer service, asset protection, finance, information technology, inventory control, distribution, marketing, or merchandising. These individuals will eventually fill middle- and upper-level management positions. New employees are usually exposed to all facets of the retail business before they select a specific track—usually in merchandising or operations. Many department stores train new managers in this way.

Saks Fifth Avenue in New York City provides an elite Executive Excellence Training Program for highly motivated and talented college graduates. Management trainees learn cross-functional skills and work directly with merchants, planners, and store managers. In addition to a four-year degree from an accredited university, candidates must have a 3.0 GPA, top-notch analytical skills, high energy, and leadership ability, among other attributes. Those that successfully complete the nine-month program go on to merchandising positions as a stepping stone to further skills training, and then eventually executive positions.[25]

Target's executive training program is one of the best in the United States and the selection process is highly competitive—only one in ten candidates is chosen. Target's corporate culture is team-centered and all efforts at training and development engage this spirit. The company mandates that service be delivered by team members in a "fast, fun, friendly" manner and refers to

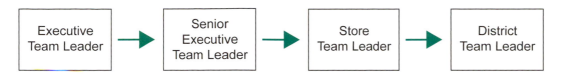

its managers in ways that reinforce team spirit.[26] The typical career paths for store leadership and human resources positions at Target are illustrated in Figure 13.5.

Executive trainees in most stores advance according to their abilities and the needs of the company, not on a predetermined schedule. Training programs require both effort and time investment on the part of trainees. For that reason, many who are unwilling to wait for the rewards leave in their first year. Others who enter management from training programs may move to positions with other retailers or other industries within a few years.

Training in small retail businesses is much more informal, since owners wear many hats. Entry-level employees learn the retail business from a unique perspective if they choose to enter the industry in this way. The desire to become a generalist, rather than a specialist, is usually strong in individuals who take this path. The intrinsic rewards are significant when learning many phases of a business concurrently. A sense of ownership, used here in a figurative sense, grows deeper in a small store than in a large organization. These advantages are important considerations for individuals contemplating a business of their own.

Opportunities to participate in special training indicate to employees that the company cares. Programs take many forms and are held either on or off the premises. Sending branch-store home electronics sales managers to vendor-sponsored product information sessions is a form of off-site professional development. Seasonal visits made by department store sportswear buyers to fashion trend presentations at resident buying offices and trade shows are other examples. Many retail executives attend annual conferences of the National Retail Federation and some of its specialized seminars. Individuals have many opportunities to participate and learn.

Levi Strauss takes a global perspective on management training. The company has established a list of global leadership competencies and expects its managers to spend time working in its foreign operations as they progress on their career paths.[27] This policy is not an unusual expectation of retailers with international divisions.

Online universities offer tremendous potential for training at all levels. Many retailers have their own learning programs, and the NRF University offers programs in all phases of retail business that are used by member stores to augment their training programs.

Assessment

The process of evaluating an individual's progress on the job is called **assessment**. Assessment ensures job security for those who meet predetermined standards and provides rewards for those who surpass those standards.

Assessment Objectives

Assessment tools are intended to measure employees' performance in order to determine salary increases, promotions, or other rewards. Viewed as progress reports, they also indicate areas in which improvement is needed. Ineffective workers need to be retrained, reassigned, or removed. In some retail stores, time is wasted tolerating repeated infractions made by employees at all levels. However, dismissing an employee still ranks as one of the most unpleasant aspects of being an owner or manager. No one wants to hear—or say—"You're fired!"

Assessment Methods

Retailers use several different methods to evaluate employees:

- *Performance records.* These are quantitative ways of measuring performance of sales associates and managers using criteria such as the total dollar sales, total number of sales transactions, units sold per transaction, number of customer complaints, number and dollar value of returns, net sales per hour worked, and number of days absent or late. Performance records are useful in identifying effective or ineffective salespeople and their managers.

- *Management by objectives.* **Management by objectives (MBO)** is a process by which a superior and a subordinate jointly set measurable performance goals for the subordinate and then meet periodically for performance reviews. Formal appraisals of an employee's work done quarterly, every six months, or annually are called **performance reviews**. Because managers are aware of their performance goals from the moment they start their jobs, this method encourages self-development and self-evaluation.
- *Rating scales.* Scales are used to identify and evaluate specific performance criteria. Ratings systems range from the simple (satisfactory/unsatisfactory appraisal checklists) to the complex (evaluation forms that designate employee performance as poor, fair, average, good, or excellent). Supervisors find that rating scales provide a quick and easy way to rate their employees. On the other hand, this method is often too simple or nebulous to be of real value. Good rating scales also require written explanation of the evaluation.
- *Shopping reports.* These are used by retailers to monitor customer service standards and honesty. Outside evaluators are hired to come into stores and behave as regular shoppers. The resulting "mystery shopper" reports are based on how the evaluators were treated and their observation of the person under scrutiny.

Assessment should be an ongoing process. It is considerate to inform the person being evaluated of a formal assessment ahead of time. To reduce anxiety and promote faith in the system, feedback should be given as soon as possible.

Compensation and Benefits

Payroll is the largest single expense item for most retailers. It reflects costs of salaries, wages, commissions, and fringe benefits. Because a good compensation package is so costly, retailers are constantly looking for ways to trim this enormous expense without losing good employees.

In some companies, part-time workers comprise as much as 80 percent of the workforce. Most part-time staff work no more than 20 hours a week, and some are paid little more than minimum wage. This dispels the legend of long hours but not of low pay, because many part-time employees receive no fringe benefits. Hiring part-timers is a major strategy among retailers to keep payroll costs under control.

Characteristics of Compensation Packages

The best compensation packages directly relate rewards to contributions to the organization. A satisfactory retail compensation plan is:

- Suitable for the functions being performed.
- Fair to the employee and the owner, whether the sole proprietor or a corporation.
- Easily calculated and understood.
- Designed to provide relatively steady income and incentive for exceptional performance.
- Related to performance without causing friction, such as fighting over customers for commission.

Because of the many different types of jobs in retailing, there are a number of compensation plans. Plans for sales associates in furniture stores differ from those for visual merchandising directors in department stores. The following sections look at nonexecutive and executive compensation plans.

Nonexecutive Compensation Plans

Retailers rely on several basic salary and commission plans as well as other income enhancement measures.

Straight Salary Plan

Straight salary is a fixed amount of compensation for a specific work period such as an hour, a day, a week, a month, or a year. For the retailer, the straight salary plan has the advantages of easy administration and a high level of employer control. For the employee, the straight salary plan has a known level of financial security and stability. One disadvantage of this plan for the retailer is a high ratio of wage costs to sales.

Retailers typically use straight salary plans for almost all staff positions in nonsales areas of the company. Hourly-wage plans are the most common form of remuneration for sales associates.

Straight Commission Plan

Under this plan, sales associates receive a percentage of what they sell. Straight commission is usually offered for big-ticket products such as automobiles, jewelry, computers, furniture, and appliances.

The major advantage to retailers of a straight commission plan is monetary incentive. It can also result in problems for the retailer, because commission sales associates sometimes only service customers who indicate an interest in high-commission products. Another problem for retailers who use this plan is the possibility of customer discontent due to high-pressure selling tactics.

The greatest disadvantage to employees of a straight commission plan is financial instability. Although they can make phone calls, send e-mails, and write notes to prospective customers, retail salespeople cannot totally control who enters the store. They also have no control over such external factors as a downturn in the economy. Because of this, some straight commission plans include a drawing account that allows employees to be paid during slow times in the business cycle. A **drawing account** is monetary compensation available to commissioned salespeople that allows them to take a fixed sum of money at regular intervals against future commissions. Car dealerships often use draw accounts to help their salespeople balance income.

Salary Plus Commission Plan

This plan combines the stability of the straight salary plan with the incentive of the straight commission plan. Generally, in the salary plus commission plan, the base salary constitutes the greatest share of the employee's total compensation; however, the employer does have the option of increasing the commission rate when additional monetary motivation is needed.

Quota Bonus Plan

Similar to the salary plus commission plan, the incentive pay in the quota bonus plan begins only after a specified sales level has been reached. Quota bonus plans vary by department within the same store. Type of merchandise, selling season, gross margins, and volume may be considered when quotas are established.

Push Money

Sales employees are motivated to sell in other ways. **Push money (PM)** is an incentive payment given to sales associates for selling certain items. As an example, an apparel store retailer may offer $25 to $50—beyond commission or bonus—to sales associates who sell a slow-selling winter coat. With push money, the salesperson, retailer, and manufacturer all benefit. The retailer or the manufacturer may provide push money.

Executive Compensation Plans

Most retail executives are amply rewarded for their hard work and long hours. Buyers, for example, earn anywhere from $35,000 to $100,000 a year depending on length of time on the job, type of store, department, volume, and bonus plan. Managers of large chain department and discount stores earn $100,000 or more. Store managers on salary are also rewarded with a yearly bonus based either on net sales or net profit. The figure depends on the amount of control they have over store operations and on the volume level of the store they manage.

In small retail stores, the human-relations function is handled by owners or designated employees; in small chains store managers may also assume human resource roles. Owners of single stores usually take a salary each week or month and then, out of profits, award themselves an annual bonus—if the year was profitable. Whether they are sole proprietors or corporate managers, executives in retailing are as well paid as executives in other industries.

Job Enrichment

The finest training in the world and monetary reward cannot guarantee a productive workforce. Constant effort on the part of management is needed to keep retention up, wage–cost ratios in line, and sales productivity up. The best way to accomplish these three goals is through job enrichment programs that are positive motivators. **Job enrichment** is a way to improve an employee's efficiency and sense of satisfaction by increasing the challenges, opportunities, and nonmonetary rewards provided by the company.

A study done for a major department store group showed that there are differences in the way managers and student interns perceive the workplace environment and their expectations regarding communication, motivation, incentives, and respect. For example, when listing factors that managers felt were most important to retention, managers chose effective communication. Tops on the student interns' list were effective training and advancement opportunities. While middle managers themselves sought supportive supervisors, interns looked for compassionate and enthusiastic managers. In fact, some respondents said they wanted "cheerleaders" for managers. Both managers and interns valued respect and recognition. Managers looked for a supportive work environment, but interns wanted fun, fun, fun on the job.[28]

Job enrichment takes many forms and fills the psychological void that exists when management offers a routine monetary reward for expected performance. People who are encouraged to be innovative and take extra steps that bring more profit to the company deserve rewards. Programs that consider all individuals' needs for respect, recognition, and fair treatment are the most effective.

Incentive Programs   Blending both monetary and nonmonetary incentives helps develop motivational programs that satisfy employees' needs for achievement and recognition. Such programs also encourage team spirit and a sense of belonging. Cash may swell the bank account of a manager whose department achieved a great increase in sales. However, offering a meaningful awards dinner, extra time off, or a free vacation trip may produce a more loyal employee.

Some companies offer employees the opportunity to suggest time- or cost-saving measures that are rewarded with a monetary sum, gift, or preferred parking spot. This type of enrichment activity encourages employee input, and builds pride and a sense of ownership in the company.

Grievance Procedures   A grievance process is another positive employee reinforcement program. A **grievance** is a complaint that is handled formally through established procedures. Employees perform much better when they know someone will not only listen to their problems, but also help find solutions. Being able to air grievances without fear of reprisal empowers employees. Grapevine chatter loses credibility when formal grievance procedures are in place.

Retailers develop procedures that best suit their particular organizations. In small stores, bringing issues directly to owners is usually most appropriate. Large, multi-store retailers have more complex hierarchies. Staff members first go to their immediate supervisors, who either solve the problem or take it to higher-level managers or human resource specialists.

In serious cases, it might be necessary for a representative from corporate headquarters to visit the store where the grievance occurred. If necessary the company may use an outside mediator. A **mediator** is an impartial evaluator hired to listen to both sides of a conflict and suggest solutions. All involved parties are interviewed and recommendations of the mediator are made to the appropriate line manager, who then discusses the proposed resolution with the disgruntled employee. Other retailers use elected grievance committees to implement this process. Occasionally cases have to go to court to be resolved.

Responsibilities of Human Resource Managers

In many retail companies, human resource managers work closely with and report to the general manager and assume a leadership position in ensuring the success of these organizations. In addition to overseeing the recruitment, placement, training, motivation, and assessment of employees, human resource managers monitor state and national labor laws, plan job enrichment programs, and so much more.

Figure 13.6
Study tours for students, like this one at Target, are a win-win situation. Students learn about the retailer and the company identifies prospects for its internship and management training programs. The store team leader and store human resource leader provide informative programs that include store and warehouse tours, meetings with staff and executives, asset protection, and interaction with other operational team leaders.

Observing health and safety practices on the premises, through standards set by a federal agency known as the Occupational Safety and Health Agency (OSHA), is another part of the human resource manager's job description. They also handle sexual harassment issues that involve employees.

Many serve as liaisons within the community, spearheading charitable functions or scheduling field visits by college classes. They may serve as guest lecturers and participate in career development activities. Figure 13.6 shows a group of students visiting with Target executives during a study tour. Much time is spent planning these and other aspects of management.

Ensuring that enough well-trained employees are on duty to satisfy the needs of customers, as well as complete the many supervisory and backstage tasks that must be fulfilled every business day, requires ongoing effort by the human resource department. Benefits may add to the appeal of compensation packages for employees, but for employers they represent much work. The benefits administration team keeps records on everything from employee attendance to health care plans. To conclude this chapter, we'll look at two key areas that are overseen by human resource managers: labor scheduling and benefits administration.

Labor Scheduling

Often initiated by the human resource manager, full-time and part-time work schedules are carefully synchronized to the store's needs, availability of workers, shopping patterns of customers, and pressures of holiday and other peak-demand periods. Heavy customer traffic days—like Saturdays in a discount store—demand careful employee scheduling so that enough cashiers are on duty when they are most needed and enough stockers are in place to handle the expected volume of items being sold.

Stocking the floor is usually done twice a day by high-volume retailers like Target, ensuring that goods that sell out on shelves are quickly replenished. Some retailers will automatically open another checkout lane when more than two people are waiting to be served. Keeping customers engaged, happy, and satisfied with the service so that they will be back the following Saturday is the objective of this managerial directive, but this can be a complex task. What happens if enough cashiers are not available for the buildup of customers, if someone calls in sick, or if someone just doesn't show up for work? Having the right employees on duty at the right time without overshooting the budget for sales associates each day requires a delicate balancing act.

Benefits Administration

Employee compensation other than cash amounted to 34.1 percent of gross income in the United States, as of September 2009.[29] The tax-free aspects of many fringe benefits add to their appeal and may contribute to high employee morale and level of performance. Low attrition also results when good fringe benefit packages are part of compensation packages. Most employees receive basic fringe benefits such as health, disability, and life insurance and sick-leave provisions. Medical benefits are one of the most costly benefits retailers extend, requiring them to pass on a portion of the cost to employees. Pension and 401k plans and paid vacations are also customary.

Extended fringe benefits often address wellness and quality-of-life issues. Paid memberships in fitness clubs, on-site child care facilities, and tuition reimbursement plans are examples. During periods of recession, many of these perks are discontinued, reevaluated, or downsized.

New perks are finding their way into benefits packages. Online grocery services and dry cleaners have partnered with businesses to offer employee discounts on orders that are placed from home or office. Some even deliver to business parking lots. Occasionally, massage or yoga is offered in corporate headquarters, and some have on-site company credit unions and company stores. At the headquarters of Burton Snowboards, every day is "bring-your-dog-to-work day."[30] In periods when the job market is tight, benefit packages usually become more appealing.

In this era of health care change, growing costs, and government intervention, human resource managers depend on skilled specialists to decipher and administer programs for all employees. Benefits administration professionals also handle the paperwork for new hires and retirees, so the full spectrum of individual lives passes through their offices on a daily basis. These professionals must be up to date about legal changes that affect insurance, pension funds, and other business-specific policies.

Human resource managers constantly evaluate the company's programs to make sure they have maximum appeal and minimum risk. Managers who are adept at thinking futuristically, emphasizing results, and seeking integrative solutions are valued. Sensitivity along with a strong ethical orientation and vigilance about employee privacy are expected of persons filling this role. Most human resource managers have a talent for communicating, listening, and mentoring. Hours spent studying, updating, and implementing change (sometimes unwanted) and attending numerous meetings—these, too, are a part of working in human resources.

Summary

Success in retailing depends on the ability to serve customers. An effective, knowledgeable workforce is needed to meet this goal. To that end, employees should be well selected and trained, and fairly compensated. Profits and a positive company image are linked to effective human resource management.

Contemporary challenges that retailers face include, but are not limited to, low and high unemployment rates, internal theft, unionization, and health care benefit costs. The amount that an inventory is reduced due to internal theft, shoplifting, and other factors is not only an inventory management issue, but also a human resource problem. Unfortunately, employee theft is a major contributor to shrinkage. Through improved testing and interviewing techniques, retailers try to increase the honesty quotient and decrease the criminal aspirations of new employees.

A solid human resource program starts with a six-step plan that includes a personnel forecast, an inventory of current employees, and an analysis of factors inside and outside the company that may affect employment needs and recruitment. Also important is planning for succession so that leadership transitions within the company will be smooth ones. Execution and evaluation of the plan are the final steps of the process. Job analysis, job descriptions, and job specifications are important planning tools. Budgeting for people is as important as it is for merchandise.

Recruitment involves attracting qualified candidates in a variety of ways. Online career sites, college recruitment, and job fairs are contemporary forms of employee solicitation. Advertising, search firms, word-of-mouth referrals, and electronic kiosks also are used. Recruitment techniques vary depending on whether staff or management is sought.

Retailers use many tools including applications, resumes, interviews, skill and personality tests, physical exams, drug screenings, and reference checks to screen new employees. Once hired, new employees are on-boarded and trained. Retailers that are high performers conduct continuous training and development programs for employees.

Objective-based assessment tools are used to judge performance in a number of areas, including sales, number of transactions, impact of returns, and attendance. Managers or supervisors give performance reviews to each employee that may include rating scales and, in the case of sales associates, shopping reports.

The best compensation packages include monetary and nonmonetary rewards, fringe benefits, and job enrichment programs. Employees need recognition and opportunities to build self-esteem on the job.

Human resource management in retailing is complex and diverse. Significant areas of responsibility are labor scheduling and benefits administration, along with the many tasks discussed throughout this chapter. Retailing, after all, is very much a people business.

Key Terms

Assessment	Networking
Displacement	On-boarding
Drawing account	On-the-job training (OJT)
Grievance	Performance reviews
Headhunters	Piracy
Job analysis	Planning for succession
Job description	Push money (PM)
Job enrichment	Referrals
Job specification	Role-playing
Line management	Shadowing
Management by objectives (MBO)	Stress interview
Mediator	Sweethearting

Questions for Review and Discussion

1. Discuss two major challenges that face human resource managers this decade. How are these challenges being met?
2. Referring to the six steps in developing a human resource budget, how would you "modify existing data" to help determine personnel needs?
3. List and discuss at least three internal sources that are useful in recruiting staff and managers.
4. What are some of the top retailers doing to recruit motivated and talented management trainees?
5. Do you feel that orientation and training should be offered to every new employee, both full-time and part-time? Why or why not?
6. How do job enrichment programs enhance regular compensation packages?
7. What are two of the key responsibilities of a human resource manager? Do you believe you possess the talents necessary to be an effective human resource manager?

Endnotes

1. "NRF Forecasts Retail Industry Sales Growth of 3.4 Percent in 2012," National Retail Federation, January 16, 2012, www.nrf.com/modules.php?name=News&_id=1291&op=printfriendly&txt=National-Retail-Federation-Forecasts-Industry-Sales-Growth-of-3.4-Percent-in-2012.
2. "Occupational Employment Statistics, 2008–2009," U.S. Bureau of Labor Statistics, www.bls.gov/oco/ocos121.htm.

3. "The Employment Situation-January 2012 (Table B3)" and "Average Hourly and Weekly Earnings of All Employees on Nonfarm Payrolls by Industry Sector, Seasonally Adjusted." U.S. Bureau of Labor Statistics, February 3, 2012, www.bls.gov/ces.

4. "Retail Industries—Employees, Average Weekly Hours, and Average Hourly Earnings: 2000 to 2010," in *Statistical Abstract of the United States: 2012*. Table 1050, U.S. Census Bureau, www.census.gov/compendia/statab/2012/tables/12s1050.pdf.

5. "Occupational Employment Statistics. 2008–2009," U.S. Bureau of Labor Statistics, www.bls.gov/oes/current/oes131022.htm.

6. "The Employment Situation—January 2010," U.S. Bureau of Labor Statistics, February 5, 2010, http://data.bls.gov/cgi-bin/print.pl/news.release/empsit.nr0.htm.

7. "The Employment Situation—January 2012," U.S. Bureau of Labor Statistics, February 3, 2012, www.bls.gov/ces.

8. "Employment of the Civilian Population by Sex and Age (Household Data, Table A1)," U.S. Bureau of Labor Statistics, February 3, 2012, www.bls.gov/ces.

9. "The Employment Situation–January 2010: Adjustments to Population Estimates for the Household Survey, Table B," U.S. Bureau of Labor Statistics February 5, 2010, http://data.bls.gov/cgi-bin/print.pl/news.release/empsit.nr0.htm.

10. "Gender Impact of the Economic Crisis in Developed Economies," in *Global Employment Trends for Women, March 2009*, Part 3, 20, International Labour Organization, www.ilo.org/pls/apex/f?p=109:3:0::NO::P3_SUBJECT:GENDER.

11. David P. Schulz, "Global Retail Theft Barometer," *Stores*, January 2012, www.stores.org/print/book/export/html/15166. (Source: Centre for Retail Researching, Nottingham, England.)

12. "Summary of the 2011 GRTB Study," in *Global Retail Theft Barometer*, Centre for Retail Researching Global Retail Shrinkage 2011, http://globalretailtheftbarometer.com/high.html

13. "Union Members—2011: Table 3. Union Affiliation of Employed Wage and Salary Workers by Occupation and Industry, 2010–2011." U.S. Bureau of Labor Statistics, January 27, 2012, 7, www.bls.gov/news.release/pdf/union2.pdf.

14. Steven Greenhouse, "Union Effort Turns Its Focus to Target," *New York Times*, May 23, 2011, www.nytimes.com/2011/05/24/business/economy/24target.html

15. "NRF Foundation Opens New Retail Skills Center in New Jersey," National Retail Federation, May 4, 2007, http://www.nrf.com/modules.php?name=News&sp_id=286/

16. J. Craig Shearman, "NRF Says 'Essential' Health Benefits Proposal Doesn't Balance Need Against Cost," *Washington Retail Insight*, February 2, 2012, www.nrf.com/modules.php?name=Newsletter&op=viewlive&sp_id=437&id=51.

17. Rex Gale. "Using Behavioral-Based Design to Encourage Healthy Behavior." Society for Human Resource Management. August 8, 2011. www.shrm.org/hrdisciplines/benefits/articles/pages/behavioral-baseddesign.aspx.

18. Nicholas Shannon Kulmac. "Reporter's Notebook: How Burgerville Made Health Care Work for Them." August 15, 2012. Vancouver Business Journal. www.vbjusa.com/er/just-business/reporters-notebook/4917-reporters-notebook-how-burgerville-made-healthcare-work-for-them.

19. "HR Kiosk, Overview," Kiosk Information Systems Inc., accessed September 30, 2009, www.kis-kiosk.com/apps/hr-kiosk.html, source: Salmon Smith Barney.

20. Rusty Williamson, "Good Help is Hard to Find and Keep," *Women's Wear Daily*, March 30, 2000, 12.

21. Vanessa O'Connell, "Test for Dwindling Retail Jobs Spawns a Culture of Cheating," *Wall Street Journal*, January 7, 2009, A1, A10.

22. Sandy Smith, "Outsourcing Seasonal Hiring a Gift for Hickory Farms," *Stores*, Human Resources, Farm System, 2009, 20–21.

23. David Moin, "Retail's Quest for Talent," *Women's Wear Daily*, April 29, 1998, 11.

24. George Anders, "Companies Find Online Training Has Its Limits," *Wall Street Journal*, March 26, 2007, B3.

25. "Executive Excellence Program." Saks Fifth Avenue. Information Sheet, Saks Inc. Career Day Presentation, Birmingham, AL, March 2006.

26. Simone Borges, Presentation, "Target Executive Team Leader—Human Resources," Southern New Hampshire University, Manchester, NH, March 22, 2007.

27. "A Roadmap for Retail Training," *Women's Wear Daily*, May 6, 1998, 10.

28. Sandra Forsythe, Carol Warfield, Lynda Gamans Poloian, Paul Shore, Roland Hearns, "Recruiting and Retailing Retail Professionals: Becoming an Employer of Choice," Presentation, National Retail Federation Conference and Expo, New York, NY, January 2002.

29. "Employer Costs for Employee Compensation-September 2009," U.S. Bureau of Labor Statistics, December 9, 2009, http://data.bls.gov/cgi-bin/print.pl/news.release/ecec.nr0.htm.

30. Jennifer Saranow, "Anybody Want to Take a Nap?" *Wall Street Journal*, January 24, 2005, R5.

Chapter 14

Financial Analysis and Management

Learning Objectives

After completing this chapter you should be able to:

- Investigate several profit management models and tools that gauge financial performance.
- Discern implications of the strategic profit model and key ratios.
- Detail the major components of income statements.
- Familiarize yourself with cash flow statements.
- Explain the significance of the retail inventory method (RIM) in retail accounting.
- Describe methods of measuring financial performance and compiling a balance sheet.
- Interpret benchmarks that are used by global and multichannel retailers.
- Survey several trends and tactics of financing domestic and international retail trade.

Figure 14.1
Financial planning requires input from many executives around the conference table as data is analyzed and discussed during meetings.

Income statements, gross margins, net profits, asset turnover, cash flow, balance sheets, and so much more comprise the world of financial managers. The popular "A" word—accountability—a distinctive feature in job performance evaluations, is also central to the process of intricate financial planning, control, and analysis. Measuring fiscal performance is a primary responsibility of the financial team.

Chief financial officers (CFOs) guide retail companies through slow growth during economic hard times, and rapid growth when the outlook is more robust. Factor in a volatile retail sales cycle and an environment where risk is omnipresent and it is easy to see that the wrong financial decisions may paralyze a company.

This chapter describes the models and tools used by financial leaders to run a retail business. Whether the company is large or small a common theme prevails: sales, growth, and profits are always high on the agenda.

Profit Management Models and Tools

Reinforcing a point made in previous chapters, performance criteria used in corporate retailing differ from those used in small single-unit stores. Likewise performance of mid-sized chains is evaluated differently than that of online stores. The common denominator? Retailers across all channels share the resolve to generate sales and profit. To meet this goal, financial models are derived and implemented, controls are modified and executed, and necessary adjustments are made. Analysis of financial data relies on input from key members of the organization, as seen in Figure 14.1.

As an entry point to this topic, we'll examine the strategic profit model, along with liquidity ratios and the five principal parts of an income statement, which enable retailers to monitor the overall financial status of their companies. With this as a foundation, we'll turn to the craft of constructing cash flow statements and the retail inventory method of accounting, which provide more specific details about the functioning of the company.

Tracking Retail Performance

Key elements that affect a retailer's financial performance are acknowledged in the strategic profit model. Liquidity ratios are also useful to retailers, because they measure the ability of the retailer to pay off debts. Both aspects are discussed next.

Strategic Profit Model

Three questions are at the heart of retailing: (1) "How much can we sell?" (2) "How fast can we sell it?" and (3) "How much money do we need to turn a profit?" The answers are arrived at sooner and more accurately if the strategic profit model and other related financial tools are used.

The **strategic profit model** is a financial paradigm that uses two components, net profit margin and asset turnover, to calculate return on assets. **Net profit margin** (or *net profit*) is the after-tax figure expressed in units of currency or a percentage, or both. In this usage, **asset turnover** refers to selling the inventory—the valuable merchandise of retailers. Also known as *inventory turnover* or *turn,* asset turnover recognizes the financial impact of the volume of sales transacted and the speed at which they occur. Asset turnover measures the productivity of dollars the retailer has invested in products and services. For example, if asset turnover is 2.5, the retailer generates $2.50 in sales for each dollar invested. Real estate property and human resources are considered assets in other situations but are valued differently.

Retail Profit Formulas Understanding how pricing decisions affect profit is complex, because retailers, manufacturers, accountants, and customers have slightly different viewpoints regarding profit. Net sales less the cost of goods sold equal **gross profit**. The resulting number after the costs of doing business are deducted from gross profit is called **operating profit**. From a retailer's perspective, gross margin—the term used in pricing and merchandising contexts elsewhere in this text—and gross profit are the same. The definitions of operating profit and net profit also concur. The following formulas are used to calculate both types of profit:

$$\text{Net sales} - \text{Cost of goods sold} = \text{Gross profit}$$

$$\text{Gross profit} - \text{Expenses} = \text{Operating profit}$$

Return on Assets Formulas Two components must be reviewed before the return on assets (ROA) formula is calculated. First, **net sales** is the gross cash value of goods sold at retail, less the allowances from vendors or suppliers and minus the value of merchandise returned by customers for refund. Net sales do not include alteration charges, sales taxes, interest charges on in-house credit cards, or transportation charges. Second, **allowances** are reductions in costs of goods that involve concessions made between supply chain members. Concessions include—but are not limited to—promotional discounts, vendor subsidies to retailers to reduce the impact of markdowns, damaged merchandise that is returned to vendors, and noncollectable bad debts.

A profitability ratio is used to assess financial performance. Expressed as a percentage, **return on assets (ROA)** indicates the relationship of sales to total assets after taxes and interest are deducted. It is used as a standard for future planning. Different types of retailers may generate similar ROA results even though they operate on vastly different net profit margins and asset turnovers.

In retail terminology, ROA is conceptually the same as return on investment or return on inventory (the acronym ROI can apply to either). The formulas used to derive ROA are:

1. Net profit margin = After-tax profit ÷ Net sales
2. Asset turnover = Net sales ÷ Assets
3. Net sales = Gross sales + Allowances − Customer returns
4. Return on assets (ROA) = Net profit × Asset turnover

Clarifying Profit   Managing the gross margin means planning markup and markdowns carefully, controlling expenses, and planning to produce profits—topics that are discussed in Chapters 15 and 16. To the uneducated customer, gross margin dollars might appear to be pure profit for a retailer. This is, of course, not true. Net profit is calculated after all expenses of doing business have been considered. The average operating or net profit of large retail organizations is about 4 percent. An example clarifies this concept. Suppose a retailer sells a piece of luggage for $100. If the profit margin is 4 percent, the retailer is making $4.00 on the item, or 4 cents on every dollar of goods sold.

Liquidity Ratios

The current ratio and the quick ratio are two computations that examine the relationship between assets and liabilities.

Current Ratio   The **current ratio** measures present financial assets against present liabilities. For example, a retailer includes revenue from sales as assets against accounts payable to vendors and suppliers, payroll, insurance, rent, and other costs of doing business as liabilities. When calculating the current ratio, the term **current assets** is used to refer to revenue from the sale of goods and services. The formula for calculating the current ratio is shown below using hypothetical numbers:

$$\text{Current ratio} = \frac{\text{Current assets}}{\text{Current liabilities}} = \frac{\$700,000}{\$300,000} = 2.3 \text{ times}$$

Quick Ratio   The **quick ratio** is similar to the current ratio but includes a provision for deducting unsold inventory from current assets. This consideration gives a more realistic view of financial status since it includes goods that have been sold, and also merchandise that is still on the floor or being warehoused. Using current assets from the previous example and assuming inventories are worth $300,000, the formula looks like this:

$$\text{Quick ratio} = \frac{\text{Current assets} - \text{Inventories}}{\text{Current liabilities}} = \frac{\$400,000}{\$300,000} = 1.3 \text{ times}$$

The quick ratio is viewed as the "acid test" for a retailer because it offers a much more stringent assessment of the company's financial position, one that can be performed quickly and at any time the results are needed.

Identifying Components of Income Statements

A variety of figures, ratios, and calculations comprise an income statement. An **income statement** is an accounting of all categories of income and expenses for a business for a specific time period—usually quarterly and annually. Gross margin, operating expenses, net profit, current assets, and inventory turn are included. Each component is summarized below. Income statements are also referred to as *profit and loss (P & L) statements.* When income exceeds expenses, a net profit is recorded; if expenses exceed income, the result is a net loss. A sample income statement for a specialty furniture retailer is shown in Table 14.1.

- *Gross margin.* The same as gross profit, introduced above, gross margin is the difference between the total cost of goods and their selling price; as noted earlier, it is calculated by subtracting the cost of goods sold from net sales.
- *Operating expenses.* The costs of doing business, including rent, salaries, supplies, insurance, utilities, and other overhead, are termed **operating expenses**. Expenses incurred through financing the business and the cost-of-goods sold do not fall into this category.
- *Net profit.* Recall that net profit (also called net profit margin), discussed earlier, is expressed as dollars or a percentage, or both.
- *Current assets.* Used in calculating the current ratio, these assets include revenue from the sale of goods and services.
- *Inventory turnover.* Whether a retailer refers to "inventory turn," "stock turnover," "turnover," or just plain "turn," the meaning is the same: The number of times merchandise available for sale was sold during a specified selling period. Introduced in Chapter 5, inventory turnover is calculated as a whole or decimal percentage.

To better understand how an income statement is compiled, consider the following example. A retail furniture store is located in an affluent, trendy suburb of Seattle. It is a single-unit, independently owned specialty store. Merchandise is unique as products are sourced from local artisans as well as vendors from Southeast Asia. Items include kitchen and bar stools made from exotic woods, many with custom-made cushions. The store also offers small bookshelves, occasional tables, wall sconces, and an assortment of window treatments. The store is freestanding and has 10,000 square feet of selling space. The husband-and-wife owners share general management duties and buying responsibilities for the store. They rely on a store manager who doubles as human resources point person, two full-time sales associates, and an interior designer who also is responsible for visual merchandising. Eight part-time or seasonal employees round out the sales, shipping and receiving, and alterations staff. Major maintenance tasks like heavy cleaning, snowplowing, and landscaping are hired out to third-party contractors; smaller tasks are handled by staff.

As you peruse Table 14.1, keep in mind that line items such as returns and allowances from customers, listed under Income from Sales, are deducted from gross sales before net sales are determined. In the Cost of Merchandise Sold entries, notice that returns and allowances are again listed. These are not the same as customer returns but signify dealings with vendors and suppliers that need to be accounted for. Returning goods to a manufacturer is not uncommon and occurs when goods are damaged, late in delivery, or do not meet quality expectations. Cash discounts are given to retailers by some vendors as incentives for early payment or when goods are considered a special purchase for promotional purposes.

Alteration costs are commonly charged for tailoring or other changes that are made to apparel purchased in-store. Some retailers charge for this service while others, including the designer departments of major department stores, offer alterations free of charge. Alteration departments are not revenue drivers and usually are considered a cost of doing business. In the case of our furniture store, alterations are made on window treatments, bed covers, and the custom upholstery that is produced on-site.

Operating Expenses, in this example, are grouped by five key functional areas. Administrative costs include salaries for the two owners and the store manager; costs of employee recruitment, training, and retention; accounting and legal fees; and so on. Occupancy costs would include rent, leasing of retail space, and paying down the mortgage on property owned by the company. In the case of our furniture retailer, the occupancy expenses listed include mortgage payments as well as insurance, utilities, and maintenance. Selling costs include salaries of sales associates and the interior designer, and travel for buying trips domestically and abroad. Costs of marketing and buying complete this section of the income statement.

Table 14.1 Income Statement for the Year Ending January 31, 2011—Hypothetical Profit and Loss Statement for an Independent Specialty Furniture Store

Data	Cost of Merchandise	Sales and Expenses	Totals	Percentages
Income from Sales:				
Gross Sales		$3,041,367		
Returns and Allowances		144,827		
Net Sales			$2,896,540	100%
Cost of Merchandise Sold:				
Opening Inventory		$604,088		
Gross Purchases	$1,905,110			
Returns and Allowances	9,478			
Net Purchases	$1,895,632			
Inward Freight	28,868	$1,924,500		
Total Merchandise Handled		$2,528,588		
Closing Inventory		619,768		
Gross Cost of Merchandise Sold		$1,908,820		
Cash Discounts		75,310		
Net Cost of Merchandise Sold		$1,833,510		
Alteration Costs		14,483		
Total Cost of Sales			$1,847,993	63.8%
Gross Margin			$1,048,547	36.2%
Operating Expenses:				
Administrative		$231,723		8%
Occupancy		139,034		4.8%
Marketing		176,689		6.1%
Buying		112,965		3.9%
Selling		251,999		8.7%
Total Operating Expenses			$912,410	31.5%
Net Profit			$136,137	4.7%

Analyzing Cash Flow Statements

A **cash flow statement** is an accounting of cash that moves in and out of a business for a specified period of time. Monthly cash flow statements are common practice, but with today's technologies, cash position can now be accessed whenever the need arises. Studying a cash flow statement is one of the better ways to quickly ascertain the health of a business. For a retailer, accounts receivable includes money due to the retailer on credit sales; accounts payable comprises remittals to vendors and suppliers from the retailer. This information is discerned by reviewing the cash flow statement. Also included in the monetary ins-and-outs are rent, mortgage or leasing costs, utilities, marketing expenses, salaries, insurance, taxes, and other costs of doing business. The cash flow statement shown in Table 14.2 works in tandem with Table 14.1 as a reflection of planned income and expenditures based on the specialty furniture store example described earlier.

Table 14.2 Cash Flow Statement for the Year Ending January 31, 2012—Hypothetical Statement for an Independent Specialty Furniture Store

DATA	Feb	March	April	May	June	July	Aug	Sept	Oct	Nov	Dec	Jan
Rent	8,000	8,000	8,000	8,000	8.000	8.000	8.000	8,000	8,000	8,000	8,000	8,000
Utilities	2,500	2,400	1,500	1,500	1,500	1,500	1,500	1.800	1,900	2,000	2,300	2,600
Maintenance	1,800	1,800	1,500	1,100	1,000	1,000	1,200	1,200	1,100	1,900	1,900	1,800
Payroll	35,000	35,000	40,000	40,000	30,000	30,000	35,000	40,000	40,000	48,000	50,000	30,000
Merchandise	40,000	70,000	85,000	90,000	40,000	35,000	80,000	150,000	200,000	75,000	90,000	35,000
Supplies	1,000	1,000	1,500	1,500	1,500	1,000	1,500	2,000	2,000	3,000	3,000	1,000
Shipping	1,500	1,200	2,000	2,000	1,000	1,000	3,000	4,000	5,000	2,000	3,000	1,000
Travel	10,000	5,000	3,000	3,000	5,000	5,000	10,000	10,000	10,000	3,000	1,000	3,000
Alterations	1,000	1,500	2,500	1,300	1,000	1,000	1,000	3,000	1,400	1,000	1,000	1,000
Marketing	3,000	8,000	14,000	15,000	5,000	5,000	10,000	13,000	17,000	20,000	18,000	5,000
Insurance	2,200	2,200	2,200	2,200	2,200	2,200	2,200	2,200	2,200	2,200	2,200	2,200
Taxes	10,300	11,300	11,300	11,300	9,300	9,300	11,000	15,300	13,300	15,300	15,300	11,000
TOTALS	116,300	147,400	172,500	176,800	105,500	100,000	164,400	250,500	301,900	177,400	195,700	107,000

Projection is based on the information detailed in Table 14.1. Selected line items represent the five major operating expense categories. In U.S. dollars, rounded for clarity.

Examining the Retail Inventory Method

While most of the tools described in this section pertain to any business, one accounting method is exclusive to retail businesses. The **retail inventory method (RIM)** measures and evaluates the worth of current inventory at retail prices. This method includes not only the retail value of goods currently available for sale—on the sales floor, at an online store, or in a catalogue—but also the total value of inventory being held in a distribution center. Its intention is to produce an approximate book value of goods at retail that is used to estimate gross margin without taking a physical inventory. The RIM technique is not used by businesses that produce goods, but rather is designed for mid- and large-size retailers that sell merchandise to customers. Note that in this context, gross margin is the term used by retailers whereas gross profit is more commonly used by manufacturers.

The model in Table 14.3 illustrates financial details of both cost and retail as they appear on a hypothetical RIM statement for a fashion accessories department of a specialty store. As you

Table 14.3 Managerial Accounting Statement Using the Retail Inventory Method (RIM)

RIM Data	Cost	Retail
Opening Balance	$30,000	$ 40,000
Purchases	$60,000	$100,000
Markups/Appreciation	NA	$ 10,000
Current Balance/Available Stock	$90,000	$150,000
Less: Sales		$ 96,000
Less: Markdown/Depreciation		$ 2,000
Inventory at Retail		$ 52,000
Cost-to-Retail Ratio		60%
Inventory at Cost		$52,000 × 60% = $ 31,200

Hypothetical statement for a specialty store, accessories classification.

From the Field 14.1   CFOs Shift Aim to Managing Slow Growth

Retailers have shifted their focus from downsizing their businesses to downsizing the risks associated with renewed but slow growth. That was among the conclusions of the third annual survey of chief financial officers (CFOs) conducted by PriceWaterhouseCoopers' Retailing Consulting Services. The study found that CFOs were using many of the skills picked up during the economic downturn to maximize sales on minimal inventory, tighten up their supply chains and even look for ways to make their investments in marketing and advertising more productive in the wake of the worst recession in more than a generation.

Survey results were gleaned from 32 retail CFOs—21 in North America and 11 abroad—and included department stores as well as apparel, jewelry, and footwear specialty stores that ranged in volume from $200 million to more than $10 billion.

Among those queried, 24 percent said that use of more precise and conservative "re-forecasts" has led to a strategic reduction in open-to-buy (funds available for wholesale merchandise purchases) quantities, with adjustments in sales plans constituting the most critical factor in managing their inventories. Nearly as many—23 percent—said that adjusting sales plans more frequently had allowed them to flow goods closer to demand rather than bringing all or most of their merchandise in at the start of a season. Assortment and vendor editing ranked third, with 22 percent of respondents selecting that option.

"The whole process of pre-season and in-season planning has become much more challenging because you have, in some cases, 25 percent less inventory and 10 percent less sales," said Antony Karabus, leader of PwC Canada Retail Consulting Services, formerly Karabus Management. "Stores had way too much inventory in 2007, but by 2009 they had great full-price selling because they cut back so far they had nothing to mark down."

Karabus noted that there is a natural dynamic tension within retail between CFOs trained to focus on the bottom line, and buyers "who tend to be optimistic and upbeat by nature. The CFOs are forcing re-forecasts on a more regular basis, looking to make sure that the store is flowing goods closer to need rather than bringing them in and stacking them high."

An exception to this emphasis on lean inventory—and certainly a hot spot for apparel discounting—is the teen market, which Karabus termed "a whole different market than it's ever been. Forever 21 created a far bigger supply of stores and goods. It's just about the only market where net square footage is still expanding, but there'll be a shakeout in time."

Marketing and advertising was also pressured during the recession. Twenty-eight percent of the CFOs surveyed said they reduced their total advertising and advertising spending, but only nine percent felt the reduction hurt traffic, sales, or both. One CFO told Karabus that he had reduced expenditures by 40 percent without a loss of outreach as the company focused more on customer retention and less on customer acquisition.

The study also showed that brick-and-mortar retailers have lots of room for improvement in the electronic retailing sector. Fully 30 percent of respondents did not have a functional e-commerce site, but were planning to develop online stores. On average, those surveyed that had sold on the Web for about four years derive about four percent of sales from their Internet presence. However, those selling online for more than four years generate about nine percent of total sales through e-commerce.

Among the CFOs questioned, 63 percent said they believed customers are feeling a bit more optimistic about their financial circumstances and have slowly begun to buy again. Karabus said CFOs are asking themselves the same questions repeatedly: "Just how much inventory do I have to carry?"

Adapted and condensed from Arnold J. Karr, *Women's Wear Daily*, October 25, 2010, 12.

---

review the statement, notice how the retail price compares with the wholesale cost of the goods. Operational costs of running the business are covered by the margin that exists between cost and retail prices. More on these topics appears in Chapters 15 and 16, which discuss merchandising management and pricing for profit.

Factors that Affect Profitability

Implementing the strategic profit model, maintaining tight financial controls, and monitoring key ratios are not the only aspects of conducting business that drive retail sales and profits. Lest we forget, it is customers that power sales, marketing efforts that propel information to customers, strong merchandise procurement and distribution policies, a stellar sales force, and competent managers that affect the bottom line just as significantly. The **bottom line** refers to the final resolution of an income statement that indicates whether a company earned a profit, broke even, or lost money during a specific time period.

CFOs are trained to concentrate on the bottom line and spearhead strategies that serve their companies well, particularly when the economy is fragile. Read about the many ways retailers have tightened expenses and revised inventory forecasts through the results of an industry study in From the Field 14.1.

Financial Performance Accountability

"Precise" and "analytical" are words that describe contemporary, well-trained financial minds adept at designing and using sophisticated information technology systems, key ratios, and performance indicators. These tools bring accuracy and foresight to today's retail financial planners. CFOs are not only well schooled in finance, but also in accounting procedures and strategic planning. The quest for accountability in all phases of the retail business is a trait of high-performing firms.

Tools and applications used in this process draw from financial and operational events that occur in the course of doing business. Measuring this year's sales against last year's, structuring a balance sheet, and developing performance standards for several retail formats are covered next.

Key Performance Indicators

Financial executives in retailing use or develop key performance indicators to help them judge the strength of the operation. **Key performance indicators (KPIs)** are statistical measurements that gauge the most critical factors for the success of a business or other organization. Progress in meeting goals and objectives can't be judged until measurement criteria are determined. This is done prior to developing and implementing quantitative tools.

Depending on the type and needs of a retail company, KPIs will vary. For example, all retailers consider the management of sales volume, gross margins, and net profit goals significant to the well being of their retail units. A brick-and mortar store chiefly is concerned with sales per square foot, but an online store is focused on customer conversion rates. A catalogue retailer measures sales per page or per square inch of page. Consider the differences in key performance indicators as you view the display in Figure 14.2. Would you measure productivity by sales per square foot or linear foot?

An apparel chain with rapidly turning merchandise measures not only inventory turnover but also sales per hour of its sales associates. A human resource department is concerned about employee attrition—also called turnover—measuring the percentage rates annually and comparing them to figures from previous years. KPIs come in different guises, but all are viable when they impart accurate information that helps executives make better decisions and run the company more efficiently.

Measuring Performance

As indicated in earlier examples and reinforced again here, performance measures relevant for an entire retail organization differ from those appropriate for a single department or a small store. Deciding which critical situations or events need measurement is the first step in developing such measures. Metrics are then selected or devised. The statistical form of a measurement tool is

Figure 14.2
Retail productivity comes in many shapes and sizes: store sales per square foot, merchandise classification, or vertical display; sales per catalogue page or square inch; and conversion rates as surfers become shoppers at an online store.

called a **metric**. Formats used for reporting information that is gathered and measured vary, and benchmarks often are used. **Benchmarks** are metrics that are compared to figures from industry or internal standards that have proved accurate and useful for forecasting and evaluating performance over time. Having a point of reference from which to work is helpful when planning budgets and other workplace needs. Two descriptors of performance categories—input and output—are explained here.

Classifying Input

Details of the retail infrastructure, human resources, merchandising, and marketing activities that form a core of measurable events are called **input**.

Elements that have an impact on a retailer's performance include, but are not limited to:

- Square footage of store selling space.
- Number of employees or sales associates.
- Promotion expenditures.
- Inventory data.
- Expenses for utilities.

Classifying Output

Financial details that describe the results of internal business initiatives to achieve sales and profits are called **output**. Contributing factors, most of which were defined in previous sections, include:

- Net sales.
- Net profit.
- Growth rates for sales and profit.
- Gross margin.
- Comparison with same-store sales.

Retail productivity increases or decreases as decisions are made and tactics are implemented in one or more of these areas. Increasing square footage for in-demand cosmetics and fragrances may have a positive impact on sales in that department. However, if an adequate number of experienced sales associates cannot be recruited for that area, customer service—and ultimately sales—could suffer.

Comparing Same-Store Sales

The measurement of **same-store sales** compares sales from the previous year with sales for the current year in stores that have been open for at least one year. This is done in order to make a more relevant comparison between stores or other units of business that might otherwise distort growth percentages. For example, a company that opens 20 new stores during one fiscal year will show inflated sales growth as compared with a retail chain that did not open any stores that year. Considering stores that have opened and also those that have closed presents a more accurate picture of the company's financial position. Table 14.4 summarizes sales for a hypothetical department store group and includes comparisons based on same-store data.

Table 14.4   Same-Store Sales Summary for a Department Store Group

$ in Millions	Fiscal Period Ended		Percentage Increase		
	April 3 2010	April 4 2009	All Stores	Comparable Stores	
				TY	LY
March	$913.5	$750.6	21.7%	0.4%	9.1%
Year-to-Date	$1,399.7	$1,191.6	17.5%	(1.5)%	11.1%

Hypothetical example. TY = this year; LY = last year.

The **4-5-4 calendar** is an adaptation of a conventional calendar used for retail planning and accounting. This tool blocks the weeks within the year into manageable periods, more equitably distributing sales data for measurement and reporting purposes. This same concept is used by merchandisers when planning sales, the focus of Chapter 15. An example of a 4-5-4 accounting calendar is shown in Figure 14.3.

Compiling a Balance Sheet

Another piece of information that records performance over time is the balance sheet. The **balance sheet** is an accounting document with a long life that shows the viability of a business from the first day it started operating to the last day of a reporting period. For example, if a retailer opened for business in 2009 and is preparing a first quarter report for 2012, the balance sheet will show the financial details of the business from opening day in 2009 through March 31, 2012. The main items included in a balance sheet are:

- Current assets—Cash, inventory, and accounts receivable.
- Current liabilities—Accounts payable, interest on debt, taxes, and dividends.
- Noncurrent assets and liabilities—Property, equipment, and long-term loans.
- Ratios and other calculations—Debt/asset ratio, current ratio, and quick ratio.
- Shareholder equity—Total assets minus total debt.
- Working capital—Current assets minus current liabilities.
- Turnover—Rate of inventory turn; high turnover of inventory is generally more favorable than low turnover, but this is dependent on the type of merchandise carried.
- Leverage—Amount of debt assumed in order to finance the business's assets.[1]

In accounting terms, the "balance" occurs when total Assets = total Liabilities + total Equity.

Corporate and Multichannel Benchmarks

At the corporate level, finance is crucial to the growth and longevity of retailers that compete in the global marketplace. Mergers and acquisitions were introduced in Chapter 3. Due diligence, the process that prepares a company to buy or sell a chain or property, begins with many number-crunching activities.

Merchants use retail mathematics to forecast sales as they prepare plans for merchandise assortments. They strive for accuracy as they derive figures prior to market trips and later as they control inventories. Stores, online retailers, and catalogue houses sell their merchandise to ultimate consumers—that's *us.*

Retailers may require adjustments in financial controls, sales forecasting techniques, and supply chain partnerships as they add selling channels. Pressures on supply chains—and those who finance their initiatives—are compounded when firms deal internationally and through multichannel companies. Maintaining the flow of goods under these circumstances requires advanced planning measures, astute financial capabilities, and teamwork.

Measuring Corporate Performance

In large retail companies, the same-store sales metric is most commonly used to compare performance from one year to the next. However, retail strategies advocated by a firm greatly affect the type and variety of financial analysis tools that are needed. For example, short-term sales goals were notably more important to retailers during the recession. Retailers aspire to long-term profitability, but the uncertainty of the economy influenced the immediate direction taken by many companies. Some retailers added new services during this period. For example, pharmacies added health clinics and some even offered medical procedures such as flu shots on the premises.

Several other actions that potentially affect financial affairs in the corporate sector are routinely followed. Two examples are stock market performance, domestic and global, and market capitalization figures. Why global, you might ask? The parent company of the New York Stock Exchange (NYSE), NYSR Euronext and Deutsche Boerse were in talks regarding the merger of their businesses, which could have given them a competitive edge globally. U.S. antitrust authorities had approved the merger in late 2011, but in early 2012, the European Commission put a halt to the plan citing

NATIONAL RETAIL FEDERATION
4-5-4 CALENDAR FOR MONTHLY SALES RELEASES 2012 vs. 2011
52 vs. 53 Week Year *See Note Below

Figure 14.3
4-5-4 Calendar for Monthly Sales Releases (Source: NRF)

Week	2012 Week Ending	2011 Week Ending
FEBRUARY		
1	2/4	2/5
2	2/11	2/12
3	2/18 (Valentine's Day)	2/19 (Valentine's Day)
4	2/25 (Presidents Day)	2/26 (Presidents Day)
Publish Date	March 1	
MARCH		
5	3/3	3/5
6	3/10	3/12
7	3/17	3/19
8	3/24	3/26
9	3/31	4/2
Publish Date	April 5	
APRIL		
10	4/7	4/9
11	4/14 (Easter)	4/16
12	4/21	4/23
13	4/28	4/30 (Easter)
Publish Date	May 3	
MAY		
14	5/5	5/7
15	5/12	5/14 (Mother's Day)
16	5/19 (Mother's Day)	5/21
17	5/26	5/28
Publish Date	May 31	
JUNE		
18	6/2 (Memorial Day)	6/4 (Memorial Day)
19	6/9	6/11
20	6/16	6/18
21	6/23 (Father's Day)	6/25 (Father's Day)
22	6/30	7/2
Publish Date	July 5	
JULY		
23	7/7 (Independence Day)	7/9 (Independence Day)
24	7/14	7/16
25	7/21	7/23
26	7/28	7/30
Publish Date	August 2	

Week	2012 Week Ending	2011 Week Ending
AUGUST		
27	8/4	8/6
28	8/11	8/13
29	8/18	8/20
30	8/25	8/27
Publish Date	August 30	
SEPTEMBER		
31	9/1	9/3
32	9/8 (Labor Day)	9/10 (Labor Day)
33	9/15	9/17
34	9/22	9/24
35	9/29	10/1
Publish Date	October 4	
OCTOBER		
36	10/6	10/8
37	10/13 (Columbus Day)	10/15 (Columbus Day)
38	10/20	10/22
39	10/27	10/29
Publish Date	November 1	
NOVEMBER		
40	11/3 (Halloween)	11/5 (Halloween)
41	11/10	11/12 (Veterans Day)
42	11/17 (Veterans Day)	11/19
43	11/24 (Thanksgiving)	11/26 (Thanksgiving)
Publish Date	November 29	
DECEMBER		
44	12/1	12/3
45	12/8	12/10
46	12/15	12/17
47	12/22	12/24
48	12/29 (Christmas)	12/31 (Christmas)
Publish Date	January 3, 2013	
JANUARY		
49	1/5 (New Year's Day)	1/7 (New Year's Day)
50	1/12	1/14
51	1/19	1/21 (Martin Luther King)
52	1/26 (Martin Luther King)	1/28
53*	2/2	
Publish Date	February 7, 2013	

* Fiscal Year 2012 is 53 week year.

a probable trading monopoly in stocks and derivatives in Europe.[2] Globalization affects all sectors, and this attempted merger exemplifies the vast changes occurring in global business relationships.

The many ways in which financial leaders study movement within the stock markets, consider earnings per share and market capitalization, and formulate and analyze 10-K reports lend another dimension to the gathering of data pertinent to financial planning at retail's corporate level, which we'll explore next.

Monitoring Stock Performance   If their company is publicly traded, financial officers monitor stock market performance—not only for their firms but also for competing and other retailers. In this way, trends can be deduced early and plans altered if necessary. This element of the external retail environment provides insight for retailers and shareholders who share a symbiotic relationship. Other benefits await companies that follow financial markets. On March 10, 2011, Starbucks stock rose 9.93 percent on the news that the coffee company would partner with Green Mountain Coffee Roasters, the firm that owns Keurig, manufacturers of single-cup coffee makers preferred by many coffee devotees. Distributing Starbucks premium coffee exclusively is a first for Green Mountain, but came at a high price for one competitor: stock of Peet's Coffee & Tea fell 11.49 percent on the same day.[3]

Stock performance—or nonperformance—is followed by top executives who are scouting companies for possible acquisitions or mergers. The financial decision-makers initiate research into the inner workings of a company that may or may not be for sale. Gathering data on stock performance, market capitalization, growth cycles, openness of the takeover target's management, and availability of willing investors all precipitate strategic moves of this magnitude.

Read about Macy's financial plans and benchmarks in From the Field 14.2. The piece was written just prior to the 2010 holiday season and references many of the performance standards and benchmarks mentioned in this chapter.

Analyzing Market Capitalization   Retailers are generally ranked by size in terms of units owned and sales generated. When shareholders are involved, the rules change as companies attempt to satisfy not only their customers, employees, and the communities they serve, but also those individuals and companies that hold stock. Another way of evaluating a company is by calculating its market capitalization. **Market capitalization** is the total value of outstanding shares of stock held by a company. Also called *market cap,* it is determined by multiplying the number of outstanding shares by the stock's current market price. For example, if a hypothetical yoga apparel chain, ZZZEN, has 20,000,000 shares outstanding and the share price is $25.00, the market cap is $500,000,000. This information gives more useful information than stock price alone. The Q ratio takes this analysis a step further.

The **Q ratio** measures the relationship of a company's market capitalization to the value of its assets. If the ratio is greater than one, it indicates that financial markets are including intangible assets as well as financial assets in their evaluations of retail companies. Intangible assets include product differentiation, brand equity, market position, and customer experience. A high ranking indicates that financial markets hold the retailer in high regard and will recommend the company to potential investors. Not surprisingly, retailers with high Q ratios tend to be large with a well established track record of growth. Companies based in the United States and those in emerging markets tend to have the highest Q ratios.[4] The yardstick is used by large retail corporations as they assess the feasibility of potential mergers or acquisitions.

The top global retailers according to Q ratio in 2012 are ranked in Table 14.5, along with their country of origin. The apparel company H&M has held the top position more than once, but Coach was first in the 2012 ranking. By format, electronics specialty retailers and apparel specialty stores scored highest in the 2012 ranking; Africa and the Middle East, followed by South Africa and Western Europe, scored well by geographic region, substantiating the importance of emerging markets. However, those areas did not do as well as the United States and Sweden.[5]

Deriving Earnings Per Share   As part of a five-year plan issued in April 2010, JCPenney's then-CEO Myron E. "Mike" Ullman III stated that the company forecasted $5 billion in sales and $5.00 in earnings per share by 2014.[6] **Earnings per share (EPS)** is "a measure of how much profit a company

From the Field 14.2   Macy's Is Bullish on Holiday

Macy's Inc. executives said that third-quarter profits and sales beat their expectations, overcoming sluggishness in early October, and exuded optimism about the holiday 2010 season to a degree not seen in years. "Our results continue to build, and with each quarter come new initiatives where we haven't fully realized our potential. These just become additive," Terry J. Lundgren, Macy's chairman, president and chief executive officer told *Women's Wear Daily*. "The last couple of years we were all concerned about how the holiday season would turn out, but last year we ended up having a very good fourth quarter. I felt OK. I didn't feel good at all about 2008. Certainly, this is a better moment in time."

Lundgren said the My Macy's localization program has "firmly taken root," that Bloomingdale's has "aggressively capitalized on the return of the upscale customer," that the company has been using "significant" cash to strengthen the balance sheet by reducing debt by more than $1.2 billion (leading to lower interest costs), and that Macys.com is rapidly growing. Macy's had $6.98 billion in long-term debt at the end of 2010.

Asked about Macy's taking market share from competitors, Lundgren replied: "Our results have been good and they have been improving from quarter to quarter versus the retail index and the general landscape. I would assume we are taking market share," though he didn't say from whom. Kohl's Corp., Dillard's, Inc. and JCPenney Co. Inc. are among Macy's most direct competitors.

While Macy's may be opening some distance from other retailers, Lundgren suggested the industry in general should be improving. "We had 9.5 percent unemployment in 2009 and 9.6 percent in 2010. We still don't have the high levels of consumer confidence we've been used to, but people are feeling more secure about their income stream and the position they are in, and they are managing with some visibility into the future. A year ago they lacked that vision."

"Our organization is ready and prepared to execute the fourth quarter to a whole new level," added Karen Hoguet, Macy's chief financial officer, on a conference call after the company disclosed that net income rose to $10 million, or two cents per diluted share in the third quarter that ended October 30, against a loss of $35 million in 2009. Sales rose to $5.62 billion from $5.28 billion and 3.9 percent on a comparable store

basis. Year to date in 2010, Macy's sales were up seven percent in total and 4.7 percent based on same-store sales. Online sales (Macys.com and Bloomingdales.com combined) were up 24 percent in the third quarter and 28.5 to date in late 2010. Macy's projected same-store sales in the fourth quarter to be up 3–4 percent.

Amid all the glee, the report was not without concerns, including rising costs of sourcing products overseas. Also, Macy's acknowledged that gross margins were expected to be "flattish" for the fourth quarter, but Lundgren and Hoguet concurred that the 850-unit department store chain, which posted $23.5 billion in sales in 2009, wouldn't be running more promotions in 2010 than they did the previous year.

Macy's best-selling areas in the third quarter of 2010 were fashion watches, the INC private apparel brand, cosmetics, fragrances, menswear, and luggage. The weakest areas were cold weather–related products, tabletop items, and traditional sportswear.

Lundgren also said retailers won't be able to use weather as an excuse for weak sales much longer. "The weather issue will be a non-issue over time unless there is a big snowstorm on an important day...The coat business will come, and the scarves and mufflers and gloves and all those accessories so important at this time of year will indeed happen."

Other initiatives that Lundgren considers additive to results include the new "MAGIC selling" training program, launched in summer 2010 for the chain's 130,000 sales associates and sales managers, and seasonal hires as well. "MAGIC" is an acronym for:

1. Meet and make a connection with a customer.
2. Ask questions.
3. Give options and advice.
4. Inspire to buy.
5. Celebrate the purchase.

Lundgren also cited Macy's new in-store gift shops in 400 stores, stocked with "limited edition, fun gifts, mostly under $50" and themed around keeping warm, pampering, and exclusive celebrity products from Jessica Simpson, Kenneth Cole and Rachel Roy, among others.

Adapted and condensed from David Moin, *Women's Wear Daily*, November 11, 2010, 3.

earns for each share of stock outstanding."[7] Expressed as a ratio, EPS is calculated by dividing the company's net income by the average number of shares of common stock outstanding during a specified period of time. For example, at the end of 2009, Penney's had an EPS of $1.08.

To reach the company's EPS goal—and targets of $23 billion in sales and $250 in sales per square foot—Ullman announced that Penney's would open new stores and initiate productivity plans for fine jewelry, women's shoes, and intimate apparel departments, areas that had been identified as being ripe for growth. True to the changing currents of the retail environment, by mid-May 2011, the company's forecast had been revised. Plans for new store openings were reduced, and those stores that were still slated to open were scaled down to about half the size of current footprints. The earlier profit goal of reaching $5 per share was eclipsed by more vigorous plans to add new in-store businesses.

By the end of 2011, the company expected its MNG by Mango line of young women's fashion to grow to 600 in-store boutiques. This arrangement is similar to the one it has with Sephora, the cosmetic retailer, which had about 230 in-store shops by the end of 2010.[8] Ullman noted that the exclusive line of Liz Claiborne apparel had brought "hundreds of thousands" of new shoppers to Penney's. By March 2011, Penney's had opened 100 Call It Spring shoe stores and added 292

Table 14.5 Top 25 Global Retailers by Q ratio

Company	Format	Country of Origin	Q ratio
Coach	Luxury leather	United States	7.15
BiM (Birleşik Mağazalar A.Ş.)	Hard goods discounter	Turkey	5.81
Hennes & Mauritz (H&M)	Specialty apparel	Sweden	5.67
Amazon.com, Inc.	Books, music, general merchandise	United States	5.30
Apple Inc./Apple Stores	Computers, iPhones, accessories	United States	4.69
CP ALL Public Company Limited	Convenience, supermarkets, hypermarkets	Thailand	4.50
Inditex S.A.	Department and specialty stores	Spain	4.15
Dollar Tree, Inc.	Discount stores	United States	4.05
Woolworths Holdings Limited	General merchandise	South Africa	3.69
Tractor Supply Company	Farm, ranch, lawn, and garden equipment; apparel	United States	3.61
Dairy Farm International Holdings Limited	Multiple formats, convenience stores, supermarkets	Hong Kong	3.35
Ross Stores	Apparel	United States	3.30
Shoprite Holdings Ltd.	Multiple formats, supermarkets	South Africa	3.22
Whole Foods Market, Inc.	Specialty food markets	United States	3.00
TJX Companies, Inc.	Off-price apparel, home goods	United States	2.89
Fast Retailing Co. Ltd.	Specialty apparel	Japan	2.85
Next PLC	Specialty apparel	United Kingdom	2.69
Bed, Bath and Beyond Inc.	Home goods, small appliances, general merchandise	United States	2.65
President Chain Store Corp.	Supermarkets	Taiwan	2.53
Open Joint Stock Company "Magnit"	Convenience stores, hypermarkets, and cosmetics	Russia	2.42
AutoZone, Inc.	Automotive supplies	United States	2.41
Compagnie Financière Richemont SA	Luxury goods, jewelry, fashion	Switzerland	2.39
The SPAR Group Limited	Supermarkets, multiple formats	South Africa	2.36
Family Dollar Stores	Discount stores	United States	2.29
PetSmart, Inc	Pet food, supplies, and services	United States	2.18

Source: "Top 30 Retailers by Q ratio—Global Powers of Retailing Top 250," *Stores,* January 2012. www.stores.org/assets/Top250/2012/QRatioTop30.jpg (condensed and adapted)

MNG by Mango shops, bringing the company halfway to its 600-unit goal for 2011. The company intended to shave $50 million in expenses in 2011 in a bid to increase its bottom line. But earlier projections for annual EPS of $2.15 to $2.25 looked out of reach, since only 28 cents per share was recorded in the first quarter of 2011.[9]

JCPenney made another strategic move in late 2011, as Ron Johnson, of Apple, Inc. retail stores fame, took over as CEO. Drawing from his Apple colleagues to staff his own team, Johnson immediately began putting his stamp on the company's five-year plan.[10] The stores-within-stores—including MNG—performed well in the first two quarters of 2012, but many of Johnson's changes were not received well by customers. Doing away with coupons and frequent sales confused customers whose expectations were not being met. Total sales for the quarter ending in July 2012 were down 23 percent and online sales were down 33 percent.[11] The financials will be reviewed carefully as new strategies are developed. This example illustrates the importance of planning and the impetus needed to revise plans as the economy, market, and CEOs change. Strategic changes like these are

Figure 14.4
Expressive fashion apparel line, MNG by Mango, is part of JCPenney's plan to attract a younger audience. Mango is a Spanish retailer that expanded its U.S. presence with freestanding Mango specialty stores and in-store boutiques like the one in Penney's.

dependent upon the availability of financial resources and the careful analysis of multiple factors, including leadership change, that influence sound decision making. The MNG by Mango store in Penney's is shown in Figure 14.4.

Filing 10-K Reports   When a U.S. retail company is publicly traded, it is required by the Securities and Exchange Commission (SEC) to file a Form 10-K report annually. A **10-K report** is an audited document containing extensive financial data and information about the company, as well as its people, operations, and strategic planning. These reports are quite detailed and generally contain four main parts:

1. *General business overview.* This section contains a review of a company's strengths and weaknesses. Potential risks both inside and outside the company are revealed.
2. *Management discussion and financial statements.* The perspectives of key executives regarding the internal workings of the company lend credence to the analytical aspects of the report. Readers need to know the cash position, major investments, and capital-intensive projects that are upcoming, for example.
3. *Information about directors and officers.* Who they are, how they operate, how they are compensated, educational backgrounds, and prior experience—all lend insight into the human factor within the company.
4. *Exhibits.* Documentation of all aspects of the business is included here. Financial reports, agreements with banks and other lenders, purchase and sale agreements, and major employment agreements or changes are examples of clarification and amplification of data presented by the company.[12]

Analysis of 10-K reports is a crucial step for anyone who anticipates acquiring a company or perhaps investing in one. Information on recent acquisitions, specific business divisions, and financial initiatives is invaluable and should be examined before becoming involved with a company as partner, investor, vendor, potential suitor, or employee.

Measuring Store Performance
To ascertain store sales performance, retailers calculate sales per square foot for the entire store, and by department when appropriate. Many stores also benchmark sales per associate. Most look at the impact of inventory shrinkage, because losses caused by shoplifting, employee

////////////////////////////////
Cyberscoop
Pull the 10-K report for your favorite publicly traded retail company. It's easy and free via EDGAR, the SEC's online index, where you can download the documents in several formats. Go to www.sec.gov/edgar.shtml, take the brief tutorial, and you're on your way. (It helps if you know your company's ticker abbreviation.) Take a shortcut to Form 10-K for Children's Place (PLCE) at http://biz.yahoo.com/e/110328/plce10-k.html.

theft, and organized retail crime directly affect the bottom line. Measuring performance against the competition is customary among electronics retailers battling to meet or beat sale prices on big-screen TVs or the latest iPads. Every tactic that is implemented ultimately is felt in the retail marketplace.

Calculating Sales Per Square Foot   Sales per square foot is the standard unit of measurement for productivity in most conventional stores used as examples throughout this text. To amplify concepts introduced in Chapter 11, recall that sales per square meter is used in some foreign countries and sales per linear foot of shelf space is used under special circumstances. The formula for calculating sales per square foot for a store is:

Total square feet of selling space ÷ Net sales = Sales per square foot of selling space

More detailed information is learned about a single category of merchandise by applying this formula, particularly if it has been relocated from one area of the store to another. Another useful tool is the space productivity index.

Using Space Productivity Metrics   The **space productivity index** is an advanced tool that helps retailers determine optimal merchandise placement in a brick-and-mortar store. The index compares the proportion of a store's gross margin achieved by a specific merchandise category to the proportion of selling space used for the merchandise. A ratio of 1.0 indicates that the amount of square footage allocated to a department or merchandise category is in direct proportion to the contribution to gross margin it generates. A ratio below 1.0 indicates that the merchandise is not selling well and that space allocated to it should be decreased. A rating above 1.0 means that the merchandise category is performing better than average. This indicates that enlarging the department might be feasible, or that it at least should be monitored closely for possible changes in the future.

Comparing Product Line and Department Performance   The earlier section on profit management models and tools presaged this discussion of measurement tools and benchmarks. Some retailers use a more sophisticated version of gross margin management—called **gross margin return on investment (GMROI)**—to compare the productivity of different departments, lines of product, or placement on the selling floor. Within the store, merchandise brands, lines, and departments vie for prime selling space. Often GMROI is used to judge the real contribution of each to the organization. The data obtained are sometimes more informative than a simple sales analysis.

Using this approach, two vying product lines are compared based on their contribution to sales, use of physical resources, sales associate performance, overhead, and utilized space. This enhanced tool works on the principle that all aspects of a business should be included when determining spatial allocation within a store.

Analyzing Employee Productivity Records   There are quantitative ways to measure performance of sales associates and managers using criteria such as total dollar sales, total number of sales transactions, units sold per transaction, number of customer complaints, number and dollar value of returns, net sales per hour worked, and number of days absent or late. Comparative performance records are useful in identifying effective or ineffective salespeople and their managers.

Monitoring Shrinkage   One factor that directly affects retailers' profits is theft by employees, customers, and organized crime rings. Typical shrinkage rates for most large retail chains in the United States and Europe are less than 2 percent. This may not sound like much, but it translates to a significant loss of profits.

Research shows that a 1.7 percent shrinkage rate results in an average loss of profits of 19 percent. Add costs due to crimes against retailers and the decrease in profits escalates to 25 percent.[13]

Brick-and-mortar stores are not the only retailers facing losses due to theft. In the United States and Canada combined, all e-commerce fraud losses totaled $3.4 billion in 2011—up from $2.7 billion the previous year. This higher loss figure is attributed to the theft of more expensive merchandise such as electronic goods, even though the rate of fraud incidents was 0.6 percent in 2011, down from 0.9 percent in 2010.[14] The business costs associated with shoplifting, employee theft, internal error, supplier and vendor issues, online fraud, and organized retail crime are ones that retailers work hard to alleviate.

Measuring Catalogue and Call Center Performance

Catalogue productivity is measured in terms of sales per page or sales per square inch of a page, so valuable is the paper selling space. Most catalogue retailers and other direct sellers also operate online stores. Often, they are able to offer more products via their Web sites than they could possibly display in a single catalogue.

Although catalogue and call center sales increased 10.8 percent to $22.6 billion in 2011, Web catalogue companies with online stores rank last in growth when compared with brick-and-mortar retailers with Web sites, Web-only retailers, and consumer-goods manufacturers that sell online.[15] A major reason for this slow growth rate is that the demands of fully exploiting online selling have strained already tight budgets due to rising printing, paper, and postage costs attributed to catalogue operations.

The state of flux experienced by catalogue retailers is apparent in the shift made in trade terminology from "call" to "contact" center. With this change the industry acknowledges the change to a more integrative descriptor. Not only does the new moniker dispense with the sometimes-negative connotation given to telephone marketing, but it also suggests that customer-centric and revenue stream models must evolve when business is conducted across several selling channels.

Measuring Online Store Performance

When online stores count "hits," it's the equivalent of counting window shoppers past a brick-and-mortar storefront. E-retailers monitor conversion rates, results of search, and shopping cart abandonment—new methods for a new century of retailing.

Measuring the outcome of online initiatives is another necessary function performed by Web retailers. A variety of analytical tools used to quantify certain customer behaviors and several types of assessment tools were introduced in Chapter 7. The following measurements are most commonly used to chart and evaluate performance and ROI:

- *Traffic counts*—The number of people who access a Web site. Because this number is largely dependent on the effectiveness of the search process, search engine optimization is one of the more crucial mechanics when it comes to finding and moving prospective customers to an online store.
- *Conversion rates*—The percentage of visitors to a site who make a purchase. Recency and frequency of shopping are positively correlated to high conversion rates as is preference for the brand and past experience with the retailer.
- *Average order size*—Calculated in terms of dollars spent and number of units purchased by customers. This figure is used to benchmark future sales and analyze customers' prior purchasing habits.
- *Shopping cart abandonment rates*—The percentage of people who shop an online store but disengage their shopping carts before completing the checkout process by arranging for payment. (Industry studies show that up to 75 percent of shoppers fit into this category.)
- *Return visitors*—Numbers of people who become loyal customers. Many retailers record recency and frequency of visits and number of purchases, as well as collect detailed customer preference data so that customers may be better served.
- *Effectiveness of customer service*—Many research companies delve into behaviors and attitudes toward customer service, an aspect that is difficult to quantify but important to monitor. Using one such method, a customer satisfaction survey, Amazon topped Apple and QVC. "The Foresee E-Retail Satisfaction Index"[16]—scoring an 89, the highest ever for this index. Online polling, blogs, and customer reviews are other methods that are valuable to retailers as they evaluate their customer service programs.
- *Level of brand awareness*—Customers who have already developed a relationship with a catalogue or brick-and-mortar retailer are more likely to also shop the retailer's online store. High brand awareness helps customers form an opinion about the brand and increases the likelihood of purchase.
- *Receptiveness of customers to new features*—Progress and change are good, but only when they answer unmet needs of customers or present novel technologies or merchandise. Creative apps designed for those who prefer to order via their mobile devices are examples of positive developments that are more likely to be embraced by customers.[17]

////////////////////////////////
Cyberscoop
See how improving Web site conversion rates affects a company's total online sales. *Entrepreneur* has many tools on its Web site to help online businesses refine their financial goals. Make some assumptions about your online store (invent one if you want to!), then go to www.entrepreneur.com/calculaters/conversionrate.html and plug in some numbers. Play "what if" and see what happens.

These measurement descriptors translate directly or indirectly to revenue generation. Examples illustrating how online retailers deal with negative results after implementing some of these performance measures were presented in Chapter 7. Improving processes, increasing sales, and reducing costs of retaining customers are of interest to all retailers.

Benchmarking Multichannel Performance

Multichannel retailers have the distinction of generating revenue from several selling channels, and the dynamics of the revenue surge are changing. For several large chains, including Staples, Office Depot, Williams-Sonoma, and dELiA*s, by 2011 more than 30 percent of total company sales came from their online stores.[18]

Multichannel retailers that have fully integrated systems across all divisions, channels, and countries of operation perform the best in the industry. Sales growth changes the complexion of their revenue streams and, accordingly, their financial management strategies. For example, cannibalization of one sales channel by another has been a very real problem for some multichannel retailers. In one survey, 55 percent of retailers said they could not measure cannibalization in their companies.[19] If changes to existing technology are necessary to measure cross-channel cannibalization, a retailer must secure funding for new systems. Cannibalization in a business may have inadvertent negative effects on profitability, especially if the retailer is unaware of its extent. Researchers who conducted one cross-cultural study, which included North American and U.K. retailers, acknowledged that different parts of the world view the cannibalization issue differently.

Cannibalization is becoming less problematic as retailers fully integrate financial and operating systems in their businesses. Those that embrace the omnichannel ideal consider all revenue centers part of the greater whole.

Financial Trends and Tactics

Global trade involves adapting to existing infrastructure in countries that are less developed than one's home base, but it also involves striving for standardization so that international commerce and banking flow more efficiently. Accounting methods may differ in countries other than the United States, but multilingual, multichannel systems emerge as the retail industry demands total integration—not only in merchandising, distribution, pricing, and sourcing, but also in financial systems. The banking community services this aspect of retail finance.

Growth by acquisition of other retail companies near and far is an aspect of retail strategy that requires complex fiscal planning. The shift away from financing—or refinancing—major acquisitions through traditional banking institutions and venture capital firms, and instead turning to private-equity firms, including real estate investment trusts, has changed the parameters of indebtedness and created opportunities for new partnerships within the retail industry. These areas of growth and change are highlighted next.

Global and Multichannel Accounting Systems

A look at one state-of-the-industry example helps us gain insight into how retailers can adapt their financial systems to handle the needs of a global, multichannel business environment. Coda Financials, a division of UNIT4 CODA, Inc. is among the newest wave of technology-savvy companies that understand the needs of global and multichannel retailers. Coda provides software-based accounting systems for retailers, including department and home improvement stores; fashion, music, and hardware companies; and the global furniture retailer IKEA.

Among the benefits of Coda systems are:

- Programs that facilitate multi-country, multi-language, and multi-currency accounting.
- Web-enabled software that facilitates global financial transactions.
- Easy interfacing and real-time information that makes processes and reporting faster and more efficient.
- Cost reductions and other processes that support growth.

IKEA implemented Coda's accounting system to create a unified finance system for its global network. Details are provided in From the Field 14.3.

From the Field 14.3   Global Retailer IKEA Builds On a Single Finance System

Home furnishings giant IKEA is one of the best-known international brands worldwide. It has around 270 stores in 26 countries, and more opening every year. The stores are franchises of Inter IKEA Systems BV. Given the company's rate of expansion and globalization, it has had to invest heavily in information technology (IT) over the years. Different languages, operating environments, processes, and technology in each location made it difficult for IKEA to operate as efficiently as it wanted to.

Coda Financials, from the UNIT4 Group, was chosen some years ago to achieve IKEA's long-term goal of having a single common finance system globally that would make accounting quicker and easier. Coda was implemented in Philadelphia (servicing North America), in Sweden (servicing Europe), and in China (servicing IKEA operations in Asia).

Using a standard chart of accounts—which updates information in real time from IKEA's operational systems—means each store has on-demand access to real-time performance data. Coda Link for integrating source systems and data makes systems integration seamless; financial reports are more accurate because staff members do not spend as much time inputting manually. The risk of manual error has been reduced and month-end and year-end reporting times have improved considerably.

"Coda is excellent for obtaining performance information when you need it," said Ulrika Martensson, a Project Manager at IKEA. Forecasts are held in Coda and are used for benchmarking reported data. Information relating to transactions and performance is seen at a very detailed level.

IKEA uses shared services in the main regions, for handling invoices relating to goods and freight, which has saved time and money. Because Coda can be implemented as a "single-instance" application and accessed from anywhere, it fits the shared-services model well.

Coda's ability to support multi-language businesses is another reason why large enterprises choose it. At IKEA, everybody uses mainly English, but its Chinese finance team, for example, has the option to set up menus in Chinese.

Coda has grown with IKEA as it has evolved into a multinational business. According to Martensson: "The fact that Coda has kept up with the requirements of a growing business like IKEA shows it can stand the test of time and is a good software investment for any organization where speed and efficiency are key."

Excerpted from *Accounting for Change: Finance Technology in the Retail Industry*, UNIT4 CODA, Inc., 2010, www.unit4coda.com.

Financing Domestic and International Trade

We've probably all lost track of a bill that needed to be paid. Paying one's household and personal bills on time is a task that requires attention, and sometimes a juggling act; this is also true for retailers. Several methods are used, from cash to credit, and many are germane to retailing and global trade. Firms called factors ensure the prompt payment of many retailers' accounts payable—especially invoices presented for merchandise shipments from manufacturers. Letters of credit are used to pay for imports and exports and are accepted worldwide. The newest forms of electronic payment are growing in popularity.

Factoring

Retailers that operate on tight cash flows but must meet payments to vendors on time or even make payroll—fast—might need the services of a factor. A **factor** is a financial firm that coordinates payment between buyers and sellers by buying accounts receivable on a commission basis and assuming financial risk for the retailer. **Factoring** is the process of purchasing retail accounts receivable at discount and then collecting on the debt from the manufacturer or distributor on behalf of the retailer. For example, the seller could be an apparel manufacturer in China that has invoiced the buyer, a specialty chain in California that ordered a shipment of swimsuits. The buyer notifies the factor that the goods have been shipped. Unless a business relationship has already been established, the factor will carefully check the credit of the retailer. If good credit is confirmed, the factor assumes the financial risk for the shipment and advances 70 to 90 percent of the invoiced amount to the seller.

When the bill is paid in full, the factor remits the balance to the retailer, less the agreed upon factoring fee—usually about 2–6 percent.[20] Some retailers are notoriously slow payers, and using a factor alleviates that problem. Factors, in turn, welcome retail accounts that are credit-worthy. For their part, manufacturers relish the thoughts of being paid in 24 to 48 hours rather than the customary 30, 60, 90, or even 120 days.

According to J. Michael Stanley, managing director of Rosenthal & Rosenthal, Inc., a large factoring firm with offices on the east and west coasts of the United States, factoring has become much more complex in the last few decades. His company serves a spectrum of clients from retailers that are growing fast and require greater cash flow to those that are in trouble financially, or those that are intentionally scaling back and need money during the transition period. Stanley believes that consolidation in both the manufacturing and retailing sectors, plus the major production shift to low-wage countries, has changed the factoring business due to the challenges of financing a diverse and geographically dispersed supply chain.[21]

Internationally, if loyalty and trust are built despite the complexities of financing trade, then factoring will surely remain a financial service of choice for many retailers.

Letters of Credit

Importers and exporters have realized that to be profitable, they needed to do business internationally at less risk financially. Banks and other financial institutions responded by making such a service available. A **letter of credit (LC)** is "an instrument issued by a bank to an exporter by which the bank substitutes its own credit for that of the importer and guarantees payment provided the documentary requirements are satisfied."[22] With so many retailers now involved in global trade, the use of LCs has escalated.

There are two types of commercial LCs: revocable and irrevocable. Each is requested under certain circumstances. The importer and exporter—in this case, retailer and manufacturer—must first agree on the terms of the sale and that the means of payment will be an LC. Next the retailer asks its bank for the LC, which is processed much like a loan application. The bank may include the provision that if the retailer defaults on payment, the bank would take possession of the merchandise.[23]

Electronic Payables

Advances in technology and the age of the Internet have brought forth many new, secure, and cost-effective payment methods for multichannel, domestic, and global retailers. Electronic data interchange (EDI) systems, introduced in Chapter 1, have been the backbone of electronic shipping notices, invoicing, and payment methods and paved the way for exclusively Web-based platforms. Two constraints have hampered implementation by retailers: EDI systems are expensive and not all suppliers are online.

Most large retailers—and many small—want to receive and process vendors' invoices and remit payment online. One e-invoicing system developed by the California-based company Transcepta has serviced Canadian restaurant chain Tim Horton's since 2009, when the chain dispensed with paper invoices. The system, hosted by the company SAP, has improved billing accuracy and reduced payment processing time impressively. Instead of taking several days to receive an invoice, the new system transmits one within 24 hours.[24]

Financial Trends in Property Acquisition

The recession has been long, deep, and global. Although the economy was expected to rebound in 2010, it did not for most U.S. citizens and many retailers. By 2011, the stock market had rallied but the housing outlook remained dismal in many parts of the United States, and commercial real estate markets still operated sluggishly. Many changes in leasing practices and retail acquisitions began during 2008 and 2009—now considered the early years of the recession. Reaction was evident as retailers attempted to make property acquisition and financial management more effective. When store buildings that had been vacated by retailers like Circuit City were retrofitted for new tenants like deep discounters and video-game arcades, most retail observers admitted that the retail community had irreparably changed. Several facets of change and reactions of retailers that were presented in Chapter 9 merit additional analysis from a financial perspective here.

Acquiring Existing Companies

As you learned in Chapter 3, one of the more prominent techniques used by retailers to grow their businesses is acquisition. Many retail companies outside the United States are investing in U.S. property, due to oversaturated home markets, decline of the dollar against some currencies, and the increase in available capital in some emerging markets. European retailers have long held property in the United States, but companies from India, Brazil, China, and South Korea are now increasingly well represented in the hunt for U.S. retail real estate.

Did You Know?
Walmart's Global eCommerce division purchased 18 percent of shares in Yihaodian, a Chinese online grocery and general merchandise retailer. This venture gives Walmart an opportunity to add to its business portfolio in Shanghai, Beijing, and Guangzhou, and gain experience with next-day grocery delivery service. For many companies, buying shares is an overture to full acquisition. In 2012 Chinese officials approved an increase in Walmart's shares to 51 percent. What next? (Source: "Walmart Global eCommerce Invests in Yihaodian." Kantar Retail IQ, May 13, 2011, www.kantar retailiq.com/ContentIndex/ NewsDisplayLW.aspx?id= 333170&key=Vpa.) (Update: Laurie Burkitt. "Retail Giant Gets the Nod for China Web Partner." *Wall Street Journal.* August 15, 2012, B4)

This last trend is supported by the observations of leading retail analysts. RECon is a retail real estate conference held annually in Las Vegas by the International Council of Shopping Centers. Michael Kercheval, president and CEO of the organization, noted that 10–15 percent of companies attending the conference in 2011 were from outside the United States—a vast increase over prior years.[25]

Financial Impact of Real Estate Investment Trusts

Real estate investment trusts are involved in acquisitions of land and shopping centers. REITs were defined and several were profiled in Chapter 9, Site Selection. The financial strategizing that forms the backbone of retail acquisition plays a significant role in retailers' business goals and objectives. Case in point: Vornado Realty Trust owns all or part of many retail companies and developments in the United States and is expected to raise $1 billion for a private-equity fund to acquire or invest in properties that did not make it through the recession intact.[26]

Refinancing Tactics

Sluggish economies can wreak havoc with retail firms that were once high flyers but suffered liquidity crises along with other retailers during periods of slow revenue growth. One such company is American Apparel. A viable, trendy, specialty chain in better times, American Apparel sells edgy-artsy apparel for women, men, and children. Brightly colored dancewear, as well as mellower activewear and basics, have been the lure for young fashionistas entering the retailer's doors. The company, which operates almost 250 stores in 20 countries, is proud of the fact that it manufactures most products at its Los Angeles factory.

Despite phenomenal sales growth during its first five years in business, in the spring of 2011 American Apparel found itself looking for assistance from private investors. The company had posted losses of $86.3 million in 2010 and noted that same-store sales were off 13 percent. To finance its day-to-day business—and avert possible bankruptcy—the retailer convinced a group of investors led by Michael Serruya to purchase $15.2 million in shares; convertible warrants worth another $27 million in shares were expected to be exercised at a later date. The retailer's largest lender, London investment firm Lion Capital, had kept American Apparel founder Dov Chaney solvent through previous crises.[27]

Refinancing appears to have helped the company resume a growth trajectory. By early 2012, the company reported sales increases throughout the preceding year; store sales for January 2012 had increased approximately 11 percent, and online sales rose almost 40 percent. While full recovery may depend on a significant economic upturn, American Apparel's strategies to improve operational efficiencies and leverage corporate costs have had a significant impact on its fiscal performance.[28]

Confronting the Future

It was with "cautious optimism" that retail CFOs worldwide approached planning in the second decade of the 21st century. A survey conducted early in 2011 by the accounting firm KPMG found that most CFOs expected slow economic growth to continue. Only 24 percent expected improved financial performance in 2011 over the previous year. The more confident retailers were in Asia, followed by those in the United States.[29]

At the time of this survey, most respondents reported that the unrest in the Middle East and devastating earthquake and tsunami in Japan had had a limited effect on retail finance worldwide. As time would tell, nothing could be further from the truth. As the Japanese economy began to feel the full brunt of the post–natural disaster period, it soon became evident that the anticipated short recovery period would not ensue.

For leading Japanese manufacturers such as Nissan and Toyota, the effects of the 2011 earthquake and tsunami were far-reaching. Critical parts could no longer be manufactured in factories located in or near the disaster zone, resulting in curtailed shipments overseas. Auto dealers worldwide worried that their customers would not receive the parts they needed in a timely manner. The laws of supply and demand played out as the global economy adjusted and responded. New car

Did You Know?
Michael Serruya's entrepreneurial passions were apparent long before he led the consortium that bought $15.2 million's worth of stock in American Apparel. From running a single frozen yogurt stand in Toronto to co-founding CoolBrands International, Inc., which operated 5,000 franchises, Serruya has built a career using a mix of passion and persistence. True to form, Serruya purchased stock in the now-hot health food chain Jamba Juice when its worth had plummeted during the recession. (Source: David Lipke, "American Apparel Gets Key $15M Cash Injection," *Women's Wear Daily*, April 22, 2011, 4.)

dealers stood to benefit, foreseeing that any vehicles that did ship would sell for higher retail prices. Similarly, used car dealers discovered that higher prices on used automobiles were accepted by consumers, due to the shortage of new cars.

Rebuilding had been expected to compromise the distribution cycle for at least nine months, but greater levels of contamination at the reactor site, uprooted residents who could probably never return to their homes, potential health problems for those in the immediate and peripheral areas, and the constant draining of resources made it clear that a large swath of the country was at risk. For Japan, another deep recession loomed, compromising its global standing as a manufacturing and economic leader.

Recognizing risk when it involves the solvency of retail companies is one of the key responsibilities of the financial community. Driven by the loyalty and whims of their customers, retailers require firm guidance from their financial experts as they regulate the ebb and flow of monetary resources in search of profitability.

Summary

Financial planning and control underlie the operation of retail enterprises and the quest for profitability. Many tools are available to assist retailers as they plan their financial needs. The strategic profit model uses a formula of net profit multiplied by asset turnover to calculate return on assets. Return on assets is conceptually the same as return on investment or return on inventory. Slightly different accounting terminology is used by retailers as compared with manufacturers. In the retail sector, gross profit (equivalent to gross margin) is determined by subtracting the cost of goods sold from net sales. Operating profit is determined by subtracting expenses from gross profit. What all businesses have in common is the need to determine how much money is required to earn a profit.

Liquidity ratios look at the relationship between assets and liabilities. The current ratio and the quick ratio—the so-called "acid test"—are calculations that provide this information.

Income statements have five key elements—gross margin, operating expenses, net profit, current assets, and inventory turnover—and are usually issued quarterly and annually. Cash flow statements give details about the ins-and-outs of a business's money on a monthly basis.

The retail inventory method (RIM), a unique accounting method used by retailers, considers not only merchandise in the store but also goods that are warehoused. Its purpose is to determine the book value of merchandise without taking a physical inventory. This method also allows retailers to differentiate between retail and wholesale valuations.

Everyone has heard about "the bottom line." This financial term describes the ultimate resolution of doing business as a retailer: Did the company make or lose money this week, month, or year? Accountability is an import concept for all businesses. Key performance indicators are used to measure the retailer's activities.

Metrics are used to assess retail financial performance. Information gleaned from inside the company, such as sales figures, can be compared with previous years' data and also with industry and trade association statistics obtained from outside the company. Many opportunities for performance measurement exist in two broad categories. Input covers topics such as rate of attrition of employees or effectiveness of a marketing campaign. Output looks at financial topics such as how controlling expenses affects gross margins, for example.

Same-store sales compare the preceding year's sales with current sales in stores that have been open for at least one year. The 4-5-4 calendar is used for accounting and merchandise planning purposes since it allows retailers to break up the weeks in a way that equalizes the weeks in a month. The balance sheet is a comprehensive document that shows the financial progress of a retail company since its inception. Included are current assets and liabilities, ratios, working capital, shareholder equity, turnover, and leverage.

When analysts evaluate corporate benchmarks as compared with those of the retail units represented, other viewpoints and sources of information are examined. Financial trends in the stock market provide useful information about companies that are publicly traded and those that are not. Market capitalization (or market cap) is another metric that is followed since it represents the total value of outstanding shares held by a company. The Q ratio not only looks at market cap, but also at its relationship to the value of a company's assets. Earnings per share identify how much profit a company earns per share of outstanding stock. Public firms are required to file a Form 10-K report annually. This document contains a wealth of fiscal, operational, strategic, and personnel information that is of significance to investors and the Securities and Exchange Commission, to which it is directed.

Although brick-and-mortar stores, catalogues and call centers, and online stores share many performance metrics, several unique attributes are specific to selling channel. Whereas stores use sales per square foot as a performance measure, catalogues use sales per page. Online stores look for high conversion and low shopping cart abandonment rates, among other criteria.

Inventory shrinkage is a worldwide problem that affects not only traditional store retailers but also e-retailers and multichannel businesses. Shrinkage due to shoplifting, employee theft, fraud, and organized retail crime hurts retailers by persistently chipping away at their profits.

International payment systems have changed the way the world does business. Global retailers use Web-based systems that support accounting, finance, and other business functions while lowering operational costs. Factoring helps buyers and sellers work together to hasten payment and reduce risk for retailers—for a fee paid to the factor. Letters of credit are a secure method used to finance many avenues of global trade. Newer methods of e-payment embrace accurate and fast Web-based technologies.

The financing of retail businesses worldwide, whether through acquisition, expansion, or retrenchment, has been dampened since the start of the recession. Several trends are apparent. Many overseas retailers are actively seeking opportunities in the United States. Others are refinancing so that once-workable concepts that failed can be revitalized. Real estate investment trusts (REITs) and private equity sources of capital have assumed the financial roles formerly played by investment banks and venture capitalists. It is with cautious optimism that most financial planners, retailers, and consumers are embracing the risks and rewards of this decade.

Key Terms

4-5-4 calendar	Key performance indicators (KPIs)
10-K report	Letter of credit (LC)
Allowances	Market capitalization
Asset turnover	Metric
Balance sheet	Net profit margin
Benchmarks	Net sales
Bottom line	Operating expenses
Cash flow statement	Operating profit
Current assets	Output
Current ratio	Q ratio
Earnings per share (EPS)	Quick ratio
Factor	Retail inventory method (RIM)
Factoring	Return on assets (ROA)
Gross margin return on inventory (GMROI)	Same-store sales
Gross profit	Space productivity index
Income statement	Strategic profit model
Input	

Questions for Review and Discussion

1. The fields of finance and accountancy merge when retailers ask for quantitative measures to help them run their businesses. What is the core of the strategic profit model, and what purpose does it serve for retail companies as they develop financial plans?
2. What are liquidity ratios? How do the current and quick ratios differ? What information do they contain for retailers?
3. What key elements comprise an income statement? How does an income statement compare with a cash flow statement? Why is each important to the financial health and transparency of a retail company?

4. A unique aspect distinguishes the retail inventory method (RIM) from other accounting methods. What is the essential difference, and of what value is it to retailers?
5. How do key performance indicators (KPIs) for small businesses differ from those used for large retail chains?
6. Aspects of input and output are considered when performance indicators are selected. Give two examples of each classification, and describe their value to financial planners.
7. Why do retailers use same-store sales as a basis for evaluating their monthly, quarterly, or annual financial performance?
8. How does measuring corporate retail performance differ from assessing the performance of a single division of that corporation?
9. Why are corporations concerned with the performance of stock markets? How do they use earnings per share and market capitalization data when evaluating their own performance and that of other companies?
10. Several methods are used to determine brick-and-mortar store financial performance. What is the most common form of assessment? Which method do you believe holds the most promise for increasing retail profits?
11. How do conversion rates help online retailers chart their sales performance? What aspects of online selling performance assessment are similar to catalogue retail evaluations?
12. What is the advantage of using a factor to finance a retailer's accounts payable? In what circumstances do companies use letters of credit?
13. Developers and retailers are moving away from financing expansion through loans with traditional commercial lenders or investment banks. From what sources are retailers seeking capital to acquire other retailers, expand their chains, or recapitalize a business in need? Use concrete examples from the text or your own observations in your answer.

Endnotes

1. "Investing Basics, Explanation of the Balance Sheet," InvestorGuide University, accessed May 20, 2011, www.investorguide.com/printarticle.cgi?ref=428. (Condensed and adapted.)
2. Juergen Baetz. "EU Blocks Merger of N.Y. Stock Exchange with Deutsche Boerse." *USA Today*. February 1, 2012. http://www.usatoday.com/money/markets/story/2012-02-01/nyse-euronext-deutsche-boerse/52912232/i.
3. "Stocks in the News, The Good News...And the Bad News," *Wall Street Journal*, March 11, 2011, C5.
4. "Analysis of Market Capitalization," in *Global Powers of Retailing, Stores*, 2007 (Published by the National Retail Federation in conjunction with Deloitte), G36–37.
5. "Q Ratio Analysis of the Top 250," in *Global Powers of Retailing Top 250*, Deloitte and *Stores* Media, January 2012, www.stores.org/print/book/export/html/17773.
6. David Moin. "Penney's Lays Out 5-Year Plan." *Women's Wear Daily*. April 21, 2010, 2.
7. Rona Ostrow. *The Fairchild Dictionary of Retailing*, 2nd ed. (New York: Fairchild Books, 2009), 131.
8. David Moin. "Penney's Lays Out 5-Year Plan." *Women's Wear Daily*. April 21, 2010, 2.
9. Evan Clark, "Penney's Net Up; New Store Plan Cut Back," *Women's Wear Daily*, May 17, 2011, 2.
10. Dana Mattioli, "New Penney CEO is Tapping Former Apple Co-Workers," *Wall Street Journal*, November 30, 2011, B3.
11. Karen Talley. "Sales Plunge Another 23% at Penney." *Wall Street Journal*. August 11–12, 2012, B3.
12. Mike Periu, "How to Read and Interpret a 10-K," American Express Open Forum, May 6, 2011, www.openforum.com/idea-hub/topics/money/article/how-to-read-and-interpret-a-10-K.htm.
13. Paul Demery, "Sorting Good From Bad," *Internet Retailer*, April 29, 2011, www.internetretailer.com/2011/04/29/sorting-good-bad. (Source: CyberSource Corp. Annual Report.)
14. Thad Rueter, "E-Retail Fraud Rate Hits a Record Low in 2011," *Internet Retailer*, February 2, 2012, www.internetretailer.com/2012/02/02/e-retailing-fraud-hits-record-low-2011.
15. Kevin Woodward. "Retail's Role Players." *Internet Retailer*. July 12, 2012. www.internetretailer.com/2012/07/12/retails-role-players.
16. Allison Enright. "More Than a Third of Top-E-Retailers Deliver Super Web Experiences." *Internet Retailer*. May 9, 2012. Source: "The Foresee E-Retail Satisfaction Index." (Spring Top 100 Edition) May 9, 2012. Analysis by: Larry Freed, president and CEO of Foresee.
17. "Step 1 Determine Key Metric to Improve," in *Social Ecommerce 2009 Planning Guide*, Optaros, 3. (Excerpted and embellished by author.) www.slideshare.net/optaros10/2009-Social-ecommerce-guide?c.
18. Mark Brohan, "Top 500 Chain Retailers Look After the (Web) Store," *Internet Retailer*, May 4, 2011, www.internetretailer.com/2011/05/03/top-500-chain-retailers-look-after-web-store.

19. "9. Impact on Profitability," in *Multichannel Retailing 2010, Summary of research findings*, 22. Martec International, Ltd. www.martec-international.com

20. Geoff Williams, "Factoring: 5 Things You Need to Know," AOL Small Business, January 23, 2011, http://smallbusiness.aol.com/2011/01/23/factoring-5-things-you-need-to-know/p.1.

21. Liza Casabona, "An Executive Take on Factoring's Global Future," *Women's Wear Daily*, September 17, 2007, 16.

22. Michael J. Scheller, "A Guide to International Trade and Letters of Credit." Sterling National Bank, International Banking Division, 2008, 32, www.sterlingnationalbank.com/intl/lcbook.pdf.

23. Ibid., 12.

24. Lauri Giesen, "The Next Generation of Accounts Payable," *Stores*, January 2001, www.stores.org/print/book/export/html/5747.

25. Rachel Brown, "Retail Real Estate Sees Better Times at Last," *Women's Wear Daily*, May 17, 2011, 1, 6.

26. Anton Troianovski, "Vornado Makes a Big Bet on Distressed Properties," *Wall Street Journal*, July 8, 2009, C6.

27. David Lipke, "American Apparel Gets Key $15M Cash Injection," *Women's Wear Daily*, April 22, 2011, 1, 4.

28. "American Apparel Announces January Sales, Wholesale Jumps 21 Percent," *Promo Marketing*, February 6, 2012, http://magazine.promomarketing.com/article/american-apparel-announces-january-sales-wholesale-jumps-20%.

29. Jessica Wohl, "Update 1-Retail CFOs Cautiously Optimistic on 2011-Survey," *Reuters*, May 11, 2011, www.reuters.com/assets/print?aid=USN1118709720110511.

Chapter 15

Merchandising Management

Learning Objectives

After completing this chapter you should be able to:

- List the sources of information that help retailers interpret customer demand.
- Describe the steps in creating dollar and unit merchandising plans.
- Apply the basic stock method for determining inventory needs.
- Comprehend the basics of category management.
- Identify the members of a merchandising team and discuss their responsibilities.
- Explain the importance of vendor relationships.
- Identify trends in private labeling and product development.

Planning for sales requires a clear-cut plan of action. First, all retailers determine customer demand for their products. Next, budgets are formulated. Finally, details—including quantities, colors, styles, and models—are specified. Completing these tasks and coordinating management of inventory requires strong relationships with vendors, input from all levels of the organization, and up-to-the-minute technologies.

Merchandising: The Core of Retailing

Let's cut to the core. Effective merchandising means that the popular print shirt you crave is waiting for you in your size and color, at a price you are willing to pay, on the cusp of a new selling season, at your favorite retailer. **Merchandising** is the culmination of planning, budgeting, sourcing, and procuring products for sale to identified target markets. It involves not only the purchasing of goods at wholesale to be resold to retail customers, but also product development, which is the melding of designing, buying, and sourcing goods with technological expertise—often from offshore markets. Merchandisers also select goods for placement on the selling floor before the visual team works its magic.

Who's in Charge?

Although general and divisional merchandise managers in large retail organizations set priorities and develop financial plans, retail buyers mastermind the actual purchasing of goods for resale. In small retail stores, the owner is frequently responsible for all phases of planning and buying. More detail on the responsibilities of the merchandise team appears later in this chapter.

Figure 15.1
Finding the perfect hat requires patience on the part of the customer and a well-planned assortment of styles, which are in stock and available on time, by the retail buyer.

Introduction to Dollar and Unit Planning

Standard operating procedures used in the merchandising planning process are dollar and unit planning. A **dollar plan** is a forecast used by retailers to determine how much money they need to invest in new merchandise. A **unit plan** is a detailed list of all items being purchased by color, style, size, and price. This configuration constitutes an appropriate merchandise assortment.

When developing merchandise dollar and unit plans, store image, changes in the global economy, and distribution practices are also documented. Most important, the procedure begins and ends with customers. Translating their needs and wants into merchandise is at best a tedious task. The rewards come when the goods sell.

Collecting information at the level of stock-keeping unit enables buyers to compare actual figures to planned figures on a daily or hourly basis. Retail planning software provides sales, reorder, markdown, gross margin, and sell-through data. **Sell-through** is the percentage of stock sold against the total of stock remaining in a store or department after a specific period. For example, if your stock consists of 30 T-shirts and you sell 15 in one week, your sell-through is 50 percent. If 15 of the 30 T-shirts sell in eight weeks, your sell-through is still 50 percent but the excessive time on the selling floor indicates that the merchandise is not moving well. Sell-through is used in monitoring of both quantity and time perspectives.

Approaches to Merchandising

Store policies influence the kinds of goods or services the store will sell, the quality of products, and the details of the merchandise assortment. Merchandising objectives differ by company. For example, Express is a well-known national fashion chain that limits its merchandise to apparel and accessories geared to fashion-conscious, young, middle-class women and men who want the latest in smart fashion at moderate prices. Target, the upscale discount retailer, has a different approach to merchandising because the store carries everything from pet supplies to notebook paper, food to fashion. It is primarily young married women that comprise the store's target market. Barnes & Noble uses category management to manage its extensive book inventory. **Category management** is an eight-step method of inventory management used primarily by supermarkets, category killers, and other big-box retailers that carry large inventories of staple foods like sugar and frozen vegetables and consumer goods like toothpaste. Understanding merchandising objectives provides a framework for planning.

Sources of Customer Information

Retailers use many sources of information to learn more about their customers. Amassing as much data as possible and synthesizing that information into meaningful reports that facilitate the planning process is necessary. When interpreting customer demand, both in-store and out-of-store information and resources are used.

In-Store Information

Analyzing past and current sales is the usual starting point for retail merchandise planners. In addition, examining returned goods, credit, and loyalty program data also provides valuable information. Retailers also do research to determine specific customer spending habits.

- *Past and current sales.* Both past and present data are important when interpreting customer demand and estimating sales. Analyzing past sales lets the buyer know exactly which backpacks, in which colors, from which vendors were sold in a specific time period. Because all items do not have a history, selection of new items is much more subjective. Scanning devices instantly record a wide variety of information that is useful for capturing sales and inventory figures for planning purposes.
- *Returned goods and adjustments.* The unspoken message from customers who return goods is displeasure. Retailers may reject items, entire classifications of goods, or vendors on the basis of heavy returns from customers. Rate of return varies by type of store, but in general customers return very little to grocery stores, approximately 10 percent to home-electronics

stores, and more than 10 percent to women's apparel stores. This information is useful to retailers planning new stores or classifications.

- *Credit and loyalty program data.* Analysis of store credit and loyalty data provides important information on records of purchases and customer profiles. Because credit sales make up a large proportion of total sales, transaction receipts are an excellent source of both quantitative and qualitative data. Loyalty card data supplies similar information, not only regarding kinds and prices of merchandise purchased, but also customers' lifestyles and spending habits.
- *Internal research.* Both customer inquiries and suggestions made by customers, salespeople, and staff offer additional input to merchandise planning. Many retailers use customer suggestion boxes, conduct exit interviews with shoppers, and utilize want slips. **Want slips** are notations gathered by sales associates about merchandise requested by customers but not carried by the store. Often computer tallies are used.

Out-of-Store Information

Moving out of the box is also important. Studying the competition, talking with vendors and buying offices, attending trade shows, reading trade and consumer publications, and utilizing online resources are necessary. Expert opinions gleaned from consulting firms, external research, and testing laboratories are useful.

Competition

Useful information is obtained by studying the competition, both in and out of the trading area. In any fashion marketplace, one is sure that in the case of Charlotte Russe and Forever 21, featured in Figure 15.2, each is shopping the other's stores on a weekly—if not daily—basis. Small retailers that cannot afford costly market research learn by scouting similar stores in other market areas and visiting major stores in metropolitan areas for fresh ideas. Identifying hot items they may have overlooked is another motivation to shop the stores. Retailers also study the competition so they can avoid the same or similar merchandise. Analyzing the competition is not done to encourage

Figure 15.2
Charlotte Russe and Forever 21 compete for the same young fashion-conscious female market and share similar merchandise selections.

"me-too" merchandising, but to have more ammunition on hand. It is an excellent research method whether the goal is to meet, beat, or avoid the competition.

Vendors

Although not unbiased, vendors' and manufacturers' sales representatives contribute valuable information. Vendors know what is selling and the dynamics of demand in many geographic areas. Most vendors are reliable sources of information, because lying to retail clients is detrimental to building long-term relationships. However, their suggestions should be considered in the light of one's own market conditions.

Resident buying offices

Resident buying offices, also called central market representatives, study trends for clients and send them a constant flow of information. **Resident buying offices** are companies that facilitate market coverage for retailers by acting as their eyes, ears, and legs in the marketplace. Most retailers belong to buying offices and use their services when preparing for and while on buying trips. A small retailer in South Dakota may find it difficult to go to market more than once or twice a year, or keep abreast of trend information and available resources. Buying offices provide valuable services to large and small retailers.

Trade Shows

Two to four times annually, manufacturers who supply the retail industry hold huge business expositions. Convening in major cities worldwide, trade shows bring together under one roof a variety of manufacturers and distributors showing their wares. Because so many manufacturers take booths at these events, retailers can compare and contrast offerings in the marketplace. They can also see what is new in their particular venue, enjoy one-stop shopping, and place orders on the spot. The WWDMAGIC trade show in Las Vegas is illustrated in Figure 15.3.

Consumer Publications

Business strategists react to information conveyed in the President's State of the Union address, as well as global economic conditions, tariff reductions, and reports of unrest or piracy in various

Figure 15.3
Trade show MAGIC has lured buyers to Las Vegas for decades. Originally a menswear show, WWDMAGIC added women's fashion in the 1990s.

parts of the world. Business newspapers like the *Wall Street Journal* are a great source of current data, as are their online editions. Retailers in all locations, large and small, have this quick form of research available. Reading print and online articles from news magazines like *Time* or *Newsweek* and business periodicals such as *Forbes* or *Business Week* also contributes to a retailer's bank of knowledge.

Trade Publications

Trade papers that are directed toward a business rather than a general consumer audience are another information resource. Fairchild Publications is one of the most respected sources of data for merchandise planning and the fashion industry in general. Many retailers consider *Women's Wear Daily* invaluable. In addition to offering all the latest industry news, the newspapers and online editions carry fashion trend and merchandise resource information. *Stores* and *Chain Store Age* are monthly trade magazines that also provide general retailing data and articles. *Supermarket News* and *Vending Times* carry articles specific to these fields. Most online versions of trade publications also offer blogging for subscribers.

Consulting Firms

Business consultants concentrate on specific or general management issues. Firms from either group are helpful to retailers in the merchandise planning phase. Small retail companies are wise to hire a consultant when planning their first merchandise budgets. Large retailers often use consulting firms when planning global expansion, upgrading technology, or considering major merchandising changes. Deloitte Touche Thomatsu, Kurt Salmon Associates, and PricewaterhouseCoopers are three of the best-known large consulting firms. Focused primarily on retailing are Kantar Retail, based in Columbus, Ohio, and Toronto-based J.H. Williams. In smaller cities, regional firms are helpful because they understand their markets so well.

External Research

Mail and telephone surveys are other ways to collect customer patronage information. Results of random surveys conducted with current and prospective customers are useful to retailers in pinpointing product preferences. Many companies use their Web sites not only to capture merchandise preference information, but also to develop their databases for future promotional purposes. Also helpful are focus groups, made up of representative customers from a store's clientele. **Focus groups** are panels of 5–15 people who are invited to discuss a product, service, or market situation. Selected participants consider a variety of business issues in an informal but controlled setting. For example, participants might be asked by a moderator to pass judgment on merchandising, customer service, or advertising effectiveness. National research organizations, such as ACNielsen Company, use customer surveys to develop valuable information for the industry. Nielsen Reports are commercial reports providing information on market share, sales, and trends, and may be purchased by retailers.

Testing Laboratories

The offer of quality is something that customers have the right to expect from retailers. To ensure the quality of the goods they offer for sale, some large retailers like Sears or JCPenney do extensive testing in their own laboratories. Retailers that do not have their own testing facilities can hire outside testing bureaus like Underwriters Laboratories, Inc., to test products for them. **Underwriters Laboratories, Inc.** are large, independent, nonprofit testing groups whose trademarked UL mark means the product has been safely tested against national standards. Many vendors also seek product certification from publications such as *Consumer Reports*. Retailers like to purchase goods from vendors who have good reputations because they know how important this is to their customers. Manufacturers and other supply-chain members also generate research studies that are provided to the retailers they service.

Gathering information appropriate for evaluating past and current conditions in and out of the store is only the first step in merchandise planning. General financial aspects were addressed in Chapter 14. The specific needs of merchandisers require concise timing, accurate forecasting, and deep knowledge of the ebb and flow of both their own inventories and customers' changing tastes and ability to pay.

The Dollar Merchandise Plan

Retailers plan sales differently depending on the type and size of store, merchandise, and inventory turnover (or "turn"). They plan long term and short term, by chain, division, store, department, and classification. Most retailers work from two six-month plans that are updated on a monthly basis. Retailers are prepared to adjust their business on a daily basis if necessary. Seasonal operations may operate only for a four-month period, but that time span is carefully planned. Swimsuit shops in summer resort areas are examples. A six-month plan worksheet is illustrated in Figure 15.4.

The dollar plan is a forecast for buying and controlling the amount of goods purchased to meet customers' needs during a specific time period. The five major aspects of any dollar merchandise plan are:

1. Estimated sales.
2. Planned stock (inventory).
3. Planned reductions.
4. Planned purchases.
5. Planned gross margin.

Analysis and management of these pieces of merchandise planning are crucial to the success of large and small retailers.

Estimated Sales

Estimating future sales is the starting point in any budgeting process. At this stage, past-year sales are analyzed and percentage changes are projected. In determining the percentage change, several factors are considered. The state of the economy, specific retail growth indicators, changes in competition, and department square footage all affect the forecast. Retail trade associations are excellent sources of comparative sales figures and other statistics vital to the planning process. Whether the product is a fad or classic item, its place in the product life cycle also is considered.

Most retailers plan sales in dollars regardless of the economy. In an inflationary economy, some retailers estimate sales first in units and then in dollars. This is done because future dollars will not always buy as many units as past or current dollars and the projected figures might represent an insufficient number of planned items. Once units are planned, dollar amounts are estimated by building in a currency fluctuation factor if the company is involved in international sales. On the other hand, future dollars may buy more units than past or current dollars.

Buyers who purchase in global markets closely monitor currency fluctuations. The deflation of the dollar against the euro during the recession illustrates the importance of this practice. In November 2009, €1.00 bought almost $1.50, enabling European retail buyers of American apparel to purchase much more merchandise than they could have earlier that year, when €1.00 bought about $1.37. After a roller-coaster two years that brought gains and losses against the dollar, by March 2012, the exchange stood at €1.00 to $1.32, slightly lower than the earlier value due to significant financial crises in several eurozone countries. This volatility emphasizes the necessity for retail buyers to monitor shifts in currency exchanges.

As a general rule, if a retailer is not planning a sales increase, it probably should not be in the business. Of course, there are exceptions to this rule. Departments and classifications vary greatly. For example, Webkins stuffed animals and related products had become very popular with children by 2007, providing reliable sales for retailers that carried the merchandise. Retailers that were strong in this product line did not drop the items in response to the economic downturn, but they also did not project increases in business. With business conditions so uncertain, it was very difficult to predict sales. Scenarios such as this raise additional concerns for retailers, as inaccurate future sales can result in too much or too little merchandise being purchased. When this happens, the steps of the planning process that follow do not fall into place smoothly and the entire budget is of little use.

Six Month Merchandise Plan								
/___/ Total Store /___/ Department /___/ Classification	Department #_____			Classification #_____				
/___/ Spring, 20__ /___/ Fall, 20__	Feb. Aug.	Mar. Sept.	Apr. Oct.	May Nov.	June Dec.	July Jan.	Total	
Net Sales								
Last year								
Plan								
Revision								
Actual								
Beginning of Month Stock (At Retail)								
Last year								
Plan								
Revision								
Actual								
Reductions (Markdowns + Shortages + Discounts)								
Last year								
Plan								
Revision								
Actual								
Purchases (At Retail)								
Last year								
Plan								
Revision								
Actual								
Purchases (At Cost)								
Last year								
Plan								
Revision								
Actual								

Figure 15.4
Six-Month Planning Document

Planned Stock

The second step in the budgeting process is to plan the correct amount of merchandise to meet sales expectations and inventory requirements. Changes in store locations or layout may affect plans. The addition of new stores, the closing of others, or an enlarged selling floor can change inventory requirements radically. For example, during the 1990s, retailers who specialized in the music business had to consider vast shifts in customer preferences and manufacturing trends as they planned their cassette tape and compact disc (CD) assortments. In the early 1990s, vinyl record albums still accounted for nearly 10 percent of all music sales. By the mid-1990s tapes made up about 60 percent and CDs 40 percent. Because tapes and CDs took up much less space than albums, inventory needs and space requirements changed. By the late 1990s, the bulk of sales were CDs, with cassette tapes rapidly phasing out of the merchandise assortment. In the 2000s, CD sales fell because of the shift to iPods and other MP3 players.

Sephora, the French cosmetics retailer, offers hundreds of different makeup items and colors as illustrated in Figure 15.5. Accommodating quantities of diverse colors and ensuring adequate space to display the merchandise presents unique merchandise planning challenges for this retailer. Stock plans help keep inventory investment at an acceptable level. Planners know that the end-of-month stock is just as important a figure as estimated sales. **End-of month (EOM) stock** refers to the dollar amount of stock remaining at the end of a month's selling period. Because standard practice may change from one year to the next, it is difficult to create the perfect plan. Several methods are useful to retailers depending on their specific needs and their type of store.

Two methods of stock planning that are most frequently used are the weeks-of-supply system and the basic stock method. The **weeks-of-supply method** is an inventory planning system in which stock on hand is kept at a level representing projected sales for a predetermined number of weeks. The **basic stock method** is an inventory planning system in which estimated sales for the month are added to a minimum stock to determine merchandise needs for the planning period. The method chosen depends on the type of merchandise, the turnover, and other factors. However, the basic stock method has the most universal applications. The mechanics of this method are emphasized in this section.

Smaller retailers may find using simpler stock-to-sales ratios adequate for their needs. A **stock-to-sales ratio (SSR)** reflects the relationship between goods on hand at the beginning of the month

Figure 15.5
Makeup assortments are difficult to build because there are so many different products and colors to display, like these in Sephora.

and merchandise sold during the month, expressed in dollars or units. SSR is also used for other time periods depending on the retailer's preferred method of inventory planning.

Weeks-of-Supply Method

The weeks-of-supply method is frequently used when planning fast-moving fashion merchandise or supermarket packaged goods. Optimal conditions exist when turnover rates are high and selling periods are short. Goods on hand might equal sales estimates for several weeks.

The formula for calculating weeks of supply is:

$$\text{Weeks of supply} = \frac{52}{\text{Turnover}}$$

Once calculated, the weeks-of-supply number is used to determine the amount of inventory needed to achieve sales goals. This is done by multiplying the planned sales figure by the weeks-of-supply number. The weeks-of-supply method is used when sales of a product are relatively stable over time. It would not be the best method to use for fads.

Stock-to-Sales Ratio

The SSR expresses the numerical relationship between stock on hand at the beginning of a period and sales for the period. The ratio is used as a guide so that a classification will not be in an under-bought or overbought condition. Over time, the SSR is used to identify sales trends. The formula is expressed in this way:

$$\frac{\text{Beginning-of-month stock at retail}}{\text{Net sales for the month}} = \text{SSR}$$

Once calculated the ratio is used to determine beginning-of-month stock for a new period—usually a month. For example, if the stock for a particular classification of merchandise on November 1 is worth $40,000 at retail, and sales for November are $20,000, the SSR is 2.0. If sales for December are projected at $35,000 and the SSR is 1.5, then beginning-of-the month stock should be $52,500. By observing changes in the SSR on a monthly basis, retailers are able to monitor sales levels and revise plans for forthcoming months if necessary. As a rule of thumb, fast-selling periods demand lower SSRs than slower sales periods, which require higher SSRs.

The SSR can also be used to plan inventory needs for specific merchandise items. If a store is selling men's oxford shoes it may determine that it needs 20 pairs on hand to sell one pair. This ratio may seem high, but it is not. Because of variants in sizing (length in whole and half sizes as well as width), plus considerations for color (for example, black, brown, or cordovan), large inventories are typical in this product classification. The store must be prepared for the next customer who may want a black shoe in size 13½, DD width. And the customer has not yet even mentioned brand name!

The SSR is a planning tool for all retailers and is also used in conjunction with other methods of planning as it adds another dimension of analysis to the process. For retailers, there is no such thing as too much information or accuracy when planning to profit from their labors.

Basic Stock Method

The basic stock method is useful for determining inventory levels for most types of merchandise, particularly staple goods. Items of merchandise that are routinely purchased are called **staple goods**.

In spite of fluctuations in demand, the basic stock method helps retailers meet sales goals and avoid out-of-stock conditions. Stock levels at the beginning of each month equal the estimated sales for that month, plus a cushion in case actual sales exceed estimated sales. If retailers provide a balanced merchandise assortment, it is less likely that customers will go elsewhere because they can't find the right size, color, or model. The cushion also acts as a regulatory mechanism by helping retailers maintain an optimum stock level. **Optimum stock level** means having the right amount of merchandise on hand to satisfy customer needs without being under- or overstocked. Using this method also protects against stockouts if future shipments of merchandise are delayed or returned to the vendor because of damage.

Did You Know?
Speaking of men's shoes, the trend in some fashion circles is to denote men's apparel and accessories using the letter "M" to modify the female-linked word for an item. The trend gained prominence when President Barack Obama was spotted wearing a pair of mandals in the summer of 2011. What, the uninitiated among us might ask, are *mandals*? Simply sandals for men that are more constructed and shoe-like than flip flops.
(Source: Christina Passariello and Ray A. Smith, "Grab Your 'Murse,' Pack a 'Mankini' and Don't Forget the 'Mewelry,'" *Wall Street Journal,* September 8, 2011, A1, A12.)

There is a downside to using the basic stock method. Building in a cushion increases the inventory carried by a retailer. Because margins are small on some items, this could cut into profits if products don't sell as well as expected.

The basic stock method involves calculating inventory needs for each month based on two important dimensions—volume and time. "How much can you sell?" and "How fast can you sell it?" are the chief questions the basic stock method answers. Average sales per month reflect the volume portion of the equation. Average stock is a function of turnover and represents the time factor. Turnover rates translate to average days in inventory. For example, in a store with a 4.0 turnover, the inventory sells completely in about 90 days. This is a typical turn for department stores. A jewelry specialty store might operate on a turn of 2.0. This would mean that it takes approximately 180 days to achieve total sell-through of merchandise.

Once calculated, basic stock remains the same for each month of the planning period unless buyers choose to revise their plans. In an ideal merchandising world basic stock is the same as planned EOM stock. Formulas used when calculating basic stock are expressed as follows:

$$\text{Average stock} = \frac{\text{Total planned sales} + \text{Prior month's sales}}{\text{Turnover}}$$

$$\text{Average monthly sales} = \frac{\text{Total planned sales} + \text{Prior month's sales}}{\text{Number of months in sales period} + 1}$$

$$\text{Inventory needs} = \text{Planned sales for one month} + \text{Basic stock}$$

Planned Reductions

Reductions are inevitable; consequently, retailers must build a planned figure into their merchandise budget. Markdowns, stock shrinkage resulting from customer or employee theft, discounts, and human error all contribute to the reductions category. For example, if a retailer grants discounts to senior citizens every Tuesday, this reduction must be anticipated in advance.

A logical percentage for reductions, based on past performance and current trends for each merchandise group, must be used. If a reasonable percentage for reductions is not included when planning sales, retailers could lose potential sales, having underestimated needed stock. Reductions are calculated by multiplying the reduction percentage by planned sales. Reduction percentages are charted by trade associations and can be used by retailers for comparative purposes, when adding new merchandise classifications or opening new stores.

Planned Purchases

The next step in the process includes adding planned sales, planned reductions, and the planned end-of-month (EOM) stock, and then subtracting planned beginning-of-month (BOM) stock. When planning far in advance of a selling season, retailers do not have merchandise on hand (OH).

Using the Planned Purchases Formula

To see how the formula works, assume that you are the owner of a snow and skateboard shop that targets male and female teens and young adults between the ages of 14 and 26. Usually retailers plan per month, but you are planning snowboard sales for the winter season. Because of your choice location (Colorado), favorable economy, and demographics, you estimate that the shop should be able to sell a total of $200,000 worth of items. Your worksheet looks like this:

Planned sales	$200,000
+ Planned reductions (10.4%)	20,800
+ Planned ending inventory (EOM)	58,000
	278,800
− Planned beginning inventory (BOM)	83,000
= Planned purchases	$195,800

It is important to note that when using the basic stock-planning method, planned ending inventory (EOM) is the same as basic stock. If actual sales go as planned, you will be left with stock equivalent to the basic stock figure at the end of the selling period. Using the formula, planned purchases for the selling period amount to $195,800.

For a new store, department, or classification, there is no beginning inventory to subtract:

Planned sales	$200,000
+ Planned reductions	20,800
+ Planned ending inventory (EOM)	58,000
	$278,800
− Planned beginning inventory (BOM)	—
= Planned purchases	$278,800

If the store had been new, the planned purchases figure for the month or season would be $278,800.

Calculating Open-to-Buy

The amount of money a buyer has allocated for purchasing merchandise for a designated period of time is called **open-to-buy (OTB)**. The OTB figure should always be thought of as a guide, not an absolute.

Planned purchases are equivalent to the OTB figure if there are no goods already on order. Because retail buying is never nice and neat, often a buyer has already committed funds to merchandise on order but not yet received. The planned purchase and OTB figures are also the same when the season or month being planned is not yet underway.

Once the selling period begins, the situation changes. Buyers must be able to calculate an OTB figure at any time during a season or month. Goods already on order will affect OTB calculations. The following example again uses the skateboard store:

Planned sales	$200,000
+ Planned reductions (10.4%)	20,800
+ Planned ending inventory (EOM)	58,000
	278,800
− Beginning inventory (BOM)	83,000
= Planned purchases	195,800
− Goods on order (OO)	30,000
= Open-to-buy (OTB)	$165,800

To find the OTB figure, it is necessary to estimate how much merchandise is needed, then determine how much of it is already available. The mid-month or mid-season OTB figure is found by subtracting available goods from needed goods.

Converting Retail Open-to-Buy to Cost

Budgets are planned using retail dollars for all categories. The OTB figure is also computed at retail, but actual purchases from vendors are made at cost. Conversion is necessary. If the markup is 55 percent, cost is 100 percent less 55 percent, or 45 percent. In the example given earlier, the OTB figure at retail is converted to cost in this way:

$$45\% \times \$165,800 = \$74,610$$

The OTB figure is flexible. Conditions often change between the plan and its implementation. Remember, OTB is not an absolute.

Planned Gross Margin

The difference between the retail selling price and the cost of goods sold is called the gross margin. This concept was introduced in Chapter 3 and discussed in Chapter 14 in the context of retail profit formulas. Gross margin is an extremely important figure that accounts for the expenses of doing business and earned profit. Recall from Chapter 14 that gross margin (i.e., gross profit) is calculated as follows:

$$\text{Gross margin} = \text{Net sales} - \text{Cost of goods sold}$$

If the initial price put on merchandise is not high enough, factors such as reductions or the rising costs of doing business may result in a loss rather than a profit. On the other hand, if the initial price is too high, customers will not respond. In both scenarios, profit will be affected. Gross margin also is perceived as the cost of doing business plus a reasonable profit. Retail markup, which affects gross margin, is discussed in detail in Chapter 16.

Retail Planning Calendar

The best way to plan sales is to use a calendar that offers some uniformity. The 4-5-4 calendar, introduced in Chapter 14, is an adaptation of a conventional calendar used for retail planning and accounting. When preparing assortment plans and budgets, merchants compare planned sales to past sales for equal periods of time. On a regular monthly calendar, this is not always possible because months may end or begin in the middle of a week. Using a 4-5-4 calendar, each season has the same number of weeks and days for two consecutive years. In the third year, the last season has an extra week in the last month, and so it is a 4–5–5 rather than a 4–5–4 quarter.

With many uncontrollable factors affecting profit, it would be disastrous to attempt to buy merchandise without advance planning. Once the merchandise budget is completed, buyers turn their attention to the actual assortment of products, outlined in a unit plan.

The Unit Plan: Building the Assortment

Whether buying fashion or basic goods, most retailers begin by breaking down the total inventory for a department into manageable units. For example, the classification *jackets* could include knee-length wrap coats and hip-length fleece-lined hoodies. This classification might be part of an outerwear or sportswear department. Some buyers start at the classification level and build up to the major department requirements. Either way, dollars are allocated to specific groups of merchandise.

Classification Planning

With classification plans, dollars are allocated to give the best possible return on investment. For example, if private-label goods are selling better than designer brands, this is considered when determining stock levels. Without classification planning there is a greater chance of running low on one item and overstocking another. Benefits of planning by classification are highlighted in Table 15.1.

Planning by classification guarantees proper representation of items at planned prices, helps channel purchases to preferred vendors, and provides an opportunity for customers to experience the best the store has to offer. Some retailers choose to plan their inventories in even greater detail by using subclassifications. Groups of merchandise in a classification that are defined more

---

Table 15.1   Benefits of Planning by Classification

- Enables dollar sales and units to be planned well.
- Permits the development of a realistic open-to-buy (OTB) figure.
- Allows buyers to evaluate each segment of their business in order to locate areas for future growth, greater profitability, and cost savings.
- Permits associates in each selling area to understand what merchandise is to be stocked and at what prices.
- Allows department sales managers and buyers to identify merchandise areas that have unmet or insufficient demand.
- Prevents duplication of merchandise.
- Encourages optimum timing for each classification on the selling floor.
- Presents the right colors, styles, prices, and models when customers want them.
- Calls attention to the most productive classifications.
- Assures coverage of each key merchandise area.

narrowly are called **subclassifications**. For example a classification would be *outerwear* and sub-classifications might include wool pea coats, down parkas, or raincoats.

Figure 15.6 illustrates a Ralph Lauren Corp. in-store branded-concept shop. Different manufacturing processes are used to produce the woven and knit shirts on display. The many color variations for each style lend another dimension to building the assortment. Most likely, the knit and woven goods are handled as subclassifications for these reasons. Other retailers may select styling nuances or end use as criteria for subclassification. For many retailers, more detail equals better planning.

Also used to plan merchandise assortments are model stock plans. **Model stock plans** are lists that show specific stock levels needed for a selling period. The model stock method for planning inventory levels is used for staple as well as fashion goods because it takes into consideration the variations that occur not only from season to season but also within a season.

Three types of data are gathered:

1. Specific information such as classifications, subclassifications, prices, colors, and sizes.
2. Important dates in the season for which model stocks are to be constructed.
3. Sales estimates for the months preceding and following the date for which the model stock is set in units are calculated. The total is translated into dollars and then checked against the dollar plan.

In preparing a model stock plan, the amount of goods needed in each classification is determined by past sales and current trends. Several additional factors that affect assortment planning are also considered, as discussed next.

Factors Affecting Merchandise Assortments

Detailed tracking of customer purchasing habits provides additional information that retailers use to modify their merchandise plans. Some are also changing their merchandise formats to better capitalize on changing demographics and the increasing demands placed on them by customers and the economy.

Figure 15.6
This Polo Ralph Lauren in-store shop shows the scope of available colors, sizes, and styles in the woven and knit shirt subclassifications.

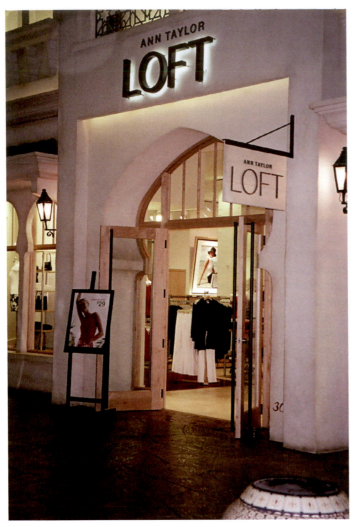

Figure 15.7
Loft is a lower priced spin-off from master brand Ann Taylor. This tactic draws new customers and is particularly effective during difficult economic times.

Predictive Modeling

Retailers analyze current customer behavior in order to prepare better merchandise assortments for the future. Knowing that the customer who purchased a home computer this year may be interested in new peripherals next year has a direct effect on the buying process. Research suggesting how inactive customers can be brought back into the fold can temper merchandise plans.

Creating Spin-Offs and Outside Labels

Retailers are creating spin-off formats to better meet the needs of customers. This is also true of their merchandise. Walmart developed its Sam's Club, and Toys "R" Us opened Babies "R" Us stores, necessitating new directions in merchandising tactics. Ann Taylor Corp. opened its Loft stores, illustrated in Figure 15.7, which present merchandise at lower price points and with a more casual focus than at its Ann Taylor stores.

Looking to expand its assortment of athletic footwear, Nine West teamed with the manufacturer New Balance to create a New Balance for Nine West line. In a twist that was hard to predict, apparel retailer Club Monaco, owned by Ralph Lauren Corp., brought in Royal Gazelle bicycles from the Netherlands to add interest for customers and drive sales.[1]

Economic Concessions

As retailers prepare for holiday selling seasons it is usually with high spirits that they will beat the previous year's sales figures. During economic downturns, the survival instinct causes buyers to scale down merchandise assortments and sometimes bring in goods at lower price points. As examples:

- As part of its plan to revamp its image and counter lagging sales, in 2011 Sears introduced 400 in-store Kardashian Kollection boutiques to spiff up its apparel lines that target younger fashion customers.[2]
- Designer Joseph Abboud moved his JOE menswear collection from Macy's to JCPenney in 2009.[3]
- Both J. Crew and Gap opened accessories boutiques not only to sell more high-margin goods, but also to present impulse items to customers who might have deferred purchasing more expensive apparel.[4]

Proactive approaches like these are indicative of thoughtful strategic planning. The days when retailers reacted only to competitive pressures as they formed their merchandise plans are over. Other visions of assortment planning include:

- Developing merchandising niches with definable differential advantages.
- Reacting to market conditions without trying to serve a broad market.
- Selling limited but distinctive product assortments.
- Remaining solvent during good or bad times.
- Exceeding customer expectations.

Large and small retailers alike strive to carefully analyze customers, determine needs, and plan well in dollars and units.

The Merchandising Team

An efficient system of planning dollars and units is vital to profits. Equally important is the selection of merchandise. As retail purchasing agents, buyers are charged with many responsibilities including gathering market information, shopping the market, preparing detailed orders, negotiating terms, and undertaking other related tasks. However, buyers are not the only members of the team responsible for implementing merchandise plans.

Team Members

Titles may change from store to store, but all retailers perform the same functions. Starting from the lowest level of responsibility to the highest, key merchandising positions include assistant buyers, buyers, divisional merchandise managers, and general merchandise managers.

Assistant Buyers

Considered an entry-level position in many organizations, assistant buyers:

- Provide merchandising and administrative support for buyers.
- Set up market trips for buyers.
- Monitor delivery of merchandise.
- Communicate with vendors via Web-based systems.
- Provide product information to sales promotion departments.
- May initiate markdowns.
- Report to buyers.

Buyers

Retail buyers take chief responsibility for the procurement of merchandise as they:

- Gather and interpret customer information.
- Develop dollar and unit plans for their department or classification.
- Shop major and secondary markets, and select and purchase merchandise.
- Negotiate terms of delivery.
- Arrange for cooperative advertising money, trade discounts, and markdown money.
- Cultivate and maintain vendor relationships.
- Communicate product information to department sales managers.
- Monitor competition.
- Report to the divisional merchandise manager.

Qualities of effective retail buyers are summarized in Table 15.2.

Table 15.2   Qualities of an Effective Retail Buyer

- The ability to handle pressure in a variety of forms, including long hours on the job, frequent travel, and achieving management's financial goals.

- An eye for quality, taste, and value—based on customer preferences, not always personal ones.

- Excellent human relations skills; the ability to deal favorably with many different personality types.

- Sharp negotiating skills.

- Superior math and computer skills.

- The ability to read and interpret financial and merchandising reports.

- The ability to be flexible and juggle many tasks at once.

- An indefatigable nature.

- A desire to maintain high ethical standards.

Divisional Merchandise Managers

Overseeing multiple departments, usually in either soft or hard goods areas, divisional merchandise managers:

- Initiate financial planning.
- Supervise higher-level buying functions for a major store division.
- Give directional and trend input to buyers.
- Work with information technology to utilize appropriate merchandise information systems.
- Report to the general merchandise manager.

General Merchandise Managers

Controlling fiscal and merchandising decisions on a store-, region-, or chain-wide basis, depending on the size of the organization, the general merchandise manager:

- Initiates dollar and unit planning on a storewide basis.
- Conducts strategic planning in the merchandising area.
- Reports to the vice president or president of the company, depending on the size of the organization.

Support Staff

Several staff members assist with the flow of information and technical data to other members of the merchandising team and branch stores. Allocators and merchandise analysts play important roles in the merchandising process. College graduates with retail experience and excellent analytical skills are often recruited for these positions. More information on opportunities in merchandising appears in the Appendix at the end of this text.

Allocators

Acting as a liaison between merchandising and distribution, allocators have assumed very important roles in large specialty chains, department stores, and discount operations. **Allocators** are individuals who support merchandise teams by providing detailed distribution information. Their duties include:

- Ensuring that each store has the optimal assortment of merchandise to maximize sales, profits, and customer satisfaction.
- Making distribution recommendations to buyers based on their close monitoring of stock levels.
- Staying abreast of regional and local needs and competition.
- Communicating merchandise information to stores.

Allocators technically work on the distribution side of the company, but their interaction with the buying team is imperative if the retail organization is to achieve a smooth flow of goods.

Merchandise Analysts

Merchandise analysts perform additional functions in large organizations. Their responsibilities include:

- Planning detailed stock levels by utilizing database and other computer-generated reports.
- Communicating information to other merchandising team members.
- Facilitating the distribution of goods to stores.

Sources of Market Information

Earlier in the chapter, several methods for gathering customer data were discussed. This is the foundation of a buyer's job. However, there is much more work to be done. Sources of information must be probed more deeply. In this way, retail buyers build confidence in their ability to make the correct choices.

Shopping the Market

Manufacturers show merchandise in major cities at specified times of the year in advance of a selling season. Scheduled seasonal showings of merchandise by manufacturers in market centers around the globe are called **market weeks**. Although different industries show their wares at different times, the objective remains the same—to provide the opportunity for buyers to see the best and the brightest new merchandise. In most cases, market week showings are held in manufacturers' showrooms four times per year. Sometimes hotel suites are used. In the case of the designer fashion market, more elaborate arrangements are made and showings are held twice a year. Many of these extravaganzas can now be viewed online by retail buyers, as well as the general public.

Manufacturers' Showrooms

Going directly to the market offers an opportunity for buyers to see many different lines of merchandise. Major manufacturers lease space in established market centers in major cities throughout the world. Major markets in the United States include New York City, Dallas, Los Angeles, Atlanta, and Chicago. In Europe, Paris, London, and Milan are significant. Sydney, Australia, has a trade mart, and Japan and China also hold key markets. Attending markets offers several advantages to buyers. They can:

- Identify new lines that appear stronger than lines presently carried.
- Determine which current resources have added new products to their lines.
- Comparison-shop more vendors with ease.
- Make decisions based on seeing the big picture.
- Increase awareness of significant trends in their industry.
- Give undivided attention to the task of purchasing products.

Many of the cities mentioned above have large, well-planned buildings in which to showcase manufacturers' wares. Apparel trade marts are freestanding or linked to other trade facilities. In New York City—considered by many to be the fashion capital of the world—buildings are spread through the garment district and other parts of the city that accommodate showrooms. Seventh Avenue, called Fashion Avenue on street signs, is considered the heart of the garment district.

Sales Representatives

Sales representatives operate from permanent or temporary showrooms in major markets during market weeks. Some manufacturers also go on the road to meet with buyers in their stores. Some independent sales representatives operate without showrooms and travel limited geographic areas, calling on smaller retailers. Multi-line sales reps carry anywhere from a few to 25 or more lines of related merchandise. Many are able to reduce their traveling commitment yet offer personalized service through their Web sites. The biggest advantage to the retail buyer is convenience.

Trade Shows

Concurrently, or close to market weeks, trade shows are held several times per year in all merchandise categories. They are a major source of product information and serve as an arena for exchange for retail buyers. There are two distinctly different types of trade shows in the fashion apparel industry: those that are dedicated to ready-to-wear and those that are designer showings. **Ready-to-wear (RTW)** is mass-fashion apparel that is sold at low, moderate, and high prices at retail companies ranging from discounters to department and specialty stores. Goods are manufactured in factories all over the world. Prêt-à-porter is the French phrase for RTW. **Designer fashion collections** are made in smaller quantities and sold at higher prices in high-end retail stores globally. Gucci, Armani, Versace, Dolce & Gabbana, Marc Jacobs, and Brioni are examples. Designer fashion collections should not be confused with couture fashion. **Haute couture** fashions are made-to-order high-fashion garments by major design houses, priced extremely high by average consumer standards.

Among the important trade shows in the fashion industry are the following:

- Première Vision is a textile trade show held in Paris where hundreds of mills from France and Italy show their goods to manufacturers, designers, and product developers.
- Fashion Coterie, for buyers of trendy upmarket women's apparel, is held in New York City. Labels including True Religion, Trina Turk, Resin, and Prairie New York are shown.
- MAGIC International is one of the first and most important of the ready-to-wear trade shows. Held in Las Vegas twice a year, it featured menswear initially and extended to women's wear in 1995 when a unique partnership was formed with *Women's Wear Daily.* WWDMAGIC indicates the women's apparel trade event.
- Milano Moda Donna in Milan, Italy is where designer fashions are shown, usually in late September and February. Established names from Armani to Zegna, as well as new designers, show their merchandise at fashion shows, presentations, and by appointment.
- Smaller trade shows that feature newer designers and unique specialty items include Intermezzo, Fame, Moda Manhattan, and AccessoriesTheShow. Chances are the floppy hat worn by the fashion maven in Figure 15.1 was discovered by a buyer for a boutique working one of these shows.

Most retailers concur that trade shows provide opportunities to find new resources that add spark to merchandise assortments. With several hundred to more than 2,000 vendors represented, trade shows run 3–5 days and are held in all major cities of the world.

The role of the trade show in merchandise procurement has changed. In the past, many retailer buyers would "leave paper" while attending a trade show. **Leave paper** is a slang expression for writing an order on the spot. Today, most buyers and small storeowners peruse vendor booths collecting trend and preliminary planning information for later use.

Assortment planning software makes it easier for manufacturers and retailers to communicate. Whether initial contacts were made in showrooms and trade shows or the companies have been doing business together for decades, technology enables more efficient planning. Read about a system from 7thOnline in From the Field 15.1.

Resident Buying Offices

The nature and purpose of resident buying offices was explained earlier in this chapter. Details on their structure, formats, and the services they provide retailers are included here.

Organization

Buying offices are set up so that staff members can work with their retail counterparts. Senior executives of buying offices are equivalent to vice presidents of merchandising in retail organizations. General and divisional merchandise managers are comparable on the next levels. Resident buyers are counterparts to store buyers. They are responsible for a department or single classification of merchandise and fully immerse themselves in the stores they serve. Retail image, target markets, company objectives, and geographic areas served are carefully studied so that buying offices can provide effective service.

Services Rendered

The primary role of buying offices is market coverage. Resident buyers spend most of their time visiting vendors in the market. They gather information on trends, new resources, best sellers, prices, and delivery dates. The information is made available to store buyers through a variety of reports, hot sheets, vendor evaluations, catalogues, or via the Internet. Most buying offices are compensated on a percentage of sales.

Some buying offices are empowered to place merchandise orders for member stores. This practice allows stores located far from the market to test items immediately without traveling to the market.

Changes in attitudes, lifestyles, and patterns of consumption tend to move across the globe in uneven waves. Buyers may learn of advancing trends from a resident buyer and be better prepared when it reaches their markets.

Types of Buying Offices

There are three basic kinds of resident buying offices:

1. *Independent firms.* Companies that represent a variety of noncompeting retail stores are the most common. The buying office and the stores are separate entities that work together for mutual gain. The Doneger Group in New York City is an example of an independent firm. The company provides full services for retail clients including Nordstrom, Belk, Kohl's, ShopNBC, and House of Fraser in the United Kingdom. Creative director David Wolfe has been with the company since 1991 and provides seasonal fashion trend reports for Doneger clients and the fashion industry. Check out From the Field 15.2 to evaluate how close his predictions for Spring 2010 came to hitting the target.

///////////////////////////////

Cyberscoop
The Doneger Group provides information for retailers and buyers on future trends, the latest merchandising techniques, and overall analysis of the retailing business. Midsized and smaller retailers use the services of groups like Doneger when they cannot afford or do not have the time to conduct trend research. Check out www.doneger.com to learn more about the activities of this independent research firm.

2. *Company-owned or affiliated offices.* These are buying offices that serve only one company. JCPenney maintains its own buying office. Target Corp. purchased Associated Merchandising Corporation (AMC) in 1998. The office serves only stores that belong to the corporation. Divisions of holding companies that operate chains of retail companies are slightly different. Macy's and Bloomingdale's use the services of what once were Federated's (now Macy's) buying offices around the world. These are also called syndicated offices.

3. *Specialty offices.* Smaller offices may focus on specific types of stores or merchandise classifications. For example, buying offices that serve only stores selling women's larger sizes fit this category. Occasionally larger store chains that are not affiliated with other buying offices maintain their own offices in New York or other major markets.

There has been much consolidation among buying offices in the last decade and that trend is expected to continue.

Additional Sources of Buying Information

Effective buyers are aware of every whisper of a trend. One of the best ways to identify new opportunities is to simply observe people. Buyers who know what music people are listening to in London, what is being worn on the streets of Milan, or what Japanese anime film characters will affect merchandise sales in other global cities may be able to use this information to gain a market advantage. Celebrity information, trade association research, and trend forecasting firms are other good resources.

Celebrity Influences

Several examples illustrate how celebrity influence affects merchandise assortments. If we were lucky and walked through Target's fashion departments at the right time, we might have spotted Missoni's special offering of Italian apparel and home furnishings. A visit to Kohl's brings us the new Vera Wang, Daisy Fuentes, Jennifer Lopez, and Marc Anthony lines. Compare the newer Martha Stewart lines at JCPenney with her company's merchandise lines in Macy's. And let's not forget the Taylor Swift Store at Walgreens. Celebrity endorsement and star designer influence add excitement to the merchandise presentation and put dollars into the pockets of retailers.

Trade Associations and Publications

Trade associations help retail members define their markets and forecast sales. They provide information on market share, customer preferences, and sales and merchandise trends. For instance, the skateboarding trend, which began a decade ago, is expected to have an impact on sales for years to come. Information of this sort helps sporting goods retailers refine their merchandise plans. Conversely, if the National Sporting Goods Association reports that sales of sports equipment and footwear are relatively flat, this is of note to sporting-goods retailers. An announcement like this could be attributed to the lack of emergence of a new sport to drive sales.

Women's Wear Daily releases its WWDList many times a year. The list is a compilation of key research on a variety of topics that are of use to fashion merchandisers. Research showing what the top apparel product categories are for a particular period or year, would prove useful to retail buyers as they planned future assortments. Information provided at the brand level is equally as important. Through May 2011, jeans garnered $1,316.9 million in sales in the United States, a decrease of 0.1% over the previous year.[5] The top brands preferred by consumers are listed in Table 15.3. Retailers that carry this classification need to know what brands are selling best and preferred by consumers so they can make selections that will help them remain competitive. Trade and industry publications provide this information.

Color and Trend Forecasters

Many manufacturers and retailers use the services of forecasting firms to clarify and detail trends that are occurring in style, direction, and color. Companies like Nigel French and Promostyl are international trend prognosticators. The Color Association of America (CAUS) and The Color Box are smaller, independent firms that deal primarily with color palettes and do their predictive research

Table 15.3 Consumers' Favorite Denim Brands 2011

Rank	Brand	Percent of Survey Participants
1	Levi's	34%
2	Lee	12%
3	Wrangler	11%
4	Old Navy	6%
5	Gap	5%
6	Lucky	4%
7	Calvin Klein	3%
8	American Eagle	3%

Cotton Incorporated. "The 'Jeaneology' of a Wardrobe Favorite: Denim's Enduring Popularity." May 24, 2012. p. 2. Lifestyle Monitor(tm) Survey. From article published by *Women's Wear Daily*. www.wwd.com/markets-news/textiles/the-jeaneology-of-a-wardrobe-favorit-denims-enduring-popularity-5923983.

18–24 months in advance of retail selling seasons. Although this type of research may seem most appropriate in the fashion industry, other businesses also make use of it. Automobile, appliance, home furnishing, and furniture manufacturers and retailers all use color forecasting. Figure 15.8 shows a color consultation in session at CAUS.

Many designers are finding valuable trend forecasting services online. The director of trend and concept for the apparel retailer White House Black Market uses Stylesight, a proprietary Web site for the fashion industry. The subscription-based service offers photos, sketches, articles, and color and fabric swatches for inspiration. Stylesight has 1,000 clients, including Macy's and Victoria's Secret, and shares with them a library of three million images, many from around the globe.[6]

Merchandising is not a "me-too" business. All team members carefully read their customers before they make radical changes in a fashion category. It is not enough to know what the competition is doing. Buyers evaluate all information according to their market, image, policies, past trends, and future business objectives.

Did You Know?
Color forecasters predicted that a new red, called "oxblood," would be the hot color in men's and women's apparel for the 2012 fall fashion season. Tommy Hilfiger, Derek Lam, and 3.1 Phillip Lim all showed garments in a rich deep-red hue that resembled the tone of a ripe Bing cherry. How close were the experts' predictions to the color trends you observed in retail stores during that period?
(Source: Christina Binkley, "Next Fall, There Will Be Oxblood," *Wall Street Journal*, February 10, 2012. D1–D2.)

Figure 15.8
A color forecasting session in progress at the Color Association of the United States, in New York City.

Vendor Relationships

Vendors also are good sources of information. Retailers' relationships with vendors are second only to their interaction with their customers.

Building key resource relationships helps increase bargaining power and gains many advantages for retailers. To evaluate vendors, buyers consider the following factors: quality of merchandise, location and reputation of the firm, brand policy, terms of sale, return policies, sales and profit potential, and ethical business practices. Preferred vendor lists and the power wielded by large retailers on vendors have changed the way business is done.

Preferred Vendor Lists

Giant retail companies expect that vendors will do business on their premises and establish preferred vendor lists to facilitate this process. Being on this list means that a manufacturer is capable of communicating via Internet systems and has established a partnership program with the retailer. Retailers like Walmart, Target, and major specialty and department store companies operate on this basis.

Pressures in the Supply Chain

The great power exerted by giant retailers in the supply chain causes conflict between retailers and manufacturers. Although retail companies are large in terms of volume generated, most manufacturers are relatively small. Manufacturers must meet stringent criteria in order to do business with large retailers. For example, retailers may specify that goods are shipped on hangers in certain cartons, labeled precisely, routed to the store in an exact manner, or documented according to detailed instructions. If manufacturers fail to comply exactly, retailers penalize them by increasing distribution costs or imposing chargebacks on the vendors. **Chargebacks** are financial penalties imposed on manufacturers by retailers. These fees are often reversed by the retailers, but in the meantime they can cause ill feelings in what should be a mutually beneficial relationship.

Pressure escalated in the mid-1990s as retailers faced sluggish sales in many soft goods areas and cut their resource lists. Heavy consolidations in the industry and erratic customer behavior also contributed to the malaise. Afraid of being removed from preferred vendor status, manufacturers found themselves in the uncomfortable position of having to acquiesce to retailers' demands or face losing their business. In addition to stiff logistical demands, retailers increased pressure in other areas. Manufacturers were expected to share the retailers' risk in uncertain markets by providing guaranteed profit margins and increased remuneration should merchandise not sell in their stores.

A decade later, vendors deemed the chargeback practice worse than ever and had rallied to bring lawsuits against retailers. One industry study found that many of the issues deemed unfair by vendors were in the areas of customer returns, shipping time infractions, mislabeling, and problems with advanced shipping notices (ASNs). Retailers, for their part, believed vendors primarily complain about chargebacks to cut costs they are legitimately responsible for paying. However, retailers also admitted that too many of their counterparts abuse the practice.[7] More information on practices involving the supply chain appears in Chapter 18.

Key Trends in Merchandising and Sourcing

Retailers try to find the best products for their stores wherever advantageous buys can be made. Global sourcing, private labeling, licensing, and product development are all ways retailers can increase margins and profits. Private labeling and product sourcing are two directions that have been adopted by most large retailers, whether domestic or global. Category management as a mode of inventory planning is included in this section, since it is of particular concern to retailers that sell food products or great quantities of consumer goods. In many instances, firms sharing these characteristics tend to be global retailers.

Global Merchandise Sourcing and Management

Positive and negative aspects of global sourcing continue to challenge retailers. Using offshore labor is a standard practice for most retailers, but it prompts plenty of stimulation for the decision makers.

Advantages and Logistics of Global Sourcing

Through importing, retailers are able to offer well-designed products that their competitors are less likely to have. Sound relationships with vendors and contractors need to be established before exclusive production runs are feasible. Retailers are able to achieve higher markups on imports because they usually cost less to produce offshore. This is true of most fashion apparel, since it is labor-intensive to produce. Today's emphasis on private labeling is another reason product developers turn to production facilities for the most lucrative arrangements. A typical workroom located in a country where the labor rate is low is illustrated in Figure 15.9. When a good working relationship is established with foreign suppliers, lower inventory levels can be kept and initial markups on products can be higher.

Some countries, such as Italy, are known for their high quality and strong design work. Others in Asia are famous for the production of volume merchandise. Some parts of the world are important for specialty merchandise—Peru for sweaters and knits, Haiti and Africa for carved woodenware, and Malaysia and Indonesia for batik. Despite the shrinking globe, materials that inspire are still being discovered in parts of Africa, South America, and Asia. However, to find and develop these resources, buyers must have the patience and time to work closely with small manufacturers or cottage industries.

Buying offices can be instrumental in planning foreign trips for retail buyers. Many have branches or affiliates in key international cities. Some large retail organizations such as Limited Brands have their buyers travel in groups accompanied by a merchandise manager, looking for fast-breaking and, they hope, profitable trends.

Overseas market representatives may facilitate entry into foreign markets and might also become a retailer's best link to the optimal providers of merchandise. Knowledge is power, in this case, and can affect a buyer's success in the marketplace. Local representatives can also make appropriate introductions and help arrange for exclusive merchandise. Beyond being represented in foreign countries, retail buyers should be knowledgeable about tariffs discussed in Chapter 2, as well as international finance and shipping standards.

Ethical Conflicts

Ethical issues that arise when doing business abroad also affect people who source products globally. Counterfeit goods, labor abuses, and environmental issues bring challenges of a different nature.

Figure 15.9
Product developers head to Asia where contract manufacturers are prolific, labor rates are low, and quality is high.

Bogus goods are a universal problem that ultimately contributes to increased costs for vendors, retailers, and customers. In some cases, complete underground industries have cropped up, replicating Louis Vuitton handbags, Versace belts, or Levi's jeans. Often skilled workers are lured into the trade, working nights on fake goods after their legitimate day jobs in the fashion sector. Figure 15.10 shows counterfeit goods being sold on the streets of Pisa, Italy.

The value of counterfeit and pirated merchandise was about $600 billion in 2011 and is expected to double by 2015. Over 60 percent of counterfeit products seized by U.S. Customs and Border Protection authorities in 2011 emanated from China. Chinese apparel and accessories workers are known for their high skill levels and produce quality goods for reputable companies. However, some take their skills under-the-table and make counterfeit products. Many apparel companies use advanced technologies to help curb counterfeiting. As examples, Levi's employs anticounterfeiting teams that authenticate branded products through special labeling devices. Chanel handbags bear a unique identification number that travels with each handbag from the start of production to its sale to a retail customer. Any Chanel boutique can verify that a handbag is authentic.[8]

Some counterfeit goods sold in the United States are made here as well. Apparently increased border security since 2001 has made it more difficult for foreign shippers to pass goods through U.S. Customs. As a result, they have gone into business inside the United States.

Respect for intellectual property rights, including trademarks and copyrights, is of concern to industry leaders worldwide. The problems won't subside, however, until the level of education about ethical issues rises, more monitoring programs are developed, and stiffer penalties are enacted. Raising consciousness levels is also important so that people will recognize the negative impact purchasing counterfeit goods has on their own wallets.

Figure 15.10
Counterfeit goods being sold by an African immigrant near the Leaning Tower of Pisa and the Piazza del Duomo in Italy. The practice is illegal, but the law is not strictly enforced.

Private Labeling

Because so many stores sell the same merchandise to the same customers in the same market, private labeling has affected merchandising greatly. Private label programs are initiated when a store contracts with a manufacturer to produce exclusive items. The items bear the name developed by the retailer rather than the name of the manufacturer. This is a successful tactic when the store name or its invented brand carries an image of quality, fashion, or value. Private label goods account for the majority of sales in specialty stores such as Barneys New York, Diesel, Benetton, and J. Jill.

Private labels can achieve widespread recognition and loyalty. Macy's INC (International Concepts) women's apparel label and Charter Club apparel and home goods are other examples of private labels created for their respective markets. Catchy brand names may emanate from anywhere in the world. Metrojaya department stores in Southeast Asia developed a label for its line of nautical-inspired sportswear called "Cape Cod Massachusetts."

Figure 15.11
One of Target's private labels is Archer Farms. Customers look for this name, which embellishes many food products, as well as bottled water, in the retailer's stores.

Private labeling also is an important strategy for discounters. Top U.S. discounters Walmart and Target, and warehouse club Costco, use private labeling to position their stores as desirable destinations for exclusive merchandise and to increase their profits per unit. Brands are important in apparel, grocery, health and beauty aid, and general merchandise categories. As examples:

- Walmart's Great Value brand extends to food and nonfood items; George is one of its many fashion labels.
- Costco uses its Kirkland brand across many merchandise categories from automotive products to vitamins.
- Target's Merona men's and women's apparel lines and Archer Farms food products attest to the popularity of this strategy. The Archer Farms brand is illustrated in Figure 15.11.

Licensing

In this brand-conscious world, product licensing has become the chief way major designers, sports teams, and entertainment businesses have expanded their brands worldwide. **Product licensing** is a contractual relationship between a designer—or other holder of rights to a brand—and a manufacturer to produce items under that name or brand. Ironically, when companies grow in this manner, they lose some control over the very thing that made them successful in the first place: their names. Fragrances and underwear bear the Calvin Klein logo, but companies other than the CK parent manufacture it all. For example, fragrances are licensed to Unilever and underwear to Warnaco.

A license is a legal contract between the holder of rights to a name or product and a manufacturer. Often holders are designers who license their names to other parties to produce and distribute merchandise to select retailers. This method has become a popular and profitable way for companies to extend their brand internationally. Designers such as Tommy Hilfiger, cartoon characters like Hello Kitty, and sports heroes including snowboarder Shaun White bring handsome profits to retailers that stock merchandise bearing their names.

The typical royalty fee paid to designers is 5–7 percent. Because many customers are brand- and status-conscious, licensed goods are another option buyers consider in their assortment plans. If you are still unsure of the power—and extremes—of brand licensing, consider this example: Gucci has licensed a dog bed.

Product Development

Taking the buying function a step further, dependence on global sourcing has spawned a new retail career position—product developers. **Product developers** are individuals or teams that generate ideas, design prototypes, and arrange for production of exclusive products for retailers. Product developers are very knowledgeable about material specification, textile performance standards, manufacturing procedures, and quality control. Many speak the languages of countries where they do business. In these areas, their expertise usually goes beyond that of buyers.

As retailing has changed so have job functions on a small planet with worldwide connected-ness. Product developers are multi-skilled members of the merchandise team since their roles meld buying, private label development, product sourcing, and technological skills into one pack-age. In the last decade more companies have developed product development divisions for the express purpose of producing well-constructed, exclusive goods less expensively. Asia is one of the prime areas for product development, especially Taiwan, China, Sri Lanka, Thailand, Malaysia, and South Korea. Because many contractors are in remote parts of the globe, extensive travel may be necessary. On the other hand, much work regarding the specification of garments—details includ-ing sizing, fabric, fit, and so on—is done remotely using Internet-based technologies.

Figure 15.12 shows an example of a "mood board" for an eventual line of menswear for a department store group. The design work is done in-house and involves extensive contact with contractors. Ideas for designs are shopped around the world, as merchandising at this level is a very competitive part of retailing. New ideas must come forth each season without disengaging from customers' needs and wants.

Category Management

Category management has been a leveling force in the aggressive arena of competition between retailers that sell high-demand goods that are purchased frequently by customers. The objective of category management is "to help retailers and their manufacturer partners succeed by offering

Figure 15.12
A "mood board" is a tool product developers use to formulate ideas for forthcoming private-label merchandise lines. Color, lifestyle, and fashion direction merge as the designs take form and shape. One of the objectives of building in-house lines is exclusivity.

the right selection of products that are marketed and merchandised based on a complete understanding of the consumer they are committed to serving."[9] The method of inventory planning and control is infused with marketing principles and voices a strong consumer focus.

The concept originated in the early 1990s when manufacturers Coca-Cola and Phillip Morris worked with companies like Safeway and Kroger supermarkets to "turn marketing basics into an organized process."[10] Category management is used primarily by retailers that sell grocery products or large quantities of consumer products. Supermarkets, superstores, warehouse clubs, and category killers particularly benefit from this type of merchandise planning. Some of the retailers now involved include Costco and BJ's wholesale clubs; Walmart, Dollar General, and Family Dollar discounters; Home Depot, the home improvement retailer; and Supervalu and Publix supermarkets.[11]

Specially designed software is used by retailers that rely on category management. Ensuring that shelves are never empty is a goal that can only be achieved if very advanced systems are in place. A local independent drugstore may manage the flow of two or three brands of toothpaste and sales of 1,000 units annually. Compare this with Costco, which carries six or more major brands in multiple sizes and feature preferences plus its own private label, selling millions of units annually. That's when category management is most useful.

Merchandising strategies are profoundly complex and encompass thinking both globally and locally to provide customers with the merchandise they want in a timely fashion. The buyer's job is not complete, however, until the details of the purchase are negotiated and finalized.

Finalizing the Purchase

After merchandise selections are made, the next responsibility of retail buyers is to negotiate the terms of the wholesale transaction. The purchase terms include some or all of the following: discounts, completion dates, shipping arrangements, point of transfer of title, prices, exclusivity agreements, cooperative advertising, return policy, markdown money, and reorder capabilities.

Time and Money Incentives

So much in business revolves around time and money. A manufacturer urges a retailer to pay early and rewards the retailer by giving a discount. Longevity in business, payment record, and position in the supply chain also dictate more favorable terms.

Cash Discounts

Almost all lines of merchandise carried by a store are purchased with cash discount terms, commonly ranging from two to eight percent. Consequently, obtaining cash discounts is of great importance to gross margin management.

Discounts taken as a percentage of the total purchase price are offered in return for prompt payment. For example, under terms of "2/10 net 30," the first numeral designates the percentage discount rate, the second the time period. In this case, a two-percent discount is offered if the bill is paid within ten days of the invoice date. After ten days, the full amount of the invoice is due. Net 30 indicates that the retailer has 30 days from date of invoice to pay the bill in full, even if it chooses not to take advantage of the discount period. After that period, the company seeking payment can impose a finance charge on the outstanding balance.

Savvy retailers use advanced or extra dating to extend their payment terms. This is advantageous to retailers that purchase coats in June for an August preseason sale but do not want to pay for those goods until they have had ample opportunity to sell them. For example, on terms of 8/10 net 30X (extra) 60 (days), the retailer would be entitled to deduct the eight percent discount within approximately two months of the original remittal date.

Retailers also ask for another early payment incentive called anticipation. **Anticipation** is an additional discount that is sometimes allowed when the invoice is paid before the expiration of the cash discount period. Anticipation is also deducted from the invoice price. There are other nuances to discounts based on invoice dating that extend credit to retailers as they juggle cash flow. Although beyond the scope of this discussion, all are important in the negotiation process.

The reality of discounting is sometimes quite different and the issue of ethical business practices is often raised. Early payment discounts offered are usually worked into the wholesale price.

Even if a time-dependent discount is agreed upon, some retailers do not adhere to the terms. Large, powerful firms have been known to pay at will and still take their discounts, even if payment occurs six months later. This certainly puts pressure on manufacturers. Better partnership arrangements, based on mutual concern and respect, are alleviating this problem. However, disrespect of the discount period still exists in some sectors of the industry. Growing acknowledgment that all supply chain members are responsible for the satisfaction of customers should further combat this negative tendency.

Trade Discounts

Deductions from an agreed price, usually granted by manufacturers to other supply chain members, are called **trade discounts**. Trade discounts are quoted in a series and commonly occur between manufacturers and wholesalers or other members of the supply chain. The amount of the discount is dependent on the market prices at the time of the sale, the size of the order, and the payment record of the retailer. An invoice might carry terms of "less 25 percent, less ten percent, less five percent." This would mean that one company might pay 75 percent of an invoice, or take a 25 percent discount. Another might be allowed an additional ten percent, and a third company might receive another five percent off. However, large chains and department stores buy much larger quantities than some wholesalers and also secure trade discounts. The buying power of large retailers has changed the way business is done.

Shipping Terms and Title Issues

Retailer buyers also discuss completion dates with vendors. A **completion date** is the date promised by the manufacturer for total receipt of goods by the retailer. Although all goods on the same order might not arrive on the same day, they must arrive by the completion date. Retailers can choose to cancel the order if goods do not arrive on time.

In addition, the mode of delivery—U.S. Postal Service, Federal Express, UPS, DSL Global, by rail, truck, air, sea, for example—should be specified. The party responsible for paying the shipping charges is also specified. **Free on board (FOB)** is a term identifying the point from which the retailer assumes responsibility for goods and payment of transportation charges. It usually indicates where title to the goods passes to the retailer. Usually, terms are FOB factory, meaning the retailer pays for transportation charges to the store or distribution center. FOB destination indicates that the manufacturer is picking up the shipping costs.

Because there are several alternatives for transfer of title, retailers assume different levels of responsibility under each. Retailers may take ownership of merchandise at various points in the purchase process: upon purchase, when the merchandise is loaded for delivery, when the shipment is received, or at the end of the billing cycle. Another possibility is that the retailer does not own the goods at all, but accepts them on consignment. In this arrangement, the seller retains ownership, requiring the retailer to pay only after the goods are sold. This might occur when the manufacturer needs the retailer as an account, when products are new and untested, or in the case of unusually high-priced merchandise such as furs or fine gems. This practice is common in Japan and other parts of the world.

Merchandising and Advertising Incentives

Other items open to negotiation before the purchase is officially complete include markdown money and cooperative advertising. Taking advantage of one or both options extends the retail gross margin.

Markdown Money

In an attempt to share the risk, many buyers ask for and get markdown money from vendors. **Markdown money** is extra reimbursement allowed the retailer if a manufacturer's goods do not sell well. Some buyers might negotiate to return to the vendor all items in an order that did not sell in the store after a specified time on the floor. But more are turning to markdown money as a way to receive cash for slow-moving merchandise. This may put pressure on the vendor, but create leverage for the retailer.

Did You Know?

The mode of delivery for merchandise has a big impact on the cost to a retailer of merchandise, as well as the retailer's overall profit. Have you ever ordered products online that you wanted to have delivered quickly and then rethought the delivery options when you saw the cost of expedited shipping? Retailers face similar situations. Because the fastest modes of delivery are usually the most expensive, most retailers prefer to ship their goods using inexpensive methods such as sea or rail.

Cooperative Advertising

Vendors often make advertising allowances available to the retailers they service. **Cooperative advertising** is a program under which retailers and manufacturers agree to share costs for retail advertising. Based on a percentage of sales—usually about five percent—funds accrue on an annual basis and can be used as a draw account for advertising expenses. For example, if a retailer chooses to run a newspaper ad, co-op funds can be used to pay 50–100 percent of the cost, provided criteria set by the manufacturer are met. Although sales promotion departments administer co-op programs, buyers are at the table with manufacturers. They are responsible for inquiring about co-op opportunities at the time they are negotiating the sale.

When selecting merchandise intended to meet the needs of customers and secure profits for retailers, there are no guarantees. Retail merchandising teams can increase the odds—and thereby, their gross margins—by planning dollars wisely, being aware of worldwide trends, seeking input from a variety of professional resources, synthesizing that information into a workable assortment plan, and negotiating carefully. Buyers provide the vital artery between retailers and manufacturers. All are in business to satisfy their customers.

Summary

Retailers' primary function is to generate a profit by buying and selling merchandise. Inventory management is the most critical issue faced by all retailers, from giant chains to the smallest shopkeepers.

Retailers begin the process by analyzing past and current information from both in-store and out-of-store sources. Accurate interpretation of customer demand is crucial at this stage. Dollar planning requires consideration of sales, stock levels, reductions, purchases, and gross margin. Unit plans are made for each classification or subclassification of goods.

No formula guarantees that the optimum number of items will be on hand to meet the demands of the market. Adherence to a planning process—and approaches such as the weeks-of-supply method, stock-to-sales ratio, as well as basic stock and model stock plans—reduces risk. Stock planning software from a number of resources makes merchandise planning more efficient.

The merchandising team is responsible for the creation and control of the merchandise budget and buying plan. Many sources of market information are available for retail buyers who are on the front line of the purchasing process. Buyers shop the market by attending trade shows and visiting manufacturers' showrooms, multi-line sales representatives, online sites, and buying offices.

Cultivation and maintenance of vendor relationships is important. Global sourcing has become particularly important because of increased retail competition and the resulting need to develop exclusive products that are less costly to manufacture. Product developers are taking buying to new levels as experts design and manufacture products in the locations where the best deals are struck. Ethical issues such as counterfeiting are global problems. Private labeling and product licensing continue to play important roles in merchandising. Food retailers, superstores, and other big-box retailers use category management to control large quantities of staple goods.

Cash and trade discounts are some of the incentives offered retailers by manufacturers. Before a purchase commitment is made by a retailer, shipping terms, title issues, markdown allowances, and cooperative advertising are also finalized.

Key Terms

Allocators	Free on board (FOB)
Anticipation	Focus groups
Basic stock method	Haute couture
Category management	Leave paper
Chargebacks	Markdown money
Completion date	Market weeks
Cooperative advertising	Merchandising
Designer fashion collections	Model stock plans
Dollar plan	Open-to-buy (OTB)
End-of month (EOM) stock	Optimum stock level

Product developers
Product licensing
Ready-to-wear (RTW)
Resident buying offices
Sell-through
Staple goods
Stock-to-sales ratio (SSR)

Subclassifications
Trade discounts
Underwriters Laboratories, Inc.
Unit plan
Want slips
Weeks-of-supply method

Questions for Review and Discussion

1. What internal and external sources of information do retail buyers seek when planning their merchandise assortments?
2. Why is it necessary for retailers to plan sales in dollars and units? What steps are taken to create a dollar merchandise plan?
3. Give examples of a classification and a subclassification. How do retailers use these concepts to merchandise their stores?
4. Describe the members of a merchandise team and explain their principal duties.
5. What are resident buying offices? How do they act as the eyes, ears, and legs of a retail buyer in the market?
6. What is the main purpose of a trade show? How does a buyer use information acquired at a trade show?
7. What are the advantages to retailers of developing products globally?
8. Why are vendor relationships important to retailers? What areas of friction exist between retailers and manufacturers?
9. What impact does private labeling have on merchandise assortment planning? Discuss examples of private labeling you've observed in retail stores in your market.
10. What characteristics should an effective retail buyer possess?

Endnotes

1. Andria Cheng, "Retailers Seek Outside Labels," *Wall Street Journal,* June 29, 2009, B3A.
2. Sears. "Sears to Launch Kardashian Kollection. Fall 2011: Exclusive Agreement with Kardashian Sisters and Jupi Corp." January 12, 2011. PRNewswire. http://searsholdings.com/pubrel/pressOne.jsp?id=2011-01-12-0005382440.
3. Ray A. Smith, "Men's Fashion Line Trades Down," *Wall Street Journal,* April 15, 2009, B6.
4. Elizabeth Holmes., "Retailers Highlight Accessories," *Wall Street Journal,* July 24, 2009, B6.
5. Ross Tucker, "Denim Jeans: State of the U.S. Market," *Cotton Incorporated Supply Chain Insights,* 2011, http://lifestylemonitor.cottoninc.com/Supply-Chain-Insights/Denim-Jeans-US-Market-07-11/Denim-Jeans-US-Market-07-11.pdf.
6. Claire Cain Miller, "Fashion Designers Go Online for Latest Trends," *International Herald Tribune,* September 8, 2008, www.iht.com/bin/printfriendly.php?id=15970412.
7. Vicki M. Young and Arthur Zaczkiewicz, "Chargebacks Survey: Vendors Claim Abuses Worse than Ever in '05," *Women's Wear Daily,* December 28, 2005, 10. (Study conducted by Demographix for WWD.)
8. Elizabeth Holmes, "The Finer Art of Faking It," *Wall Street Journal,* June 30, 2011, D1, D4
9. ACNielsen with John Karolefski and Al Heller, *Consumer-Centric Category Management* (Hoboken, NJ: John Wiley & Sons, Inc., 2006), v–vi.
10. Ibid, 15.
11. Ibid, 19–20.

Unit Four: Global Retail Profile
Hennes and Mauritz (H&M), Sweden

Fast fashion, cheap chic, call it what you will, H&M has been practicing the merchandising and selling concept for decades. With apparel for men, women, and children and an eye for trendy, appealing fashion, it's no wonder the company is one of the top three apparel chains in the world.

Prologue

I first became acquainted with H&M in the mid-1980s. I was teaching in London and particularly interested in getting my fill of everything retail. Since I wanted to find out more about the company and needed an outfit for a holiday party, I visited a store near the Kensington High Street tube station. As I browsed, it occurred to me that there were few places in London where a trendy aquamarine blue satin pantsuit was priced for under £30. That was about $45 at the time and a good value. A simple silk shirt completed the outfit and cost the equivalent of $14. I spoke to people in the store, scoured trade publications, and picked the brains of my teaching colleagues in London, and then began to piece together some material for my classes.

History and Leadership

H&M was a pioneer in the fashion industry. Here's how it happened. Hennes (Swedish for "her") was founded in Västerås, Sweden in 1947 by Erling Persson. Initially, stores sold only women's clothes, but by 1968 Persson was ready to add menswear. That year Hennes acquired Mauritz Widforss, an outdoor sporting gear store that carried men's apparel. It was a match made in retail heaven, and the company name was changed to Hennes & Mauritz. Since then the company has been known as H&M.

In 1974 family-owned H&M went public with a listing on the stock market. Growth and expansion continued as more markets were opened and more merchandise lines added, including cosmetics. In 1980, the company became a dual-channel retailer when it began selling apparel by mail order. During the early 1980s, Erling Persson retired as chief executive officer (CEO), appointing his son Stefan as the new leader. Stefan held that position until he stepped down to become chairman of the board in 1998. That year the company began selling apparel online, joining the ranks of multichannel retailers.[1]

Two non-family CEOs ran the company briefly during the late 1990s and early 2000s. In 2009 Karl-Johan Persson became CEO of a much larger company than his father, Stefan, and his grandfather, Erling, had operated.

International Growth

H&M was an international retailer long before many of today's fast-fashion retailers appeared on the scene. Those retailers, including Forever 21, Zara, Mango, Uniqlo, Topshop, and others, are now H&M's competitors.

Neighboring Norway was the site for the company's first international store, which launched in 1964. A decade later, H&M opened in England and Switzerland. Between 1974 and 1996, H&M entered five more European countries as its international stable grew. H&M's expansion strategy was typical of that of many retailers that open their first international stores close to home and then branch out geographically to countries in close proximity before venturing to other continents.

It wasn't until 2000 that H&M opened its first store in the United States. By then the company had gained popularity and an international buzz. Its flagship store on Fifth Avenue at 51st Street in Manhattan continues to be a magnet for fashionable individuals and is often where the custom-concept lines developed by famous designers are launched. During the period between 2000 and 2011, the company extended its reach to Eastern Europe, Russia, Turkey, Israel, Japan, South Korea, and China.

By 2012, H&M had 2,500 stores in 44 countries and was preparing to enter Latin America. That year, one of its largest stores was scheduled to open in the Centro Santa Fe Mall in Mexico City. This upscale mall is the largest in Mexico, and Saks Fifth Avenue is one of the anchors.[2] Further expansion was planned for 2012, with store openings scheduled in Bulgaria, Latvia, Malaysia, and Thailand. H&M also announced its intent to introduce its Collection of Style (COS) private-label chain into its stores in Hong Kong, Italy, Finland, and Kuwait as it tracks the luxury market.[3] COS, an upscale designer-inspired chain of boutiques, was developed in 2007 by Karl-Johan Persson.

Financial Position and Corporate Culture

The Persson family owns about 37 percent of H&M's capital stock and controls almost 70 percent of shareholder votes. After successfully running a business of his own, Karl-Johan Persson worked in operations in 2005 before joining the board in 2006. He headed the expansion and business development segment before assuming the position of CEO.[4]

Shortly after he assumed the leadership position, the new CEO—the youngest executive to head the company—spoke about the company's culture, which values teamwork, encourages constant improvements, and is cost-conscious. Karl-Johan's involvement with the company began when he was a young child, and he noted that his father and grandfather had instilled in him certain qualities, including being open to new ideas. As CEO, he spends much of his time visiting the company's global stores, monitoring operations, and keeping track of competition in the retail apparel market.[5]

H&M may have done better than some of its competitors during the economic downturn because of the company's low-price policy. The slump also created opportunities that allowed the retailer to find new store locations and gain market share.[6] In 2009, Persson spearheaded the launch of H&M's first home furnishing line in one of its Stockholm stores. That same year the company opened its first freestanding store for Cheap Monday, a jeans wear chain that H&M acquired as part of its controlling share in Fabric Scandinavian AB, which also owned apparel chains Weekday and Monki. This was the first acquisition consummated by H&M since it was founded in 1947.[7]

In mid-2011, as profits fell, Persson voiced concern that other retailers were cutting their prices as rising interest rates and energy prices—and unpopular austerity measures in many European countries—took their toll on consumer spending. Increased costs related to product sourcing were also negatively affecting many retailers' margins. At H&M, gross margin fell to 62 percent in the second quarter of 2011 from 70 percent in the comparable quarter of the previous year.

It was during this period that Japan experienced a devastating earthquake and tsunami, which led many retailers including H&M to close their stores temporarily as the populace dealt with the ensuing nuclear crisis. H&M closed nine out of ten stores in the Tokyo area and postponed the imminent opening of another. This left only one store open, in Osaka. As you read in Chapter 2, unanticipated events can instantly change the course of lives and streams of revenue for businesses. This crisis would have affected H&M during its 2011 fiscal period, contributing to the altered profit picture.[8]

Despite these hurdles Persson remained optimistic, noting: "We continue to gain market share in a very challenging market, which proves H&M's strong position."[9] H&M's annual sales excluding VAT (value-added tax) were approximately $16 billion in 2011. At the end of that year, there were 233 H&M stores in the United States. The company has come a long way since 2000. Online shopping is available in 18 European countries, and the United States was expected to be added to the global network by the end of 2012.[10]

Merchandising Strategies

H&M maintains a staff of more than 140 designers, buyers, and pattern-makers in its Stockholm design studio. Designers have many age groups, sizes, and fashion preferences to inspire them. In the children's category there are three age groups: zero to 18 months; 18 months to eight years; and 9–14 years. True to tradition, clothing for kids shows the same balance between basics and fashionable styles as that for men and women.[11] So, whether it's a pair of black yoga pants or a special collection item by Jimmy Choo or Madonna that you want, it's probably available.

Through sheer serendipity, a group of students and I passed the H&M store on Fifth Avenue in Manhattan on our way to Bendel's, further up the Avenue, early one morning in 2004. A line of shoppers stretching around the block awaited the store's 9:30 a.m. opening, eager to claim items from H&M's Karl Lagerfeld collection. This was our chance to see firsthand the drawing power that H&M's special designer collections can generate. Since that opening in 2004, the company has collaborated with many other designers who have global appeal, including Roberto Cavalli, Viktor & Rolf, Sonia Rykiel, Rei Kawakubo of Comme des Garçons, Stella McCartney, and Lanvin. Excitement runs high when these collections arrive, and H&M's Facebook page and YouTube presentations stoke the frenzy through preliminary postings and video clips.[12]

The company's designers are careful not to knock off an item spotted on a runway in Milan, but use the experience to grasp fashion direction, accessory trends, color, and fabric. By taking a general silhouette, adapting it, and cutting it in a vibrant color or unusual fabric, they make it their own. Whether the item can be produced at a saleable price point to meet customers' expectations is always a consideration. The designers work with buyers and sometimes customers as they finalize their lines, which are then shipped to one or more of the company's 700 contractors, located primarily in Asia. H&M saves on outlay by not owning the factories outright, yet benefits greatly from low-cost labor.

H&M's first fully sustainable line of garments made using organic cottons and linens was shipped to U.S. stores for the spring season in 2010. Appropriately named The Garden Collection, items also incorporated material such as recycled polyester and Tencel. The 80-piece line featured dresses, skirts, jackets, and accessories ranging from pure white to more vivid prints. Special features included embroidery, appliqués, and other value-added features. When H&M began producing apparel made from organic cotton in 2004, it set a goal of increasing organic cotton use by 50 percent each year until 2013. According to the company, organic garments are no more expensive to make than those that use less earth-friendly textiles.[13]

Call it fast-fashion or cheap chic, it's all about satisfying customers who want good value and fantastic style for their money. The designer collection strategy brings a rush of publicity and shoppers into the markets that H&M serves. If the garments are better made than the competition's and not just Saturday-night-specials that wear well once but barely withstand the first washing, all the better for H&M, one of the world's top three apparel chains.

Profile Discussion Questions

1. How have three generations of the Persson family shaped the corporate culture of H&M and defined its values?
2. What is the company's strategy for international growth? Where did H&M expand first? Is this an established practice used by other retailers that enter international markets?
3. Why do you think H&M waited until 2000 to enter the United States?
4. By the time you read this, H&M will have begun opening stores in Latin America. Collect information on the challenges and successes H&M experienced during this strategic move to discuss in class.

5. What were Karl-Johan Persson's sentiments regarding opportunities that were available to H&M in the early stages of the global economic downturn?
6. What economic factors contributed to H&M's falling profits and margins in mid-2011? Do you believe the closure of stores in Japan during the nuclear crisis significantly affected company performance that quarter? Why or why not?
7. What impact has H&M's designer-collection collaborations had on sales, promotions, and image?
8. How do you define a fast-fashion apparel retailer?

Profile Notes

1. "Our History," H&M, accessed May 5, 2012, http://about.hm.com/content/hm/AboutSection/en/About/Facts-About-HM.html.
2. Lydia Dishman, "H&M's Expansion in Latin America Begins in Mexico," *Forbes*. April 23, 2012, www.forbes.com/sites/lydiadishman/2012/04/23/hms-expansion-in-latin-america-begins-in-Mexico.
3. Ibid.
4. Ola Kinnander, "H&M Scion Named As Retailer's Chief," *Wall Street Journal*, February 12, 2009, B6.
5. Miles Socha, "H&M's Persson Details Growth Plan," *Women's Wear Daily*, December 2, 2009, 9.
6. Ola Kinnander, "H&M Scion Named As Retailer's Chief," *Wall Street Journal*, February 12, 2009, B6.
7. Miles Socha, "H&M's Persson Details Growth Plan," *Women's Wear Daily*, December 2, 2009, 9.
8. Associated Press, "H&M Temporarily Closes 9 out of 10 Stores in Japan," *ABC News*, March 18, 2011, http://abcnews.com/CleanPrint/cleanprintproxy.aspx?1300723347265.
9. Joelle Diderich, "H&M Profit Drops 18%," *Wall Street Journal*, June 23, 2011, 2.
10. *H&M Hennes & Mauritz AB Full Year Report* (December 2010–30 November 2011), 2, H&M, http://about.hm.com/content/dam/hm/about/documents/en/cision/1573157.en.pdf.
11. "The Personality of Cheap," *Women's Wear Daily*, August 20, 2010, 1, 10–11.
12. Miles Socha, "Lanvin Next for H&M?" *Women's Wear Daily*, September 1, 2010, 4.
13. Sharon Edelson, "H&M Goes Sustainable With Garden Collection," *Women's Wear Daily*, February 10, 2010, 4.

Unit Five

Marketing the Merchandise

Eventually, it all comes down to product, pricing, distribution, and promotion. The marketing mix is the framework for understanding how, when, and where the merchandise is sourced. You learned about product in Chapter 15. In this unit, the three remaining elements are presented:

1. How price is determined and administered is the magic engine that drives sales—*if* the price of the merchandise constitutes value to customers.

2. Promotion gets the word out to customers that a retailer has the best merchandise in the world—or, so the retailer contends.

3. The supply chain through which merchandise moves from producer to consumer is the capstone to the myriad functions that make up the practice of retailing.

It's not surprising that this last unit emphasizes a marketing perspective, acknowledging once again the role that customers play in all retail activities.

Chapter 16

Pricing for Profit

Learning Objectives

After completing this chapter you should be able to:

- Articulate how customer behavior and elements of the retail environment influence pricing objectives.
- Examine passive, aggressive, and neutral pricing methods used by retailers.
- Assess pricing strategies and techniques being used by retailers.
- Discern the use of markup and markdown as pricing tools.
- Explain the relationship between pricing and profitability.

Figure 16.1
Major markdowns are taken during semi-annual sales at Selfridges in London. Regular displays are put on hold as racks of red-tag sale merchandise take center stage.

Many customers refuse to pay full retail prices. They shop at discount and off-price stores, membership warehouses, and category killers, and search online for the best deals. At department and specialty stores, they wait for promotional prices. For many, telling friends where they scored a great buy has become more significant during the recession than relating an expensive designer handbag purchase. Yet some customers spend more to get better service, quality, or status.

Customers perceive price differently based on individual concerns and priorities. Quality, value, ambiance, convenience, source, and services rendered by retailers influence customers' interpretations of fair prices. Price comparisons between retailers are made easily—particularly online. In fact, the pricing policy of some stores is to beat competitor's prices at all costs. They encourage customers to shop around and will match competitors' prices, or in some cases offer an additional bonus.

Pricing objectives are set before detailed pricing strategies and techniques are determined. Chances are few products will sell at the price first ticketed. Therefore, the management of

////////////////////////////////////
Cyberscoop
The advent of Google has made it much easier for consumers to do price comparisons. Pick up your smartphone or tablet and log on to www.google.com. Try several consecutive searches for specific products that interest you. What kinds of Web sites are pulled up during these searches? How do the sites compare based on the types of products you search for?

markups and markdowns is strategically imperative to retailers. This chapter considers several aspects of pricing.

Pricing Objectives

Earning profits is the ultimate goal of retailers, but the ways of achieving profitability vary. Some retailers strive to gain market share, some to reach specific sales volumes, and others to achieve high gross margins. Goals for department and specialty retailers differ from those of discount retailers. Some of the most common pricing objectives are:

- *Profit-maximized.* Retailers that advocate this objective set prices that ensure high profits. In theory, this approach sounds admirable; in practice it is unrealistic in highly competitive markets.
- *Volume-driven.* Retailers that opt for volume-oriented sales goals are intent on dominating a retail category. Best Buy's successful campaign to erode Circuit City's market share illustrates this pricing objective. Walmart is a master at volume pricing, as evident in the checkout photo in Figure 16.2.
- *Image-driven.* Some retailers set pricing objectives that cement a specific image in the minds of their customers. It's not unusual to find a DVD for $3.00 at Family Dollar, a discounter that has made its name selling inexpensive products in low-income markets. With prices on small leather goods starting at $250, Louis Vuitton takes the opposite tack. Both retailers use pricing to communicate image.
- *Performance-based.* This method works well for some retail service businesses and professional services such as independent personal shoppers. Rather than charging by the hour, service providers charge only when the pre-established provider's and client's goals are met.
- *Status quo.* Some retail companies pride themselves on offering the same or similar prices over a period of time. For example, 99-cent stores or those where everything is $10 fit this category.

Figure 16.2
An abundance of goods and services at Walmart suggests the volume of sales at the world's largest retailer. Note the scores of customers and overfilled shopping cart at checkout.

Retailers change objectives as market demands require. The California-based chain 99 Cents Only was one of the first companies to introduce the status-quo concept. Survival tactics today may become image issues tomorrow.

Factors Affecting Retail Pricing

Before choosing a retail pricing strategy, several factors that affect decisions are considered by executives: customers, competition, government regulation, business design, merchandising strategies, and, of course, the state of the economy, which has been discussed at several junctures throughout this text.

Customer Lifestyles and Perceptions

Unless retailers know the economic status and lifestyles of their customers, they can't make appropriate pricing decisions. For example, a factory worker earning $38,000 a year would spend money differently and have different tastes than a teacher earning the same salary. Not all customers buy with price as their first priority. Visual merchandising and store ambiance also influence purchasing behavior. Image might be as important as price, or price more important than any other factor, depending on the situation.

The worth that customers place on merchandise, which may be different from true value, is called **perceived value**. People pay a higher price to have Starbucks coffee on their morning commutes and designer labels in their closets. Starbucks coffee costs approximately five times as much as a cup of home-brewed coffee. Can the difference in price and quality be fully justified in terms of production and marketing costs? If not, is Starbucks' product better than coffee brewed at home? How much better?

A revealing exercise is to ask a roomful of people to indicate what they are willing to pay for a hotel room in a major city for one night during the business week. The responses usually vary greatly, because everyone has different ideas of a suitable accommodation, varied experiences renting rooms, and diverse notions of how much it should cost. Many variables intertwine. For example, a major brand such as Westin charges more than lesser-known hotels. Location plays a role, as do the services offered, time of year, duration of stay, and whether promotional offers are in effect. How we perceive a product or service largely determines what we are willing to pay for it.

Certain individuals are quite inflexible about price. People who insist that they have never paid more than $20 for hair styling and refuse to do so are not necessarily in the minority. When retailers contemplate raising prices, they consider their customers' habits and ability to pay, as well.

Competition

Overstored marketplaces are discussed throughout this text. Too many retailers are chasing the same customers. Target competes with discounters such as Walmart and Kmart. However, Target's position as a high-end discounter justifies the price differential on products that are priced slightly higher. Large retailers pressure smaller companies with limited resources. Small retailers learn to compete in different ways by offering personalized service, innovative merchandise concepts, or great depth in a single product category.

Large retailers employ people whose sole responsibility is to collect pricing information from competitive stores. Those stores, catalogues, and Web sites that have the potential to become competitors are also monitored.

In preparation for the 2011 holiday season, competition among Amazon.com, Barnes & Noble, and Apple intensified, although prices for their tablets and e-books varied considerably. Amazon's Kindle Fire, with 8 GB of memory and free cloud storage, retailed for $199. Barnes & Noble's Nook tablet, with 16 GB of memory and the capacity to record stories read aloud for future use by children, sold for $249. Apple's iPad with 16 GB of memory, slightly larger size, and two cameras went for $499. Pricing may have been less binding on consumers than product attributes, service, and branding.[1]

It is less expensive to purchase some products—such as books, stocks, newspapers, cars, golf clubs, and airline fares—online. Because they are a powerful source of consumer information, online comparative pricing sites will continue to influence retail pricing. The trend toward value pricing that began in the 1980s will accelerate as more customers find electronic ways to continue the mission: never pay full price.

Government Regulation and Stimulation

Horizontal and vertical price fixing have been issues for retailers and manufacturers for well over a century. If regulation doesn't always wear well with the parties involved, government-sponsored rebates and incentives surely do. This section visits both sides of the fence.

Price-Fixing Issues

In the 19th century, small retailers that were hurt by larger firms with greater purchasing power needed protection. The Sherman Antitrust Act was passed in 1890 to prevent horizontal price fixing that might take place in any kind of business. The law, aimed at keeping competition open, makes it illegal for manufacturers, wholesalers, or retailers to fix prices.

The Robinson-Patman Act prevents manufacturers from price discrimination when selling goods of like quality. Although the act permits manufacturers to establish different prices based on sales volume differences, they must prove that specific price agreements do not hinder retail competition. Individual states also have enacted unfair trade practice laws in efforts to protect smaller retailers.

You read about the role competition plays in pricing and are familiar with retail strategies in the tablet and e-book markets. Antitrust issues can provoke much discontent between major retailers and book publishers allegedly involved in price-fixing and the accompanying secretiveness and innuendo.

The announcement in 2012 that the Department of Justice was suing five major book publishers and Apple based on alleged collusion between Apple and the publishers shocked many competitors. Parties involved were accused of setting their own prices on e-books and deriving clandestine policies that implied no bookseller would undercut Apple's prices. Shortly after the news release, three publishers settled with the government.

Concurrently, industry leader Amazon, which controls approximately 60 percent of the e-book market, said it would lower prices. That decision could reduce the price of some books from $14.99 to $9.99, seemingly to the delight of customers who value price cuts. Amazon can afford to sell all types of books at lower prices and is more concerned about gaining market share for its Kindle reader. For several years, Barnes & Noble and its Nook have been pummeled by competitors' e-book popularity and lower-priced products, and the pricing spectrum appears to be moving further apart.[2]

Some publishers and booksellers believe that the antitrust suit did little more than switch a perceived monopoly by Apple for a real one by Amazon. The impact of further court decisions will be interesting to follow. Customer attitudes toward pricing are transitory and dependent on industry decisions and government rulings as well as supply and demand.

Government Rebate Programs

When Congress endorsed and funded the U.S. Department of Transportation's $3 billion Car Allowance Rebate System (popularly known as the "Cash-for-Clunkers" program) in 2009, consumers, auto dealers, and manufacturers cheered this bold attempt to infuse cash into the economy. Ragged from the effects of the recession, shoppers lined up to trade in their vehicles for rebates up to $4,500—if they met gas-guzzler criteria. The overwhelming majority of customers parted with trucks, SUVs, and vans, and some traded in passenger cars. The top three new models purchased under the rebate program were Toyota Corolla, Honda Civic, and Toyota Camry.[3]

The successful "Clunkers" program inspired other industries to institute significant rebate programs. Pushing energy savings as the primary motivator, appliance companies offered rebates ranging from $50 to $200 on washing machines, dishwashers, refrigerators, and other home appliances under the U.S. government's $300 million program funded by the economic stimulus plan. Consumers who purchased Energy Star–rated washing machines and dishwashers showed an average

30 percent reduction in energy usage.[4] Implemented in 2010, the incentive was expected to boost sales for the depressed home appliance sector of the economy.

Other countries implemented similar stimulus programs aimed at improving sales for retailers. Brazil offered consumers a tax break on household appliances that precipitated a 20 percent increase in sales following a spring 2009 promotion.[5] Japan also started a Cash-for-Clunkers program to spur sales of green cars.

Business Design

Retailers have different operating philosophies, called **business designs**, based on factors that include gross margins, turnover, and other financial metrics. Generally, retailers with high gross margins, such as jewelers, operate on a low-turnover basis. Retailers with high gross margins and high turnover include convenience stores and some vending machine operations. On the other hand, low margin retailers, such as grocers or warehouse clubs, operate on a very high turnover basis. Average food retailers achieve net profits of one percent. Typical soft goods retailers earn net profits of 2 percent—10 percent or more for high achievers. Gross margin, and its relationship to the retailer's ability to turn a profit, is the final topic in this chapter. This concept was discussed in Chapter 14 in the broader context of financial management. Discount and department store pricing policies vary as the following sections illustrate.

Discount Stores

Today's discounters differ from their predecessors, which sold a wide variety of lower-priced (and often lower-quality) merchandise. The philosophy of discounting is based on high-volume, low-margin sales.

Kmart has combined fashion appeal and attractive price points with its celebrity-endorsed Jaclyn Smith sportswear collection. Other private-label merchandise, such as its Route 66 sportswear and Smart Sense products, is priced lower than national brands. Kmart also features nationally branded jeans such as Lee at competitive prices. Other discounters keep demand high and prices low by adopting similar strategies.

Off-price discount retailers sell name-brand merchandise at lower prices than department stores. Services, ambiance, and assortments are limited. Turnover usually runs double that of traditional apparel stores. Prices are 20–60 percent less than those in department stores for the same merchandise. Part of the growth in off-price sales comes from the sharp increase in the number of outlets. The off-price chains T.J. Maxx and Marshalls sell predominantly first-quality, in-season merchandise at higher margins than traditional discounters. Parent company TJX operates over 2,900 stores in the United States, Canada, and Europe and expects to grow to 4,500 stores long term.[6]

Department Stores

Department stores traditionally prioritized high gross margins. That focus changed as the most aggressive department stores adapted to the promotional frequency and pricing tactics of discounters. Department stores and other retailers are often criticized for their policies of marking goods up at a higher-than-customary percentage in order to bring prices down for a sale or special purchase. Knowledgeable customers perceive this method of establishing prices akin to a scam. Retailers insist it is a legitimate pricing technique. Both make strong points.

Retailers recognize that not all products will sell at the price initially tagged on the merchandise. Fashion apparel classifications may be marked down three or more times before the end of the season. With a retail calendar that includes a plethora of one-day sales, three-day sales, pre-holiday sales, and post-holiday clearance sales, it's a wonder anything sells at the original retail price. In fact, retailers are fortunate if 30 percent of their ready-to-wear items sell at the full retail price. Usually another 30 percent of stock sells at a first markdown, and a final third at a second markdown. The remainder sells well below wholesale costs of the merchandise.

Almost inevitably, pricing policies create tension between retailers and customers. Retailers are most concerned with the average retail selling price, and if they have to mark up to mark down,

Did You Know?
TJX Companies is opening Marshalls Shoe Shops in urban areas where full-size stores are very costly to operate. Most shoes sell for $29.99 to $39.99, with some merchandise—like a pair of Kate Spade sandals that were regularly $298.00, now only $169.00—priced to attract designer customers at the off-price specialty store. One of the store's slogans, "Our prices never pinch," is part of the décor. (Source: Excerpted and adapted from Joan Verdon, "Marshalls Chain Jumping Into New Concept, Feet First," NorthJersey.com, March 3, 2011, www.northjersey.com/templates/fdcp?1299362135734.)

Did You Know?
Many European retailers have only two major sale periods per year: January and July. The ensuing pent-up demand encourages customers to shop early for the best buys. But this early? When Harrods on Brompton Road in London opened at 9:00 a.m. for business, customers were already on queue ready to charge—and this time we mean dash—to their favorite department. Two committed shoppers who had waited since midnight in freezing temperatures to see Victoria Beckham (a.k.a. Posh Spice) cut the ribbon were the first customers to enter the store. (Source: Excerpted from: *Daily Mail Online.* "Posh Opens the Harrods Sale," www.dailymail.co.uk/news/article-92708/Posh-opens-Harrods-sale.html.)

Figure 16.3
There is no doubt in any customer's mind that De Bijenkorf is having a sale. Its location in Amsterdam's central square, where people gather day and night, helps draw traffic to the department store.

they do. Customers are concerned that merchandise may be overpriced. It is no surprise that many wait for goods to be marked down before making a purchase.

Throngs of customers traditionally shop department stores like Amsterdam's De Bijenkorf, illustrated in Figure 16.3, during peak sale periods in the Netherlands. Pricing appears less aggressive in many European retail stores, which hold fewer sales than their American counterparts but offer significant savings when they do.

Merchandising Strategies

Pricing is closely related to certain merchandising practices. Private-label merchandise allows retailers to achieve higher profits. Bridge lines are a way retailers merchandise their stores based on specific price levels.

Private Labeling

Retailers have developed their own lines of merchandise with their store label as a way of competing with stores selling national brands at discounted prices. Private labeling was discussed in Chapter 15 in the context of merchandising and sourcing of products. One of the main reasons for using private-label programs is to increase gross margins. Economies of scale created by large production runs and increased control over the manufacturing process generate cost savings. Retailers are then able to price private label goods lower for their customers. Private-label pricing advantages are realized by retailers at all stages of the price/quality continuum. Costco, also mentioned in Chapter 15, produces items—including automobile tires, apparel, bakery goods, and household cleaning products—under its Kirkland label that are sold at prices considerably lower than those of nationally branded items. A comparative display of laundry detergent at Costco is shown in Figure 16.4.

Barneys New York does extensive private-label work under its store label. Fashion products are invariably well made, of quality fabrics, and with fine styling details. They are not inexpensive but are well received by Barneys' upmarket clientele.

Bridge Lines

Some groups of women's apparel are designed to fit a specific price zone. Apparel that is priced lower than designer fashion but higher than better lines is called a **bridge line**. Price zones in the industry range in descending order from designer to bridge, better, moderate, and budget. Donna Karan's DKNY line and designer Emanuel Ungaro's Emanuel line are examples of bridge lines. Bridge lines have a price range several hundred dollars below the regular designer collections. If a Donna Karan jacket costs $1,000 in the designer line, for example, one in the DKNY line might be priced at $400.

Dana Buchman bridge apparel, once manufactured by Liz Claiborne, went downmarket to find a new niche in Kohl's department store. The label no longer makes goods at bridge-line price points but expects to do more volume in the moderate price zone.

Factors such as store location, quality, and fluctuation of wholesale prices or transportation costs due to shifts in the economy or other factors in the retail environment also affect pricing. The complex nature of pricing brings forth a profusion of practices.

Retail Pricing Practices

The method chosen for determining retail prices depends on a variety of factors. New products are treated differently than products that have been in the market for several seasons or years. Customer demand plays a role, as does product availability. Competition and customer sensitivity

Figure 16.4
Prices for national brands such as Tide and Cheer are higher than the price of Costco's private-label Kirkland laundry detergent. Costco uses similar packaging colors for its private label product and positions it in close proximity to competitors' brands on the shelves.

to price also have a bearing on pricing. Pricing methods fit into three categories: passive, aggressive, and neutral.

- **Passive pricing** is based on a retailer's differential advantage rather than on beating competitors' prices. Location or unique merchandise might constitute a differential advantage.
- **Aggressive pricing** is based on undercutting competitors' prices rather than concentrating on the company's strengths. It can be very risky to implement.
- **Neutral pricing** is based on adding a fair amount of money to the cost of products to cover overhead and profit. Products are priced independently of competition, as when a fixed margin is added to the cost of products.[7]

Retailers use different strategies and techniques based on these three ideologies. Several variations on each method are explained here. Two basic pricing strategies culled from marketing theory are skimming and penetration pricing. They are used during the introduction stage in the product life cycle and have important retail applications.

Passive Methods

Skimming, differential, and blind-item pricing are passive methods that prove useful to retailers in certain circumstances.

Skimming

Setting a high initial price on a product when competition is low is called **skimming**. This strategy is used in circumstances when:

- Customers are insensitive to price.
- There is little competition.
- Customers know little about the costs of producing and marketing a product.
- The product is targeted toward a small market segment.

High margins and the development of a prestige image are advantages gained by using a skimming strategy. Skimming attracts competition, however, and may endanger the life cycle of a product. If sales volume builds and competition increases, prices are adjusted downward.

The progression of Blu-ray players through the product life cycle illustrates the benefits and consequences of a skimming strategy. Median prices were $800 when Samsung Electronics first introduced its disk player in 2006.[8] Innovators and early adopters who first purchased Blue-ray did not mind paying a high price to experience advanced technology. They couldn't compare Blue-ray to comparable technologies because the player was produced by only one manufacturer and sold in few retail stores. Less knowledge about the merchandise made customers less sensitive to price. As Blue-ray gained customer acceptance, demand grew.

Median price dropped appreciably by 2007, when it was $497. In 2008, this had fallen to $388; by 2009, it was $322; and as of Black Friday 2009, $221. Units sold for $130 and as low as $80 by the end of December 2009.[9] By this time, more manufacturers including Sony and Panasonic had entered the market and more retailers carried the product, intensifying the competition.

As Blue-ray approached the maturity phase of the product life cycle, competition was most intense and production costs had decreased. When customers began to replace older models with Internet-capable models prices stayed competitive. As sales of newer Blu-ray models grow, and more entertainment applications are added, prices of less-equipped models will decline further. What began as a passive, skimming strategy evolved into a more aggressive one.

By 2011, new movies that came out on Blu-ray disks cost on average 35 percent more than DVDs.[10] Touting exclusivity and better quality to justify higher prices on disks apparently are strategies designed to compensate for declining gross margins on Blu-ray players. Skimming serves a slightly different objective in this case.

Differential Pricing

Using this method, prices are set based on past sales history. Research involving vendors, retail sales associates, or customers is used to determine whether a new product under consideration is priced more or less than a similar product that sold well last season. Toys priced for a holiday season are examples of products that probably have a close comparison. Suppose another version of a Batmobile toy were to be released this year. Most likely, the pricing history will suit the new toy because the track record was established over time as a result of the cross-generational acceptance of Batman-themed products.

Differential pricing is more difficult to use on fashion merchandise owing to the inherent nature of seasonal change in these products and planned obsolescence of most fashion trends.

Blind-Item Pricing

Products that are rare or not easily found in other stores are candidates for blind pricing. Sometimes this method is used in conjunction with private labeling as retailers build their own brands on untested but potentially sound products. Those involved in the decision-making process determine the highest price customers could be expected to pay. Prices are treated as though they were being evaluated in a test market. If the item doesn't sell in a respectable amount of time, the price is lowered until a more acceptable level is reached.

Aggressive Methods

Alternative viewpoints on pricing encompass penetration, experience curve pricing, and matching the competition. Choice of method is circumstantial and dependent upon retail goals and objectives.

Penetration

Setting a low initial price on a product when competition is high is called **penetration**. The goal is to generate demand for the product through mass merchandising. This also lays the groundwork for repeat purchases. Penetration pricing is used when:

- Customers are sensitive to price.
- Competition is intense.
- Large groups of initial users are sought.
- Market share growth is the object.

Initial losses are anticipated when using penetration pricing. Supermarkets use penetration to introduce new food products. After the initial period, prices are raised or lowered further depending on the reactions of customers and competitors.

From the Field 16.1   Consumers Driving Harder Bargains for Price

Kiss full price goodbye. With deep discounts continuing after the holidays, shoppers battered by the recession aren't as likely to buy much at full price for spring and beyond, particularly when they can find lower-cost equivalents. "This is the moment in time when you have to wow people for the price," said Candace Corlett, a principal partner in WSL Strategic Retail, echoing the "wow" word that was associated with "price" in a Target TV spot. "That's what H&M does: a great piece for $79. Highly recognizable brands can do that."

The bottom line is that fashion consumers are reevaluating what they think goods are worth. In this environment, a growing group of shoppers is more willing to spend $30 or $40 for a polo shirt from Lands' End or L.L. Bean than, say, part with $80 for a Lacoste polo or with $100 for a polo shirt from Ralph Lauren.

Unless they're hooked by a discount or a significant value—something well made and well priced—many shoppers could stay on the sidelines, marketing experts and consumer analysts said. That kept the pressure on retail profit margins, as lowered forecasts for Walmart, Macy's, Gap, and others confirmed.

A resumption of robust buying also hinges on the emergence of "pent-up demand" for apparel, spurred by growth in jobs and wages, the kind of purchasing consumers with ample closets can postpone, said Marshall Cohen, chief industry analyst at the NPD Group. However, an employment-based shot in the arm from President Obama's economic stimulus plan is uncertain. Federal Reserve chairman Ben Bernanke said that more "strong measures to further stabilize and strengthen the financial system" are needed for a lasting recovery.

The public is "a bit mercenary," said Marian Saltzman, chief marketing officer at Porter Novelli. "We've read of retailers' troubles and want to exploit it. We know they're stuck with the goods. Price is elastic, and we've learned that means down as well as up."

A case in point: the shopping experience of Paco Underhill, on the hunt for a favorite pair of Ecco classic, casual slip-ons. The first time Underhill bought the shoes, seven years ago, he paid $155 for them at an Eneslow shoe store in Manhattan's Flatiron district. The next time, three years ago, he paid $79 at a DSW store in Battery Park City. Three weeks ago they were just $23.99 when Underhill bought them at the same DSW. "Am I ever going to pay $155 again?" he asked rhetorically.

"We are watching the evisceration of the concept of value," Underhill said. "The only thing people will pay full price for again are crafts: unique artisan products. No one understands the concept of full price anymore. We are addicted to the sales."

Some people are anticipating a fundamental change in the world of promotional pricing, now voiced by shoppers newly skeptical about the original cost attached to a growing array of products. "People want to wear as a badge of honor—a sense of themselves as being wise by saving money," said Robert Passikoff, president of Brand Keys research consultancy. "But a greater reckoning is coming. A lot of the promotional sales toolbox is going to go the way of the dodo," he added, alluding to the likelihood of lower initial price markup. Retailers have to become accountable first to their customers, rather than to their boards of directors, the consultant suggested, acknowledging that it will require "a fundamental shift."

A prescription for price-resistant shoppers was suggested:

- Replace blowout sales with reasonable everyday prices.
- Make technical improvements to raise the quality of more apparel items, like applying stain-resistant finishes and moisture-wicking treatments.
- Tell shoppers about an innovative product feature or a brand's heritage via hangtags, sales associates, or online.
- Take more fashion risks, rather then focusing largely on limiting financial risks.

Adapted and condensed from Valerie Seckler, *Women's Wear Daily*, January 14, 2009, 10.

Experience Curve Pricing

Used by major discount retailers and category killers, this method depends on retailers' ability to reduce prices consistently for the duration of the products' stay on the selling floor. The philosophy is based on the vast purchasing power of giant companies, the volume they generate, and the pressures they exert on vendors to reduce costs.

Matching the Competition

Many retailers advertise their policy to meet or beat competitors' prices. Usually customers who challenge a specific price provide proof such as an advertisement or a receipt before the retailer adjusts pricing. It is difficult to determine how many customers take advantage of these offers. However, it is certain that meet-the-competition policies keep prices more level and lower for customers. Retailers that sell home electronics have been engaged in price wars on LCD/HDTV screens for several years. Best Buy, Walmart, Target, and online stores slash prices and honor customers' pricing research as shoppers scout for the lowest ticket prices.

Even gasoline prices are affected by competition. Customers are sensitive to changes in price per gallon or liter—especially when price fluctuates widely in a relatively brief span of time. For these reasons, price wars may ensue when gas stations attempt to meet or beat competitors' prices.

In deeply competitive situations, including those imposed by economic downturns, customers become more sensitive to price and are not willing to accept face value on price tickets if they believe they can negotiate a better price. From the Field 16.1 addresses some of the changes in consumers' behavior and suggests how retailers cope with price-resistant shoppers.

Neutral Method

When retailers determine price by adding a fixed percentage to the cost of their merchandise, they are using a cost-plus method. This is considered a neutral pricing approach. The method allows them to cover expenses and make a profit. Fluctuating prices of competitors matter less than negotiations with vendors to secure more advantageous buys at wholesale. Most small independent retailers and some specialty stores use this method.

Retail Pricing Techniques

Expressing the price in a way that invites customer response more rapidly is a pricing objective of many retailers. Several techniques enable retailers to do this. Some are difficult to differentiate from straight promotional techniques. Others are related to customer psychology and merchandising strategies.

One Price Versus Flexible Pricing

When all customers pay the same price and purchase an item under similar conditions, a **one-price policy** is in use. Early department store retailer John Wanamaker was the first merchant to mark each piece of merchandise with its own price. This policy eliminated bargaining and led to the newer concept of unit pricing. Quoting prices in terms of standard units of measurement such as ounces, pounds, or kilograms is called **unit pricing**. Supermarkets use this technique. The exact cost per pound or pint is computed for every item in the grocery and dairy departments. Labels with unit prices are attached to shelves where merchandise is displayed.

In contrast to the one-price approach, flexible pricing occurs in automobile showrooms, jewelry shops, antique shops, and at flea markets. Setting prices that are open to negotiation and bargaining is called **flexible pricing**. To deal successfully, customers who are knowledgeable about the merchandise and the competitive market have an edge.

Psychological Pricing

Custom, habit, and repetition have influenced many pricing techniques in use today. All capitalize on customers' perceptions of price, value, and sales and include several variations.

Multiple Unit Pricing

Offering a discount for buying in quantities of more than one unit is called **multiple pricing**. When socks that normally sell for $1.00 per pair are marked at six pairs for $4.99, multiple pricing is in effect. Even more savings accrue if you buy 12 pairs for $8.99. Grocery stores offer lower prices on bulk packaging, often called family packs. Customers might save 10–20 cents per pound when they buy 12 pork chops versus the customary four.

Offering customers two products at a lower price than would be paid if each was purchased separately is called a **twofer** in retail slang. This is a special type of multiple-unit selling. A retailer that advertises shoes for $20 per pair or two pairs for $34.99 is using psychological pricing to encourage multiple sales. With both bulk packaging and twofers, retailers achieve increases in unit sales, although profit per unit is reduced.

Odd-Ending Pricing

Selecting a price point below the even dollar value is another form of psychological pricing. The setting of prices that end in an odd number such as $9.99 rather than rounding off to $10.00 is called **odd-ending pricing**. For customers who have a budget of $300 for a North Face parka, a price of $299 has immediate drawing power. Retailers hope customers will sense a bargain, as shown in Figure 16.5. Consumers are conditioned to expect that an odd ending signifies a promotional price or sale, even though a retailer, for the sake of a cent or two, is achieving a full margin. A classic odd ending on a backyard/recreational item at Cabela's is illustrated in Figure 16.6.

Promotional Pricing

Setting prices below a level that is usual or customary with the intention of having a sale or offering a special purchase is called **promotional pricing**. Suggesting that customers shop for specially priced items with the intention that additional items at regular prices will be purchased is the objective. In this way, total retail sales volume and profits increase. Using loss leaders, advertising

Figure 16.5
Odd pricing is used to ensure that the customers at the Wild Animal Park outside San Diego know they are getting a good deal when they purchase an elephant at a wild animal farm kiosk.

Figure 16.6
A price doesn't get any more odd than $99.99—but for those looking to relax in a hammock, it sounds like a much better deal than if the retailer had rounded off to $100.

branded merchandise with time-sensitive implications, and using coupons to drive sales, retailers magnify the close link between pricing tactics and promotion.

Loss Leaders

Items that are priced below cost to increase store traffic are called **loss leaders**. They are restricted by minimum price laws in some states, but these laws are rarely enforced. Advertised loss leaders bring customers into the store. For this reason, items priced in this way are also called *traffic builders*. When a photo shop offers a memory stick for $7.99 that is worth $19.99, it doesn't earn a profit on that item but anticipates a significant increase in digital camera sales during the promotion.

Time-Sensitive Tactics

Supermarkets that price 12-packs of Coca-Cola at $2.99 for one week only rather than selling them at the usual $3.99 are using a time-sensitive pricing tactic. Some customers plan their entire weekly food shopping expeditions based on promotional prices. Since soda is promoted 35 out of 52 weeks per year, profits are securely built into the pricing structure. Coke, however, earns its biggest profits from vending machine sales. This raises the question of whether the company's promotional pricing is really large-scale loss leader pricing.

Couponing

When we hear about ardent coupon clippers who boast that they save small fortunes on their grocery bills by being thrifty and snipping coupons, we may wonder if they really do. The answer is yes; diligent shoppers are able to clip from newspapers, magazines, and flyers and save money. Most now use manufacturers' and retailers' Web sites, downloading some savings coupons directly to their shoppers reward cards or smart phones, and printing others. Several examples show how retailers are using technology to drive customer traffic while using a pricing model that provides savings for shoppers who buy wisely.

- Kroger launched a digital coupon service at www.kroger.com. Customers can download coupons to their Kroger Plus Card or print them at home.
- Stop & Shop and Giant Foods, divisions of Royal Ahold, the Dutch supermarket company, have made hand-held scanners available for their customers in many stores. The scanners subtotal the bill and make a cash register sound when they offer shoppers coupons for something related to a past purchase.
- Dellaria, a chain of hair salons and spas, found it attracted repeat customers after offering coupons through online services EverSave and LivingSocial.

Figure 16.7
Value pricing is evident at Walmart, where there are "Always Low Prices."

Approximately $470 billion in coupon savings was available to U.S. shoppers in 2011, but only 1 percent of potential savings was redeemed. Usage of online and mobile coupons is growing rapidly; however, 89 percent of coupons are accessible through traditional print media.[11] Predictions indicate that by 2012, 96.8 million adults in the U.S. will redeem an online coupon.[12]

Unethical Tactics

An unethical promotional pricing technique that attempts to lure customers into the store on false pretenses is called **bait and switch**. If a furniture retailer advertises a sofa priced at $549, a customer who visits the store would expect to see the advertised item. Suppose the customer is greeted by a sales associate advising that the $549 model is out of stock, but that a $799 model would be perfect. If a $549 model never existed and the retailer's intent is to deceive the customer, this is an unethical pricing policy. On the other hand, if the store is legitimately out of the product, a rain check could be offered. On a related note, it is not unethical to practice trade-up selling. Using this strategy, the sales associate could show the $549 sofa but point out the enhanced features of the more expensive style and let the customer decide.

Other types of promotional pricing techniques include percentage off sales, twofer (buy-one-get-one-free) offers, or those that suggest customers purchase one item at full price and receive another at half off. A 50-percent-off sale is illustrated in Figure 16.1.

Merchandise-Driven Techniques

Retailers also use techniques that put merchandising policies at the center of pricing decisions. Value pricing and price lining are examples.

Value Pricing

Value pricing has dominated the strategies of retailers and the preferences of customers since the 1990s. Providing the best-quality product for the lowest price as viewed by customers is called **value pricing**. Walmart and Sears both offer everyday low pricing to their customers. Just so we don't forget, signage near the entrance to a Walmart superstore with its emphasis on the company's philosophy is illustrated in Figure 16.7. Most discount and off-price stores apply the concept to their pricing policies. True value is available in any price zone and is not confined to low-price retailers.

Price Lining

The practice of setting distinguishable price levels, according to store policy and pricing objectives, is called **price lining**. Merchandise assortments are purchased specifically to meet price line standards. For example, prices on iPhones could be set on the basis of few, many, and maximum options. When using price lining, retailers are confident that customers will pay the asking price before merchandise is ordered. Price is thoughtfully set to cover expenses and make a profit. If price lines are wisely established, they afford some range of choice for customers at various income levels. They should be far enough apart to make differences of quality and style distinguishable.

Price lines are set for various merchandise categories. A customer who is prepared to pay $400 for a watch may be interested in looking at items priced at $800 or $200, the next higher and next lower price levels. If timepieces were offered at random prices, the retailer would find it more difficult to justify differences in price. Customers might lose confidence and not make a purchase.

One of the advantages of limiting price lines is that past sales data help plan future assortments more effectively. Another is that price lining allows a retailer to adopt a good-better-best merchandising strategy and, in doing so, attract more customers.

Setting a price that will be viewed as fair by customers yet earn an equally fair return for the retailer is not easy. Establishing markup and managing pricing during the time merchandise is on the selling floor is an important part of retail operations.

Methods of Price Setting

Buyers go to market with the purpose of finding items that can be priced with confidence. There are several methods for determining prices, but the most common in retailing is the markup method.

Markup Method

Markup is the figure that covers fixed and variable costs of doing business plus a fair profit. It is the amount that is added to the wholesale cost of merchandise to determine the selling price. Markup is expressed as a percentage or dollar amount. A **keystone markup** is calculated by doubling the cost of an item to determine its retail price. Expressed in another way, it is the same as a 50 percent markup on retail.

The terms markup and markon are frequently used interchangeably. Technically, **markon** refers to the target, or first, markup placed on a retail product. In its most basic form, the retail selling price is calculated like this:

$$\text{Selling price} = \text{Cost} + \text{Markup}$$

Because nothing is quite that simple in retail pricing, several methods of manipulating the markup to better serve customers and profit motives are used.

Additional Markup

Under certain circumstances, retailers take an additional markup. An **additional markup** is a price increase taken after the original markup has been determined. Retailers may decide, after initial prices are set, that higher prices will make goods appear more attractive and desired. Alternatively, an item may become scarce, justifying a higher retail price. Occasionally, a retailer may adjust a price upward to meet the competition or because inventory costs went up. For example, the cost of merchandise might have increased when it was reordered.

Markup Cancellation

On occasion, goods are marked up additionally and then returned to their original price. When the additional price increase is removed and the original price is restored it is called a **markup cancellation**. It is not a markdown until the price dips below the original retail price.

Dimensions of Markup

Three types or stages of markup are used in retail pricing and control. They are initial, maintained, and cumulative markups.

Initial Markup

The difference between the gross delivered cost of merchandise and the original retail price for a single item or a total assortment of goods is called the **initial markup**. The gross delivered cost is the wholesale price of an item plus transportation charges. The formula for calculating initial markup is:

$$\text{Markup percentage} = \frac{\$ \text{Retail} - \$ \text{Cost}}{\$ \text{Retail}}$$

Did You Know?

In early 2011, L.L. Bean announced: "Free Shipping Is Here to Stay." When the company made the commitment to ship to its customers in the United States and Canada, it guaranteed two- to five-day delivery, emphasizing that no minimum order was needed and there was no end date to the free offer. A reasonable charge was added for express shipping. Since distribution is a significant cost for a retailer, how would this decision affect markup? The service might be reflected in higher prices on merchandise. Alternately, the company could maintain its existing price structure in anticipation of higher sales volume. Would absorbing shipping costs add a valuable customer service and good will, or is it done simply to keep up with the competition? Decisions that affect pricing require research and reflection on questions like these before permanent changes are implemented. (Source: "Big News: Free Shipping is Here to Stay + Maine Isle Flip-Flops," L.L. Bean E-Mail Updates, March 29, 2011, llbean@e.llbean.com.)

To illustrate, if the invoice cost of a shipment of athletic footwear reflects a cost of $59 per pair and the transportation cost is $1.00, the delivered cost is $60. If the buyer then places an original retail price of $100 on the article, its initial markup is $40, expressed as 40 percent. Applying the formula:

$$\text{Markup percentage} = \frac{\$100 - \$60}{\$100} = \frac{\$40}{\$100} = 40\%$$

The initial markup may be placed on an entire shipment or on a single item. Markup percentage is based on the retail price that must be sold to generate profit and not the wholesale price to the retailer. Retailers prefer this approach because it accurately reflects the changes in retail prices of merchandise during a selling season.

Maintained Markup

Maintained markup is calculated on a group of merchandise or a department at the time the goods are sold. To continue the example, let's assume that there were 500 pairs of shoes in the shipment of athletic shoes. Three hundred pairs were sold in the first four weeks, then sales tapered off. The retailer decided to mark the goods down to $80 to promote sales. At that price, the remaining shoes sold. The maintained markup reflects the reduction in retail price.

Cumulative Markup

After all goods are sold or at the end of the selling season, markup is calculated once again. The average markup for an entire department or classification after a selling period is called **cumulative markup**. A target percentage is determined by the merchandising divisions after analyzing past records and the outlook for the coming period. Retailers use these figures for comparative purposes. Continuing the earlier example, assume that the athletic footwear retailer intends to reach a cumulative markup of 35 percent on sales for a season. The retailer understands that if less than 35 percent is achieved on some sneakers, it is necessary to take more than 35 percent on others. Cumulative markup is calculated for an entire department or classification.

Global considerations regarding markup are worth following. Markup policies differ by country, retailer, local economies, volume sold, and sales taxation. For example, retail prices for a brand-name special-edition soccer ball in cities around the world, expressed in U.S. dollars, vary from a high of $170 in Paris to a low of $86 in Singapore.[13]

Markup Calculations

Retailers use other formulas to calculate markups in special situations. One situation arises when original retail in dollars and desired initial markup in percent are known, but it is necessary to determine wholesale cost in dollars. As an example, the buyer for an accessory department is ready to buy silk scarves to be sold at a $90 retail price point. The initial markup goal is 50 percent. The buyer needs to determine the highest wholesale price that can be paid for scarves while still maintaining pricing policy.

Original retail price in dollars multiplied by the initial markup percentage gives the initial markup in dollars. This figure subtracted from original retail price in dollars gives the cost in dollars. This relationship is expressed in these two formulas:

$$\text{Original retail (dollars)} \times \text{Initial markup (percentage)} = \text{Initial markup (dollars)}$$

$$\text{Original retail (dollars)} - \text{Initial markup (dollars)} = \text{Cost (dollars)}$$

The original retail in dollars may also be multiplied by the percentage of original retail that represents cost of merchandise. The cost percentage of original retail is the complement of the initial markon percentage; namely, 100 percent minus the initial markup percentage. Translating this into a formula, cost in dollars is found this way:

$$\text{Original retail (dollars)} \times \text{Initial markup 100\% (percentage)} = \text{Cost (dollars)}$$

Suppose the buyer is purchasing $90 scarves and is projecting a 50 percent cumulative markup. The required cost is determined by the following calculation:

$$\$90 \times .50 = \$45 \text{ Markup}$$

$$\$90 - \$45 = \$45 \text{ Cost}$$

The following alternative method also can be used:

$$\$90 \times 50\% = \$45 \text{ Cost}$$

The buyer can afford to pay no more than $45 for a silk scarf to be retailed at $90, if an initial markup of 50 percent is specified. This is easy to understand when a keystone markup is involved, but slightly more complicated when a markup of more or less than 50 percent is used. Pricing breakdown for the scarf used in the preceding examples is given in Table 16.1.

Markdowns

Reducing a retail price below its original level is called a **markdown**. Markdowns are taken only after a thorough analysis of business is completed. If markdowns are kept in check, they are useful

---

Table 16.1 Pricing Breakdown for One 42-inch Jacquard Hand-Painted Batik Silk Scarf

Fixed and Variable Costs

CONTRACTOR'S	$6.00	Fabric
MARGIN	$5.00	Labor
	$1.50	Contracted Services
	$4.00	Overhead
	$3.50	Profit
	$2.00	Export Expenses
	$22.00	CONTRACTED COST
WHOLESALE	$3.00	Payroll
GROSS	$3.00	Rent
MARGIN	$1.00	Utilities
	$1.00	Taxes and Insurance
	$2.00	Custom Fees, Tariffs, Shipping
	$10.00	Sales and Advertising (Includes travel, and trade show expenses)
	$2.50	Profit
	$44.50	WHOLESALE PRICE TO RETAIL STORES
RETAIL	$10.00	Payroll
GROSS	$10.00	Rent
MARGIN*	$5.00	Utilities
	$2.00	Taxes and Insurance
	$2.00	Advertising
	$5.00	Profit
	$10.00	Markdowns
	$1.00	Shipping
	$90.00 to $100.00	RETAIL PRICE TO ULTIMATE CUSTOMERS

*Based on 50% to 60% initial markup on retail.

merchandising tools for a retailer, because they facilitate the flow of goods. However, excessive markdowns can keep the retailer from achieving a target gross margin. Markdown money as a negotiable aspect of merchandise planning was discussed in Chapter 15.

Typical markdown percentages vary by merchandise category and type of store. This is another figure that is tracked internally and for comparative purposes. Markdowns help stores achieve their sales plans without hurting gross margins. They are taken for a variety of reasons:

- Having a sale or special promotion.
- Stimulating customer traffic.
- Clearing stocks of out-of-season or obsolete merchandise.
- Moving slow-selling goods faster.
- Clearing stocks of damaged goods that cannot be returned to vendors.

The formula for calculating a markdown percentage is:

$$\text{Markdown percentage} = \frac{\text{Markdown dollars}}{\text{Original retail price}}$$

Calculating a markdown percentage is a confusing issue for retailers and customers. Customers' perceptions of the price on which a markdown is based may not match the retailer's reality. To the retailer, the markdown percentage is related to sales obtained. Therefore, the markdown formula looks more like this:

$$\text{Markdown percentage} = \frac{\text{Markdown dollars}}{\text{Current retail price}}$$

Markdowns are sometimes taken in accord with a sale or special promotion effort using what is called a markdown cancellation. A **markdown cancellation** involves restoring a price to its pre-markdown level.

Pricing and Profitability

As stressed in Chapter 14, managing gross margin means planning markup and markdowns carefully, controlling expenses, and planning to produce profits. Pricing strategies and techniques expedite a retailer's journey to profitability, but they are not the only factors. Management of many fixed and variable costs of doing business is equally important. Payroll, rent, costs of distribution, taxes, insurance, and promotion also contribute.

Table 16.1, referenced earlier, shows the pricing breakdown for a hand-painted batik silk scarf that was manufactured in Malaysia. The scarves were distributed by Silk Accent, an American company, to specialty stores in the United States, South America, and the Caribbean, and a sample is illustrated in Figure 16.8. Expenses incurred at manufacturing, wholesaling, and retailing levels are expressed in the three sections of the table. In the retail example, figures are based on a keystone markup method using a five percent operating profit model.

Achieving sales and profits in a booming economy is easy. Almost any pricing strategy works in such a business climate. The real test comes when business cycles are down. Profit is a tenuous and fleeting element. Its place in a sinking retail ship is nonexistent. The next chapter emphasizes the importance of informing customers about new products through advertising, sales promotion, publicity, public relations, personal selling, and customer services that comprise the promotional mix.

Summary

Pricing objectives differ among retailers and may include volume, market share, image, or growth opportunities. Factors that retailers consider when deciding on a price strategy are customers, competition, government regulation and incentives, business design, and merchandising strategies. Perceived value is often the criterion for purchase decisions. Web sites are making it easier for customers to comparison shop.

There are three general methods for determining pricing practices: passive, aggressive, and neutral. Market saturation has led to retail market share battles that in turn have generated diverse

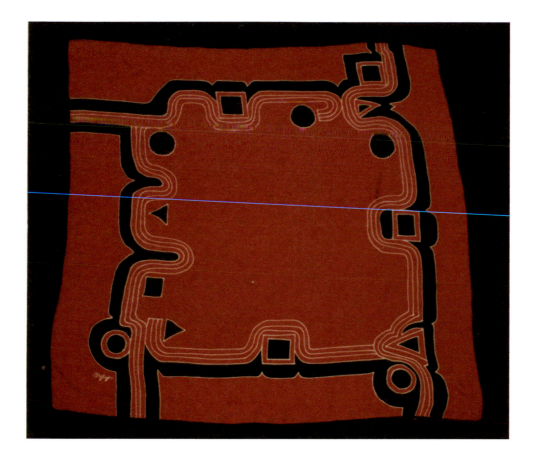

Figure 16.8
Low labor rates in Malaysia make it possible to manufacture hand-painted silk batik scarves for much less than it would cost in fully industrialized countries. The hand-painting process is time-intensive but the result is unique, marketable goods. The scarf shown is indicative of those represented in the pricing breakdown in Table 16.1.

pricing strategies. When choosing pricing techniques, one price or variable pricing, psychological, promotional, or merchandise-driven pricing are options for retailers.

After selecting methods and techniques, retailers calculate markup, taking into consideration the cost of the item, operating costs, and profit goals. Markdowns are useful pricing tools when not taken in excess. They make it possible for retailers to sell merchandise, replenish inventory, and increase turnover.

Retail profits are difficult to achieve in good economic times and close to impossible to earn in bad times. Many fixed and variable expenses challenge retailers to run a highly efficient business. Well-chosen pricing strategies help retailers earn profits.

Key Terms

Additional markup	Markup cancellation
Aggressive pricing	Multiple pricing
Bait and switch	Neutral pricing
Bridge line	Odd-ending pricing
Business design	One-price policy
Cumulative markup	Passive pricing
Flexible pricing	Penetration
Initial markup	Perceived value
Keystone markup	Price lining
Loss leaders	Promotional pricing
Maintained markup	Skimming
Markdown	Twofer
Markdown cancellation	Unit pricing
Markon	Value pricing
Markup	

Questions for Review and Discussion

1. Discuss three major factors that influence retail pricing strategy today.
2. How do pricing policies of discount and department stores differ? Draw on examples from your own shopping experience.
3. What are the important differences between passive, aggressive, and neutral methods of determining pricing policies? What types of retailers use each method?
4. In what circumstances are initial, maintained, and cumulative markup used by retailers?
5. Why does a retailer take markdowns? Are they considered positive or negative to maintaining smooth retail operations?
6. What is the difference between a markup cancellation and a markdown?

Endnotes

1. Jeffrey A. Trachtenberg and John Kell, "B&N Joins the Tablet Fray," *Wall Street Journal*, November 8, 2011. B6.
2. David Streitfeld. "Cut in E-Book Pricing by Amazon is Set to Shake Rivals." *New York Times.* April 11, 2012. p. 1–4. www.nytimes.com/2012/04/12/business/media/amazon-to-cut-e-book-prices-shaking-rivals.
3. Judith Burns, "'Clunkers' Lifts Foreign Cars," *Wall Street Journal*, August 27, 2009, B9.
4. Timothy Aeppel and Paul Glader, "'Clunkers' Sequel Rattles Appliance Producers," *Wall Street Journal*, August 27, 2009, B1, B9.
5. Ibid.
6. About Us. "A Message from Our CEO." accessed June, 2012, www.tjx.com/about.asp.
7. Roger Dickinson, "Pricing at Retail," Paper Presented at American Collegiate Retailing Association Spring Meeting, Dallas, Texas, April 9, 1992.
8. Yukari Iwatani Kane and Miguel Bustillo, "Dreaming of a Blu Christmas," *Wall Street Journal*," December 23, 2009, D1–D3. (Source: The Envisioneering Group.)
9. Ibid.
10. Martin Peers, "Hollywood: The Price is Wrong," *Wall Street Journal*, Heard on the Street, February 9, 2011, C14.
11. Selena Maranjian. "Guess Who Clips the Most Coupons?" February 22, 2012. Source: Coupons.com. www.dailyfinance.com/2012/02/22/guess-who-clips-the-most-coupons/.
12. eMarketer Digital Intelligence. "Quick Stat: 88.2 Million US Adults Will Redeem an Online Coupon This Year." June 2, 2011 Source: US Adult Coupon users, 2009–2013. www.emarketer.com/blog/index.php/quick-stat-3/ (Posted by Stephanie Reese).
13. "Arbitrage, Retail Prices Around the World," *Wall Street Journal*, August 7, 2008, D8.

Chapter 17

Planning Retail Promotion

Learning Objectives

After completing this chapter you should be able to:

- Identify the elements of the retail promotional mix.
- State several methods used to formulate a promotional budget and ways to evaluate the results.
- Contrast the advantages and disadvantages of the major media.
- Identify several types of sales promotion activities.
- State why personal selling is a key promotional technique.
- Discuss customer service in the context of customer relationship management.

a

b

Figure 17.1
A profusion of sale signs outside (a) and inside (b) indicates a major event at Galeries Lafayette in Paris. Typically, department stores in France have two major sale periods annually, so there is lots of pent-up demand for the promotion.

The finest products in the world go unsold if customers are unaware of them and the benefits they offer. The goals of retail promotion are to inform customers where, when, and how they may purchase merchandise, and to create a favorable impression in customers' minds. Promotion comes from the Latin word *promovere,* meaning "to move forward." Major media and other promotional tools are explained in this context.

Advertising, sales promotion, publicity, public relations, personal selling, and customer services comprise the **promotional mix**. Most retailers spend between 1 and 5 percent of sales on the promotional mix. This estimate does not include personal selling costs that run approximately 8 to 10 percent of sales. Publicity is not paid for directly.

Retailers track the results of their efforts, and sometimes it is difficult to discern whether a promotion was effective. An aesthetically appealing full-page print ad, an online fashion show, or a seductive billboard is pleasing to the eye but may not produce immediate sales. On the other hand, a simple flyer, jam-packed with savings on name-brand ski equipment, proves effective when the merchandise sells out in three days.

Small retailers do not have the financial resources of major chains. Their promotional tactics are more localized to serve their customers well. Both From the Field boxes in this chapter speak from small business viewpoints.

The objectives of promotion open this chapter, followed by descriptions of the promotional mix, major advertising media, and sales promotion tools. Personal selling and customer relationship management round out our survey of retail promotion.

Setting Objectives and Budgets

Promotion is the voice of the store—whether it's brick-and-mortar or online, permanent or temporary. Few merchants rely on their locations and reputations alone to build traffic. Communicating image and merchandise information to the public is a significant part of retail branding. Promotion is also multichannel, as when catalogue retailers advertise their publications on their Web sites and direct sellers supplement their personal touches with print and electronic media advertising. Effective customer engagement is achieved after setting promotion objectives, budgeting for expenditures, and planning the promotional mix.

Objectives of Retail Promotion

The true worth of a promotion is measured by how much merchandise it sells and how positively it reflects and reinforces retail image. Every promotion is designed to build the brand through customer awareness, education, and sales.

Selling Products and Services

Promotion is deliberately planned and created to elicit a response. It sells an idea, a service, an item, or the retail brand to customers. The reaction is an immediate one when a person clicks on Bluefly.com intending to order a discounted sweater. Sometimes the impetus to indulge is delayed. Seeing a giant butterfly flapping its wings on the Rainforest Cafe façade generates a joyful emotional response that encourages families to return later for dinner.

Attracting Attention

Promotions encourage customers to stop, look, listen, taste, touch, smell, or otherwise tune in. Customers notice print advertisements through their layout, illustration, or provocative headline. Numerous stations in Apple stores invite customers to try out new products. Promotions have only a few seconds to capture customers' attention. There is no question in our minds that the store in Figure 17.1 is having a huge sale—even if we don't read French.

Educating Customers

Customers want to know how merchandise benefits them. In-store demonstrations show customers how to operate food processors, polish their cars, or prepare Thai lemon chicken. Facts necessary to make a buying decision—such as sizes, prices, options, fabrication, and colors—are presented clearly on retail Web sites. Fashion shows inform customers how to put together the latest trends, dress for the job, or transition to a new season.

Home improvement stores teach do-it-yourselfers how to lay tile or install lighting fixtures. If you've completed a workshop at Home Depot, chances are you'll purchase your supplies there.

Presenting a Differential Advantage

Attributes including uniqueness of location, fashion orientation, value pricing, or special services are worth presenting clearly to the public. Identifying a reason to visit Best Buy rather than a competitor is one reason why the company uses strong promotions that focus on its low prices. If online stores are offering free shipping during a holiday period, they'll let customers know through multiple media.

Reflecting Brand Image

A way to test the strength of a brand is to have a friend cover the logotype in a newspaper, magazine or home page ad and then see if you recognize the retailer sponsoring the promotion. Promotions that exude the branding and personality of the retailer over time are more likely to be remembered and to produce sales.

Increasing sales and profits, maintaining loyal customers, and attracting additional customers are worthy objectives, but are not met without adequate funding.

Promotion Budgets

Planning the budget means considering promotion objectives and specifying the funds needed to implement campaigns. The type and amount of media used have a direct bearing on promotion allowances and vary greatly by the size of the business. In small stores, when money is spent on advertising, owners may feel it is coming directly out of their pockets—and it probably is. In large stores, marketing executives budget for advertising space, production expenses, and sales promotion materials. There are several methods for setting budgets.

Unit-of-Sales Method

The unit-of-sales method for establishing a budget is based on numbers of sales rather than on dollar amounts. A fixed sum is set aside for each unit the merchant expects to sell. For instance, if it takes ten cents' worth of promotional materials or events to sell a bottle of perfume and the retailer plans to sell 15,000 bottles, the store must plan to spend 15,000 times $0.10, or $1,500 on promotion. Because the amount of promotion needed to sell a particular unit must be known, the key to unit-of-sales planning is past experience. This method is effective for retailers of specialty goods like fine jewelry and rugs.

Percentage-of-Sales Method

The percentage-of-sales method for establishing a budget uses a percentage of past sales, anticipated sales, or a combination of both. Past sales are the figures from the previous year or an average of several years. Anticipated sales are estimates. A combination of the two is preferred for establishing a budget during periods of fluctuating economic conditions. Percentages of sales spent on promotion are lower for large retailers and higher for smaller or newer retailers.

Objective-and-Task Method

The objective-and-task method relates the advertising budget to sales objectives for the coming year. This is the most accurate method. The merchant reviews the total marketing program and considers store image, size, location, and business conditions. The task method stipulates exactly how to meet the objectives. The level of advertising expenditure is directly related to what it will cost to do the job; knowledge of media rates and schedules is implied. This method is effective when a new retail business is opening.

Whichever method is selected, retailers then determine each month's percentage of annual sales. Promotional expenditures coincide with or precede the sales curve. Next, department or classification allocations are identified. As a rule of thumb, if apparel accounts for 20 percent of sales, the department receives 20 percent of the promotion budget. Promotion budgets need to be flexible so they can be adapted as market conditions change.

Components of the Promotional Mix

Many promotional strategies are used both in and out of retailers' stores, through catalogues, or on online sites. The major components of the retail promotional mix are considered in turn here. Advertising, sales promotion, publicity, and certain public relations activities are dependent on **media**, which are communication methods used to deliver news, information, and promotional messages to viewers and listeners.

Internal and External Promotion

Promotional tools include signs and posters, digital sound and visual systems, and electronic kiosks and displays. These are considered internal promotion. **Internal promotion** communicates ideas to customers inside the store. Major broadcast and print media are forms of external promotion. **External promotion** communicates ideas to potential customers with the objective of bringing them into the store. Broadcast media include radio and television. Print media such as newspapers, magazines, and magalogs are in this category. A **magalog** is a combination magazine and catalogue published by a retailer and distributed through stores or direct mail. Web-based communications are used for both internal and external promotion.

Advertising

Businesses use advertising to build their brands, generate traffic, notify customers of sales, present new merchandise, and maintain a favorable image in the eyes of customers. Their advertising campaigns may encompass national, trade, or retail avenues and focus on a product, promotion, or institution.

Categories of Advertising

Three major categories of advertising concern retailers: national, trade, and retail. Companies use one or more of these types depending on their role in the supply chain and their objectives.

National Advertising   To encourage brand awareness and ultimately sales, national advertising is done. **National advertising** is advertising placed in major media by manufacturers, distributors, and retailers, usually on a broad geographic basis. Manufacturers' national magazine advertisements and Web sites often list local retail stores where customers can purchase popular brands. This application of advertising helps retailers by combining brand awareness with store location—although it is not the main objective of the manufacturer. It is a form of cooperative advertising and is discussed later in this chapter.

Trade Advertising   Mailing list brokers routinely advertise in *Direct Marketing News* to reach decision makers in catalogue companies. Apparel manufacturers and trade show sponsors run ads in *Women's Wear Daily* that are directed to retailers. These are examples of **trade advertising**, which is business-to-business advertising used among supply chain members and not directed to final consumers.

Retail Advertising   Retail advertising differs in several ways from national and trade advertising. **Retail advertising** is advertising specifically directed to final consumers by retailers. Other characteristics that differentiate retail advertising include:

- *Trading area specificity.* Retail advertising for most small businesses is usually confined to the immediate trading area. Retailers with national or international distribution and online retailers draw customers from a larger trading area.
- *Relationship to customers.* Because many retailers draw business from limited geographic areas, those retailers direct advertising to succinct target markets more efficiently. In this way, they develop closer relationships with their customers. Many people pride themselves on supporting their local retailers whenever possible.
- *Reader interest.* When customers trade locally, they focus on retail advertising more intently than national advertising. This tendency is particularly true for frequently purchased products such as groceries. Most grocery advertisements are placed in newspapers.
- *Response expectations.* Retail advertising encourages customers to purchase items promptly—usually within a one-day to one-week timeframe.
- *Use of price.* Because retail advertising generates an immediate response, price is a key element and usually is included in print advertisements.

Approaches to Advertising

Advertising is broken down into three further classifications: product, promotional, and institutional.

Product Advertising   Advertisements that feature specific merchandise at regular prices and are designed to encourage timely sales are called **product advertising**. Occasionally retailers focus on product but do not specify styles or prices. These advertisements are considered brand-enhancing. Frequently the items chosen are new arrivals.

Promotional Advertising   Advertisements that feature merchandise at sale prices are called **promotional advertising**. Clearance merchandise or goods that were bought as special purchases are considered promotional items. Most retail advertising is promotional in nature.

Institutional Advertising   Advertising designed to convey a positive image of the company or brand, rather than present specific merchandise, is considered **institutional advertising**. Some-

Figure 17.2
Product advertisements for Tiffany illustrate the consistency of the jeweler's branding. Opulent white space indicates the high-end status of this famous retailer.

times this method is called image or brand advertising. Institutional advertisements concentrate on building the reputation of the company by focusing on unique qualities and services, and aim for long-range sales results as opposed to immediate sales. Some advertisements attempt to build an image of fashion leadership. Others promote unique services, position the store as a community leader, or focus on the retailer's stance on social responsibility. Marketing the brick-and-mortar store, online store, or shopping center is as important as advertising specific items. All advertisements are institutional to the extent that they promote company and brand image. A product advertisement for Tiffany & Co. is illustrated in Figure 17.2.

Major Advertising Media

Advertising uses many forms of communication to reach potential customers. Facts and benefits of a product, service, or company are presented to target markets through print media such as newspapers, magazines, direct mail, yellow pages, or flyers. Broadcast media include television and radio. Digital media include Web sites, electronic kiosks, and mobile commerce. Outdoor billboards and transit advertising comprise special media categories.

Across all of these media categories, global advertising expenditures were expected to reach $485.9 billion in 2012. The United States, Japan, and China are the top three advertising markets in the world. It is impressive that four out of the top ten ad markets are the four BRIC countries explained in Chapter 3. In fact, Brazil, Russia, India, and China are expected to account for 33 percent of total global growth by 2014.[1] The advantages and disadvantages of major media are compared next and are summarized in Table 17.1. Direct mail advertising was covered in Chapter 6 and is not detailed in this section.

Newspapers

Historically, the most common medium for retail promotion was newspaper advertising, but media reports have indicated a gradual slowdown in advertising revenue for several years. Total global advertising expenditure on newspapers is expected to decline from $94.6 billion in 2010 to $88.4 billion by 2014. In terms of share of total ad spending by medium, newspapers held 18.7 percent in 2012, second to television's 40.4 percent share. Internet advertising, continuing a growth trend, was a close third with 17.6 percent share.[2]

Did You Know?
Expecting 4.9 percent growth of advertising revenue worldwide, analysts speculated that several events of global consequence would boost figures in 2012: The U.S. presidential election, the Olympic Games in London, the European Football Championships, as well as Japan's recovery from the 2011 earthquake. Time will tell if they were on target. (Source: Leika Kawasaki, "Global Forecast 2012 Q1," Strategic Analytics. February 24, 2012, www.strategic analytics.com/default.aspx?mod=reportabstractviewer &a0=7129.)

Table 17.1 Comparison of Major Media Categories

Advantages	Disadvantages
Newspapers	
• Low cost.	• Quality of reproduction and color not as good as direct mail and magazines.
• Short lead time needed by publisher.	• Wasted circulation possible depending on target market strategy.
• Flexible market coverage.	
• Recall potential.	• Short carryover time.
• Layouts, graphics, and typefaces convey brand image.	• Dependent on immediacy of customer response.
• Immediacy of customer response.	
Magazines	
• Market segmentation used to reach audiences based on lifestyle, gender, age, ethnicity, or interests.	• High cost.
	• Long lead time—usually 2–3 months needed by publisher.
• Long life; high pass-along rate.	• Circulation rates greatly affected by economy.
• National or regional editions available.	
• Top-quality color and graphics.	
Direct Mail	
• Personalized offers possible.	• Moderate lead time needed.
• Long life.	• High costs of printing and mailing.
• Careful targeting avoids wasted circulation.	• Considered "junk" mail by some customers.
• Good reproduction and color.	
• Flexible sizes and types of mail pieces.	
Radio	
• Widespread coverage; ubiquitous medium.	• No visual stimulus.
• Quick and easy to change or adapt message.	• Poor listener recall.
• Immediacy and urgency stressed.	• Need for repeated identification of brand, location, store name, and contact information.
• Low cost to produce.	• Losing share to new media.
• Station formats support market segmentation.	
Television	
• Multidimensional—strong visuals, action, drama, color, sound.	• High total costs for production and air time.
• Glamour and prestige medium.	• Poor viewer recall.
• Large audience.	• Zapping: many viewers change channels when a commercial airs.
• Numerous networks and stations provide market targeting opportunities.	
• Home shopping networks.	
Electronic	
• Lower cost than other media.	• Online sales responsible for less than 10% of all retail sales.
• High socioeconomic markets accessed.	• Web 2.0 and 3.0 capabilities still being perfected.
• Great advances in reach and penetration.	
• Improved graphics, navigation, and search.	• Broadband not available in all geographic areas.
• Growing numbers of Internet users and shoppers.	• Limited sensory capabilities; can't touch, smell, or physically inspect products, or try on apparel.
• Access to international markets.	• Privacy and security issues.

Newspaper advertising remains important to retailers large and small seeking to reach specific target markets. Results of one study showed that people aged 50 and older were more likely to make price comparisons using the newspaper rather than any other medium. However, those under 30 were less than half as likely to use the newspaper to research prices.[3] Although the print version has declined in popularity, online edition readership has increased steadily as readers access news, information, and retail advertising from a variety of traditional and digital sources.

Newspapers offer a variety of editions including daily, weekly, Sunday, and weekend versions, as well as multipage advertising inserts, and they provide many other advantages to retail advertisers. Short lead times allow retailers to submit advertisements close to publication. **Lead time** is the amount of time required between receipt of an advertisement by print, broadcast, or electronic media and its appearance in the respective medium. Although retailers might pay a premium price, the benefits of placing advertisements on short notice are noteworthy. If a late-breaking news story occurs, such as the results of a major sporting event or the Academy Awards telecast, retailers react with appropriate advertisements. If a city is bogged down by heavy snow, rainfall, or heat, retailers can release ads for snowblowers, umbrellas, or air conditioners, respectively. Merchandise test market results are assessed swiftly through newspaper advertising. Retailers tailor messages and request special placement to reach select target markets. For example, sports enthusiasts, entertainment buffs, and home and garden devotees read corresponding newspaper sections regularly. People rank newspapers high in terms of easily finding product information, prices, and money-saving offers.

Some ethnic markets do not display the same demographic patterns or reading habits as mainstream populations. A research study comparing retail advertising in Spanish-language and English-language newspapers showed some significant differences. For example, retailers that advertised in *El Diario,* a Spanish-language newspaper published in New York City, featured products ranging from used clothing to expensive watches. Several advertised furniture and floor coverings, indicating that customers were intent on furnishing and improving their homes. In contrast, other retailers advertised power generators. It was understood that customers usually shipped generators to their homelands, indicating a more transient existence or perhaps the long tradition of supporting family members back home.[4]

Global statistics and trends are insightful when comparing different regions of the world. Changes in newspaper circulation and reading habits are not consistent in all countries. A study by the World Association of Newspapers and News Publishers (WAN-IFRA) illuminated several points:

- Print circulation is increasing in Asia, but decreasing in mature Western markets.
- There are approximately 14,800 newspapers in the world, but the number of newspapers is shrinking, especially those in Eastern Europe, and the free daily newspapers in Europe that were favored by young readers aged 15–24.
- Newspapers typically reach 20 percent more readers per day worldwide than the Internet reaches.
- The new digital business is not the same as the traditional newspaper business. Digital users are only about a third of the print readership for newspapers providing both print and online versions. [5]

When markets with diverse incomes, tastes, lifestyles, or ethnicity are targeted, it is more difficult to judge the effectiveness of newspaper advertising. Another challenge to global retailers is to monitor media habits in the countries they enter.

Magazines

Superior color reproduction and unlimited target marketing opportunities are reasons why magazines are used to reach customers. Magazines have the advantage of reaching specific age and interest groups. Many manufacturers and retailers advertise in women's fashion magazines to reach key markets for apparel and cosmetics.

In a typical fashion magazine such as *Vogue,* more than 70 percent of the pages are advertisements. But over the last few years, advertising revenues in top magazines have declined largely due to burgeoning economic problems. For example, *Vogue*'s advertising revenue was down

Did You Know?
The highest newspaper readership rate in the world is held by Iceland, where 96 percent of the population read a daily newspaper. A close second in the readership race is Japan, with 92 percent readership rate.
(Source: "World Press Trends: Newspapers Still Reach More Then Internet," World Association of Newspapers and News Publishers (WAN-IFRA), October 12, 2011, 3, www.wan-ifra.org.)

26 percent during 2009 while *InStyle* experienced a similar slump at 21 percent. The declines primarily were caused by budget cuts of apparel marketers, resulting in much thinner magazines.[6] By 2011, advertising spending on magazines was generally flat with slow growth anticipated.[7] Although luxury-goods companies including Louis Vuitton Moet Hennessy (LVMH) traditionally have relied on magazine advertising to build their brands, many are shifting some of their budgets from magazines to more-frequently updated online digital advertising.

The use of magazine advertising by retailers was limited in the past. Now, discounters like Target and strong regional department stores like Macy's and The Bon-Ton are turning to magazines to reach lucrative teen markets. Walmart, Dr. Martens, Benetton, DKNY Jeans, and Diane Von Furstenberg are examples of international retailers that have used this medium. Magazines are too expensive for local merchants with limited drawing power. The high costs of ad production and placement make magazines a medium of choice primarily for large retailers. For example, top photographers command $100,000 or more for a 3–5-day fashion shoot.[8] That figure does not include styling, model, production, or media costs. A full-page, full-color advertisement in *Cosmopolitan* runs about $237,000, which might seem steep—but approximately three million copies are sold each month in the United States. To snare a similar page in *Glamour,* which sells 2.3 million copies per month, an advertiser would pay slightly more than $200,000.[9]

Many national magazines and newspapers have editions called split runs that extend regional retailers' advertising budgets. A **split run** is the practice of selling advertising space at reduced prices to regional advertisers. The publisher divides the national circulation into smaller sections, and merchants pay only for the geographic areas specified.

Magazines require long lead times before publication, usually two to three months. This limits retailers' placement of product ads. Either brand or institutional ads are run—or those featuring merchandise that is guaranteed to be in-store at the time the magazine reaches customers.

Radio

Radio is capable of reaching very select markets based on customer preferences in music, talk, or news shows. This medium requires repetition of messages and key information within commercials. The opportunity to use drama verbally to create an intimate relationship with customers makes radio a creative and useful medium for retailers.

Reflecting shifts in media habits and budget reassessment, radio's retail advertising revenues were expected to increase slightly from $32 billion in 2010 to 35.9 billion in 2014; however a decline in share by medium from 7.2 percent to 6.7 percent in the same timeframe was anticipated.[10]

Television

The impact of action, sound, and color is undeniable—television is the medium for retail advertisers that want to maximize exposure for their stores and brands. Buying national network or cable television time is costly. Most people are awestruck when the annual multimillion-dollar, 30-second spot rates for the Super Bowl are announced. Retail industry consolidation has created larger domestic and international companies that have the buying power to advertise via television. Although television was once known for its mass-market appeal, broadcast networks are now adept at segmenting their markets by age, gender, special hobbies, and interests. Because of its international presence, cable network CNN is a good choice for advertisers intent on reaching a global audience.

Retailers targeting a young audience weaned on television have increased their television advertising. Cable networks like MTV and Nickelodeon reach young customers on most every continent. It is not surprising that global manufacturers and retailers use this medium.

It is refreshing to note that even small retailers benefit from television advertising in their local markets. Most cities have local-access cable stations and network affiliates whose rates are not prohibitive. Many encourage retailers to advertise by providing production assistance and offering cost-effective airtime packages.

The big decisions retailers are making involve where, when, and how viewers are watching television programming. It might be on a 52-inch LCD screen, but also via PC, iPhone, tablet, or other yet-named digital devices. Consolidation and ownership changes in the television sector are bound to change the tactics of retail advertisers as new programming and opportunities present themselves.

When federal regulators approved cable communications company Comcast's acquisition of the NBC television network in 2011, the act signified a media milestone. It was the first time a cable company had owned a major network, now called NBC Universal.[11] Speculation is strong that more acquisitions of television networks by unanticipated suitors could occur.

On a related note, advertising revenues increased 11.8 percent for cable TV and decreased 7.6 percent for network TV from 2010 to 2011.[12] Concurrently, cable TV subscriptions declined for the first time in late 2010 as online video grew.[13] Retail promotion planners will be taxed as they allocate funds for visual media.

Digital

The many ways online stores are changing how customers shop and retailers do business were addressed at length in Chapter 7. Reinforcing the importance of the new media, other applications of digital retail advertising are highlighted:

- Justice targets 'tweens and teens using video merchandising for in-store promotions and entertainment. Sears has featured Disney Channel performer Selena Gomez in a series of upbeat videos on its microsite, ArriveLounge.com.
- Demonstration of new garden tools, the qualities and uses of bamboo fiber, or a fashion collection is enhanced by online video and convenient in-store electronic kiosks.
- Technology that enables retailers to send video messages along with promotional messages is being perfected. Earlier attempts were thwarted by aggressive spam filters. The company Goodmail Systems developed a secure video e-mail system for companies to use when customers opt in. One example is Comcast's e-mail fashion newsletter DailyCandy, which has added video segments.[14]
- Kmart filmed a six-episode comedy show called "First Day" in which actors were decked out in Kmart apparel. Geared to teenage girls, the film ran on Facebook and other Web sites during September 2011.[15]
- Three-Dimensional digital images are finding their way into more applications as the technology evolves. Papa John's International used augmented reality to reach pizza customers through an unusual marketing campaign. **Augmented reality (AR)** is the technology behind interactive images that appear like holograms and are accessed through Webcams on enabled sites. Papa John's attached an AR image to its pizza boxes. Customers placed the image in front of a Webcam, then used their keyboards to simulate driving a vintage Camaro on the screen. Discount coupons for pizza were available through further interaction with a billboard in the car animation.[16]

As a means to inform, educate, and entertain, online video and its newest incarnations are used to promote many products and services. This is only the beginning.

Outdoor

Designed to appeal to general audiences, billboards and signs are located along highways, in strategic metro areas near stores, or on stores themselves. Increasingly, shopping centers are the venue of choice for interior billboards. Mall marketers see this as a revenue-generating strategy.

Many companies are using digital billboards and other signage that allows messages to be changed easily and frequently. Walgreen's pharmacy announces new products in this way in Figure 17.3.

Billboards embedded with mobile phone codes are another example of merged media. The car service franchise EZ Lube ran a "One Year of Free Oil Changes" contest. Motorists who text-messaged the short code were then automatically sent a discount coupon for an oil change and entered into the contest.[17]

Inventiveness reigns in the outdoor advertising field. As retail storefronts "went black" due to the recession, advertisers rented their window space for huge product ads. Companies including

Red Bull, Verizon Wireless, and General Motors have used the service, spending $1,000–$8,000 per month, depending on the size of the ad and amount of foot traffic passing the window.[18]

The emphasis has been on major media in this section, but that is not to discount the variety of other promotion vehicles available. Although the popularity of yellow pages print advertising has waned in comparison to other media, it still holds an important place in small business advertising. The move online for Yellowpages.com opened up more competition with Web sites like Google and Superpages.com. Globally, revenues for digital yellow pages are expected to overtake print versions by 2015. By then, 53 percent of yellow pages will be digital, compared with 29 percent in 2011.[19]

Transit

Transit advertising exploits commuters' boredom in order to gain readership. Advertisements are placed in and around transportation terminals and within trains, buses, and taxis. Taxi Grams, positioned in full view of cab riders, are crawling red lights carrying 20-word messages in repeated bursts of advertising. Advertising messages on buses have almost become an art form. They serve as a means to reach international customers and travelers, as seen by the Mango broadside ad on a double-decker London bus in Figure 17.4. Bus stop shelters and benches also provide advertising venues for captive audiences.

Theater advertising has also come of age. The standard popcorn box parade has been supplanted by local retailers, national companies, and military recruitment ads filling the gap between finding your seat and beginning the movie trailers.

The assessment of how each type of promotion can perform most effectively is the next task for retailers. The development of a media mix that is well conceived and executed is crucial.

Media Selection

For retail advertising to generate sales, the message must reach the correct target market. The specific configuration of media selected by an advertiser for a campaign is called the **media mix**. There is no one successful formula for selecting media, because businesses, markets, and customers dif-

Figure 17.4
Transit advertising reaches
a broad spectrum of
customers around the
world. The broadside of a
double-decker London bus
shows branding ingenuity
by Mango.

fer. Media availability and circulation also vary. Some of the questions asked during the decision-making process, and how cooperative advertising extends the budget follow.

Media Decision-Making Process

Questions retailers consider before making media mix decisions include:

- Which medium reaches the greatest number of well-targeted people at the time the retailer wants to reach them?
- Which medium (or combination of media) is most affordable?
- If one medium is not capable of reaching a large share of the market, what other medium will? At what cost?
- Will a greater expenditure in the present media generate a bigger dollar share of the market?
- Will a greater expenditure in additional media in the same market area bring extra business? At what cost?

A sound principle for buying media is to avoid spreading advertising dollars too thin. Making a maximum impression in one medium before considering others is a sound plan. When evaluating each medium, reach and coverage are important considerations. **Reach** is the number of actual readers, listeners, or viewers in an audience. **Coverage** is the geographic area in which advertising messages potentially are seen or heard.

An option for retailers is the media buying service. **Media buying services** are media specialists that buy blocks of advertising time and space on behalf of several businesses. In contrast, an advertising agency media department generally buys time and space to advertise a client's products or store. Media buying services wield considerable clout and make cost-effective media buys for retailers.

Small businesses use a variety of marketing methods. Smaller retailers cannot make extensive media buys but some are very creative. From the Field 17.1 looks at the many ways City Music, a two-store retail business, makes the most of limited promotion funds.

Cooperative Advertising

Supply-chain members sometimes share the costs of advertising with retailers. Among the several benefits to retailers of cooperative advertising are cost savings, the ability to run larger or more frequent advertisements, and the opportunity for more exposure in the marketplace. Disadvantages include

From the Field 17.1 Creative Promotion at City Music

How does a brick-and-mortar, nonfranchised enterprise increase the impact of its limited advertising funds? With information sources shifting from local papers to the worldwide Internet, how can mom-and-pop retailers ensure that their advertising reaches the public in their trading areas? Nancy Rines has been co-owner of City Music for 20 years. Also a vocalist and musician, she shares her experience developing cost-conscious and effective promotions for the business.

City Music LLC is a music lesson and retail musical instrument store with two locations serving two of Boston's northwest bedroom communities (62,000 people, 30–35 percent of households with children under 18). The Leominister store is featured in the figure on the left. City Music's clientele ranges from beginning players to local professional musicians. As people turn to the Web for their news and information, our store feels the added competition of the Web for musical instrument purchases and even music lessons, as illustrated in the figure on the right. To compete, we find that establishing goodwill as a community-based organization with a multilevel promotion helps us target the audience we most want to reach—families with school-aged children.

Enlisting the support of other music-based local businesses, City Music hosts concerts featuring local teen musicians aged 18 and under. These teen bands get to perform for friends and family with expert sound and stage support on a popular professional concert stage. Proceeds from the event are donated to support local public school music programs. Each step of the event preparation brings City Music opportunities to connect with qualified buyers.

The announcement of the concert and a call for participants is the first opportunity to reach our market through community calendars in print and online, posters and invitations to local schools (public, charter, and private), and Web site announcements that stimulate search engine

hits. Applications to participate must be picked up in person, increasing awareness of our locations.

Press releases announcing the bands chosen to perform and participating musicians create a new opportunity to update community calendars with names and event dates. Noteworthy participants inspire newspapers to feature individual groups and performers in articles. Teen musicians enjoy using their own social networks on the Web—MySpace and Facebook pages—to advertise the event. The posting of names and photos creates new stimuli for search engines. Participants are required to appear at the store for photo opportunities and event orientation, reinforcing store location and sponsor awareness.

In the weeks leading up to the event, the supporting businesses willingly publicize their participation and support. The participating teen musicians self-promote the occasion by selling tickets to the performance to friends and family. The venue's 300 seats are generally sold out. Families, proud of their children's efforts, appreciate the safe, supervised program in a professional all-ages venue.

Finally, announcing the total proceeds and presenting the check to the local school music director—ideally at a school music event—creates a newsworthy photo opportunity as well as material to update our Web site.

Each step of the program targets new customers for City Music. By contributing to the local schools, we reach an audience in the schools by offering support as they strain to meet budgets, and open the door for a cooperative relationship as a direct vendor to their music program. The results of our advertising efforts are clear as these young musicians, families and friends, and their schools become the regular customers vital to our business.

By Nancy Rines

the need to comply with vendors' advertising design and placement criteria. At times, a vendor's advertising philosophy may not be in accord with the store's. In addition, securing cooperative agreements, administering accounts, and maintaining standards set forth by vendors is time-consuming.

Arrangements for cooperative advertising are either vertical or horizontal. **Vertical cooperative advertising** is an advertising arrangement by which a manufacturer or other supply chain member agrees to share costs with a retailer. An example of a vertical cooperative promotion involving Walmart and Tyson meat is illustrated in Figure 17.5.

Cooperative agreements are based on a percentage of business—usually around five percent—transacted by a retailer and vendor annually. Retailers use funds from the cooperative account to pay all or part of an advertisement. Agreements vary, but are usually done on a 50-50 share between vendor and store. The manufacturer sometimes supplies materials, such as artwork and advertising copy containing open space for the retailer's name.

Retailers are reimbursed after the advertisements appear in print or are aired. Invoices or documents from the media, such as tearsheets, are required as proof that the advertisements appeared. A **tearsheet** is a page torn from a publication and sent to an advertiser, vendor, or agency to prove that an advertisement has run.

Small merchants are often unaware of the existence of cooperative funds and unaware of the procedure for accessing them. Manufacturers encourage large retailers to use joint advertising, but may not do so with small merchants. Administering programs that involve many small merchants is more costly and provides less media exposure for vendors. The Robinson-Patman Act, however, requires vendors to give the same promotion allowance to all retailers on a proportionate basis. Therefore, if a vendor gives a large department store chain a five percent advertising allowance, all other retailers are entitled to the same arrangements. Retailers benefit because cooperative advertising helps increase their gross margins.

Horizontal cooperative advertising is joint advertising by a group of businesses, usually at the same level of the supply chain, with the objective of increasing traffic or interest in a product or special event. When a ski resort teams with local restaurants and retail shops to promote a big weekend, it is using horizontal cooperative advertising. Shopping centers and downtown merchants' associations sponsor promotions with local businesses. The sidewalk event illustrated in Figure 17.6 drew together downtown retailers, outside vendors, a band, and community theater and art groups to stage a summer sales promotion event.

Figure 17.5
When we notice that a visit by country-western singer Mark Wills is sponsored by Walmart and Tyson, a major supplier, vertical cooperative advertising is at work.

Figure 17.6
Take a sidewalk sale, add outdoor vendors, local artisans, theater groups, and a marching band, and you have a well-attended horizontal cooperative advertising event in Harlingen, the Netherlands.

Measuring Results

Not every advertisement has immediate and measurable impact. How impact is measured is related to whether the advertisement was designed to sell the brand or specific products. Through institutional advertising, a retailer creates and maintains its brand image over the long term. However, the results of institutional advertising are not quantitatively measured. Long-term goals of institutional advertising include:

- Gaining respect for the store from its customers, suppliers, stockholders, and the community.
- Reinforcing the company and its brands in the marketplace.
- Increasing sales and profits over time.

Whether the price featured in a product advertisement is regular or promotional influences customer reaction. Regular product advertising creates and maintains a company's reputation through its merchandise. Response is measured over a period of a week or a season, not necessarily the day after the advertising appears. Sale, clearance, and special purchase advertising are all promotional. Planned for immediate response, promotional advertising is measured the next day or the next week, depending on the length of the event.

Response varies depending on business location, type, time of year, and intensity of campaign. Factors that contribute to the success or failure of a campaign include weather change, the economic climate, or an unexpected occurrence in the news. The announcement of an outbreak of avian flu curtails the best promotions of chicken in Asian supermarkets. In North America, tainted fruits and vegetables made people hesitant to visit supermarket produce departments despite appealing colored flyers. The aversion to buying hamburger that was processed with "pink slime" caused many regular beef customers to alter their shopping and consumption habits despite well-advertised sales. Circumstances like these are considered when measuring advertising results.

Retail Sales Promotion

The list of sales promotion activities is as vast as retailers' imaginations. Promotional techniques change with the retailer, market, competition, and the position of merchandise in the product life cycle. Some retailers offer loyalty programs, gifts, or prizes; others even display messages in the sky to get attention. Most utilize some of the following techniques: special events, coupons, sampling, demonstrations, contests, premiums, and giveaways—online, in-store, through catalogues, and via your cell phone.

Like advertising, sales promotion helps retailers attract and retain customers. Various forms of visual merchandising and advertising pique our attention, but we won't take action unless we feel strongly about the merchandise. This is difficult to achieve when product differentiation is not apparent or when customers are price sensitive. With careful selection and use of promotional activities, sales are stimulated.

Today, little difference exists between sales promotion activities in department stores and those in discount stores or online. A look at several techniques suggests the diversity and ingenuity of retail sales promotion.

Special Events

Fashion shows, art exhibits, parades, marathons, and celebrity appearances generate great enthusiasm. Special events promote the company whether they are held on- or off-site. One of the best-known retailer-sponsored special events is the annual Macy's Thanksgiving Day parade, viewed on television coast to coast by many who have never visited Macy's flagship store in New York City's Herald Square. This parade made Macy's name synonymous with the best in retailing and draws customers to its stores across the country.

Bringing unique entertainment and traffic to shopping centers, special events draw crowds and are considered worthwhile by most retailers' standards. It is difficult, however, to measure direct return on investment.

Couponing

Individuals clip coupons from magazines, newspapers, and direct mail pieces. They print them from Web sites, pick them up at supermarkets, or find them on product packages. A little work

//////////////////////////////////
Cyberscoop

For close to 90 years, Macy's has been holding a retail extravaganza known to the multitudes as the Macy's Thanksgiving Day Parade. For a sample of what goes on behind the scenes to prepare for the event, as well as an assortment of photos and videos from the latest parade, go to: www.macys.com/parade.

achieves price reductions on many specific items. We looked at a few facts and figures regarding couponing and how it affects pricing in Chapter 16. Here we see how it behaves as an element of sales promotion.

Renewed interest surfaced during the recession when people from all walks of life were seen with wads of coupons at supermarket checkouts. Some supermarkets and home improvement centers encourage coupon exchange between customers by providing bins or bulletin boards for this purpose. Most supermarkets have on-site electronic devices that dispense coupons at checkouts based on purchases customers are in the process of making. Receiving a 75-cents-off coupon for kitty litter after purchasing a supply of canned cat food is not unusual.

Many retailers use coupons to stimulate sales on their Web sites. Coldwater Creek and J. Jill enclose coupons with their apparel catalogues for use only at their online stores. Using a paid search campaign, outdoor retailer Cabela's placed coupons on its Web site that were designed to drive customers into the company's stores. The retrieval rate for customers clicking through to obtain coupons from the site was ten percent, and of those who had coupons, 40 percent redeemed them in Cabela's stores. These figures exceeded the predicted retrieval and redemption rates.[20]

To keep customers coming back, the 99 Restaurant chain urges customers to use its Web site for retrieving coupons, reading announcements of special events, and learning of new menu items. It generates special coupons for a free dessert for your birthday once you've registered. Couponing is an established institution that changes with the needs and shopping habits of customers.

Sampling

Placing products in customers' hands for trial use is called **sampling**. Manufacturers of products such as cereal, detergents, and health and beauty aids promote their products by mailing introductory-sized samples to households or packaging them with magazines or newspapers delivered to target customers. Receiving a sample of Quaker cinnamon shredded wheat cereal and accompanying coupon with the Sunday newspaper encourages a trip to the supermarket for more.

Demonstrations

In-store product demonstrations attract potential purchasers. Customers whose senses are aroused in a store by the smell of perfume, taste of pizza, or feel of facial tissues often purchase the item on impulse. Cosmeticians draw interest when demonstrating how to apply new makeup. The smell of nachos being prepared in a warehouse club causes many shoppers to try a package. Trader Joe's has something to offer, whether it's baked beans or a new beverage, every time you visit the store. Nine times out of ten, I'll try, and then buy, whatever they are promoting. Often when these demonstrations are combined with sampling and couponing, customers cannot resist a product they hadn't noticed previously.

Contests, Sweepstakes, and Awards

Contests and sweepstakes are similar in intent, but in a contest the customer must demonstrate some skill in order to win, while participation is all that is required to win a sweepstake. Both are used to attract and keep customers by encouraging participation and additional purchases.

The beauty industry uses honors and awards to promote products. Magazines, trade associations, and retailers themselves devise contests or ask the public to vote on their favorite brands. For example, the trade group Cosmetic Executive Women asked its 4,000 members to evaluate products, and then pare down the field to determine finalists that were voted on by board members. Sephora used an online format for customers to vote for the "Best of Sephora" awards.[21]

Awards are displayed in stores, on the Web, and in magazines, and are a promotional tactic with a high degree of credibility.

Premiums and Giveaways

Desirable items are offered to customers at substantially reduced prices or, in some instances, for free. The idea behind giving premiums is to generate immediate sales. A special-edition toy or trading card that a seven-year-old takes home after lunch is often the deciding factor in selecting one fast food restaurant over another. When both parent and child are happy, repeat business is the result.

Pens, calendars, and T-shirts bearing the names of retailers often are given away to shoppers. Freebie Frisbees are visible reminders of a store, ensuring that sales promotion continues long after the event.

Cosmetic companies consistently use gift-with-purchase techniques. Purchasing a specific dollar amount of product and receiving a reusable cosmetics case full of product samples and full-size lipsticks is a typical incentive. With the purchase of a men's fragrance, the gift is more likely to be a travel or gadget bag.

Many customers time their purchases to coincide with premium offers. Most spend more money than they intended during the promotion.

Publicity

Nonpaid news or editorial comment about ideas, products, services, or stores is called **publicity**. Some retailers hire specialists or use staff publicists to get their names and messages in the public eye. Publicity that is current, credible, and newsworthy is most appropriate to enhance branding. If the story or message is dramatic and has human interest, it is much more likely to be used. The value of nonpaid publicity is priceless when positive, less so when negative.

Public Relations

Promotional activities that enhance or reform retail image, and support charitable foundations or important social causes, are called **public relations**. Goodwill generated by participating in fund-raising activities goes a long way. Donating to medical research aiming to cure devastating diseases helps a worthy cause and positions the retailer as a caring member of the community. For example, Macy's supported the American Heart Association's Go Red For Women movement by offering a sensational red dress designed by Irina Shabayeva, season six's winner of Project Runway. For the Valentine's Day promotion, the dress was offered for $99, with five percent going to the Association to fund education and research on heart disease. But that's not all. Macy's partnered with Facebook to donate $1 to the movement for each special Valentine sent to a loved one.

Public relations work is needed when a retailer announces a store closing, store break-in or accident, or other negative but newsworthy occurrence. The test for a good public relations team is to cover the event with compassion, dignity, truth, and transparency.

Other Promotional Techniques

Other paid forms of promotion include endorsement advertising, slotting fees, and product placement. Viral marketing and guerilla tactics are contemporary versions of word-of-mouth advertising that lend excitement and buzz to a campaign. All elicit mixed emotions from consumers and provide benefits to retailers.

Celebrity Endorsement

For many customers, identifying with a favorite sports hero, musician, actor, or model increases the propensity to purchase. Since many circumstances and motivations affect consumer behavior, it is difficult to gauge the effectiveness of celebrity endorsement advertising. If performer Miley Cyrus lends her name to a line of apparel, tennis ace Venus Williams touts Reebok, or golfer Tiger Woods extols the virtues of Nike, Gillette, and Gatorade, does it translate to more sales for the retailers that carry these brands?

Conversely, if that person behaves in his or her public life in a way that detracts from the manufacturer's or retailer's brand image, will it be detrimental to the advertising campaign? Two examples provide insight. In late 2009, Tiger Woods' domestic discord and subsequent traffic accident made headlines. Speculation on whether his lucrative endorsement contracts would be jeopardized fueled media coverage. As the incident unfolded, Gatorade cut Woods' television commercials and announced that it was discontinuing the beverage he endorsed—although the company intimated that the decision was made well before his personal problems surfaced.[22]

When Olympic medal winner Michael Phelps was photographed smoking marijuana—an action that deviated from his image as an all-American athlete—his endorsements with many sporting goods companies and consumer products were questioned. Cereal and snack manufacturer Kellogg's concurred that his behavior did not befit the company's brand image and cancelled his

Figure 17.7
Celebrity visits add excitement to department store promotions and generate favorable publicity. Tom Ford promoted his new fragrance, Bois Marocain, at Selfridges in London.

sponsorship contract.[23] While the behavior of celebrities affects their status as role models, many people inside and outside the industry believe that the emphasis should be on the individual's performance as an athlete, actor, designer, or supermodel, and not on his or her personal life.

Most retailers and manufacturers believe that endorsement works and pay large sums per advertisement to celebrities that lend their image to products. Some retailers believe that the success of celebrity endorsement depends on the degree to which customers relate to the celebrity. To celebrate the launch of a new fragrance that coincided with Selfridges' 100th anniversary, designer Tom Ford appeared at the store to sign autographs and have photos taken with customers. Drawing in a diverse London crowd ranging from preteens and college students to older women, the event, illustrated in Figure 17.7, was deemed a success.

Pay-to-Play Tactics

The supermarket industry historically has charged manufacturers **slotting fees** for select shelf locations. This concept has spread to other retail institutions. For example, music stores charge distributors listening-post fees to secure placement on the devices for CDs they want to promote. Music ownership and listening habits are changing rapidly as iTunes and Spotify refine their cloud-based music streaming. Pay-to-play tactics will change as well.

Advertising and sales promotion take various shapes and forms, but all are carefully planned and evaluated.

Product Placement

In addition to print, broadcast, and electronic media, manufacturers and retailers are using product placement as a way to increase brand exposure. A Dunkin' Donuts coffee cup, American Eagle T-shirt, or BMW automobile spotted in films or television shows are examples.

In a ranking of prime-time programs that have the most product placements, several TV shows had hundreds in 2011. The top three shows, their networks, the number of episodes and occurrences, and key products were:

1. *American Idol*; FOX; 39, 577; Coke, AT&T wireless phones.
2. *The Biggest Loser*; NBC; 34, 533; Subway, 24-Hour Fitness Gyms.
3. *Celebrity Apprentice*; NBC; 391; Camping World, Australian Gold's brand.[24]

Cyberscoop
To check out the top ten major TV network shows that ruled the product placement promotion game in 2011, Google: "Primetime Shows with the Most Product Placement." Explore the content and learn who the major advertisers are. Nielsen Research Group compiles this list annually.

Product placement grew in popularity as viewers' inclination to skip commercials—aided by digital video recorders—became more common. Advertisers believe that product placement offsets losses from TV commercial zapping, but government and consumer organizations support full disclosure of placements as paid forms of advertising.

The range of companies using product placement for promotional purposes is diverse. We see product placement informally on YouTube and wonder: what's next?

Viral and Guerilla Marketing

Word-of-mouth is a powerful promotional tool when it occurs one-on-one. But when a company multiplies this method of contact by hundreds or thousands of recipients, it is using viral marketing. **Viral marketing** uses customers to generate "buzz" to help sell a product. Using on-the-street delivery, online social networks, e-mail, video sharing, and customer panels to spread the word about a company, brand, or retailer is effective. Crank this tactic up a few levels, add exuberance, outrageousness, and the suggestion of spontaneity, and you have guerilla marketing. Creative street promotions and online events implemented by hired groups of outgoing people to raise brand awareness are considered **guerilla marketing**.

Sometimes viral and guerilla marketing gurus enhance the buzz by giving away free samples at fairs, in schools, at parks, or in highly visible locations like New York City's Times Square. In other circumstances, products are demonstrated and tied into online social networking groups. When the company Batter Blaster introduced its organic pancake and waffle batter—which is packaged in an aerosol can—customers responded by blogging and posting YouTube videos of the product in use. Some fans created a Facebook group called "The Church of Batter Blaster."[25] Slightly irreverent, irrelevant, or both, extreme measures of word-of-mouth advertising are effective promotional tools because they are easily remembered and highly believable.

Personal Selling

Employees who work with customers individually, or communicate with them on the phone or online, greatly affect retail business. We expect managers, sales associates, gift-wrap clerks, door greeters, personal shoppers, and customer service experts to extend gracious service to customers. Retailers hope customers that are satisfied will return again and again.

Personal selling is viewed as both a service and a form of sales promotion. Good salespeople expedite sales as they direct their attention to shoppers who might become loyal customers. Customer service bridges the gap between the immediate sale and long-term satisfaction.

The selling floor is the key to productivity and profit for retailers that consider personal selling part of their promotional mix. As you learned in Chapter 13, retailers plan for and compensate employees with the same gusto they use to manage other retail functions. These details are not reiterated here; instead, the steps of a sale, training of sales associates, and qualities attributed to effective sales personnel are covered.

Steps in the Selling Process

The seven steps in the retail selling process are: (1) customer approach, (2) need determination, (3) presentation of merchandise, (4) overcoming objections, (5) closing the sale, (6) suggestion selling, and (7) post-sale follow-up.

1. *Customer approach.* Approaches vary, but most retailers agree that when customers enter a store or department they should be recognized. In the past, when a salesperson asked, "May I help you?" customers automatically responded, "No, I'm just looking." It was considered pushy and offensive to some customers if a salesperson continued to pursue the question. A more contemporary approach is a greeting: "Hello, how are you today?" or "Good morning, please look around, I'm here to help you if you have any questions." Regardless of the exact words, the greeting is meant to make customers feel welcome and show a friendly interest in being of service. Promptness counts when approaching customers, even if only to indicate awareness of their presence. Nothing is more discouraging to retailers and customers than when customers wait in vain and end up as walkout statistics.

2. *Need determination.* To determine customers' needs, the salesperson needs an understanding of human behavior. Underlying reasons may exist for the purchase of a Razor scooter. Is one being considered as an alternative urban transportation, a way to revisit childhood memory, or a gift for a favorite child? Even direct questions may not bring out the real reasons. A combination of observation and questions, plus the ability to empathize, helps determine customers' true needs.

3. *Merchandise presentation.* Faced with too many items to choose from, many customers become overwhelmed. If a decision is not made from three products presented, removing one item that appears less desirable to the customer may help bring the sale to closure. Salespeople who make it easy for customers to make decisions are more effective.

4. *Overcoming objections.* Most customers have some sales resistance and ask questions that demand answers before they agree to purchase. Others have genuine objections. Salespeople with in-depth product knowledge deal with these more easily than with ambiguous objections such as "I'm not sure my spouse will like it" or "I really like it, but I don't feel like trying it on." These are only excuses. Objections can be met head-on and cast aside if the salesperson:

   - Does not argue with the customer.
   - Anticipates objections when presenting the merchandise and addresses them before they are raised.
   - Shows respect for customers' opinions.
   - Offers tactful answers and gently suggests alternatives.
   - Does not belittle the competition.

5. *Closing the sale.* Some salespeople know instinctively when the time is right to conclude a transaction. They realize that when a customer keeps coming back to the same item, it is time to ask: "Will you charge this, or do you prefer to use your debit card today?" Salespeople know that once objections are overcome, it is time to close. Directing customers to this conclusion by physical maneuvers such as moving toward the checkout station or even starting to wrap the merchandise is acceptable. Talking too long after an appropriate closure point can delay or lose the sale. If the steps in selling are followed, the closing happens naturally. The more experience a person has, the easier this becomes.

6. *Suggestion selling.* A sale does not always end with the purchase of the one item the customer has originally requested. Customers are led into multiple purchases by creative promotions and personal selling. For instance, before completing the transaction, a salesperson usually suggests a few extra ink cartridges to go with a new printer. All retailers are interested in increasing sales volume in all classifications, yet many create barriers to multiple sales through their organizational structure and store layout. When a salesperson cannot cross department lines in order to add athletic footwear or hand weights to a workout outfit, it is unfortunate. Momentum is lost if merchandise is not readily available.

   An obvious way of practicing suggestion selling in apparel stores is to bring additional merchandise into the fitting room. Busy shoppers with limited time not only appreciate suggestion selling, they expect it.

7. *Post-sale follow-up.* Even though sales associates devote a great deal of time to the selling process, all customers do not make a purchase. Regardless of the outcome, if the customers are left with a feeling of goodwill they are likely to return to the store. The memory of a smile and a friendly good-bye is often the reason. Sincerity and a pleasant manner are prerequisites for success in selling. This is especially true at the conclusion of a sale. Some upscale stores follow up a sale with a personal note to the customer. Other retailers continue the customer relationship and follow up long after the sale was closed. From the Field 17.2 chronicles the experience of a shopper who, over a 14-year period, had problems with a product that were eventually—and graciously—resolved.

Training the Sales Force

Salespeople are expected to exert a positive influence on the behavior of customers. In many retail establishments, titles such as sales associate, sales consultant, or fashion representative are given to those who sell. Job titles help explain role, responsibilities, or status, but title alone does not

From the Field 17.2   There's Gold in Customer Service

Supposedly when we have a bad experience with a retailer, we tell a dozen of our friends, family, and associates; when we have a good experience, we tell far fewer individuals. I'd like to change that ratio by telling a few thousand readers about the amazing customer service I've received from jewelry retailer A.G.A. Correa & Son over a period of 14 years.

The business was founded in 1968 and operates out of an unpretentious, quintessential cottage in Edgecomb, Maine, that is illustrated in the figure on the left. Through its catalog and Web site (www.agacorrea.com) it reaches enthusiasts of distinctive hand-braided gold jewelry worldwide.

In a recent catalog, third-generation proprietor Andy Correa mentioned that the vast economic and lifestyle changes happening around the globe had affected business. In response to customer requests for more sterling silver jewelry, the company is producing silver designs that were popular 40 years ago. In his introductory piece, Andy quoted designer Coco Chanel who once said, "Fashion fades, only style remains the same." A.G.A. Correa jewelry is timeless and that is one of the reasons my husband and I selected wedding bands from the company in 1996.

We purchased matching double-strand 18-karat gold Turk's-head rings from the catalog. After some collaboration on size and shipping the rings arrived, beautifully packaged, in time for our wedding. We were pleased with the results and to this day receive many compliments on our rings.

Approximately four years into our marriage, I noticed that one of the gold strands on mine had broken, so I called Correa and told them of my plight. I mailed the ring to Maine and within days I received the repaired ring back intact and shinning like new. The shipping invoice read, "Repair made. No charge." Several years later a similar problem occurred and the ring went back to Maine with a note. Again, it was returned expediently with the same notation. In 2009, sure enough, my ring had to make the trip for repairs once again. I couldn't understand why the ring had broken. In my cover letter I noted that although it is a fragile-looking

piece it should withstand normal wear and that I am careful with all of my jewelry. I asked if it could possibly be a flaw in the gold. I joked that my husband and I were debating whether our marriage at least would outlive my ring. As a side point, he has had no problems with his in all this time.

The ring arrived back 2 days later, only it wasn't my ring. It was a brand new one. The handwritten note said, "We are so sorry. This should never have happened." Sure enough the company stood by its product. I gasped when I saw the invoice. It read, "Ring replaced. Invoice value, $940. No charge."

I wrote and thanked the company for services far above the call of duty and asked if I might include this story in my textbook. Andy called and said they would be delighted as long as anything in my letter to them could be used in their publicity. Talk about mutually beneficial dealings.

A photo of a catalog cover featuring a few precious pieces of jewelry is illustrated in the figure on the right. Remember that customer service is not a one-time affair; building lifelong value is the mission of the best retailers. I'm saving up for my matching earrings!

By Lynda Rose Poloian

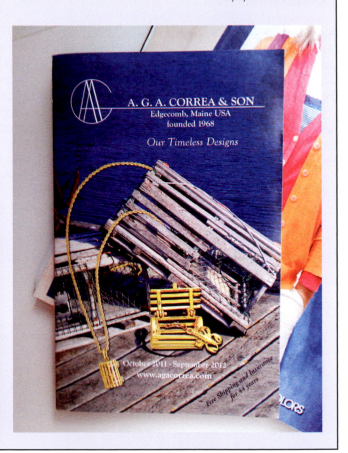

make an expert salesperson. The key is good training that looks beyond the basics. To the customer, salespeople *are* the store.

Researchers from Michigan State University noted the positive correlation between the training and performance of new sales associates. Results of their study indicated that higher levels of learning led to better performance on the selling floor.[26]

Profile of a Retail Salesperson

It's important for the salesperson's appearance, product knowledge, and selling techniques to match customers' expectations. One trait common to all successful salespeople is enthusiasm for the company and its merchandise. Two sales associates at Abercrombie & Fitch, shown in Figure 17.8, project an impression congruous with the company's merchandise and image.

Successful salespeople earn an excellent living. Those who serve regular customers well call or e-mail them when new merchandise arrives, check on items not in stock and order them online, make personal deliveries when appropriate, and help family or friends select gifts.

Selling is a very rewarding job, which is why some people make sales their career. Others see it as the first step to becoming a buyer or merchandise manager. Still others aspire to open their own businesses. What better way is there to learn the intricacies of a particular market than to sell to it?

Seeing retail customers' reactions to merchandise firsthand, some sales associates take their experience to other firms in the supply chain. Many work for sales representatives or in manufacturers' showrooms. When sitting on the other side of the counter, speaking to retail buyers, they speak with authority.

Sales associates are on the front line of customer service. They are much more than a conduit to a checkout terminal. Qualities of an ideal retail salesperson are listed in Table 17.2.

Figure 17.8
Sales associates are carefully chosen by Abercrombie & Fitch to be compatible with the company's merchandise and image.
Courtesy of Joseph Hancock.

Customer Relationship Management

Customer relationship management has grown in importance in the last two decades. The customer-centric attitude of retailers has increased respect not only for customer service, but for all activities that are undertaken to identify, satisfy, and retain customers. Customer relationship management (CRM) was introduced in Chapter 3, which stressed the importance of building a

---

Table 17.2 Qualities of an Ideal Salesperson

- High level of product knowledge that is constantly updated.
- Enthusiasm for the selling process and the products and services being sold.
- Excellent oral communication skills, including the knowledge of when to talk and when to listen.
- Good business etiquette, including prompt, friendly attention to customers.
- Positive attitude and the ability to handle rejection.
- Adaptable to diverse customer types.
- Credible, sincere attitude; high ethical standards.
- Appropriate appearance; wardrobe compatible with target market.
- Respectful, responsible, and reliable professional behavior toward co-workers.

database of information about customers. Providing customer-oriented programs generates return on investment for the retailer and serves long-term goals of keeping loyal customers. Customer service is a big part of this initiative.

Customer Services
Service retailing was introduced in Chapter 1. You will recall that some pure services are also customer services because of their inextricable involvement with merchandise in brick-and-mortar as well as online stores.

Several types of customer services that relate to retail marketing initiatives are examined in this context. Retailers deliver services that:

- Gain knowledge about their customers so that they are better served.
- Enhance their merchandise presentation.
- Promote their brand.
- Expedite the selling process.
- Facilitate fulfillment.
- Precipitate return visits by customers.

To meet the increasing demands of customers, retailers offer a wide variety of services. An appliance retailer that services products in-store and maintains high standards can succeed despite the lower prices on products at a nearby discount store that does not provide repair services. Some retailers offer personal-shopping services or a high degree of customer counseling and interaction. Astute online stores think beyond basic selling skills and delivery of amenities to work with customers effectively through e-mail and chat. All realize the necessity of including customer service as a promotional technique.

Customer Service Goals
Retailers provide customers many value-added services that serve common goals. They may choose to:

- *Embellish services.* Retailers that provide body-scanning technology to help customers get a better fit while shopping for apparel online take that extra step to expedite a sale and ensure customer satisfaction. Offering new credit arrangements to customers who would rather not defer purchases, or delivering a new car to a customer at home, are examples of extended services that go beyond simple product purchases.
- *Increase convenience.* Examples include in-store restaurants and banks, and full-service photo kiosks. Drive-up food service and prescription windows are services that ease customers' hectic lifestyles. Pet daycare services that pick up and deliver companion animals back home are growing in popularity because they provide more convenience than other daycare companies that don't offer transportation.
- *Enhance image.* Some retailers create a competitive advantage by offering an array of outstanding services. In contrast, other stores might intentionally offer few services if self-service and low prices foster the desired image. Cabela's, the outdoor enthusiasts' store, offers many innovative customer activities. The stores feature dioramas of animals, aquariums, a gun museum, and even video games to occupy the time of young people who tire of shopping. A game kiosk is illustrated in Figure 17.9.

With goals in mind, retailers consider other factors: type and size of store, location, type of goods and services sold, service levels of competitors, and financial resources. Economic conditions also affect the type and extent of services rendered. Credit programs are essential to retail services—whether the economic outlook is robust or challenging.

Credit Programs
Most all retailers offer the convenience of cashless shopping and deferred payments—that is, credit. Credit is a way of life for people, and retailers need only decide what types to offer. Offering credit is a valuable aid to both retailers and customers.

Types of Credit Plans

Three types of basic credit plans are:

1. *Regular or open account.* This plan allows customers who hold a store's own charge card to buy merchandise from that retailer and to pay within a specific time period without charges or interest. Usually this is within 30 days of the billing date. Some retailers extend the due date to 60 or 90 days to promote special events or identify a competitive advantage. Beyond the due date, a finance charge is assessed if the balance is not paid in full. Retailers generally reduce both credit costs and risks by limiting open accounts to customers with established records of good credit.

2. *Installment credit.* Installment credit is used to buy large-ticket items such as computers, automobiles, furniture, and appliances. The installment credit plan lets consumers pay the total purchase price plus interest charges in equal installment payments over a specified period, usually monthly. Retailers sometimes request down payments on installment purchases, but rather than lose a sale, some ask for none. Installment credit agreements are legal contracts between retailers and customers. Installment credit plans administered by third-party financial institutions are common in the retail industry.

3. *Revolving credit.* Probably the most frequently used account, revolving credit incorporates features of the regular account and the installment plan. Several variations of revolving credit plans are used but the most common is the option term plan, which provides customers with two payment options. Customers either pay the full amount of the bill before the due date to avoid finance charges, or they make a minimum payment and are assessed finance charges on the unpaid balance. Customers are assigned credit limits and can make purchases up to this limit as long as they continue to pay an agreed-upon minimum payment each month.

Types of Credit Cards

Different forms of credit cards include:

- *Universal credit cards.* These include bank cards such as Visa or MasterCard, and travel and entertainment cards such as American Express.
- *In-house charge cards.* These bear the retailer's name and are handled by store credit departments or third-party firms. Increasingly, retail companies are offering Visa or MasterCard to their customers, co-branded with the store name. Costco, for example, co-brands with American Express; Sears co-brands with MasterCard.
- *Business-sponsored credit cards.* Gasoline company- or airline-sponsored credit cards are used routinely. Others are backed by university alumni organizations or other special-interest groups. Most are managed by third-party financial firms.

Figure 17.9
Computer gamers can have some fun at the entertainment kiosk in Cabela's while the rest of the family shops. Outdoor enthusiasts find services, displays, and exhibits that keep the excitement level high in the store.

The uses and abuses of credit are an evolving retail saga. Retailers closely monitor outstanding consumer debt figures, since the dynamics of this economic measure affect sales. During the recession, outstanding consumer debt shrank and savings rates grew, constraining the cash flow from consumers to retailers and slowing sales considerably during this period.

Imaginative ways to obtain and use credit are available online. Shopping sites geared to teenagers engage parents to establish credit limits for their children. Using their own credit cards, parents set up accounts with pre-established balances for their teenagers. Once assigned passwords, teens can shop on the sites. Parents monitor balances using their own passwords.

As an alternative to credit, Macy's offers ReadyCARDS, which offer the same loyalty benefits as Macy's in-store Star Rewards cards, through kiosks in its stores. Prepaid cards bearing the Master-Card brand were introduced in several Macy's stores in 2009.[27]

Practices like these encourage customers who are ineligible for regular credit cards to participate in the retail experience.

Common Retail Services

Many retailers offer gift-wrapping, bridal and other gift registries, alterations, delivery, and rest areas in the store. Some offer amenities like valet parking, coat checking, or complimentary refreshments. Others provide necessities such as strollers and wheelchairs. Some typical customer services include:

- *Delivery.* Delivery methods and availability depend on the market, the merchandise, the distribution practices of the retailer, and the mode of transportation used by the customer. Customers who shop in an urban flagship store and use public transportation cannot easily take a new microwave oven home with them. Those who drive to a nearby regional mall and buy the same microwave oven in one of the company's branch stores can readily transport the product. The fact that not all customers require delivery becomes a major determinant when retailers make a decision concerning the extent of their delivery services. Stores that sell major appliances and furniture offer delivery, as must catalogue and online merchants. Few retailers offer free delivery unless it is used as an occasional special promotion. Delivery and return policies of catalogue and Web-based retailers are more liberal in this respect. During the holiday season, most online retailers and many catalogue retailers offer free shipping, and during the recession, many increased their offers of free shipping and express delivery as a way of spurring sales.
- *Alterations and repairs.* Alterations to apparel are offered as a supplement to sales or as revenue-generating services by many retailers. Some upscale stores offer free alterations if the item is from a designer department. Retailers usually charge for repairs of durable merchandise they have sold, such as home electronics and computers, unless products are under warranty by manufacturers. Repair service is completed in-store or done by independent firms. The alterations room at a Saks Fifth Avenue store is illustrated in Figure 17.10.
- *Returns/Complaints.* All retailers have a system for handling customer complaints and returned merchandise. How a retailer handles customers' complaints or returns is more important to the customer than the solution itself. Willingness to listen and help goes a long way in retaining the goodwill of distressed customers. Some companies establish corrective action teams that are empowered to cut through red tape to reach solutions to customer problems in a rapid, positive manner.

According to several consumer behavior studies, people who have had a particularly good retail experience will tell three or four people. People who have had a particularly horrible experience will tell many more. Despite these tendencies, more customers actually leave a store's patronage due to indifference than outright poor treatment.

Retailers overcome this ennui by responding to customer needs in a variety of ways. They institute suggestion boxes, feedback cards, online chat, and Twitter options. Training associates in human-relations skills and initiating customer advisory panels also are helpful. Retailers use

Figure 17.10
There is more than meets the eye for customers that expect and receive top-shelf service from Saks Fifth Avenue. The alterations department builds brand image behind the scenes, through flawless tailoring and service.

hotlines and interactive Web sites to their advantage. To encourage flexibility, employees are cross-trained: when a need arises, they are able to pitch in and never say, "It's not my department." Managers also lead by example if they too help out on the selling floor when customers have particularly urgent requests or problems. The Home Depot manager in Figure 17.11 exudes enthusiasm for his position.

Promovera: Where Do We Go From Here?

To maintain and grow their markets, retailers recognize and serve the most important aspect of their business—their customers. Retailing during the 21st century is characterized as much by the provision of services as by the sale of products.

Other trends change the types and intensity of media retailers use to communicate with customers. We are bombarded with promotional messages, news, and information from traditional media as well as online social networking sites. Our expressed need to be closely connected to one another surely helps retail sales. Ideas about life and products are shared universally with the blink of a cursor or touch of an iPhone. Consumer-generated content is changing the face of advertising: blogs, viral marketing, and YouTube "commercials" are encouraged and valued by viewers everywhere, even if quality—and perhaps good taste—are sometimes lacking. Never let it be said that marketers force us to buy; we're doing that to and for each other.

Competitive advantages are gained by technological measures, but profitable sales also depend on effective customer relationship management. Service that is delivered in a prompt, competent, and caring manner is appreciated worldwide. That aspect of retailing should never change.

Figure 17.11
When the manager of Home Depot steps in to assist a shopper or backed-up cashier and does it with a smile, you know you are seeing customer service at its best.

Summary

The primary purpose of retail promotion is to sell something: brands, merchandise, services, or the store as a wonderful place to shop. The retail promotional mix consists of (1) advertising, (2) sales promotion, (3) direct mail, (4) publicity, (5) public relations, (6) personal selling, and (7) customer services.

Internal promotion tools include methods of communication used inside the store. External promotion methods entice customers into the store. Retail advertising differs from national and trade advertising, although all are valuable to retailers and other supply-chain members. Two broad classifications of advertising are product and institutional.

Retailers formulate promotion plans and budgets to return a projected sales volume for the money invested. Budgets are established on the basis of the unit-of-sales method, the percentage-of-sales method, or the objective-and-task method. Retailers measure promotion results.

The media mix is the unique combination of promotional vehicles used by retailers. Major media categories include print, broadcast, and digital. Cooperative advertising is vertical or horizontal. Both methods imply strong relationships between supply chain members.

Sales promotion activities depend to a great extent on target market, type of company or service, merchandise, and the competition. They include a variety of activities such as special events, couponing, sampling, demonstrations, contests, sweepstakes, giveaways, and premiums.

Personal selling is an important form of promotion in many retail stores. Salespeople who are adequately trained in the seven steps of the selling process are the most effective.

Customer relationship management involves all activities that lead to the total satisfaction of customers. Customer service is one way retailers provide necessary interaction with their customers. Customer services include the availability of credit plans, handling returns, and resolving complaints. Valet parking, child-care facilities, bridal and gift registries, and personal-shopping services are some of the special customer services that retailers offer. Included in the income-producing category are alterations, shoe and jewelry repair, fur storage, gift-wrapping, and on-premises restaurants, beauty salons, and banking. The many faces of retail promotion are changing, but one thing is certain: the top retailers advocate effective customer-centric programs. Promovera.

Key Terms

Augmented reality (AR)	Promotional advertising
Coverage	Promotional mix
External promotion	Publicity
Guerilla marketing	Public relations
Horizontal cooperative advertising	Reach
Institutional advertising	Retail advertising
Internal promotion	Sampling
Lead time	Slotting fees
Magalog	Split run
Media	Tearsheet
Media buying service	Trade advertising
Media mix	Vertical cooperative advertising
National advertising	Viral marketing
Product advertising	

Questions for Review and Discussion

1. Is sales the only objective of retail promotion? Discuss this in your own context of shopping, selling, browsing, or "just looking."
2. Describe the three major promotion budgeting methods. Which type works best? Why?
3. What is advertising and how does it differ from other types of promotion? How does retail advertising differ from national and trade advertising?
4. In what circumstances are institutional advertising, regular product advertising, and promotional product advertising used? Give examples of each from print, broadcast, online, or other sources.

5. What is meant by the term *media mix*? What are the choices available to a retailer? How does a retailer determine which medium will be emphasized?

6. What is the difference between vertical and horizontal cooperative advertising? Bring examples of each to class for your discussion.

7. How does negative publicity affect celebrity endorsement of products and services? Do you believe celebrities should be judged on the basis of their personal lifestyles as well as their professional performance? Does negative publicity affect your retail purchasing habits?

8. What five qualities should the ideal retail salesperson possess? Which one is most significant to you?

9. Identify the seven steps in the retail selling process. Which stage is most crucial to the successful completion of a sale? Why?

10. How does customer service affect the performance of successful retail companies? Which aspects of customer service are most important to you as a customer? Justify your choices.

Endnotes

1. "Quadrennial Events to Help Ad Market Grow in 2012 Despite Economic Troubles," ZenithOptimedia, December 5, 2011, 2–3. http:// zenithoptimedia.blogspot.com/2011/12/quarrennial-events-to-help-ad-market-.html.

2. Ibid, 6.

3. "Consumers Comparison Shop Using a Variety of Channels," comScore. November 11, 2012, www.com scoredatamine.com/2011/11/consumers-comparison-shop-using-a-variety-of-channels. (Source: Survey results, *Buy Down Study, 2011*, Graph: "Methods Used For Price Comparison: % of Respondents).

4. Marilyn Lavin, "Retail Advertising in the Spanish-Language Press: Evidence from El Diario/La Prensa," American Collegiate Retailing Association Conference, New York. January, 1994,10.

5. "World Press Trends: Newspapers Still Reach More Than Internet," World Association of Newspapers and News Publishers (WAN_IFTA), October 12, 2011, 1, 3, www.wan-ifra.org/print/press-releases/2011/10/12/world-press-trends-newspapers-still-reach-more-than-internet.

6. Emily Steel, "Thick Fashion Magazines Are So Last Year," *Wall Street Journal*, August 17, 2009, B1.

7. Suzanne Vranica, "Agencies Brace for Slowdown," *Wall Street Journal*, September 12, 2011, B4.

8. Amy Wicks, "Photographer's Ad Game," *Women's Wear Daily*, November 2, 2007, 10.

9. "Circulation Averages for All ABC Magazines 2010," The Association of Magazine Media, www.magazine.org/ASSETS/27160E54028546CABBEE508C1EEA2BED/2010FYALLCIRC.xls. (Source: Audit Bureau of Circulation.) Bobbye Alley. "The Average Cost of Advertising in a Fashion Magazine," EHow.com, accessed April 8, 2012, www.ehow.com/print/info_10016643_average-cost-advertising-fashion-magazine.html.

10. "Quadrennial Events to Help Ad Market Grow in 2012 Despite Economic Troubles," ZenithOptimedia, December 5, 2011, 6, http:// zenithoptimedia.blogspot.com/2011/12/quarrennial-events-to-help-ad-market-.html.

11. Cecilia Kang, "Federal Regulators Approve Comcast's Acquisition of NBC Universal, With Asterisks," *Washington Post*, January 18, 2011, 1, www.washingtonpost.com/wp-dyn/content/article/2011/01/18/AR 2011011806440_pf.html.

12. "Kantar Media Reports U.S. Advertising Expenditures Increased 3.2 % in the First Half of 2011," *Direct Marketing Newswire*, September 30, 2011, 2, http://mediadecoder.blogs.nytimes.com/2011/09/30/a-bright-forecast-for-direct-marketing/?pagemode=print.

13. Cecilia Kang, "Federal Regulators Approve Comcast's Acquisition of NBC Universal, With Asterisks," *Washington Post*, January 18, 2011, 1, www.washingtonpost.com/wp-dyn/content/article/2011/01/18/AR 2011011806440_pf.html.

14. Emily Steel, "Video Gets Entrée Into Email," *Wall Street Journal*, April 2, 2009, B6.

15. Sam Schechner and Lauren A.E. Schuker, "Lights, Camera, Advertisements," *Wall Street Journal*, September 14, 2011, A1, A14.

16. Suzanne Vranica, "Madison Avenue Flirts With 3-D," *Wall Street Journal*, May 26, 2009, B10.

17. Dianna Dilworth, "Billboards Come to Life by Adding Mobile," *DMNEWS*, August 17, 2009, 10.

18. Kris Hudson, "This Space for Rent—to Advertisers, if Not Retail Tenants," *Wall Street Journal*, October 22, 2008, B4.

19. "Global Yellow Pages: Digital Revenues Overtake Print by 2015," Print in the Mix, December 6, 2011, http://printinthemix.com/Fastfacts/Show/514. (Source: BIA/Kelsey, *BIA/Kelsey Estimates 2011 Global Yellow Pages Revenues at 23.4 Billion*, December 6, 2011.)

20. "Cabela's Bags In-Store Traffic With Online Coupons," *Internet Retailer*, May 5, 2009, www.internetretailer.com/printArticle.asp?id=30337.

21. Ellen Byron, "Awards Promote Beauty Contest," *Wall Street Journal*, Media and Marketing, March 4, 2008, B4.

22. Corey Dade and Emily Steel, "PepsiCo Drops Tiger Drink," *Wall Street Journal*, December 8, 2009, B1.

23. Reed Albergotti, David Biderman, and Dana Mattioli, "Woods Aims to Stem Damage," *Wall Street Journal*, December 3, 2009, A3.

24. "Primetime Shows with the Most Product Placement in 2011," CNBC.com, January 5, 2012, www.cnbc.com/id/45884892/Primetime_Shows_with_the_Most_Product_Placement. (Source: Nielsen Media Research.)

25. Raymund Flandez, "Entrepreneurs Strive to Turn Buzz Into Loyalty," *Wall Street Journal*, July 21, 2009, B4.

26. Nettavia D. Curry and Linda K. Good, "Factors Influencing Training Effectiveness for New Retail Sales Associates," American Collegiate Retailing Association Conference. Detroit. April, 1994, 12.

27. Jacob Bennett, "Macy's Kiosks Issue Prepaid Cards as Alternative to Credit," *Kiosk Marketplace*, March 17, 2009, www.kioskmarketplace.com/article.php?id=21911.

Chapter 18

Monitoring the Supply Chain

Learning Objectives

After completing this chapter you should be able to:

- Describe the three main areas of the supply chain and the activities that occur in each.
- State several reasons for the formation of strategic partnerships between retailers and other supply chain members.
- Detail the components of an efficient physical distribution system.
- Relate how supply chain members work together using technology-based systems.
- Determine the impact of radio frequency identification (RFID) on the supply chain.
- Evaluate different types of inventory control methods and shrinkage deterrence systems.

Figure 18.1
This DHL Global fulfillment center in Germany is equipped to move parcels expediently and safely. The movement of goods from distribution centers to transportation carriers is an important aspect of supply chain management.

Thirty years ago, it took retailers 30 days to get merchandise from domestic manufacturers onto their selling floors. Today, it takes about 30 hours, and the manufacturers are all over the world. Supply chain efficiencies and strategic partnerships powered by information technology made this possible. The supply chain was introduced in Chapter 1. An industry-wide program referred to as CPFR forms the backbone of distribution practices. **Collaborative planning, forecasting, and replenishment (CPFR)** is an initiative to develop distribution efficiencies throughout the supply chain. CPFR encompasses several aspects of quick response—getting products on the selling floor as rapidly as possible—a strategy that was introduced in Chapter 3.

The distribution process is customer-centric and the supply chain responds to consumer demand for better products delivered faster. No loyalty is given to retailers that do not fulfill customers' needs. If a shoe store does not have tall black Ugg boots in size eight at the time customers want them, they'll go elsewhere. If a convenience store does not stock your favorite cola drink, will you opt for a competitor's brand or go without? Chances are you'll quench your thirst with the competitor's brand.

Distribution includes all activities required to physically move the product through the supply chain from manufacturer to final customers. It includes transportation, warehousing, inventory management, and shrinkage control.

It takes cooperation from all members to track and move merchandise through the supply chain. Building strategic partnerships is crucial to the process. The roles and interdependencies of key retail supply-chain members are discussed in this chapter.

Supply Chain Overview

Coverage of the composition of the supply chain, performance objectives, and the many ways supply chain management minimizes costs and maximizes services begin the overview.

Supply Chain Membership

The supply chain comprises three main areas: production, distribution, and customer interface. Production activities include product sourcing, manufacturing, and related activities. Distribution involves logistics such as transportation and warehousing. Supply chain members that are part of distribution include transportation companies, wholesalers, and distribution and fulfillment centers. At the point-of-sale (often called point-of-service), people, systems, equipment, and technologies that maximize customer satisfaction complete the supply chain.

Performance Objectives

Members of the supply chain work in harmony to meet many objectives including:

- On-time merchandise delivery.
- Complete shipments of orders.
- Accuracy of orders shipped.
- Equal accuracy of domestic and foreign-sourced products.
- Customer satisfaction.

Retailers who were surveyed about supply chain management were asked to describe their strategic emphasis for 2012. Controlling costs was the top priority, coupled with customer service. Next in importance was a supportive growth strategy.[1]

Supply chain members use technology-based supply chain management systems to achieve these ends. Several ways these and other performance objectives are met are discussed in the next section.

Supply Chain Lean Practices

Reduction in the number of participants in the retail marketing channel, as well as several new lean practices designed to increase efficiency and save money, began in the 1990s. **Lean practices** are methods of doing business that facilitate cost reductions, cycle-time efficiencies, and increased inventory turns. Chapter 12 introduced this approach as the basis for management strategies such as Lean Six Sigma. Several practices in supply chain management are described here.

Cost Savings

Distribution costs are reduced by:

- Determining the optimum number and location of warehouses.
- Improving materials handling to speed deliveries.
- Upgrading inventory management systems.
- Implementing quick response systems.
- Streamlining human resource needs.

Figure 18.2
Considered state-of-the-art when it opened in 2001, this former Saks distribution center in Alabama was designed to receive and ship 75,000 cartons per 16-hour day with 90 percent accuracy or more. The facility was sold to Belk stores in 2006 and subsequently purchased by a manufacturing and distribution company.

A distribution center designed to minimize merchandise handling, expedite flow, and save money is illustrated in Figure 18.2. Throughout the supply chain, cost savings are apparent. Large retail chains use their purchasing power to persuade vendors to make substantial contributions. When vendors assume responsibility for packaging and preticketing merchandise, supply chain costs are kept down. Carrying excessive inventories or warehouse space were luxuries of the past. Economies in both areas create savings for retailers and distribution centers.

Shortened Cycle Times

The period of time that elapses between production of goods and order fulfillment is called **cycle time**. For example, the typical cycle time for private label goods is generally six months. That period would comprise designing, sourcing raw materials, securing textile products, and the manufacturing process. It also includes transit times between manufacturer, distribution center or fulfillment hub, and retailer. A new breed of company has emerged, specializing in solutions for supply chain efficiency, including cycle-time optimization. The company i2 Technologies, considered a leader in supply chain management, found that eight to ten weeks could be shaved off the six-month cycle by sharing design information with other supply chain members earlier in the cycle.[2] In 2010, i2 was acquired by JDA, another supply chain software and services company.[3]

If we look only at the segment of the cycle that represents the time it takes to move merchandise from fulfillment center to consumer we see that 81 percent of goods are shipped in one or two business days.[4] This statistic measures fulfillment time of online retail businesses, but is similar at this level to the cycle-time pattern in catalogue selling, as well as brick-and-mortar stores. Much more time is spent in the early stages of product development than when the goods are ready to be shipped to consumers or retail stores. Time spent in a holding facility is time not spent on the selling floor. The cost of storing merchandise until it is sorted for delivery to individual stores is high.

Contemporary systems minimize or eliminate the time merchandise spends in distribution centers. Consider your own experience with mail order or online purchases. If you expected your shipment of sweet Comice pears within three days after placing an order, but delivery took two weeks, you'd be dissatisfied with the service. You might even stop buying from the retailer if the fruit was spoiled upon arrival.

Increased Inventory Turns

Advanced information technology improves distribution practices. Tighter distribution tactics contribute to lower inventory levels, better in-stock position, and faster stock turns. The number of times inventory turns into sales annually is an important performance measurement tracked by all retailers because it greatly affects profitability.

Upgraded Management Systems

Fine-tuning just-in-time and total-quality management systems also encourages distribution efficiencies. **Just in time (JIT)** refers to efficient logistical systems that allow for reduced inventory levels and timely distribution, resulting in cost savings. JIT systems are specific quick-response applications. Using JIT systems, retailers stock minimum inventory, but rely on frequent shipment of goods. On-target forecasting is crucial to the success of this method. **Total quality management (TQM)** refers to management systems that encourage teamwork and ownership of the production, distribution, or retailing processes. Achieving total-quality status means manufacturing and delivering the product in optimum condition. If products are damaged, or if the wrong sizes or colors are shipped, TQM goals are not met. When other variables are equal, retail buyers will buy from vendors that consistently deliver undamaged products the fastest.

Strategic Directions

To support the development of lean practices, supply chain members are forming partnerships to encourage efficiencies, better communication, lower costs, and greater profitability. Effective distribution techniques, consolidation, and power within the supply chain influence the development of new standards and advancements.

Supply Chain Partnerships   Both large and small retailers seek fruitful working arrangements with other supply chain members. Strategic partnerships vary depending on size of business, degree of involvement, and available technology. For example, large retailers need more sophisticated information technology systems and distribution methods because of the volume of merchandise they ship and the number of stores and customers they service. Smaller retailers that are more involved with customers on a personal basis need finely tuned merchandise assortments and flexibility. Both require on-time, accurate, and cost-effective delivery. In the past, supply chain members were concerned primarily with performing their functions independently. Now, working together to achieve mutual goals is the aim of partnerships.

Many retailers are reluctant to share financial performance and other sensitive data with vendors—and vice versa. Building trust is necessary when forming this relationship: success is more likely if retailers and vendors are more concerned with the improved performance of all crucial supply chain members involved in transactions, rather than committed to secrecy and privacy of proprietary information.

Efficient Distribution Techniques   Developing and improving distribution techniques influences lean practices. Cross-docking and customer-direct shipments are operating methods designed to move goods faster by eliminating unnecessary stops requiring more steps in the physical distribution systems. **Cross-docking** is the practice of moving goods in and out of a distribution center with minimal handling of merchandise. Shipping all pieces of a coordinated apparel group to stores simultaneously rather than in small increments is made possible with cross-docking. Mass merchandisers have used this technique for some time, but specialty store chains were slower to implement it. To move goods expediently, companies using cross-docking expect vendors to pack goods by stock keeping unit (SKU) according to company specifications.

Polo Ralph Lauren took over its Southeast Asia wholesale and retail distribution from Dickson Concepts International Ltd., on January 1, 2010. Dickson Concepts served as Polo's licensee for the region prior to the changeover. At Polo, the Southeast Asia region is made up of China, Hong Kong, Malaysia, Indonesia, Singapore, Taiwan, the Philippines, and Thailand.

The move is in line with Polo's overall corporate strategy to take licenses back in-house, which has proven a successful strategy to better control the quality, distribution, image, and growth of the company as a whole. In recent years, Polo has taken back licenses for footwear and Polo jeans, Lauren by Ralph Lauren, and its European and Japanese businesses. "[This change] represents a significant strategic step for our company as we continue to develop our business globally," Lauren, the company's chairman and chief executive officer, said. "The appetite for our brand and products in Southeast Asia is strong and growing, and we expect to build on the momentum by reinforc-ing our luxury lifestyle positioning and elevating our distribution in the region."

In Southeast Asia, Dickson Concepts sold Polo merchandise through approximately 40 freestanding stores and nearly 100 shop-in-shops. Roger Farah, Polo's president and chief operating officer, called the region, "a dynamic emerging market with incredibly strong growth characteristics."

"We are grateful to Dickson Concepts for enabling us to establish Polo Ralph Lauren as a premier lifestyle brand throughout the region over the last two decades, and we look forward to working closely with them on a smooth transition," Farah said. "The work we will undertake to develop Southeast Asia is similar to what we've done successfully in Europe and are executing in Japan. With control of our distribution, we intend to leverage our world-class managerial, marketing, and merchandising capabilities to deliver significant revenue and profit growth over the long term."

Adapted from Marc Karmizadeh, Women's Wear Daily, February 17, 2009, 2.

Consolidation and Control   Consolidation in the retail industry also affects the supply chain. As retailers merge with or acquire competitors, larger, more powerful companies are created. Some companies seek greater efficiencies by taking on manufacturing and distribution responsibilities through vertical integration. Other retailers that have distributed goods through third-party companies are taking the supply side back under their corporate umbrellas. Read about the decision Ralph Lauren Corp. made to take back control of its wholesale and retail distribution in Southeast Asia, in From the Field 18.1.

Dominant retailers pressure suppliers into changing distribution procedures because they are able to exert control. Retail companies that control the supply chain change the way business is done. Limited Brands has its own procurement arm, Mast Industries, to source and distribute merchandise. This has cut down the number of supply chain members needed by the company.

In the 1980s, Walmart pioneered electronic links from its headquarters to stores using satellite networks. The company introduced electronic data interchange (EDI) links with its vendors in the 1990s that made it possible to track sales and inventory in real time. In the 21st century, Walmart became a leader in radio frequency identification (RFID) technology. We'll review both practices later in the chapter. The great purchasing power of the world's largest retailer pressures suppliers to adapt their business practices to the market leader.

Apple was recently ranked number one in a listing of top companies that exemplify supply chain best practices. Companies were judged in several categories using several weighted financial measures, as well as peer and pollster votes. The results were used to create a composite score for all supply chain leaders.[5]

Every time a customer tries to buy a product that is not available and buys a competitor's product, the retailer has lost a sale. The cost of that lost sale is profit the company would have made. By practicing best physical distribution practices through greater use of information technology, retailers minimize these costs.

Physical Distribution and Logistics

Effective supply chain management requires meticulous physical distribution and logistics planning. **Physical distribution** is the process of transporting goods from producer to retailer. Operations include receiving, processing, storing, picking, packing, shipping, and stock replenishment.

During the picking and packing stages of the process, individuals select merchandise listed on an inventory sheet or electronic device from shelves in the distribution center. The goods are then

Figure 18.3
Picking and packing is still a manual function in many distribution centers. At Mothers Work, Inc.'s headquarters and distribution center in Philadelphia, the warehouse receives goods from all over the world and distributes them to the company's several maternity fashion apparel chains at 98 percent efficiency.

packaged and sent to the appropriate retail store or customer. Figure 18.3 shows a picker assembling goods for shipment to one of the retail stores owned by Mothers Work, Inc. The company prides itself on its environmental stance regarding the use of reusable canvas totes rather than cardboard boxes. A recycling center on the premises is used for cardboard boxes that come into the facility from contractors and suppliers worldwide.

Selecting an appropriate delivery network, scheduling transportation, and managing traffic are parts of logistics planning. Other aspects include import and export processing and the utilization of technology for decision making.

Domestic and international chains share three basic concerns:

1. Managing great distances between stores.
2. Moving merchandise quickly from suppliers to customers.
3. Keeping distribution costs down.

Smaller retailers share the latter two concerns. To deal with these issues, retailers need considerable merchandise and logistics information. They also need to respond quickly to changing market conditions.

Efficient logistics make it possible for businesses to specialize in products that best fit the natural resources, climate, and other local characteristics of a geographic region. For example, in the United States, avocado growing is concentrated in Florida and California, but world-class distribution systems deliver these fresh fruits almost anywhere, anytime, both safely and efficiently. While planning and distribution functions expedite the flow of merchandise to stores, choice of transportation mode is equally important.

Transportation Providers

Four principal means of transportation are used to physically transport goods domestically or globally: rail, truck, sea, and air. The characteristics of each mode of transportation are explained here, as well as their economic impact on the industry. The strengths and weaknesses of these modes are summarized in Table 18.1.

Table 18.1 Strengths and Weaknesses of Major Transportation Modes

Mode	Strengths	Weaknesses
RAIL	• Medium cost • Able to transport containers • Feasible to ship heavy, bulky products • Often used in conjunction with intermodal systems	• Dependent on existing rail systems • Low frequency of scheduled runs
TRUCK	• Extensive areas served; globally available • Flexibility of scheduling • Speedy, local delivery; reliable long-distance routes • Multiproduct potential	• High to medium cost • Pricing vulnerable to increases in fuel costs
SEA	• Medium to low cost • Able to ship large quantities of goods using containers • Best when used in conjunction with intermodal systems	• Slow delivery times • Limited ports served • Not feasible for perishable items
AIR	• Many locations served • Fast delivery times • Feasible for lightweight, high-ticket, or perishable merchandise	• High cost • Security concerns • Potential carbon-based environmental factors

Land Transport

Participants in land transportation include railroads and trucking companies. Fewer rail and more truck deliveries are the general rule in domestic transportation of retail goods. Both rail and trucking shipping rates were expected to increase approximately four to six percent in 2012, largely due to rising fuel costs in the United States.[6]

In the United States, rail is used extensively to move container loads of goods that were shipped by sea, often from Asia to ports in California, for example. Upon arrival in port, the containers are transferred to railroad cars. Stacktrains are preferred by many transportation firms. These high-speed trains feature rail cars with two piggybacked freight containers per car.

Railroad shipping experienced a decline during the recession but had regained momentum by 2010–2011. Union Pacific, one of the top rail companies in the United States, reported a net income increase of 18.4 percent and a 6 percent increase in volume growth of general merchandise cargo from 2010 to 2011.[7]

Larger trucks and specialized vehicles handle all types of merchandise effectively. The two major categories of truck transportation are line-haul and short-haul delivery. Moving goods long distances between cities and towns is called **line-haul delivery**. Moving goods to customers locally is called **short-haul delivery**. Line-haul normally involves large trucks, usually tractor-trailers that deliver large quantities to major distribution centers. Some trucking firms work long-distance routes but do not fill trucks to full cargo capacity; they are referred to as **LTLs**, which stands for less-than-truckload capacity, in contrast to **TIs**, which service routes at full truckload capacity. Two of the major LTLs in the industry are YRC Worldwide and Old Dominion.[8] Logistics managers evaluate routes to find better ways to dispatch carriers and reduce mileage.

Several small shipments are much more expensive than a single large one. In the independent trucking and rail industries, freight forwarders and consolidators bring together products

Did You Know?
According to the International Transport Forum, the outlook for domestic road and rail freight in the European Union's 27 countries is weak. Trucking within the EU is eight percent below its pre-recession peak, indicating a slow recovery. In the first quarter of 2012, railroad freight had declined to nine percent below pre-recession levels. Monitoring this type of state-of-the-supply-chain data is important to retailers worldwide.
(Source: "Global Freight Volumes Remain Stagnant," *International Transport Journal (ITJ)*, April 4, 2012, www.transportjournal.ch/index.php?id=425&tx_ttnews[pS]=1333547899&tx_ttnews[backPid]=4158cHash=3750c5609601ab55ed304be86b05dab65.)

manufactured by several small firms and transport them as one shipment to major retailers. **Freight forwarders** are firms that group shipments of several manufacturers into truckload, rail car, or container shipments. This service saves freight costs for shippers and retailers. Some trucks have specialized fittings to accommodate specific products; for example, apparel is often hung on racks during shipment. Shipping and delivery are more efficient when merchandise is consolidated and shipped appropriately.

The trucking industry is not without its problems. The economic downturn coincided with heavy increases in fuel costs. Retailers that relied on truckers were forced to increase their shipping rates at a time when customers were cutting their own budgets. The same issues challenged the transportation industry in 2012. Transportation firms like United Parcel Service (UPS) also add surcharges and understandably have to pass these on to retailers. In 2012, UPS rates for ground, air, and international shipments originating in the United States increased 4.9 percent. Decreases in fuel surcharges were 1 percent for ground and 2 percent for air and international, which balanced the overall rate for all shipments from the previous year's rates.[9]

The experience of catalogue and online retailer Harry & David illustrates the fine line that companies tread as they price shipping for their gourmet food and fruit products. When the company prepared for the 2008 holiday season, it was well aware that consumers were distressed by the high costs of shipping and the state of the economy. They were also aware of the competitiveness between retailers regarding shipping rates at this time of year. Typically, customers pay $8.99 to ship a $30 box of pears. Harry & David reduced shipping costs by about one-third for the 2008 season.[10] Harry & David offered free standard delivery on some of its popular gifts including Royal Riviera Pears and its Fruit-of-the-Month Club gifts. The company also offered late billing on online orders over $99, according to the company's *Christmas Gifts 2009* catalogue. Revenue plummeted that holiday season and again in 2010.

In response, chief executive office (CEO) Steve Heyer cut prices drastically on gourmet pears, fruit baskets, and Mouse Munch caramel corn during the 2010 season. Competition from companies like Amazon.com increased. Huge debt, the departure of two CEOs (including Heyer), and the perils of recession led the company into bankruptcy in March 2011. Fortunately, after securing financing, the company came out of Chapter 11 in September 2011 and continues to do business under several brands and through catalogues, a call center, online selling, and 67 retail stores.[11] During the second quarter of fiscal 2012, earnings increased 75 percent to $62.6 million compared with $35.8 million the previous year.[12]

There are lessons to be learned from this saga. Even when a retailer reduces product prices, adds service incentives, implements creative marketing tactics, and drops shipping charges, these actions do not ensure that the retailer can regain momentum once internal and external factors intercede. Tightening up an organization by closing poor-performing stores and growing a business through better inventory controls and fulfillment practices are some of the ways retailers can heal a sick company.

Figure 18.4 shows how another retailer, L.L. Bean has dealt with the recent recession. This popular retailer, operating primarily online and through its catalogues, recognized free shipping as a major appeal to its customers.

Sea Transport

When speed is not a main criterion for the delivery of goods produced overseas, containerships are the main carriers of cargo. **Containerships** are sailing vessels that are outfitted with large numbers of cargo holders that are roughly 20 to 40 feet long and shaped like a tractor-trailer bed. The volume of containers is measured in **20-foot-equivalent units (TEUs)**. Using this system, a 40-foot container would measure twice as many TEUs as a 20-foot container. Containerships carry retail products from and to major ports. Ocean crossings are slower than air cargo flights, but costs are low and huge quantities of goods can be shipped at one time. A container dock is illustrated in Figure 18.5.

Newer ships carry as many as 10,000 TEUs and cross the Pacific from Los Angeles to Tokyo in nine days. In 2010, the global containership fleet consisted of close to 4,700 vessels. More than half handled 2,000 TEUs or less. Although the number of craft is expected to grow only marginally, the size of ships now being built will differ radically. Shipping consultants estimate that approximately

Figure 18.4
L.L.Bean's catalogue celebrates the retailer's 100th anniversary in business as well as the company's major change to free shipping. Competitive pressure during the economic recession prompted shipping-cost strategy changes for many retailers.

Figure 18.5
Containerships are the least costly but most time-consuming way to ship retail goods overseas. Containers are 20–40 feet long and comprise the bulk of cargo. This container dock and terminal is in Boston Harbor.

163 ships of 10,000 TEUs will be in service by 2014.[13] This will significantly change the dynamics of shipping everything from dog collars to automobiles, and most likely reduce the costs of shipping for those on the receiving end.

Beginning in mid-2008, the shipping industry experienced the same deep slump as other supply chain members worldwide. Many shipping companies reduced the fees they charged customers to fuel-only just to keep the sea lanes moving and delivering goods to market. By the end of 2009, business was improving but many major lines predicted large losses. Shippers of raw commodities were less affected by the declines than those that primarily carry manufactured goods destined for the retail sector.[14]

Ocean transport is driven by import and export rates. By November 2011, import container traffic had contracted six months in a row in the Ports of Los Angeles and Long Beach. On a year-over-year basis exports decreased 1.9 percent and imports declined 3.6 percent. Because the California ports account for the bulk of imports entering the United States by sea, they are considered a bellweather of the economy.[15] Subsequently, ships serving trade lanes from Asia and the Indian subcontinent to Canada and the United States announced a General Rate Increase (GRI) for all North American-bound cargo. The rate increases per container ranged from $320 per 20-foot standard container up to $510 for larger units and took effect in March 2012.[16] The cost of containers traveling an Asia–to–United States lane was about $3,000 per TEU in 2008 as the volatility of recession pricing commenced.[17] Consider this in the context of the GRI, and you will see that this is a significant increase. Rates are beginning to rebound toward pre-2008 levels.

These traffic and rate figures are not good news for shippers or retailers. Likewise, increases in fuel costs negatively affect all members of the supply chain—including customers. However, the long-range expectations for container traffic appear buoyed by gradually improving vital signs in the United States, and we hope, the rest of the world.

Air Transport

Although air transportation is six to ten times more expensive than sea transport, it is the fastest option for international or cross-country shipping.[18] It is the least utilized method of cargo transportation but still reigns as the safest and most efficient mode for several product categories. Air transportation is cost-effective for small, lightweight merchandise classifications such as apparel and accessories. Jewelry and small high-ticket items like iPads also travel well by air, as do perishable products.

One of the results of a freight industry study showed that 23 percent of shippers plan on switching some heavy air cargo to ocean transport and only 4 percent said they would switch from sea to air carriers. These statistics indicate that more shippers are interested in cost savings than speed to market.[19]

Much retail-bound merchandise is shipped via UPS, Federal Express, DHL Global, and government mail services—all of which maintain their own air carriers as well as ground transport systems. Partnerships have formed between government mail services and independent companies. The German postal service, Deutsche Post AG, owns DHL Global. A DHL Global fulfillment specialist at work at one of the company's distribution centers is shown in Figure 18.1. Another DHL Global employee, seen in Figure 18.6, ensures that all retail shipments are carefully processed and expedited. These examples indicate the growing number of alliances between public and private delivery services and the increase in global trade.

Air cargo businesses see growth ahead, but cautioned that fuel and energy costs, proposed carbon-trading laws in the EU, and ongoing air security issues will continue to challenge the industry.[20]

Intermodal Transport

A high volume of imported merchandise creates a need for improved transportation logistics. Companies that integrate transportation by land, sea, and air command physical distribution channels. Shipping goods via more than one transportation conveyance owned by the same company is called **intermodal transport**. Several transportation providers have the capability to move freight from Asia to all of North America using ship, train, and truck, for example. The Danish firm A.P.

Figure 18.6
Computer systems facilitate the flow of goods from source to customer. An order processor at a DHL Global fulfillment center in Germany makes sure that documentation for a shipment is in order.

Moeller-Maersk owns the world's largest container shipping company, the Maersk Line.[21] Sea-Land Service Inc., the largest U.S. shipping line, has intermodal capabilities and an alliance with Maersk. Shipping line partnerships create greater presence in global trade routes.

Under normal circumstances, once ships arrive, containers are stacked on trains and delivered to major U.S. cities. At that point, trucks take over the distribution process. However, when times are not usual, methods of operation must be rethought. During the recession, some trucking firms began to utilize coastal shipping. Three reasons for this move were compelling: (1) The high price of fuel, deteriorating condition of roadways and bridges in the United States, and highway gridlock in several regions of the country precipitated intermodal alternatives; (2) most ports already contained special ramps accommodating huge tractor-trailer trucks; and (3) while the $155.5-billion estimated annual price tag to revive the surface infrastructure was high,[22] coastal shipping had long been used to move goods from the South to cities in the North, making this route a worthwhile option.

Environmental and economic concerns have aligned in encouraging shippers and retailers to evaluate the carbon impact of the many modes of shipping. As they attempt to incorporate more green practices into their operations, it is quite possible that solutions will come from intermodal strategies that minimize use of higher-polluting fuels by maximizing water transportation. Rail transportation is considered one of the lesser contributors to carbon emissions due to new technologies that power engines with significant lower distress to the environment. Advances in the use of electric power for trucks are just a step behind those that are spurring the introduction of high-mileage, low-emission cars on today's roadways.

Economic malfunction affects distribution. The recession paralyzed trade in many parts of the globe as manufacturers and retailers cut production and inventories in response to consumers' tightened grip on their wallets. Because of the decrease in demand, business was lost. The physical distribution process is complex and greatly affected by uncontrollable elements in the global environment.

Warehousing

Warehousing is the process of housing merchandise at various stages of the physical distribution process. Warehouses are publicly or privately owned. Major retailers rely on a network of strategically placed warehouses called distribution centers. These are football field–sized facilities, fully automated for efficient handling of merchandise. In an automated system at a department store distribution center, human hands touch merchandise cartons no more than twice—unless there's a problem. Major decisions regarding warehousing include number, location, size of centers, and level of customer service and technology required.

Optimization of Distribution Centers

Whether a retailer utilizes one or more distribution centers depends on several factors. One distribution center per country or major trading area is efficient or cost effective under certain circumstances:

- When customers don't mind waiting for products, such as furniture or items in high demand.
- When companies sell bulky, heavy products with high per-pound values.
- When the fulfillment center belongs to an online retailer.
- When highly secure inventory organization is necessary.
- When a retail chain is not geographically dispersed.
- When some pre-shipping services such as ticketing or shrink wrapping are completed in the distribution center.

Category killers typically have three or more distribution centers in operation. The sheer size and scope of national and global mass merchandisers, specialty and department store chains justifies the presence of multiple distribution facilities.

Customer Service Standards

Customer service requirements in terms of turnaround time for delivery and minimum acceptable order fill rates are guiding factors. **Turnaround time** is the time that passes between an action and the response to it such as the placement of an order and the receipt of it. **Fill rate** is the metric that evaluates the ability of manufacturers or distributors to ship all goods ordered. It is expressed as a percentage. A fill rate of less than 100 percent means sales are lost at retail. Locating a warehouse in a particular region or country involves weighing whether additional transportation costs will be needed to reach customers efficiently from that geographic point in order to meet fulfillment goals. When this information is known, the feasibility of meeting target turnaround times and fill rates can be better judged.

Almost 94 percent of retail inventory moves through company-owned distribution centers. The average performance for store order fill rates is 95.9 percent.[23] Table 18.2 charts fill rates as well as other important metrics.

Table 18.2 Performance Data for Retailer-Owned Distribution Centers

Metric	Average Performance Percentage	Range of Performance Percentage
Store on-time delivery	96.7	90 to 100
Store order fill rates	95.9	88 to 99
Store in-stock availability	94.3	80 to 99
Annual inventory turnover	6.5 times	2 to 22 times
Delivery cost as % of sales	2.2	<1 to 9
DC cost as a % of sales	3.3	<1 to 9

Source: Brian J. Gibson, C. Clifford Defee, and Wesley S. Randall, "The State of the Retail Supply Chain, Results and Findings of the 2009 Study," Auburn University College of Business and Retail Industry Leaders Association (RILA), sponsored by Fortna, 7–8.

Efficient Warehouse Systems

Computer models help determine efficient use of space. Using random storage, warehouse space is not assigned needlessly to products that do not need it during specific time periods. **Random storage** is a computer-generated model for optimal use of storage space. Automated storage and retrieval systems reduce both aisle space and manpower required. **Automated storage and retrieval (ASR)** refers to warehousing systems that combine the use of computer control of stock records with mechanical handling. In the stock-holding area of a grocery distributor that uses ASR, one might see pallets of soda next to paper towels and canned beans above bags of rice because it is more efficient. The capital cost of automation is measured against labor savings, better inventory control, and better customer service.

Push–Pull Distribution Strategies

Chapter 1 introduced two methods of distributing goods to stores. A **push strategy** also is used when a distribution center initiates shipments to a retailer in anticipation of sales. A **pull strategy** is used when a retailer initiates shipment from a distribution center in response to sales. The method selected depends on the type of goods carried, inventory turnover rates, type of store, and retailer preference. For example, grocery stores almost invariably use a pull method and specialty apparel chains mainly use a push method.

Warehouse professionals have maintained their commitment to redesigning facilities and upgrading warehouse management software amid the economic convulsions of the past few years.[24] Effective physical distribution methods and logistics management methods depend heavily on state-of-the-art technology, modern facilities, and close supply chain relationships, and an efficient and timely delivery to the retailer, as illustrated in Figure 18.7.

Supply Chain Decision Systems

Information technology has made significant contributions to supply chain management in the area of inventory control. Complete merchandise and financial control systems support all retail functions in large as well as many small retail stores.

Key Inventory Control Functions

These systems make it possible for retailers to:

- Use electronic purchase orders.
- Print sales tickets.
- Hold purchase orders for invoice matches.
- Facilitate physical distribution of merchandise.
- Monitor point-of-sale systems.
- Highlight slow-selling merchandise and initiate markdowns.
- Highlight transfers, reorders, fast sellers, and age of stock.
- Compile SKU, classification, and department reports.
- Integrate financial data.
- Extract historical sales data.
- Create online linkages with suppliers.
- Better manage multichannel operations.
- Generate advanced shipping notices.

Figure 18.7
On the last leg of the distribution process, packages are delivered to a retail store by the DHL delivery service. Final destination in the supply chain: onto the selling floor and into customers' hands as soon as possible.

Advanced shipping notices (ASNs) are electronically generated documents that alert receivers to impending shipments of goods. Retailers and vendors share information in order to provide more effective decision making and better service. Many exchange data regarding units and inventory, and increasingly supply chain members are sharing more sensitive financial information such as gross margin figures. Standardization of point-of-sale technology streamlines communication of sales information from retailers to manufacturers and other supply chain partners.

Collecting and Analyzing Data

Retailers collect and analyze information in several ways. Internet technology is outpacing other types of communication between supply chain members. Wireless technology increases efficiencies for retailers and customers. Quick response systems that incorporate CPFR information form the core of supply chain management. Finally, inventory counts take on new importance as retailers streamline procedures, increase accuracy, and reduce shrinkage.

Inventory control systems depend on two technologies—UPC and EDI. **Universal product codes (UPCs)** are series of printed stripes found on most products encoding product identification information. The stripes and SKU numbers identify vendors, departments, classifications, and style numbers, for example. Barcoding is used for data entry. **Barcoding** is the capture of information at the point of service by scanning the UPC with an electronic device. Electronic data interchange (EDI), introduced in Chapter 1, links retailers, manufacturers, and other supply chain members. Inbound merchandise is marked with UPCs, and the information contained in these codes is then communicated via EDI systems. From this point shipping notices (ASNs) are prepared.

Retail companies with global vision interact with more supply chain members. It is imperative for them to adopt global standards. An annual survey done by IBM Corp. addressed supply chain efficiencies through compliance with global standards. The study compared company participation and performance of manufacturers and retailers in several categories in 2006 with 2010–2011 results. For example, in 2006, 45 percent of orders were transacted by EDI whereas in 2010–2011, the percentage had grown to 60.7 percent. The percentage of invoices transacted via EDI increased from 32 to 46.3 percent in the same period.[25] Efficiencies in the supply chain are particularly important for companies that deal with fast-selling goods like health and beauty products, groceries, and fresh and frozen foods. Apparel, books, music, and video categories also depend on timely movement through their respective channels.

Quick Response

In the past, high inventory levels of slow-selling goods significantly hindered the flow of goods. As a result, cash flows of both retailers and manufacturers were affected. When retail sales were sluggish, open-to-buy was not available to purchase new merchandise from manufacturers. Or, retailers were forced to cancel orders already placed. A negative cycle of sales and replenishment ensued. Vendor-managed inventory systems are becoming more popular as retailers and manufacturers become partners rather than adversaries. **Vendor-managed inventory (VMI)** shifts the responsibility of keeping track of merchandise to the manufacturer.

Quick response helps refine CPFR procedures, which benefits the entire supply chain. When quick response premiered in the 1980s, its main objective was to increase the speed and accuracy of retailers' orders and manufacturers' shipments. Cycle times that once took weeks are reduced to days when quick response is used. Other attributes of quick response systems include:

- Increased inventory turnover.
- Lower costs of carrying inventory.
- Improved gross margin.
- Better customer service.

Supply chain members that use quick response have a vested interest in continuing to work together. The concept merges well with Internet-based systems and applications.

Internet-Based Technologies

Manufacturers and retailers are making supply chain management more efficient through online communications technology. Product developers keep in touch with scores of mills, factories, and offices globally. In some countries, wireless systems are more advanced than highway systems, encouraging digital alternatives to tedious business travel.

Microsoft developed a program called Value Chain Initiative that brings together scores of software, hardware, and logistics companies. The group developed a set of international standards to aid communication between supply chain members. Better communication allows companies to track merchandise shipments globally.

The computer language supporting inventory control and business-to-business functions evolved from EDI to the more advanced XML technology used on the Internet. **Extensible markup language (XML)** is an electronic message format that integrates different forms of hardware and software and allows data sharing by multiple users. It is becoming the standard since it is more versatile, accurate, and easy to use than older formats.

Online strategic partnerships necessitate compatible information technology systems. New standards ease the transition to better supply chain communication.

Wireless Tools

State-of-the-art wireless information technology tools provide retailers with a wealth of decision-making and customer service tools. Some are designed to make receiving, price management, and inventory control more accurate and efficient. Others are security and customer service oriented. Most we take for granted, while others still impress. For example:

- Robots are used by growing numbers of retailers to expedite the distribution process.
- Auto identification systems electronically capture customer signatures—and even photographs—for credit and check verification transactions.
- Self-scanners allow customers to check prices before getting to the checkout lane.
- Shopping cart–mounted touch screens provide information on product locations, video promotions, and offers tailored to customers' past shopping behavior.
- Electronic shelf labels and signage, and instant coupon dispensers promote products and aid customers.
- Digital information kiosks in supermarkets let customers post their deli orders instead of waiting in line.

Other improvements are occurring in labor management software, voice recognition technology, automated storage and retrieval, heavy-duty mobile computers, and slotting optimization.[26]

Inventory Management

Controlling the ebb and flow of inventory makes it easier for retailers to satisfy customers' needs. Several mechanisms help maintain the flow of goods. There are two basic inventory management systems, periodic and perpetual. Shrinkage adversely affects inventories and is calculated and controlled.

Periodic and Perpetual Systems

A **periodic inventory** is a physical count of all merchandise, usually taken annually or semi-annually. A **perpetual inventory** is an ongoing measurement of merchandise in stock as sales and purchases occur. The perpetual system provides retailers with several advantages including:

- Increased revenues.
- Reduced out-of-stock positions.
- Reduced inventory levels.
- Identification of slow-selling goods.
- Reduced markdowns.
- Higher inventory turnover.
- Fewer internal transfers.

Because a perpetual system is a book or estimation method, discrepancies occur. For example, a scanner-based point-of-sale system used for inventory control records actual sales, but it does not have the capability to record shoplifted items. Inventory is charted by units or dollars in both perpetual and periodic systems.

Some retailers choose to outsource the physical inventory process. They do this to utilize the expertise of specialists in the field and provide objectivity.

Shrinkage Deterrents

Efficiencies elsewhere in the supply chain are veiled when inventory shortages run high. Shoplifting, employee theft, damaged goods, organized retail crime, and human error all contribute to shrinkage rates. Shrinkage is determined by subtracting actual stock on hand from the book inventory. A comparison of the two counts will yield an inventory shrinkage rate.

Electronic article surveillance (EAS) originated in the mid-1960s, when cumbersome plastic-encased electronic devices were invented and used to deter potential shoplifters. Most retailers feel that EAS is the most effective means of shrinkage control. This concept was discussed briefly in Chapter 11.

Throughout the world, suppliers are combating the shrinkage problem by devising new deterrents. Norprint Labeling Systems, based in the United Kingdom, combines hangtag and merchandise security essentials into one device. Its paper tags, incorporating product information and magnetic labels, are used by British retailers Selfridge's department store and Boots drugstore chain. Two garment label companies in South Africa have joined forces to produce sewn-in fabric labels incorporating Norprint's advanced technology. During a 3-month test in a South African retail store, shrinkage rates decreased 85 percent.

Radio frequency identification (RFID) triggering devices hidden in mannequins can help keep shrinkage rates in check. One example, the Anne Droid mannequin, has concealed video cameras behind its eyes and a microphone in its nose. Read more about this and other uses of RFID in From the Field 18.2 and in the section that follows.

Radio Frequency Identification

Not limited to loss prevention, RFID technology has many retail applications. **Radio frequency identification (RFID)** is the use of radio waves to detect merchandise, people, and other discernable elements. It activates our SpeedPass at the gas pump and alerts stock-keepers to the flow of goods in stores. We'll examine its evolution, explain the technology, and review the benefits of RFID over existing inventory management systems.

Evolution

The advances that made UPC and EDI possible set the stage for the next technology to evolve: automatic identification devices, also called auto ID. **Auto ID** uses wireless devices to capture and identify information. RFID is a form of auto ID that dates back to the 1970s. Radio waves are used as the medium, and the technology is dependent upon a microchip antenna, an electronic product code, and a wireless computer. An **electronic product code (ePC)** is the RFID version of the UPC. There is potentially a unique number for every item in the world.

Types of Tags

There are two basic types of tags, active and passive. **Passive RFID tags** are very small microchips that are attached to a paper-like antenna. Encoded information is read when chips are scanned from a pallet, a case, or an individual product. The reader converts the code to recognizable data. The code contains information such as producer, manufacturer, or unique number. It also tells where the item is and where it is going. **Active RFID tags** require a power source and are larger, more expensive, and have a longer range than passive tags. E-ZPass highway toll payment devices use active tags.

Advantages

RFID is being adopted by many large retail companies because the technology helps eliminate stockouts, control shrinkage, and integrate the supply chain. RFID technology is superior to UPC barcodes in several ways:

- Capture of information is not limited to a line of sight; 360-degree detection is possible over a relatively wide range.
- Data are transferred without physical contact.
- Items are distinguished from one another in groups, as in a shopping cart.

From the Field 18.2   Retail RFID Today, As Seen Through the Eyes of an Expert

When it comes to RFID in retail, "There is much more happening than would be apparent to the casual observer, and it has been this way for almost two years," says Marshall Kay, founder of the consulting practice RFID Sherpas and former director of the North American RFID program for Kurt Salmon Associates.

"Item-level RFID is drawing increasing interest from luxury retailers and big-box discounters alike. This reflects a growing recognition of the many ways that value is generated once an item has been tagged."

Kay spoke with *Stores* contributor David P. Schulz about the state of RFID.

Schulz: What has changed in the world of RFID over the past 12 months?

Kay: I can think of several big changes. First, the number of retail CEOs that have taken an interest in RFID has grown, and they are taking the time to educate themselves and ask the right questions. They tour their test stores, meet directly with RFID experts, and receive briefings from their people on the progress of internal projects.

Second, we now have disposable RFID tags being used in the United States on items that retail for under $5. We have shattered the myth that an item needs to cost at least $15 in order to warrant attaching a disposable tag to it.

Third, there are reports that auditors are now willing to waive the requirement of laborious physical inventory counts if retailers instead track their inventory throughout the year with RFID. Not only can retailers save the money they pay outside parties to perform these counts, they can also save the overtime wages they pay to their own employees to shadow these people.

Schulz: Many people still associate RFID primarily with Walmart. Is that an accurate assessment?

Kay: Walmart's RFID program has to-date focused on carton-level visibility and efficiencies; this is very different from the item-level visibility and efficiencies being achieved today by several retailers. Since each item has a serialized tag, these retailers now have much better visibility into the merchandise they receive and its location within the store,

allowing them to keep their sales floors properly stocked and use store labor more effectively. Item-level RFID is even being used to expedite the checkout process.

Executives at companies like Brooks Brothers and American Eagle Outfitters should pay attention to the progress of retailers like Bloomingdale's, Dillard's, and Nine West; Office Depot, OfficeMax, and Best Buy can similarly learn a lot by tracking the success that Staples is having with item-level RFID in Canada.

Schulz: Why do you believe it is imperative for department stores to collaborate on RFID?

Kay: It's really quite simple. Flash-forward five years to a period where the majority of specialty clothing retailers are using RFID on their garments [and] put yourself in the shoes of the average consumer. Those stores are more likely to have your size in stock, are more likely to have amenities like "smart" fitting rooms with interactive video screens that make your visit more interesting and productive, and they will be using RFID to expedite checkout.

If department stores cannot offer you a similar shopping experience, you will spend less and less time in their stores. Specialty retailers will also be reaping the rewards of inventory efficiency and visibility across their supply chains, further strengthening their balance sheets and making them even more dangerous competitors.

Schulz: Source-tagging seems to be relevant to both retailers and branded vendors. What is happening on that front?

Kay: Source tagging—which often amounts to little more than asking your overseas factory to apply a smarter RFID label or ticket than the one they are accustomed to attaching—has been happening for several years. One retailer routinely has its suppliers tag more than 100 million garments a year. While this doesn't yet constitute 100 percent of that retailer's merchandise, this is a large-scale tagging program that has been up and running for some time. Factories that choose to use RFID to check the contents of their outbound shipments are exhibiting higher levels of order accuracy.

Adapted and condensed from David P. Schulz, *Stores,* October 2009. www.stores.org/ InformationTechnology/2009/10/Edit06/index.asp.

- Shipping efficiency is increased and distribution center management enhanced.
- Product recalls occur faster.
- Spoilage of perishable goods is decreased.
- Tags can be rewritten, reused, or destroyed.
- Labor costs are reduced.

Future Applications

Several retailers have tested or are conducting tests of RFID technology. Some of the first to develop and use retail applications were supermarket and superstore retailers Metro AG of Germany, Tesco of the United Kingdom, and Walmart in the United States. Other retailers involved in RFID programs include Target, Home Depot, Lowe's, Ace Hardware, Best Buy, Costco, Levi Strauss, and Zara. Retailers often work in partnership with key vendors, including Procter & Gamble, Gillette, Johnson & Johnson, Purina, and Kimberly-Clark.

Retailers are escalating their adoption of RFID because of the improvements in collaborative planning, forecasting, and replenishment that are enabled by this technology. Although the economic downturn and supply chain reticence have shifted RFID adoption lower on the priority list, many industry members see RFID as a risk-aversion tool as well as an inventory-control function.

As markets mature and globalization intensifies, retailers compete to increase supply chain effectiveness. Technology-driven supply chain improvements create differential advantages and

Did You Know?
To maintain accurate inventory and prevent out-of-stock problems, Lord & Taylor is using hand-held RFID readers in its upscale department stores. The technology, from Motorola Solutions, lets retailers quickly determine how much RFID-tagged inventory is in a specific place at a specific time. There are many RFID applications for retailers. (Source: "Lord & Taylor Deploys RFID Inventory Tracking System," *Retail Information Systems News,* February 13, 2012, http://risnews.edgl.com/ print?printpath=/RIS/retail— news/Latest-News/LatestNews/ Lord-&-Taylor-Deploys-RFID- Inventory-Tracking-System.)

cost savings for retailers. Findings from research conducted specifically on the retail supply chain indicated that 83 percent of shippers planned to maintain or increase IT spending levels in 2012. The four areas of prioritization mentioned were inventory management, warehouse management, demand planning, and transportation management.[27] It appears that members of the supply chain are on the right track as they invest in the future.

Postscript: Destination 2020

In this world of multichannel retailing, you are only as successful as your next sale—whether that is through traditional, contemporary, or future selling channels. In fact, let's make that *omnichannel* retailing, since the buzz in the industry is leaning toward that more expansive term. **Omnichannel retailing** is the optimal practice of aligning merchandising, logistics, technologies, and all other functions fully in order to serve customers consistently well across all selling options. Notice that this term was used by Saks' Steve Sadove in the Did You Know? margin box, earlier. Expect that it will be fully ensconced in the lexicon for the next edition of this book.

The Aberdeen Group's study, "The 2012 Omni-Channel Retail Experience," substantiates the importance of this powerful movement. Despite the gravitational pull on retailers in the last decade, 74 percent of multichannel retailers still operate their respective channels separately. The omnichannel approach seeks to dispel this inertia. It is time for retailers to once again embrace change.[28] To accomplish this, all things retail—from product sourcing, pricing, and fulfillment to customer service and human resources management—must converge. Let retail leaders welcome open-forum discussions and full participation of all constituents. New and stronger methods and lines of communication will inaugurate omnichannel retailing: All things for all customers, all of the time.

Summary

The goal of distribution from the standpoint of the retailer is to move products from manufacturers to customers efficiently and at the level of service expected by customers. Industry lean practices address cost savings, timeliness of delivery, increased inventory turnover, upgraded management systems, and the formation of strategic partnerships.

The components of a physical distribution and logistics system include transportation, warehousing, inventory, and shrinkage control. Transportation systems include rail, truck, sea, and air. Intermodal companies combine two or more transportation methods for maximum efficiency. Crises in the global retail environment such as economic downturns affect logistics management.

Warehousing involves the temporary storage of goods during the fulfillment process. Retailers operate with one or many distribution centers depending on their size, objectives, and product categories. Physical handling of goods is kept to a minimum in order to achieve cost effectiveness. Through cross-docking, replenishment cycles are shortened significantly.

Inventory control methods rely on the integration of information technology and partnerships between retailers and vendors. Quick response is the umbrella term for the marriage of EDI and UPC systems. Newer message formats such as XML are making supply chain communication more robust. Wireless communications networks help retailers streamline operations and customer service. Controlling shrinkage caused by employee theft, shoplifting, organized retail crime, and human error is an ongoing issue. Theft deterrents are plentiful, and the development of RFID is expected to help avert shrinkage and control inventory more effectively.

Understanding the service levels expected by all members of the supply chain is critical to the evolution of distribution methods and supply chain partnerships.

Key Terms

Active RFID tags
Advanced shipping notices (ASNs)
Auto ID
Automated storage and retrieval (ASR)
Barcoding
Collaborative planning, forecasting, and
    replenishment (CPFR)

Containerships
Cross-docking
Cycle time
Electronic product code (ePC)
Extensible markup language (XML)
Fill rates
Freight forwarders

Intermodal transport	Push strategy
Just in time (JIT)	Radio frequency identification (RFID)
Lean practices	Random storage
Line-haul delivery	Short-haul delivery
LTLs	TLs
Omnichannel retailing	Total quality management (TQM)
Passive RFID tags	Turnaround time
Periodic inventory	Twenty-foot-equivalent units (TEUs)
Perpetual inventory	Universal product code (UPC)
Physical distribution	Vendor-managed inventory (VMI)
Pull strategy	

Questions for Review and Discussion

1. In what businesses are members of the supply chain involved? Discuss the major performance objectives of supply chains.
2. What are lean practices? How do retailers benefit from increased distribution efficiency?
3. Why do supply chain members such as manufacturers and retailers form strategic partnerships?
4. How does cross-docking make physical distribution more cost and time effective?
5. How do retailers evaluate transportation systems? If you were shipping silk scarves from Asia, what mode(s) of transportation would you use to get your goods to your hometown store? What if you were shipping electronic keyboards?
6. Why might radio frequency identification (RFID) make universal product code (UPC) bar code systems obsolete? Discuss several advantages of RFID.
7. Discuss several ways RFID is used to facilitate distribution and control inventory shrinkage.

Endnotes

1. Brian J. Gibson and Clifford Defee. "The State of the Retail Supply Chain, Essential Findings of the Third Annual Report," Auburn University and Retail Industry Leaders Association (RILA), Sponsored by Accenture, 4. www.rila.org/supply/Documents/2012StateoftheRetailSupplyChainReport.pdf.

2. "Cycle-Time Optimization: From Concept to Cash Register Faster—and More Profitably," *Supply Chain Leader*, 2009, www.i2.com/supplychainleader/issue 4/html.

3. "i2 Acquisition," JDA, January 2010, www.jda.com/company/i2-acquisition.

4. " The Internet Retailer Survey: Fulfillment and Order Management," *Internet Retailer*, February 2008, 40.

5. "The Gartner Supply Chain Top 25 for 2011," Gartner, Inc., June 1, 2011, 5–6, www.gartner.com/supplychain top25.

6. "Logistics News: Latest State of the Freight Report Finds Rate Expectations Rising Again Across Most Modes," *Supply Chain Digest*, March 14, 2012, www.scdigest.com/ontarget/12-03-14-2php?cid=5607. (Source: Wolfe Trahan." State of the Freight" quarterly report. December 2011.)

7. " Rail Carriers Full 2011: Logistics News: Rail Carriers Enjoy Another Strong Quarter and Year, as LTLs Make Progress," *Supply Chain Digest*, March 7, 2012, www.scdigest.com/ONTARGET/12-3-07-1.php?cid=5575.

8. "LTL Carriers Q4 2011: Logistics News: Rail Carriers Enjoy Another Strong Quarter and Year, as LTLs Make Progress," *Supply Chain Digest* December 1, 2011, www.scdigest.com/ONTARGET/12-3-07-1.php?cid=5575.

9. "2012 Rate Change Information," United Parcel Service, January 12, 2012, www.rates.ups.com.

10. Jayne O'Donnell and Sarah Butrymowicz, "Despite Higher Fuel Costs, Retailers Cut Shipping Rates," *USA Today*, September 4, 2009, www.usatoday.com/money/industries/reetail/2008-09-04-free-shipping-holiday_N.htm.

11. Anthony Effinger, "Wasserstein Haunts Harry & David in Buyout Doomed to Bankruptcy," *Bloomberg Markets Magazine*, October 12, 2011, 1–9. www.bloomberg.com/news/print/2011-10-12/wasserstein-haunts-harry-david-in-buyout-doomed-to-bankruptcy.

12. "Reports Second Quarter Fiscal 2012 Results," Harry & David Holdings, Inc., February 13, 2012, 1, www.hndcorp.com/investor/financial-information.html.

13. "Table 14-5: Global Container ship Fleet, February 2010 and Table 14-6: Global Container Ship Orderbook, 2010–2014," in *Ocean Transportation*, Chapter 14, 448-449, USDA, www.ams.usda.gov/AMSV1.0/getfile?d DocName=STELPRDC5084098. (Source: Drewry Shipping Consultants.)

14. Ainsley Thomson and Art Patnaude, "No Quick Fix for Container Shippers' Woes," *Wall Street Journal*, October 9, 2009, B4.

15. "November 2011 Container Shipments Not Good," Econintersect, April 10, 2012, http://ecinintersect.com/worldpress/?p=17017.

16. "Transpacific Carriers Announce GRI for March 15, 2012," Omnitrans, February 20, 2012, www.omnitrans.com/news_article_print.aspx?news_id=2110.

17. "Ocean Transportation" Chapter 14. "Figure 14-3: Container Rated for Trans-Pacific Trade Lanes," in *Ocean Transportation*, Chapter 14, 452, USDA, www.ams.usda.gov/AMSV1.0/getfile?dDocName=STELPR DC5084098. (Source: Containerization International.)

18. Evan Clark, "Speed vs. Cost: The Economics of Shipping by Air," *Women's Wear Daily*, July 2007, 24.

19. "Logistics News: Latest State of the Freight Report Finds Rate Expectations Rising Again Across Most Modes," in *State of the Freight Quarterly Report, Supply Chain Digest*, March 14, 2012, www.scdigest.com/ONTARGET/12-03-14-2.php?cid=5607. (Source: Wolfe Trahan, December 2011.)

20. Patrick Burnson, "Air Cargo: Is 2012 the Turnaround Year?" *Supply Chain Management Review*, March 6, 2012, www.scmr.com/article/Air_Cargo_Is_2012_the_Turnaround_Year.

21. Ainsley Thomson and Art Patnaude, "No Quick Fix for Container Shippers' Woes," *Wall Street Journal*, October 9, 2009, B4.

22. Ross Tucker, "Traffic, Oil Prices Spur Interest in Coastal Shipping," *Women's Wear Daily*, October 7, 2008, 17. (Source: The American Society of Civil Engineers.)

23. Brian J. Gibson, C. Clifford Defee, and Wesley S. Randall, "The State of the Retail Supply Chain, Results and Findings of the 2009 Study," Auburn University College of Business and Retail Industry Leaders Association (RILA), Sponsored by Fortna, 7–8.

24. "Aberdeen: Most Warehouses Planning Redesign by 2010," *Multichannel Merchant*, July 1, 2008, www.multichannelmerchant.com/opsandfulfillment/advisor/aberdeen-most-warehouses-planning-redesign-2010. (Source: Aberdeen Group.)

25. "Findings of the 2011 Global Compliance Study," in *The Consumer Goods Forum*, 24, 2012, IBM Corporation, www.globalscorecard.net/live/download/CGF_Compliance_Survey_2011_Analys.pdf.

26. "Aberdeen: Most Warehouses Planning Redesign by 2010," *Multichannel Merchant*, July 1, 2008, www.multichannelmerchant.com/opsandfulfillment/advisor/aberdeen-most-warehouses-planning-redesign-2010. (Source: Aberdeen Group.)

27. Jeff Berman, "Retail Supply Chain Study Paints an Optimistic Outlook for Future Growth," *Supply Chain Management Review*, March 8, 2012, 3, www.scmr.com/article/retail_supply_chain_study_paints_an_optimistic_outlook_for_future_growth. (Source: "Third Annual State of the Retail Supply Chain," Study by RILA and Auburn University, sponsored by Accenture Consulting, 2012.)

28. Chris Cunnane, "The Omni-Channel Retail Experience," Aberdeen Group, January 2012, 1, www.aberdeen.com.

Unit Five: Global Retail Profile
Uniqlo (Fast Retailing Co. Ltd.), Japan

Uniqlo, with its totally hip, Asian influenced, affordable, and casual apparel in on-trend colors, is well positioned to be a full-fledged global fast-fashion chain. With aggressive expansion plans, watch for a store opening in a city or country near you.

Prologue

When a parent company's name is Fast Retailing, you can be sure its campaign for a strong international presence is anything but slow and stodgy. Although it has not yet surpassed the number of stores and annual revenues of its three top fashion competitors—Zara, H&M, and Gap—Uniqlo thinks, acts, and performs like it is already number one. The company is based in Yamaguchi, Japan, and is headed by chief executive officer (CEO) Tadashi Yanai.

Yanai gained his early retail experience selling kitchen gadgets and men's clothing at a Jusco supermarket in Japan. He left that position in 1972 to work in his father's tailoring business and became president of the family business in 1984. It was at this juncture that he opened the first Uniqlo store, then-called Unique Clothing Warehouse. Eventually Unique became Uniqlo, and in 2010 Fast Retailing became the holding company for Uniqlo and Yanai's other investments. Fast Retailing has been a top performer on the Nikkei (Japanese stock market) for the past five years.[1] With a 22 percent share in Fast Retailing, Yanai is the largest shareholder—and a billionaire.[2] Sales totaled $11.8 billion for the fiscal year that ended August 31, 2012.[3]

Merchandise and Other Competitive Advantages

What makes Uniqlo so special?

- Apparel is hip but infinitely wearable, with an Asian spin that gives the retailer a competitive advantage.
- Designers are usually a half-step ahead of the color forecasters. Think orange skinny stretch jeans the year before they were popular in most fashion markets.
- Textiles are of very good quality.
- The company experiments with heat-retentive, moisture-wicking, and other high-tech fabrics for ultra-serviceable outdoor and casual clothing.
- Modest prices on well-made basics for men and women are at the crux of Uniqlo's fashion story.
- Parent company Fast Retailing is vertically integrated and designs, manufactures, and distributes its own products.

Finally, the meaning of the abbreviated name Uniqlo says it all: "unique clothing."

Growth and Acquisition Strategies

Since 2003, Fast Retailing has acquired or bought shares in several businesses. The following examples illustrate the complexity of growth plans in retailing and underscore how the economy, and a company's timing, can make or break such plans.

Fast Retailing bought out Link Theory, an apparel manufacturer, in two transactions spanning 2004 and 2009. Link Theory owned the apparel brands Theory and Helmut Lang. It had been an early participant in the bidding process when Barney's New York went up for sale in 2007. Ultimately, however, the Japanese company was outbid by Dubai-based Istithmar.[4]

As a side note, although Istithmar allocated significant amounts of money and resources to build up the business, increasing debt caused by the economic crisis soon made restructuring necessary. Perry Capital now owns the majority share (over 70 percent) in Barney's, and Yucaipa Companies about 20 percent, with Istithmar retaining 10 percent. As this book went to press, Barney's was close to filing Chapter 11, as it had done in the late 1990s.[5] We can assume that Fast Retailing is relieved it did not win that bid.

In a more successful effort, Fast Retailing acquired a modest stake in Nelson Finance, owner of Comptoir des Cotonniers, in 2005, and a year later bought another 64 percent of the French brand. It now controls the French fashion brand Princesse Tam Tam, having purchased 95 percent of its owner, Petit Vehicule, that same year.[6] Because Fast Retailing is cash strong and sells at low price points, the long recession in Japan did not adversely affect sales in the company's 800-plus stores. This meant it was well placed to go global with plans for Uniqlo's expansion.

Part of the global thrust may include the acquisitions of other fashion chains. CEO Yanai has dropped many hints that U.S. and European acquisitions are part of his strategic plan for growth.

Uniqlo Enters America—and the World

Fast Retailing's premier brand is Uniqlo, the agent of change that is expected to take the world by storm. In 2010, the company announced that it intended to open a minimum of 200 Uniqlo stores in the United States by 2020, when it expected to be earning $60 billion annually through 4,000 stores.[7] This prediction displays a lot of bravado for a company that entered the United States in 2005 with three tiny mall stores in New Jersey and a few scattered in the Northeast—test-market stores that closed within a year.

In November 2006, the company opened its first landmark store in New York City's SoHo. I remember it well as I happened to be across the street during the preopening event for dignitaries and the press. The three-story building glowed with bright red lighting. Onlookers might have mistaken it for a sushi restaurant—until they spotted the piles of clothes in wonderfully edgy colors, revolving mannequins, and the requisite greeter at the door.

Including the SoHo location, there are three Uniqlo stores in Manhattan, the latest two being an 89,000-square-foot store on Fifth Avenue, and another on 34th Street at Herald Square. Both opened in 2012. The Fifth Avenue flagship exudes a futuristic theme at every turn. For starters, the store has custom LED video installations in the windows and in four glass elevators. There are 100 dressing rooms in the three-level store as well as 45 checkouts, plus an escalator that takes customers directly from the entrance to the third level if they wish.[8] Training of sales staff is extremely important to Uniqlo. Before opening day, 50 employees from the Fifth Avenue and 34th Street stores were sent to Japan to participate in a 6-month manager training program allowing them to fully internalize the Uniqlo concept.[9]

The parent company expects to launch flagships in several other U.S. cities, including Boston, Chicago, Philadelphia, and Washington, D.C., and to secure 10–20 additional locations in the near future, according to Shin Odake, U.S. chief executive. A 29,000-square-foot store opened in San Francisco in 2012, and other California locations are being studied.[10] The first mall location has opened in Paramus, New Jersey.

In addition to brick-and-mortar stores, Uniqlo built an online store for the United States, its "digital flagship," which launched late in 2012. The company expects to increase U.S. revenues to $10 billion, with 20 percent of sales coming from the online store. Although plans are still tentative, Uniqlo believes that there is sufficient customer demand in the United States to warrant the million-dollar investment.[11]

Global Expansion Strategies

One of Fast Retailing's main goals is to increase international sales by 2015 to the point where they exceed domestic revenue. To do this, the company will expand in China and Southeast Asia as well as in the United States. Uniqlo currently has over 1,000 stores in 12 countries; about 800 of them are located in Japan.

Other countries where growth is apparent include the United Kingdom, Russia, South Korea, Taiwan, Singapore, and France. A sampling of recent Uniqlo openings follows:

- Russia, April 2010—Moscow is the site for the first Uniqlo in the country. The 13,000-square-foot store is in the upmarket Atrium shopping center.[12]
- Taiwan, March 2010—Fast Retailing opens a Taiwanese subsidiary in Taipei in preparation for major expansion in that country, with the first Uniqlo store scheduled to open that fall.[13] Yanai plans to open 30 more stores in Taiwan by 2014.[14]
- France, October 2009—Referencing the high-tech vibe of its other stores, Uniqlo locates its Paris flagship near the Paris Opera House in the heart of the city. The retailer already has smaller stores in other areas of Paris, but the flagship fills 23,000 square feet of a refurbished 1866 building whose façade contrasts well aesthetically with the modern interior's clean lines.[15]

Future areas of interest include South America, Australia, New Zealand, and eventually India. Yanai forecasts that the company's sales worldwide will reach $22 billion in the fiscal year ending in August 2015.[16]

Pricing and Promotion

Fast-fashion does not always equate to discount prices, but it does herald styles that younger fashionistas can comfortably afford. Uniqlo's motto, "Made for All," truly represents its philosophy, which can also be seen in its pricing techniques. A women's V-neck cashmere sweater might be regularly priced at $89.90. On sale, the item would be about $49.90. For $59.90, a customer could purchase a men's or woman's lightweight down jacket.[17] Note the rounded-off, yet not-entirely-odd pricing method.

Fast Retailing has also developed a low-cost clothing branded store called "g.u." The apparel lines were developed to meet the intense competition in Japan, where even supermarkets have joined the cheap-chic brigade. Prices are about half those found in Uniqlo branded stores. For example, jeans sell for about $12.00 and tee shirts for under $6.00. The company predicts the "g.u." chain will grow to 200 stores by 2013 and eventually roll out to international markets.[18] The Ginza flagship store opened in 2012 and has substantially increased sales and the "g.u." brand profile.[19]

When Uniqlo's two flagship stores opened almost simultaneously in New York City, the requisite splash was not accomplished without a flurry of creative promotional events. For several weeks before the openings, six "pop-up" stores rotated throughout the city. Brightly lit mobile Uniqlo Cubes were sent to city events and street fairs—anywhere people gathered. The campaign was supported by transit ads in subways, on buses, and in high-traffic locations throughout the city.[20]

To promote its line of Heattech innerwear, Uniqlo gave away a few thousand free samples in Times Square with all the theatrics the company could conjure up. A structure that looked like a human vending machine housed two professional mimes, who could be seen through the windows. Uniqlo representatives dressed in brilliant silver body suits attracted potential volunteers by chatting them up and demonstrating a thermograph scanner that identified cold spots in their bodies. Once the scan was completed, participants were directed to the human vending machine—one side for men, the other for women—to pick up their innerwear while the mimes danced on. The one-day event generated publicity on TV, Web sites, and via print media.[21] Not a bad day's work to promote a product whose average price tag runs about $18.[22]

Tadashi Yanai was named International Retailer of the Year in 2010 by the National Retail Federation. If accolades like this are already his, then surely the ultimate success of Uniqlo is not far behind. Number one may not be such a stretch of the imagination. In fact, it may be inevitable. Yanai has this to say about globalization: "Companies that sell only in Japan will eventually not be able to sell even in Japan. Corporations have to go global in order to survive."[23]

Profile Discussion Questions

1. What is the basis for Fast Retailing's aggressive plans for future global expansion?
2. Summarize the key components of the Uniqlo brand. What strengths and weaknesses are apparent?
3. Not only does Uniqlo sell fast-fashion, it is on a fast-track to surpass competitors like H&M and Zara. What other apparel retailers do you see as competition for Uniqlo?
4. Although the company has been in business since 1984, it made no overtures to enter the United States until 2000. Does this approach make sense strategically?
5. The bulk of Uniqlo stores are in Japan. How does the company intend to change that balance other than by opening wholly owned stores?
6. What promotional tactics were used to alert customers to the opening of the two flagship stores in New York City? Do you agree with the media selections?
7. How would you justify to Uniqlo the expense that introducing an online store for U.S. customers would cost? If launched, do you believe sales will grow to the extent mentioned in the profile?

Profile Notes

1. Dana Mattioli, "Uniqlo Plans Store On U.S. Coast," *Wall Street Journal*, April 9, 2012, http://online.wsj.com/article/SB10001424052702304587704577333740754213030.html.
2. Shunichi Ozasa and Cheng Herng Shinn, "Fast Says it May Buy U.S., European Rivals," *Bloomberg*, November 6, 2011, 2–3. www.bloomberg.com/news/print/2011-11-04/fast-retailing-seeking-acquisitions-in-europe.
3. Hiroyuki Kachi and Kenneth Maxwell, "Uniqlo Woos the World but Falters at Home, *Wall Street Journal,* October 12, 2012, B8.
4. Ozasa and Shinn, 1–2.
5. Mike Spector, "Barney's Skirts Bankruptcy," *Wall Street Journal*, May 8, 2012, B3.
6. Shunichi Ozasa and Cheng Herng Shinn, "Fast Says it May Buy U.S., European Rivals," *Bloomberg*, November 6, 2011, 2-3. www.bloomberg.com/news/print/2011-11-04/fast-retailing-seeking-acquisitions-in-europe.
7. "Uniqlo May Open 200 Stores in the U.S. by 2010," *Chain Store Age*, December 10, 2010, www.chainstoreage.com/article/uniqlo-may-open-200-stores-us-2020.
8. J. Mosscrop, "Uniqlo's Manhattan Flagship," *Chain Store Age*, October 26, 2011, www.chainstoreage.com/article/uniqlo%E2&80&99s-manhattan-flagship.
9. Marianne Wilson, "Expansion-Minded Uniqlo Aims Big," *Chain Store Age*, November 18, 2011, www.chainstoreage.com/article/expansion-minded-uniqlo-aims-big.
10. Dana Mattioli, "Uniqlo Plans Store On U.S. Coast," *Wall Street Journal*, April 9, 2012, http://online.wsj.com/article/SB10001424052702304587704577333740754213030.html.
11. Kunur Patel, "Japanese Retailer Uniqlo Exploring Online Store for U.S.," *Advertising Age*, April 23, 2012, http://adage.com/article/digital/japanses-retailer-uniqlo-exploring-online-store-u-s/234326.
12. Katya Foreman, "Uniqlo Set to Open in Moscow," *Women's Wear Daily*, March 24, 2010, 13.
13. "Uniqlo to Open a Unit in Taipei," *Women's Wear Daily*, February 19, 2010, 22.
14. Hiroyuki Kachi, "Uniqlo Fashions Global Push," *Wall Street Journal*, September 15, 2011, B8.
15. Elena Berton, "Uniqlo Paris Flagship Set to Open," *Women's Wear Daily*, September 29, 2009, 3.
16. Ibid.
17. Liz Parks, "Fashion for the People," *Stores*, December 2011, www.stores.org/print/book/export/html/11806.
18. Elena Berton with contributions from Kelly Wetherille, Tokyo, "Fashion Eyes New Avenues of Growth," *Women's Wear Daily*, December 29, 2009.
19. "Uniqlo's Sales Up 4.4% for Nine Months Period." Fashion United Group. July 9, 2012. www.fashionunited.com/executive/report/uniqlo-japan-records-sales-growth-of44-for-nine-months-on-y/y-basis-20120907489557.
20. Liz Parks, "Fashion for the People," *Stores*, December 2011, www.stores.org/print/book/export/html/11806.
21. Amy Odell, "Uniqlo to Stage Best Promotion Ever in Times Square," *New York Magazine*, October 24, 2008, www.nymag.com/daily/fashion/2008/10/uniqlo_to_stage_best_promotion.html?mid=fashion-alert-20081024.
22. Ayai Tomisawa "High Temperatures Cause Sales Drop at Uniqlo," *Wall Street Journal*, October 25, 2010, B6.
23. Miki Tanikawa, "Japanese Clothing Retailer Lives Up to Its Name," *New York Times*, September 26, 2009, www.nytimes.com/2009/09/26/business/global/26uniqlo.html.

Appendix

Retail Career Directions

Learning Objectives
After completing this appendix you should be able to:
- Identify retail career options.
- Discern why technological expertise is important for a career in retailing.
- List the benefits of work experience programs.
- Describe the personal characteristics important for success in retail management.
- Discern the important components of a résumé and the interview process.
- Develop a self-marketing plan for your job search.

If you enjoy diversity, new challenges, a fast pace, and geographic and career mobility, retailing *could* be the field for you. If you also enjoy being with people, being creative, and helping others to make decisions; are comfortable with information technology; and enjoy working in an industry where no two days are ever exactly alike, retailing is *probably* for you. Even if you want a nine-to-five desk job where the work requirements at ten o'clock each day are exactly like the previous day, retailing *may* still be for you. In any case, before making a decision, investigate all of the retailing career options.

Although many retailers use online job boards, including Monster.com, to recruit prospective employees, most applicants for retailing positions come to a retailer's attention through the company's Web site or personal referral. Salaries and benefits for management positions in retailing match and may surpass those in other industries. Yet retailing suffers from a public perception that this is not so. The industry has not always conveyed the fact that highly motivated people with skills can advance from entry level to executive ranks in ten years or less and achieve major compensation. Yet this is true.

Today an increasing number of industry human resource managers are promoting retailing as a worthwhile and rewarding career. Informational programs occur on many college campuses, and proactive retailers recognize the importance of partnering with educators on fertile recruitment ground. The goal is to overcome the lingering negative image that hinders many college graduates from pursing a career in retailing.

Many colleges and universities offer retailing courses as an integral part of curricula leading to bachelor's, master's, and doctoral degrees. Many also sponsor one or more retail executive seminars annually. The American Collegiate Retailing Association, a professional organization composed of educators from the United States and several other countries, lists member schools that offer retail programs at www.acraretail.org. The National Retail Federation maintains career information on www.nrf.com and partners with major colleges and universities through its NRF Foundation.

When thinking about a career in retailing consider your own qualifications as well as job opportunities. Look into the various managerial positions open to you as an employee; also explore retail ownership possibilities. However you begin, think about the directions that spring from your first job. Where can you expect to be in five years? In ten years? Which retail companies are growing? What functional areas provide the best opportunities? What skills do you need? The sections that follow will help you answer these questions as you learn how to prepare for a career search.

Retail Career Options
The opportunities for qualified employees in this dynamic industry are strong despite economic woes. Retailing offers a multitude of career opportunities: in stores; with e-retailers, catalogue companies, and direct sellers; and in service businesses. Retailers of every size and type are found globally. There are careers for those who want to be in business for themselves, and careers for those who prefer to work in corporate environments.

Experience is transferable from one business format to another because the basic functions are the same. The retail options are endless.

Opportunities with Retail Stores

Store retailers encompass every type of operation from superstore to drive-through pharmacy. As you have learned, some retailers are huge companies in which functions are divided by specialty. In contrast, sole proprietors manage their stores, performing most functions themselves.

Employees are needed for merchandising and real estate activities; in operations, promotion, human resources, fulfillment, and credit management; and for designing inventory management systems or private label merchandise. From chief executive officers to sales associates, traditional retailers recruit people with a variety of skills. Target has forged links with colleges and universities for locating executive management leadership trainees with bachelor's degrees for its store operations. Services such as interior design and rental stores require personnel. Part-time jobs for students are available in stores, telemarketing firms, and distribution centers. Despite downsizing, retail consolidation, and economic volatility new retail jobs are predicted worldwide.

Opportunities with Nonstore Retailers

A nonstore retailer is one who does not sell through traditional brick-and-mortar facilities. Career opportunities are available in direct marketing and selling operations and online divisions of multichannel firms. For example, Amway, a global direct seller, gives generous rewards to its consultants who reach certain sales quotas through direct sales. Vending companies offer new ownership or franchise opportunities, or both, to those who are interested in dispensing everything from food to DVDs.

Technology has a great impact on retailing, as it has on every other industry. Distribution centers are fully automated and inventory, payrolls, credit systems, databases, accounting, and financial controls are powered by information technology. Streaming video features online shows promoting designer fashions. Systems experts, programmers, analysts, technicians, Web designers, and Webmasters complement the retail career spiral. At all levels of retail distribution, technological expertise is the standard.

Preparing for Your Retail Career

Before you commit to a retail career, explore the many formal and informal programs as you expand your knowledge of retailing. This can be accomplished in several ways including work experience programs, management training programs, and promotion from within—all of which include on-the-job training.

Work Experience Programs

Internships, cooperative education programs, and part-time employment are three ways that individuals sample the retail industry before deciding on a career. Work experience programs help enthusiastic and talented students get the jump on competition for the best jobs.

Internships

Many colleges and universities offer students an opportunity to sample careers while still in school. As interns, individuals work in selected jobs in their chosen field. **Interns** are students in formal training programs that encourage learning on the job while working closely with professionals. Students may work part-time during a semester, full-time for an entire semester or summer, or in other combinations. Internships may be paid or unpaid. In either case, college credit is usually earned because the internship is treated as a learning experience.

Typical retail internships take place on a selling floor, in a merchandising office, or in the areas of human resources or product development. One student may run the temporary Christmas decoration shop in one of Bloomingdale's branch stores. Another may assist the buyer in Debenham's department store in London. A third may work at headquarters for a manufacturer/retailer such as Timberland or Reebok. Others learn from the owner how to completely merchandise a local hardware store or set up a Web page for a vintage clothing business.

The value of an internship varies because training is only as good as the trainer, the motivation and maturity of the student, and the demands of the academic institution. Most interns follow a syllabus and do academic assignments that enhance their experience while employed and help them reflect upon and integrate what they've learned upon completion.

A good internship often precipitates a retail career since many retailers hire previous interns as management trainees. Employers like to hire from this group, because its members are familiar with both the company culture and retail procedures. There are few surprises for the new employee who has had previous experience with his or her employer. Attrition is much lower, training is easier, and advancement is faster. **Attrition** is the reduction of employees within an organization due to resignation, retirement, or death. Depending on their experience, some former interns start in management positions.

Cooperative Education

Although the terms are often used interchangeably, there are differences between internships and cooperative education. **Cooperative education** is an educational methodology that uses alternate periods of formal study and work experience as a requirement for graduation. The major difference is in the number of work experiences. Students may have as few as two work periods in a two-year community college or graduate program, or as many as five in a five-year bachelor's degree program. Because students usually return to the same employer, it is possible to move from the lowest level during the first work term to a full-fledged managerial position by graduation. Cooperative education is offered in over 1,000 colleges and universities in the United States, Canada, United Kingdom, Australia, Europe, Japan, and other countries committed to the philosophy.

Part-Time and Temporary Jobs

Even if a college or university has no formal work program, some students begin their retailing careers while in school. Many of the most successful retail executives began working part-time in stores while in high school and continued working part-time and during summers through college. They dedicated themselves to a retail career long before receiving their degrees. Long hours and low pay are typical when starting out in retailing. Those that accommodate these inconveniences and continue to pursue retail careers are likely candidates for success.

Management Training Programs

Most large retail companies have formal management training programs. Whether in merchandising, store operations, or online divisions, these programs offer college graduates a route to junior executive positions. Recruitment, training, and development of selection criteria are important to retailers and management training candidates as they begin the search process.

Recruitment

Major retailers around the world recruit on selected college and university campuses annually. They also invite graduating students from all colleges to submit their résumés.

Competition for slots in these programs is fierce, and it is not unusual for 800 students to be interviewed for 80 openings. Applicants with experience have a better chance of being selected, and of surviving the demanding first years.

Training

Most training programs produce both merchandising and operations executives. Trainees move ahead as quickly as their interests and skills develop. Programs combine intense work experience with structured seminars and study using computer modules, video, and training manuals.

Management training programs vary in length from several months to two years, depending on the company. Focus of training programs also differs. Training in management skills may be more important to some companies, while others place a higher premium on customer relations and technology skills.

Starting salaries vary according to the experience and educational background of the candidate and the geographic location of the employer. Most companies conduct periodic reviews of trainees and award salary increases based on merit. Starting salaries for management trainees usually range from $30,000 to over $50,000 per year. Although retailing salaries are somewhat low at the beginning, salaries for middle- and upper-management employees become comparable to, if not higher than, those in other fields. After five years of experience, it is possible for executives to more than double their salaries.

Qualifications for Selection

Recruiters differ on the academic degrees they prefer for candidates seeking entry into their management trainee programs. Some seek general business majors or those specializing in marketing, management, retailing, fashion merchandising, finance, and information technology. Others recruit liberal arts graduates. Most favor business majors over humanities majors, if all else is equal. Some recruiters will accept graduates of two-year programs.

Candidates with MBA degrees are viewed favorably because of the increasing importance placed on strategic planning, quantitative analysis, and information technology, including Web analytics—areas in which those with advanced degrees are more adept. For individuals with a fashion orientation who are interested in earning a master of business administration degree, the Laboratory Institute of Merchandising offers one of the first programs of its kind at its New York City campus. The accredited MBA program expects candidates to have at least two years of experience in the fashion industry, among other requirements.[1]

Recruiters agree on the attributes necessary for success in an executive training program:

- Individuals with an outgoing personality, effective communication skills, and a sincere interest in retailing have an edge.
- Intelligence and demonstrated leadership skills are necessary.
- Candidates with high levels of energy and the ability to think on their feet do best.
- Mature, assertive decision-makers are prized.
- Above-average technological skills and analytical abilities are expected.
- Previous experience is necessary.

Promotion from Within

Although executive training programs offer the fastest route to management positions, there are other alternatives. Selling is a starting point for many executives in retailing. From sales associate, an individual moves to assistant department manager, group manager, assistant buyer, and possibly store manager. Some retailers offer special training programs for employees who show management potential. These programs generally take longer to complete than executive training programs.

Because everyone who applies cannot possibly be selected for a firm's management training program, the sales route, although slower, is an alternative road to a top management job. Often, a good person who is passed over by executive placement recruiters, and who is willing to start in sales, becomes a more valuable executive in the long run than some individuals in formal training programs. Radio Shack and Enterprise Rent-a-Car are retail companies that promote from within regularly.

Specialty store chains offer management positions in which employees have responsibilities ranging from staff supervision to merchandising duties, human resource functions to total store operation. In addition to store management, specialty chains provide skill enhancement opportunities for those interested in becoming district managers, regional managers, and training directors.

At the Gap, management trainees go through several steps on their career path. Advancement is based on job performance, not the amount of time spent in each position. The first promotion for a management trainee at the Gap is to assistant manager; the next, to store manager. At that point, some individuals become training store managers and teach other managers who are on their way up the career ladder. Ultimately, some Gap managers are promoted to area managers, district managers, and regional managers. At these levels their responsibility for overseeing several to many stores grows incrementally.

The impressions of an Express store manager are related in From the Field A.1, and she is featured in the accompanying figure. Her insight on learning, gaining experience, and developing patience while working for promotion is valuable to those considering a retail career.

From the Field A.1   Management Training at Express

Years ago when I took a part-time job in retailing for the summer, I never imagined the impact it would have on my life. After that summer, I returned to college as a sophomore and changed my major from Hotel/Restaurant Management to Retailing. I feel it was the right choice. People say you either love retailing or you hate it. I love it, but trust me, I have my days—and sometimes even weeks—when things do not go smoothly. I have learned firsthand the stresses of working retail, such as the long hours, understaffed stores, and rude customers. As for the benefits, there are the great clothes, cutting-edge fashion tips, valued coworkers, wonderful customers, flexible schedules, and the opportunity to learn skills that will help you get ahead.

I began my career in retailing as a sales associate and quickly was promoted to assistant manager. Fortunately, I was taking business classes and was able to use the information and tools to help me do my job better. Often I heard students say that they felt that what they were learning in the classroom was going to be useless once they got a job. I am very grateful that I did benefit from my education. Money well spent!

College classes and my internship prepared me well for my career. Four months after graduation, I was promoted to a higher-volume Express store and given a raise while in my position as assistant manager. When Express was still owned by the Limited, the general store manager was called the sales manager. I worked closely with her, performing operations such as opening and closing the store; executing inventories, shipments, and transfers; and managing the cash wrap with various customer service issues and the computerized point-of sale (POS) systems. I coordinated in-store contests and special promotions, helped re-merchandise the store, and assisted with hiring and training sales associates. All managers offered customer service by assisting customers on the sales floor. I was content with this position at the time, but aspired to bigger things. The pay was adequate for my needs and I received small raises with each promotion to a higher-volume store. The experience I gained made up for what was missing in my paycheck.

After two years as an assistant manager in three other large-volume Express stores in my region, I was promoted to sales manager of a lower-volume store. Finally, my own store with a larger salary! Wouldn't you know it, Express was acquired by Golden Gate Capital in 2007. The transaction went more smoothly than we expected, and I adapted to new management directives, company mission, and the title of co-manager.

Not a demotion—as I first thought by the sounds of my shared title—but rather an effective way of developing a management hierarchy for vast stores with women's apparel on one side and men's on the other. After 18 months, I was promoted to a much higher-volume store, also as co-manager.

I've been a retail manager for 10 years and my skills continue to develop. Finding and keeping good personnel and dealing with the problems that accompany staffing a store with young part-time workers are challenges I routinely face. I still work long hours, but I've learned that to develop good managers you have to learn to delegate responsibility. It is also important to train your staff well, because it makes a huge impact on the overall store experience for customers.

Every day is different. One afternoon, a price tag hanging close to a display light unexpectedly caught fire and burned a pair of jeans. Mall security and the local fire department responded immediately, and no real damage was done, but the event certainly reinforced the point that managers have to be ready to react to almost anything and stay calm under pressure.

When I graduated from college, I had realistic expectations. I did not expect a set schedule and a high salary. I knew I would receive both eventually, but the first few years are when the most blood, sweat, and tears are shed. At one point, I didn't believe that I could be a successful manager. It took a wise professor to point out that I could. For this I am ever grateful. Self-doubt is what blocks the road to success. Don't let yourself or others put up roadblocks.

As you embark on your career in retail management, here are a few additional points to keep in mind:

- You are a leader of a team. Lead by example because people are looking to you as a role model.
- As you grow and develop in your role, you will make mistakes—you are human. Be humble and use these mistakes as valuable lessons; then move on.
- Retail is ever-changing, so be ready to adapt. You are always either trying to keep up with or beat your competition or stay on track with today's technology. Take it in stride because the company's goal is to be a leader in the industry.
- Be open to opportunities that can help you acquire new skills. Do this with a positive attitude and try to keep all professional relationships exemplary ones. You never know when new opportunities will present themselves.
- Hold high hopes that you will have a successful and rewarding career.

When I look to the future, I'm not always sure what I see myself doing, but that's all right. The training, knowledge, and experience that I have gained are enough to allow me to do whatever I choose in the retail industry.

Good luck to you!

By Sara Bilodeau Misuraca

Author's Note: Sara left Express, earned a degree in interior design, and is currently employed by Ethan Allen Furniture Galleries as an interior designer. (She's also a new mother!)

Qualities of Successful Retail Managers

Managers trained in organizational leadership skills, finance, and strategic planning are in demand, particularly when this expertise is balanced by an understanding of marketing and merchandising. It is evident that very special kinds of people are needed. Skill-based competencies of successful retail managers were listed in Chapter 13. Personal qualities, abilities, and attitudes of a successful retail manager are included in the following profile:

- *Problem solving:* To analyze financials and data used in planning, managing, and controlling.
- *Creativity:* To bring imaginative ideas to merchandising and operations and stay attuned to recognize trends.
- *Confidence:* To take action, seize opportunities, and make quick, confident decisions in the ever-changing retail world.
- *Leadership:* To show initiative, helping everyone work together to run a business smoothly.
- *Flexibility:* To be receptive to changing trends in styles and attitudes, and be adaptable to the everyday surprises in retailing.
- *Energy:* To handle the stress of the fast-paced, demanding job of retail managers.
- *Communication skills:* To practice excellent written, oral, and digital communication skills.
- *Human relations skills:* To relate well with others in a business setting. The human side of the marketplace is often neglected in the rush for profits; however, profits are sometimes lost because of this neglect.
- *Ability to function under pressure:* To handle multiple tasks and make decisions effectively and expediently.
- *Optimistic attitude:* To maintain an optimistic outlook, and inspire and motivate others.

Managers frequently give verbal instructions to those who work for them and send written reports—including e-mails and tweets—to those for whom they work. Good verbal and writing skills are thus important. Students sometimes ignore the professor who emphasizes the need for communication skills in business. Listen well, future retailers; few lessons are more important. Although possession of these and other qualities does not guarantee success, without them a retail manager is less likely to succeed.

Many retailing students aspire to open their own stores one day. All of the qualities required of a retail executive hold true for an entrepreneur. In some areas, emphasis shifts and some new traits emerge. Sole proprietors perform multiple tasks concurrently. When you own your own store, you can never say, "That's not my department." Ownership brings a great sense of involvement to an entrepreneur both professionally and personally. Knowing that you are responsible for generating not only your own salary, but also those of your employees, lends a new meaning to the word *responsibility.* Being a storeowner is totally time-consuming. You are a professional multitasker and your business becomes your whole life.

The Career Search

Whatever the career choice, planning is essential when identifying jobs and employers. Without a plan, graduates can easily end up in the wrong occupation, in the wrong location, and with the wrong firm. They must begin their search with a goal in mind, a self-analysis, and a self-marketing plan. Before setting your own goals, ask yourself four questions about the career field you are considering:

1. Does it have a future? Consider trends in the retail environment such as technology, the economy, social change, and competition.
2. Will it be financially rewarding?
3. Does it have growth potential to accommodate a large number of new recruits in the future?
4. Do you absolutely love it?

If retailing is your choice, then the answer to all four questions must be yes—in spite of the mergers, acquisitions, bankruptcies, and growth pains of the past decade. As you start your strategic career search, look at the growth potential in the industry. This is more important than the door through which you enter an industry or company. No one wants a dead-end job or one that barely provides a living wage, but because too many people think only of the starting salary and job title, some miss the best opportunities. Thinking about your goals helps you stay on target as you develop, learn, and implement skills in your entry-level position.

Make an honest appraisal of your interests, abilities, and weaknesses. Do they fit the picture you are painting of your future? If not, you must reappraise your goals before going any further. They have to be realistic in terms of who you are, your interests, and your aptitudes. Part of self-analysis is determining what knowledge or skills you have acquired through your educational and work experiences and judging how this knowledge will transfer to your desired career path.

Set goals and relate them to who you are, what you desire, and how your capabilities and interests relate to the world of work. Then, you are at least one step ahead of the competition. Most candidates only seek a job. They do not think about the long-range implications of planning for a career.

Career Search Preliminaries

Now the real work begins. Seek information on companies that interest you through research, interviews, and networking.

Seeking Information and Encouragement

Explore online job sites, or write or call companies and ask about jobs, the company, and future opportunities. Telephone or e-mail executives you know and ask if you can take a few minutes of their time for an informational interview. An **informational interview** is an informal meeting between an executive and a person seeking information on an industry, company, and career opportunities. Many people are flattered to be asked, and if you do this in a polite way, you may get an appointment. Talk to family friends, alumni of your college, and summer or part-time employers. Armed with information, you will be better prepared to present yourself to potential employers.

Turn to faculty, friends, relatives, and others to learn about employment opportunities and to let people know you are in the job market. Not surprisingly, most positions are found by personal referral. Networking is an excellent preliminary strategy that often leads to employment. A good tip when networking: never leave one contact without getting the names of one or two more people. Because they know the first contact, they are more likely to receive you. This method helps build a wonderful resource file of potential employers. Attending job fairs is another way to build your list of prospective employers.

You can obtain lists of employers from such sources as the College Placement Council, chambers of commerce, directories from professional associations, and references like Standard & Poor's register, Moody's manuals, and the Dun & Bradstreet directories. Specialized career publications such as *Job Postings* magazine are often available from career development offices. The yellow pages and many online resources are also valuable. In fact, Web sites have become a primary means of alerting prospective employees about opportunities within a company. The Direct Marketing Association publishes on its Web site an annual listing of companies that provide paid summer internships. Material such as this may often pave the way to full-time positions as well. Job-search Web sites range from the general to the highly specific. Several retail and fashion, domestic and international Web sites are listed in Table A.1.

Seek out someone who will offer encouragement and support during the job search. It is helpful to have a friend, adviser, or approachable faculty member to whom you can report weekly and discuss progress or frustration. Consider offering the same support to friends or colleagues when they seek a position in retailing.

Anticipating the Expense

Try to plan for the necessary monetary investment in the job search. You will need a smartphone or tablet, e-mail access, and voicemail capability or a telephone answering machine. Other costs may include transportation, interview clothing, résumé development and printing charges, and postage—if you have been asked to mail rather then e-mail your documents.

A part-time job serves as a bridge to allow time for job-search activities. Depending on the circumstances, one creative approach to job hunting is to offer to work for free as an intern. One

///////////////////////////////////
Cyberscoop
When you're ready to research job options, log onto the List of Search Engines Web site and spend some time browsing its resources. The list is compiled from traffic rank data, only, but represents a variety of career fields and includes profiles of each job search engine. Go to www. listofsearchengines.info/job-search-engines and start planning your future.

Table A.1 Retail Focused Online Job-Boards

Web site	Key Attributes
www.retailcrossing.com	• Division of Employment Crossing • Full-spectrum retail postings • Current retail news on site • Worldwide reach
www.workinretail.com	• Retail and restaurant listings • Easy to navigate all aspects • Many sales associate and store manager positions, locally and nationally • Partner of National Retail Federation
www.allretailjobs.com	• Approximately 50,000 retail jobs available, from corporate to sales associate levels • Direct links to well-known retailers • Search by functional areas
www.retailjob.ca	• Attractively designed and navigable site for Canadian job seekers • Jobs listed immediately on home page
www.inretail.co.uk	• Focus on retail and hospitality sectors • Directed to job seekers in the United Kingdom and European Union • Major retail advertisers sponsor site
www.the.dma.org/careercenter	• Directed to job seekers and employers • Sponsored by the Direct Marketing Association • Site advertises 500 multichannel positions
www.fashioncareercenter.com	• Dedicated to fashion merchandising, design, apparel, and retail postings • Useful career and training information • New York City–based site
www.wwd.com/wwdcareers	• Savvy fashion industry site • Can register at site or sign in through Facebook • Career videos available

college graduate with a marketing degree and a postgraduate certificate in Web design who was job hunting during the recession used this strategy. Frustrated with the tight job market despite good experience, she took a position as an intern. A few months later she was offered a full-time job with benefits and now does graphic work for a direct marketing agency. Don't get discouraged!

Developing a Plan of Attack

Usually the greater the number of contacts and interviews you have, the greater the number of job offers you will receive. College placement offices offer on-campus interviews, résumé assistance, employer and alumni contact lists, job opening information, and Internet access.

Direct mailings and e-mails are useful in a long-distance job search. Letters addressed to a specific individual are more likely to be read, and a cover letter should always accompany a résumé.

A long-distance search involves visits to your area of interest, subscriptions to the major newspaper, and inquiries to colleges that might offer reciprocal placement services.

For individuals contemplating a major move, consider some of the top geographic markets for young people. Leading trade and business publications like the *Wall Street Journal* and *Forbes* magazine frequently publish lists of the best cities for specific careers or entry-level positions, including cost of living, lifestyle, real estate options, and other useful information. Others, like the job board CareerCast.com, publish a list of the best jobs, ranked according to five criteria: income, work environment, stress, physical demands, and hiring outlook. Its 2012 listing ranked human resource managers in third and online advertising manager in eighth—both potential job categories for those with business interests.[2]

Creative approaches to the career search include placing a position-wanted ad in newspapers or online, distributing business cards at professional meetings, or developing a one-of-a-kind résumé. Cold calls or walk-ins involve visiting companies in person, without an appointment, to try to make contacts where you have had difficulty lining up an interview or getting the name of a contact person. Sometimes attracting attention in an innovative way is the best way to get a foot in the door.

Online-Specific Tactics

Job boards like Monster.com, CareerBuilder.com, and CareerCast.com are only three of thousands of job boards on the Web. Blogs are useful as you try to digest other people's experiences on job boards, and those written by retailers themselves can be useful sources of information. And then there is Twitter.

Job Boards   Monster is just that—monstrously huge. To better meet customer needs, the company partners with cities to deliver key resources to job seekers in specific geographic areas and those interested in relocating. With Monster.com as a partner, at www.boston.com/jobs you can post a résumé, explore local companies via photo galleries, as well as read about job market status, hiring trends, and other details on the area. The job blog on the site posts the latest job news and commentary. In April 2012, there were over 60,000 postings for positions in the Greater Boston area.[3] Monster acquired job search company HotJobs from its owner, Yahoo, in 2010. Under the terms of the agreement, Monster provides job information for Yahoo's U.S. and Canadian home pages.[4]

Some job sites also offer job seekers affinity assessment in the form of job-matching tools. Like a dating game, you list criteria you are seeking and they are matched with an appropriate job. CareerBuilder is one of the largest of these sites, with over 1.5 million jobs and 300,000 employer members.[5]

Though most job sites are relatively secure, caution is advised when you answer advertisements and follow through with companies, to assure they are genuine and not bogus. Most job boards are free while others are paid services. The smaller, more focused sites are useful for people looking at specific industries.

Online social and business networks like Facebook and LinkedIn are useful tools for some job seekers. The online experience broadens the reach of one-on-one networking to a vast number of potential contacts located around the country or even worldwide.

Blogs   Blogging is useful when attempting to form a relationship with a company for which you'd like to work. It is also a way to get recognition for special expertise that you may have by soliciting comments or recommendations from others. A Walmart recruitment manager said that he filled 125 corporate jobs with the aid of Web journals written by prospective candidates. If you use a blog for career-building purposes, be sure your writing is concise, grammatically correct, and pertinent to the topics addressed in the industry.[6]

Twitter   If you can write a job description or post your key attributes in less than 140 characters, you may find Twitter useful in your job hunt. Some companies find it a valuable way to detect technologically knowledgeable individuals who are proficient in and inclined to use social media.[7] If Sears is looking for a retail-oriented technical expert to design a new Web site, Twitter could be the service to use. Sears could advertise the position on Twitter and also view tweets from potential candidates who emphasize their aptitude, personality, and expertise.

Career Search Tools

Three basic tools are essential in getting the first job: (1) résumés, (2) letters, and (3) interviews. All three are approached from a marketing point of view. The marketing concept is your guide, just as if you were selling a product or a service instead of yourself.

The Résumé

A brief history of your education and experience gives prospective employers something concrete to review. Two formats to consider when you prepare a résumé are chronological and functional. Chronological résumés list past experiences in order, beginning with your current position, and then working back in time. Functional résumés stress competencies and experiences gained on the job and are not reflected on a timeline. There is no overall consensus as to what constitutes the perfect résumé. However, keep in mind that employers spend less than 20 seconds scanning a résumé to determine if a candidate is worth further consideration. A résumé that opens interview doors is organized, attractive, brief, concise, complete, truthful, and clearly written with no misspellings.

The heading gives identifying information including name, address, phone number, and e-mail contact. The job or career objective is a brief statement of short- and long-range goals. An option is a qualifications summary, a statement indicating how your skills relate to your desired objective.

In giving your educational background, work backward from your most recent degree. Include your degree, major, minor, honors, date of graduation, and the name of your school. Courses are optional. Consider omitting your grade point average unless requested; if the company screens candidates using a specific GPA and you fall just short, you don't want to be eliminated as a candidate before recruiters have the chance to meet you and learn of your many other stellar qualities.

In giving work experience, work backward from your most recent job. Include summer employment, part-time jobs, volunteer work, internships, and projects completed for companies as part of class projects. Use action verbs to describe your duties and responsibilities.

Your interests and activities indicate that you are a well-rounded person. Highlight the activities and identify interests that closely relate to your career goals or the needs of the employer. Personal details need not be included on a résumé, and it is illegal for a potential employer to ask questions about age, marital status, health, sexual orientation, or disabilities.

Include the line "References furnished upon request"—and ask permission from faculty or employers who know you well to use their names as references. Have their names, affiliations, addresses, and contact information readily available. A good résumé in itself does not guarantee that you will get the job, but a bad one easily prevents you from being considered.

The Internet provides boundless opportunities for job searching, but you will find that some Web sites are easier than others to navigate, are more industry specific, and are geared to entry-level positions. Online applicants for a position should follow any special protocols identified on the Web site as well as a few basic rules:

- Create a scannable and Internet-friendly version of your résumé by including fewer graphic accessories—such as bullets, borders, and elaborate columns—to ensure intact delivery.
- Use universal font types like Courier or Times New Roman in a size no smaller than 12 point.
- Avoid overuse of italics.
- Stick to a one-page format, with contact information at the top.

While you are in preparation mode, be sure to update your profiles on Facebook, LinkedIn, and any other social network sites you follow. Evaluate these postings as objectively as you can, putting on a fresh set of eyes to view them as a potential employer might.

Letters

Effective letters are as important in the job search as a compelling résumé. The following is a list of letters to consider as part of your personal marketing campaign. Some communications require hard-copy formats. Other forms of contact are appropriately made via e-mail.

1. *Letter of application.* Employers read the letter before they read the enclosed résumé. Be sure it is good. To maintain control of the process, end the letter with a sentence such as: "Within

ten days I will call you in order to follow up this mailing and see if we might arrange an interview." Make your letter a clean, hard-copy document suitable for mail or fax.

2. *Letter of appreciation.* It is always appropriate to say thank you after an interview. Such a letter shows that you are considerate and displays common business courtesy. This can be done by e-mail, but a hard copy note sent through the mail might make you stand out in a crowd.

3. *Letter seeking additional information.* This certainly can be done by e-mail when questions are very specific and not readily available on the company's Web site.

4. *Letter inquiring about status.* E-mail follow-up is suitable, but depending on the circumstances, a text message may work as long as you have cleared that method in advance with your contact person.

5. *Letter accepting a position.* This is a formal letter, often containing legal documents for your signature and is handled through the mail unless you are advised otherwise by the company.

6. *Letter rejecting an offer of employment.* Likewise, this is done formally. Continue to leave a good impression by including your thanks and a positive note regarding the company or the person who interviewed you. You never know if your paths will cross in the future

The Interview

Be prepared: a good résumé opens the interview door; a poor interview quickly slams it shut. You are judged on your grooming, the way you carry and express yourself, and your maturity and personality. This is the time to sell your job-related qualities. In one-on-one interviews, the job candidate meets with only one human resource manager or other executive at a time. A good first interview leads to a second interview, and often the second interview leads to the job you want.

As a job applicant, you may want to review some of the material in Chapter 13 as you learn more about the interview process. Stress interviews were mentioned there; here, we see how multi-candidate situations speed up the interview process. Panel interviews are conducted in which applicants face a barrage of questions and problem-solving situations generated by three or four company executives. Group interviews sometimes are conducted discreetly during informal meals or other events. In this scenario, social skills of prospective employees are evaluated, as well as their levels of assertiveness.

Speed interviews are growing in popularity for some retailers. When retailers meet with multiple job candidates and candidates meet with several interviewers in a compressed period, this is called **speed interviewing**. As many as 200 candidates are screened in this manner. Typically five to ten recruiters meet with each person for about five minutes. Some recruiters humorously compare it to speed dating.[8] Zappos.com has used speed interviewing to filter out job prospects that are not a good fit for the company before extensive—and expensive—interviewing takes place. The shoe retailer looks for employees who are team-oriented and often asks prospective candidates to determine where they fit on Zappo's one-to-ten "weirdness scale."

Protocol of Interviewing   Of course you will become well versed on the company and think long and hard about your own contributions to the position under offer before you interview. However, it is often little things that sway the hiring decision your way or to another applicant. Think about the following points as you prepare.

Wear Company-Appropriate Dress   Despite a world gone casual, there are still a few circumstances in which adhering to the norm displayed in a particular industry or setting is appropriate. In general, an interview for a management trainee that takes place at a retail headquarters or flagship store requires a suit or carefully selected separates for women and a suit or sport coat and slacks for men. For women it also means no plunging necklines or visible skin around the waist, and modest but effective makeup and hair. This seems rudimentary, but many job opportunities are lost because of poor personal presentation and wardrobe selection. Keep shoes simple and impeccable.

On the other hand, if an interview were with a fashion-forward company, you would want to tone down the more formal presentation and skip the suit in favor of outfits that show your interest and affinity for the company. When in doubt, try to ask someone working for the company or a person who has already interviewed there for guidance.

Rarely—if ever—is it acceptable to wear sneakers to an interview Consider it the exception if the interview is at a distribution center and you are required to wear athletic footwear. Here is another viewpoint regarding choice of wardrobe: Dress as though the company already employed you.

Prepare Yourself   Practice for your interview with members of your career development center, a trusted friend who works in business, or an objective friend or relative to see how you come across under fire. Try to get them to ask you questions you may or may not have thought about beforehand. The use of live remote video interviewing is increasing, so videotaping a practice interview is a valuable tool. Many of you can do that using your smartphone or pocket camera.

Interviewers have varied styles and your challenge is to be ready for several possibilities. After the initial greeting, some human resource managers may ask you to tell them about yourself. Others will start by sharing the job description with you or telling you something about the company. Others may give you a retail problem to resolve early in the interview or ask for your opinion on newsworthy topics in the retail industry. Sometimes the interview is extremely informal and conversant and you may not feel that you were interviewed. Be ready for all approaches—and then some.

Monitor Personal Mannerisms   Look your interviewer in the eye when you answer a question—not the floor or an appealing picture on the wall. Be expressive with your hands if that is your natural inclination, but don't fidget or use too many random or sweeping gestures. Watch your body language; tightly folded arms usually imply a closed mind or other behavior that could be viewed negatively. Sit up straight in your chair; don't slouch down and rest your arm on the back of the chair or couch as though you were settling in for an episode of *American Idol*—even if the interviewer has asked you to relax. Try not to use slang. Absolutely do not chew gum.

Talk About the Position   Although it's in the back of your mind, it's best not to talk about money—read that as salary, bonus, benefits, vacation time, company car—on the first interview. Instead talk about the position and why you are the right fit for the company and the right person for the job. Stress "team" over the sometimes overused and narcissistic "I" in conversation.

Last, but not least: be on time for your interview.

Projections: Where the Jobs Will Be

Despite economic calamities, demand will increase for the next generation of retail executives. Opportunities for new recruits in discount and off-price chains are usually greater than in department stores during periods of economic slowdown. The discounter Target prides itself on its commitment to college recruiting and tries to maintain a presence on campus in many ways. Through job fairs, on-campus interviews, internships, guest lectures to classes, and in-store study tours for retail majors the company builds relationships on campus. Taking the quest for information even further, the company provides "Beyond the Bull's-eye" programs at its Minneapolis headquarters for guidance counselors, directors of career development centers, and committed faculty. Target's executives offer an in-depth look at the company and its culture, presentations by top team members, and the opportunity to become acquainted with local and regional recruiters.

Specialty chain companies, like Limited Brands, have clearly defined career paths and good compensation packages including bonus incentive plans. They have the allure and ability to attract high-ranking graduates. Department stores like JCPenney and Kohl's do an admirable job of recruitment.

When asked to choose their ideal employer, many job-seekers cite the importance of companies that recruit heavily on campus, have jobs to offer, and are financially stable. Contrary to job-seekers in prerecession years, many young people today express the desire to find a retail position where they can stay and grow with the company. This contrasts with the former mind set that the first full-time job was a mere stepping-stone to the next big job offer. Others are rightfully concerned about the corporate culture and whether the company takes an active stance on environmental concerns. The top 12 companies ranked by how they treat employees, customers, and the planet are listed in Table A.2.

Table A.2	Top Retail Companies to Work For	
Rank	**Company**	**Score**
1	Apple	100
2	Ace Hardware	84
3	Dell	82
4	Office Depot	82
5	Staples	82
6	Whole Foods Market	80
7	Lowe's	79
8	The Home Depot	71
9	O'Reilly Automotive	70
10	Costco	67
11	Verizon Wireless	65
12	Target	65

Condensed and adapted from: Laurie Bassi, Ed Frauenheim, Dan McGuire, and Larry Costello, "2011 Good Company Retail Index," Good Company, November, 2011, www.goodcompanyindex.com.

Some companies lose a disturbing number of recruits to other firms in or out of the industry after the initial training stages. This is often due to the unrealistic expectations of young college graduates who did not have the opportunity to engage in internships or part-time work in retailing. Also a factor in recidivism: the glamour attached to apparel retailing dissipates when new recruits face the reality of long workdays, hard work, and responsibilities for which they are not ready. In an effort to retain staff, some stores move employees up the career ladder too quickly. Meaningful training programs and ongoing support are necessary for recruits in any retail organization.

As firms embrace omnichannel retailing, opportunities in e-commerce divisions offer another avenue of growth for skilled individuals. Some global retailers actively recruit foreign students studying in the United States. The tactic is to identify and train qualified management candidates before they graduate and return to their home countries to work for that retailer. There are job prospects with direct marketing firms including catalogues and direct mail, and in the food/supermarket industry. These examples are only some of the possibilities in a rapidly evolving industry. Whatever the setting, retailing is an exciting and rewarding profession. Discover this for yourself.

Endnotes

1. Whitney Beckett, "Laboratory Institute of Merchandising Offering M.B.A. Program," *Women's Wear Daily*, October 31, 2008, 9.
2. "Top of the Heap: Job Board CareerCast Released a List of the Best Jobs in 2012." *Wall Street Journal*, April 11, 2012, B6. (Source: CareerCast.com.)
3. "Jobs," Boston.com and Monster.com, accessed April 16, 2012, www.boston.com/jobs.
4. "Monster Completes Acquisition of HotJobs and Enters into Multi-year Traffic Agreement with Yahoo!" Monster Worldwide, Inc., August 24, 2010.
5. "Top 10 Job Search Sites 2012," List of Search Engines, accessed April 16, 2012, www.listofsearchengines .info/job-search-engines.
6. Sarah E. Needleman, "How Blogging Can Help You Get a New Job," *Wall Street Journal*, April 10, 2007, B1.
7. Sarah E. Needleman, "A New Job Just a Tweet Away," *Wall Street Journal*, September 8, 2009, B7.
8. John Sullivan, "Leading-Edge Candidate Screening, Interviewing, and Assessment Practices," ERE.net, April 9, 2012, www.ere.net/2012/04/09/leading-edge-candidate-screening-interviewing-and-assessment-practices.

Glossary

10-K report   Audited document containing extensive financial data and information about a company, its people, operations, and strategic planning.

4-5-4 calendar   Adaptation of a conventional calendar used for retail planning and accounting.

807 programs   Caribbean initiative programs offering low taxation on goods, among other incentives, to encourage manufacturing in selected countries.

Accordion theory   Theory that explains the way retail organizations expand and contract in response to changes in the marketplace.

Accountability   Policy that ensures that job expectations are satisfactorily met by the person or persons held responsible for the action.

Acquisition   Buying of one company by another in either a friendly or hostile manner. (See also *hostile takeover*.)

Active RFID tags   Larger tags that require a power source, have a longer range, and are more expensive than passive tags.

Additional markup   Price increase taken after the original markup has been determined.

Advanced shipping notices (ASNs)   Electronically generated documents that alert receivers to impending shipments of goods.

Aggressive pricing   Method based on undercutting competitors' prices rather than concentrating on the company's strengths.

Aisle interrupters   Signs, usually made from cardboard, that protrude into an aisle.

Allocators   Individuals who support merchandise teams by providing detailed location and distribution information for goods.

Allowances   Reductions in costs of goods that involve concessions made between supply chain members.

Ambiance   Mood evoked by the use of tangible and intangible store design tools.

Analog method   Method used to obtain a sales forecast by comparing potential new sites with existing sites.

Anchor stores   Major mall tenants occupying large, usually corner or end stores.

Anticipation   An additional discount sometimes allowed when an invoice is paid before the expiration of a cash discount period.

Aspirational wants   Products and services that people perceive will help them achieve higher status in life.

Assessment   Process of evaluating an individual's progress on-the-job.

Asset turnover   Selling the inventory—the valuable merchandise of retailers. Also called *inventory turnover* or *turn*.

Association of Southeast Asian Nations (ASEAN)   Trade alliance set up in 1967 with U.S. backing to benefit countries including Brunei, Indonesia, Malaysia, the Philippines, Singapore, Thailand, and later, Vietnam.

Asymmetrical balance   Positioning of items on either side of a center line so that they are not equally weighted optically. Also called *informal balance.*

Attrition   Reduction of employees within an organization due to resignation, retirement, or death.

Augmented reality (AR)   Interactive images that appear like holograms and are accessed via Webcams on enabled sites.

Auto ID   Technology that uses wireless devices to capture and identify information.

Autocratic leaders   Leaders who make decisions independently, then inform employees or subordinates.

Automated storage and retrieval (ASR)   Warehousing system that combines the use of computer control of stock records with mechanical handling.

Avatar   An animated digital form that portrays a person.

Baby boomers   The 76 million people born between 1946 and 1964.

Bait and switch   Unethical promotional pricing technique that attempts to lure customers into a store on false premises.

Balance of trade   Difference between a country's imports and exports over a period of time, such as a year.

Balance sheet   Accounting document with a long life that shows the viability of a business from its first operating day to the last day of a reporting period.

Bankruptcy   Legal declaration to inform the public of the financial insolvency of a company. (See also *Chapter 11*.)

Bankruptcy protection   Legal filing that gives an ailing company time to restructure debt, secure new financing, and reorganize while remaining in business.

Banners   Advertising graphics that appear on Web site pages.

Bar coding   Capture of information at the point of service by scanning the universal product code (UPC) with an electronic device.

Base rent   Fixed payment determined by retail square footage used that is due monthly or annually.

Basic stock method   Inventory planning system in which estimated sales for the month are added to a minimum stock to determine merchandise needs for the planning period.

Behavioral targeting   Strategy in which companies track customers' online behavior and use the information to personalize ads or information that is later sent to them.

Benchmarks   Metrics that are compared with figures from industry or internal company standards that have proved accurate and useful for forecasting and evaluating performance over time.

Big box   Identifies a broad spectrum of discount and other retailers that operate out of large, utilitarian stores.

Big ticket items   Merchandise that is expensive such as cars or furniture.

Biogenic needs   Physiological needs for food, warmth, shelter, and sex.

Blog   Written narrative that conveys opinions and solicits reader feedback online.

Bottom line   Final resolution of an income statement that indicates whether a company earned a profit, broke even, or lost money during a specific time period.

Brand equity   Level of consumer recognition a brand, label, or store has in the marketplace.

Branded concept shops   Store-within-a-store departments featuring internationally known merchandise.

Branding   Process of developing, building, and maintaining a name in the marketplace.

Breadth of stock   Number of different product lines carried in a store.

Bribe   Payment made to an individual, a company, or a government in order to secure special business privileges.

BRIC   Abbreviation used by the media for Brazil, Russia, India, and China—countries with key developing economies.

Bridge line   Apparel that is priced lower than designer fashion but higher than moderate lines.

Browsers   Software programs that facilitate Web navigation, the search for information, or access to a site.

Buildout   The process of implementing a design–build construction project.

Bumpback   Locating a smaller, usually temporary, tenant in the front portion of a space vacated by a larger retailer.

Business design   Different retail operating philosophies that are based on factors including gross margins, turnover, and other financial metrics.

Business intelligence (BI)   Information gathered from a variety of internal and external sources to help businesses make sound decisions.

Business-to-business (B2B)   Industrial or commercial channel such as one through which an apparel manufacturer sells to a wholesaler, distributor, or retail company.

Business-to-consumer (B2C)   Retail channel through which retail stores, catalogues, or online retailers sell goods to final consumers.

Buying power   Amount of money a family has available for purchases after taxes. Also known as purchasing power. (The Buying Power Index, or BPI, measures the retail sales potential for a specific geographic or media-based area.)

Buying power index (BPI)   Weighted value that measures the purchasing ability of households in a trading area.

Cannibalization   Loss of sales from one retail sector to another caused by the introduction of competing products or services.

Carbon footprint   Amount of carbon dioxide and other toxic emissions given off by manufacturing processes, utilities, household use, and transportation.

Carryover   Period of time between a person's receipt of a catalogue or advertisement and the actual sale.

Cash flow statement   Accounting of cash that moves in and out of a business for a specified period of time.

Category killers   Specialty superstores that focus on limited merchandise classifications and great breadth and depth of assortments.

Category management   An eight-step method of inventory management used primarily by supermarkets, category killers, and other big-box retailers that carry large inventories of food and consumer goods.

Cause marketing   Practice of staging promotions that benefit charitable organizations or communities and also build positive public relations for the sponsoring retailer.

Caveat emptor   Latin phrase meaning "let the buyer beware."

Central American Free Trade Agreement (CAFTA)   Alliance that includes the United States, Costa Rica, El Salvador, Guatemala, Honduras, and the Dominican Republic.

Central business districts   Downtown commercial areas in large and small cities where many businesses including retailers tend to congregate.

Chapter 11   Federal statute of the bankruptcy code that allows a company to enter a grace period in which it attempts to reorganize its financial affairs in order to remain in business. (Often called bankruptcy protection.)

Chapter 7   Federal statute of the bankruptcy code that allows a company—which is no longer able to sustain its business and seeks to liquidate stock and close its doors to file for bankruptcy.

Chargebacks   Financial penalties imposed on manufacturers by retailers.

Click-to-call   Web site function by which online customers seeking information can request a call from a customer service representative rather than placing the call themselves.

Click-to-chat   Web site function that takes online click-to-call contact a step further by offering live chat to customers.

Closed management   Early management method used strictly within the company without the benefits of outside considerations or input.

Cloud computing   Software applications that are accessed on the Internet rather than through PCs, tablets, or other mobile devices. Popular applications include e-mail access; data, photo and video storage; and Web hosting.

Cluster analysis   Method used to group people according to their attributes and behaviors.

Co-branding   Practice of two separate retailers (brands) joining forces for the purpose of reaching customers more effectively and increasing sales for both parties.

Cog's Ladder   Group management theory that uses five developmental stages to help assess group interaction and effectiveness.

Cognitive dissonance   Anxiety that occurs when people have mixed feelings or beliefs.

Collaborative planning, forecasting, and replenishment (CPFR)   Initiative to develop distribution efficiencies throughout the supply chain.

Collection shops   Stand-alone specialty stores that feature merchandise by international designers such as Prada or Giorgio Armani.

Common area maintenance (CAM)   Charges assessed on retailers to fund general mall upkeep internally and externally.

Community center   Neighborhood center that has been expanded to serve people in a three- to six-mile radius.

Compiled lists   Lists of potential customers' names and addresses that are prepared by commercial firms.

Completion date   Date promised by the manufacturer for total receipt of goods by the retailer.

Concessions   Independently owned and operated departments that cross all product and service lines and are less dependent on special levels of management expertise than leased departments.

Consolidation   Act of combining two or more companies for the purpose of achieving greater dominance in the marketplace.

Consultative selling   In-home or in-office selling by specialists whose expertise the customer values.

Consumer confidence   Index used to assess customers' sentiments toward making retail transactions.

Consumer cooperatives   Stores in which customers own a stake, receive lower prices on merchandise, and may participate in profit sharing.

Consumer Price Index (CPI)   "A measure of the average change over time in the prices paid by urban customers for a market basket of consumer goods and services." (U.S. Bureau of Labor Statistics)

Consumerism   Social movement advocating fair interaction between people and merchants.

Consumer-to-consumer (C2C)   Online channel for transactions completed by individuals selling to one another.

Containerships   Sailing vessels outfitted with large numbers of cargo holders that are roughly 20–40 feet long and shaped like a tractor-trailer bed.

Contingency planning   Process of seeking alternative methods for achieving goals when original plans do not reach fruition.

Convenience goods   Low-cost items that are purchased with minimum effort or time.

Cooperative advertising   Program under which retailers and manufacturers agree to share costs for retail advertising.

Cooperative education   Educational methodology that uses alternating periods of formal study and work experience as a requirement for graduation.

Core-based statistical areas (CBSAs)   Geographical areas made up of both metropolitan and micropolitan communities.

Corporate chain   A group of 25 or more stores with identical or similar formats under central ownership.

Counterfeiting   Intentional falsification of an established brand, design, or symbol for the purpose of illicit financial gain.

Coverage   Geographic area in which advertising messages potentially are seen or heard.

Criminal "flash mobs"   Pre-established groups of people that enter stores for the purpose of raising havoc, harassing sales associates, and stealing merchandise.

Cross-channel promotion   Practice of using multimedia to promote retail Web sites or other channels used by a retailer.

Cross-docking   Practice of moving goods in and out of a distribution center with minimal handling of merchandise.

Cross-merchandising   Practice of allocating the same merchandise to two or more areas of the store instead of one.

Cumulative markup   Average markup for an entire department or classification after a selling period.

Current assets   Term for revenue from the sale of goods and services that is used when calculating the current ratio.

Current ratio   A company's present financial assets measured against its present liabilities.

Customer relationship management (CRM)   Gathering and using database information to reach customers more effectively, identify their needs more specifically, and direct promotional and selling initiatives more precisely.

Customer relationship management (CRM)   Total company effort directed at satisfying the needs of all customers.

Cycle time   Period of time that elapses between production of goods and order fulfillment.

Danglers   Signs that are suspended from a shelf.

Data breach   When hackers enter a commercial or other Web site for the purpose of stealing customer information or sales transaction records.

Data mining   Probing a database for pertinent information that can be used to target future offers to customers.

Database marketing   Process of capturing and using observable and quantifiable information regarding customer behavior and aspirations.

Deep discounter   Discount store that operates on much lower markups and gross margins than conventional or other discount retailers.

Deflation   Reduction in the amount of money available in a country, creating a decline in prices and wages.

Demalling   Breaking up older enclosed malls into open concept clusters of stores and other multiuse construction.

Democratic leaders   Leaders who involve others in the decision-making process by asking for employees' opinions, which are shared and evaluated before decisions are made.

Demographics   Statistics on human populations, including age, gender, ethnic origin, education, income, occupation, type of housing, and other descriptors.

Department stores   Retail companies that occupy large facilities and carry broad assortments of goods organized by use, function, and brand.

Depth of stock   Number of similar styles or models in each product line.

Designer fashion collections   Apparel that is manufactured in smaller quantities and sold at higher prices in high-end retail stores globally.

Destination stores   Stores that have drawing power because they offer unique merchandise, cater to a specific lifestyle, or have strong brand identification.

Devaluation   Reduction in the international exchange value of a currency.

Developing countries   Countries moving out of emerging-nation status by becoming industrialized rather than dependent on agricultural economies.

Differential advantage   Unique characteristics of a business or product that may give it a superior position in the marketplace. (Also known as competitive advantage.)

Diffusion lines   Groups of merchandise that are produced and sold at lower prices than designer collections.

Direct mail   Personalized print communication that arrives via the mail providing relevant information on products and eliciting a direct response.

Direct marketing   "Integrative process of addressable communication that uses one or more advertising media to effect, at any location, a measurable sale, lead, retail purchase, or charitable donation, with this activity analyzed on a database for the development of ongoing mutually beneficial relationships between marketers and customer, prospects, or donors." (Source: Direct Marketing Association.)

Direct response television (DRTV)   An advertising medium used by direct marketers to reach customers with the intention of eliciting an immediate response.

Direct selling   Practice of selling to consumers through one-on-one situations or parties usually held in homes or workplaces.

Discounters   Retailers that buy and sell at low prices and depend on high volume and low overhead to be profitable.

Discretionary income   Amount of money that remains for nonessential purchases after life-sustaining items have been purchased.

Displace   To reduce the size of the workforce by laying off employees or granting early retirement.

Displacement   Reducing the size a workforce by laying off of employees or granting early retirement.

Disposable income   Amount of money remaining after taxes for major household expenditures such as sustenance foodstuffs, basic clothing, and shelter.

Diversification   Practice of acquiring or developing companies or stores that are not directly related to a firm's core business.

Divestiture   Selling of one business to another company.

Dollar plan   Forecast used by retailers to determine how much money they need to invest in new merchandise.

Domain name   Portion of a Web address that contains the company or other unique name and the identifier such as .com, .net, or .biz.

Domestic retailers   Companies that do business only in their home countries.

Drawing account   Monetary compensation available to commissioned salespeople that allows them to take a fixed sum of money at regular intervals against future commissions.

Due diligence   Process of preparing in-depth evaluations before a merger or acquisition can occur.

Dumping   Exporting goods that are priced lower than those manufactured in the country that imports the merchandise, thus creating unfair advantage.

Earnings per share   "A measure of how much profit a company earns for each share of stock outstanding." [Rona Ostrow, *The Fairchild Dictionary of Retailing.* 2nd ed. (New York: Fairchild Books, 2009), 131.]

Easement agreement   Agreement that allows limited use of land owned by someone else.

E-commerce   All goods and services sold on the Internet and through other electronic means, including business-to-business (B2B) and business-to-consumer (B2C) transactions.

Economic and Monetary Union (EMU)   System set up to facilitate the adoption and use of the euro among participating members of the European Union.

Economic utility   Ability of a product to satisfy consumers' needs and wants. The four basic economic utilities are time, place, form, and possession.

Economies of scale   Savings or efficiencies achieved by producing or purchasing large quantities of goods or sharing services.

Effective buying income (EBI)   Statistic that measures the availability of personal disposable income in an area.

Electronic article surveillance (EAS)   System that uses various security devices, often triggered at store exits, to deter theft.

Electronic cash (e-cash) cards   Smart cards that load and hold cash values in any currency via an ATM, computer, or cell phone.

Electronic data interchange (EDI)   Computer-guided communication network between retailer, manufacturer, and other supply chain members.

Electronic kiosks   Small computer displays or vending units in stores or other locations that help generate sales or provide extended customer services.

Electronic product code (ePC)   Radio frequency identification (RFID) version of the universal product code (UPC).

Emerging countries   Countries that are presently developing their infrastructures and economies.

Empowerment   Enabling individuals to complete tasks by providing resources, instilling motivation, and expecting them to take responsibility for the outcome.

Encryption codes   Computer programs that prevent unauthorized users from committing crimes such as fraud and access of personal information.

End caps   Display areas located at the ends of shopping aisles.

End-of month (EOM) stock   Dollar amount of stock remaining at the end of a month's selling period.

Engel's Laws of Family Expenditures   Theory developed by 19th-century German statistician Ernst Engel offering a basic view of how people spend their incomes on goods and services.

Environmental settings   Simulated rooms with three walls used to display home furnishings and accessories in a coordinated group.

E-retailing   Online and other electronic transactions involving goods and services for personal, nonbusiness use.

Ethnocentric   Perspective that views individual cultures or countries in narrow focus and perpetuates the viewpoint of one's own culture or country.

Euro   Common currency used by the European Union.

European Central Bank (ECB)   Financial institution that administers currency policy for the European Union.

European Union (EU)   One of the largest trading blocs in the world, comprising 27 member nations.

Eurozone   Countries within the European Union that have adopted the euro as their unit of currency (currently Belgium, Germany, Ireland, Greece, Spain, France, Italy, Cyprus, Luxembourg, Malta, the Netherlands, Austria, Portugal, Slovenia, Slovakia, and Finland.) Also called the *euro area.*

Experiential retailing   Retailing approach that encompasses all contemporary methods used to engage customers at emotional, sensory, and participatory levels as they shop.

Extensible markup language (XML)   Electronic message format that integrates different forms of hardware and software and allows data sharing by multiple users.

External promotion   Promotional message that communicates ideas to potential customers with the objective of bringing them into the store.

External search   Use of search engines such as Google to locate Web sites.

Extranets   Secured computer links between business partners such as retailers and suppliers.

Eye-level merchandising   Practice of displaying merchandise in the line of vision, an approximate 18-inch range of eye level, for optimal product placement.

Faced-out   When merchandise is displayed on fixtures so customers can see the product head-on.

Factor   Financial firm that coordinates payment between buyers and sellers on a commission basis by buying accounts receivable at a discount and assuming financial risk for the retailer.

Factoring   Purchasing a retailer's accounts receivable at discount and then collecting on the debt from the manufacturer or distributor.

Fill rates   Metric that evaluates the ability of manufacturers or distributors to ship all goods ordered.

Flagship store   Main store in a retail group, usually located in a city and often on the site of the original store. This definition expands as retailers, including designers and specialty stores, open additional flagship stores in the major cities in which they trade.

Flexible pricing   Setting prices that are open to negotiation or bargaining.

Floor fixtures   Display units designed to house and present merchandise.

Focus groups   Panels of 5–15 people invited to discuss a product, service, or market situation.

Franchising   Contractual arrangement by which individuals or companies agree to own and operate a business in accord with the brand standards of the host company.

Free on board (FOB)   Term identifying the point from which the retailer assumes responsibility for goods and payment of transportation charges.

Free trade   Conducting business without boundaries or taxation.

Freeform floor plan   Less structured floor arrangement with emphasis on engineered traffic flow.

Freestanding store   Self-contained building often located on the periphery of a shopping center or city.

Freight forwarders   Firms that group shipments of several manufacturers into truckload, railroad, or container shipments.

Fulfillment   Practice of using physical and electronic distribution systems efficiently to deliver products to customers in a timely manner.

Full-line department stores   Stores that carry both soft goods like apparel, accessories, and shoes and hard goods like home electronics or furniture.

Generation X   Children of early baby boomers, usually identified as those born between 1965 and 1977.

Generation Y   People born between 1978 and 1992, who include contemporary young adults, teens, and younger school-age children. (Those members who came of age early in the 21st century are called millennials.)

Generic goods   Products that do not bear brand names of manufacturers or retailers and are cheaper than comparable branded goods.

Geocentric   Perspective that views the world as a whole—the locus for ideas and decision making.

Geodemographic marketing tools   Methods that use computer-based mapping to identify consumer segments in specific geographic locations.

Geodemographics   Combination of geographic information with demographic attributes that describe a population.

Geographic information systems (GIS)   Technologies that allow retailers to analyze and map potential sites on the basis of interrelated demographic, psychographic, and geographic data.

Global retailers   Companies that do business in their home countries and in more than one other trading bloc.

Goals   Statements that indicate general company aims or end results.

Gondola   Moveable, bin-type display fixture frequently used for promotional merchandise.

Government-owned stores   Stores that are owned and operated by local, state, or federal governments.

Gravity models   Calculations used to identify customer drawing power of geographic areas.

Grid floor plan   Linear geometric floor arrangement with aisles and fixtures parallel or perpendicular to walls.

Grievance   Complaint that is handled formally through established procedures.

Gross domestic product (GDP)   Total value of all goods and services produced by a country during a specific time period.

Gross leasable area (GLA)   Amount of square footage available for lease in a shopping center, excluding common areas such as walkways, offices, and parking areas.

Gross margin   Difference between net sales and the cost of merchandise sold, expressed as a percentage.

Gross margin return on inventory (GMROI)   Sophisticated version of gross margin management that compares the productivity of different departments, lines of product, or placement on the floor. Supersedes simpler gross margin return on investment.

Gross profit   Net sales less the cost of goods sold.

Group direct selling   Method that encourages in-home or in-office selling to groups hosted by a sales representative who is also a customer.

Guerilla marketing   Creative street promotions and online events implemented by hired groups of outgoing people to raise brand awareness.

Hackers   Individuals who break into computer systems with criminal intent.

Hand raisers   Customers or prospects who initiate contact with a direct marketer after receiving a targeted direct mail piece with a special offer.

Harmonization   Process by which tax rates across several countries are brought into equilibrium.

Haute couture   Made-to-order high-fashion garments by major design houses, priced extremely high by average consumer standards.

Headhunters   Individuals or agencies who are paid to find managers or executives for a client company.

Hedonic needs   Human needs that are emotionally based and concerned with serving the ego.

Hierarchy of needs   Dr. Abraham Maslow's theory stating that people seek to satisfy needs in an ascending order of importance: biogenic, social, and psychogenic.

High streets   Busy retail thoroughfares where many retailers locate in large cities of the United Kingdom and other countries.

Horizontal competition   Competition that involves retailer against retailer.

Horizontal cooperative advertising   Joint advertisements by a group of businesses, usually at the same level of the supply chain, with the objective of increasing traffic or interest in a product or special event.

Hostile takeover   Ownership change that occurs when one company purchases large quantities of outstanding stock in another company, thereby giving controlling interest to the acquiring company.

House lists   Mailing lists that are drawn from companies' own charge account records or credit card transactions.

Hybrid center   Shopping area of mixed composition that combines the qualities of two or more basic center configurations with contemporary additions.

Hypermarkets   Stores of 150,000 square feet or more, 70 percent of which is devoted to general merchandise and 30 percent to food products. (Closely related to superstores.)

Import snobbery   Tendency for people to believe that better, more desirable products come from other countries.

Impulse goods   Items that are purchased at the spur of the moment.

Inbound calls   Telephone communications initiated by customers to companies or call centers.

Income statement   Accounting of all categories of income and expense for a business for a specific time period—usually quarterly and annually. Also called *profit and loss (P & L) statement.*

Independent retailers   Single stores, multiunit operations, and service businesses owned by an individual, a partnership, a small group, or a family.

Index of retail saturation (IRS)   Measurement tool that allows retailers to determine the degree of competition in a trading area.

Industrialized countries   Countries that have reached full production capabilities with well-developed infrastructures and technologies.

Inflation   Abnormal increase in the volume of money and credit in a country, resulting in substantial and continuing increases in price levels.

Infomercials   Television commercials that combine detailed product information, demonstration, and excitement with a sales pitch.

Informational interview   Meeting between an executive and a person seeking information on an industry, company, and career opportunities.

Information technology (IT)   Umbrella term for computer-based decision support systems that are used to make business operations more efficient.

Infrastructure   Physical facilities and services that support a specific area and include highway and transportation systems, communication networks, and public and private utilities.

Initial markup   Difference between the gross delivered cost of merchandise and the original retail price for a single item or a total assortment of goods.

In-line stores   Nonanchor stores located along corridors of enclosed malls.

Input   Details of the retail infrastructure, human resources, merchandising, and marketing activities that form a core of measurable events.

Insert media   Direct mail that reaches customers by riding along with newspapers or envelope mailers containing several offers from businesses.

Institutional advertising   Advertisements that are designed to convey a positive image of a company or brand rather than present specific merchandise.

Intermodal transport   Shipping goods via more than one transportation conveyance owned by the same company.

Internal promotion   Promotional message that communicates ideas to customers inside the store.

Internal search   Use of search within a Web site to locate information or items easily.

International retailers   Companies that operate in their home countries and in countries within their own or one other trading bloc.

Internet   Vast system of interconnected computer networks that enables computers worldwide to access and exchange information.

Internet Corporation for Assigned Names and Numbers (ICANN)   Organization that oversees Internet addresses.

Internet service providers (ISPs)   National or regional companies that provide access to the Internet for a monthly fee.

Interns   Students in formal training programs that encourage learning on the job while working closely with professionals.

Intranets   Internal computer communication systems used within a business or institution.

Job analysis   Procedure that determines the specific employment needs of a company.

Job description   Summary of the basic tasks expected of a person in a position.

Job enrichment   Way to improve an employee's efficiency and sense of satisfaction by increasing the challenges, opportunities, and nonmonetary rewards provided by the company.

Job specification   Summary of the personal qualifications and educational background required for a position.

Just in time (JIT)   Efficient logistical systems that allow for reduced inventory levels and timely distribution resulting in cost savings.

Key performance indicators (KPIs)   Statistical measurements that gauge the critical success factors of a business or other organization.

Keystone markup   Calculated by doubling the cost of an item to determine its retail price.

Lead time   Amount of time required between receipt of an advertisement by print, broadcast, or electronic media company and its appearance in the respective medium.

Leadership   Process of one person influencing another individual, team, or group of people to work toward common goals.

Lean practices   Methods of doing business that facilitate cost reductions, cycle-time efficiencies, and inventory turn increases.

Lean Six Sigma   Initiatives that specifically produce cost-saving measures; also called *lean practices* in business.

Leased departments   Merchandise or service specialty areas that are owned and operated by companies other than the host store.

Leave paper   Slang expression for writing an order on the spot.

Letter of credit (LC)   "An instrument issued by a bank to an exporter by which the bank substitutes its own credit for that of the importer and guarantees payment provided the documentary requirements are satisfied." (Source: Sterling National Bank, New York.)

Level of saturation   Degree to which retailers that trade in a common geographic area are able to maintain a fair share of business.

Leveraged buyouts   The most complicated and controversial type of acquisition or hostile takeover in which an acquiring company borrows large sums of money to finance the deal.

Lifestyle   The way people live, work, play, and spend their money.

Lifestyle center   Planned area designed to encompass retail, entertainment, and living in an expansive, themed, outdoor setting.

Limited-line department stores   Stores that focus on a few closely related categories of merchandise.

Line management   Members of the management team who are directly involved with key retail functions such as operations, finance, information technology, marketing, or merchandising.

Line-haul delivery   Moving goods long distances between cities and towns.

Liquidation   Process of selling off all inventory in preparation for closing down a company or one of its divisions or assets.

List broker   Company or individual that acts as a middleman between list buyers and sellers.

List manager   A company that is responsible for organizing and keeping a list up to date for an owner.

Live chat   Web site function by which a customer makes contact with a real person through telephone or instant messaging while simultaneously using the site.

Loss leaders   Items priced below cost to increase store traffic.

LTLs   Truckers that work long-distance routes with less-than-truckload capacity.

Luxury department stores   Department stores that operate on high gross margins, feature opulent facilities, and offer high prices to high-income customers who are more fashion-forward.

Magalog   Combination magazine and catalogue published by a retailer and distributed through stores or direct mail.

Mailing list   Collection of names, addresses, and contact information of present or potential customers complied from sources of significance to direct marketers.

Maintained markup   Retail markup that is calculated on a group of merchandise or a department at the time the goods are sold.

Mall   "A climate-controlled structure in which retail stores are architecturally connected." (International Council of Shopping Centers.)

Management   Administration of a company by leaders who are responsible for setting goals and objectives, implementing business and marketing plans, fostering innovation, guiding and motivating staff, and earning a profit through satisfaction of customer needs and wants.

Management by objectives (MBO)   Process by which a superior and a subordinate jointly set measurable performance goals for the subordinate and then meet periodically for performance reviews.

Manager   Person who controls, monitors, or directs a business or component of a business.

Manufacturer's representative   Independent businessperson who works in a specific territory selling related but noncompeting products to more than one account. (Also called a "rep.")

Manufacturer's suggested retail prices (MSRP) Prices determined by manufacturers as suitable for the market and at a level that allows a profitable retail return.

Markdown Reducing a retail price below its original level.

Markdown cancellation Restoring a price to its pre-markdown level.

Markdown money Extra reimbursement allowed the retailer if a manufacturer's goods do not sell well.

Market capitalization Total value of outstanding shares of stock held by a company. Also called *market cap.*

Market segmentation Process of breaking down a large population into smaller, accessible groups that share similar characteristics, lifestyles, or needs.

Market share Proportion of industry-wide product sales earned by one company.

Market weeks Scheduled seasonal showings of merchandise by manufacturers in market centers.

Marketing Process that uses product, price, promotion, and distribution to address customer needs effectively and turn a profit.

Marketing channel Route taken by a product as it travels from producer to final consumer.

Marketing mix Unique blend of product, price, promotion, and distribution techniques that are used to reach and satisfy a target market.

Markon The target, or first, markup placed on a retail product.

Markup Figure that covers fixed and variable costs of doing business plus a fair profit.

Markup cancellation When the additional price increase is removed and the original price is restored.

Mass merchandisers Large-format chain stores with broad geographic coverage that carry large assortments of general merchandise and food.

Master franchise Ownership arrangement in which one company buys the rights to a large region of a country, setting up scores of individual stores.

Mature retail companies Large, well-developed retailers that have the financial and managerial expertise to consider global expansion.

M-commerce Business conducted online using wireless devices such as cell phones, smartphones, and tablets.

Media Communication methods that deliver news, information, and promotional messages to viewers and listeners.

Media buying service Media specialists that buy blocks of advertising time and space on behalf of several businesses.

Media mix Specific configuration of media selected by an advertiser for a campaign.

Mediator Impartial evaluator hired to listen to both sides of a conflict and suggest solutions.

Megamall Shopping center of well over 1 million square feet, drawing from a trading area of over 100 miles and, in some cases, several states or provinces.

Mentoring Informal training given to one employee by another who is of higher rank within an organization.

Merchandise assortment All the goods in a store, defined in terms of breadth and depth of stock.

Merchandise classification A group of related goods in a store, such as all lines of jeans or all types of cell phones sold in a store.

Merchandising The culmination of planning, budgeting, sourcing, and procuring products for sale to identified target markets.

MERCOSUR Trade bloc that promotes free trade among several South American countries; full members include Argentina, Brazil, Paraguay, and Uruguay.

Merger Pooling of financial and material resources by two or more companies in order to become one.

Metric Statistical form of a performance measurement tool.

Metropolitan areas Geographic areas that contain a population of at least 50,000 people.

Micropolitan areas Geographic areas in which populations range from 10,000 to 50,000 people.

Microsites Independent Web sites that provide value-added information or activities that enhance the user's or customer's experience.

Mid-market department stores Department stores that operate on higher gross margins, provide more impressive facilities, and offer moderate prices to middle-class consumers.

Ministries of trade Government offices able to assist businesses with importing and exporting activities.

Mission statement Usually a brief paragraph that concisely describes a business and its reason for existence.

Mixed-use center Shopping center with two or more uses, such as an office building with a retail mall and residential areas.

Model stock plans Lists that show specific stock levels needed for a selling period.

Multichannel retailing Practice of trading using two or more methods of distribution concurrently.

Multilevel marketing Direct selling by firms that are set up in a pyramid-style hierarchy.

Multinational companies Corporations that conduct manufacturing, service, or retail businesses, or a mix of all three, in their home countries as well as many other countries.

Multiple pricing   Offering a discount for buying in quantities of more than one unit.

Multiunit department store   Department store organization consisting of a flagship store and two or more stores.

National advertising   Advertisements placed in major media by manufacturers, distributors, and retailers, usually on a broad geographic basis.

Natural search   Used to look up a topic of general interest or to do research on the Internet.

Neighborhood center   Convenience center, usually with a supermarket anchor, that occupies 30,000–150,000 square feet of gross leased area. (International Council of Shopping Centers.)

Net profit margin   After-tax figure expressed in units of currency or a percentage. Also shortened to *net profit.*

Net sales   Gross cash value of goods sold at retail, less allowances from vendors or suppliers and minus the value of merchandise returned by customers for refund.

Networking   Process of mingling with groups and speaking with individuals who may be in a position to offer a referral or a job.

Neutral pricing   Method based on adding a fair amount of money to the cost of products to cover overhead and profit.

Nonstore retailers   Retail businesses that sell through means other than traditional storefronts.

North American Free Trade Agreement (NAFTA)   Alliance that promotes trade among the United States, Canada, and Mexico.

Objectives   Specific goal-directed initiatives stated by a company.

Odd-ending pricing   Setting of prices that end in an odd number such as $9.99 rather than rounding off to a number such as $10.00.

Off-price retailers   Specialty discount stores that sell branded products at 20–60 percent less than traditional specialty or department stores.

Omnichannel retailing   Optimal practice of aligning merchandising, logistics, technologies, and all other functions fully in order to serve customers consistently well across all selling options.

On-boarding   Initial orientation activities and preparation sessions for new hires.

One-price policy   When all customers pay the same price and purchase an item under similar conditions.

On-the-job training (OJT)   Instructing employees during regular working hours while they also are doing productive work and are being paid regular wages.

Open management   Contemporary practice of focusing within the company and openly sharing knowledge of all internal functional areas and the external environment.

Open-to-buy (OTB)   The amount of money a buyer has allocated for purchasing merchandise for a designated period of time.

Operating expenses   The costs of doing business, including rent, salaries, supplies, insurance, utilities, and other overhead. Financing the business and cost-of-goods sold are not considered operating expenses.

Operating profit   The resulting number after the costs of doing business are deducted from gross profit.

Opinion leaders   Trendsetters whose opinions are respected within a group.

Optical weight   Amount an object appears to weigh rather than what it actually weighs.

Optimum stock level   Having the right amount of merchandise on hand to satisfy customer needs without being overstocked or understocked.

Organizational charts   Schematics that identify the chain of communication (formerly called command) and indicate the responsibility level of positions on the company hierarchy.

Organizational leadership   Umbrella term for cross-functional, team-oriented management models that encourage concensus building and formulating solutions to problems.

Organized retail crime (ORC)   Criminal activity involving groups of people in multiple locations and jurisdictions that commit planned crimes against retailers. (Source: National Retail Federation)

Outbound calls   Telephone communications initiated by direct marketers to customers or prospects.

Outlet center   Shopping center composed mainly of stores owned by manufacturers or retailers selling popular brands at a discount.

Outparcels   Tracts of land on the periphery of a shopping center or other commercial site that are often owned by the developer of the property.

Output   Financial details that describe the results of internal business initiatives to achieve sales and profits.

Outshopping   Practice of purchasing goods from retailers that are located outside of a customer's usual shopping territory.

Overstored   Condition that exists when too many retailers in the same retail trading area are competing for the same customers.

Paid search   Advertisements purchased by online retailers and located in the sponsored links boxes at the top of a Web page.

Passive pricing   Method based on a retailer's differential advantage rather than on beating competitors' prices.

Passive RFID tags   Very small microchips attached to a paper-like antenna.

Pathway floor plan   Floor arrangement that uses paths to engineer traffic from the front of the store to the rear and back again by means of designated walkways.

Penetration   Setting a low initial price on a product when competition is high.

Perceived value   Worth that customers place on merchandise, which may differ from true value.

Percentage rent   Percentage of annual sales above a threshold volume paid by the retailer to the lessor.

Performance reviews   Formal appraisals of an employee's work conducted quarterly, every six months, or annually.

Periodic inventory   Physical count of all merchandise, usually taken annually or semi-annually.

Perpetual inventory   Ongoing measurement of merchandise in stock as sales and purchases occur.

Person-to-person selling   When a salesperson calls on a customer at home or at the customer's place of business.

Physical distribution   Process of transporting goods from producer to retailer.

Piracy   Act of luring personnel from other firms.

Planning for succession   Process of identifying qualified internal candidates who will be available for promotion when an executive change is anticipated.

Planograms   Detailed scale drawings that illustrate precisely where each fixture and piece of merchandise is to be placed in a store.

Platform displays   Displays created in a prominent area using temporary or permanent low-rising units. Also called *island displays*.

Podcast   Audio file used to lend credence, opinion, or detail to Web-based content.

Point of impulse (POI)   Version of point of sale (POS) that more accurately reflects customer behavior information as well as sales data that is captured electronically when it occurs.

Point-of-purchase (POP)   Displays that use fixtures, or special racks, as well as printed materials positioned close to customer interface areas in a store.

Poison pill   Tactic that allows other shareholders the chance to purchase stock at a reduced price, thus thwarting a takeover by a major shareholder.

Polygon method   Used when determining a trading area by considering natural and human-made phenomena that apportion the space into straight-sided geometric shapes.

Population density   Number of people per square mile or kilometer in a specific geographic area.

Pop-up store   Retail operation at a temporary location that is used to test the market or fulfill a time-sensitive need in the marketplace.

Positioning   Perception a customer has of a company or product in relation to others.

Power center   Shopping center that has as many as seven anchor stores, usually discounters, warehouse clubs, or category killers.

Power node   Grouping of big-box stores—including at least one power center—located at or near a major highway intersection.

Preferred trading partner (PTP)   Status conferred by the World Trade Organization on a country that freely engages in trade with other countries.

Preferred vendor lists   Lists of prescreened manufacturers that are chosen to do business with large retail companies.

Price gouging   Taking advantage of consumers by marking up prices on retail products to an unreasonably high level.

Price lining   Practice of setting distinguishable prices determined by company policy, often part of a good-better-best approach.

Primary data   Information compiled to address specific research issues.

Primary trading area   A geographic area that encompasses 50–80 percent of a store's potential customers. Also known as a *primary service area* (PSA).

Prime rate   Interest rate charged to commercial lending institutions by the Federal Reserve Bank.

Private label merchandise   Goods that are manufactured to a retailer's specifications and bear the retailer's name or other brand names created by the retailer.

Product advertising   Advertisements that feature specific merchandise at regular prices and are designed to encourage timely sales.

Product developers   Individuals or teams that generate ideas, design prototypes, and arrange for production of exclusive products for retailers.

Product licensing   Contractual relationship between a designer—or other holder of rights to a brand—and a manufacturer to produce items under that name or brand.

Product life cycle   Process of tracing the existence of a product in the marketplace by examining the stages through which it passes and the time it spends in each stage.

Product line   A group of closely related items produced by a manufacturer.

Product management   Process by which managers break down the essential activities that have an impact on their work and reorganize staff in meaningful ways to create reactionary teams.

Product reviews   Communications generated by customers or retailers seeking input on merchandise performance, pricing, customer service, or other topics.

Promotional advertising   Advertisements that feature merchandise at sale prices.

Promotional mix   Advertising, sales promotion, publicity, public relations, personal selling, and customer service.

Promotional pricing   Setting prices below the usual or customary level with the intention of having a sale or offering a special purchase.

Prospecting   Seeking qualified potential customers through screening and analysis of database information.

Protectionism   Boycotting foreign-made products in order to support domestic manufacturers.

Protectionism   Government policy that protects domestic manufacturers by placing restrictions on foreign producers of the same goods.

Psychogenic needs   Human needs that stem from the socialization process and involve intangible aspects, such as status, acquisition, or love.

Psychographics   Classification of people on the basis of their lifestyles, activities, interests, and opinions.

Public relations   Promotional activities that enhance or rectify retail image and support charitable foundations or important social causes.

Publicity   Nonpaid news or editorial comment about ideas, products, services, or stores.

Pull strategy   When a retailer initiates shipment from a distribution center in response to sales.

Pure service retailers   Retail businesses that conduct transactions not involving merchandise.

Push money (PM)   Incentive payment given to sales associates for selling certain items.

Push strategy   When a distribution center initiates shipments to a retailer in anticipation of sales.

Pyramid format   Geometric display that follows the lines of a triangle, beginning at a broad base and progressing to an apex.

Q ratio   A company's market capitalization measured against the value of its assets.

Queue   British English term for a line of people.

Quick ratio   Similar to the current ratio but more rigorous since it includes a provision for deducting unsold goods from current assets.

Quick response (QR)   Umbrella term for integrated supply chain distribution systems that allow rapid replenishment of merchandise.

Quick response codes   Two-dimensional barcodes—usually black-and-white squares with pixels (short for picture elements)—that are scanned and downloaded to smartphones.

Quota   Limitation imposed on the quantities of a product imported from other countries.

Racetrack floor plan   Floor arrangement in which elements of grid and freeform plans are combined to direct customers around the entire store by means of oval-shaped walkways.

Radio frequency identification (RFID)   The use of radio waves to detect merchandise, people, and other discernable elements.

Random storage   Computer-generated model for optimal use of storage space.

Reach   Number of actual readers, listeners, or viewers in an audience.

Ready-to-wear (RTW)   Mass-fashion apparel that is sold at low, moderate, and high prices at retail companies ranging from discount to department and specialty stores.

Real estate investment trust (REIT)   Legal and financial arrangement by which substantial property is owned and large-scale real estate transactions are masterminded.

Recession   Period in which there is less money in the economy than there was previously.

Reference groups   Social or professional associations with which a person identifies and to which he or she looks when forming opinions.

Referrals   Names of business insiders' acquaintances who might be potential employees.

Regional mall   Shopping center consisting of at least two anchor stores and 40–80 smaller stores, serving a minimum of 100,000 people.

Resident buying offices   Companies that facilitate market coverage for retailers by acting as their eyes, ears, and legs in the marketplace.

Retail advertising   Advertisements specifically directed to final consumers by retailers.

Retail holding companies   Huge conglomerates that are composed of many individual companies doing business under a variety of names.

Retail inventory method (RIM)   Accounting method exclusive to retailers that measures and evaluates the worth of current inventory at retail prices.

Retail mix   Various activities in which retailers are engaged as they attempt to satisfy customers including location selection, facilities planning, merchandising, pricing, promoting, distributing goods, and human resource management.

Retail saturation   The degree to which a trading area is overstored or understored.

Retailing   Selling of goods or services directly to the customer for personal, nonbusiness use.

Retenanting   Finding new retailers to replace those that have gone out of business or otherwise vacated the premises.

Return on assets (ROA)   A percentage that indicates the relationship of sales to total assets after taxes and interest. Similar to *return on investment* and *return on inventory (ROI)*.

Ring analysis   When a trading radius is determined by using an existing or potential retail site as the locus. Also known as the *concentric circles method*.

Role-playing   Training exercise in which individuals experience a situation through dramatization, by participating as actors.

Sales potential   The total amount of possible sales that can be realized in a trading area.

Sameness syndrome   Tendency of some retailers to offer the same or similar merchandise or services as their competitors.

Same-store sales   Comparative measurement of sales from the previous year with sales for the current year in stores that have been open for at least one year.

Sampling   Placing products in customers' hands for trial use. (Not to be confused with sampling as a marketing research procedure.)

Scrambled merchandising   Carrying products unrelated to a store's traditional or expected merchandise mix.

Search engine   Computer program used to seek, find, and index all the information that is available on the Web.

Search engine optimization   The industry term for harnessing ways to increase the number of visitors to a site by increasing the site's ranking within the search engine.

Secondary data   Information that comes from previously published sources.

Secondary trading area   A geographic area located just outside the primary trading area that contains an additional 20 to 25 percent of a store's potential customers.

Secure electronic transmission protocol (SET)   Software that makes transactions between buyers and sellers safer.

Self-actualization   Desired result when a person becomes all that he or she is capable of being.

Sell through   Percentage of stock sold against the total of stock remaining in a store or department after a specific period of time.

Shadowboxes   Small display windows located in-store or out, often used to display luxury items.

Shadowing   Programs in which students observe exactly what happens on the job and have the opportunity to discuss their career goals with executives.

Shoppertainment   Combining retail shopping with many forms of entertainment in stores and mall.

Shopping carts   Special software features that online shoppers use to collect products and park them electronically until they are ready to check out.

Shopping center   "A group of retail and other commercial establishments that is planned, developed, owned, and managed as a single property." (International Council of Shopping Centers.)

Shopping goods   High-priced merchandise usually purchased after the buyer compares the offerings of more than one retailer.

Short-haul delivery   Moving goods to customers locally.

Shrinkage   Reduction in the value of stock due to employee theft, shoplifting, and human error. (Also called *shrink*.)

Situation analysis   Process used to determine the strengths and weaknesses of a company, specific business plan, or proposed strategy.

Six Sigma   Method developed by Motorola that uses economic metrics (econometrics) to increase efficiency and quality in businesses.

Skimming   Setting a high initial price on a product when competition is low.

Slotting fees   Charges imposed on manufacturers by retailers for select shelf locations.

Sourcing   Identification and utilization of resources for the manufacture of goods.

Sovereign wealth funds   Investment capital emanating from governments.

Space productivity index   Advanced tool that helps retailers determine optimal merchandise placement in a brick-and-mortar store.

Spatial analysis   When two or more types of data are overlaid to more accurately define the drawing power of a specific site.

Specialty goods   Products bearing name brands or products with special features that buyers will go out of their way to purchase.

Specialty stores   Retail outlets that present large selections of highly focused, limited lines of merchandise in small or large facilities.

Speed interviewing   Retailers meet with multiple job candidates and candidates meet with several interviewers in a compressed time period.

Spin-off stores   New chains launched by a retailer for the purpose of filling a market need or reaching a new target market.

Split run   Practice of selling advertising space at reduced prices to regional advertisers.

Sprinkler strategy   International entry tactic by which companies enter each country or market consecutively.

Standardization   Establishment of uniform operational, environmental, and monetary systems across several countries.

Staple goods   Merchandise that is routinely purchased.

Step format   Display that begins at a low point on one side and climbs incrementally to a higher point in a diagonal arrangement.

Stock keeping units (SKUs)   Individual inventory control numbers—indicated on bar codes—which distinguish one product from another.

Stock-to-sales ratio (SSR)   The relationship between goods on hand at the beginning of the month and merchandise sold during the month, expressed in dollars or units.

Store image   Combination of concrete and esoteric factors that is the total impression of a retailer retained by its customers.

Strategic planning   Process of gathering and analyzing information from a variety of internal and external sources for the purpose of reducing risk before special business plans are executed.

Strategic profit model   Financial paradigm that uses two components, net profit margin and asset turnover, to calculate return on assets (ROA).

Strategies   Action plans that prescribe tactics used by a company to reach common goals and objectives.

Stress interview   Screening tool in which a panel of interviewers fires questions requiring quick, thoughtful answers and looks for evidence of problem-solving ability by the candidate.

String streets   Retail thoroughfares located away from central business districts that retain thriving clusters of retail shops in or near residential neighborhoods.

Strip center   "An attached row of stores or service outlets managed as a coherent retail entity." (International Council of Shopping Centers.)

Striping   Practice of displaying merchandise in vertical formats to bring attention to deep assortments carried by the retailer.

Subclassifications   Groups of merchandise in a classification that are defined more narrowly; if a classification is outerwear, subclassifications are jackets, parkas, long coats, or rain coats.

Super regional mall   Shopping center consisting of three or more anchor stores and as many as 350-plus specialty and service retailers.

Superette   Small grocery store that is larger than a mom-and-pop store but smaller than a supermarket.

Supermarkets   Self-service food and grocery stores of under 100,000-square-feet that may carry some nonfood items, but do not have extensive specialty departments.

Superstores   Huge retail stores, usually over 150,000 square feet, typically combining general merchandise and food under one roof.

Supply chain   All of the businesses involved throughout the marketing channel.

Sweethearting   The practice by retail employees of adding merchandise that has not been paid for to the shopping bags of relatives or friends.

Swing areas   Key areas in stores that are used for rotating promotional displays or small temporary departments.

SWOT analysis   Planning model that lists a company's strengths, weaknesses, opportunities, and threats (SWOT), which is used to determine future direction.

Symmetrical balance   Positioning of items on either side of a center line so that they are equally weighted optically. Also called *formal balance.*

Tactical planning   Detailed short-term planning in a narrow vein usually done by middle and lower management.

Target market   A group of people with similar characteristics and needs who are likely to purchase.

Tariff   Duty or tax imposed by a government on an import.

Tearsheet   Page torn from a publication and sent to an advertiser, vendor, or agency to prove that an advertisement has run.

Tertiary trading area   A wide area located outside the primary and secondary trading areas, containing 5–25 percent of the store's potential customers. Also known as the *fringe area.*

Theme/festival center   Shopping venue oriented toward entertainment as well as shopping.

Thrust areas   Prime locations in stores used for the display of new, high-margin, or seasonal items.

TLs   Truckers that work long-distance routes at full truck-load capacity.

Total quality management (TQM)   Management systems that encourage teamwork and ownership of the production, distribution, or retailing processes.

Town centers   Retail urban villages located outdoors consisting of buildings with nostalgic architectural features or theme designs.

Track lighting   Display lighting that consists of moveable units mounted on vertical or horizontal tracks.

Trade advertising   Business-to-business advertising used among supply chain members and not directed to final consumers.

Trade discounts   Deductions from an agreed price, usually granted by manufacturers to other supply chain members.

Trade embargo   Restriction set by a government on the importation of goods.

Trade sanctions   Penalties imposed on one country by another in an attempt to curb unfair trade practices.

Trading area   Geographic area from which a retailer draws its customers.

Trading bloc   Major geographic trading area that tends to have close political, cultural, or economic ties.

Transformational leaders   Leaders who motivate employees to work for the greater good of the organization rather than exclusively for personal goals.

Triple net   Leasing term that describes a retailer's responsibility for paying insurance, utilities, and internal upkeep.

Turnaround time   The time that passes between an action and the response to it, such as the placement of an order and the receipt of it.

Turnkey operation   A methodically planned retail store or service that is completely ready to begin operation.

Turnover   Number of times inventory is sold and replenished in a year. Also called *turn* or *stock turn.*

'Tweens   Girls between late childhood and the early teenage years.

Tweet   Short message of no more than 140 characters that can be sent via computer, tablet, or smartphone.

Twenty-foot-equivalent units (TEUs)   Unit of measurement for the volume of shipping containers.

Twofer   Offering customers two products at a lower price than would be paid if each was purchased separately.

Underwriters Laboratories, Inc.   Large, independent nonprofit testing groups whose trademarked UL mark means the product has been safely tested against national standards.

Unit plan   Detailed list of all items being purchased by color, style, size, and price.

Unit pricing   Quoting prices in terms of standard units of measurement such as ounces, pounds, or kilograms.

Unity   Perception that all design elements in a display belong together.

Universal product code (UPC)   A series of printed stripes found on most products encoding product identification information.

Universal resource locator (URL)   Complete Web site address that includes access protocol and the domain name.

Value center   Cross between a power center and an outlet mall.

Value megamall   Large hybrid mall containing elements of power, value, and outlet centers, with added entertainment components.

Value pricing   Providing the best-quality product for the lowest price as viewed by customers.

Value-added tax (VAT)   Tax levied at each stage of processing for a raw material or of production and distribution for a commodity or retail product.

Value-driven department stores   Department stores that operate on lower gross margins, provide modest but pleas-ant facilities, and offer lower prices to budget-conscious consumers.

Variable data printing (VDP)   Classic offset printing combined with digital printing using high-speed inkjet equipment.

Vendor-managed inventory (VMI)   Program that shifts the responsibility for keeping track of merchandise to the manufacturer.

Vendors   Specific members of the supply chain that provide goods and services to retailers. Also known as *resources.*

Vertical competition   Competition that involves a retailer against a wholesaler or manufacturer also engaged in retailing.

Vertical cooperative advertising   Advertising arrangement by which a manufacturer or other supply chain member agrees to share costs with a retailer.

Vertical integration   When two or more supply chain members are owned by the same company.

Vertical mall   Shopping center in a high-rise building, usually in an urban location.

Video datacasting   Technology that uses digital television to send Internet data.

Viral marketing   Using customers to generate "buzz" to help sell a product.

Viral video   Online video campaigns featuring appealing brands that are shared with friends and family.

Vision statement   Detailed and forward-thinking descriptive piece written by a company.

Vlog   Blog that has a video component.

Wall systems   Full-height perimeter partitions and high partitions placed between departments.

Want slips   Notations gathered by sales associates regarding merchandise requested by customers but not carried by the store.

Warehouse clubs   Large format, bare-bones retail stores that sell a broad assortment of merchandise to small businesses, as well as families and individuals.

Waterfall strategy   International entry tactic by which companies enter several countries or markets concurrently.

Web 2.0   Advanced technologies that enable high-level user interaction, and offer rich media, heightened graphics, and 3D capabilities.

Web 3.0   Technically advanced systems that mesh online shopping and offline services.

Web site   Specific location of a business, organization, or person on the World Wide Web.

Weeks-of-supply method   Inventory planning system in which stock on hand is kept at a level representing projected sales for a predetermined number of weeks.

Wheel of retailing theory Description of retail evolution as a cyclical pattern consisting of three phases: entry, trading up, and vulnerability.

White space Portion of an advertisement that is not used for type or illustration.

Widgets Embedded code that users can insert into Web sites, blogs, or social networking pages to provide information, interactive activities, and items for sale.

Wobblers Signs on spring assemblies that jiggle to attract attention.

World Trade Organization (WTO) International governing body made up of representatives from over 150 countries that grants preferred trading partner status, regulates trade, and settles disputes among members.

World Wide Web The totally integrated informational and commercial electronic services accessible via global computer networks and wireless technology. Often shortened to "the Web."

Index

public relations, 482
publicity, 482
as retail business function, 11
in retail mix, 6
retail sales promotion, 480–82
Twitter, 182, 195, 200–201
viral marketing, 484
promotional advertising, 470
promotional funds, 281
promotional mix, 467, 469
promotional pricing, 458–61
property leasing. *See* leasing property
property ownership, 279, 303t, 406–7
proportion, 323
prospecting, 163
Protect IP Act (PIPA), 209
protectionism, 44, 229
PSAs (primary service areas), 267
PSOEs (privatized state-owned enterprises), 257
psychogenic needs, 94
psychographics, 97, 101–3
psycholinguistics, 376
psychological pricing, 458
PTPs (preferred trading partners), 43
public information, 208
public relations, 482
publications, consumer, 416–17
publicity, 482
publishing industry, 45, 190, 452
Publix, 439
pull strategies, 206, 215, 507
purchase, 112
purchase decision, 111–14
purchase terms, 439–41
purchases, planned, 422–23
purchasing power, 40, 53, 225, 266
pure catalogue companies, 170
pure service retailers, 13
pure services, 13
pure-play retailers, 192
Purina, 511
push money (PM), 381
push strategies, 206, 507
push-pull distribution, 507
PVH (Phillips-Van Heusen) Corp., 430
PwC (PricewaterhouseCoopers), 225, 393, 417
PWS, 13
pyramid format, 326
pyramid hierarchy, 180

Q

Q ratio, 398, 400t
QR (quick response) codes, 216
QR (quick response) distribution systems, 74
QSRs (quick-service restaurants), 153–54
quads, 321
quality control, 238
quality expectations, customer, 167
quality-of-life issues, 374, 384
Quelle, 133
queues, 106
quick ratio, 389
quick response, 508

quick response (QR) codes, 216
quick response (QR) distribution systems, 74
quick-service restaurants (QSRs), 153–54
Quicksilver, 181
quota bonus plan, 381
quotas, 42
QVC, 61, 213–14

R

racetrack floor plans, 316, 317f
radio advertising, 474
radio frequency identification (RFID), 106, 499,
    510–12
rail transport, 501
Ralph Lauren
    Club Monaco, 88, 426
    global expansion, 245–46
    in-store branded-concept shops, 425, 425f
    trickle down dissemination, 18
    vertical integration, 9
Ralph Lauren Polo, 88, 216
Ralphs, 150
random storage, 507
rate of adoption, 109–10
rating scales, 380
Ray, Rachel, 459
RBM Venture Company, 87
reach, 477
ready-to-wear (RTW) apparel, 429
Real, 202
real estate industry, 281–84
real estate investment trusts (REITs), 282,
    284, 407
recession, defined, 38
recession, effects of
    advertising, 393
    apparel industry, 8, 37, 431
    chain stores, 28
    consumer spending, 38–39, 40, 57–58
    customer behavior, 38–39, 40, 110, 132, 142
    department stores, 131
    direct mail, 173
    discount retailers, 39, 110, 121, 142, 148
    EU members, 241
    exchange rates, 40
    global capital availability, 230
    global effects, 41
    high-end retail markets, 56, 56f, 105–6
    job outlook, 54
    merchandise planning, 426
    online retailing, 189–90
    property leasing, 281–82
    retail industry, 35, 36, 38–39, 41, 70–73
    shipping industry, 504, 505
    shopping centers, 304–5
    strategic planning, 70–73
    unemployment, 366–67
    vending industry, 181
recession, precipitating factors, 38, 70, 189
RECon, 407
recruitment, 372–76
recyclables, fashioning, 83
Red Bull, 476

Redbox, 212
reductions, planned, 422
Reed, Shenan, 196
reference checks, 375
reference groups, 96
referrals, 373
refinancing, 407
regional malls, 292, 306
regression analysis, 269
regular accounts, 489
REI, 10
Reilly, William, 269
Reilly's Law of Retail Gravitation, 269
Reis, 282, 306
REITs (real estate investment trusts), 282,
    284, 407
religion, 103–4, 242
renewable energy, 84
renewal, 360
rent, 275, 280, 283
Rent-a-Center, 86
rented-goods services, 14
repair services, 490
repetition, 323, 323f
Republic of China (ROC), 108, 255, 438, 517
Rescue, 73
research, external, 417
research, internal, 415
resident buying offices, 416, 430–32
residential analysis, 266
resorts, 277–78
resources (vendors), 5, 416
restaurants, ethnic, 54
restaurants, full-service, 153–54
restaurants, quick-service, 153–54
results-oriented metrics, 211
resumes, 375
Retail, Wholesale, and Department Store
    Workers Union, 368–69
retail advertising, 470
retail business functions, 11, 12f
retail careers, 519–31
retail competition. *See* competition
retail crime, 82, 329
retail dissemination, 17–19
retail evolution, 15–19
retail holding companies, 21
retail inventory method (RIM), 392–93, 392t
retail jobs, U.S., 339–40
retail location types, 272–75, 275–79
Retail Macro Space Management software, 314
retail marketing channels, 5, 6–10, 7f
Retail MarketPlace Profile, 271
retail mix, 6
retail ownership. *See* ownership, retail
retail planning calendar, 424
retail profit formulas, 388
retail sales promotion, 480–82
retail saturation, 268
retail sectors, 10
retail services
    classification of, 13–14, 109
    convenience stores, 150
    drugstores, 142
    effect of gas prices on, 39